The Collected Works of
James M. Buchanan

VOLUME 14
*Debt and Taxes*

*James M. Buchanan, Middle Tennessee
State University, Murfreesboro, 1988*

*The Collected Works of*

# James M. Buchanan

VOLUME 14

## *Debt and Taxes*

LIBERTY FUND

*Indianapolis*

| 04 | 03 | 02 | 01 | 00 | C | 5 | 4 | 3 | 2 | 1 |
| 04 | 03 | 02 | 01 | 00 | P | 5 | 4 | 3 | 2 | 1 |

*Library of Congress Cataloging-in-Publication Data*
Buchanan, James M.
Debt and taxes.
p.   cm. — (The collected works of James M. Buchanan ; v. 14)
A collection of 35 journal and book articles previously published
1960–1997.
Includes bibliographical references and index.
ISBN 0-86597-239-7 (alk. paper). — ISBN 0-86597-240-0 (pbk. : alk. paper)
1. Taxation.   2. Tax and expenditure limitations.   3. Debts,
Public.   4. Social choice.   I. Title.   II. Series : Buchanan, James M.
Works.   1999 ; v. 14.
HJ2305.B79   2000
336.2—dc21          99-41677

LIBERTY FUND, INC.
8335 Allison Pointe Trail, Suite 300
Indianapolis, IN 46250-1684

# Contents

## 3. Analytical and Ethical Foundations of Tax Limits

## 4. The Fiscal Constitution

## 5. Confessions of a Burden Monger

## 6. Ricardian Equivalence

## 7. The Constitution of a Debt-Free Polity

# *Foreword*

Although James Buchanan's interests are wide-ranging, the core of his professional reputation as an economist and the origin of much of his broader thinking lies in public economics—in engagement with the questions of what governments should do and how governments should properly finance what they do. It has been a persistent theme in Buchanan's approach that these questions cannot be satisfactorily handled separately: specifically, that the issue of the appropriate methods of revenue-raising must be fully integrated with consideration of the general purposes to which the revenue is to be put. For much of Buchanan's career, this integration went somewhat against the practices of the economics profession. The tradition was that public finance divided itself fairly neatly between those who saw their expertise as lying in tax analysis and those who engaged the more abstract welfare economics issues of the economic theory of the state. And though there has been some change in professional attitudes on these matters, much of that change attributable to Buchanan's own influence, the division of intellectual labor still tends to fall along this fault line. For this reason, as editors, we feel somewhat uncomfortable about the division of Buchanan's public economics papers between this volume and the next along essentially equivalent lines. That is, in the current volume, we present the papers on taxation and debt; we then deal with the public expenditure papers in volume 15, *Externalities and Public Expenditure Theory.* We want, therefore, to emphasize the importance of reading the material in these two volumes in tandem. The emphasis here goes somewhat beyond more general urgings elsewhere about the overall coherence of Buchanan's thinking and the desirability of seeing his work as a whole. In an important sense, the essential *point* of Buchanan's worldview is caught up in the insistence, which he derives originally from Knut

Wicksell, that public spending and revenue-raising are inextricably linked aspects of the same politically constituted action.

In the same spirit, it is as well to draw attention to the tax and debt papers in the representative collection of papers in volume 1 of the Collected Works, *The Logical Foundations of Constitutional Democracy.* It is an obvious concomitant of the centrality of debt, taxation, and public expenditure as topics in Buchanan's thought that some of the significant papers on those topics would need to be included in the initial introductory volume. Accordingly, the reader should be alerted to the selections in part 3 of volume 1, and particularly to "Taxation in Fiscal Exchange," which is in some ways the most overtly contractarian/Wicksellian treatment of tax questions in Buchanan's work.[1]

Equally, the books *Public Principles of Public Debt, Public Finance in Democratic Process, Democracy in Deficit,* and *The Power to Tax,* appearing in the present series as volumes 2, 4, 8, and 9, respectively, are all centrally relevant to the papers collected in this volume.[2] There is much of Buchanan's thinking about taxation and debt, for example, that is only lightly represented in the papers in the current volume. There is no concentrated version of the central argument in *Public Principles of Public Debt;* there is relatively little account in the papers of the central ideas advanced in *Public Finance in Democratic Process;* and we have deliberately omitted several papers whose argument is directly replicated in the book-length treatments.[3]

The papers included here divide themselves quite naturally into two parts

---

1. James M. Buchanan, "Taxation in Fiscal Exchange," *Journal of Public Economics* 6 (1976): 17–29, reprinted in volume 1 in the series, *The Logical Foundations of Constitutional Liberty.*

2. James M. Buchanan, *Public Principles of Public Debt* (Homewood, Ill.: Richard D. Irwin, 1958), volume 2 in the series; *Public Finance in Democratic Process: Fiscal Institutions and Individual Choice* (Chapel Hill: University of North Carolina Press, 1966), volume 4 in the series; James M. Buchanan and Richard E. Wagner, *Democracy in Deficit: The Political Legacy of Lord Keynes* (New York: Academic Press, 1977), volume 8 in the series; Geoffrey Brennan and James M. Buchanan, *The Power to Tax: Analytical Foundations of a Fiscal Constitution* (New York: Cambridge University Press, 1980), volume 9 in the series.

3. This consideration explains, for example, the omission from the representative papers of the Leviathan account of earmarking, "Tax Instruments as Constraints on the Disposition of Public Revenues"; the argument appears without serious modification as chapter 7 of *The Power to Tax.* Geoffrey Brennan and James M. Buchanan, "Tax Instruments as Constraints on the Disposition of Public Revenues," *Journal of Public Economics* 9 (June 1978): 301–18.

and correspond with the two elements of the title. It seems logical, however, to present the two elements in the opposite order from that in which the title announces them. Euphony dictates titles; logic dictates arrangement. The first four parts of the book, therefore, deal with tax analysis. Part 1 offers six general papers concerning the characteristic features of the Buchanan approach. Two of these examine explicitly the connection between public choice theory and public finance—"Public Finance and Public Choice" and the subsequent "Public Choice and Public Finance." The former treats the influence of emergent public choice theory on developments in public finance scholarship, while the latter traces the public finance origins of public choice theory. The next two papers, "Democratic Values in Taxation" and "Tax Reform as Political Choice," focus on other general aspects of Buchanan's method of tax analysis: as the titles imply, both papers emphasize the central *political* character of tax policy.[4] The final two papers in this section are included to highlight the difference between Buchanan's approach and the conventional "public economics" approach, as represented by the work of Richard Musgrave.[5] It was Musgrave's work during the 1950s that synthesized and refined orthodox public finance—most notably in his treatise *The Theory of Public Finance*.[6] In that sense, Musgrave's contribution and Buchanan's reactions to it form the perfect backdrop against which to assess the distinctiveness of Buchanan's conceptual framework.

Part 2 includes five papers on specific issues in tax analysis—earmarking, indirect versus direct taxation, and tax incidence—all within the context of an essentially democratic model of political process.[7] Part 3 treats tax questions in

4. James M. Buchanan, "Public Finance and Public Choice," *National Tax Journal* 28 (December 1975): 383–94; "Public Choice and Public Finance," in *What Should Economists Do?* (Indianapolis: Liberty Fund, 1979), 183–97; "Democratic Values in Taxation," in *Freedom in Constitutional Contract: Perspectives of a Political Economist* (College Station: Texas A&M University Press, 1977), 243–53; "Tax Reform as Political Choice," *Journal of Economic Perspectives* 1 (Summer 1987): 29–35.

5. James M. Buchanan, "The Theory of Public Finance," *Southern Economic Journal* 26 (January 1960): 234–38; "Richard Musgrave, Public Finance, and Public Choice," *Public Choice* 61 (June 1989) 289–91.

6. Richard A. Musgrave, *The Theory of Public Finance: A Study in Public Economy* (New York: McGraw-Hill, 1959).

7. James M. Buchanan, "The Economics of Earmarked Taxes," *Journal of Political Economy* 71 (October 1963): 457–69; "The Constitutional Economics of Earmarking," in

what has come to be known as the Leviathan model of political process in which ordinary electoral constraints are ineffective and where government discretion is interpreted in terms of access to economic rents. There are six papers in this section, including the original statement of Leviathan tax theory and several that deal with the normative and political logic of tax limits.[8]

The papers included in part 4 are a more diverse set. "The Tax System as Social Overhead Capital" offers a constitutionalist perspective on the tax system. "Tax Reform without Tears" is a piece of more or less conventional efficiency-oriented tax analysis, though with a characteristically contractarian edge. In "The Political Efficiency of General Taxation," Buchanan lays out a justification for more or less conventional tax norms as a means of avoiding essentially *political* distortions. And in "Rational Majoritarian Taxation of the Rich," we see the application to tax analysis of Buchanan's development of Smithian ideas relating to increasing returns.[9]

---

*Charging for Government: User Charges and Earmarked Taxes in Principle and Practice,* ed. Richard E. Wagner (London and New York: Routledge, 1991), 152–62; James M. Buchanan and Francesco Forte, "Fiscal Choice through Time: A Case for Indirect Taxation?" *National Tax Journal* 17 (June 1964): 144–57; James M. Buchanan, "Externality in Tax Response," *Southern Economic Journal* 33 (July 1966): 35–42; James M. Buchanan and Mark V. Pauly, "On the Incidence of Tax Deductibility," *National Tax Journal* 23 (June 1970): 157–67.

8. Geoffrey Brennan and James M. Buchanan, "Towards a Tax Constitution for Leviathan," *Journal of Public Economics* 8 (December 1977): 255–73; "The Logic of Tax Limits: Alternative Constitutional Constraints on the Power to Tax," *National Tax Journal* 32 (June 1979): 11–22; James M. Buchanan and Roger Congleton, "Proportional and Progressive Income Taxation with Utility-Maximizing Governments," *Public Choice* 34 (1979): 217–30; James M. Buchanan, "The Ethical Limits of Taxation," *Scandinavian Journal of Economics* 86 (April 1984): 102–14; "Coercive Taxation in Constitutional Contract," in *Explorations in Constitutional Economics,* comp. Robert D. Tollison and Viktor J. Vanberg (College Station: Texas A&M University Press, 1989), 309–28; "Constitutional Constraints on Governmental Taxing Power," *ORDO* Band 30 (Stuttgart: Gustav Fischer Verlag, 1979): 349–59.

9. Geoffrey Brennan and James Buchanan, "The Tax System as Social Overhead Capital: A Constitutional Perspective on Fiscal Norms," in *Public Finance and Economic Growth,* ed. Karl Roskamp (Detroit: Wayne State University Press, 1983), 46–56; James Buchanan and Geoffrey Brennan, "Tax Reform without Tears," in *The Economics of Taxation,* ed. Henry Aaron and Michael Boskin (Washington: The Brookings Institution, 1980), 33–54; James M. Buchanan, "The Political Efficiency of General Taxation," *National Tax Journal* 46 (1994): 401–10; James M. Buchanan and Yong J. Yoon, "Rational

The papers in the remaining parts of this volume are concerned with public debt but, as already emphasized, constitute only a small part of Buchanan's writing on this topic: the more extensive and systematic treatments are in the book-length discussions.[10] However, we can detect in the debt papers the same prevailing themes and anxieties—in particular, the need to see debt-financing in terms of its effects on political processes and a general Wicksellian concern about the justice and political efficiency of current generations of citizens voting for themselves expenditures for which future generations will have to pay. Because these anxieties depend for their coherence on the idea that debt does indeed transfer tax burdens intertemporally in a relevant sense, sustaining this prior analytical claim has been a central part of the Buchanan agenda in the area. Buchanan's early argument for this claim is contained in *Public Principles of Public Debt,* and in part 5 of this volume we include several supporting statements from that earlier period.

Questions about debt-incidence enjoyed a resurgence of attention following the appearance of Robert Barro's paper "Are Government Bonds Net Wealth?" Although Barro's paper was developed out of a concern broadly with the micro foundations of macroeconomics, and although his argument makes no reference to either the original Ricardian version or the public finance literature on debt-incidence, the debate on the effects of social security entitlements on private savings that surrounded his paper involved claims about public debt incidence rather at odds with Buchanan's. The three papers that make up part 6 are all concerned, one way or another, to address Barro's "neo-Ricardian" position. (The quotation marks in this context are used to signify that though Ricardo originally exposited the logic of the position he explicitly rejected its real-world relevance.)[11]

Part 7 contains seven papers oriented in various ways to the constitu-

---

Majoritarian Taxation of the Rich: With Increasing Returns and Capital Accumulation," *Southern Economic Journal* 61 (April 1995): 923–35.

10. See, in particular, volumes 2 and 8 in the Collected Works, *Public Principles of Public Debt* and *Democracy in Deficit.*

11. James M. Buchanan, "Barro on the Ricardian Equivalence Theorem," *Journal of Political Economy* 83 (April 1976): 337–42; Geoffrey Brennan and James M. Buchanan, "The Logic of the Ricardian Equivalence Theorem," *Finanzarchiv* 38 (1980): 4–16; James M. Buchanan and Jennifer Roback, "The Incidence and Effects of Public Debt in the Absence of Fiscal Illusion," *Public Finance Quarterly* 15 (January 1987): 5–25.

tional politics of debt-financing.[12] What implications does access to public debt have for the conduct of democratic politics? asks Buchanan. And with those implications in mind how might we rationally constrain the operation of in-period politics? The final paper in this section involves a particularly astounding possible solution to excessive use of the debt option: Buchanan has not lost his capacity to be controversial![13]

> Geoffrey Brennan
> *Australian National University*
> 1998

12. Viktor Vanberg and James M. Buchanan, "Organization Theory and Fiscal Economics: Society, State, and Public Debt," *Journal of Law, Economics, and Organization* 2 (Fall 1986): 215–27; James M. Buchanan, "The Moral Dimension of Debt Financing," *Economic Inquiry* 23 (January 1985): 1–6; "The Economic Consequences of the Deficit," *Symposium on Budget Balance,* ed. Carol Cox (Washington, D.C.: Committee for a Responsible Federal Budget, 1986), 11–18; "Budgetary Bias in Post-Keynesian Politics," in *Deficits,* ed. James M. Buchanan, Charles Rowley, and Robert Tollison (New York: Blackwell, 1987), 180–98; "The Balanced Budget Amendment: Clarifying the Arguments," *Public Choice* 90 (1997): 117–38; James M. Buchanan and Richard E. Wagner, "Dialogues Concerning Fiscal Religion," *Journal of Monetary Economics* 4 (July 1978): 627–36.

13. James M. Buchanan, "The Ethics of Debt Default," in *Deficits,* ed. James M. Buchanan, Charles Rowley, and Robert D. Tollison (New York: Blackwell, 1987), 361–73.

## PART ONE

# Taxation, Politics, and Public Choice

# Public Finance and Public Choice

*Abstract:* Public finance has undergone major transformation since World War II. This paper surveys this transformation, particularly from a public choice perspective. Post-Marshallian public finance had two major gaps: the expenditure side of the fiscal account, and the public decision-making process. Both of these gaps have been partially filled, although much discussion of policy continues to take place in a now-outmoded setting. Social security financing is used as an illustration of the separate methodologies.

"Public finance," as a quasi-independent subdiscipline in the American academic setting, has been substantially transformed in the thirty years after the ending of World War II, although heritages of the earlier tradition remain, and notably as these affect practical political discussion. From its relatively minor role as one among many fields of applied microeconomic theory—akin to industrial organization, agricultural economics, or labor economics—public finance emerged to become "public economics," which, at least conceptually, is on all fours with "private economics," or, more familiarly, the economics of the private sector. If relative weights are assigned in accordance with relative shares in GNP, public economics promises, for better or for worse, to grow still more important in decades ahead.

My purpose in this survey paper is to discuss this transformation of public finance from a public choice perspective, one that reflects my own meth-

From *National Tax Journal* 28 (December 1975): 383–94. Reprinted by permission of the publisher.

I am indebted to my colleague Gordon Tullock for helpful comments.

odological presuppositions. I shall not include reference to the "theory of fiscal policy," which bloomed brightly in the early post-Keynesian environment only to fade somewhat in the face of political realities. The macroeconomic policy emphasis derived from Keynes is a causal element in the relative growth of the governmental sector and, as such, one source for the increasing attention to public economics. But there is no direct relationship between this emphasis and the fundamental paradigm shift that is the primary subject of my treatment in this paper.

## Post-Marshallian Public Finance

I can commence by describing the content of public finance in post-Marshallian economics, as limited to English-language discourse. Positive analysis was restricted almost exclusively to theories of tax shifting and incidence. And, indeed, as Marshall himself explicitly recognized,[1] the theory of tax shifting becomes almost the ideal instrument for applying the principles of competitive price theory. Comparative statics offered a plausible predictive framework for analyzing tax alternatives. Within limits, and for certain simple forms, the economist could confidently predict the effects of a tax on the behavior of persons and firms in the private economy, and, through this, on the aggregate effects on such variables as relative prices, outputs, profits, and industry structure in particular sectors. For this strictly positive analysis, which could also yield empirically refutable propositions, the economist had no reason to inquire about the political purpose of taxation, no reason to introduce external evaluation of alternative tax instruments.[2] This subarea of public finance, which is essentially applied price theory, has continued to be developed through more sophisticated technical analysis which has now moved beyond the Marshallian partial-equilibrium framework to general-

---

1. ". . . there is scarcely any economic principle which cannot be aptly illustrated by a discussion of the shifting of the effects of some tax. . . ." Alfred Marshall, *Principles of Economics*, 8th ed. (London: Macmillan, 1930), 413.

2. Beginning attempts were made to extend an analogous positive analysis to the expenditure side of the fiscal ledger (see, for example, Earl Rolph, "A Theory of Excise Subsidies," *American Economic Review*, 42 [September 1952], 515–27). But, as noted, the predominant emphasis was, and remains, on taxation.

equilibrium settings, including extensions to open economies. No basic paradigm shift has occurred here, but this subarea has necessarily been relegated to a relatively less important role in the larger theory of public economics which has emerged.

Alongside this post-Marshallian positive theory of taxation, there existed what I may label as the post-Pigovian normative "theory" of taxation. This unfortunate and somewhat confused discussion stemmed vaguely from the utilitarian philosophical tradition and had as its purpose the derivation of normative "principles" for taxation. The most sophisticated of these, developed most fully by Pigou,[3] was that of "equi-marginal sacrifice," which was based on a simplistic application of the calculus in a context of assumed interpersonal utility comparability. This normative discussion was much less rigorous intellectually than the positive analysis of tax incidence, and, indeed, the normative treatment of taxation among English-language economists was almost a half-century out of phase from the more sophisticated discussion on the European continent. The normative "principles" of taxation that were seriously discussed may seem bizarre when viewed in a modern post-Wicksellian or public choice paradigm. But these principles assume continuing practical importance as soon as we recognize that observed institutions of taxation find their intellectual origins in these norms, which also, to a large extent, inform modern political criticisms of tax structures, along with continuing calls for tax reform. For example, the most vocal modern advocates for reform, notably Joseph Pechman and Stanley Surrey, base their arguments on presupposed norms for the distribution of tax shares, norms which are derived independently.

There are two related, but quite distinct, gaps in the normative public finance of the post-Marshallian, post-Pigovian tradition. There is, first, the long-continued, and methodologically inadmissable, neglect of the expenditure side of the fiscal account. The necessary interdependence between the two sides of the public-sector budget must be incorporated into any analysis, even if the purpose is to lay down ideal standards drawn from some external scale of evaluation. Secondly, there is the neglect or oversight of the collective decision structure itself. The shift in paradigm which has occurred involves the incorporation of both these elements.

3. A. C. Pigou. *A Study in Public Finance* (London: Macmillan, 1928).

## The European Theory of the Public Economy

Following the central contributions of the early 1870s, the economic theory of markets assumed a unified structure. The simultaneous operation of productive input and final product markets accomplished evaluative, allocative, and distributive functions. The European attempts to extend this aesthetically satisfying logic structure to "explain" the operation of a public as well as a private sector now seem to represent predicted increments in scientific progress. The puzzle in intellectual history does not concern these efforts; the puzzle lies in the long-continued failure of English-language economists to make comparable extensions of their basic framework or to acknowledge an interest in the continental efforts.

As early as the 1880s, Mazzola, Pantaleoni, Sax, and de Viti de Marco made rudimentary efforts to analyze the public economy within an exchange framework. Sax and Mazzola discussed the demand side of public goods by identifying collective wants as distinct from private wants. Pantaleoni extended the marginal calculus to apply to the legislator who makes choices for both sides of the budget. De Viti de Marco explicitly constructed a model in which the consumers and the suppliers-producers of public goods make up the same community of persons.[4]

The most sophisticated contribution was made by Knut Wicksell in 1896.[5] He explicitly identified the fundamental methodological error in the then-orthodox approach, and he combined positive criticism with normative suggestions for reform. Wicksell recognized the necessity of bridging the two sides of the fiscal account, and he noted the indeterminacy of any proposed normative principles that were limited to tax-side considerations. More importantly, Wicksell admonished economists for their failure to recognize the

4. For a brief summary discussion of the early continental contributions, see Richard A. Musgrave, *The Theory of Public Finance* (New York: McGraw-Hill, 1959), 68–80. For a more extended discussion which is, however, concentrated largely on the Italian contributions, see my *Fiscal Theory and Political Economy* (Chapel Hill: University of North Carolina Press, 1960), 24–74. For translations of most of the important contributions here, see *Classics in the Theory of Public Finance*, ed. R. A. Musgrave and A. T. Peacock (London: Macmillan, 1958).

5. Knut Wicksell, *Finanztheoretische Untersuchungen* (Jena: Gustav Fischer, 1896). Major portions of this are translated and included in *Classics in the Theory of Public Finance*, op. cit.

elementary fact that collective or public-sector decisions emerge from a political process rather than from the mind of some benevolent despot. His suggestions for reform were concentrated on the institutional structure for fiscal decision-making, on the institutions of public choice. The unanimity rule was presented as the normative benchmark for efficiency in public-sector decisions, and a clear distinction was made between those situations where genuine gains-from-trade might emerge and those which involve zero-sum transfers. Despite the essentially normative setting for Wicksell's reform suggestions, the groundwork was laid for subsequent positive analysis of political decision structures.

Subsequent to these early contributions, work was carried forward, notably in Sweden and in Italy. Erik Lindahl's attempt to examine more closely the relationship between standard efficiency norms and the political bargaining process offered a halfway house between Wicksell's seminal effort and modern analyses of public finance in democratic process.[6] Lindahl's proposed solution, the set of so-called Lindahl tax-prices, or Lindahl equilibrium, has come to occupy the attention of several sophisticated analysts who have attempted to extend the modern theory of general competitive equilibrium to include the public sector.[7]

The Italian tradition, following the early work by Pantaleoni and de Viti de Marco, was characterized by an emphasis on the necessary political assumptions required for either a positive or normative theory of the public economy. The Italians devoted much more attention to the implications of nondemocratic political structures for the emergence and viability of fiscal institutions, on both the tax and the expenditure sides, than did their continental counterparts. These aspects, in particular, become helpful in the analysis of the supply institutions of the public economy, an analysis that remains in its formative stages. Apart from these substantive contributions, Barone

---

6. Erik Lindahl, *Die Gerechtigkeit der Besteuerung* (Lund, 1919). A central portion of this has been translated and is included in *Classics in the Theory of Public Finance*, op. cit.

7. See, for example, Duncan Foley, "Lindahl's Solution and the Core of an Economy with Public Goods," *Econometrica*, 38 (January 1970), 66–72; T. Bergstrom, "A Scandinavian Consensus Solution for Efficient Income Distribution Among Nonmalevolent Consumers," *Journal of Economic Theory*, 4 (December 1970), 383–98; D. J. Roberts, "The Lindahl Solution for Economies with Public Goods," *Journal of Public Economics*, 3 (February 1974), 23–42.

and Einaudi, in particular, were sharply critical of the naive utilitarian framework of the English-language normative discussion of tax principles.

## The Transitional Setting

The substantial transformation in American public finance did not spring full blown from some rediscovery of the European theory of the public economy, although it might legitimately be claimed that this theory, appropriately modernized, was sufficiently complete to have allowed for this as an alternative intellectual scenario. The transformation emerged slowly and in bits and pieces, influenced by several sources other than the strict analysis of the continental scholars. Precedence in presenting the central ideas of what he called the "voluntary exchange" theory of the public economy belongs to R. A. Musgrave who, in his first paper, offered a highly critical evaluation.[8] However, Musgrave's analysis was not such as to attract independent and complementary attention to the body of work discussed. And Howard Bowen, in his original and much-neglected 1943 paper, showed no signs of having been influenced by the European analysis.[9] Bowen's paper combined two elements that were to be more fully developed later as separate strands of analysis, the theory of demand for public goods and the theory of voting. Although flawed by minor analytical errors, Bowen's paper was perhaps neglected because it was too much in advance of the analytical mind-set of its time. My own efforts, in my first substantive paper in 1949, one that was also largely neglected, were concentrated in a methodological critique of the post-Pigovian normative framework. In this, I was influenced almost exclusively by a fortuitous discovery of Wicksell's basic work.[10]

8. R. A. Musgrave, "The Voluntary Exchange Theory of Public Economy," *Quarterly Journal of Economics,* 53 (February 1938), 213–37.

9. Howard R. Bowen, "The Interpretation of Voting in the Allocation of Resources," *Quarterly Journal of Economics,* 58 (November 1943), 27–48.

10. See my "The Pure Theory of Government Finance: A Suggested Approach," *Journal of Political Economy,* 57 (December 1949), 496–505, reprinted in my *Fiscal Theory and Political Economy,* op. cit., 8–23.

I may add here an autobiographical note concerning this discovery that will be familiar to my students and former colleagues but which may deserve wider dissemination. In the summer of 1948, having finished my dissertation and fresh from having passed the German-language requirement, I spent some weeks wandering about the stacks in Harper

Developments of note came rapidly during the 1950s and 1960s. These may be discussed initially in terms of their independent emergence, with little or no direct interconnection one with another and with the corpus of public finance theory. In what follows, I shall discuss briefly four lines of inquiry or analysis: (1) the theory of demand for public goods; (2) the theory of voting; (3) the theory of constitutions; and (4) the theory of supply of public goods. In each of these, I shall attempt to distinguish positive and normative elements of analysis. After these strands are separately examined, I shall try to integrate these as they relate to modern public finance theory. Finally, I shall use a single example to demonstrate how the modern public choice paradigm in public finance differs from the post-Marshallian, post-Pigovian paradigm which, although conceptually flawed, continues to inform some policy discussion.

## The Theory of Demand for Public Goods

As previously noted, there were two gaping holes in the pre–World War II normative analysis of taxation, a neglect of the expenditure side of the fisc and a neglect of the collective decision process. Modern public finance theory incorporates both of these elements, but they remain conceptually distinct and they were, to an extent, independently developed. An internally consistent set of principles for efficiency in the public economy may be elaborated with no attention to the political decision process. This was the framework for Paul A. Samuelson's seminal paper in 1954,[11] in which he laid down the necessary marginal conditions for allocative efficiency in the provision of public or collective goods to a defined community of persons. Samuelson extended the accepted norms of theoretical welfare economics from the private to the public sector of the economy, using individual evaluations as the building blocks. Perhaps his primary contribution lay in his rigorous definition

---

Memorial Library at the University of Chicago. By chance, I picked up Wicksell's *Finanztheoretische Untersuchungen,* a book that had never been assigned or even so much as mentioned in my graduate courses, and, as I later ascertained, one of the very few copies in the United States. Quite literally, this book was responsible directly for the paradigm shift that I experienced.

11. Paul A. Samuelson, "The Pure Theory of Public Expenditure," *Review of Economics and Statistics,* 36 (November 1954), 387–89.

of a "collective-consumption" good, embodying both complete nonexclusion and complete efficiency from joint consumption, the two acknowledged attributes of "publicness." Early criticisms of the polarity features of Samuelson's classification were, in my view, misplaced because this initial step seemed essential before the further elaboration of taxonomic detail could take place.

The Samuelson mathematical formulation of the conditions for public-sector efficiency did not contain a comparable normative theory of the distribution of tax-shares. Income-effect feedbacks of tax-shares on individual evaluations of collective-consumption goods were incorporated in the analysis, but the tax-share distribution itself was arbitrarily selected by resort to a social welfare function. This normative construction is quite different from that which is required for the definition of the allocative conditions for efficiency. Within Samuelson's conceptual framework, resort to the social welfare function for tax-share distribution was an implication of his unwillingness to close the model in a manner analogous to the exchange process of the private sector. He did not conceive the fiscal process as one of "exchange," even at the level of abstraction that the formal statement of the necessary marginal conditions for efficiency required.

Nonetheless, the Samuelson analysis can readily be interpreted positively, which necessarily implies an exchange framework. In this case, the necessary marginal conditions for allocative efficiency become conditions that must be satisfied for an equilibrium solution to the complex "trades" that the political or collective choice process embodies. One such solution is the Lindahl equilibrium, which meets the basic Samuelson requirements, although it is arbitrarily restricted in its distribution of tax-shares inframarginally. The more general Wicksellian approach makes no attempt to specify particulars of an equilibrium. Instead this approach concentrates on the institutions for "trading," and implicitly defines efficiency to be present when all gains-from-trade are exhausted. In a setting of zero transactions costs, including bargaining costs, unanimous agreement will be possible on both marginal tax-share distribution and on the quantity of public goods to be purchased, although the position of agreement will not be unique and its characteristics will depend strictly on the path of adjustment.[12]

---

12. My book *The Demand and Supply of Public Goods* (Chicago: Rand McNally, 1968) develops public-goods theory in the Wicksellian framework. The book's title is somewhat

## The Theory of Voting

The Wicksellian paradigm for fiscal exchange, ideally operative under a decision rule of unanimity without prior constraints on tax-share distribution, places the public economy, methodologically, on all fours with the private economy. The importance of this Wicksellian benchmark or starting point for the developments that have followed cannot be overestimated. But the world is not characterized by zero transactions costs, and these loom especially large when many persons must agree on single outcomes. The two-party dimensionality of private-goods training, especially as constrained by the presence of numerous alternatives on both sides of exchange, allows the costs of reaching agreement to be minimized, and, because of this, to be largely neglected in analysis. No such neglect is possible for the complex trading process that politics embodies. Necessary departures from the idealized models become much more apparent, and enter analysis even at the level of institutional design. Wicksell himself recognized, in his discussion of qualified majorities, that the ideal political constitution could not embody a strict unanimity rule, even for the legislative assembly. And, of course, historical experience in democratic politics includes a wide variety of voting and decision rules-institutions, only a few of which approximate the unanimity-rule benchmark.

Once the ideal is abandoned, as necessary for the operation of political decision structures in accordance with more inclusive efficiency norms, what rules for collective choice should be chosen? Before this question can be addressed at all, there must be positive analysis of alternative voting rules and institutions. From a current vantage point, in 1975, it seems almost incredible that American public finance economists completely ignored analysis of voting rules prior to World War II, even though they must have recognized that fiscal outcomes were related directly to the political structure. Aside from the paper by Bowen, noted above, there was no discussion of voting rules prior to the seminal contributions of Duncan Black and Kenneth Arrow, in the late 1940s and 1950s.[13]

---

misleading; the analysis is almost exclusively devoted to the demand side; the supply side is neglected.

13. Their first papers appeared in 1948 and 1950, respectively. See Duncan Black, "On the Rationale of Group Decision Making," *Journal of Political Economy*, 66 (February

Black's earlier efforts had been strictly within the post-Marshallian tradition of incidence analysis.[14] His reading of the Italian works was an acknowledged source of his shift of emphasis to an analysis of voting rules. Black's major work was largely confined to an analysis of majority rule as a means of reaching decisions in collectivities. In his analysis, which included the discovery of precursory work by Borda, Condorcet, and, most notably, Lewis Carroll, Black noted the possibility of the majority cycle, but his emphasis was placed on the workability of majority rule rather than the reverse. This emphasis led him to examine restrictions on preference domains that might produce unique majority solutions. He discovered that if all individual preferences could be arrayed over alternatives so as to appear as single-peaked, the majority-rule outcome will always be that which meets the preferences of the median voter in the group. This median-voter construction was to emerge as an important tool in the public choice theory of the 1960s, and especially in public finance applications. Single-peakedness in preferences becomes a plausible assumption for many fiscal decision variables.

Kenneth Arrow's work exerted far more influence on economic theory generally than did the closely related work of Duncan Black. However, the specific effects on public finance theory are less direct. Arrow placed his analysis squarely in the social welfare function discussion that had emerged from theoretical welfare economics, and he demonstrated that there existed no collective decision rule for amalgamating individual preference orderings into a consistent social or collective ordering. This rigorous generalization of the cyclical-majority phenomenon, along with Arrow's emphasis on the impossibility of generating a social ordering meeting plausible criteria, had the effect of putting the analysis of collective decision rules directly on the research agenda of modern economists. Faced with results that they did not welcome, and with their somewhat naive political presuppositions exposed, economists were slowly forced to acknowledge that social welfare functions

---

1948), 23–34; Kenneth Arrow, "A Difficulty in the Concept of Social Welfare," *Journal of Political Economy*, 58 (August 1950), 328–46.

These were followed by their full-length works. See Kenneth J. Arrow, *Social Choice and Individual Values* (New York: Wiley, 1951); Duncan Black, *The Theory of Committees and Elections* (Cambridge: Cambridge University Press, 1958).

14. Duncan Black, *The Incidence of Income Taxes* (London: Macmillan, 1939).

do not exist. Only two alternatives remained open. They might become public choice analysts and examine the operation of alternative decision rules, no one of which is ideal. Or, they might revert to the normative post-Pigovian stance which requires the explicit introduction of private and personal value standards that bear little or no relationship to the decision-determining institutions of the real world.

## The Theory of Constitutions (Voting Rules)

Once positive analysis of the operation of alternative voting rules was placed on the agenda, along with the Wicksellian recognition that no nonunanimity rule could guarantee efficiency in the narrow sense, the way was open for the development of a theory of constitutions, based on an analysis of the choice among a set of less-than-ideal institutions for generating collective outcomes. This was the setting for *The Calculus of Consent,* which I jointly authored with Gordon Tullock, and which was published in 1962.[15] This work carried forward the analysis of alternative decision rules, with emphasis on the political external diseconomies inherent in any less-than-unanimity rule and on the prospects for vote trading as a means of mitigating the results of differential preference intensities. Our central purpose was, however, that of analyzing the choice among collective decision rules, and of deriving criteria for "optimality" at this constitutional level. Our procedure was to shift backwards, to the level of choice among rules, the Wicksellian unanimity or general consensus criterion. The transactions costs barrier to general agreement may be fully acknowledged at the stage of reaching collective decision on specific fiscal (tax and spending) variables. But this need not imply that persons cannot agree generally on the rules or institutions under which subsequent decisions will be made, whether these be majority rule or otherwise. To the extent that individuals' future preference positions are uncertain and unpredictable under subsequent operation of the rules to be chosen, they may be led to agree on the basis of general criteria that are unrelated to economic position.[16]

15. James M. Buchanan and Gordon Tullock, *The Calculus of Consent* (Ann Arbor: University of Michigan Press, 1962).
16. The setting for our analysis has an obvious affinity to that which is used by John Rawls in his derivation of the principles of justice, a setting that has been made familiar

Our analysis was positive in the conceptual sense, and we made few suggestions for institutional reform. Nonetheless, our discussion was admittedly informed by a vision or model of constitutional process that embodied individualistic norms. This vision was, in its turn, used to "explain" features of existing political structures, features which might, with comparable methodological legitimacy, be explained with alternative normative models. Our analysis of constitutions was not sufficiently complete to allow us to discriminate among widely varying explanations for the emergence and existence of observed political institutions.

## The Theory of Supply of Public Goods

This gap in our analysis of the choice among constitutional rules stemmed, in part, from our neglect of the supply side of the public-goods exchange process. The theory of demand for public goods, the theory of voting, and the theory of voting rules—each of these lines of inquiry initially embodied the implicit assumption that individual demands for public goods, once these could be articulated and combined through some collective choice process, would be efficiently and automatically met. It was as if the alternatives for public choice were assumed to be available independently from some external source; there was no problem concerning the behavior of the suppliers or producers. Governments are, however, staffed by persons who make up only a subset of the community, and any full analysis of fiscal exchange must allow for differences between the behavior of persons in producing-supplying roles and in consuming-demanding roles.

Precursors of supply-side analysis can, of course, be found in the Italian theory of public finance in the nondemocratic or monopolistic state. Models of this political structure were developed in some detail, models in which some ruling group or class collects taxes from the masses who are ruled and utilizes the proceeds to its own maximum advantage. But attention was also paid to the feedback or reaction effects on the behavior of those who were

---

since the publication of Rawls' treatise (John Rawls, *A Theory of Justice* [Cambridge: Harvard University Press, 1971]). Although our approach was independently developed, Rawls had employed the "veil of ignorance" in earlier papers in the 1950s. Other scholars have used essentially similar devices as a means of moving from the individual's short-term interest to what may be called, in one sense, the "public interest."

exploited. At the turn of this century, Puviani developed the interesting and still-relevant concept of "fiscal illusion," which he applied to both the taxing and the spending side of the fiscal account.[17] However, aside from my own summary of some of these elements, which I did not sufficiently stress, there was no direct linkage between the monopolistic-state analysis of the Italians and the emergence of the modern theory of public-goods supply.

American scholars have operated within a continuing presupposition that their own political institutions remain basically democratic. Even within this structure, however, the demanders and the suppliers of public services must occupy differing economic roles, and the interests of the two groups need not coincide. The seminal American contribution toward the ultimate development of a theory of public-goods supply was made by Anthony Downs. In his book *An Economic Theory of Democracy,* published in 1957, Downs presented a model of political party competition analogous to the competition among firms in an industry, with vote-maximization serving as the analogue to profit-maximization.[18] The predictive power of Downs' model was sharply criticized by William Riker, who introduced a game-theoretic framework to suggest that political parties, even when treated as monolithic decision-taking entities, will seek to organize winning coalitions of minimal size rather than to maximize vote totals.[19] For purposes of this survey, however, the central contribution of these efforts lay not in the explanatory potential of the models themselves but rather in the fundamentally different setting offered for viewing the activities of governments. Once governments came to be viewed as collectivities of persons who were themselves maximizers—whether these persons be party organizers, political representatives, elected officials, judges, or bureaucrats—the emerging paradigm involving the passively efficient supply response to public-goods demanders was dramatically changed in course.

The Downs-Riker models of interparty competition, which have been

---

17. For a summary discussion of Puviani's contribution, along with a treatment of fiscal illusion more generally, see my *Public Finance in Democratic Process* (Chapel Hill: University of North Carolina Press, 1967), Chapter 10. An English translation of Puviani's basic work will be published in 1976, under the supervision of my colleague Charles Goetz.

18. Anthony Downs, *An Economic Theory of Democracy* (New York: Harper, 1957).

19. William H. Riker, *The Theory of Political Coalitions* (New Haven: Yale University Press, 1962).

carried forward and elaborated in more sophisticated forms by other scholars, were paralleled by the development of a theory of bureaucratic behavior,
both at the level of the individual member of the hierarchy and that of the
agency or bureau itself. Gordon Tullock introduced the maximizing bureaucrat, who responds to his own career incentives like everyone else, and analyzed the implications of this behavioral model for the control problem faced
by those at the top of the hierarchy.[20] Even on the extreme assumption that
the agency head desires to meet the demands for public goods efficiently,
Tullock's analysis suggests that this objective could not be met in organizations requiring personal services.[21]

William Niskanen boldly challenged the orthodox conception of bureaucracy by modeling separate bureaus as budget-maximizing units.[22] The implication of his polar model is that bureaus, acting as monopoly suppliers of
public services, and possessing an ability to control the elected political leaders through a complex and interested committee structure in the legislature,
fully drain off the potential taxpayers' surplus that might be possible from
public-goods provision. Once again, it is not the particular predictive power
of Niskanen's analysis that is relevant for our purposes; what is relevant is
the contrasting setting within which the operations of agencies and bureaus
may be examined.

The theory of public-goods supply has not been fully developed, and efforts to integrate this theory, as it exists, with the theory of demand, including the theory of voting and voting rules, have only commenced.[23]

20. Gordon Tullock, *The Politics of Bureaucracy* (Washington: Public Affairs Press,
1965).

21. Tullock's analysis of the bureaucrat represents perhaps the closest that public
choice analysis comes to a parallel, but quite different, development in modern economic
theory, that which has been called the theory of property rights. The latter work of Alchian, McKean, Demsetz. Pejovich, and others has been concentrated on predicting the
effects of differing reward-penalty structures, as defined in terms of rights to property, on
individual behavior. For a summary, see Eirik Furubotn and Svetozar Pejovich, "Property
Rights and Economic Theory: A Survey of Recent Literature," *Journal of Economic Literature,* 10 (December 1972), 1137–62.

22. William Niskanen, *Bureaucracy and Representative Government* (Chicago: Aldine,
1971).

23. Two introductory attempts should be noted: Albert Breton, *The Economic Theory
of Representative Government* (Chicago: Aldine, 1974); and Randall Bartlett, *Economic
Foundations of Political Power* (New York: Free Press, 1973).

## The Expanded Domain for Positive Analysis

In the four preceding sections of this paper, I have briefly summarized four main lines of inquiry or analysis that have combined to form the still-emerging subdiscipline of "public choice."[24] My purpose has not been that of describing the substantive content of these separate but closely related bodies of analysis; this would have required further treatment of the specific modern contributions in each area.[25] My purpose has been the more restricted one of sketching with a broad brush the separated strands of public choice theory in order to suggest how these have combined to effect the transformation in public finance theory during the decades after World War II.

Methodologically, the central element in this transformation is the dramatic expansion in the scope or domain for positive economic analysis. The subject matter of public finance has shifted outward; the economist now has before him many more questions than his counterpart faced a half-century ago. This expansion in the set of opportunities for applying the economists' tools, both conceptual and empirical, may be discussed in terms of specific categories.

### I. The effects of alternative fiscal institutions, existing and potential, on the behavior of persons and groups in the private economy

As I have noted earlier, this is the only domain for positive economic analysis in post-Marshallian public finance. The results of the public choice transformation have been to remove this still-important avenue for investigation from its place of exclusive dominance and to put it alongside other significant and equally legitimate applications of economic theory. This does not,

24. Because of space limits, I have not included a fifth line of analysis, that of locational public choice, or "voting with the feet," which has exerted a significant influence on public finance theory, especially as applied to local governments and to the interrelations among levels of government. The seminal paper which stimulated much of this analysis was that by Charles Tiebout, "The Pure Theory of Local Expenditure," *Journal of Political Economy*, 64 (October 1956), 416–24.

25. For a more extensive survey paper which does have this as its objective, see Dennis Mueller, "Public Choice: A Survey," *Journal of Economic Literature* (forthcoming).

of course, suggest that the theory of shifting and incidence, with expenditures added to taxes, has been reduced in absolute importance. The hard questions in incidence theory have not all been resolved, and these will, and should, continue to command the attention of economists.

## II. The effects of alternative fiscal institutions, existing and potential, on the behavior of persons and groups in the public economy, in public choice

In a relative sense, however, traditional incidence theory must be reduced in significance because other questions beckon. If the effects of a designated fiscal institution, say a specific excise tax, on the behavior of persons in private markets may be analyzed, what is to deter the intellectually curious and competent economist from examining the effects of this tax on the behavior of persons in "public markets"? If persons pay for public goods through such a tax, might they not be predicted to "purchase" differing quantities than they would do under alternative taxing schemes? Once such questions are raised, the need for answers along with the opportunities for research seem self-evident. An implicit assumption of invariance in fiscal choice over widely divergent institutional structures will simply not stand up to scrutiny.

The whole set of questions raised here stem from the publicness of the goods as these are demanded and consumed and as these are supplied through political or governmental institutions. Individuals do not pay "prices" for partitionable units of these goods. They pay "taxes," which are coercively imposed upon them through a political process, and this coercion is, in turn, made necessary by the "free-rider" motivation inherent in general collective action. Few persons will voluntarily pay taxes if they expect to receive the benefits of generally available public goods. But what quantity will persons, when they act collectively in public choice capacities—as voters, actual or potential, as members of pressure groups, as elected politicians, as government employees—choose to provide and to finance? This choice depends on the bridge that is constructed between the benefits or spending side of the account and the costs or taxing side. Differing fiscal institutions influence the weighing of accounts. What are the implications for budgetary size if taxes are spread more generally than benefits? And vice versa? Quite apart from the "true" distribution of tax shares and benefit shares, the "perceived" distribution matters. Fiscal perception becomes an important and relevant area for positive analysis. By necessity, "fiscal psychology" merges with fiscal economics. The research potential for positive analysis seems almost unlimited, and relatively little has been done.[26]

## III. The effects of alternative political or collective choice institutions, existing or potential, on the behavior of persons and groups in the public economy, in public choice

A closely related, but somewhat different agenda for positive analysis and one that is more central to what might be called "public choice theory," as such, involves the choice-making institutions themselves, as these may be predicted to generate fiscal outcomes. This is the public finance application of the theory of voting, summarized above.

What budget characteristics can be predicted to emerge under simple majority rule? What differences in size and composition might emerge when general-fund budgeting is compared with separate-purpose budgeting, with earmarked tax revenues? What differences in the willingness to issue public debt can be predicted when the effective voting franchise is expanded from local property owners to all members of the local electorate? What will be the comparative levels of public outlay on, say, education, when these services are provided through a set of monopoly school districts and through the market response to educational vouchers provided directly to families? What are the effects of school-district consolidation on budget size? What are the effects of franchising bureaucrats on the level and growth of public spending?

These are only a few of the questions that have been, and are being, asked by those who approach public finance from the general public choice paradigm. As these sample questions suggest, the domain for positive analysis here includes institutional analysis at a level where explanatory hypotheses

---

26. My own book *Public Finance in Democratic Process* (1967), op. cit., is largely a call for such research, along with a summary of some initial efforts, and the provision of a suggested research agenda.

are derived deductively from extract models, and also at a level where these hypotheses are tested empirically.[27]

## IV. ANALYSIS OF THE BEHAVIOR OF PERSONS AND GROUPS IN THE COLLECTIVE CONSTITUTIONAL CHOICE AMONG FISCAL INSTITUTIONS

This area for positive analysis is the direct public finance application of the theory of constitutions, previously summarized. As they may be historically observed, certain fiscal institutions take on quasi-permanent or constitutional characteristics. For example, basic changes in the tax code are discussed as if these are expected to endure over a sequence of periods. Neither taxes nor spending programs are chosen carte blanche at the onset of each budgetary period. Indeed one of the primary difficulties in reducing the explosive rate of increase in federal outlays in the 1970s is alleged to be the high proportion of uncontrollable spending in the budget. Once the quasi-permanence of institutions is recognized, the analysis of fiscal choices is modified. Differing criteria for choice must be invoked, criteria which may be less directly identified with self-interest of persons and groups. The models which are designed to derive hypotheses become different in this context.

I shall not attempt to suggest research opportunities that exist in this extension of positive analysis, one that is perhaps less fully developed than the others. My point of emphasis in this listing is to indicate that at least three areas of actual and potential positive analysis now exist over and beyond the severely limited post-Marshallian field of shifting and incidence.

## The Modified Domain for Normative Discussion

The domain for positive analysis in public finance has been greatly expanded. But what about the domain for normative discourse? So long as the economist proffers his advice as if some benevolent despot is listening to him, he may

27. Some of the early applications are contained in the separate studies included in the volume *Theory of Public Choice,* edited by James M. Buchanan and Robert Tollison (Ann Arbor: University of Michigan Press, 1972). For a textbook in public economics that consistently employs a fiscal choice paradigm, see Richard E. Wagner, *The Public Economy* (Chicago: Markham, 1973).

be much more willing to devote his efforts to persuasion based ultimately on his own personal, private scale of values, even if the argument is couched in quasi-philosophical terms. Despite Wicksell's clearly stated admonitions in 1896, this remains the setting for much of the normative discourse in public finance, even in 1975. If the public choice paradigm is accepted, however, the assumption of the benevolent despot cannot accompany normative advice, even at the subconscious level. The economist must recognize that collective outcomes emerge from a complex political process in which there are many participants. Almost by necessity, he will be less willing to devote time and effort to persuasion here, even though his own personal convictions about ideal outcomes may be equally as strong as in the despotic paradigm. It should come as no surprise, therefore, that modern public finance is less characterized by normative advice concerning the "best tax" program and more concerned about predicting the effects of alternatives.

The public choice paradigm does, however, allow for a parallel expansion in the normative realm of discourse. Once it is recognized that fiscal decisions emerge from a complex collective choice process, the economist may concentrate his normative advice on "improvements" in the process itself. He may, for example, say that direct taxation is preferred to indirect taxation, not because direct taxation is likely to be more or less progressive, but simply because direct taxation leads to a more rational choice calculus among voters and their representatives than indirect taxation. Similarly, he may suggest that withholding, as an institution, tends to reduce the rationality of the choice process because it tends to make the taxpayer somewhat less conscious of his costs. These are admittedly normative suggestions that emerge from a paradigm of the political world, one that embodies the democratic-individualistic standard that persons should get what they want so long as each person counts for one. This seems a more secure normative base than that which lays down criteria for choosing among separate persons and groups, in which one man must somehow count for more than another. These comments may, however, reflect my own personal normative biases and I shall not pursue them further in this survey.[28]

---

28. My methodological views are developed in several of my books, some of which have been noted. In my most recent book, I try to examine some of the problems that-

## An Example: The Provision and Financing of Social Security

I shall conclude this paper by a brief discussion of a single example, one that is of current importance. I shall demonstrate that the transformation in public finance produced by the public choice paradigm allows different and additional questions to be asked. In the process, policy discussion must be improved, independent of this or that economist's preferred set of norms.

Consider, first, the application of the post-Marshallian theory of shifting and incidence, along with the post-Pigovian norms for taxation. The social security system is financed by payroll taxes, and the shifting and incidence of these, both the employees' and the employers' shares, are proper subjects for inquiry. These taxes are, when viewed in isolation, "regressive," and this characteristic leads the post-Pigovian to denounce it on normative grounds.

Strictly speaking, this is all that public finance might have contributed to the policy discussion in the methodological mind-set prior to World War II. Straightforward extension of analysis to the other side of the budget, quite apart from the public choice extension, would have allowed positive analysis of the effects of public pension commitments on the rate of private saving in the economy.[29] Similarly, the effects of the public pensions on retirement behavior might be analyzed. The normative strictures arising from the regressivity of the payroll tax might also have been tempered somewhat by the extension of simple incidence analysis to the benefits side, where progressive elements are significant.

The public choice paradigm draws direct attention to the bridge between the tax and the spending side of the account. As noted earlier, this bridge is influenced by perception, and even within the confines of payroll-tax analysis, the effects of the structural features on voter-politician attitudes become important. In the first place, the public choice analyst would note the earmarking features of the financing; payroll taxes are earmarked for the social security trust fund account. This fact, in itself, strongly suggests that these

---

emerge in trying to define "an individual," including the preliminary distribution of rights. See my *The Limits of Liberty* (Chicago: University of Chicago Press, 1975).

29. See Martin Feldstein, "Social Security, Induced Retirement, and Aggregate Capital Accumulation," *Journal of Political Economy*, 82 (September/October, 1974), 905–26.

taxes are viewed differently from other general-fund revenue sources. Secondly, the public choice theorist would suggest that the withholding feature of the employee share makes payroll taxes less influential on behavior than orthodox incidence analysis might imply. More importantly, he would suggest that the employers' share of payroll taxes, even if ultimately paid by the workers, may not directly influence the attitude of workers. The suppliers of pensions, the authorities of the social security administration, may have been privately quite rational in their early arguments for making this employee-employer tax separation.

The public choice theorist would try to predict the effects of a proposed shift of the financing of social security, in whole or in part, from earmarked payroll taxes to the sources of general-fund financing, notably to personal and corporate income taxation. Rudimentary analysis would suggest that the direct linkage between tax and benefit sides would be severed by such a change, and that both sets of institutions would be subjected to wholly different political criteria. Could pensions be kept related to earnings (and contributions) under such a change? Could a means test for benefits be avoided? Even if the existing structure does not reflect the operation of genuine "insurance" principles, taxpayers-voters, and their political representatives, may acquiesce in its continuance so long as the intergeneration transfer process which the system seems to embody is plausibly acceptable. Young workers who enter the system may not worry when they are told that the present value of tax obligations exceeds manyfold the present value of future pension benefits provided that they continue to expect that future legislatures will insure a reasonable rate of return on their total contributions. Such continuing support may depend, however, on maintaining the separation of the system from the government's general fiscal account and also on insuring that severe limits are imposed on departures from earnings-related benefits.

The public choice economist, to the extent that he is willing to make suggestions for reform, seems more likely to suggest institutional adjustments designed to insure against the "political bankruptcy" of the system than he is to suggest that the payroll taxes be made more progressive. Whether the discussion takes the form of positive analysis or normative statement, the public choice economist looks on the fiscal process as a complex exchange, which must involve two sides of the account simultaneously. Those who pay the ultimate costs of public goods need not, of course, be identical with those who enjoy the ultimate benefits. But, in democracies, the intersection be-tween these two sets must be large, especially when the budgets are considered in composite totals and over a sequence of time periods. Regardless of political structure, the proportion of the community's membership that shares in genuine "fiscal surplus" is related inversely to the size and coercive power of the government's police force.

# Public Choice and Public Finance

In an earlier survey paper, "Public Finance and Public Choice,"[1] I traced the developments in American public finance in the years after World War II, and I demonstrated how the emergence of public-choice theory has been influential in affecting these developments. To an extent, my discussion in this paper must parallel that of my earlier effort. I shall, however, emphasize somewhat different points here. I shall first briefly discuss the public-finance origins of public-choice theory. I shall argue that public finance is, indeed, the parent discipline out of which the more generally applicable public-choice theory, now sometimes called the "economic theory of politics," emerged. Following this introductory look at the origins, my two main sections concentrate on the effects of public-choice theory on positive and normative public finance. I shall show how the introduction of public choice dramatically expands the scope for positive analysis and how it shifts the focus for normative understanding and evaluation of fiscal institutions. In the discussion of these two main sections, several public-finance applications of public-choice theory will be mentioned, along with what seem to me to be promising directions for research.

## The Public-Finance Origins of Public-Choice Theory

"Public finance" is about taxing and spending. Both of these are activities rather of governments or collectivities than of individuals as private persons.

From *What Should Economists Do?* (Indianapolis: Liberty Fund, 1979), 183–97. Reprinted by permission of the publisher.

This chapter was initially prepared for presentation at the Thirty-fourth Congress, International Institute of Public Finance, Hamburg, Germany, September 4–8, 1978.

1. *National Tax Journal* 28 (December 1975): 383–94.

This feature alone distinguishes public finance from the other traditional subdisciplines in economics, those which concentrate largely if not entirely on the activities of nongovernmental decision-makers, on the behavior of consumers, producers, entrepreneurs, workers, etc. Viewed in this basic perspective, it would seem neither surprising nor inappropriate that in the European tradition public finance should have occupied a position related more closely to law than to economic theory. There is no cause for wonderment, therefore, in the fact that the important precursors of modern public-choice theory are to be found among the works of those economists who were trained within the European public-finance tradition. In a summary definition, public choice is the analysis of political decision-making with the tools and methods of economics. For specific precursors, we look to the works of Continental scholars like Sax, Mazzola, Pantaleoni, de Viti de Marco, and, most important, Knut Wicksell, all of whom wrote before the end of the nineteenth century. The works of these scholars differed substantially one from another, but all shared a common objective, which was to bring the public economy within the analytical framework that had seemed so successful in explaining the working of the private economy. To do this, these scholars almost necessarily were forced to pay some attention to the political decision structure within which taxing and spending choices were made.

It is interesting to speculate on why these seminal works were so much neglected for half a century, especially in Britain and America, but also to an extent on the Continent itself, only to be "rediscovered" and extended in the decades since World War II, not only in public-choice theory strictly defined but also in the theory of public goods. The unproductive state of classical political economy, Benthamite utilitarianism, and idealist political philosophy—these may be introduced as partial causes for the British neglect of the Continental literature. But the mystery remains: Why were economists generally so slow in extending their basic tools of analysis to the behavior of persons who act in public-choice rather than in private-choice capacities?

It is not surprising that several scholars who made early contributions in public-choice theory came to the subdiscipline by way of public-finance theory, and, for the most part, reflected some influence of the Continental writings mentioned. Duncan Black and I both provide good examples. Black's first book was on the incidence of income taxes, strictly within the subject matter of traditional public finance. But Black read the Italian writers in public finance, and he also read Wicksell. From this background emerged his now classic work on the theory of committees, which, of course, has general applicability extending much beyond public-finance problems. In my own case, I was trained initially as a standard public-finance economist, but a chance reading of Wicksell, followed by an examination of the Italian works, turned my attention increasingly to analysis of political decision structures, to constitutional rules, and away from the set of problems in public-finance orthodoxy. I found myself less interested in the old question, How should tax shares be allocated? and at the same time more interested in the new question, How are tax shares allocated in a democracy? There seemed to me to be little value or purpose in normative discourse about optimal or efficient taxation until we achieved a better understanding of how political structures produce fiscal outcomes. In my case, I was not specifically motivated by the scientific superiority of this sort of positive analysis over the normative discussion of the traditional question.

## The Expanded Domain for Positive Analysis in Public Finance

The positive-normative dichotomy does, however, provide a useful way of classifying the impact of public choice on public finance. One of the most important effects has been that of expanding the domain for positive analysis in public finance. Public choice opens up new sets of questions to be asked; the subject matter of the discipline has been dramatically increased. It will be useful to be quite specific on this point. Several categories of positive analysis may be distinguished.

### 1. THE EFFECTS OF ALTERNATIVE FISCAL INSTITUTIONS, EXISTING AND POTENTIAL, ON THE BEHAVIOR OF PERSONS AND GROUPS IN THE PRIVATE ECONOMY, IN *PRIVATE CHOICE*

This category offered the *only* domain for positive economic analysis in post-Marshallian public finance in the English-language tradition. Even when broadly defined, this category includes essentially the theory of shifting and incidence, applied to taxes and to public outlays. As such, and as Marshall himself recognized and noted, the subject matter is applied price theory, which is precisely where it was located in American doctoral curricula before World War II. Comparative statistics offered a plausible predictive framework for analyzing the effects of alternative tax arrangements. Within limits, the economist could predict how particular taxes would affect the behavior of persons in the market economy, and through this could predict aggregate effects on such variables as relative prices, outputs, profits, and industry structures. This positive analysis also enabled the economist to derive empirically refutable propositions. Restricted to these questions, the public-finance economist had little reason to extend his inquiry to the purposes of taxation and public outlay.

Research in this traditional area of positive public finance has continued to be developed through more sophisticated analytical techniques in the decades since World War II. Work has moved beyond the Marshallian partial equilibrium framework into general equilibrium settings, including the extension of analysis from a closed to an open economy. The area of inquiry remains important; the hard questions in incidence theory have not all been resolved, and these will continue to command the attention of economists. What public choice has done is to remove this area of analysis from its position of exclusive dominance in positive public finance. Other significant and equally legitimate applications of positive economic analysis have been opened up, areas of inquiry that were foreclosed in the Marshallian regime.

## 2. The effects of alternative fiscal institutions, existing and potential, on the behavior of persons and groups in the public economy, *in public choice*

If the effects of a designated fiscal institution—say, a specific excise tax—on the behavior of persons in private markets may be analyzed, what is to deter the intellectually curious economist from examining the effects of this tax on the behavior of persons in "public markets"? If persons pay for public goods through such a tax, might they not be predicted to "purchase" or to "demand" differing quantities from those that they would demand under alternative financing schemes? Once such questions are raised, the need for answers, along with the opportunities for productive analytical and empirical research, seems self-evident. An implicit and unquestioned assumption to the effect that the level and the composition of budgetary outlays must remain invariant under widely differing tax arrangements surely cannot be either analytically or empirically legitimate.

The whole set of questions here stems from the "publicness" of the goods and services as these are demanded and consumed and as these are supplied through political or governmental institutions. Individuals do not pay "prices" for partitionable units of these goods. They pay "taxes," which are coercively imposed through a political process, and this coercion is, in turn, made necessary by the free-rider motivation inherent in general collective action. Few persons will voluntarily pay taxes if they expect to receive the benefits from generally available public goods. But what quantity will persons, when they act collectively in public-choice capacities—as voters, actual or potential, as government employees—choose to provide and to finance? This choice depends on the bridge that is constructed between the benefits or spending side of the fiscal account and the costs or taxing side. Differing fiscal arrangements, different tax rules, will influence the weighing of these accounts. What are the implications for budgetary levels if taxes are spread more generally than benefits? And vice versa? Will more or fewer public goods be generated under a regime of indirect taxation or under one of direct taxation? Will the number of tax sources influence the size of the budget? Fiscal perception becomes an important and relevant part of positive analysis in public finance. By necessity what has sometimes been called "fiscal psychology" merges with fiscal economics.

This area of inquiry remains perhaps less well developed than any other in positive public finance, and the potential for productive research seems almost unlimited.[2] But there is a significant methodological block to be surmounted here, one that warrants brief discussion. Tradition-bound economists react negatively to the notion that individuals may be influenced in their choice behavior by institutional structure. Economists are prone to extend their postulate of individual rationality to include the ability of persons

---

2. My own book *Public Finance in Democratic Process* (Chapel Hill: University of North Carolina Press, 1967) is largely a call for such research, along with a summary of some initial efforts.

to "see through" the institutional maze and to reject attempts to explain patterns of outcomes by resort to such things as "fiscal illusion," that institutions may be alleged to create. In my view, this attitude is based on a failure
to appreciate the differing analytical settings for market and for public choice.
In ordinary markets, the presumption that all persons choose rationally does
little to distort empirical reality because the rationality of only a few participants who can affect results at the appropriate margins of adjustment guarantees the equivalence of outcomes as between what we might call the full
rationality and the partial rationality models. The situation in "public markets" is not at all analogous. Solutions do not emerge as the outcome of the
mutual interactions of many participants who make private and independent decisions. Instead, public-market solutions are the result of the interactions of many persons who are necessarily involved in the unique public
or collective decision. The result reflects the choice of the median voter, or
his representative, who may or may not be fully rational in the sense that
informs traditional price theory. The presumption of fully informed rationality here is much more severely restrictive than in any other market setting.
Fiscal economists should not be deterred by methodological criticism that is
essentially without foundation from going ahead in research efforts to find
out just how differing fiscal structures might indeed affect the information
and perceptions of the relevant public choosers.

3. The effects of alternative political or
collective-choice institutions, existing or
potential, on the behavior of persons and
groups in the public economy, *in public choice*

This area of positive inquiry is related to, but quite different from, that discussed above, and this area is more central to what might be termed "public-
choice theory" in the narrow sense. Analysis here involves the working
properties of the choice-making institutions themselves, as these might be
predicted to generate taxing and spending results. Research here involves the
public-finance applications of the theory of voting.

What budget characteristics can be predicted to emerge under the operation of simple majority voting rules? What difference in the size and composition of outlays might emerge when general-fund budgeting is compared

with separate-purpose budgeting, with earmarked tax sources? What differences in the willingness to issue public debt can be predicted when the effective voting franchise is expanded from local property owners to all members of the electorate? What will be the comparative levels of public spending on, say, education, when these services are provided through a set of monopoly school districts and through the market response to educational vouchers supplied directly to families? What are the effects of school-district consolidation on budget size and quality of service? What are the effects of franchising bureaucrats on the level and the growth of public spending?

These are only a few of the questions that have been, and might be, asked by those who approach public finance from the generalized public-choice paradigm. As these sample questions suggest, the domain for positive analysis here includes institutional analysis at a level where explanatory hypotheses are derived deductively from abstract models, and also at a level where the implications of these hypotheses may be tested empirically.[3]

## The Modified Domain for Normative Public Finance

As the above discussion suggests, public choice has expanded the domain for positive analysis in public finance. But what about the domain for normative discourse? Here, too, the effects of public choice are both interesting and important. As I shall demonstrate, these effects serve, in one sense, to restore legitimacy to much of the age-old discussions in normative tax theory, a legitimacy that seems absent in the public-finance extension of the norms from theoretical welfare economics.

It will be useful to commence with the latter, which may be summarized under the rubric "theory of public goods." This development, like public-choice theory, has roots in the Continental tradition, but for my narrative summary it will be useful to start with Samuelson's seminal formulation in

---

3. Some of the early applications are contained in the separate papers included in the volume *Theory of Public Choice*, ed. James M. Buchanan and Robert Tollison (Ann Arbor: University of Michigan Press, 1972). For a textbook that employs a fiscal-choice paradigm, see Richard E. Wagner, *The Public Economy* (Chicago: Markham, 1973).

1954.[4] He posed the normative question, What are the necessary conditions for efficiency that must be satisfied in the public economy? Having defined these conditions in aggregative terms, Samuelson turned to a "social welfare function" to determine the final distribution of welfare among persons net of the public-goods production and subsequent benefits. There is no scope for normative tax theory, as such, in this basic Samuelson model.

Less general norms for the marginal imputation of tax shares are found in the earlier model developed by Erik Lindahl, norms which also meet the Samuelson allocative requirements. The concept of Lindahl equilibrium in the public economy has emerged to command the attention of general equilibrium theorists in the last decade, and notably those theorists who are primarily interested in establishing existence proofs and in assessing stability properties of solutions. Given an initial set of endowments, and extending the Lindahl imputation of marginal tax shares over inframarginal ranges for individual quantity evaluation, the allocation of tax payments among persons becomes unique in the Lindahl solution. Once this allocation is formally defined, there is once again no scope for normative tax theory in terms of relative evaluations of traditional tax instruments.

The traditional questions in normative tax theory have, however, witnessed something of a modern revival, beyond the limits of either general equilibrium welfare theory or public-choice theory. I refer here to the work in "optimal taxation," which has come to occupy the attention of several competent young practitioners in public finance during the 1970s. In a very general sense, this work examines the old questions of normative public finance with the sophisticated tools of modern mathematical economics. Those who have worked in this area have been willing to look at the allocation of tax shares independent of globally efficient solutions to the fiscal process; they have been ready to ignore the efficiency norms derivative from the theory of public goods. Hence, despite its sophistication in technique, "optimal tax theory" is something of a methodological throwback to the pre-Wicksellian framework of Anglo-American public finance.

So much for a hurried, and necessarily incomplete, discussion of normative public finance as it stands today, independent from and outside the nor-

---

4. Paul A. Samuelson, "The Pure Theory of Public Expenditure," *Review of Economics and Statistics* 36 (November 1954): 387–89.

mative domain that is offered in the context of the public-choice paradigm. Let me now turn to the question as to how public-choice theory has changed and can change the whole setting for normative analysis in public finance.

My answer claims a great deal for public choice, but I think that its potential for productive normative work can scarcely be overly estimated. Properly introduced and interpreted, the public-choice paradigm enables us to combine the logical realism of Wicksell with the obvious political relevance of some of the traditional questions that normative tax theory has addressed.

In any community in which the government is not wholly divorced from the citizenry, the fiscal process must logically be modeled as a two-sided exchange. Taxes are payments made for benefits received. But how is it possible to envisage the collective-choice process, in the context of observed political structures, as a positive-sum game? How can we model the participation by individuals in the complex network out of which taxing and spending results finally emerge?

Here we must return directly to Wicksell, to look at his basic insights along with his normative arguments. Wicksell was interested in reform, and he recognized the essential absurdity of proffering normative advice on the assumption that some benevolent despot would listen. Wicksell stressed that fiscal results emerge from political institutions, and that if reform was to be introduced, the institutional structure must be modified. He recognized, further, that there was some substitutability between the institutions for making political choices and those for taxing and spending. As we know, he aimed most of his normative argument at political structure. He was quite willing to relax many of the rigidities of tax rules in exchange for efficiency-increasing changes in political decision rules.

In one sense, we may say that the normative public-finance implications of public-choice theory involve the other half of this Wicksellian duality. In the context of established political institutions, how can fiscal institutions be modified so as to produce more acceptable results? How can the taxing and spending *process* be improved? This is the normative issue to be addressed, as opposed to the more direct, but also empty, issue concerning specific allocations of outlays and of tax shares.

Empirically, we observe individuals, in their public-choice capacities as voters, politicians, bureaucrats, choosing, not among tax-share allocations in each period, but among alternative tax institutions that, as they operate, will produce tax-share distributions as a result. Legislatures choose among alternative financing instruments—among such instruments as personal income taxation, progressive or proportional in rates, corporate or company taxation, turnover taxation, commodity taxation, wealth taxation, etc. In real-world settings, tax arrangements or rules, once these are settled, are expected to remain in place for a long succession of budgetary periods, in each one of which outlay allocations are made. The choice among tax institutions is, properly considered, analogous to the choice among rules, or to *constitutional* choice.

Once we begin to think of the choice among tax arrangements in constitutional terms, however, we escape the zero-sum implications that tax-share imputation in any single budgetary period necessarily invokes. It becomes conceptually possible to think about tax-sharing arrangements, which could never be accepted by all persons in the community in a single-period context, as commanding consensus at some prior constitutional stage of deliberation and argument. It becomes possible to establish criteria for potential agreement on tax institutions, including some of those that we have historically observed, in a constitutional or contractual setting. At least ideally, it is now possible to derive norms for the fiscal structure that are internal to the utility functions of the members of the community and not externally drawn from ethical principles.

I am not suggesting that the constitutional approach which the public-choice paradigm implies necessarily removes all elements of interpersonal or intergroup conflict from tax-share allocation. But the analysis does allow departure from the pure conflict model that orthodox normative theory must introduce. The question becomes, What is the structure of taxation upon which individuals might agree at some constitutional stage, in the knowledge that once implemented this structure is to remain in force over a succession of periods? To establish some sort of contractual agreement here, the quasi-permanency of the institutions is necessary, since only in this way can the necessary uncertainty be introduced regarding the identity of individual economic status. In the limit, the potential taxpayer-beneficiary, asked to participate in the constitutional selection process, is behind a complete veil of ignorance as regards his own future position.[5]

5. In our book *The Calculus of Consent* (Ann Arbor: University of Michigan Press, 1962), Gordon Tullock and I used the quasi-permanency of constitutional rules as a

I shall not try here to elaborate on this constitutional approach to normative public-finance theory. I hope that my cursory comments have been able to suggest that exciting work remains to be done. I am currently working on what we call the "tax constitution," or, more broadly, the "fiscal constitution," for a community under specific assumptions about the workings of the political process. This research has already yielded results that turn much of the traditional normative theory on its head. I shall not summarize this research here. But I should note only that it is necessary to call on the positive analysis from each of the three separate areas of inquiry listed above before any attempt is made to derive plausibly acceptable norms for fiscal reform. We must know or at least make some predictions about who bears the burden of taxes. We must know or at least make some predictions about how various taxes affect public as well as private choices. We must know or at least make some predictions about how political processes work. Only then can we even begin to ask questions about justice in taxation, the ultimate normative issue. Wicksell called his treatise a new principle for justice in taxation. Public-choice theory can, following his lead, help in the elaboration of the Wicksellian precepts.

---

means of introducing the uncertainty necessary to produce agreement on rules. In his more general, and more explicitly normative, discussion of principles of justice, John Rawls invokes the veil of ignorance which all persons face in the original position, before basic social institutions are settled (Rawls, *A Theory of Justice* [Cambridge, Mass.: Harvard University Press, 1971]).

# Democratic Values in Taxation

## Justice and Democracy

There are several ways of approaching the subject matter suggested by the title of this chapter. One projected focus of attention is on the possible inconsistency between ethically derived criteria for imposing taxes and the political process through which taxes must be levied and collected. This approach immediately confronts the philosopher-economist with the question that he often tries to escape or to evade. Many economists, along with other social scientists and social philosophers, enjoy playing God, by which I mean laying out in detail their own private versions of the "good society" without being required to suggest ways and means of implementing their precepts or even to defend the consistency of these precepts with democratic political processes.

Once the question of implementation through democratic politics is raised, however, the possible contradiction between two sets of values becomes apparent. Should we continue to adhere to what we might call "democratic values," even if these values, when institutionally represented, generate results that we do not acknowledge to be "just"? Or do we go along with Plato and drop democracy as a political process if it fails to generate the "just society" that our ethical precepts dictate?

My own position on these matters is at least partially familiar. I think that as economists we spend far too much time worrying about what is "justice" in taxation and far too little time trying to predict the results that will emerge

From *Freedom in Constitutional Contract: Perspectives of a Political Economist* (College Station: Texas A&M University Press, 1977), 243–53. Reprinted by permission of the publisher.

from the political process that we observe to be operating, one which may, in many respects, be labeled as "democratic." My plea is for more positive analysis of taxes and tax institutions, of the taxing process, and for less espousal of personal, private norms for taxes and taxation. In an indirect sense, my position might be interpreted as one that places democratic values above those of "justice" or "equity," putting me in the anti-Plato group. I am willing to accept this classification and, if needs be, to defend the primary role of democratic values in my own scheme of things, provided, of course, that you allow me to use my own definitions.

In my view, democratic values must be founded on the basic Kantian notion that individual human beings are the ultimate ethical units, that persons are to be treated strictly as ends and never as means, and that there are no transcendental, suprapersonal norms. From this idea it follows as a natural corollary that each person counts for one and only one in the determination of collective constraints that are to be imposed on all. This conception of political equality is central to any meaningful definition or formulation of democratic values, but in and of itself it scarcely insures against the coercive treatment of man by man, treatment that could remove all content from such values. Political equality, in its pure form, may mean little more than a right of franchise of all persons in a plebiscitary voting process which is unlimited in range. In such a case democratic values may be of small note to the persons or groups who are subjected to possible majority oppression through the abrogation of rights to life and property. The equal right to the voting privilege, even as an ideal, must surely be complemented by other precepts, which must also find their way into institutional reality. Equality before the law is a necessary condition that must be observed, regardless of how, by whom, and through what process law is made or changed. The majority coalition that imposes its will on the minority must do so within the strict constraints of this precept. The income tax law, for example, cannot be applied differentially to Democrats and Republicans, no matter how much the self-serving bureaucrats of the IRS might want that to be the case. They cannot endorse Lyndon Johnson's actual use of the IRS against Goldwaterites in 1964 while objecting strenuously to Nixon's attempts to use the IRS in 1972. To the extent that observed governmental processes are not bounded by the precept of equality before the law, we have departed from democratic values.

## Norms for Taxation

So far, so good. But we must turn more specifically to issues of taxation. Taxes are and must be coercive instruments of the state; they require that persons transfer to the state valued resources or purchasing power. Most of us, save for a few anarchists, recognize the need for the state to exist and also recognize that there are goods and services which can best be provided by the government. Such goods and services must also be financed, and this financing requires taxation in one form or another. Some persons or groups in the economy must give up private command over resources, over values, if the state is to secure the ability to provide public goods and services. But what rules, what precepts, must be followed if the levy of taxes is to satisfy the criterion of equality before the law?

There is no answer to this question that suggests a unique principle for tax sharing. At one level of consideration, only equal-per-head taxes would seem to qualify. At another level, proportional taxes on income or wealth might plausibly be accepted as fulfilling the equality requirement. But what about progressive taxes? The original constitutional requirement for uniformity in taxation was held by successive courts to prohibit the imposition of progressive taxes, and this requirement was written, and interpreted, in the context of the principle of legal equality. As we know, the Constitution was explicitly amended to allow the use of progressive income taxes. But this fact does not answer the philosophical question. Is tax progression, in itself, a departure from "equality before the law," or can such taxation be reasonably interpreted as falling within the constraints of that fundamental precept?

We cannot really begin to answer this basic question until we bring in the public expenditure side of the ledger, until we recognize explicitly that there are benefits to be enjoyed from governmental provision of goods and services, benefits that are of value to the same persons who are taxpayers. Once we look at this side of the fiscal account, however, the applicability of the principle of legal equality to the tax side is called into question. It seems simple enough to talk about taxes in legal terms provided that we forget about public expenditure benefits. If, for example, taxes should in fact represent deadweight losses for the whole economy—if they should be required, let us say, to finance reparations to a foreign country—the simplistic legal criterion of equality might be tolerable. But taxes do not finance reparations payments; they finance public or governmental outlays, and these outlays increase individual utilities. Taxes become a necessary part of a genuine "fiscal exchange," and they become, in one real sense, the public-sector equivalent of private-sector prices.

## Taxes and Prices

This analogy between taxes and prices warrants further discussion. What does legal equality mean with respect to prices? This question becomes relevant only under the institutional absence of competition, for example, in the pricing policy of public utilities. But it seems clear that a regulated monopoly would violate this basic legal principle if, say, electric power should be sold to me at a lower rate per kilowatt hour than the rate charged to my neighbor across the street. Nondiscrimination in prices for the same commodity is surely required to satisfy the criteria for legal equality. If this line of reasoning is extended directly to the provision of public goods and services, what is implied about taxes? All persons in the sharing group receive the same quantity of public goods, and this equivalence in consumption is the dominating characteristic for "public goods" in the quasi-technical meaning given to this term. The national defense is equally available to each one of us, as is the whole legal system. Since all receive the same quantity of a public good, would not legal equality require that each person pay the same price, in this case a tax price? Something is amiss here, however, since the equality of consumption need not emerge from individual choices. In the private sector individuals adjust quantities of consumption to uniform and nondiscriminatory prices. But in the public sector, either technologically or institutionally, the equal quantities are not chosen by persons. At a fixed and uniform tax price, different persons would optimally prefer widely differing quantities, but this sort of adjustment is precluded. Equality of tax prices among persons will not, therefore, insure the presence of individual adjustment equilibrium, as is the case in the nondiscriminatory pricing of private goods.

There is no need to elaborate the technical details here, but the discussion is perhaps sufficient to suggest some of the difficulties that arise when we try to put meaningful economic content into simplistic legal norms. Once we abandon uniformity of tax prices among persons, however, how are we to confine the range of tax-price variations or differences? What ranges are appropriate under the plausible limits defined by "democratic values"? Let me return to the two-person setting and consider the comparative tax treatment of me and my neighbor across the street. We secure the same quantity of police services from our municipal government, in this case the town of Blacksburg, Virginia. What set of tax structures will satisfy the criterion of legal equality? If I place a higher value on police services than my neighbor does, it seems reasonable that I should pay more for the same quantity than he does. To tax him more highly than me would seem out of bounds on almost any criterion of reasonableness. Therefore, as long as the basis for taxation offers a good proxy for individual evaluations of the public goods and services offered, serious violation of legal precepts might be kept within broadly acceptable limits. If my property commands a higher market value than that of my neighbor, the assessment of taxes on the basis of property values may correspond roughly to relative evaluations. But how much higher should my taxes be? There seems to be nothing sacrosanct about the rule of proportionality here, and rate structures that are progressive, or even regressive, might be equally tolerated. At base, the ideal here would emerge only from an empirical estimate of relative evaluations for publicly provided services and from the empirical relationships between these and the tax bases under consideration.

How far have we gotten? What sort of taxes can be accepted and what sort ruled out from the somewhat abstract perspective developed? For general-purpose public goods and services, and especially for such services as external and internal defense, the legal system, and the like, the familiar bases for taxation fare reasonably well under our appraisal. Individual evaluations on such services are presumably related directly to individual wealth and incomes. Hence, taxing persons on the basis of these objectively measurable proxies may be justified on broad grounds of legal equality. But what about special-purpose government services? Is there any justification at all in legal principle for the use of general tax revenues, collected from levies based on proxies for evaluations of general-benefit services, to finance the provision of goods and services for special groups, regardless of the means of classification?

## Fiscal Asymmetry

Somewhat surprisingly, we find that the application of legal principle to the fiscal structure has been asymmetrical. Uniformity or nondiscrimination in the levy of taxes has been embodied in "the law" as it has developed, but there has been no comparable extension to the expenditure side of the fiscal account. Legally, constitutionally, legislatures are able to provide benefits of public goods to special groups and to finance those benefits from general taxes. Congress has been notorious in its willingness to spend billions on pork-barrel projects. The Arkansas River navigation project is the most flagrant recent example, but regional benefit legislation has been the order of the day for decades. And special benefits for specific occupational and functional groups in the economy are characteristic features of the American fiscal landscape. If the legal principle of equality of treatment is to be applied at all in fiscal matters, symmetry between the tax side and the spending side must be present. Special-benefit and discriminatory spending has no more place in a system reflecting democratic values than does discriminatory taxation.

We have at least come part of the way in our attempt to determine the limits on the fiscal structure that are suggested by consistent adherence to democratic values, as we have interpreted them. The fiscal reforms that would be required to incorporate these limits would be dramatic, but they would not, it seems to me, present issues of conflict with precepts for fiscal "justice." In fact, quite the opposite seems to be the case. The introduction of symmetry between the two sides of the fiscal account should be fully consistent with almost any conception of fiscal justice. But the major issues posed by this subject matter remain unresolved.

Let us suppose that all taxes are levied in a nondiscriminatory fashion on bases such as personal incomes and wealth that do, in fact, serve as reasonable proxies for individual evaluations of general-benefit government goods and services. Suppose further that tax revenues are devoted exclusively to the financing of just such general-benefit goods and services. Within broad limits, as we have suggested, the precepts of legal equality and nondiscrimination would seem to be met.

## Transfers

But there seems to be no place in such a fiscal structure for *transfers* of income and wealth among different social and economic groups, whether these transfers be direct or indirect. And when discussions introduce the notion of justice in taxation, these transfers are what the talk is about. Many observers hold that the fiscal system should be used to achieve distributional objectives, quite apart from the provision and financing of public goods and services. In this view, taxes should be levied with the purpose of redressing prevailing differences in incomes and wealth among persons and families in the economy. Great confusion in discussion often arises because the tax structure is simultaneously conceived as serving two separate social functions.

What can be said about the possible incorporation of democratic values in a fiscal structure that is designed primarily to implement real income and wealth transfers? Almost by definition, a fiscal transfer system must be discriminatory in effect. If transfers take place, some persons and groups must be net losers and other groups net gainers. The fiscal exchange paradigm used earlier in the discussion of governmental provision of real goods and services is inapplicable here. Once this fact is recognized, how can we begin to reconcile overt fiscal transfers with any semblance of legal equality? I do not think that reconciliation is possible within the ordinary understanding of democratic polity. To the extent that the fiscal structure comes to be conceived as a transfer mechanism, legal equality must be deliberately sacrificed.

There are several points that may be made here. Once any precept of legal equality is dropped, and once the fiscal system is thought by citizens and by politicians to be a transfer mechanism, how can transfers be restricted to those that might be deemed ethically desirable? It is precisely at this point that the workings of unbounded democratic politics may violate all precepts of fiscal justice. If constitutional constraints are dropped, what is to prevent self-interested political entrepreneurs from carrying fiscal measures far beyond those which might be suggested by ethical criteria, or, more likely, from using the fiscal system to implement transfers that bear little or no relationship to the objectives that might be dictated by norms of equity or of justice? Should social scientists and social philosophers really be surprised when their idealized schemes for income transfers to the demonstrably poor are converted by the legislating process into schemes which produce benefits for members of dominant political coalitions while the poor secure assistance largely as a by-product? If the whole fiscal structure, taxes and benefits alike, comes to be viewed as the instrument through which zero-sum income and wealth transfers can be produced, simplistic economic theory should tell us that attempts will be made to use this instrument to secure political profits. A public-choice approach to politics allows us to make the positive prediction that unconstrained democratic process will generate results that satisfy neither the precepts for fiscal justice nor those which can be meaningfully interpreted as incorporating democratic values.

Is there any way to resolve the dilemma? We can hardly expect political decision makers to become enlightened ethical leaders and, in so doing, to insure their own replacement by others more in tune with constituency preferences. And despite the continuing mythology about liberal education's overriding social values, it is surely naïve to expect that individual citizens, privately or in groups, will voluntarily forego the political and economic profit opportunities that modern fiscal systems appear to offer them.

## Constitutional Rules

I think that the dilemma posed can be resolved, at least at the level of conceptual discussion, although practical steps toward resolution may be extremely difficult. Resolution must be based on the introduction of a sharp categorical distinction between what I call the *constitutional* level of collective decision making and the *operational* level. To summarize before I discuss it in detail, "justice," as an attribute of a fiscal structure, must be implemented exclusively at the constitutional level, when institutions that also reflect meaningful democratic values are incorporated into the rules for operational political action. Fiscal institutions that will insure some net redistribution can be constitutionally selected, while at the same time effective constraints can be placed on the range of action taken operationally by dominant political coalitions. Day-to-day exploitation of the fiscal process to seek income and wealth transfers must be abandoned in favor of quasi-permanent and built-in features of the structure which will implement transfers while at the same time restricting legislative authority.

The approach that I take, and have taken, to these matters is essentially contractarian, in the social-contract meaning of this term. Basic decisions on the structural institutions of society, including the limits on governments, must be made in a setting in which, to the maximum possible extent, the identifiable interests of persons and groups are not known. At this genuine constitutional level persons must try to select and to agree upon preferred "rules of the game," and they must use criteria of fairness and efficiency in the selection and evaluation process. The affinity between my general position and that of John Rawls has been discussed in chapter 9.

For purposes of discussing fiscal structure, the Buchanan and Rawls formulations are interchangeable. The question concerns the characteristics of the fiscal structure that would emerge from such genuine constitutional deliberation and agreement. More specifically, how much income and wealth transfer would be built into the structure? As Tullock and I argued in *The Calculus of Consent: Logical Foundations of Constitutional Democracy,* and as Rawls also argues, fiscal transfers would predictably be embodied in the constitutional structure. I think that Rawls, in his book as distinguished from his early papers, made a serious error when he tried to be overly specific and limit himself to predicting the emergence of his so-called difference principle, or maximin principle in the terminology of game theory. It seems to me that any of several institutions of redistribution might emerge from genuine constitutional process, and we should not, it seems to me, be particularly concerned about the uniqueness of our conceptual solution. The important point is not that of describing the specific characteristics of the institutions that would emerge, but that of emphasizing the characteristics of the *process* through which these institutions are chosen—the constitutional process. By this process I refer to the deliberate act of selecting quasi-permanent rules and institutions within which day-to-day operational choices, both private and public, are to be made and implemented. The important practical corollary of this constitutional approach is the implication that once chosen, the fiscal structure should not be subject to year-to-year manipulation and change by shifting coalitions in democratic legislative assemblies. A structure of progressive income taxation, extending over both negative and positive rate ranges, might well be consistent with constitutional process, as here defined, but it must be conceived to be, by the public and politicians alike, a quasi-permanent feature of the social setting and not subject to discussion in terms of current operationally determined economic and social policy. Nothing could do more toward promoting nonconstitutional attitudes than continued readjustment of basic income tax rates. Such readjustment surely furthers the view that the political process, as it operates, is after all little more than a complex profit-and-loss system.

In conclusion, a basic structure of rate progression in taxes on incomes and wealth might be plausibly defended on genuine constitutional contractarian grounds. This structure may guarantee some fiscal readjustments in net economic differences between persons in the economy. To this structure there may be appended constraints on the use of tax instruments for financing collective goods and services, constraints that should rule out arbitrary discrimination both in taxation and in the distribution of public goods benefits. Political majorities must be placed within effective constitutional limits, both with respect to the basic institutions of the fiscal system and to the degree of arbitrary discrimination that is allowable. In this conceptual manner "fiscal justice as fairness," to use Rawlsian terminology, may be fully compatible with genuinely meaningful "democratic values."

Honesty forces me to acknowledge, however, that reconciliation in conception is a far different thing from reconciliation in actuality. Anyone who observes American political process today cannot fail to sense the continuing and perhaps accelerating erosion of what I have called the "constitutional attitude" on the part of our legislators, our courts, and, sadly, our legal philosophers. Until we get our thinking straight at the fundamental and even elementary philosophical level, we can hardly criticize working politicians and judges to do anything except carry forward the prevailing attitudes. Honestly described, these attitudes seem to be that, effectively, the government is not really bounded except by the expediently derived gut feelings of the accidentally appointed Supreme Court, which we have allowed to become our supreme legislative authority in a perversion of its historic role. "Constitutional anarchy" instead of "constitutional order" seems characteristic of our time. In my view, "democratic values" have long since been distorted out of all meaning, and anything that might be labeled as "fiscal justice" seems likely to emerge only as a by-product of an ongoing game of political profit and loss.

# Tax Reform as Political Choice

Public choice theory explains and interprets politics as the interaction between constituents and agents seeking to advance or to express their own interests. Applied to an observed political event like the 1986 tax reform legislation, any such analysis must identify the effects on separate interests and make some presumption concerning the perception of these effects. The linkage between assigning gains and losses from the 1986 tax changes and explaining these changes depends critically on the model of political choice. Political reality presumably embodies some mix of models of consensus, conflict, and agents' discretion. These three models are examined separately, with features from each retaining some explanatory value.

## A Consensual Calculus: All Taxpayers Secure Utility Gains

The salient features of the 1986 tax legislation are rate reduction and base-broadening for both individual and corporate taxpayers. The overall revenue-neutrality constraint implies that the trade-off or exchange between lower rates and a broader tax base occurs within the inclusive set of taxpaying units; there is no direct cross-budget "exchange" with expenditure program beneficiaries. Within aggregate revenue neutrality, there may be gainers and losers in terms of estimated tax payments before and after the change. Although the gains of low-income earners whose income tax liabilities are

From *Journal of Economic Perspectives* 1 (Summer 1987): 29–35. Reprinted by permission of the publisher.

I appreciate comments from my colleagues Jennifer Roback, Robert Tollison, and Viktor Vanberg.

eliminated by the reform are exaggerated in the political rhetoric due to the neglect of how increased corporate taxes affect them, these low-income earners are clearly net gainers. The existence of pecuniary gainers implies the existence of offsetting pecuniary losers, but need not suggest the existence of utility losses on the part of any taxpayers. *All* taxpayers may possibly secure utility gains. This consensus model is examined first since it implies that the reform legislation may have secured broad support by taxpayers.[1]

Consider an individual who is fully informed as to the incidence and effects of taxation and can assign to himself an accurately estimated share in overall tax liability. This taxpayer may be assumed to be in a position of full equilibrium, before the reform. His after-tax risk-adjusted rate of return is equalized between taxable and nontaxable earning or investment opportunities.[2] The rate of return on nontaxable opportunities is lower than the pretax rate of return on the taxable opportunity by the rate of tax. The taxpayer's resources are not efficiently allocated; he suffers the excess burden of altered earning and investment choices in addition to the direct burden of tax payments.

The change in tax law reduces the rate of tax on taxable opportunities and, at the same time, makes earnings from previously untaxed opportunities fully taxable. This exchange will, under plausible values for response elasticities, make possible a post-reform equilibrium in which tax payments are the same as before, but in which the taxpayer's resources are allocated more efficiently. In this setting of individual revenue neutrality, the taxpayer's excess burden is reduced; the taxpayer enjoys net utility gains while paying the same amount.

If individual revenue neutrality is possible, however, there must also exist some range over which the taxpayer attains equilibrium after the reform

---

1. For a more formal presentation of the consensus model, see James Buchanan and Geoffrey Brennan, "Tax Reform without Tears," in *The Economics of Taxation*, ed. Henry Aaron and Michael Boskin (Washington: The Brookings Institution, 1980), 33–54.

2. The nontaxable opportunities may be those that are legally exempted or those that arise in the underground economy. Analytically, these two categories are identical. For expositional simplicity, I limit discussion to adjustment among income sources, which presumes that taxes are levied on sources rather than uses of income and that the base-broadening involved in the change consists in making previously nontaxable sources taxable. The analysis is, of course, identical in the case of income uses, whether as a base of tax, or as a means through which, pre-1986, tax liabilities were reduced.

with both increased payments and increased utility. The increased revenue collected from taxpayers in this position may be available to allow for a class of taxpayers who secure net pecuniary gains from the reform through lowered tax payments. The latter will, of course, also enjoy utility gains. In this setting, all taxpayers support structural shifts in the tax structure along the general lines of the 1986 changes.

The possible applicability of this consensus model to the changes in personal income taxation may seem clear, while extending it to changes in corporate taxation may appear more questionable. Note, however, that taxpaying units in both sectors experience a rate-reducing, base-broadening "exchange." Corporations, like individuals, will be led to allocate resources more efficiently. Despite the substantial increase in tax payments projected for the corporate sector, the rate of return on investment need not be reduced after 1986 if the offsetting gains in allocative efficiency are sufficiently large.

Corporations do not vote, but the model of political consensus must allow some method of translating corporate tax liabilities into individual gains and losses. If individual taxpayers are presumed to be unable to trace out the incidence and effects of alternative corporate tax structures, the observed support for the 1986 tax law changes may have reflected a failure to make the translation from corporate to individual tax accounts. This possibility raises the interesting issue, however, of whether perceived or "genuine" fiscal interests should be relevant for evaluating tax reform.

## Nonconsensus: Utility Gainers vs. Utility Losers

The consensus result sketched out in the previous section emerges, of course, only with a limited set of rate-reducing, base-broadening proposals, and the 1986 changes may or may not fall within such a set. For some taxpayers, the rate reductions do not fully offset the greater revenue raised by broadening the tax base. Despite the reductions in their excess burden, they will suffer net utility losses. These taxpayers would have opposed the change, provided only that they acted on the basis of an informed consideration of their own interests. In contrast, the reform would have been supported by those who secure reductions in payments, along with utility increases, and by those who secure utility gains even when making higher tax payments.

In this setting, the rate-reducing, base-broadening tax reform separates taxpayers into three distinct groups, those who will experience: (1) lowered tax payments and increased utilities; (2) increased tax payments and unchanged or increased utilities; (3) increased tax payments and reduced utilities. These three sets of taxpayers may be considered to correspond to differences in their capacity to take advantage of nontaxable income-earning or income-using opportunities under the pre-reform tax code. Persons in Group 1 may have been unable to shift resources into nontaxed uses; members of this group lose nothing from base-broadening and gain from the rate reduction. Persons in Groups 2 and 3 pay more from the broadening of tax base, but will have a post-reform incentive to allocate resources under their control more efficiently. Persons in both Groups 2 and 3 will secure reductions in excess burden, but only those in Group 2 will benefit enough to offset the higher tax payments from base-broadening.

In a majoritarian political setting, persons in Group 2 may find themselves in the median position. Taxpayers in Group 1 support any rate reduction; taxpayers in Group 3 oppose any base-broadening. Taxpayers in Group 2 insure that the rate reductions are sufficiently large to maintain or increase their utilities. Any proposal to reduce tax rates by a smaller amount, along with the same broadening of base, might have been opposed by taxpayers in Group 2. The widely observed difficulties in generating political support for any post-reform maximum rate of personal income tax much beyond the 30 percent range may well have reflected some such calculus, at least indirectly.

As with the consensus model, the observed behavior of taxpayers in supporting the 1986 reform may not have embodied unbiased information concerning the incidence, effects, and assignment of post-reform taxes. To the extent that people fail to sense themselves as bearing part of the burden of corporate taxation, whether as owners of capital assets or as consumers of final products, their behavior might suggest that they perceive themselves as members of Group 1 or 2, whereas their genuine interests might place them in Group 3.

*Post-1986 predictions.* The 1986 changes allow the same aggregate revenue to be collected at a smaller efficiency loss, at least for a majority of taxpaying constituents. The benefits from federal spending are now available at a reduced opportunity cost. This shift in the terms of "fiscal trade" may generate subsequent changes in both taxing and spending levels.

If political pressures for increased spending were roughly matched by those for reduced taxation under the pre-reform tax structure, then the 1986 legislation can be interpreted as displacing the budgetary equilibrium with predictable consequences. The disequilibrium will be corrected by expansion in spending and tax rates (under the post-reform tax structure) and a new budgetary equilibrium will be attained with a somewhat larger budget.

By contrast, if the 1986 legislation was itself a response to an emerging political disequilibrium, no such prediction can be made. If under the pre-reform tax regime pressures for tax reduction were becoming relatively more effective than pressures for expanded spending, and if further recourse to nontax sources for financing (such as public debt and inflation) was not available, the tax structure changes become the instrument for correcting the political disequilibrium without cutting spending. In this scenario, the 1986 fiscal action was equilibrating rather than disequilibrating, and political efforts to increase budgetary expenditures in the next few years should not be successful.

## The Interests of Political Agents

The preceding analysis has assumed that taxing choices reflect constituency interests and that political agents seeking to further interests of their own exert no independent influence. But any public choice interpretation with plausible claim to generality must allow some consideration of these agents. Their self-interests may differ very substantially from the interests of constituents, and electoral control instruments may be too crude to bring the two sets of interests into correspondence. Within broad threshold constraints, those empowered to take political action may exercise discretionary authority, with respect to taxation or anything else.

Political agents seek to maximize their rents, subject to the general legal constraints against corruption, and to the temporal and survival constraints imposed by the electoral and institutional structure. The magnitude of rents will be positively related to the size of public outlay, and to the frequency of shifts in the pattern of this outlay and the pattern of financing. Budgets will be larger than they would be in an ideally constrained "democratic" decision procedure, and the rules for budgetary allocation and for the distribution of tax shares will be modified more often.

If the pre-reform political equilibrium embodied an excess spending bias because of the influence of agents' interests, agents would have had a related interest in the rate-reducing, base-broadening enterprise of 1986. Whereas political agents might have preferred base-broadening alone, with the concomitant revenue and spending enhancement, they may have interpreted the "exchange" as a necessary way station toward revenue enhancement in a post-reform budgetary equilibration. This interpretation of the events of 1986 suggests that the reform exercise may have been promoted by political entrepreneurship of self-interested agents who exploited the temporary coincidence between their own and general constituency interests. Some of the discussion that followed the passage of the legislation supports this argument.

If political agents are presumed to be totally unconstrained by electoral constituency feedback, the pre-reform tax structure should have approached its revenue-maximizing limits; that is, higher tax rates would lead people to respond by choosing less efficient but less taxed investment and earnings options, with little revenue gain. Given the availability of nontaxable opportunities, this model predicts that pre-reform rates would place some classes of taxpayers even beyond maximum revenue limits. The 1986 revenue-neutral trade-off served to relocate all classes of taxpayers on their response functions in such a way that, in the near future, rates can again be increased with secure and substantial revenue gains, above and beyond the possible limited spending increases that might emerge from genuine constituency demands.[3]

The rents of political agents are related also to the frequency of political change, most notably changes in the patterns of spending and taxing. Long-term stability in fiscal structure is a highly desirable feature for institutional efficiency because of the reduced costs of taxpayer-beneficiary adjustments. In this sense, an old tax is, indeed, a "good" tax. But such long-term stability need not be in the interests of those who make decisions as agents, especially when electoral turnover is allowed as a means of shifting the set of agents. At

---

3. For analysis that models government as revenue-maximizing, see Geoffrey Brennan and James M. Buchanan, *The Power to Tax* (Cambridge: Cambridge University Press, 1980). For analysis that relates revenue-maximizing to the time period of taxpayer adjustment, see James M. Buchanan and Dwight R. Lee, "Politics, Time, and the Laffer Curve," *Journal of Political Economy* 90 (August 1982): 816–19, and James M. Buchanan and Dwight R. Lee, "Tax Rates and Tax Revenues in Political Equilibrium: Some Simple Analytics," *Economic Inquiry* 20 (July 1982): 344–54.

the date of any initial change toward favored treatment, agents have an interest in conveying the idea that changes are permanent. Once in place, however, any part of the structure is vulnerable to the temptation of agents to renege on the earlier "promise" of permanency.

The 1986 broadening of the tax base by closing several established loopholes and shelters offers potential rents to those agents who can promise to renegotiate the package, piecemeal, in subsequent rounds of the tax game. The special interest lobbyists, whose clients suffered capital value losses in the 1986 exercise, may find their personal opportunities widened after 1986, as legislators seek out personal and private rents by offering to narrow the tax base again. In one fell swoop, the political agents may have created for themselves the potential for substantially increased rents. This rent-seeking hypothesis will clearly be tested by the fiscal politics of the post-1986 years. To the extent that agents do possess discretionary authority, the tax structure established in 1986 will not be left substantially in place for decades or even years.

As Puviani noted, political agents find it in their interest to modify the fiscal consciousness of citizens, and to do so in predictable fashion.[4] Tax impositions will be made to seem less onerous than might otherwise be the case. A disturbing feature in the rhetoric of 1986 was the impression that fiscal illusion was deliberately fostered by rent-seeking politicians, aided and abetted by journalistic discussion. Although overall revenue neutrality was maintained, the ultimate incidence of the corporation tax was almost totally neglected. Public choice considerations suggest that, to the extent that the shift from personal to corporate taxation stems from fiscal illusion, there will be some efficiency loss in the allocation of resources between the private and public sector.

## Normative Evaluation

This public choice explanation or interpretation allows for a normative evaluation of the legislation if we accept the desirability of correspondence between the preferences of citizens and the patterns of fiscal outcomes. From

---

4. Amilcare Puviani, *Teoria della illusione finanziaria* (Palermo: Sandron, 1903).

this democratic-individualistic perspective, it is the process of fiscal choice that must be tested rather than the particular results this process generates.

Have the changes in tax law enacted in 1986 made the fiscal choice process more "rational" in the sense that they have promoted a less wasteful and better informed matching of the costs and the benefits of governmental programs? The answer seems necessarily to be mixed. The broadening of the bases for taxation in both the personal and corporation income tax will reduce excess burdens. The marginal costs of payment for public program benefits should be lower than they were before the 1986 changes for all taxpayers, even for those who may have suffered utility losses in the exercise. On the other hand, the major shift of taxation from the individual income tax to the corporate tax base will reduce, perhaps substantially, the individual voter's ability to perceive the costs of program benefits. This effect may be especially pronounced for those taxpayers whose individual income tax liabilities were eliminated in the 1986 changes. Program benefits will seem to be available without tax-cost if these people do not effectively translate increased corporate tax liabilities into their individual accounts.

After 1986, fewer economic resources will be wasted through efforts to avoid taxes, but a higher value of resources will tend to be channelled into public sector outlay. To the extent that this budgetary expansion is a result of fiscal illusion generated by the 1986 changes, the new political equilibrium may embody more rather than less overall distortion and "waste." Before the 1986 reform, taxpayers generally may have been paying "too much" for the program benefits they enjoyed; after the reform, taxpaying citizens may approve levels of program benefits higher than those that would be dictated by their illusion-free preferences.

# The Theory of Public Finance[1]

In the English-language tradition, public finance has represented, on the one hand, a pragmatic study of fiscal institutions, and, on the other, an application of Marshallian partial equilibrium analysis. This sub-discipline has not contained, nor have its scholars been concerned with, a theory of collective choice, either positively or normatively considered. In comparison with continental scholarship this has long been anomalous; but quite apart from this, the tradition could not have been continued in an era characterized with so large a public economy as that which we have experienced since World War II. Within the last decade, the need for developing some theory of collective choice, some pure theory of public finance, has become obvious to many scholars, and important initial advances have been made. Perhaps even more significantly, scholarly interest seems to have been kindled with a promise for further developments. Professor Richard A. Musgrave's place in this emerging field is best demonstrated by the association of his name with both of the full-length works now available. In the *Classics in the Theory of Public Finance,*[2] Musgrave and Peacock have made available to English-language readers the most notable of the European contributions. And, with *The Theory of Public Finance,* Musgrave has written the first English-language treatise in the field. This book, about which this paper will be especially concerned, should become obligatory reading for all serious students of public finance,

From *Southern Economic Journal* 26 (January 1960): 234–38. Reprinted by permission of the publisher.

1. This is a review article of Richard A. Musgrave, *The Theory of Public Finance: A Study in Public Economy.* New York: McGraw-Hill, 1959. Pp. xvii, 628. $12.50.

2. International Economic Association, *Classics in the Theory of Public Finance.* Edited by R. A. Musgrave and A. T. Peacock (London: Macmillan, 1958).

and it should remain the standard reference work for graduate study and advanced scholarship for many years.

The book is divided into four parts: (1) Statement of Issues, (2) The Satisfaction of Public Wants, (3) Adjustments to Budget Policy: Classical Aspects, and (4) Compensatory Finance. The last part, which occupies a third of the book, includes a careful treatment of the theory of fiscal policy. While I should differ with Musgrave somewhat in general emphasis here, and perhaps quibble with him over certain points in his analysis (e.g., some aspects of debt theory), this part of the book seems to be systematically developed and analytically competent. The third part of the work, as the title suggests, deals with some of the classical problems in public finance. The impact on individual behavior resulting from changes in fiscal variables is examined and analyzed. Some of Musgrave's contributions to these topics are reasonably well known from his earlier published articles.

In this short review paper, I propose to leave aside further comment on Parts Three and Four in order to discuss more fully Musgrave's approach to fiscal theory which is developed in the first two parts of the book. The reader should be doubly warned that in so doing I am leaving out of account two-thirds of the volume, including the part which contains, by Musgrave's own statement, the original design of the work. The provocative ideas, at least to this reviewer, are to be found in the first parts of the book. It is here that Musgrave is grappling with conceptions, issues, and analyses that may ultimately lead to an acceptable theory of collective choice. And the discussion here becomes especially interesting in that it has not, as yet, become stereotyped.

I shall first summarize briefly Musgrave's approach. Following this, I shall discuss separately a few aspects of his argument in some detail.

## The Musgrave Approach to Fiscal Theory

The "fisc" is engaged in the performance of several functions, and any comprehensive theory of public finance must incorporate all of these activities. To accomplish this, Musgrave develops his fiscal theory in terms of a multibranch conception of the governmental budget. There are three branches specified: The Allocation Branch, The Distribution Branch, and The Stabilization Branch. The first of these is charged with the function of providing for the satisfaction of social or public wants of individuals as contrasted with private wants that are satisfied through the market mechanism. The second branch has as its only function the implementation of the adjustments in individual incomes and assets that are necessary to secure the appropriate norms of distributive justice. The instruments here consist solely of positive and negative transfers among individuals. The third branch is responsible for manipulating the budget when necessary to insure the maintenance of desired values for the standard macro-economic variables: employment, the price-level, and the rate of growth. The three budgetary branches are, of course, interdependent, and any decision actually made must be based on a recognition of this interdependence. The separation of the whole budget into the three branches serves a conceptual and methodological purpose, not only for students of fiscal affairs, but also for the actual decision-maker. Normatively, the three-branch approach leads directly to the conclusion that the share of economic resources devoted to the satisfaction of social wants should not be directly dependent on either distributional or fiscal policy considerations.

The allocation branch is organized to satisfy "social wants." These are defined as those wants "satisfied by services that must be consumed in equal amounts by all." The *exclusion principle* cannot be applied. The single individual's share in the benefits received from the services cannot be isolated or separated from the benefits received by other individuals; hence, others cannot be excluded from simultaneous consumption. The inapplicability of the exclusion principle, which characterizes private market transactions, makes collective or governmental action necessary. Private individuals, acting independently, will not be able to make the required connection between contribution and reward to insure adequate satisfaction of social wants. The individual, because he is aware that he cannot be excluded from sharing in the benefits, will try to escape his share of the costs. He will be led to conceal his "true" preferences for the services provided, and there is no mechanism analogous to the market which can be employed to force him to reveal these preferences. By necessity the political process must be introduced along with its inherent compulsion. And voting rules must be adopted which will secure the closest approach to some "optimal" results. Although the solution is acknowledged as imperfect, Musgrave concludes that the satisfaction of social wants through the use of majority voting rules for collective choices represents perhaps the single best compromise.

In addition to social wants, there are "merit wants" which the allocation branch, presumably, may be called upon to satisfy. Merit wants are those which individuals may not be willing to express by their overt actions, but which informed leaders of the social group consider important enough to be deliberately encouraged and promoted.

## The Three-Branch Budget

Musgrave's conceptual breakdown of the budget into three separate branches enables the student to understand more quickly the distinctions among the different functions performed by the fiscal organization. In this approach, Musgrave is extending to fiscal theory an orthodox tradition of economic policy analysis where the distinction between the "efficiency" and the "distributive" aspects of specific changes has long been found to be useful. For purposes of descriptive clarity, the three-part budget has much to recommend it. And Musgrave is quite successful in relating the different approaches to taxation directly to concentrations on single aspects of budget policy. In two of the best chapters in the book, he discusses the benefit theory of taxation and the ability-to-pay theory. The first arises somewhat naturally from the allocation-branch approach to the budget whereas the second emerges for the distribution-branch approach.

Governments do provide for the satisfaction of social wants, redistribute incomes, and use the budget to achieve stabilization objectives. For the purpose of explaining this varied activity and of understanding better some of the past discussion of it, the three-part budget is an extremely helpful analytical tool. As such, it seems likely to become a permanent part of the fiscal theory literature. But Musgrave seeks to do more than to describe or to explain. His purpose goes beyond this to that of constructing a "theory" for fiscal organization. His stated interest is in developing a normative theory of the whole budget. He is concerned, not so much with predicting what will emerge from fiscal activity, but with finding out what *should* emerge, given certain basic value postulates. This desire to develop a normative theory for fiscal organization is, of course, fully legitimate. For this purpose, however, the three-branch budget approach may be interpreted in such a way as to introduce internal inconsistencies. In the following argument, I shall show that Musgrave's three-part budget leads to positions which seem inconsistent with each other at the most fundamental philosophical level. I shall then propose an alternative approach which can incorporate all public activity under only one of the three branches.

A decade ago I published an early, exploratory paper in which I called for the recognition of two separate and alternative approaches to fiscal theory.[3] The first, which I there called the organismic approach, aims directly at providing a set of norms to be followed in establishing values for the tax-expenditure variables. Clearly normative, this approach requires first the definition of a fixed value scale. This scale may or may not include some recognition of individual values. The second approach, which I called the individualistic one, explicitly denies the existence of a single value scale for application to collective decisions. Collective activity is viewed as a form of individual behavior, and social wants are satisfied through individuals choosing to act collectively rather than privately in certain areas. This approach, by definition, cannot be normative in the same sense as the first. At best, it can examine the process through which individual values may be translated into social decisions, and it can define the conditions which must be satisfied for "equilibrium" to be established. This individualistic approach can be directly related to the Paretian constructions in modern welfare economics, but it cannot go beyond these to the employment of any "social welfare function."

The use of the Musgrave three-part budget seems to involve both of the two approaches simultaneously. The theory of the allocation branch, which Musgrave develops at some length, allows individual evaluations of services provided in the satisfaction of social and private wants to be the relevant factors in determining the amount of resources to be devoted to the public sector. If individual preferences are known, the necessary marginal conditions for Pareto optimality can be defined. And, in moving from an "inefficient" to an "efficient" position, everyone can be made better off. It is conceptually possible, therefore, that unanimous consent can be attained for making the change. Therefore, leaving aside for the time being the very real problems involved in collective decision making itself, the theory of the allocation

---

3. "The Pure Theory of Government Finance: A Suggested Approach," *Journal of Political Economy,* December 1949, 57, 496–505.

branch is fully consistent with the individualistic approach to the whole fiscal process. There are no external norms laid down; the theory is normative only in the sense that it implies that individual values are the only ones which should be counted.

It seems clear that if individual evaluations are to count in the determination of the share of resources to be devoted to the public sector, they should also be counted in determining the amount of redistribution that is to be carried out through the fiscal process and also in determining the degree to which stabilization objectives are to be promoted by fiscal activity. Consistent application of the individualistic approach would extend the theory of the allocation branch to the other two budgets; there would, for this purpose, be no need for a three-part breakdown. Both "redistribution" and "stabilization" can be treated as satisfying "social wants." Unless they are so treated, the three-part budgetary approach implies that individual values are to be used in one sector of the budget but not in the other two. Such a position can, of course, be stated as an explicit value judgment. But the acceptance of this position would seem to make the whole problem of getting individuals to reveal their true preferences relatively unimportant.

## The Exclusion Principle

Musgrave explicitly states his preference for an individualistic approach at the outset of his work. This being the case, why has he failed to appreciate fully the implied inconsistency in the normative application of the three-part budget? I suggest that this failure may be explained, at least in part, by Musgrave's unnecessary reliance on the exclusion principle as the appropriate criterion for distinguishing between private and social wants.

A more fruitful approach would seem to be one which recognizes that any externality, any external effects stemming from individual behavior, must to some degree introduce certain extension to third parties of either the costs or the benefits of private action. These externalities, negative or positive, range from those of negligible importance to those where the externality is complete, that is, goods which must be consumed equally by all. But the possibility of *exclusion* does not remove the externality, as Musgrave's treatment may appear to suggest. Individual decisions to purchase tickets for the circus involve external effects so long as the production of circus services is in the range of increasing returns to scale. The possibility of exclusion is a necessary but not sufficient condition for insuring that a market solution is appropriate. By the same token, the impossibility of exclusion is not a necessary condition for collective action in satisfying a genuinely social want. A somewhat broader approach to the whole problem of "public goods" or social wants removes the necessity that the services be consumed in equal amounts by all individuals. Once this extreme or polar case is incorporated into a more general framework, and the more important intermediate cases introduced, the limited usefulness of the exclusion principle as the criterion is evident, as Musgrave seems to recognize in certain passages.

A sounder approach would suggest that any attempt to define public goods or social wants be dropped. Once this is done, the way is opened for developing the appropriate criterion for choosing between private market action and collective action. The solution is to be found in a rather straightforward extension of the orthodox analysis of external economies, as Baumol has emphasized. Whenever the action of a single individual modifies the "individual production function" of another individual, an external effect is present. With the polar case of equal consumption, the externality is complete. When the single individual purchases a unit of such a good, a unit is made available to other individuals at zero cost. In such cases, collective action over a sufficient number of individuals to remove the externality may be indicated. If the collective goods problem is viewed in this way, there is little distinction between the pure public good and those which are partially private and partially public. No sharp dividing line between social wants and private wants is present, but the apparent advantage derived from drawing such a line is offset by the greater generality achieved. In this modified approach, the allocation branch may be extended to cover all of the activities of government, including redistribution and stabilization.

## Merit Wants

The advantages of the more general approach are perhaps clearest in application to Musgrave's discussion of "merit wants." These wants are to be satisfied by collective action, even though individual evaluations do not reveal them. Musgrave mentions such things as school lunches, free education, and public housing as satisfying merit wants. Since there are individual beneficiaries of such services, the principle of exclusion applies. These are clearly not purely collective. Yet Musgrave recognizes that the provision of such services falls within the proper sphere of government. In order to accommodate them, he is forced to depart sharply from his individualistic value postulate, and to suggest that, in these areas, individual preferences be modified.

In the more comprehensive approach to collective activity that I have suggested, it is relatively easy to bring such items as public housing, public education, and free school lunches into the legitimate range of collective provision. The external economies that arise from individual behavior may, in such cases, be more than sufficient to warrant collective action. There is no need to depart from the acceptance of individual evaluation in these decisions, and the special category of merit wants may be discarded. The fact that the externalities are not complete suggests only that efficiency considerations may dictate the use of both a market price and a tax in the financing of the services involved.

## The Revelation of "True" Preferences

In his discussion of the allocation branch, Musgrave stresses the point that individuals will not reveal their "true" preferences for public goods, since they will assume that these goods will be paid for by other beneficiaries. Perhaps I reveal my own confusion here, but I remain unconvinced by the Musgrave-Samuelson arguments on this point, and I think that the basic Wicksell contribution in this respect has not been fully appreciated. When will an individual find it advantageous to conceal his preferences? He will do so whenever a bargaining range exists, that is to say, whenever there is a net gain to be made in a transaction, when the buyer's maximum demand price exceeds the seller's minimum supply price. Transactions made at the margin involve no net gain of this sort. Only if an exchange is extra-marginal will a bargaining range be introduced. But bargaining does not eliminate the possibility of this gain being realized. It does eliminate the possibility that an independent observer can predict a unique solution. But uniqueness will be produced; the contract locus will be reached.

The same analysis seems to apply to the bargaining process that is involved in the political behavior through which the group decides on what and how much collective action shall be taken. If the decisions are extra-marginal, individuals will try to conceal their preferences. Those who are successful will be able to secure the proportionately larger share of the gains to be made by the "trade." But the group will attain the Pareto frontier without anyone in the group being required to reveal his own "true" preferences except at the margin. All true preferences *for the marginal unit* must be revealed. But the implication of the Musgrave argument seems to be that the revelation of preferences must embody the whole marginal rate of substitution (MRS) schedules of the individuals. If this is the case, the market analogy breaks down. The market also requires that preferences be revealed only at the margin. There is no way in which the market can force consumers or producers to reveal the surpluses secured by the parties to the whole exchange. This is not to suggest that there is not an important difference between the market process through which decisions on private goods are made and the political process through which decisions on public goods are reached. In the latter, all action must be group action, and the attainment of the Pareto frontier is much more difficult.

## Voting and the Unanimity Rule

Wicksell's great contribution to the theory of public finance lies in his showing how group action can, in fact, be organized to insure that the Pareto frontier will be attained. Despite his familiarity with this Wicksell contribution, Musgrave does not apply the principle of unanimity in tax-expenditure decisions. Let us suppose here that individuals' true preferences are known, and that this knowledge shows that an incremental unit of a collective good (say the development of an additional operational ICBM) is Pareto-efficient. What does this mean? It means that the aggregated MRS schedules exceed the marginal cost of producing the collective good. There is a *positive* gain in individual welfare, in accordance with the Pareto measure, which will result from the sacrifice of private goods for the production of the public good. Since this is true, there must exist a *dominant* solution to the "game" involved in the political exchange of private goods for public goods. That is to say, there must exist a solution to which all parties can agree. The Wicksell rule of unanimity allows this solution to be found, or rather it allows one from among the whole set of dominant solutions to be located. The recognition of this point makes it very difficult to understand the following Musgrave statement. "The result of majority voting is optimal in the sense that it is *the* solution agreed to by more people than any other" (page 127). Or, quite similarity, consider the following. "Wicksell's case for qualified majority has the advantage of protecting minorities and serving as a stabilizing factor. At the same time, it encourages a policy of inaction and interferes with the interests of the majority" (page 128). The Wicksell rule does, of course, interfere with the interests of the majority in the sense that these interests include coercing the minority into accepting welfare losses, as expressed by individual evaluations. But what is the purpose of the construction in the first place? Is the purpose that of defining the "optimal" solution to the "game," a solution which, once defined, can be adjusted as necessary to accommodate the facts of the real world? Or is the purpose something else?

## Conclusions

The rather sketchy and incomplete comments made in the separate sections above suggest, I hope, the wealth of provocative ideas that Musgrave's work introduces. Although I specifically limited this paper to one-third of his book at the outset, I find that I should like to discuss the few topics mentioned in considerably greater detail and also that there are many other topics upon which I should like to comment. This is, perhaps, the best single measure of the book's stature. It is a book that will inspire books to be written. If this prediction holds true, Musgrave's work will mark the formal beginning of a new and stimulating branch of American scholarship.

# Richard Musgrave, Public Finance, and Public Choice

The two volumes under review allow us to look at the half-century's scholarship of the leading public finance economist of that half-century. The papers included are well organized into major categories, even if not precisely those indicated in the volumes' titles, and, within each category, the selections are arranged chronologically. Volume One is prefaced by a teasingly short autobiographical essay, which is supplemented, in part, by Chapter 8 which is the lecture delivered on the occasion of an honorary degree at Heidelberg (1983), Musgrave's first academic home.

The first paper in Volume One is, appropriately, Richard Musgrave's first publication in a major journal, his 1939 evaluation of the voluntary exchange theory of the public economy. As surprising as it may seem, this paper represented the very first introduction of the extensive, and productive, European scholarship in public finance theory to English-language readers. And it was this European scholarship that provided the foundations for both the formalization of normative public finance by Paul Samuelson and the somewhat later emergence of public choice, as an independent subdiscipline.

The second paper in Volume One is an early introduction of Musgrave's tripartite budgetary classification, a taxonomy that he successfully imposed on public finance economics through the publication of his 1959 treatise,

From *Public Choice* 61 (June 1989): 289–91. Reprinted by permission of the publisher, Kluwer Academic Publishers.

Richard A. Musgrave, *Public Finance in a Democratic Society,* Volume One: *Social Goods, Taxation, and Fiscal Policy;* Volume Two: *Fiscal Doctrine, Growth, and Institutions* (New York: New York University Press, 1986). xiii + 391 pages, and 400 pages.

*Theory of Public Finance.* In retrospect, it is, I think, fair to say that public finance was in intellectual disarray in the early 1950s. Marshallian incidence theory along with Pigovian-Edgeworthian utilitarian normative principles of taxation had characterized pre−World War II English-language public finance. This structure had already been shocked by the Robbins critique of utilitarianism, by Keynesian fiscal policy, and by Samuelson's formal theory of public expenditure emerging from theoretical welfare economics. Richard Musgrave, almost alone, was able to re-establish intellectual order through his treatise, a book that was, almost literally, waiting to be written. His three-part breakdown of the budget allowed economists to separate conceptually the allocative function of the public economy, to which the norms of theoretical welfare economics could be applied, from the transfer or redistributive function, to which utilitarian or other social welfare function apparatus might be extended (whether successfully or not), and from the stabilization function emergent from post-Keynesian usage of the budget as an instrument for aggregative control. This structural framework for analysis allowed specialist researchers in the three separate branches to proceed more or less independently, one from the other.

As Musgrave has always acknowledged, then and now, the three-part classification is a conceptual rather than an operational tool for analysis. Even as a normative exercise, there is relatively little assistance provided in integrating the three functions into some final budgetary adjustment. And, as a predictive theory of how budgets are, in fact, actually made in any democratic structure of governance, the conceptual framework may confuse rather than enlighten unless it is very carefully introduced.

The second and third parts of Volume One contain papers on taxation and fiscal policy. The first part of Volume Two covers fiscal federalism; other parts of this volume include papers on social security, development finance, government growth, and, finally, Musgrave's generalized overview of public economics. There are, in total, twenty-nine papers in Volume One and twenty-three papers in Volume Two.

I shall not attempt to evaluate Musgrave's contribution from the perspective of a modern public finance economist. I am neither competent to do so nor interested in making such an effort. I suspect that Musgrave would agree with my assessment that there have been technical advances and conceptual retrogressions. My evaluation here is explicitly constrained by the location for publication of this review and by its potential readership. I shall try to examine Richard Musgrave's contribution from the limited perspective of a public choice analyst.

Given the combination of cultural and educational heritage, language comprehension, normative interests, and research concentration, Musgrave might have been expected to be highly sympathetic to public choice efforts to analyze public-sector decision structures. He maintains a life-long interest in what is sometimes called "fiscal sociology," and he has never been entranced by either the intricacies of mathematical economics or the scientism of the empiricists. His position toward public choice has been what I should call sympathetically critical (less well defined than a more familiar love-hate relationship). I should place Musgrave neither among the ranks of the adversaries of public choice nor among those whose interests dictate inattention and neglect.

I share with Musgrave the frustration at the efforts of many of our peers in economics when they make too much of the positive-normative distinction in our inquiry. The way that we look at, or model, the complexities of social interaction depends upon our ultimate normative ideals, and, in turn, these ideals themselves are shaped, in part, by the way we look at the interaction process. Musgrave's central and continuing criticism of public choice theory rests squarely in his residual unwillingness to model "public choosers" analogously to the way that we model "private choosers." He suggests that, descriptively, persons who make decisions as political agents do not always act in furtherance of their own interests. Of course he is correct, but the difference lies, not in an interpretation of the empirical behavioral reality, but in the appropriateness or inappropriateness of introducing an abstract model that facilitates explanation and understanding. Musgrave considers many of us who work with interest models of political behavior to be motivated by normative precepts that he does not share. We may, I think, acknowledge that he is at least partially on target, but, at the same time, we should expect Musgrave to acknowledge, in turn, that our norms, at least at the instrumental level, are shaped by our visions of social reality, which have some empirical grounding. There is room in an inclusively defined "political economy" for both the insider-Harvard-Musgrave vision of socio-political reality and the outsider-Chicago-Virginia-public choice vision.

A second strand of Musgrave's criticism of public choice is not so readily accommodated. Like many of his academic peers who emerge directly from the European rather than the American tradition, Musgrave has never understood or appreciated the relevance and importance of the constitutional structure of a polity, with the categorical separation between rules of constitutional order and behavior that takes place within such rules. This failure to appreciate the whole constitutional exercise provides yet another basis for criticism of the seemingly cynical models of in-rule political behavior, a criticism that is developed at some length in a long paper, "Leviathan Cometh— Or Does He?" in Volume Two. This paper is explicitly directed at the revenue-maximizing models of government introduced in a book, *The Power to Tax* (1980), that Geoffrey Brennan and I had previously published. This Musgrave criticism along with others of a similar nature prompted Brennan and me to write a second book, *The Reason of Rules* (1985), in which we tried to defend the whole constitutionalist enterprise.

The contrast between the Musgrave and the constitutionalist perspective can be sharply defined. If political agents act in furtherance of some "public interest," and agree on what this is, then constitutional constraints on their behavior are both unnecessary and unproductive. If political agents act in their own identifiable interests to exploit any opportunities that their authority offers, constitutional constraints are essential to insure the functioning of any political order. The abstract models yield categorically differing implications for political structure. The choice between the alternatives depends both on an assessment of empirical reality and on estimates of political opportunity gain-and-loss functions.

The fact that these two volumes span a half-century of productive scholarship by an economist who has always been contemporary is worth re-emphasis. The enthusiasm of the bliss years of Keynesian economic policy is conveyed in several of the early papers. But the public finance theory of the 1959 treatise was sufficiently encompassing to allow stabilization policy to move out of the central role initially assigned, while transfer and allocative policy shifted to more-important status. The long paper that concludes Volume Two offers Musgrave's own history of the developments in fiscal doctrine over the half-century.

The public finance of Richard Musgrave emerged more or less in parallel

with public choice. As I have noted, Musgrave has been sympathetically critical of the public choice enterprise. If his peers among the academic stars,
defined in terms of age, location, and influence, should have been equally
attentive, many issues could have been more thoroughly discussed. As things
stand, the inclusively defined political economy that might embody contributions from scholars with alternative visions remains to be developed.

## PART TWO

# Earmarking and Incidence in Democratic Process

# The Economics of
# Earmarked Taxes[1]

Economists do not agree on the effects of earmarking. For example, Julius Margolis and Walter Heller suggest that the earmarking or segregating of fiscal accounts tends to reduce the willingness of taxpayers to approve expenditures on specific public services.[2] By contrast, Earl Rolph and George Break, along with Jesse Burkhead, discuss earmarking as one device for generating taxpayer support for expansion in particular services.[3] The staff of the Tax Foundation, in a more comprehensive study, have expressed views in accord with the latter position.[4]

From *Journal of Political Economy* 71 (October 1963): 457–69. Copyright 1963 by The University of Chicago. All rights reserved. Reprinted by permission of the University of Chicago Press, publisher.

1. The background research on this paper was done in connection with a more comprehensive project on fiscal institutions that is supported by the National Committee on Government Finance, organized through the Brookings Institution. I am indebted to my colleagues James M. Ferguson and W. Craig Stubblebine, whose persistent skepticism forced me to remove several errors from earlier drafts of this paper.

2. Margolis, in his stimulating paper, provides empirical support for this hypothesis in the case of expenditures for education (see Julius Margolis, "Metropolitan Finance Problems: Territories, Functions, and Growth," in *Public Finances: Needs, Sources, and Utilization* [New York: National Bureau of Economic Research, 1961], esp. 261–66).

Heller criticizes the institution of the attached mill-levy because it serves to restrict unduly the willingness of taxpayers to support mosquito control programs and the like (see Walter Heller, "CED's Stabilizing Budget Policy after Ten Years," *American Economic Review,* 47 [September 1957], 650, esp. n. 39).

3. In both cases here, the argument is applied to the financing of special functions in underdeveloped countries (see Earl Rolph and George Break, *Public Finance* [New York: Ronald Press Co., 1961], 62, and Jesse Burkhead, *Government Budgeting* [New York: John Wiley & Sons, 1956], 469).

4. Tax Foundation, *Earmarked State Taxes* (New York: Tax Foundation, 1955).

This paper develops a theory of earmarking that "explains" the divergent predictions and also suggests certain hypotheses, the implications of which should be testable through the observation of political processes. In order to construct this theory, it is necessary to introduce models of the political decision process that are not consistent with those that have been implicitly assumed in the orthodox normative evaluation of earmarking. The near-universal condemnation of the institution by experts in budgetary theory and practice is familiar and need not be summarized here.[5] This position cannot be supported on the basis of the efficiency considerations that may be derived from the models emphasized in this paper.

"Earmarking" is defined as the practice of designating or dedicating specific revenues to the financing of specific public services. It is discussed under such headings as "special funds," "segregated accounts," "segregated budgets," "dedicated revenues." Normally, earmarking as a term is used with reference to the dedication of a single tax source to a single public service within a multitax, multiservice fiscal unit, but the identical effects are produced by the creation of special-purpose fiscal units, such as school districts, fire districts, and sanitation districts, each of which is granted independent, but restricted, taxing powers. Quantitatively, earmarking is important in the over-all United States fiscal system. At the local government level, the special-purpose units remain predominant in the financing of important services, education being the notable example.[6] At the state level, one study suggested, one-half of all state collections in 1954 were earmarked.[7] At the federal level, the modern growth of the trust-fund accounts, such as that for

---

5. For statements of the argument in standard works, see M. Slade Kendrick, *Public Finance* (Boston: Houghton Mifflin Co., 1951), 331; W. J. Schultz and C. Lowell Harriss, *American Public Finance* (7th ed.; New York: Prentice-Hall, Inc., 1959), 107; Philip E. Taylor, *The Economics of Public Finance* (rev. ed.; New York: Macmillan Co., 1963), 28; Harold M. Groves, *Financing Government* (New York: Henry Holt & Co., 1958), 500.

"Classical" statements of the standard position are to be found in C. F. Bastable, *Public Finance* (2d ed.; London: Macmillan & Co., 1895), 689; Paul Leroy-Beaulieu, *Traité de la Science des Finances*, II (2d ed.; Paris: Guillaumin, 1906), 30 ff.; Gaston Jeze, *Cours de Science des Finances: Théorie Générale du Budget* (6th ed.; Paris: Marcel Girard, 1922), 82–103.

6. Independent school districts account for almost four-fifths of total school enrolment in the United States (see Margolis, op. cit., 263).

7. Tax Foundation, op. cit.

highways, suggests that, proportionately, earmarked or segregated revenues are assuming increasing significance.

## I

The standard normative "theory" of earmarking adopts the reference system of the budget-maker, the budgetary authority, who is, by presumption, divorced from the citizenry in the political community. An alternative working hypothesis of political order is the individualistic one in which the reference system becomes that of the individual citizen. In this model, the only meaningful decision-making units are individual persons, and the state or the collectivity exists only as a means through which individuals combine to accomplish collective or jointly desired objectives. The state is not an independent choosing agent, and "collective choice" results from separate individual decisions as these are processed by constitutional rules. The analytical device of the social welfare function, which guides the judgments of an independent budgetary authority, has no place in this model. The earmarking of revenues must be re-examined in the context of individual participation in the formation of collective decisions. When this approach is taken, it becomes apparent that the restrictions that such practices as earmarking may impose on the independence of a budgetary authority need not produce "inefficiency" in the fiscal process. Some such segregation of revenues may provide one means of insuring more rational individual choice; under some conditions earmarking may be a "desirable" rather than an "undesirable" feature of a fiscal structure.

Institutionally, earmarking provides a means of compartmentalizing fiscal decisions. The individual citizen, as voter-taxpayer-beneficiary, is enabled to participate, *separately*, either directly or through his legislative representative, in the several public expenditure decisions that may arise. He may, through this device, "vote" independently on the funds to be devoted to schools, to sanitation, and so on, given the specified revenue sources. Only in this manner can he make "private" choices on the basis of some reasonably accurate comparison of the costs and the benefits of the specific public services, one at a time.[8] By contrast, general fund budgeting, or non-earmarking,

8. The necessity of relating decisions on public expenditures explicitly to decisions on taxes through the political process, and of assigning a definite revenue category to each

allows the citizen to "vote" only on the aggregate outlay for the predetermined "bundles" of public services, as this choice is presented to him by the budgetary authorities.[9]

The appropriate market analogue to general-fund financing (non-earmarking) is a specific tie-in sale, as opposed to independent quantity adjustment in each market, the analogue to earmarking. Independent adjustment is characteristic of privately organized markets for goods and services. The individual is not normally required to purchase goods and services in "bundles" of complex heterogeneous units. Insofar as some tie-ins are observed to persist in competitive markets, these reflect the advantages of superior efficiency to the purchaser. In the absence of genuine cost-reducing aspects of marketing separate goods in "bundles," any restrictions that are placed on the ability to adjust quantities independently must move the purchaser to some less preferred position on his utility surface. For example, any requirement that one stick of butter be purchased with each loaf of bread would surely produce "inefficiency" in choice, and could be implemented only through the exercise of monopoly power.[10]

## II

The model of individual fiscal choice that is required must remain extremely simplified. It is necessary to abstract from the complexities of alternative

---

single expenditure was stressed by Wicksell in his classic statement of the individualistic theory of public finance (see Knut Wicksell, "A New Principle of Just Taxation," in *Classics in the Theory of Public Finance,* ed. R. A. Musgrave and A. T. Peacock [London: International Economic Association, 1958], 72–118, but esp. 94. The original Wicksell work is *Finanztheoretische Untersuchungen* [Jena: Gustav Fischer, 1896]).

9. Control over the budgetary allocation, at one stage removed, does exist through the voter's ultimate power to remove public officials through electoral processes. And, even for the budgetary allocation as presented, legislative power to modify the allocation of funds among the separate public service outlays is normally exercised. However, these powers to change the uses to which general-fund revenues may be put do not modify the basic "tie-in" features of the model until and unless the tax structure is simultaneously considered in the same decision processes.

10. For recent statements of the theory of tie-in sales see M. L. Burstein, "The Economics of Tie-in Sales," *Review of Economics and Statistics,* 42 (February 1960), 68–73, and his "A Theory of Full-Line Forcing," *Northwestern University Law Review,* 55 (1960), 62–95 (see also Ward S. Bowman, Jr., "Tying Arrangements and the Leverage Problem," *Yale Law Journal,* 67 [March 1957], 19–36).

political decision rules and at the same time to retain for the model some relevance for collective results. To accomplish this, the "median" voter-taxpayer-beneficiary is introduced. "Median" here characterizes the individual's preference structure as typical of that describing his fellows' in the group. With single-peaked preferences the median individual becomes decisive under simple majority voting rules.[11] Hence, the behavior of the single median individual mirrors that of the effective decision-making group in the community. Through this device, collective results can be discussed in terms of the behavior of the single individual. The conception is similar to, although somewhat broader than, the community-of-equals assumption that has been employed frequently in fiscal analysis.

I shall assume that the goods or services provided publicly utilize a sufficiently small share of total community resources to allow income effects to be neglected in the behavior of the individual. Collective goods are assumed to be produced at constant marginal costs, and, finally, the costs of reaching collective decisions are neglected. Initially, I shall assume that the collective goods, whether supplied singly or jointly, are to be financed through the imposition of a particular form of lump-sum tax. This tax is designed so that the "terms-of-trade" between the individual and the fisc cannot be affected by the behavior of the former. The "tax price per unit" of the collective good made available to him is invariant over quantity, although the total tax bill is, of course, dependent on the quantity chosen by the community. This relatively pure model allows us to discuss the behavior of the individual free from any elements of strategic bargaining with his fellows that might be present were the terms of trade subject to influence by his own actions.

The choice calculus of the individual can now be analyzed in familiar terms. He is confronted by a fixed "supply price"; the supply curve, to him, for the collective good, singly or in a bundle, is horizontal at some predetermined "tax price." This tax price, to the individual, is some share of the total supply price or cost price of the good to the whole community. The quantity of collective goods made available to one person is assumed equally available to everyone else in the group. The distribution of taxes among the separate individuals is assumed to have been determined outside the model. In a world-of-equals model, an individual share might be taken simply as a pro rata part of total

---

11. See Duncan Black, *The Theory of Committees and Elections* (Cambridge: Cambridge University Press, 1958).

unit cost. In this more general setting, any distribution of taxes is possible so long as this distribution is independent of the particular choice analyzed.

Consider first a single collective good. We can think of an individual marginal evaluation schedule or curve, which in this instance is equivalent to a demand curve for this good, in the same manner that we think of such a schedule or curve for a privately marketed good or service. Individual or private "equilibrium" is reached at a point where the demand price equals the individual supply price or tax price. In this collective good case, there is no opportunity for the individual, acting alone, to adjust quantity purchased to price. Hence, the attainment of his equilibrium position is possible, even for the median consumer, only through "voting for" or "voting against" extensions or contractions in public goods supply. The construction enables us to depict the voting choices of the individual with respect to the collective good in a manner analogous to the standard treatment of market choice, so long as we assume that marginal adjustments in public expenditure programs are possible. If marginal adjustments are not possible, and the voter is presented with a final choice of voting for or against specific expenditure proposals, elements of all-or-none offers enter his calculus, and the treatment requires modification.

The analysis is straightforward when we consider a single collective good or service. Since, however, we want to introduce the tie-in "sale" that general fund financing implies, a two-good model becomes the simplest one that is helpful. For descriptive flavor, think of a community that supplies both police protection and fire protection services collectively. We seek to determine the possible differences between financing these two services separately, through a system of earmarking where each service is supported by revenues from a tax of the sort indicated above, and financing them jointly, with revenues from a general-fund budget derived from only one tax. In either case, the total amount of public expenditure is assumed to be determined by the rationally motivated choice of the voter-taxpayer. Will general-fund financing result in a larger or a smaller provision of one or both public services than that produced under an earmarked revenue scheme? Will total public outlay, on both services, increase, decrease, or remain the same as an institutional change from one revenue system to the other is made?

The answers to these, and other, questions must depend upon the particular form that a general-fund budgetary tie-in takes. It would be possible to define this tie-in with respect to physical units of service, such as, for example, the requirement that the same number of policemen and firemen be supplied. It will, however, be descriptively more realistic and analytically more convenient if we define the tie-in with respect to a budgetary allocation between the two services. In other words, general-fund financing takes the form of a specific proportion of the total budget devoted to each of the two services. There will always exist one budgetary allocation that will insure identity of solution as between the two institutions. That is, there is always one budgetary ratio that will cause the median individual to "vote for" the same relative quantities of the two services and the same public outlay with or without earmarking. This unique solution, which I shall label "full equilibrium," provides a starting point for a more careful analysis.

It is convenient to illustrate the analysis geometrically. In Figure 1 quantity units are measured along the horizontal axis, but these units are defined in a special way. Under the tie-in arrangement, a unit of quantity is defined as that physical combination of the two services available for one dollar, one hundred cents. Thus, the number of dollars expended is directly proportional to the distance along the horizontal axis. Now assume that the "full equilibrium" budgetary mix prevails, and that this is defined by the forty-sixty ratio. Forty cents out of each budgetary dollar is devoted to providing fire protection and sixty cents to providing police protection; each service is supplied at constant cost. We may now derive demand curves for fire protection services, $D_f$, and police protection services, $D_p$, respectively. These demand curves must be defined with respect to the dimensions indicated by the budgetary ratio. A unit of fire protection is defined as that quantity available to the individual for an outlay of forty cents, and a unit of police services is defined as that quantity available for an outlay of sixty cents. For expositional simplicity, I shall use linear demand functions. The vertical summation of the two demand curves, $D_f + D_p$, represents the demand for the bundle of services, available for one dollar per unit, when the forty-sixty ratio prevails. By definition of "full equilibrium," this composite demand curve cuts the tax-price curve, drawn at the one-dollar level, along the same vertical line measuring the independently chosen equilibrium quantities of fire protection and police protection, respectively. The elements of circularity that are present in this whole construction are not damaging since the purpose is illustrative only.

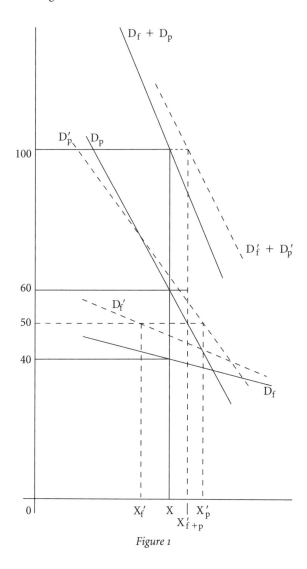

*Figure 1*

Given the conditions of demand shown in Figure 1, there is no differential effect as between earmarking and general-fund financing of the two services at the forty-sixty budgetary ratio. The individual will choose the same quantity of services and the same over-all public outlay under either one of the two institutional forms. If the services are presented separately, he will vote for an amount, $0X$, of fire services, defined in forty-cent units, which can readily be translated into any other physical dimension. Similarly, he will choose an amount, $0X$, of police services defined in sixty-cent units. Or, if forced to take these two services in bundles, defined by the forty-sixty ratio, he will choose an amount, $0X$. In either case, he will vote for a total budget outlay that is directly proportional to the horizontal distance, $0X$.

Differential effects arise only when some budgetary ratio other than that required for "full equilibrium" is introduced. Assume now that the budgetary ratio is exogenously determined, and that a proposal is made to shift from a system of segregated financing to general-fund financing under, say, a fifty-fifty ratio, with underlying demand conditions for the two services remaining as depicted in Figure 1. It is necessary to translate the demand curves, $D_f$ and $D_p$, into the modified dimensions, with physical units now being defined as the quantities available at fifty cents. The new demand curves, drawn in the fifty-cents dimensions, are shown as $D'_f$ and $D'_p$. The effects of general-fund financing at this non-equilibrium ratio, which has been shifted in favor of fire protection services, can be clearly indicated. As might be expected, more fire protection is demanded and less police protection than under earmarking. In the new dimensions, $0X'_f$ represents the "full equilibrium" or earmarking quantity of fire protection services, and $0X'_p$ the corresponding quantity of police services. In other words, $0X$, in the old dimension, is equivalent to $0X'_f$ in the new; both represent the same physical quantity of fire protection services. General-fund financing under the new, fifty-fifty budgetary ratio will produce a "tie-in equilibrium" at a quantity measured by $0X'_{f+p}$, which is determined by the intersection of the newly drawn composite demand curve, $D'_f + D'_p$, with the composite supply curve.[12]

Any shift in the budgetary ratio away from that required for "full equilibrium" will insure that general-fund financing introduces some distortion in the choice pattern of the individual. Forcing him to purchase the two services in a bundle, rather than separately, will move the individual to some less preferred position on his utility surface, given our framework assumption that decision-making costs are zero. Since, under independent quantity

---

12. The geometrical constructions in both Fig. 1 and Fig. 2 are drawn on the basis of a specific numerical model that will be supplied upon request.

adjustment, he could always, should he desire, select quantities of fire and police services indicated by the second solution, the fact that he does not do so in the first solution suggests that such a combination must be less preferred than the initial combination chosen. The distortion produced by the non-equilibrium budgetary ratio will take the form of an expansion in one of the two services beyond the "full equilibrium" quantity and a contraction of the other to some less than "full equilibrium" quantity. Relatively, the service expanded will be that one that is differentially favored by the ratio. The analysis remains incomplete, however, until and unless further questions are answered. Will over-all public outlay tend to increase or decrease, and under what conditions? What are the characteristics of those services most likely to be substantially increased as a result of favorable-ratio general-fund financing?

Total public outlay need not remain the same under earmarking and non-earmarking when a non-equilibrium budgetary ratio prevails, and the direction of change will depend on the configuration of the demand functions. Examination of the model produces the following conclusions: If the ratio turns in favor of the service characterized by the more elastic demand at the full equilibrium quantity (as in the example), total public outlay will be expanded as earmarking is replaced by general-fund financing. Conversely, if the ratio shifts in favor of the service characterized by the less elastic demand at the full equilibrium quantity, total public outlay will be reduced as a result of a similar shift in institutions. These results hold, however, only for limited shifts in the ratio away from the full equilibrium one. As the construction of Figure 1 suggests, the relative elasticities of demand may change as the "tie-in equilibrium" quantity changes. When and if relative elasticities change, the direction of change in total expenditure is reversed. Utilizing the linear demand curves of Figure 1, this point may be illustrated readily. As the ratio shifts initially in favor of fire protection, characterized by the more elastic demand at the initial quantity, total outlay will be increased by the tie-in scheme. However, beyond some critical value, the elasticity of demand for fire protection, at the tie-in quantity, becomes less than that for police services, and total public outlay diminishes as the budgetary ratio continues to shift in favor of fire protection.[13]

13. Note that these conclusions can be stated in terms of relative elasticities only in the model that allows the quantity dimensions to shift as the budgetary ratio changes. This

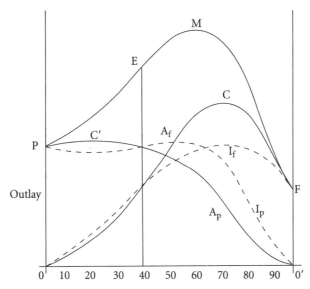

*Figure 2.* Percentage of general-fund outlay devoted to fire protection

Several of the relevant relationships are illustrated in Figure 2. On the horizontal axis is measured the percentage of fire protection services in a tie-in budgetary mix, from zero to one hundred. On the vertical axis is measured total outlay, on both and on each service, as determined by the demand pattern of the individual and the assumed cost conditions for the two services. Specifically, Figure 2 is derived from the same configuration as Figure 1, which embodies linear demand functions, although a similar set of relationships could be readily derived from any postulated initial conditions of demand. The full equilibrium ratio, defined previously as the forty-sixty one, must involve a total public outlay equal to the sum of the spending on the two services when "purchased" separately. If a ratio with zero fire protection

---

shifting of quantity dimension insures that for both services the quantity taken is the same. This, along with the additional requirement that the absolute changes in price for the two services must be precisely offsetting, allows shifts along two separate demand functions to be evaluated in terms of relative elasticity coefficients. Without these constraints, shifts along two separate demand functions could not be compared with respect to changes in total outlay solely in terms of relative elasticities. The latter would remain important, but some relative price factor would have to be added.

services is introduced, total spending will be on police services alone; conversely, if a one hundred per cent ratio is present, all spending will be for fire protection. Thus, income effects being neglected, the vertical distance, $E$, at full equilibrium, must equal the sum of the distances, $0P$, and $0'F$. As the ratio shifts in favor of fire protection services, total outlay expands, as shown by the rising portion of the top curve to the right of $E$, Total outlay reaches a maximum at $M$, and then falls sharply to $F$ as the ratio becomes more and more favorable to fire protection. As the ratio shifts in favor of police protection services, total outlay falls, as is indicated by the top curve to the left of $E$. It continues to fall to $P$, where no part of the budget is devoted to providing fire protection.

The additional curves in Figure 2 break down this total outlay as between the two services and into actual and imputed components. Actual outlay is, of course, computed by taking the indicated percentage of total outlay as shown by the ratio on the horizontal scale. "Imputed outlay" on a service is defined as that part of total outlay on a bundle that is attributed to the service by the individual at each particular tie-in equilibrium. Imputed outlay on a service equals actual outlay only at the full equilibrium budgetary ratio. For all other ratios, imputed outlay differs from actual outlay, and the difference reflects the degree of "exploitation," negative or positive, that non-equilibrium ratios can generate. Imputed outlay falls below actual outlay on the service that is favored in the budgetary mix; it exceeds actual outlay on the remaining service. This is shown in Figure 2. To the right of forty per cent, imputed outlay on fire protection services, $I_f$, falls below actual outlay, $A_f$. To the left of forty per cent, the opposite relationship holds. And, of course, the relationships for police services are the inverse of those for fire services.

Maximum total outlay is reached at $M$. As the ratio shifts beyond this point, total expenditures fall although the share of this total devoted to fire protection continues to increase. At some point, $C$, to the right of $M$, these two factors become mutually offsetting, and some maximum outlay on fire protection services alone is reached. Increasing the share in the budget beyond this "critical ratio" will result in fewer resources devoted to fire protection, always on the assumption that the voter-taxpayer retains the basic power of determining the level of total spending.

As the ratio shifts in favor of police services in our model, total outlay falls continuously. However, because of the increasing share, the quantity of police services supplied increases to some critical ratio, $C'$, where actual outlay reaches a maximum.[14]

## III

The analysis, to this point, has been based on the choice calculus of the single median individual. Even before generalizing this analysis, we are able to draw some interesting implications for political group behavior. In any community specific individuals and groups will find particular interest in the performance of one or the other public services provided. Using the two-service model we can examine the predicted behavior of groups organized in support of either fire protection or police protection services. If both services should be initially financed through independently designated taxes, that is, if earmarking prevails, then groups in support of either service would have some incentive to attempt to secure a general-fund budgetary scheme favorable to its own service. Conversely, either group would try to retain earmarking if it predicts an unfavorable budgetary allotment under general-fund arrangements.

The characteristics of demand, however, make for considerable differences in the expected gains to be secured under favorable general-fund ratios. Relatively, the group that is organized in support of the service characterized by the more elastic demand stands to gain more by favorable tie-ins. In this way, sizable amounts of "taxpayers' surplus" can be captured from the relatively less elastic demand service that is tied into the budgetary bundle.[15] Not only will the favored service be allotted a larger share of each

---

14. The rising portion of the $I_P$ curve at the left in Fig. 2 requires some explanation. As the budgetary mix shifts in favor of police services, imputed expenditures on both services fall, as indicated. However, as a smaller and smaller share of the budget is allotted to fire protection, the degree of exploitation that consumers of police services can attain reaches some maximum. Beyond this point, the "relative price reduction" that the tie-in involves is progressively diminished.

The derivation of this construction is clarified in the numerical example upon which both Figs. 1 and 2 are based. It should be emphasized, however, that the general results do not depend upon the particulars of the example or on the shapes of the curves derived therefrom.

15. This is, in general, consistent with the conclusions of Burstein with respect to the tie-in sales of the monopolist. As he suggests, the monopolist, selling a product that is

budget dollar, but also total spending on both services increases. By comparison, the pressure group organized to support the relatively inelastic demand service will not be able to secure so much advantage even from comparably favorable shifts in the budgetary ratio. A higher share of the budgetary dollar will be advantageous, but the degree of exploitation from "taxpayers' surplus" on the other service is severely limited. This group, therefore, stands to gain less and possibly to lose more from a general change in institutions leading away from segregated revenue sources. It will be much more likely to opt for the continuation, or the introduction, of segregated budget accounts.

Note that *both* pressure groups could never be observed to approve a shift from segregated to general-fund financing or vice versa if the budgetary ratio is known in advance, and known to be a non-equilibrium one. If the model has predictive value at all, observation should reveal that some groups support one financing arrangement and some the other. There is an appropriate market analogue. Rational monopolists producing two separate goods could never be observed to join in a mutually agreed tie-in sale without the pooling of revenues. Any particular tie-in, other than the full equilibrium one, must benefit one and harm the other.

As mentioned, Margolis refers to data that suggest somewhat larger expenditures on education under general-fund than under segregated financing schemes. If the analytical model presented here is valid, these facts suggest that education is favored in general-fund budgetary ratios. It seems probable, also, that total municipal spending is larger in those cases where education is included in the general-fund budget. This supplementary hypothesis, if confirmed by observation, would imply that, over the relevant ranges, educational services are characterized by a relatively higher demand elasticity than companion services in the budget. There is independent evi-

---

necessarily price elastic, will seek to tie in the sales of an inelastic-demand product. The monopolist can, of course, control the relevant ratio (see Burstein, "The Economics of Tie-in Sales," op. cit.).

The analysis of earmarking, as developed here, is simpler than the comparable analysis of monopolistic tie-in sales. In the earmarking model, the unit cost of supplying services, either jointly or separately, is always equal to the "tax price" charged to "purchasers." In other words, the government does not seek to make profits. With the monopolist, the difference between unit cost and price is a central variable that the fiscal model need not include.

dence to support this implication. Public services, like education, that provide differentially higher benefits to particular subgroups in the community (in this case families with children) will tend to be relatively more demand elastic than services that are more "general" in benefit incidence (say, police protection). By requiring taxpayers who do not secure direct benefits from publicly provided educational services to purchase general community services such as police only through a tie-in arrangement with education, some "taxpayers' surplus" is captured, as Margolis has suggested. The bachelor who might vote against additional school district taxes (and expenditures) may vote for additional taxes to finance a bundle of services that includes education. The analysis does not imply, however, even if further research should confirm fully the hypotheses involved, that school superintendents and P.T.A. groups take no chances in pushing for the abolition of segregated financial sources. Such plans would, of course, backfire unless favorable budgetary ratios are secured.[16]

The behavior of subgroups in the political community that are not organized to support specific expenditures may also be noted briefly. Taxpayer groups, those whose primary objective is that of reducing the level of tax rates independent of any consideration for public spending levels, will tend to favor earmarking schemes if they expect that general-fund budgeting implies shifts in favor of the more elastic demand services. For the same reason, these groups would desire general-fund financing in the converse case. Since, however, the gain to be expected in the latter institutional arrangement is likely to be slight, taxpayer groups normally might be predicted to support earmarking.

By comparison and contrast, the "bureaucracy," whose objective is primarily that of expanding the size and importance of the public sector, independent of costs, will directly oppose the taxpayer groups. If voter-taxpayer response is presumed, ultimately, to determine the total public expenditure level while the bureaucracy chooses the budgetary mix, the model that seems to be implicit in much of the orthodox discussion emerges. Here the budget-

---

16. As W. C. Stubblebine has pointed out, the analysis here seems appropriate to the behavior of certain charitable organizations. The model "explains" why the Boy Scouts seek to be included in general-fund Community Chest revenue-raising drives, while the Red Cross and the Cancer Society prefer independent (earmarked) financing.

makers "should" try to select a mix that approximates the full equilibrium ratio. If, however, these officials include consideration of bureaucracy objectives in their decisions, they will be biased toward shifting general-fund allocations in favor of the relatively elastic-demand services, and, in this way, toward insuring some over-all expansion in public spending.

## IV

The first step toward generalizing the model involves the extension to more than two public services. Basically, the same propositions hold. The departures from independently determined or "optimal" levels of provision for particular services become larger as more services are included in the budgetary bundle. Partial segregation of fiscal accounts, with each including several services that are commonly financed, can be shown to be more "efficient," from the reference system of the voter-taxpayer-beneficiary, than over-all integration into a comprehensive budgetary system, given the restrictions imposed on the model. Similar conclusions apply to the effects of segregated budget accounts created by special-purpose governmental units. Incorporation of decision-making costs into the model could, of course, modify these initial conclusions.

In the model discussed, the separate services were assumed to be wholly independent. Extension of the analysis to cover those cases where services are either close substitutes or close complements will not affect the results. Services were also assumed supplied at constant cost, but this simplification does not affect the conclusions.

A major step toward generalizing the analysis is that which relaxes the specific tax assumptions. The individual, whose decision processes are examined, is confronted with a fixed "tax per unit." Only a form of lump-sum tax satisfies this requirement. Under most real-world taxing institutions, the tax price per unit at which collective goods are made available to the individual will depend, at least to some degree, on his own behavior. This element is not, however, important under the major tax institutions such as the personal income tax, the general sales tax, or the real property tax. With such structures, the individual may, by changing his private behavior, modify the tax base (and thus the tax price per unit of collective goods he utilizes), but he need not have any incentive to conceal his "true" preferences for public goods. His own tax liability, per unit, is to such a small extent modified by his own choice for public goods that he will not normally include this factor in his decision for or against public spending proposals. His behavior in participating in collective choice can remain broadly analogous to his behavior as a purchaser of goods and services in the market place.

In the formal model, it was assumed that the distribution of taxes among separate persons is in some way determined independent of the particular fiscal choices analyzed. The tax price per unit that the individual confronts does not depend on the outcome of the choice. This, in itself, seems "realistic." Local communities, for example, make decisions on expansions and contractions in public spending programs in the expectation that costs will be placed on the ratepayers, and the distribution of these costs does not normally depend on the pattern of public services chosen. Similarly, assemblies at higher governmental levels vote on appropriations measures independent of the given tax structure. Conversely, tax reform does not imply change in budgetary allocation. The model employed can, therefore, apply equally to the calculus of the low-income citizen who, presumably, is required by the tax structure to pay a differentially low tax price for units of collective good and to the high-income citizen who is required to pay a differentially high tax price for the same good.

Complications produced by distributional elements must be faced when the results of the individual-behavior model are applied to fiscal experience. In the normal order of events, collective goods and services are "priced" to individuals in a discriminatory fashion. This fact makes it necessary that we interpret the conclusions concerning the relative elasticities of demand for public services quite carefully. In ordinary market analysis, when the demand for a good is classified as relatively elastic over a relevant price range, this conveys specific meaning since, presumably, all buyers confront the prevailing price. If, however, separate consumers buy at different prices, as they do in the case of collective goods, the elasticity of total demand depends on the pattern of discrimination that happens to be present. It becomes impossible to classify public services, even at known relative cost levels, into elastic- and inelastic-demand categories independent of the tax structure.

A further reference to Margolis' interesting evidence on educational spending illustrates this point. As suggested above, the data indicate that education secures favorable ratios in general-fund budgeting arrangements. If, in addition, municipal spending on all goods is higher when general-fund financing is adopted, the demand for educational services, *at the prevailing tax structures,* is relatively more elastic than that for companion services. But a shift or change in the tax structure can modify this relative demand elasticity, since any change in the distribution of costs among individuals amounts to a shifting of relative prices, as these are confronted by the separate individuals in the group. Margolis suggests that a shift to general-fund financing for education may be needed in many localities in order to generate political support for expanded expenditures. However, this expansion would be secured at the expense of some additional distortion in individual fiscal choice, along with a necessary contraction in accompanying services. A more fruitful, and more "efficient," means of securing the same objective may lie in some modification of the structure of taxes imposed by special-purpose governments, some change in the pattern of discriminatory rates.

## V

The theory of earmarking presented in this paper may be criticized on many grounds. Any formal model based on individual behavior in collective choice processes must remain remote from real-world political experience. Even when this approach to political decisions is compared with models of market behavior, a high degree of abstraction remains. Testable implications of the theory are difficult to derive, and testing itself presents serious problems. Defense of the approach comes down, quite simply, to the faith that "some theory is better than nothing."

The analysis developed is intended only as a first step toward understanding this important fiscal institution. A more complete and more complex treatment may lead to normative conclusions that would be somewhat more in conformity with ruling opinion. The most important element omitted has been that of decision-making costs, in its various institutional manifestations. If this is given due weight, the basic individualistic model may indicate that the segregation of revenues remains "inefficient" relative to consolidated revenue schemes. The point to be stressed here is only that, if this conclusion should be forthcoming, the added features must be demonstrated to outweigh the distortions upon which the model of individual fiscal choice focuses attention.

# The Constitutional Economics
## of Earmarking

During the first half of this century, the conventional wisdom in normative public-finance theory was highly critical of the earmarking of tax revenues. Any restriction on the budgetary flexibility of the fiscal authority was adjudged to be undesirable, almost by definition. Such normative condemnation of earmarking was a consequence of the implicit acceptance of a political model that excluded all elements of democracy. The introduction of electoral feedbacks generates categorically different understandings of the fiscal process, which may lead to quite different evaluations of revenue earmarking. In one limiting case the taxing-spending operation can be modelled as an idealized exchange. In this analytical setting, sectoral budgeting, a form of earmarking, emerges as a necessity in any fiscal process that meets standard efficiency norms. A somewhat less restricted, but still limiting, model may incorporate pure majoritarianism. Such a model departs from that of pure fiscal exchange and allows for politically coerced transfers. In its idealized form, however, this majoritarian model does not introduce the independent existence of the "fisc," as such. The normative implications for the desirability of earmarking institutions are far from clear.

Finally, effective electoral constraints on fiscal outcomes may again be removed from consideration, but with categorically different presumptions concerning the motivations of political agents than those which were implicitly embodied in the first model noted, that which informed the conventional wisdom early in this century. Political agents may be largely, if not wholly,

From *Charging for Government: User Charges and Earmarked Taxes in Principle and Practice,* ed. Richard E. Wagner (London and New York: Routledge, 1991), 152–62. Reprinted by permission of the publisher.

exempted from direct electoral controls, but these agents may be modelled as independent utility-maximizers on their own account.

The first four sections examine the four separate models of fiscal process: those of (1) the benevolent fisc, (2) fiscal exchange, (3) fiscal transfer, and (4) revenue-maximizing Leviathan. The examination and analysis is concentrated on the normative evaluation of earmarking institutions, as potential *constitutional* variables, in each of the models. The fifth section shifts analysis towards fiscal-political reality, in which there exists explanatory potential in each of the four models. Relatively robust conclusions may be reached with reference to the earmarking of tax revenues for spending on programmes that embody no complementarity with the generation of tax bases. Such earmarking is not supportable on normative grounds upon acceptance of any mix among the fiscal models. Earmarking that does relate tax-base generation to complementary publicly supplied services (for example, motor fuels tax revenues earmarked to finance roads) may be included in a normatively acceptable fiscal constitution, especially as a means of checking the potential overreaching of the transfer process and, at the same time, a means of introducing an incentive for political agents to provide desired levels of public goods and services.

## 1. The Benevolent Fisc

Intellectual development has been so rapid since mid-century that it seems difficult in the 1990s to recapture the image or model of governmental fiscal authority that informed and dominated the thinking of the economists of the whole reform era, roughly between the 1880s and the 1960s, an era that I have extended a little and sometimes called "the socialist century." Perhaps a more descriptive term would be "the Hegelian century," since this attribution would directly call attention to the philosopher whose influence on ideas was so great. The romantic mind-set was such that the model of government as potentially omniscient and benevolent went unchallenged for decades, and this despite the wholly contrasting set of attitudes towards the state that was dominant in the eighteenth and early nineteenth centuries. During the whole of the reform era, social scientists concerned themselves almost exclusively with alternative policy options that a benevolent authority might face and among which selection would be made.

The argument can be clarified if the model of government or the state within this paradigm is presented in its extreme, or idealized, form. In such presentation, the collectivity has an independent, organic existence and possesses a consciousness, a will, and an ability to choose, as A. C. Pigou explicitly suggested in his inquiry in normative public finance, a "fiscal brain."[1] In its utilitarian variant, this decision-making authority organizes its taxing and spending activities so as to maximize total utility in the political community, total utility as represented by the summation of the utilities of the separate persons in the collectivity. In this idealized construction, government has no difficulty in securing the requisite knowledge concerning the utility schedules of persons, and it faces no barriers in being able to add utilities over persons. The simplistic logic of maximization dictates equalization of utility increments, negative and positive, over all margins of adjustment. Taxes are to be levied so as to ensure equi-marginal sacrifices in utility; benefits are to be allocated so as to generate equi-marginal utility gains; and, finally, marginal sacrifices in utility due to taxes are equated with marginal increments to utility due to benefits and/or transfers.

In this idealized construction there is clearly no basis for *any* constitutional limits on the authority of government, whether we restrict attention to fiscal activities or extend attention more widely. And, in one sense, of course, the earmarking of tax revenues is always effectively a constitutional limit, whether or not it is explicitly discussed as such. Earmarking involves a prior dedication of revenue collections from specified taxes. And any such dedication necessarily reduces the discretionary authority of the spending agent or agency. Since this agent or agency aims to (and does) maximize total utility by equalizing utility per dollar's worth in all uses, any shift from the unique utility-maximizing allocation that may be induced by earmarking constraints must impose loss in total utility. Earmarking, as a fiscal institution, shifts the community to a position inside its utility possibility frontier.

When the model of the omniscient and benevolent state is presented in the idealized manner just outlined, its absurdities become apparent. But features of this model continue to exert normative influence even when the descriptive properties of the model are largely discarded. Governments, as they are observed to operate, may be acknowledged to lack omniscience, and, fur-

---

1. A. C. Pigou, *A Study in Public Finance*, 3d ed. (London: Macmillan, 1947).

ther, claims that governments act monolithically to further some abstractly imagined public interest may be dropped. But those persons who do assume roles as political agents, charged with making decisions on the part of the collectivity, may still be modelled to behave, even if quite imperfectly, so as to promote their own best interpretations of some generalized interest. This vision of politics and governance is a substantially watered-down model of benevolent authority, and its proponents may also acknowledge explicitly that utility, as such, is neither cardinally measurable nor interpersonally comparable in any objective or agreed-on basis.

In this more widely held conceptualization of the state and, specifically, fiscal authority, earmarking, as an effective constitutional constraint on the budgetary usage of tax revenues, may still be judged to be normatively undesirable. Despite epistemological limits, political agents charged with making decisions on outlays are seeking to promote citizens' well-being, as best that well-being can be ascertained and estimated. And any overtly imposed constraint on the ability of such agents to choose freely among spending options, in the large or in the small, must reduce the efficiency of the overall fiscal process. Earmarking, as an institution, remains categorically "bad" in a fundamental, normative sense.

## 2. Fiscal Exchange

In all variants of the benevolent fisc model, the decision-making authority of the collectivity is separated from the persons *for whom* choices are made, those persons who qualify for membership in the polity, and upon whom taxes are imposed and to whom governmental benefits are offered. The "for the people" leg of the Lincoln triad receives exclusive attention; there is no room for any direct "by the people" emendation.

The idealized model of fiscal exchange lies at the opposing end of the imagined analytical spectrum from the benevolent fisc. In the exchange model, considered in its pure form, the "by the people" leg of the triad takes on a central role, and both the "for" and the "of the people" criteria are necessarily satisfied. The state, or government, exists only as a structure or process through which citizens (taxpayers-beneficiaries) make decisions collectively (publicly) rather than separately (privately), with the idealized division between individualized and collectivized choices being determined by choices also made by citizens themselves.

In this model, individuals effectively "purchase" the goods and services that are supplied jointly to all members of the community by the payment of "tax-prices" that are analogous to the prices paid for ordinary goods that are supplied separately to purchasers in markets. As distinct from market prices, tax-prices are differentiated among separate persons, but the structure of tax-prices is settled in a process of bargaining and ultimate contractual agreement, which also includes determination of the level or quantity of the collective good or service to be purchased. In the idealized solution (sometimes called the Lindahl equilibrium), the marginal tax-price confronting each person equals the marginal evaluation of that person for the good or service at the quantity purchased, and, of course, the summed marginal evaluations over all persons equals the marginal cost of supplying the good or service (sometimes called the Samuelson conditions). In this idealized model of fiscal exchange, note that government, as such, does not exist.[2]

Note that taxes, as such, are not *imposed* on citizens. Tax-prices emerge as voluntarily agreed-on elements in the many-person exchange contract. The operative rule for making collective decisions is that of unanimity or general consensus. As Knut Wicksell recognized, only the existence of such a rule would guarantee that collective fiscal action precludes the coercion of some members of the political community. In a seminal article, R. A. Musgrave labelled this model the "voluntary exchange theory of public finance."[3]

The conditions outlined above must be met separately for each good or service that is "purchased" jointly by the members of a collectivity. If there is more than one good or service, a conceptually separate evaluation-agreement process must take place for each good. Any arbitrary bundling of several goods and services that would then require collective purchase of "baskets" rather than item-by-item adjustment would clearly reduce the efficiency of the whole fiscal operation.

The analogy with the market purchase of private goods is straightforward. The individual buyer-consumer makes purchase decisions separately for each good. Confronted with a market price, the individual selects an op-

---

2. E. Lindahl, *Die Gerechtigkeit der Besteuerung* (Lund: Gleerupska, 1919); P. Samuelson, "The Pure Theory of Public Expenditure," *Review of Economics and Statistics* 36 (November 1954): 387–89.

3. K. Wicksell, *Finanztheoretische Untersuchungen* (Jena: Gustav Fischer, 1896); R. A. Musgrave, "The Voluntary Exchange Theory of Public Economy," *Quarterly Journal of Economics* 53 (February 1938): 213–37.

timally preferred quantity. Any single good may, of course, be a complement or substitute for other goods, but such interdependencies are effectively incorporated in the independent adjustments made as each good is purchased. Any introduction of a tie-in sale of two or more goods necessarily reduces buyers' satisfaction. The endowment of the purchaser, summarized in a budget constraint, provides the revenue source for potential outlay on all goods in the market. But rational purchasing choice dictates that this common source be separately drawn on for the purchases of each good.

In fiscal exchange, the analogy to efficient decision processes in private goods markets is *earmarking*, at least of a sort. To allow for the separate consideration of each spending item, the collective contracting-bargaining process must involve examination and comparison of revenue requirements and preferred outlays simultaneously, but along each single dimension. If this idealized norm is translated into institutional reality, even to some first approximation, we should observe sectoral rather than general-fund budgeting. While the tax or revenue source for specified items of outlay would not be earmarked in advance of fiscal decision, there would exist a direct relationship between the structure of tax-prices incorporated in any proposed outlay and citizen evaluations of those outlays. In this fiscal exchange model, there is no flexibility allowed to any decision taker, whether this be the whole citizenry or some agent, to use revenues for other than spending on the good or service under consideration in isolation.

As we shift attention away from the idealized normative construction and move more towards feasible political-institutional arrangements, we may retain a generalized interpretation of the fiscal process as one involving imperfect fiscal exchange. And, in this framework, the relevance and importance of structural features akin to earmarking and sectoral budgeting become more apparent, even than in the idealized construction. Each proposed spending programme must be matched up against its projected tax costs in order for any semblance of a rational fiscal calculus to be present. So long as the overall fiscal process is conceived in the exchange paradigm, there is no normative argument to be advanced for a unified budget, from which several programmes of public outlay are to be financed and into which revenues flow from separate tax sources.

As the discussion suggests, sectoral budgeting, which allows separate proposals for spending to be considered separately and in relation to alternative tax-financing sources, emerges in any institutional approximation of a fiscal exchange process. Note, however, that the emergence of an institutional similarity to earmarking does not imply that in the fiscal exchange model constitutionally directed dedication of revenues is efficiency enhancing. Any prior constraint on the potential sources for financing a spending programme might inhibit the reaching of agreement, as Wicksell emphasized. Separate tax financing for each and every programme is a necessary feature of fiscal exchange, but a constitutional linkage between specific taxes and designated spending programmes may not be desirable.

## 3. Fiscal Transfer

As noted, an operative decision rule of unanimity is a necessary element in the idealized model of fiscal exchange. Only the presence of such a rule, or its equivalent, can ensure that those members of the community who pay for the jointly demanded and collectively supplied goods are those who actually secure the benefits provided by these goods. Only in this setting can the fiscal process be conceptually modelled as voluntary exchange. And, as a corollary, only in the matching of the two sides of the fiscal account can there be any meaningful guarantee that the exchange increases value.[4]

If the effective unanimity rule is dropped, as it must be in any approach to political reality, the model of the fiscal process dramatically changes, even if we retain the electoral democratic feature and continue to presume that an independently motivated "fisc" does not exist at all. Consider, then, a model in which taxing and outlay decisions are made strictly by the operation of a majority voting rule, either in a direct democracy or in a representative democracy setting. In this political framework, a dominant majority coalition will tend to form, and members of this coalition will aim to use the fiscal process to impose coerced tax charges on non-members of the opposing minority, with the proceeds of these taxes used to finance benefits enjoyed by members of the majority. The limiting case of this model becomes the pure

---

4. Wicksell, *Finanztheoretische Untersuchungen;* James M. Buchanan, "Taxation in Fiscal Exchange," *Journal of Public Economics* 6 (Fall 1976): 17–29. Reprinted in J. M. Buchanan, *Freedom in Constitutional Contract* (College Station: Texas A&M University Press, 1977).

fiscal transfer, in which members of the minority, and only these persons, pay taxes that finance cash transfers to members of the majority coalition, and to no one else, in the polity. It is evident that any semblance of an exchange disappears in this transfer operation, and that any modelling of fiscal institutions in the exchange paradigm would generate misleading results.

The proclivity of majoritarian political competition to degenerate towards the pure transfer process should be noted. Members of successful political majorities may, initially, limit their fiscal demands to the financing of collective-consumption goods and services while imposing all costs of these goods and services on members of the unsuccessful minority. It will become clear, however, that the benefits from direct transfers will dominate those expected from collective-consumption goods and services. The transfer elements in the majoritarian political game will emerge to swamp the public-goods elements.[5]

Constitutional limits on the direction and magnitude of pure fiscal transfers would seem clearly to be desirable in majoritarian settings, limits that may take the form of requiring *generality* in both taxing and spending. Taxes that discriminate between separately classified members of the polity would be constitutionally prohibited, along with spending programmes that offer benefits or direct transfers only to designated groups of the citizenry. Note that we have observed such constitutional limits on the taxing side but not on the spending side of the budget in the United States.[6] These inclusive constitutional limits are not, however, my primary concern here. I want to concentrate attention on the possible efficiency of revenue earmarking in the pure fiscal-transfer model.

Assume that there are no general-taxation–general-benefit constitutional constraints in existence. Would a constitutional restriction on revenue earmarking reduce or increase the potential for fiscal exploitation? In this setting, and absent constitutional attention, the dominant majority would use any available means of imposing taxes on members of the minority while absolving themselves from tax burdens. Revenue earmarking or dedication

---

5. M. Flowers and P. Danzon, "Separation of Redistributive and Allocative Functions of Government," *Journal of Public Economics* 24 (August 1984): 373–80.

6. D. Tuerck, "Constitutional Asymmetry," *Papers on Non-Market Decision-Making* 2 (1967): 27–44.

might well be descriptive of the workings of the transfer process. The successful imposition of taxes on specifically classified groups in the population might be accompanied by dedication of revenues from these taxes to programmes that concentrate benefits on members of the majority. Both sides of the account may be institutionally manipulated to ensure some approximation to the ultimately desired pure transfer. When such prospects are viewed constitutionally, as if behind some veil of ignorance or uncertainty as to membership in majority or minority coalitions, constitutional specification as to the directed use of tax sources might offer one means of constraining fiscal exploitation. If majority coalitions are prohibited, constitutionally, from the imposition of taxes on designated sources other than for the purpose of raising revenues for outlays on publicly provided goods and services that are either general in nature or are *complementary* to the activities that generate the source of the tax, the ever-present temptation to tax for transfer spending is inhibited.

Examples come readily to mind. If a majority coalition is not allowed access to, say, a motor fuels (gasoline) tax except for spending on roads, the usage of the revenues to finance cash transfers is simply out of bounds. In this setting, the pure tax-transfer process can be boxed in, so to speak, and limited to the exploitation of those general tax sources that ensure the presence of some tax costs on majority members.

## 4. Constrained Leviathan

In both the fiscal exchange and the pure fiscal-transfer models discussed in Sections 2 and 3, there is no independently existing "fisc" or fiscal authority that has an interest in and exerts an influence on fiscal outcomes. Both of these models, in sharp contrast to that model of the benevolent fisc discussed in Section 1, embody the workings of idealized democracy, even if in dramatically differing forms. The model of fiscal exchange is, of course, one of idealized cooperation, whereas the model of fiscal transfer is one of idealized majoritarian conflict. The first model is positive sum, for all players; the second is negative, zero, or positive sum in the aggregate, but is necessarily negative sum for some players.

Any move towards recognition of fiscal-political reality will surely involve some departure from these idealized constructions. In its fiscal as well as in its other activities, government operates only through choices made by political agents, who are able, within limits, to pursue objectives that may not correspond directly to those of citizens, either those in the all-inclusive coalition or in the limited coalition of a political majority. In the benevolent fisc model treated in Section 1 these objectives were postulated to be defined by the agents' perceptions of some "general" or "public" interest. By contrast, in this section I propose to examine a model in which agents are postulated to act in furtherance of their own separately defined interests—that is, to behave as ordinary utility-maximizers.

It is useful, initially, to assume that the political agents acting as the fiscal authority are not subject to electoral constraints at all. They are simply empowered to act on behalf of the collectivity in fiscal matters, bound only by whatever constitutional constraints may exist. It is clear that, under these conditions, the agents possessing such authority will seek to *maximize* revenue collections from any and all tax sources they are authorized to exploit and, at the same time, will seek to *minimize* outlays devoted to the supply of goods and services and transfers to others than members of their own preferred set of recipients, again within the constitutionally allowable limits.[7]

In dramatic contrast to the benevolent fisc model of Section 1, where *any* constitutional limits are undesirable, the Leviathan model suggests that constitutional constraints are necessary if any semblance of an exchange relationship between citizens as taxpayers and as beneficiaries is to be preserved. Such constraints must be directed towards ensuring against overextension of the taxing authority and towards ensuring that tax revenues, once collected, are expended in providing benefits to citizens over and beyond those in the agents' preferred sets. The first objective can be secured, in some degree, by careful constitutional limits on tax bases or tax sources. The second objective can be achieved, in part, by constitutionally earmarking revenues for specific spending programmes that are designed to exploit the incentive structure offered in the complementarity between the generation of the tax base and the utilization of publicly provided goods and services.

The example introduced earlier remains applicable here. If the fiscal authority is constitutionally permitted to impose a motor fuels tax only if the

7. G. Brennan and J. Buchanan, *The Power to Tax* (Cambridge: Cambridge University Press, 1980).

revenues are dedicated to spending on roads, there is an incentive for the authority, even if it seeks to maximize revenues, to provide reasonably efficient levels of road services. Suppose, however, that the fiscal authority is empowered to levy a motor fuels tax without the required dedicated spending on complementary road services. For instance, the revenues from this tax might be dedicated to spending on toxic-waste clean-up. In this case, Leviathan will, of course, maximize expected revenue collections as before, but the share of these revenues expended on the designated outlay will be minimized, since there is no economic relationship between such spending and the revenue generation. The earmarking of revenues will not constrain the excesses of Leviathan unless the potential complementarity between tax sources and spending programmes is constitutionally exploited.

## 5. Towards Fiscal Reality

As we observe the fiscal process to operate in modern political democracy (the United States *c.* 1990) there are, of course, elements of each of the four models at work. To an extent, political agents who are responsible for making choices among taxing and spending options do, indeed, try to further the "public interest," as best they can define and interpret this vaguest of objectives. But these agents are always sensitive both to actual and potential pressures from electoral constituencies, who seek to ensure that the taxes paid to government are exchanged for governmental goods and services that are broadly worth their costs. At the same time, much effort is devoted to attempts to secure differentially advantageous fiscal treatment, either via exemptions from taxes or via special benefits and/or transfers. And, finally, the natural proclivities of political agents are surely directed towards maximizing the size of the fiscal sector, which implies revenue collection beyond either plausible "public interest" or potentially expressed exchange limits.

Given the mix of descriptive models that seems to characterize the fiscal activity that is observed, what normative conclusions may be drawn with reference to the institutions of earmarking revenues for specific programmes of outlay? Note that the possible constitutionalization of earmarking imposes directionally different effects in the first two models than in the last two models. Under either a benevolent fisc or a fiscal exchange model, earmarking, when imposed as a prior constitutional constraint, restricts budgetary flexibility, and, because it does so, tends to be efficiency reducing. This result is evident in the benevolent fisc model, but it is less obvious in the fiscal exchange model due to the emergence of something like sectoral budgeting in the idealized agreement process. Only in the third and fourth model of fiscal process, that is, only under the fiscal transfer model and the Leviathan model, does the constitutionalization of earmarking offer efficiency-enhancing potentiality. It does so, in both cases, because revenue dedication may offer one among several instruments designed to keep fiscal exactions within the limits that would be constitutionally preferred.

To the extent that either or both of the last two models is considered descriptive of fiscal reality, revenue earmarking may be one component of an effectively operating fiscal constitution, provided that the institution is used to exploit the complementarity between the generation of tax bases and the utilization of publicly provided services. On the other hand and by contrast, we can reach more robust conclusions concerning the possible earmarking of tax revenues for outlay programmes that are not complementary with the generation of tax bases. Such non-complementary dedication of tax revenues does not, and cannot, serve efficiency-enhancing purposes, and should be constitutionally prohibited, in any and all models of fiscal process.

# Fiscal Choice through Time

## A Case for Indirect Taxation?

*James M. Buchanan and Francesco Forte*

## I. Introduction

How should taxes be paid? This question has been discussed for centuries. It has not been resolved, either in the formal theory of public finance or in the institutional structure of modern fiscal systems. The direct-indirect tax comparison continues to occupy a central position in the literature of fiscal theory, and the choice between these two institutions of taxation confronts governments of all states, new and old.

We do not propose to develop further refinements in the analytical models that have become familiar to scholars in public finance. The familiar "excess-burden" theorem, initially stated by Barone,[1] along with the more recent criticisms that have been advanced against it, will not concern us here except insofar as the theorem proves useful in explaining our own model. Broadly speaking, it seems correct to say that despite the acknowledged relevance of "second-best" arguments, most modern theorists accept the view that, other things equal, direct and general taxes are to be recommended over indirect and specific taxes on both equity and efficiency criteria. We shall challenge this position, and we shall demonstrate that from a different, and apparently new, approach to fiscal choice, a case can be made out for specific commodity

From *National Tax Journal* 17 (June 1964): 144–57. Reprinted by permission of the publisher.

1. E. Barone, "Studi di economia finanziaria," *Giornale degli economisti* (1912), 2, 329–30 in notes.

taxation. We do not claim that the case is a definitive one, and, as is noted, other considerations can be introduced that tend to oppose those stressed in this paper. Our primary purpose is not that of defending specific indirect taxation, *per se,* but instead that of utilizing this traditional problem to illustrate the efficacy of a proposed analytical approach to fiscal institutions.[2]

## II. A Methodology for Tax Analysis

There are two separate, but closely related, elements in our approach which contrast sharply with methods traditionally employed. First, we base the analysis on an individual calculus; that is to say, on the choice of the individual as he participates in a collective decision process. We examine his behavior as he tries to choose the "preferred" means of meeting his tax obligations. In one sense, this method is implicit in much Paretian welfare analysis, including the Barone theorem, but the central position of individual choice is made explicit in our model. Instead of conceiving the fiscal problem as that of determining the results of alternative institutions on individual and group behavior patterns, we conceive it as the choice confronted by the individual when he is required to choose among these alternative institutions.

In this setting, the second major element emerges as a natural order of events. By concentrating initially on the individual's choice among tax instruments, we are led, almost necessarily, to think of these instruments as *institutions,* and not as mere analytical devices without spatial or temporal dimension. This should not suggest that we propose to lapse into the methodology of traditional "institutionalism." But we do propose to incorporate into the analysis the quasi-permanency of fiscal institutions, and to recognize the lasting impact of fiscal decisions once they are made.

Almost without exception, the direct-indirect tax discussion has proceeded from the assumption that a choice must be made only in a one-period setting. To our knowledge, no attempt has been made to extend the comparison to the multi-period setting; no one has assumed that the tax instrument chosen

2. Essentially the same approach employed here has been applied, more generally, to the choice among various political decision rules by Buchanan and Tullock. See James M. Buchanan and Gordon Tullock, *The Calculus of Consent* (Ann Arbor: University of Michigan Press, 1962).

shall remain in effect over several income or accounting periods. The model that introduces such a temporal sequence is both more logical and more realistic than the orthodox one-period model. If we look, however casually, at the fiscal experience of almost any government, we must recognize that decisions tend to be relatively long-lived in effect. Tax institutions and spending programs alike tend to remain in force over a series of accounting and budgetary periods. Nor does this observed political history reflect irrational collective choice. The making of collective or group decisions is costly and time consuming. The agreements and the compromises that may be finally incorporated in a single apparent decision emerge from a many-stage process of discussion, debate, bargaining, mutual and marginal adjustment to complex circumstances. Quite similarly, it is costly to organize changes in institutions that are in being. If the results of analysis are to have even remote applicability to real-world problems, collective choice, and individual participation in its formation, must be examined in a long-run institutional context.

## III. The One-Period Argument Summarized

Barone demonstrated that for the individual a direct tax "should" rationally be preferred to an indirect tax of equal yield if a one-period model is accepted. The argument has been elaborated many times through the indifference curve apparatus, and it need not be repeated here. Little demonstrated that, strictly speaking, the Barone conclusions follow only when a lump-sum tax is compared with a specific commodity tax.[3] Friedman[4] and Rolph and Break[5] showed that the Barone theorem could be extended from the single individual to the community only if all of the remaining conditions necessary for Pareto-optimality should be satisfied. These latter criticisms of the basic analysis need not concern us here, however, since, initially at least, we shall remain at the level of individual choice. In this restricted one-period

3. I. M. D. Little, "Direct versus Indirect Taxes," *Economic Journal*, 61 (September, 1951), 577–84.

4. Milton Friedman, "The 'Welfare' Aspects of an Income Tax and an Excise Tax," *Journal of Political Economy*, 60 (1952), 25–33, reprinted in *Essays in Positive Economics* (Chicago: University of Chicago Press, 1953), 100–116.

5. Earl E. Rolph and George F. Break, "The Welfare Aspects of Excise Taxes," *Journal of Political Economy*, 57 (1949), 46–54.

model, the rational individual will always prefer the direct tax over the indirect tax, of equal yield, for the simple reason that he can, in this way, enjoy the widest range of choice.[6]

In order to relate it to our subsequent analysis, we shall state the problem, applied in the one-period setting, as follows: "Should" the rational utility-maximizing individual, confronted with a determined tax obligation, choose to meet this obligation through a lump-sum payment, a proportional tax levied on his income, a progressive tax on his income, a general tax on total consumption expenditure, or a specific tax on the consumption of one commodity? In such a model as this, the first alternative provides the individual with the widest area of choice. It will be preferred over the proportional tax on income which does, of course, discriminate between measured and non-measured income. This proportional tax will, in its turn, be preferable to the progressive tax which introduces an additional element of discrimination. This tax alternative will, in its turn, be rationally selected over the even less general tax on expenditure. And, finally, the tax on the single specific commodity or service becomes the least desired of the lot. These familiar conclusions are relevant, however, only if the individual is allowed to select among alternatives in each discrete period of time, or if the results of the one-period model can be generalized to apply for a sequence of periods.

## IV. The Introduction of Time

Let us now ask the same question as before; only now let us assume that the individual recognizes that the tax instrument, once chosen, will remain in force, not for a single period only, but over a whole series of periods, which we can identify as $t_0, t_1, \ldots, t_n$. The results may be different from those in the one-period model.

We want, first, to develop a model under the assumption of certainty. The individual, whose choice calculus we examine, is assumed to know with certainty, at $t_0$, the time or moment of decision, what his income will be in

6. Lancaster has shown that the whole analysis can be derived in terms of expanded individual choice instead of the more usual indifference curve apparatus. See K. Lancaster, "Welfare Propositions in Terms of Consistency and Expanded Choice," *Economic Journal,* 68 (September, 1958), 464–70.

each of the periods, $t_1, t_2, \ldots, t_n$. We shall also assume that his current decision process reflects some consideration of expected fluctuations in wants or needs over time. Viewed from $t_0$, his wants in each of the subsequent periods is also known with certainty, although these need not be stable over time.

Before posing the fiscal choice issue specifically, it will be useful to establish some general principles of rational behavior for the individual. For convenience, we may assume that the individual saves only in order to retire debt or to accumulate funds for future consumption. This is in accord with a life-cycle model of saving behavior that has been suggested by several economists in recent years.[7] In such a model, the present value of the income stream, at $t_0$, is equal to the present value of the consumption expenditures stream.

To avoid confusion, it is first necessary to distinguish spending on items of consumption and actual consumption of such items. For simplicity, we shall assume that these acts are simultaneous. This implies that the services of all durable consumption items are purchased or leased as consumption actually takes place. Let us now break down consumption into two categories, which we do not propose to define rigorously at this time. The first category includes those services that are aimed at fulfilling what may be called "basic needs." The second category includes those services that are purchased with a view toward fulfilling what may be called "residual needs," which are in some sense less urgent than those in the first category. Despite the arbitrariness of any specific dividing line, some such division exists for each individual or family. Some needs must be met in the normal order of affairs; others may be met only if the opportunity (largely determined by income) should arise.

Orthodox rationality criteria suggest that the individual will equalize the utility per dollar spent on each consumption service in each period. This may suggest that any attempt to distinguish between "basic" and "residual" services is misleading. If income fluctuates over time, however, casual observation indicates that residual items may be consumed only during periods of relative affluence. Such behavior will be irrational in a certainty model, how-

---

7. For a summary discussion that contains references to the other works, see M. J. Farrell, "New Theories of the Consumption Function," *Economic Journal*, 69 (December, 1959), 678–96.

ever, since the individual "should," through his saving activity, attain results approximating those observed under a stable income flow. He should, in other terms, equalize the marginal rates of substitution between any two items of consumption service for all time periods, viewed from $t_0$, independent of predicted fluctuations in income or in needs, on the assumption that price ratios remain constant. If needs should vary as among separate periods, this equalization need not, of course, imply equal consumption flows of either service in each period of time.[8] Viewed from the moment, $t_0$, the indi-

---

8. For each period, the standard necessary conditions hold. That is,

(1)     $$\frac{MU_i}{p_i} = \frac{MU_j}{p_j}, \quad \text{for any two goods, } i \text{ and } j,$$

$$i \neq j, \text{ in a set } i, j = 1, 2, \ldots, m.$$

In the model that includes several periods, the standard income constraint does not apply. Over the periods of the appropriately determined life cycle, the individual acts so as to satisfy (1) in each period. If we assume that the price ratios among separate goods or services are to remain constant over time, necessary conditions for multi-period "equilibrium," at the moment of planning, become

(2)     $$\left(\frac{MU_i}{MU_j}\right)_{t_0} = \left(\frac{MU_i}{MU_j}\right)_{t_1} = \ldots = \left(\frac{MU_i}{MU_j}\right)_{t_n} = \frac{p_i}{p_j},$$

where the subscripts outside the parentheses refer to periods of time, $t_0$ to $t_n$.

No explicit discounting factor need be introduced in (2), since, by assumption, prices are not paid until consumption takes place. Thus, for periods later than $t_0$, marginal utilities and prices are discounted by a common factor. Note particularly that the satisfaction of (2) does not require that tastes remain constant over time. The equalization of the marginal rates of substitution can be achieved by widely differing "mixes" of the two items.

If we assume that the individual has no control over the income to be earned, and, further, that income payments are lagged by one period, the overall income constraint becomes

(3)     $$A_{t_0} + \frac{Y_{t_1}}{(1+r)} + \frac{Y_{t_2}}{(1+r)^2} + \ldots + \frac{Y_{t_n}}{(1+r)^n} =$$

$$\left[\sum_{i=1}^{m} p_i q_i\right]_{t_0} + \ldots + \frac{\left[\sum_{i=1}^{m} p_i q_i\right]_{t_1}}{(1+r)} + \ldots + \frac{\left[\sum_{i=1}^{m} p_i q_i\right]_{t_n}}{(1+r)^n},$$

where $A_{t_0}$ measures initially held assets, $p$, $q$, and $r$, the prices, quantities, and rate of discount, respectively.

If the individual is allowed to vary his income (earnings) over time, (3) is not relevant, and it must be replaced by a set of production constraints. The fundamentals of the anal-

vidual will plan a pattern of saving and spending over the several periods such that in each period the marginal rate of substitution between any two goods, say, bread and coal, is equal to the price ratio. If as an example, we consider a two-season year as a sequence, the rational individual will plan his spending over the whole year to insure that his needs for bread and coal will be equally satisfied, in a relative sense, in each season. He will not skimp on bread during the winter season merely because his needs for coal are great. Nor will he gorge himself in the summer because he need make no expenditure on coal. He will, of course, save some portion of his income during the summer in order to meet his varying need for coal over the sequence. This example suggests that either income or need can vary over a temporal sequence and that the individual must take these variations into account as he attempts to maximize the present value of expected utility.

Now return to the problem of individual fiscal choice. We ask the same question as before, but this time in the multi-period setting. How will the individual choose to pay a specific tax obligation? In order to simplify the issue, assume that the government must service a deadweight public debt. This allows us to isolate the tax question, *per se,* from the public expenditure side of the fiscal account. Secondly, we seek to eliminate the problem of the distribution of the tax load among separate persons in the group. We assume here that each person has assigned to him a pre-determined share in the aggregate tax liability. By this set of assumptions, we arrive, finally, at a model which substitutes an equal-present-value tax obligation for the equal-yield obligation in the one-period, orthodox analytical model.

If he is allowed full freedom of choice, the individual should prefer to pay the tax when and how he wants to pay it, without temporal or institutional restriction. This undesignated tax is equivalent, in this multi-period model, to the more familiar lump-sum tax introduced in the discussions of the one-period model. If he can select both the timing and the method of payment, the individual can adjust his spending plans over time optimally. Aside from the income effects that result from any payment of net taxes, no temporal distortions are introduced.

This most preferred alternative is explicitly ruled out in the problem as

---

ysis do not, however, require this generalization. Hence, in the discussion the individual is presumed to act on the basis of the income constraint defined by (3).

posed to the individual. We allow him to consider only the following: (1) a tax of equal sum each year, defined independent of fluctuations in income or need, (2) a proportional tax on income received in each year, (3) a progressive tax on income received in each year, (4) a proportional tax on all consumption spending in each period, and, (5) a proportional tax on a specific item of consumption spending in each period. Under either one of these second-best alternatives, some distortion will be introduced in the consumption-saving pattern over time. The question is which of these institutions, each of which describes a real-world tax instrument, involves the minimum distortion? Which alternative "should" the individual select?

## V. Exchange through Time

If the capital market works perfectly, and costlessly, in a restricted sense that we shall define in a moment, the orthodox conclusions are not modified. The specific tax on a single item of consumption remains the least desirable of the lot. If the individual should be able, without additional institutional cost, either to borrow or to lend at the rate that is used in discounting the aggregate tax liability—that is, at the government borrowing-lending rate— there need be no temporal distortion introduced under any of the tax institutions. Hence, they can be arrayed in order of preference based on minimizing behavioral or pattern distortions within each single period, the setting for the one-period model. By entering the loan market, the individual can borrow or lend funds so as to maintain an undistorted pattern of consumption spending over time; he will be uninfluenced by the form of the tax instrument.

The required assumption of perfection in the capital or loan market is, however, extremely severe. Individuals may be able to lend funds, and thus to employ saving for future consumption, at the government borrowing rate. They do so by purchasing government securities. On the other hand, it seems wholly unrealistic to assume that as individuals they can also borrow at this same rate even when incomes are predictable with certainty. Lenders need not have access to the sources of information possessed by potential borrowers, and, if they do not, risk considerations alone make private borrowing rates exceed those for government. In addition, institutional factors make borrowing against future income expected from human capital possible only at differentially higher costs than borrowing against nonhuman capital. Also, in normal circumstances, the very process of entering the capital market, either as a lender or as a borrower, involves some positive conversion cost for the individual.

When such imperfections as these are allowed in the model, the private or individual rate of discount that is appropriate for the decision among the tax alternatives may be different from the "objective" rate that is employed by government in presenting the alternatives. In such circumstances, the rational man must try to select that tax instrument which requires the least amount of conversion through the capital market; that is to say, requires that he make the smallest number of exchanges of income through time. The objective of the individual is not changed. He will try, after the imposition of the tax, to retain, insofar as is possible, the desired equalities through time for the relevant marginal rates of substitution.[9]

Let us now assume that before the imposition of any tax the individual has attained a position of "planning" equilibrium. That is to say he has formulated a pattern of saving and spending over time that will equalize the relevant marginal rates of substitution in the different periods, always viewed from the moment, $t_0$.[10] We now confront him with the tax obligation, which we define in present-value terms computed on the basis of the government discount rate. The rational individual will try to select that tax alternative which minimizes resort to the market. He will choose that tax instrument that introduces the least initial disturbance in his planned "equilibrium" pattern of consumption over time. If both income and needs are expected to be equal in each period, the orthodox conclusions continue to hold. If, however, we allow for some predicted fluctuations in either incomes or needs, these conclusions must be modified in the light of specific temporal distortions. If needs are expected to be more stable over time than income, the progressive tax on income earned in each period will tend to be preferred over either the

9. The type of imperfections in the capital market that are introduced here are similar to those discussed in a recent paper by Frank H. Hahn. See his "Real Balances and Consumption," *Oxford Economic Papers*, 14 (June, 1962), 117–23.

10. We are concerned here only with the individual's calculus at $t_0$. The fact that when $t_1$ arrives he may have a different set of "optimal" plans need not concern us. On this latter point, see Robert H. Strotz, "Myopia and Inconsistency in Dynamic Utility Maximization," *Review of Economic Studies*, 23 (1956), 165–80.

annual tax or the proportional tax because of the temporal distortion factor. Here the intrusion of possible temporal distortion must be added to the "pattern distortion" that has commanded almost the exclusive center of attention in orthodox analysis of the relative efficiency of the various tax instruments. It is, of course, impossible to state, *a priori,* which of these two elements will be the more important in any particular circumstances. It is clear, however, that when the temporal distortion factor alone is considered, the progressive tax will be preferred over alternative taxes levied on income. This tax allows the tax liability to be concentrated in periods when, failing recourse to the loan market, the marginal utility of spending is expected to be low.[11] The question we seek to examine now is whether or not the general or the specific tax on consumption expenditure might not be preferred, on similar grounds, even to the progressive income tax. The answer seems clearly to be in the negative. Either of these taxes on consumption would, in this case where needs are expected to be more stable over time than income, clearly introduce the familiar pattern distortions. And, at the same time, they would not be preferred over the progressive income tax in terms of the temporal distortions introduced.

If, however, we should assume that predicted needs over time fluctuate more than predicted income, these conclusions do not follow. For simplicity, assume that income is expected to be the same in each period, but that consumption needs are predicted to vary sharply from one period to the other. The second factor insures that without recourse to the loan market the marginal utility of spending will vary sharply over time. If imperfections in the capital market introduce differential costs, the final adjustment made by the individual may involve a consumption sequence over time which allows for considerable variation in the per period consumption of residual services. In this case, the specific consumption tax, levied on an item of residual consumption, may well involve less overall distortion than even the progressive income tax due to the possibility that it allows for reducing temporal distortion.

It is rational for the individual, who expects both his needs and his income to fluctuate over time, to adjust temporally his consumption of resid-

11. This "defense" of progressive income taxation is developed and discussed at some length in a forthcoming paper by James M. Buchanan.

ual consumption services so as to "bunch" these in periods when the marginal utility of spending is low. That is to say, he will plan to satisfy residual consumption needs only when his overall level of needs is, relatively, low or when his level of income is high. This behavior need not violate rationality norms, even in the most restricted sense, when it is recognized that substitution among services in different periods is clearly possible in many instances. Certain items of residual consumption are postponable, necessarily so. For example, the individual "needs" only one holiday a year. It is rational for him to plan this holiday for a period when either income is higher than usual, or "needs" for remaining services are lower than usual.[12]

If we allow for such bunching of residual consumption, which is surely descriptive of human behavior, it is clear that when the fiscal choice is posed the tax on specific consumption services may, in certain cases, be the most desirable of the alternatives. The orthodox pattern distortions may be more than offset by the added advantage of bunching tax payments, which only this tax makes possible, during periods of low expected marginal utility for spending, and, in this way, minimizing temporal distortion. When specific consumption taxes are discussed, a familiar theorem states that distortion is minimized when the tax is levied on an item characterized by a relatively low price elasticity of demand. When some recognition of temporal distortion is made, this theorem must also be amended. The most preferred tax should be that levied on an item that combines low price elasticity of demand, thus reducing pattern distortion, with high income elasticity of demand, thus minimizing temporal distortion.

As compared with a progressive tax on income in each period, a tax on a single item of postponable residual consumption can allow adjustment in tax liability due not only to fluctuating incomes over time but also to fluctuating levels of need for basic consumption goods and services. To demonstrate this point, assume, initially, that income is expected to be stable, but that needs for basic consumption services are predicted to fluctuate. Let us say that a family expects to receive an annual income of $15,000 over the next decade,

---

12. Care should be taken to distinguish postponable items of residual consumption from durable consumer goods. The durable goods–nondurable goods distinction need not concern us here, and we have assumed that all services are purchased as they are used. A postponable service is characterized by nonrecurrence of "need" over time.

which is the assumed relevant period for planning. During this decade, $t_1$ through $t_{10}$, a son is expected to be in college during the years $t_3$, $t_4$, $t_5$, and $t_6$. Without adjustment through the capital market, the marginal utility of spending in these four years will be higher than during the other years of the decade. The progressive tax would, in this model, require payment of the same sum each year. But the family, if allowed to choose, might well "prefer" to bunch tax payments in the years $t_1$ and $t_2$ and then again in $t_7$, $t_8$, $t_9$, and $t_{10}$. They may be able to do so, without recourse to the capital market, either as net lenders or net borrowers, if the tax could be imposed on some item of residual consumption that they plan to postpone for purchase and use only in those years. For example, holidays in Europe may be "planned" only for those noncollege years. Despite the orthodox pattern distortions that a tax on holiday expenditure would surely involve, such a tax might, over time, actually expand the range of choices open to the individual as compared with the other tax instruments considered.

Interestingly, in this model, when the various tax instruments are arrayed in terms of the temporal distortions introduced, the general tax on all consumption expenditure becomes the least desirable of all instruments. The specific tax on an item of residual consumption allows tax liability to be bunched in periods when the predicted marginal utility of spending is low. The income tax, whether proportional or progressive, allows the liability to be spread equally over time. The general expenditure tax, by comparison, requires a higher total payment precisely in those years when the need for basic consumption items may be greatest. This conclusion is perhaps noteworthy for it runs counter to the argument that the general expenditure tax may be more "efficient," in some ways, than the income tax because of the removal of the discrimination against savings. This contrast in result illustrates the basic difference in our approach and the more traditional one.[13]

13. The relationship between our analysis and the "double taxation of savings" argument should be explained. This argument, as developed by J. S. Mill, Irving Fisher, Luigi Einaudi, and others, supports the imposition of a general expenditure tax relative to a general income tax on grounds of efficiency because the income tax discriminates against savings. This argument assumes meaning only when the *distribution* of the tax load among separate persons in the group is introduced. It is not relevant to our model since we limit the analysis, specifically, to the calculus of the single person when faced with a determined tax obligation defined in present-value terms. In the life-cycle pattern of sav-

Many other models, or examples, could be constructed by using different assumptions concerning predicted fluctuations in incomes and in needs for basic consumption services over time. These need not be elaborated here, however, since our main purpose is that of demonstrating that under some conditions the individual may choose to meet a tax obligation through the payment of a specific commodity tax.

These conclusions are, of course, strongly reinforced when we relax still further the rationality assumption. If moral scruples influence behavior in the direction of making individuals "live within their incomes," and causing them to consider "eating up capital" or "going into debt" to be repugnant, or, at best, imprudent, the marginal adjustments necessary for achieving any "equilibrium" pattern of planned consumption do not take place. The marginal rates of substitution between items of consumption will not be equal in separate time periods, even when viewed from a single moment. As such departures from any rationally planned equilibrium become more significant, the advantages of the specific consumption tax become greater.

The rationally planned equilibrium pattern of consumption spending is, of course, the normative version of the permanent-income hypothesis, either in the limited horizon, life-cycle version, or in the unlimited Ricardian version. To the extent that empirical data lend support to the hypothesis, in either form, the advantages of the specific consumption tax in minimizing temporal distortions are reduced. To the extent that empirical data suggest that individuals plan consumption on the basis of measured income in each period, and not on permanent income, the relative advantages of an indirect tax instrument are enhanced.

## VI. Certainty Relaxed

To this point we have assumed that the individual, whose calculus we examine, chooses under certainty regarding future income prospects, future needs, and the expected life of the fiscal institutions considered. In any plau-

---

ings behavior postulated, the present value of expenditure must equal the present value of income. If the individual is taxed on income received in each period, including the fruits of income saved in previous periods, the rate of tax will tend to be somewhat lower than the rate that would be necessary to produce the same present value under the general expenditure tax.

sible real-world situation, such choices would not be possible. Yet individuals must, in some manner, make selections among fiscal instruments as participants in some collective decision process. It will be helpful to see how the general conclusions reached under the assumption of certainty may be modified when this assumption is dropped.

When the individual is uncertain as to future income prospects and as to future needs or wants for goods and services, it is not possible to present him with a choice among a set of equal-present-value fiscal alternatives. If his income is expected to fluctuate, but the magnitude and the directions of such fluctuations are not predictable, there is no means of determining the present value of an income tax obligation. Similarly, if his consumption pattern is expected to change over time, but in some unpredictable way, we cannot determine the present value of either a general or a specific tax on consumption. The individual must choose among the several possible fiscal institutions without knowing which of these will, in fact, impose the greatest overall tax liability upon him. Obviously, this factor becomes important in his choice calculus. Quite apart from those considerations discussed above as well as those present in the more orthodox tax analysis, the individual will, other things equal, try to minimize aggregate tax liability. His behavior in so doing will depend on his expectations concerning future income and future needs. It is significant, however, that precisely to the extent that the individual is uncertain as to his prospects, he will also be uncertain as to which fiscal instrument will minimize his own personal liability. Thus, distributional considerations, which admittedly cannot be eliminated, even conceptually, from any uncertainty model, loom less important than they might appear. If the individual does not know which tax alternative will, in fact, minimize his aggregate tax liability, he will tend to choose on the basis of nondistributional considerations, such as the temporal "efficiency" calculus previously discussed.

The time element alone tends to reduce the importance of purely distributional considerations. The longer the period over which the institution chosen is expected to remain in force, the less important distribution becomes relative to the more limited criterion of efficiency. For this reason, the analysis that we have developed under the assumption of certainty retains its relevance for an uncertainty model. An example may be useful. Assume that the individual is uncertain as to his income prospects over time, and also as to his basic expenditure needs. He may, however, accept that there are certain criteria which will, roughly and approximately, measure his unadjusted marginal utility of income in particular future periods. He may say that, for instance, "if either my income is high enough or my needs for basic consumption items low enough, I shall probably find myself wearing tailored suits and my wife wearing mink capes. Such items seem to me to be reasonably good independent measures of the marginal utility of income. Hence, if a tax is placed on such items, I can maintain some insurance against being subjected to burdensome tax liability during periods when the marginal utility of income is highest, either because my needs of basic services are unexpectedly high or because my income is, for some reason, unexpectedly low." In one sense, the choice of the indirect tax on residual and postponable consumption items reflects the same sort of mental calculus that might go into a decision to exempt from income taxation certain basic consumption items. We consider this point further below.

In the uncertainty model, we need to make no particular assumption about the perfection or the imperfection in the capital market in order to derive a logical individual preference for the specific commodity tax. With future income and needs uncertain, the whole conception of an "optimal" or "equilibrium" pattern of consumption over time loses much of its meaning. The individual will, more or less as a natural order of events, expect the marginal utility of his expenditures to vary from one period to another. In the case of complete certainty, the individual may prefer, because of the orthodox in-period distortions, the direct tax to the indirect tax because his resort to the loan market can effectively remove the temporal distortions and smooth out his consumption pattern as desired. If uncertainty is introduced, however, he may be observed to select the indirect tax.

To this point, the individual has been assumed to be motivated by ordinary, utility-maximizing considerations. A somewhat broader conception of individual choice allows us to introduce other elements into the analysis that tend to support the conclusions reached. The first concerns the subjective or the "felt" burden of tax payment over future time periods. At the moment of choosing among various tax instruments, the individual may be influenced in this choice by his predictions regarding his own reactions, in later periods, to the decision that he makes at present. He may realize, for example, that on each payment date, the income tax will impose upon him a genuine "felt" burden. On the other hand, he may recognize that since he pays the tax along with the price of a specific commodity such a burden may be absent in the consumption tax. This is a fiscal illusion, and the individual, in his more rational moments, may recognize it as such. But he may, nonetheless, deliberately choose to impose future taxes on himself in such a way that the subsequent subjective burden of payment is minimized.

A second consideration involves the individual's own ethical attitudes toward his consumption of residual items. He may well recognize that he is, on occasion, the slave of his passions, and, because of this, he may, quite rationally, choose to place obstacles in the way of specific consumption patterns. Sumptuary taxation can be derived from an individual calculus of choice. Nevertheless, great care must be taken here to distinguish this attitude from the paternalist one, through which the individual attempts to lay down standards, not for himself, but for others in the social group.

## VII. Problems of Aggregation

Individuals are not, of course, allowed to choose separately and independently the fiscal instruments through which their collective financial obligations may be discharged. At best, they are allowed to participate, directly or remotely, in the group choice which must, once made, impose standard or uniform institutions on all members of the collectivity. To what extent can an analysis of individual choice, as described above, be employed in a discussion of group choice?

The consistency of individual decisions, one with the other, must be examined. While it may be rational for the isolated individual to prefer a privately levied tax on a specific commodity, he may not want the collectivity to impose uniform taxation on the consumption of specific items. Substantial agreement on the commodity or the service to be taxed may not be present. What one man considers as a superfluous or "luxury" good, and its purchase a reasonably good independent criterion for the marginal utility of income, a second man may consider to be a basic consumption item, essential to life, happiness, and well-being. If wide divergencies of this sort exist, the individual participant in group choice may well abandon any support for indirect taxation. On the other hand, social groups are reasonably homogeneous in many respects, and substantial, if not total, agreement might be attainable on a relatively small group or set of specific commodities that might be subjected to a set of specific consumption levies. To the extent that such homogeneity exists, indirect taxation of specific commodities may emerge from a group choice process, in part at least based on considerations such as those we have discussed. The individual participant in such choice may, for example, consider his own consumption of champagne to be a good indicator of his relative "welfare" position. On the other hand, another individual may consider his wife's consumption of mink capes or French perfumes a better choice. After the predicted discussion, argument, and compromise, they may well agree that a bundle of commodities, including champagne, mink capes, and French perfumes, provides a reasonably good index for the marginal utility of expenditure for the average man.

The problem of aggregating individual choices in attaining group decisions suggests the relatively greater applicability of indirect tax institutions for local units of government. The smaller the collective group, the more homogeneous are its members, and hence agreement on the specific commodities or services to be taxed. In addition, the open-ended nature of small collective groups provides the safety valve that is essential to prevent sumptuary exploitation of dissident minorities.

Elements of paternalism cannot, of course, be wholly eliminated from a collective choice among tax instruments. Each participant in a collective decision, be he voter, political leader, or bureaucrat, has a set of preferences, of "values," not only for himself but also regarding the behavior of others in his social group. The point to be stressed here is not the absence of such elements, but rather the fact that these need not be present to derive a collective preference for specific commodity taxation. "Externalities" of this nature are not necessary. Alcohol may be taxed heavily in most jurisdictions because voters and political leaders think that the average man "should" be discouraged from drinking. But, also, alcohol taxes may be accepted because the average man, himself, knows that he can always escape taxation by refraining from drink. In a basic, philosophical sense, indirect taxation of specific commodities allows the taxpayer more ultimate choice than direct taxation precisely because it is specific. He retains an additional faculty of choice over time, so to speak, because he has available a wider range of alternatives than he would retain under direct taxes. This faculty may never be exploited; indeed, the individual will hope that he will never find it necessary to reduce his tax obligation in this way. But the existence of this wider range of potential choice may be decisive for the individual.

## VIII. Taxes and Public Spending

The argument has been developed within the orthodox setting for tax analysis. By assuming that the government is obligated to meet a fixed interest charge on a deadweight debt, we have been able to discuss the choice among tax instruments independent of the choice among public expenditure programs. In a more general setting, taxes and expenditures are simultaneously selected. If the latter are considered to be such that they can be appropriately financed by "general charges against the whole community," such as, for example, spending for national defense, much of the analysis remains valid. However, additional elements enter into the individual calculus, even in these cases, and these should be discussed briefly. We shall limit the discussion to the financing of general-benefit programs. We assume that total spending is not, however, fixed in advance, as in the interest-charge model, but that the level of spending may be at any level that the group chooses.

Here the individual must consider the additional question concerning the *aggregate* tax liability. His own share will depend, in part, on how much the group chooses to spend publicly. And there may exist important interdependencies between the decisions made on tax institutions and the decisions made on the size of public expenditure programs. The individual wants, *ceteris paribus,* the largest possible general-benefit program combined with the lowest possible personal tax liability. If he values public spending benefits relatively more than his fellows, he may choose indirect taxation, quite independent of other considerations, if he thinks that the fiscal illusion involved will lead to an expanded public sector. On the other hand, should he be relatively more interested in his own personal tax liability, he may support direct taxation for the same reasons.

These, and other, considerations are important, but they can only be noted, not examined, in this paper. Only one further element should be mentioned. The individual may recognize that collective decisions to spend are likely to be more favorable when revenues from existing taxes are available. The indirect tax on specific commodities or services of residual consumption becomes, in this light, a means of insuring an automatic or quasi-automatic expansion of public spending along with the expansion of private spending on residual consumption items, and, similarly, a quasi-automatic reduction in public spending when private spending on residual items is reduced.

## IX. Generalizations

This paper does not present a generally applicable normative theory of indirect taxation. We have shown that a case can be made out for the imposition of specific consumption taxes on the basis of an individual choice calculus. The departures from orthodox fiscal analysis are represented by this concentration on individual choice and upon the introduction of fiscal instruments as institutions that are costly to select and costly to modify once they are selected. The explicit introduction of time into the model, and the individual's choice among institutions that are expected to remain in being over time, allows us to show that the indirect tax may be the most preferred instrument under certain conditions. The result may be generalized for the community, but this step depends critically on the existence of some reasonable consensus on a set of commodities or services, the consumption of which provides a criterion for the marginal utility of income in separate periods.

At one point the close similarity between the imposition of specific levies on items of residual consumption and the exemption of items of basic consumption from the income tax was noted. It will be useful to examine these two devices more carefully, since both are to be found in modern fiscal systems. Both of these schemes have been introduced to include some recognition of fluctuating needs for basic consumption goods and services in the tax base. The exemption of such basic consumption items as medical care and education from the income tax base involves the acknowledgement that during the periods when such expenses are high, income alone does not provide an adequate criterion for computing relative tax liabilities. In either case, the taxpayer retains somewhat greater freedom of action than he would have retained under the general income tax without exemptions. The freedom of the taxpayer to adjust his own liability through a modified pattern of consumption is present, but different, in the two cases. Under the exemption scheme, the individual can reduce his tax liability only by consuming the specific items, say, medical services. Under the specific commodity tax, he can reduce his liability by reducing his consumption of one or a few items, leaving him a broad range of alternatives upon which to spend.

One of the interesting by-products of the analysis is the relatively low ranking that is placed on the *general* consumption or expenditure tax. The case that has been made out for specific consumption taxation depends, strictly, on the specificity of the objects taxed. On the basis of an individual choice calculus, it is difficult to see how any argument for general indirect taxation could be derived. The orthodox distortions in static consumption patterns are, of course, smaller than they would be with specific levies. But such distortions can always be minimized with taxes on income which are also preferred on the temporal distortion scale.

# Externality in Tax Response

## I. Introduction

Theoretical welfare economics and theoretical public finance should be closely related fields of inquiry. Specifically, the implications for changes in behavior that stem from the Pigovian and post-Pigovian analysis of external economies and diseconomies should find some application in the discussion of tax institutions and in proposals for tax reform. Surprisingly, the bridge between these two areas has not been fully developed, and results that seem obvious have not been noted. Theoretical welfare economics has been developed largely on the assumption that a public sector of the economy does not exist, while theoretical public finance has continued to embody a serious neglect of the essential two-sidedness of the fiscal account. If these defects in both models are removed, the theorems of Pigovian welfare analysis can be extended directly to the web of fiscal interdependence that the very existence of a public sector normally introduces.

The notion of externality has been central to Pigovian welfare economics. The fundamental theorem is that when individual actions impose relevant external effects on parties outside a market-like contract, the necessary conditions for Pareto optimality are violated. Recent contributions have clarified the policy implications of this theorem, notably its relation to what has been

From *Southern Economic Journal* 33 (July 1966): 35–42. Reprinted by permission of the publisher.

This paper originated as a digression from a general analysis of the effects of tax institutions on individual behavior in political process. For the latter, see my *Public Finance in Democratic Process* (forthcoming, University of North Carolina Press).

called "market failure."[1] The point to be noted here, however, is that almost exclusively the discussion of externalities has been confined to individual decisions or actions taken in the private sector on the assumption that a public sector does not exist. In an earlier paper,[2] I traced out some of the simple implications of the externality aspects of individual behavior as a participant in public choice. I shall not be concerned with such collective-choice behavior here. The analysis is confined to individual choice in the market or private sector of the economy, but under the plausible assumption that a public sector exists and that familiar institutions of taxation are used to finance public goods and services. The fiscal structure in this setting introduces complex interdependencies among individuals' behavior as they respond to tax changes by modifying their market choices.

I shall not be concerned with the normative problem of deriving the necessary marginal conditions for optimality in public-goods supply. I assume, realistically, that public goods are financed through the familiar institutions of taxation which embody little or no attempt to relate individual marginal evaluations to individual marginal taxes. Most of the discussion will be limited to income taxation, although extension to other taxes is straightforward.

The analysis to be developed is closely related to, but also quite different from, that which has carried the label "excess burden" to scholars in public finance. Well-known theorems here state that any tax which causes individual behavior to be different from that which would prevail under the imposition of lump-sum levies generates an "excess burden," an "unnecessary" welfare loss that could be eliminated if the same revenues should be collected through the lump-sum alternative. The ideally efficient tax, in this context, is the lump-sum tax which, by definition, exerts no substitution effects; this is normally used as the benchmark for measuring the relative efficiency of alternative tax institutions.

The feature that distinguishes the analysis here from the traditional excess-burden discussion lies in the sharply different political setting for the two models. Implicitly, excess-burden analysis assumes that taxes are collected

---

1. See R. H. Coase, "The Problem of Social Cost," *Journal of Law and Economics,* October 1960, 1–44; J. M. Buchanan and W. C. Stubblebine, "Externality," *Economica,* November 1962, 371–84.

2. "Politics, Policy, and the Pigovian Margins," *Economica,* February 1962, 17–28.

from the economy in complete independence from the financing of public-service benefits. By contrast, I shall assume that taxes are collected solely for the purpose of financing public service benefits that are enjoyed by the same set of persons as those who pay the taxes.

Let us now examine somewhat more specifically the results attained in the externality and the excess-burden discussions before introducing the variations. The whole policy emphasis of the Pigovian literature is placed on the relative desirability of encouraging marginal extension in the output of those activities that exert relevant external economies and of encouraging marginal contraction in output of those activities that exert relevant external diseconomies. Recent contributions have raised questions as to the efficacy or even the possibility of accomplishing these desired ends through any simple or straightforward instruments of policy (e.g., taxes and subsidies) and, also, they have emphasized the necessity of comparing the institutional processes carefully before recommending specific policy actions.[3] The underlying logic of the central theorem has not, however, been essentially modified and, within all of the necessary limits, the economist who is called upon to provide policy advice would surely recommend against public or governmental measures that clearly encourage persons to behave in such a way as to impose external diseconomies on each other.

Consider now the familiar results of the standard excess-burden analysis applied to a single tax institution, say, proportional income taxation. Because the individual is led by the introduction of the tax to substitute nontaxable income (e.g., leisure) for taxable income, his utility is reduced to some level below that which could have been maintained under an equal-yield lump-sum tax because the latter, by definition, generates no substitution effects. Note that the emphasis here has been almost exclusively on the welfare losses suffered *by the individual who is taxed*. This is accomplished through the equal-yield assumption under which the comparative analysis has always been conducted. If equal revenues are collected from an individual under either of two tax alternatives, the positions of others in the community remain the same under either of the two. Somewhat strangely, or so it now seems to

---

3. In addition to the works previously cited, see also O. A. Davis and A. Whinston, "Externality, Welfare, and the Theory of Games," *Journal of Political Economy,* June 1962, 241–62.

me, no one has examined the prospect that the behavior of the individual, at the margin of adjustment, may be imposing Pareto-relevant externalities on his fellow taxpayers-beneficiaries. In responding to any nonefficient tax levy, the individual acts so as to reduce the tax base. It may be, and normally will be, to the advantage of others, as a group, to work out compensations with the individual in exchange for an agreement on his part to limit his base-reducing behavior. Therefore, even if others are totally unconcerned with the "excess burden" or welfare loss that the nonefficient tax imposes on the individual himself, they may find it to their own interest to "trade" with the individual with respect to his activity that imposes the external diseconomy. As a result of such trades, the individual will contribute more to the public treasury than the comparable equal-yield taxes allow.

The analysis here seems complex only because of the arbitrary restrictiveness imposed by the equal-yield assumption. Once this is dropped, and individual behavior in response to the levy of a single nonefficient tax is examined, the relationship becomes clear. As a result of the imposition of the tax, say a proportional income tax, the individual acts so as to reduce taxable income. The aggregate tax base for the revenue is reduced. Necessarily, all citizens in the group who are simultaneously taxpayers and public service beneficiaries are harmed. To secure the same quantity of public services as before, tax rates must be increased. Or, conversely, at prevailing rates of tax, the level of public benefits must fall. The precise distribution of external diseconomies among individuals as taxpayers and as public-goods beneficiaries depends, of course, on the rules through which the two sides of the fiscal account are tied together. If the budget is fixed and tax rates must be adjusted residually so as to produce the necessary revenues, the tax response of an individual in reducing taxable income does not impose external diseconomies on his fellows who are beneficiaries but not taxpayers. In this case, the diseconomies are limited to his fellow taxpayers. On the other hand, if tax rates are fixed and the budget is residually determined, the tax response of the individual generates external diseconomies only for individuals in their capacities as beneficiaries and not as taxpayers.

The interdependence becomes less direct when government borrowing is introduced, although the basic effects are not changed. If, in order to maintain a constant level of public service supply in the face of revenue-reducing behavior, government borrows, individuals need not experience *current* spillover harm. Insofar as they anticipate the future taxes that will be required to service and amortize the debt, they will suffer current reductions in utility. If they fail to capitalize future taxes, because of some fiscal illusion, the external diseconomy involves individuals as *future*, not current taxpayers.

Before examining some of the implications that the recognition of this quite evident interdependence involves, it will be interesting to discuss briefly why it has been largely absent from the standard analysis of taxes. As suggested, most tax analysis has been based on a conceptual separation between the two sides of the fiscal account. If, in fact, taxes represented net drainages from the economy, of the sort aptly labeled as *imposte grandine* by Einaudi, no external effects of the sort described above would arise, provided, of course, that the amount of revenue collection is not predetermined. In this sort of model, the behavior of the single taxpayer in reducing the tax base in response to some nonoptimal levy does not affect, in any way, the position of other taxpayers in the political group. And, in such a model, there are no public service beneficiaries since there are no public goods financed. The welfare loss from the nonoptimal tax is concentrated strictly on the person who is led by the tax to change his behavior and there are no spillover effects of his action on others. The external diseconomy arises only in a model that imposes the essential two-sidedness of the fiscal account.[4]

The question is, of course, whether or not the *imposte grandine* model is at all relevant for analyzing fiscal institutions in the real world. I have argued that it is not and that it is necessary to incorporate the interdependence between taxes and benefits in any analysis claiming applicability. Individuals, as participants in democratic decision processes, directly or indirectly, impose taxes upon themselves to provide public goods to themselves. In this fundamentally democratic model of political activity, the externality that is inherent in tax response must be recognized.

---

4. The interdependence will be present in all models which incorporate both sides of the budget account except for the extremely restrictive one in which the demand for public goods is directly related to the amount of taxable income earned, and to nothing else. In this model, an individual's decision to reduce taxable income reduces the aggregate tax base, but, at the same time, it reduces the demand for public goods. In any reasonable model, some relationship between public-spending needs and the amount of taxable income earned in the economy probably exists, but this seems only to reduce somewhat the particular interdependence discussed here, not to eliminate it. (I am indebted to Professor Francesco Forte, University of Turin, Italy, for this point.)

## II. Implications for Policy

At one level, the analysis here does little other than to supplement and to strengthen the familiar efficiency or excess-burden theorems. The nonoptimal tax imposes a welfare loss on the individual who responds directly, but, also, and because of his response, upon other members of the community. The incidence of nonoptimality is more diffused than is implied from orthodox fiscal theory. But there is more to it than this relatively straightforward extension. As recent contributions have made clear, the existence of relevant externalities will, necessarily, set up situations that make further "trades," "exchanges" or "rules changes" profitable to all affected parties. In small-number groups, individuals suffering damages from external diseconomies imposed by the behavior of others can directly initiate arrangements through which they offer appropriate compensations in exchange for some contraction in the scope of the activities in question. In the large-number group, the "free-rider" phenomenon arises to make individual initiation of direct action unlikely, but unexploited "gains from trade" here may be secured from general agreement upon changes in the rules through which activities are allowed to take place.

In examining tax responses, it is appropriate to limit consideration to the large-number case; fiscal jurisdictions normally include many citizens. This suggests that pressures for the reduction or elimination of externalities in tax response may not spontaneously emerge from the private initiative of individuals, but that widespread agreement may be forthcoming on properly designed modifications in the rules that govern interpersonal interaction. As some of the recent contributions have indicated, however, small-number models may be useful in deriving constitutional-institutional changes to be presented in large-number settings.

Consider an extremely simplified two-person model, which we use solely as an analogue to a large-number model. It is to be assumed that some previously established "constitutional" rule, binding on the collectivity, requires that public goods, which are shared equally by both citizens, be financed by the levy of a proportional tax on personal incomes. In the absence of any tax, individual A will earn an income of $1000 per period, and individual B will earn $500. Now assume that a collective decision is made to finance the purchase of three units of a public good, at a cost of $50 per unit. The precise rule through which this collective decision is reached is not relevant for our analysis; it is specified only that the decision, once made, is binding on both citizens. If both persons earn their pretax incomes, a rate of 10 per cent will finance the chosen quantity of public goods. A would pay a total tax bill of $100 and B would pay $50.

Some allowance for individual response to the imposition of the tax must, however, be introduced. Suppose that individual B finds it almost impossible to substitute nontaxable for taxable income, whereas individual A can make such a substitution with relative ease. Let us say that, in response to a prospective tax rate of 10 per cent, individual A will reduce his taxable income receipts to $500. He will do so, let us say, by working only one-half as much as before, taking his nontaxable psychic income in the form of added leisure. The tax levy of 10 per cent would now produce revenues of only $100, and this would finance only two units of the public good, not three. In order to finance the additional unit, the rate of tax must now be increased, or the collectivity must accept the shortfall in quantity. Clearly, A's behavior in response to the tax, his action in reducing taxable income from $1000 to $500, imposes an external diseconomy on B. This diseconomy may be measured in terms of B's evaluation of the third unit of public good, if we assume that the shortfall is to be accepted. In one sense, of course, A also imposes an "external" diseconomy on himself, in his role as a beneficiary of the public good. However, this aspect of A's action may be left out of account; this would not influence his own behavior in a large-number setting, and, recall, we employ the two-person model here only as an analogue of the large-number case.

Recognizing that A's anticipated response to the imposition of the tax will exert a diseconomy on him, B will find it advantageous to look for means to persuade A to act differently. Assume that B values the third unit of the public good at $10. He would, therefore, be willing to offer, as compensation to A, any amount up to $10 in exchange for some agreement on A's part not to reduce taxable income. In the context of this example, some bargaining range is clearly present, and some agreement should emerge that would be advantageous to both parties. Independent of any offer of compensation, A's behavior reveals only that he prefers the alternative: (1) $500 taxable income under the tax, to the alternative: (2) $1000 taxable income under the tax. His behavior, or predicted behavior, does not reveal whether he prefers, say, $500 taxable income under the tax to, say, $1005 under the tax. His elasticity of substitution between taxable and nontaxable income may be very high.

Let us presume that some bargain is struck. In exchange for a $5 payment from B (which for numerical simplicity we shall assume is nontaxable), individual A agrees to earn taxable income in the amount of $1000. Net of tax, therefore, A will now get $900 plus $5, or a total of $905, whereas B will receive, net of tax and compensation paid to A, $445. For the three units of public good that can under this arrangement be made available to both persons, A has paid a net tax of $95, while B has paid a net tax of $55. The rule of proportionality to income is violated. But, as the example clearly demonstrates, *both* members of the group have benefited from the departure from strict proportionality; both persons are better off than they would have been under simple proportional income taxation without compensation. Individual B, in the bargain, pays more than a proportionate-to-income share in the costs of the public goods, but he is better off by so doing because, in the bargain, he secures a larger supply of public goods. In the absence of "trade," B gets two units of public good for $50, or a "tax-price" per unit of $25. With "trade" he secures three units for $55; his "tax-price" falls to $18.33.

The numerical example is, of course, quite an arbitrary one. The roles of the two persons in the model could as well have been reversed. If B, with the lower income, finds it more convenient to substitute nontaxable for taxable income than does A, then a departure from proportionality in the opposing direction, in exchange for some agreement on the part of B to earn more taxable income, would be indicated. The general result of the model should, nonetheless, be clear. If individuals differ with respect to the opportunities and the tastes for substituting nontaxable for taxable income, some mutually advantageous "exchanges" involving individual tax responses and appropriate compensations are likely to be possible.

## III. Illustrative Proposals for Reform

How might this general result be applied to the reform of tax institutions? Individuals are not, of course, classified exogenously by the elasticities of substitution between taxable and nontaxable income. If some means could be found to determine just what each person would earn in potentially tax-

able income in the absence of taxation, then these data could be used to determine, ideally, the allocation of taxes among persons. Of course, no such
means exists. What is required seems to be some institutional recognition of
the direction of the fiscal interdependence that is present. Certain steps toward this objective may be suggested.

The example in the preceding section, as well as most of the general discussion, concentrated on the external diseconomy that the individual's change in
behavior imposes on his fellows. This diseconomy stems from his response
to the imposition of a tax, a response that involves the reduction in the aggregate tax base. The obverse relationship among individuals is equally obvious. In the face of an existing tax structure, a change in an individual's
behavior in the direction of earning a higher taxable income, and hence expanding the aggregate tax base, exerts an external economy on his fellows.
Institutionally, recognition and reward for changes in behavior that exert
such external economies may be more readily introduced than recognition
and penalties for changes in behavior that exert external diseconomies.

I propose here to examine only one suggestion for possible reform in
some detail. No attempt is made to explore other possible steps in reforming
tax institutions to incorporate some recognition of the fiscal interdependence analyzed here. Let us suppose that the existing personal income tax is
changed so that individuals are taxed, not on measured taxable income in the
year $t$, the period during which the income is earned, but instead are taxed, in
year $t$, on income that is earned in the year $t - 1$. In this case, the individual
whose income increases from $Y_{t-1}$ in year $t - 1$ to $(Y_{t-1} + \Delta Y_{t-1})$ in year $t$,
is allowed the increment $(\Delta Y_{t-1})$ free of tax. In this extreme, of course, other
members of the political group receive no gain from the decision made to increase income; no external economies are exerted here since other taxpayers-
beneficiaries secure no gain via the fiscal interdependence process. In this extreme, the individual who earns the income increment is allowed to secure all
of the potential "gains from trade" that the interdependence generates. However, at any tax rate on the income increment greater than zero, such spillover benefits do accrue to other taxpayers-beneficiaries. This suggests that a
more appropriate institutional change may be one that imposes some tax on
the income increment, but at some rate less than the maximum marginal
rate on base income. For simplicity, think now of the individual as being
subjected to a rate equal to one-half of his maximum marginal rate on

the increment to income. This change alone would clearly provide individuals with a strong incentive to increase taxable income through time.

Note especially that such a proposal for change in the personal income tax need not be subject to the standard criticism concerning a reduction in progressivity of the system. The rate structure, which would be applied to base or standard income, could be regressive, proportional or progressive at whatever scale the community desires. What is required here is that this standard or base rate structure, applied to income in the period immediately past, be supplemented by a second rate structure applicable only to income increments. If the measure of income for applying the base rate structure is that earned in year $t - 1$, individuals who suffer income reductions would, of course, be worse off than under current-year assessment. To some extent, such differentials might be considered as appropriate penalization for the genuine external diseconomies that are imposed. However, consideration should perhaps be given to those individuals whose income reductions are largely fortuitous. This suggests a modification of the proposal. The individual may be allowed a choice as to the base year for determining income for tax purposes. He can choose between (1) the base rate structure applied to income earned in the current period, $t$, and (2) the base rate structure applied to income earned in the period, $t - 1$, plus one-half of the maximum marginal rate applied to the income supplement, the difference between income in $t - 1$ and income in $t$. Those persons whose income increases over the two periods will, of course, always choose the second alternative. Those whose income decreases over the two periods will choose the first alternative, which is, of course, the standard current-period income tax.[5]

In an economy characterized by increasing aggregate income, a large share of the population will, of course, experience personal income in-

---

5. Protection might have to be provided against deliberate income reduction aimed at securing tax advantage. Under the unqualified option rule suggested, the individual has some incentive to reduce income in $t$, in order to exhibit income growth between $t_1$ and $t_2$, and, because of this, a lowered marginal rate of tax in $t_2$. This potential loophole might be closed effectively by disallowing the differentially lower marginal rate on recovery-growth in income to some trend path. Again, I emphasize that the analysis is intended for illustrative purposes, and I am not primarily concerned with the possible virtues or defects of the proposal as a practicable scheme for tax reform. As an editorial reader has pointed out, the proposal would reduce the adaptability of income taxation for fiscal policy purposes.

creases through time. To the extent that individuals would have earned higher incomes through time, apart from any change in income tax, the differential reduction in marginal taxes represents an "unearned reward." No such "institutional bargain" need be made to secure the increments to income in this case. On the other hand, the proposal will surely have the effect of causing some individuals to increase their earnings of taxable income over time. Since these two shares in incremental personal income cannot be effectively distinguished, any decision to introduce proposals along the lines suggested would have to be based on some balancing off of the two; some estimate of the net change in income growth that the proposals would induce must be made. To the extent that aggregate income growth, in and of itself, is considered to be an important policy objective, quite apart from the fiscal interdependence elements stressed in this paper, additional and supplementary argument is provided for the introduction of the change that has been suggested. The effects would surely be some increase in the rate of aggregate income growth in the economy.

In this strict sense, the change would violate horizontal equity in the tax if the criterion for equality among persons is defined as equality in present values for future income streams. The individual whose pattern of income earnings over time starts from a low relative base would be subjected to a lower tax (also measured in present-value terms) than the individual whose present value of future income is identical but whose time pattern of earnings exhibits less growth. This does not seem to provide a formidable objection to the proposal. When problems of comparing different time patterns of income are introduced, the questions as to just "who are equals" among taxpayers seem largely open.

The existing social consensus with respect to vertical equity among income classes need not be changed by the proposal. The change introduces differential rewards to those persons whose incomes increase through time, not to those whose incomes are "high" or "low" at particular points in time. Note, however, that this reward or compensation stems from a recognition of the essential interdependence of the fiscal structure and not on some exogenously postulated objective such as "growth," although, as mentioned, the acceptance of such an objective can provide supplementary support. The interdependence suggests that the introduction of the proposal could benefit not only those whose incomes rise over time, but also those whose incomes are not expected to rise. The latter secure benefits because of the external economies that income growth generates via the fiscal mechanism. Properly conceived, some such change can be, in itself, Pareto optimal in the sense that all persons in the group can either be made better off or left undisturbed. This is not, of course, the same as saying that the position attained, after the change, would be Pareto optimal, globally considered.

## IV. Conclusions

The discussion has been limited to one specific illustrative proposal that would embody some recognition of the fiscal interdependence among separate members of the taxpayer-beneficiary group. Other, and more elegant, proposals might be made. What is required is some differentially favorable treatment for individual behavior that exerts "fiscal" external economies and/or some differentially unfavorable treatment for behavior that exerts "fiscal" external diseconomies. The proposal suggested uses the temporal pattern of income to distinguish base-period from incremental income. Some such arbitrary device seems necessary in order to prevent undue conflict with norms for vertical equity in modern tax systems. Even for single-period models, however, explicit modifications in progressivity may, in certain cases, prove worthy of consideration because of the arguments that have been advanced. Vertical equity norms should be balanced off against other values. Some reduction in the rate of progressivity may prove beneficial, even to those who stand to pay a higher proportionate share of their own income as a result. Some implicit recognition of the externality here has perhaps been present in the orthodox discussion of the effects of taxation on incentives. The externality analysis explicitly makes it clear why the incentive effects are important, even to those in groups that are not directly able to modify income-earning patterns, and even if the growth objective is overlooked.

The argument can be applied to other suggestions for fiscal reform. A case for differentially favorable tax treatment of the incomes of working wives is provided here, wholly apart from equity considerations. Similarly, income earned in moonlighting, in overtime, during holiday periods, can be treated as supplementary income, and it may become advantageous for *others* than those who earn such incomes to grant differentially favorable treatment to such incomes.

As suggested several times, the central point of this paper is an extremely simple one. The man who sits on his sunlit patio when he could be earning taxable income is levying costs on his fellows. The man who labors and thereby earns taxable income when he could be sitting in the sunlight is providing his fellows with benefits. Discussions for fiscal reform should explicitly recognize the existence of this interdependence.

# On the Incidence of
# Tax Deductibility

*James M. Buchanan and Mark V. Pauly*

Who gains and who loses from tax deductions? Economists have considered this question to be so elementary that a specific answer is not required. The introduction of a deduction is presumed to shift some part of the cost of the activity subsidized to the general taxpayer regardless of his income. The gainers are allegedly those who take advantage of the deductibility feature. In this paper, we challenge these conclusions. We shall demonstrate that those who take advantage of tax deductions may lose and some general taxpayers may gain. This apparently paradoxical conclusion is attained by the incorporation of political feedbacks in the analysis.

## I

Tax deductions are quantitatively important. In fiscal 1967, American taxpayers reported $82 billion in deductions on adjusted gross incomes of $505 billion. Itemized deductions made up $60 billion of the $82 billion total. The four significant categories of itemized deductions, in decreasing order or quantitative importance, are: State and local taxes, interest, contributions, and medical expenses. Each of these could be examined in detail, and, as we should expect, several arguments could be advanced in support of each. In summary, however, deductions find their logical justification either in "adapting the income tax to individual circumstances" or in "advancing socially important objectives."[1] Under the first of these, the income base crite-

From *National Tax Journal* 23 (June 1970): 157–67. Reprinted by permission of the publisher.

1. Richard Goode, *The Individual Income Tax* (Washington: Brookings, 1964), 156.

rion, taken alone, is deemed insufficient evidence for determining horizontal equity. Specific deductions from income are allowed in order to make the definition of "equals" for tax purposes more meaningful. The medical expenses deduction, from among the four main categories, perhaps fits this description best.

The second objective for tax deductions is that of encouraging specific kinds of private activity deemed to be in the "social interest." Here the charitable deduction provides the best example. The effect of this deduction is to cause individuals to increase their contributions to eligible non-profit organizations[2]—those performing charitable, religious, and educational activities that are generally thought to be desirable. Presumably, the deduction is permitted because the activities yield benefits to others than those who make the contributions; they generate external economies.

The recent revival of tax reform proposals aimed, at least in part, at reducing the scope for eligible deductions has been accompanied by an offsetting discussion of an extended use of the tax structure to promote specific objectives via the mechanism of deductions and tax credits. The basic difference between the tax deduction and the tax credit should be kept in mind. A deduction allows the prospective taxpayer to reduce the base upon which the tax is levied; a credit allows the taxpayer to reduce the tax that has already been computed on a determined base. So long as the taxpayer confronts a marginal rate of less than 100 per cent, a dollar's worth of tax deductibility is worth less than a dollar's worth of tax credit. For the very reason that marginal rates of tax differ as among persons, however, tax deductions are not uniform as among persons; tax credits of given amounts are, by contrast, normally uniform in this sense. Empirically, deductions are much more important than credits. Aside from the investment credit enacted in 1962, tax credits are more talked about than enacted.

As suggested, the widespread notion has been that deductibility tends to shift a part of the cost of the activity for which a deduction is allowed onto the shoulders of the general taxpayer. Due's statement is typical:

> For persons in higher tax brackets the net cost of making contributions is greatly reduced by the tax (deduction) . . . the principle of deductibility

2. There seems to be some disagreement as to the predicted elasticity of contributions with respect to the tax deduction feature. The directional effect of the deduction is, however, clear.

has widespread support even though primary direct benefit concentrates in the higher income groups.[3]

Implicit in this statement, and other similar ones, is the assumption that tax rates will remain the same with and without the deduction in question. But it is important to examine the reasonableness of any such *ceteris paribus* assumption. If the removal of the deduction should, through the increase in revenues generated, allow a general tax-rate reduction, it seems quite possible that the rich, as a group, might pay no higher and perhaps even lower total taxes than they pay before the change. The deduction need not reduce the "net cost of making contributions" to upper income groups generally, nor need it provide direct benefits to higher income groups.

In general, once it is recognized that removal of a deduction option implies some readjustment in tax rates and, further, that tax rates are determined by voters-taxpayers in a political process, any blanket predictions as to the distributional consequences of tax deductions become more difficult to make. In this paper, we shall develop a theory of tax deductions which incorporates behavioral readjustments through the political-decision process. When such feedbacks are introduced, distributional implications are often quite different from those that emerge implicitly and explicitly from the more limited standard approach. We shall show, for example, that the groups which save relatively more taxes by a deduction feature are not necessarily the groups that gain, relatively, from the existence of the deduction. It is possible that, as between two groups, one of which takes advantage of a tax deduction while the other does not, the group which uses the deduction is made worse off in a welfare sense. Finally, we shall examine the prospects for specifying an optimal set of deductions in the presence of external economies.

The argument proceeds through the construction of a series of simple models. We first consider a case where a deduction is permitted for individual expenditures on activities that yield no spillover benefits of the ordinary sort. Equity-motivated deductions can be considered as examples. Next, we develop two models in which deductions are allowed for private activity

---

3. John Due, *Government Finance: Economics of the Public Sector* (Homewood, Illinois: Richard D. Irwin, Inc., 1968), 408.

which yields some public or collective benefits but which does not substitute for currently provided public goods. We show how this sort of deduction can be adjusted so as to satisfy the necessary conditions for optimality. The last section contains our conclusions.

Our method is strictly that of comparative statics, but with a difference. This difference is that we go beyond adjustments in market equilibria to treat adjustments in political equilibria. Those who choose to defend the orthodox approach may deny the relevance of political equilibrium as a meaningful tool for analysis. Anticipating this sort of criticism, we should state at the outset that the relatively restricted usefulness of political adjustment models can be acknowledged at the same time that the comparative advantages of such models in pointing toward pressures for political change are stoutly defended.

## II

Consider a situation where a tax deduction is introduced for spending on a good or activity that yields no benefits to other than the taxpayer who utilizes the deduction. This deduction could be considered to be introduced because of political trading or because of some newly discovered equity norm. Before the deduction is introduced, the economy is in full equilibrium, both in the supply of private goods and public goods.

It is useful to discuss the model in a two-person context. This allows us to treat in simple terms an analysis that can be extended without difficulty to apply to the many-person situation. Suppose there are only two spending units, A and B, with A's income being higher than B's. Each individual is assumed to adjust parametrically to tax-rate changes: that is, he does not consider the effects of his private behavior on the tax rate. This assumption seems to violate criteria for rational behavior in the strict two-person setting, but it is fully acceptable when we accept the two-person setting only to the extent that it yields conclusions applicable to the many-person case. In the latter, of course, such parametric behavior is fully rational.

Let us suppose, further, that the existing equilibrium is generated through the use of a proportional income tax, the proceeds of which are employed to finance a purely collective or public good. The equilibrium is complete in the Pareto-Wicksellian sense; each person is paying a marginal tax-price that is

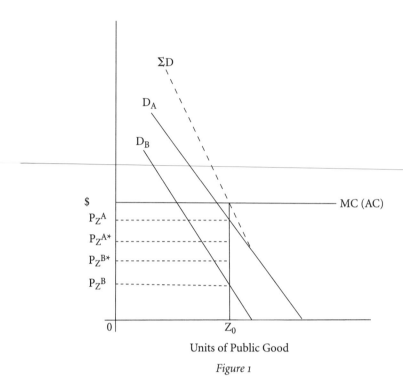

Figure 1

equal to his own marginal evaluation of the good. Tax-price is also assumed to be uniform over quantities of the public good, and for each individual. The public-goods equilibrium is depicted in Figure 1, where $D_A$ and $D_B$ are the two demand curves, and where $\Sigma D$ is their vertical summation.[4]

We now introduce a deduction for a purely private good, say, good X. Assume that only individual A will take advantage of the deduction. The orthodox analysis would suggest that A secures an increase in disposable real income because of the net reduction in taxes that he pays for the public good.

---

4. We can treat these as orthodox demand curves here, and, in this way, no problem arises in their vertical summation. This is facilitated by the simplifying assumption that tax-price is constant over varying quantities to each person. Without this assumption, marginal evaluations of the good would be dependent on how costs are shared over inframarginal ranges. Unique demand curves would, in this case, be impossible to derive.

A's taxes will fall by $tP_x X$ dollars, where t is the marginal tax rate, $P_x$ is the price of X, and X is the number of units that A purchases after the deduction. These conclusions arise, however, only because the analysis is not extended beyond first-stage reactions.

If tax collections at some initial proportional rate, $t_0$, were just sufficient to cover the total cost of providing $Z_0$ units of the public good, the introduction of the deduction would have three separate effects: (1) a shortfall in total tax collections at rate $t_0$ below that which would be required to provide $Z_0$ units of public good; (2) a reduction in A's tax base from $Y_a$ to $(Y_a - t_0 P_x X)$; (3) an increase in A's purchases of X in response to the lower effective price. These effects will set in motion forces leading to some new equilibrium.

If the community attempts to return the quantity of public goods financed to the initial level $Z_0$, and if it attempts to do so through increases in the existing proportional income tax, the new tax-price per unit of the public good that A will confront must be less than his initial tax-price. This is necessarily true because of the tax-base reduction generated by the deduction. In the two-person model, this means that the tax-price to B must be higher than in the initial equilibrium. Suppose that the two new tax-prices required to produce-supply $Z_0$ are $P_Z^{A*}$ and $P_Z^{B*}$; these imply a new tax rate, $t_1$, and a return to the previous public-goods quantity, $Z_0$.

A glance at Figure 1 is sufficient to show that equilibrium could not prevail at this new situation. A would desire an increase in the quantity of public goods; his marginal evaluation would exceed the marginal tax-price that he confronts. On the other hand, B would now desire to reduce the quantity of Z below $Z_0$. In the new position, his marginal evaluation of Z would fall below the marginal tax-price that he faces. It becomes clear from the construction that some new equilibrium in public-goods supply will be attained, if at all, only when the tax structure has been altered so as to confront A with a tax rate higher than $t_1$, and B with some rate lower than $t_1$. In other words, equilibrium will be attained only by some shift from a proportional to a progressive tax on the effective income base. The equilibrium tax-prices per unit of the public good, Z, would have to return to $P_Z^A$ and $P_Z^B$, since these are the only prices that can possibly satisfy the necessary conditions for optimality. In terms of rates of tax on the income base, A will now pay a rate on his income minus his deduction which will be less than the rate that B will pay on his total income. Since we have assumed that marginal tax-price remains unchanged over varying quantities of the public good, the new equilibrium is identical with the old one, except for the change in nominal tax rates.

This conclusion arises only under the restriction that tax-prices remain unchanged over varying quantities of the public good. If this restriction on the model is dropped, the analysis becomes considerably more complex, but the basic elements of the result are not changed. The precise quantity of public goods provided may be different in the two equilibrium positions because of the operation of income effects, and, in the net, distributional gains from the deduction may be secured by one party. However, it remains true that the amount of tax reduction continues to overstate the gains to A and, also, that at the margin, tax rates must shift against A to attain the new equilibrium.

Under the simplified conditions outlined, and without the complexities just mentioned, it can be shown that A will suffer a welfare loss. The tax deduction has the effect of lowering the effective market price of X, from $P_x$ to $(P_x - tP_x)$. As a result of this price reduction, he will purchase more X. As we have shown, however, his total tax bill in the new equilibrium will be the same as before the deduction was introduced. Figure 2 will be helpful at this point. The abscissa measures units of the private good, X. As shown, Mr. A extends his purchases from $X_0$ to $X_e$ in response to the deduction. There is a welfare loss from this extension that is approximately measured by the area FGH. This loss arises because the price reduction is illusory rather than real. In the market for good X, the price remains at $P_x$. The individual acts as if he confronts a lower price because he expects that he will secure the public good on more advantageous terms. On balance, the effect of the deduction for the person who uses it becomes similar to the granting of a per unit subsidy on an item of consumption combined with the levy of an offsetting lump-sum tax.

The argument places the whole notion of using tax deductions to secure horizontal equity norms in a new light. Insofar as individuals are able, through their own behavior, to change the quantity of the particular good or activity for which the deduction is allowed, whether this be medical care or borrowing at interest, there must arise an excess burden of the sort indicated.

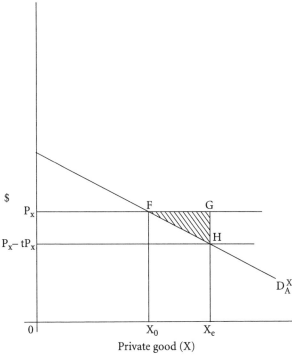

*Figure 2*

There will be a welfare loss involved in trying to achieve further equity; the efficiency-equity conflict appears in yet another form.

It becomes relatively easy to extend the model to allow both persons to utilize the deduction. The basic conclusions are not modified. A more relevant shift in the model involves the starting point. If we should commence with full public- and private-goods equilibrium, *with* the tax deduction, the model could be employed to analyze the effects of removing the deduction. Descriptively, this is applicable to some of the current discussion of tax reform. If an existing deduction is removed, the results will not necessarily be to subject the groups currently utilizing the deduction to relatively larger tax-shares. But if the existing deductions are such that only particularized subgroups, within income categories, can effectively utilize them, the orthodox analysis comes into its own.

# III

We shall now consider two cases in which a deduction is allowed for private outlay on goods which are close substitutes for public expenditures. First, suppose that a pure public good is being provided in Pareto-Wicksellian equilibrium, so that the necessary conditions for optimality are fully satisfied. Let the cost-price of this good, whether to public or private buyers, be $1, and let the publicly supplied quantity be $Z_0$. Suppose that a deduction is introduced which allows the individual to reduce his tax base one-for-one with private purchases of Z. An individual will take advantage of this if his marginal tax-price (which is, in equilibrium, equal to his marginal evaluation of the good) exceeds one minus the marginal tax rate that he confronts. (Note that if the marginal tax rate t is less than 50 per cent, there can, at most, be only one person who could use a deduction since, at most, only one person could have a marginal evaluation which exceeds $.50. Similarly, if it is 90 per cent, there can at most be only ten persons who will use the deduction. This restriction insures that the model here is useful largely in providing the groundwork for more realistic models in which the good provided publicly is not Samuelsonian pure.)

Suppose that the initial public-goods equilibrium includes marginal tax-prices of $.67 and $.33 for A and for B, these being equal to marginal evaluations. Public-goods units are measured in "dollar's worths." The deduction is introduced, and suppose that only A takes advantage of it. He will make private outlays on the good, Z, because he will think that, in so doing, he can improve his own position. By expending $1 privately on Z, A's tax bill is reduced by $.67; hence, the apparent price per unit of Z falls to $.33. In taking this action, A presumably ignores the erosion of the tax base and also the perfect substitutability of the good as between private and public provision. At the old tax rate, funds will no longer be sufficient to allow the public purchase of the previously existing supply. This decline will be less than the increase in private outlay, however, since taxes are reduced by only some fraction, t, of private outlays on Z. In our numerical example, tax revenues fall by $.67 whereas private outlay goes up by $1.

In the parametric model of behavior, the other person, B, will treat the collective-consumption good provided by A's private purchase (and, by definition, equally available to both A and to B) as an exogenous increase in his real income along a single dimension. Hence, B will be thrown out of equilibrium at the old tax rate. The tax-price that he pays for a unit of the good that is purchased publicly will have increased because of the fall in total tax base; B will, therefore, want less than the $Z_0$ units provided in the previous equilibrium. He will find, however, that he is being provided with *more* units than before, when he considers both public and private supply. Tax-rate readjustments or readjustments in the quantity of public supply are required in order to bring B back into some new equilibrium.

When we look at A's position, however, tax-rate adjustments which would satisfy B are ruled out. The marginal evaluation for A, as well as for B, will be lower than in the initially prevailing equilibrium because of the increase in gross quantity of Z. A would, therefore, be unwilling to accept any higher tax-share for publicly supplied units. Any approach toward an equilibrium that would satisfy both parties must involve cutbacks in the quantity of the collective-consumption good that is publicly supplied. The net results of the tax deduction can be seen in their starkest form if we neglect possible income effects. In this case, we should expect B to be satisfied only after the public supply is reduced by precisely the amount of the private supply increase. In our numerical example, B then secures the same quantity of Z with a total tax bill that is \$.33 lower than before. A secures the same quantity with a total outlay, tax bill plus private purchase, that is \$.33 more than before. The person who has taken advantage of the deduction has been trapped by what we may call a "tax deduction illusion."

To this point, we have analyzed only the effects of a discrete and initial usage of the deduction option. We have not traced through the behavioral adjustments that would produce a new equilibrium. Rigorous analysis becomes difficult here because of the necessity to allow for income-effect feedbacks on marginal evaluations. As A expands his private purchases of Z under the tax deduction illusion, he transfers real income to B. This will reduce A's marginal evaluation and increase B's, so long as Z is a normal good. Even when income effects are incorporated, it remains possible that equilibrium is attained only when all public supply of the good is eliminated, the whole supply being purchased privately by A. There seems to be nothing in the behavioral adjustment process that generates movement toward a position that would satisfy the conditions for optimality. In the new equilibrium, the total supply of the collective-consumption good may be above or below that of the optimal public supply before the deduction is introduced.

## IV

Again we want to consider a two-agent model, but in this case we assume that the public good is initially supplied by some combination of public and private expenditure.[5] For example, families may be making some outlay on the college education of their children at the same time that this education is being financed also by the community at large. Assume, as before, that family A's income is greater than family B's income, and that only family A takes advantage of the tax deduction when this is offered.

We assume that a pre-deduction equilibrium exists, but in this respect this model differs somewhat from those considered earlier. *Given* the outlay that is made by the family, it will be true that equilibrium prevails in the Pareto-Wicksell sense. Similarly, *given* the outlay made by the community, the position of the family is in equilibrium concerning its own private supplements. Since, however, each of these interacting units, the family and the community, reaches its equilibrium position independent of the actions of the other, the final equilibrium will not fully satisfy conditions for Pareto optimality. Under the circumstances outlined, the gross supply of the good will generally be sub-optimal.

We now permit a tax deduction for *additional* private expenditures on college education. Only family A takes advantage of this option. Orthodox theory suggests that family A benefits from this new feature in the tax law while family B does not benefit directly, and benefits indirectly only to the extent that there remain external marginal benefits from the extension in the education of A's child. As in the earlier models, we can show that this line of reasoning is in error.

When family A is permitted to deduct from its tax bill (which finances

---

5. This model is described in more detail in M. V. Pauly, "Mixed Public and Private Financing of Education," *American Economic Review* 57 (March, 1967), 120–30.

supplements to other families' children) its own incremental outlay on education, the effective price of education is reduced. A will, therefore, extend its private purchases. This will, in turn, cause the rest of the community (B in the limited two-family model) to reduce the collectively financed supplements to child A's education.

In addition to this feedback, there will be a second effect. Because of the deduction, A's taxes will no longer be sufficient to finance the contribution to B's education that A desires. A will be agreeable to an increase in its tax rate to return to some sort of equilibrium with respect to the community's purchase of education for child B.

In sum, who benefits from the deduction? Family A has not reduced and may have increased its tax payments for child B's education, but it has been induced to increase its own private outlays on its own child's education. There has been a net loss to family A, the only family in the model that took advantage of the tax deduction. The model can be illustrated diagrammatically in Figure 3.

We measure private expenditures by family A on the education of its own child on the abscissa; we measure the collectivity's outlay on the education of family A's child on the ordinate. The line AA' indicates the expenditure levels preferred by family A for every level of public supplement; RS indicates the similar locus of preferred outlay for the collectivity. The independent adjustment equilibrium is found at E; here, family A spends CC privately and the community supplements this with a spending level of 0U.

The deduction has the effect of changing family A's locus of preferred combinations from AA' to AB. A new equilibrium is shown at E'. Family A is induced by the deduction option to make additional expenditure in the amount CG because of the expected reduction in its tax burden. But, as the analysis has indicated, the tax bill for A remains the same or rises so that family A suffers a net welfare loss because of the "tax deduction illusion" as in the earlier models. Overall efficiency in the community may, however, be increased in this model, by contrast with the earlier ones examined. This is because we specified that the initial equilibrium was one in which the gross quantity of the good or activity was suboptimal. Family A's increased outlays resulting from the deduction illusion generate welfare gains to family B, and these may more than offset the net welfare losses suffered by family A.

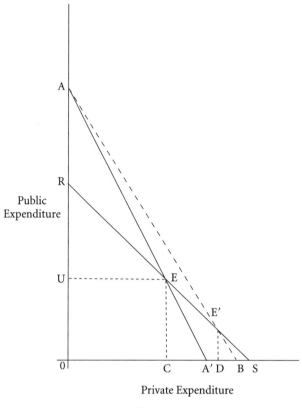

*Figure 3*

## V

The main point developed in the several simplified models discussed has been one of demonstrating that the predicted distributional effects of tax deductions may be different from those which the orthodox analysis implies. When the concept of political equilibrium is introduced, and when full readjustment through the political-decision structure is incorporated in the models, some of those who seem to gain from the introduction of tax deductions may lose.

In this section, we shall consider the possible use of the tax deduction as a means of satisfying the conditions for optimality in the presence of external economies. Suppose that taxes are paid for a public good, but that there exists another good or activity that is not provided publicly which would yield significant marginal external benefits to all members of the community. Let us assume, for simplicity, that the two goods are not close substitutes and that private *production* of the unprovided good (as distinct from private provision) is as efficient as or more efficient than public production. A practical example might be the activities of churches or religious organizations which, for constitutional reasons, are not carried out publicly, but which are alleged to yield external economies, at least to large numbers of citizens.

The introduction can lead individuals to increase the activity to the point at which an optimal quantity is generated. With a given tax rate t, a tax deduction is equivalent to a cut of t per cent in the effective price of the eligible activity. There will exist some pattern of price cuts which will cause purchasers to expand provision out to the optimal amount. Distributionally, the effects will remain as we have indicated earlier. But, if distributional considerations are neglected, efficiency in the provision of externality-generating goods can be secured through the deduction illusion.

At this point, it may be useful to contrast the deduction, as a means of securing efficient quantities of such goods, with more direct methods. It is sometimes argued that the use of tax deductions avoids public or collective control which follows upon direct public expenditures.[6] Such an argument is largely invalid, however, because it will generally be possible to provide governmental funds *directly* to individuals to spend as they please, through earmarked part- or full-payment vouchers. Instead of being allowed a deduction for medical expenses, individuals could receive part or full payment of their expenses, as is indeed now in practice for those over 65 through Medicare. There need be no change in the degree of public control. Ordinarily providing full-payment vouchers to all regardless of income would not be very efficient in encouraging expenditures on particular goods or services; such vouchers would take the form of income supplements and would induce offsetting reductions in private outlays on the parts of the recipients. What is needed for efficiency is a pattern of effective price reductions varying with incomes. Vouchers which will provide *partial* payment for desired quantities of the particular good or service are equivalent to excise subsidies.

A tax deduction is behaviorally equivalent to an excise subsidy. And it is

6. Goode, op. cit., 170–71; Due, op. cit., 408.

useful to contrast these two devices. Under an excise subsidy, individual purchasers of an externality-generating good are faced with net price reductions which will cause them to expand their rates of purchase. In this case, the results are identical with those that can be secured with tax deductibility. With the excise subsidy, however, revenues for the subsidy must be collected through an explicit increase in taxes. The tax deduction feature accomplishes an expansion of purchases without the necessity of this step. This may have major advantages in terms of political strategy, but, more importantly, the distributional results are different. Under the tax deduction device, those who are existing and potential purchasers of the externality-generating good may be deluded into paying substantially all of the net cost of internalizing the external economy. Those who are neither actual or potential purchasers of the good but who secure the external benefits from the extension of its usage or provision, may, through the deduction, secure something for nothing.

We have made no attempt here to present a complete theory of tax deduction when the political as well as the market structure is conceived as being modified by individual choice behavior. What we have done is to suggest that the incorporation of political adjustments modifies the standard predictions about the effects of deductions. We have demonstrated our analysis in terms of very simplified models. The analysis was necessarily abstract, and, as is usually the case, the assumptions will need to be examined and conclusions qualified if the results are to be applied. Nevertheless, these models should provide the basis for developing more complete models which might then be used for the derivation of empirically testable hypotheses.

## PART THREE

# Analytical and Ethical Foundations of Tax Limits

# Towards a Tax Constitution
# for Leviathan

*Geoffrey Brennan and James M. Buchanan*

*Abstract:* This paper attempts to derive normative tax rules based on the constitutional calculus of the typical voter-taxpayer when he predicts that post-constitutional political processes will be dominated by a budget-maximizing Leviathan-like bureaucracy. In this setting, selection of tax institutions becomes part of the apparatus by which Leviathan is constrained. Such an approach generates tax rules strikingly at variance with more conventional norms. In particular, the goal of a "comprehensive" tax base, which informs standard analysis, gives way to a preference for specific limitations on the width of the tax base: moves towards a greater comprehensiveness will lead inexorably to larger public spending, and beyond some point are clearly undesirable. The analysis also implies a rather unconventional defense of progression in the tax structure. An attempt is made to relate the discussion to contemporary tax reform issues.

## 1. Introduction

In this paper we analyze *constitutional* choice among tax institutions under a specified set of political assumptions. That is to say, we examine an individ-

From *Journal of Public Economics* 8 (December 1977): 255–73. Copyright 1977. Reprinted with permission from Elsevier Science.

We are grateful to members of the Public Choice Seminar at Virginia Polytechnic Institute, and in particular our colleague E. G. West, for helpful comments on an earlier version.

ual's choice among tax rules and tax instruments when it is known that such institutions, once selected, will remain in being over an indeterminately long sequence of budgetary periods, and in a setting in which the individual is presumed to be unable to predict with precision what his own position will be at any particular moment in this post-constitutional sequence.[1] Our analytical framework differs from that which informs much of the conventional wisdom in normative tax theory as well as from that which has informed much of the Wicksell-inspired, public-choice alternative.

Neoclassical normative tax theory is, in all essential respects, institutionally vacuous.[2] Abstract normative criteria for a "good" tax system are derived in response to the problem posed by the requirement to raise some exogenously determined amount of revenue for governmental use within a single time period. Emphasis is placed on the familiar efficiency and equity characteristics of alternative tax instruments. Within this traditional perspective, the influence of the tax instrument chosen on the amount of revenue demanded or required is neglected or obscured by the "equi-revenue" comparison within which the whole analysis is conducted. In a constitutional setting, by contrast, such possible feedback effects over a sequence by budgetary periods must be explicitly considered: the interdependencies between the form of tax institutions and the revenue demands placed on these institutions cannot be ignored. And, of course, predictions of such relationships will necessarily be embodied in the individual's choice. In this paper, we shall introduce an institutional model within which these interdependencies assume critical importance.

Modern public-choice theorists have already gone some way towards incorporating these effects of tax instruments on public goods supply into the

---

1. In the limit, we may assume that the individual is in some Rawlsian "original position" and behind the "veil of ignorance." (John Rawls, *A Theory of Justice* [Cambridge: Harvard University Press, 1971]). We do not need to impose such rigid requirements, however, for the constitutional setting to be relevant. Somewhat more plausibly, we may assume only that the individual is highly uncertain about his own future position. Cf. James M. Buchanan and Gordon Tullock, *The Calculus of Consent* (Ann Arbor: University of Michigan Press, 1962).

2. We would include under this rubric the recent "optimal taxation" literature, virtually all of which is explicitly set in this framework. For a useful summary, see David F. Bradford and Harvey S. Rosen, "The Optimal Taxation of Commodities and Income," *American Economic Review*, 66 (May 1976), 94–101.

analysis of constitutional choice.[3] Almost exclusively, however, the public-choice model of constitutional fiscal choice has embodied the assumption, explicitly or implicitly, that post-constitutional or in-period budgetary decisions conform to the public goods demands of the median voter or his representative in a legislative assembly. Our analysis differs critically from this in that we substitute the model of a revenue-seeking Leviathan for the demand-driven and essentially passive government characteristic of early public-choice analysis.

The norms for taxation suggested by the analysis seem to accord more closely with some of the empirically observed attitudes of the taxpaying public than those which emerge from either of the alternative paradigms. Furthermore, the institutional model is in apparent consistency with a large, rapidly growing and uncontrollable public sector. This is in dramatic contrast with the implied setting from which the traditional reform suggestions emerge, a setting that retains residues of the classical economists' assumption of nonproductive public expenditures along with the implicit notion that the governmental share in national product is severely limited. Our model is also sharply at variance with the naively optimistic public-choice perspective which incorporates the productiveness of a possibly large public sector but which does not allow for a supply-side influence on fiscal outcomes.

Our paper is intended to be a contribution to the ongoing discussion of real-world tax reform, rather than an exercise in deriving the logical properties of yet another set of arbitrarily selected assumptions. Indeed, in some sense, the point of departure for our discussion is the observation that tax reform is a quasi-constitutional exercise. Tax institutions are usually intended to be moderately permanent features of the political framework: they set the context within which in-period decisions about public goods supply are made. Furthermore, the major tax reform process (say of the Carter-type in Canada, or the British Royal Commissions) is perhaps more like an attempt at a genuinely "constitutional convention" than any other

---

3. Notably by James M. Buchanan in his book *Public Finance in Democratic Process* (Chapel Hill: University of North Carolina Press, 1967). The relationship is implicit in Knut Wicksell's whole analytical framework. See Knut Wicksell, *Finanztheoretische Untersuchungen* (Jena: Gustav Fischer, 1896).

common aspect of political life (at least in the public finance specialists' experience).

Once this is acknowledged it becomes natural to think of devising tax institutions by appeal to the constitutional calculus of the typical taxpayer-voter rather than by reference to abstract ethical norms. On the other hand, it should be borne in mind that tax reform is *not* the full constitutional arrangement envisaged for example in *The Calculus of Consent*:[4] the mandate is necessarily much more restricted. For this reason, although we acknowledge the possibility of nontax institutions which might perform a similar role to the tax rules we discuss and perhaps do so more efficiently, we do not consider such alternatives in this paper.[5] To do so would be to move outside our basic tax reform orientation.

The central structure of the institutional model is set out in section 2. In section 3, we examine the choice of an individual as he compares a comprehensive and a noncomprehensive tax base as well as alternative rate structures within these. The analysis is extended to many tax bases in section 4, and to a many-person setting in section 5. Finally, in section 6, the discussion of the paper is related to commonly held views on tax reform.

## 2. Government as a Revenue-Maximizer Subject to Constitutional Tax Constraints

As Knut Wicksell noted, no persons would approve the imposition of taxes, either at a constitutional or a post-constitutional stage of decision, unless

---

4. Buchanan and Tullock, *The Calculus of Consent*.

5. One such possibility is that of explicit constitutional limits on the proportion of national product available for public use (or on maximum rates of tax)—the national analogue of the recent tax limitations proposals in California and Michigan. It is worth noting in passing that restrictions on maximum rates would tend to cause Leviathan to aim at comprehensiveness, which restrictions on revenue as a proportion of GNP would not do. Insofar as comprehensiveness is viewed as desirable in such a context, this might be seen as suggesting a case for rate restrictions rather than revenue restrictions. Because such policy options lie outside the range of those typically available in the standard tax reform exercise, we do not focus on them in this paper. The ensuing discussion is conducted on the (practically relevant) assumption that such explicit rate and/or revenue constraints are not operative. (Of course, restrictions on nontax means of securing bureaucratic surplus [use of laws, commandeering without compensation, etc.] would be required, both in the case of tax liability and in our discussion, to ensure that the fiscal constraints are operative.)

they expect to secure some benefits from the goods and services that they predict will be financed from the revenues collected. Taxes are coercive instruments that allow governments to levy charges upon persons without any corresponding individualized expression of current willingness to pay. Furthermore, in post-constitutional stages of decision, political consent through the action of legislative representatives will not, typically, be extended to more than a simple majority of the citizenry.

What is a reasonable model of post-constitutional fiscal decision-making by governments, a model that might be appropriate in informing the constitutional-stage choice among fiscal instruments? Perhaps at one period in history, it may have seemed reasonable to rely on the operation of majority-rule in legislatures to hold governmental fiscal activities in bounds. And majority-rule models remain in both the analysis of median-voter behavior and in popular discussion of democracy. Confronted with public sectors of modern scope, and with bureaucracies that demonstrably possess power quite apart from specifically legislated authority, the democratic-limits model of governmental fiscal constraint seems to become increasingly naive. A more acceptable model would seem to be one in which the political-bureaucratic process, as it is predicted to operate post-constitutionally, involves the maximization of revenues within the tax constraints imposed in the fiscal constitution.

This is what might loosely be termed a model of "Leviathan." The citizenry has no effective or operational control over government, once established, beyond the constraints that are imposed at the constitutional level; in-period or post-constitutional fiscal decisions are made entirely by the budget-maximizing or revenue-maximizing politician-bureaucrat.[6] The model here is in several respects similar to the "monopoly" or "noncooper-

---

6. There are evident similarities between our model and that developed by William Niskanen. See his *Bureaucracy and Representative Government* (Chicago: Aldine, 1971).

We should note that the assumption of the revenue-maximizing politician is not inconsistent with the assumption that the politician is constrained by the political process. In the absence of effective constraints on the domain of public spending, or on the government's ability to redistribute private goods among voters, majoritarian democracy may simply involve "maximum" transfers from minority to majority, along with or independent of the provision of genuinely public goods. Our discussion is, however, *phrased* largely in terms of a "monopoly" government in which revenue-maximization arises from the utility-maximization of the partially unconstrained politician-bureaucrat rather than from the democratic political process itself.

ative" state theories developed by earlier continental writers, notably some of the Italian fiscal theorists.[7] These monopoly-state conceptions, however, assume that the governmental powers have emerged from some coercive seizure of the state apparatus at some period in history. By contrast, in our model, government is voluntarily established by general agreement in a constitutional contract among potential taxpayers-beneficiaries.[8,9] The problem faced by persons in such a setting involves securing and ensuring the benefits of governmentally provided goods and services (including the enforcement of contracts and claims to property titles, without which market trading would hardly be feasible), while avoiding vulnerability to exploitation by the Leviathan-like institutions that may be uncontrollable once they are established.

Many different types of constitutionally derived constraints are conceivable, and these need not be mutually exclusive. Here we focus on the subset embodied in the *tax system*. In doing so, however, we assume that there exist some effective constraints on the disposition of tax revenues. Specifically, we assume that the uses of tax revenues must include the financing of at least some goods and services that cannot be provided noncollectively. Without this assumption, as previously noted with reference to Wicksell's statement, a constitutional contract establishing a coercive tax-levying authority could not be assumed to have emerged.

Our stylized constitutional setting is characterized by the further, and familiar, assumption that each person has well-defined predictions about the aggregate level and the distribution of incomes and consumption patterns in all post-constitutional periods, but that he possesses no knowledge about his own future position within the distribution or about the characteristics of his own taste pattern. This general, nonindividualized, knowledge is sufficient for him to make some estimate, within broad limits, both of the "efficient" levels of budgetary outlay on public goods, and of the aggregate revenues to be

7. For a summary of the Italian contributions, see James M. Buchanan, *Fiscal Theory and Political Economy* (Chapel Hill: University of North Carolina Press, 1960), especially pp. 24–74.

8. It is perhaps necessary to add the comment that the relevance of our analysis does *not* critically depend on whether or not governments have been, in fact, established in such a manner. The object of the contractarian exercise is to develop acceptable criteria for normative evaluation.

9. In this respect, the model resembles that which is familiar to economists in their analysis of the granting of franchises to monopoly enterprises.

obtained under alternative tax systems. Since the individual remains ignorant concerning his own predicted income or tastes, he cannot identify a cost-share for himself under any particular tax system. He cannot, therefore, predict whether, in-period, he might prefer a larger or a smaller public goods quantity than that which he predicts to be "efficient" for the whole community. Thus, each individual rationally prefers institutions that will generate the "efficient" quantity, $\overline{G}$, given an independent estimate of the costs of provision. The actual level of outlay on desired public goods and services is given by

$$(G) = \alpha \cdot R, \tag{1}$$

where $\alpha$ is the predicted proportion of tax revenue spent on the desired budgetary component, and $R$ is aggregate tax revenue. Throughout this discussion, the value of $\alpha$ is taken to be exogenous, by which we mean that it is fixed by the operation of constraints other than those incorporated in the tax system.[10] As we have indicated, $\alpha$ is such that

$$1 > \alpha > 0. \tag{2}$$

Hence, the outlay on desired public goods and services is some direct function of total revenue raised, and the problem that the individual faces at the constitutional stage is to organize tax arrangements so that the revenue raised, when adjusted by $\alpha$, will yield roughly the quantity of public goods and services estimated to be "efficient," at the given estimated net costs— costs that will, of course, be dependent on the value of $\alpha$.

Thus, $R$ will be chosen so that

$$\alpha \cdot R = \overline{G}. \tag{3}$$

The characteristic assumption of our Leviathan-type model is that, in each post-constitutional budgetary period, the government will attempt to maximize total revenue collections (and hence total spending), within the constitutionally appointed tax regime—that is,

$$R = R^*(b,r), \tag{4}$$

---

10. Interesting questions arise if we allow the revenue yield to vary with $\alpha$. In particular, there is the possibility of choosing tax institutions so as to constrain the disposition of revenues as well as the aggregate level. These are issues which we take up in a subsequent paper.

where $R^*$ is the maximum revenue that can be raised from the tax regime, and is a function of $b$, the tax base, and $r$, the allowable rate structure. Formally, then, the problem facing the individual is to select $b$ and $r$, so that

$$R^*(b,r) = \frac{\overline{G}}{\alpha}. \tag{5}$$

What this implies in terms of the desired tax constitution is elaborated in ensuing sections.

## 3. Tax Base and Tax Rate Constraints in a Simple Model

Initially, we restrict the analysis to a single individual who is assumed to be exercising his constitutional choice between only two potential definitions of the tax base—the one fully "comprehensive," the other falling short of this. We relax these assumptions later, but at this stage the simplification is convenient. It is immaterial for our argument precisely what the noncomprehensive base is, and whether the tax is levied on the "uses" or the "sources" side (that is, whether it is an "income" or an "expenditure" tax). Let us suppose, however, that the noncomprehensive base is money income from labor effort in the market, and that the comprehensive base includes this money income and also the money equivalent of the individual's nonmarket production of valued end-products; in other words, the comprehensive base is full income. The question we examine is whether the person would prefer a tax constitution that embodies the comprehensive base over the one that restricts the base to money income.[11]

The situation is depicted in fig. 1. The indifference curves, labeled with $i$'s, indicate the individual's preferences as between money-income–earning activity $Y$ and, say, leisure activity $L$. These preferences exhibit the standard

11. The basic conclusions hold equally for the case in which full "neutrality" is precluded, and the choice must be made between the narrower base and the "second-best" alternative, in which different goods are taxed at different rates according to their complement-substitute relationships with leisure (the question of interest in most of the recent "optimal taxation" literature). Our argument is thus equally with "optimal tax" and "comprehensiveness" proponents.

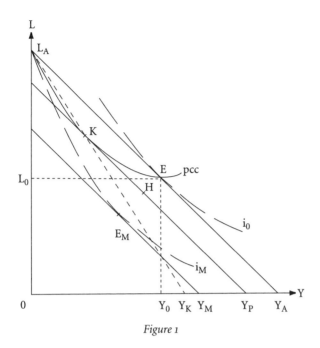

*Figure 1*

properties.[12] The pretax situation is characterized by a relative price between *L* and *Y* reflecting the productivity of income-earning activity; the initial equilibrium is at $E(Y_0, L_0)$ on $i_0$.

Consider now the prospect that the individual would face here if the government should be granted access to the fully comprehensive tax base. In this event, the individual would be exploitable up to the full limits of his potential earning ability, over and above some minimal subsistence. Apart from this minimal limit, all of the "income equivalent," $0Y_A$, is potentially available for governmental use. The government could levy a lump-sum tax that appropriated the individual's *maximum* potential earnings, beyond the subsistence level.[13]

---

12. By the assumptions of our model, the individual cannot predict his precise preference pattern as between money-income–earning and alternative activity in post-constitutional periods. All that is required for our analysis here is that these preferences are predicted to be standard.

13. It should perhaps be emphasized that the "comprehensive" *tax* is levied on the income side only: the surplus which accrues to the bureaucrat-politician, the excess of rev-

Since it is inconceivable that anyone could ever anticipate an "efficient" public-private–sector mix that would require all potential income above subsistence for governmental purposes, it seems clear that a potential taxpayer-beneficiary would *not* select the comprehensive tax base at the constitutional level if he predicts post-constitutional governmental behavior of the type that we have postulated. He will seek to impose constitutional constraints on the fisc, on the ability of the government to tax. He can do so, in our simple case, by allowing the government to levy an income tax only on the ordinary sources of earnings. This constraint, alone, will reduce the potential maximum revenue collections of government drastically—from $0Y_A$ to $Y_MY_A$ in fig. 1. Clearly, if the government imposes a tax on money income the revenue from which exceeds $Y_MY_A$, then the individual will be better off if he ceases to earn income at all: if he switches to $L_A$. If limited to the money-income base, the government can secure revenues up to this maximum limit, $Y_MY_A$, only by levying an "ideally" structured *regressive* tax, in which the rate for each level of $Y$ is equal to the slope of $i_M$. This involves creeping down $i_M$ to the maximum revenue equilibrium at $E_M$, allowing the taxpayer a minute slice of surplus to ensure only that the position $E_M$ is actually preferred to $L_A$.

Recognizing this prospect, the taxpayer may wish to impose the further constitutional constraint that the income tax should not be regressive in its rate structure. This would clearly be the case if the money-income base, along with the predicted value for $\alpha$ and the revenue-maximizing regressive rate structures, should be predicted to generate outlays on desired public goods and services in excess of the efficient levels of provision. If, for example, the government should be required to stay within a rate structure that is at least *proportional,* it would be effectively confronted with a locus of potential equilibria along the individual's price-consumption curve for varying "prices" of $Y$, depicted by $L_AKE$ in fig. 1. The revenue-maximizing arrange-

---

enue collections over public spending (as distinct from the bureaucrat's *income,* more narrowly conceived), is assumed to lie outside the coverage of the tax system. This assumption can be rationalized in a variety of ways, depending on the particular conception of Leviathan that one adopts. In the simple conception of "Leviathan" as the ruling class or monarch, the assumption is tantamount to allowing the king not to pay taxes. In a dominant majority conception, the comprehensive tax may be presumed to fall on all income, but not to fall on the special benefits, transfers, etc., that accrue to the majority coalition as a result of disbursement of the total revenue.

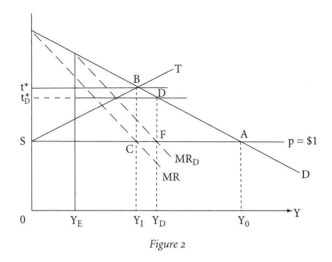

*Figure 2*

ment in this case occurs at the point where a line drawn parallel to $L_A Y_A$ is tangent to the price-consumption curve, as indicated by $K$, with the associated revenue-maximizing proportional rate of tax being, $Y_K Y_A / 0 Y_A$. The precise characteristics of this case, and the analytic resemblance to familiar results in price theory can be isolated by appeal to the corresponding partial equilibrium diagram in fig. 2.[14,15]

The curve, *DD,* in fig. 2, indicates the individual's demand for the income-

14. The construction in fig. 1 can be used to show how the constitutional-choice setting under our political assumptions transforms the familiar excess-burden argument in favor of the general or comprehensive-base tax. A solution at point $K$, in the neoclassical argument, is demonstrated to be inferior to that which might be attained with a comprehensive-base or general tax that will yield the *same* revenue, producing an ideal solution at some point like $H$ in fig. 1. This argument presumes, however, that the government, once empowered to levy the general or comprehensive-base tax will, in fact, restrict its attempts to raise revenue to the collections dictated by the equi-yield comparison.

15. The partial equilibrium version, based on the Marshallian demand-curve construction, can be used to illustrate the revenue-maximizing regressive structure, but by virtue of income effects will indicate a different rate structure than that derived from $i_M$. For similar reasons, the area under the demand curve does not accurately reflect consumer surplus; nor does the standard welfare triangle accurately reflect the welfare loss, or at least will do so only when the income-consumption curve $E_M HE$ in fig. 1 is a horizontal line. In what follows, we set such problems aside as being of no particular relevance to our discussion.

yielding activity; this might be derived from a preference mapping exhibiting the properties depicted in fig. 1. Confronted with the requirement that it must levy a proportional tax, what tax rate will the revenue-maximizing government impose? The question is obviously analogous to that asked of the monopolist who will seek to maximize profits, with the same answer. We derive a "marginal-revenue" curve, MR in fig. 2, and the maximum revenue is given where this cuts the horizontal dollar-price line (the marginal cost line), determining a post-tax equilibrium at $Y_1$.

This construction reveals the precise analogy between our model of post-constitutional governmental process and monopoly theory—in an analytic as well as a conceptual sense, our model is appropriately called a "monopoly theory government." The revenue-maximizing tax rate, $t^*$, can be derived as follows:

$$R = tY_1, \tag{4}$$

$$Y_0 - Y_1 = Y_0 \cdot \eta t, \text{ since } \eta = \frac{-\Delta Y}{Y_0} \bigg/ \frac{\Delta P}{P}, \tag{6}$$

where $R$ is government revenue; $t$ is the proportional tax rate and equals $\Delta P/P$

$$\therefore R = tY_0 (1 - \eta t), \tag{7}$$

$$\frac{\partial R}{\partial t} = Y_0 (1 - 2\eta t). \tag{8}$$

Setting (8) at zero, we have,

$$t^* = \frac{1}{2\eta}, \tag{9}$$

and, substituting $t^*$ in (7), we have,

$$R^* = \frac{Y_0}{4\eta}. \tag{10}$$

Hence, as we might expect, maximum revenue is directly related to the initial size of the taxable base, and inversely related to the value of the elasticity.

As we have indicated, the revenue raised from the given base under a *proportional* tax is less than that which might be raised from the same base under an ideally *regressive* rate structure. We are led to ask what might be the influence of a *progressive* rate structure here. The revenue-maximizing government will have no incentive to shift from the equilibrium proportional rate to any rate structure that embodies progression, since this latter would imply increasing rather than declining marginal rates of tax. The revenue effect can be demonstrated most easily by thinking of the simplest of all progressive rate structures, one that involves only two marginal rates, with the first rate being zero. Consider such a structure, sometimes called a *degressive* one, where income over some initial range to $Y_E$ is wholly exempted from tax. With this additional constraint, the revenue-maximizing proportional rate on remaining units or income falls and total revenue collections fall correspondingly.

To show this, note that under a degressive structure,[16]

$$R = t(Y_1 - Y_E)$$

$$= tY_0\left[1 - \eta t - \frac{Y_E}{Y_0}\right],$$

$$\frac{\vartheta R}{\vartheta t} = Y_0\left[1 - 2\eta t - \frac{Y_E}{Y_0}\right],$$

and

$$t_D^* = \left(1 - \frac{Y_E}{Y_0}\right)\frac{1}{2\eta}, \text{ which is } < \frac{1}{2\eta}, \tag{11}$$

and

$$R_D^* = \frac{(Y_0 - Y_E)^2}{4\eta Y_0}, \text{ which is } < \frac{Y_0}{4\eta}. \tag{12}$$

In terms of fig. 2 it is clear not only that the revenue-maximizing degressive structure postulated generates less total revenue than the revenue-maximizing proportional tax, but also that the excess burden is smaller. Under proportionality, the excess burden is measured in fig. 2 by the area *ABC*. Under the postulated degressive structure, excess burden falls to *ADF*.

Not all forms of progression yield this result for the change in excess bur-

---

16. A diagrammatic derivation of this result can be indicated by drawing a new *MR* curve, $MR_D$, over the range where the nonzero proportional rate is to be applied—as in fig. 2, with the maximum revenue rate being $t_d^*$.

den. For example, a linear progressive rate schedule (of the form shown by the line $ST$ in fig. 2)[17] will yield the revenue-maximizing *marginal* rate that is equal to the proportional revenue-maximizing rate, with the same post-tax equilibrium at $Y_1$. Note that in this case the total revenue obtained under progression is a constant share of that which would be obtained under proportionality where the marginal rate levied at income $Y_1$ would be applied over the entire income range. Thus, under the rate structure, $ST$, total revenue raised under progression is one-half that raised under proportionality. But the excess burden in the two cases is identical.

It may be useful to summarize the basic argument of this section. We have observed that the constitutional decision-making calculus of the potential taxpayer-beneficiary, operating under an expectation of a Leviathan-like post-constitutional fiscal process, involves his opting for institutional devices that will limit the revenue-raising potential of the tax system. We have explored two ways that might accomplish this. One is by limiting the size of the tax base—increasing the comprehensiveness of the tax base will be, beyond some point, clearly undesirable. The other is by imposing a constitutional requirement that some degree of progressiveness be incorporated in any rate structure. This "defense of progression" is completely different from any to be found in normative tax theory. It stems both from the constitutional perspective within which our whole analysis is developed, and from the unconventional, but highly plausible, assumptions we have made about the predicted workings of the political process. The argument does *not* spring from assumed risk aversion on the part of individuals behind the veil of ignorance, from Rawlsian maximin theorems, or from the more familiar "vertical equity" norms.[18]

## 4. Maximum Revenue and Excess Burden

To this point, we have restricted analysis to the simple setting in which the individual chooses between two potential tax bases and among rate struc-

---

17. That is, one in which the marginal tax rate, $m$, is given by $m = \beta Y^1 (m)$, where $Y^1$ is equilibrium income in the presence of tax and $\beta$ is some constant.

18. The existence of these is not inconsistent with our model. Constitutional preferences for progression as such may exist, and will merely complement the arguments posited here.

tures on these bases. Generally, however, the potential taxpayer at the constitutional stage will have the option of considering many possible base and rate structures, all of which might be estimated to raise roughly the desired level of revenue, $G/\alpha$, when exploited to the maximum-revenue potential. Retaining the single-person perspective, is there any reason to expect a constitutional preference for any particular method?

Presumably, the potential taxpayer will prefer that arrangement from among the set that will minimize net efficiency loss or excess burden. We may focus initially on the proportional-rate case, and assume that the "demand curves" are linear over relevant ranges. In this setting it is interesting to observe that when maximum revenue is obtained from a source, the excess burden is a fixed proportion of revenue raised. For,

$$W = \tfrac{1}{2}t(Y_0 - Y_1) \qquad (13)$$
$$= \tfrac{1}{2}t(Y_0\eta t),$$

where $W$ is the excess burden or efficiency loss generated by the tax. Substituting $t^*$ in (13), we have

$$W = \frac{Y_0}{8\eta} = \tfrac{1}{2}R^*. \qquad (14)$$

Consequently, given the assumption of linear "demand schedules," any two bases which yield the same maximum revenue under proportional-rate structures will involve identical excess burdens, independent of the size of the base or of the elasticity. Given proportionality, then, the maximum-revenue potential becomes the dominant choice criterion—excess burden tends to become irrelevant.

Once we admit progression into the analysis, excess burden may once again assume a role. Suppose, for example, that the choice is to be made between a proportional tax on commodity (or income source) $A$, and a tax on commodity (or income source) $B$, that yields identical maximum revenue under a *linear progressive* tax schedule. In this case, the excess burden generated will be larger under the latter, and in the assumption of our geometrical model, will be exactly two times that in the former. This result stems from the fact that under linear progression maximum revenue and the corresponding excess burden are identical. Of course, not all forms of progression exhibit this property. Specifically, for the type of degressive structures analyzed in (11) and (12) above, the relation indicated in (14) holds. In this sense, a persuasive case can be made out for degression over other types of progressivity. It is also clear that with the relevant equi-yield comparison made (that based on maximum potential revenue), a proportional tax and a degressive tax are equivalent on strict efficiency or excess-burden grounds, while either tax is preferable to other forms of a progressive tax.

This result, which indicates that many progressive rate structures generate more excess burden than the equi-yield proportional tax, is not at variance with our conclusion earlier to the effect that a constitutional requirement of progression may be one way of ensuring a restriction on the total level of governmental outlay through the limits imposed by the rate structure. We are simply observing here that, compared with equi-income reductions in the tax base, if these possibilities should exist, then progression may be an inefficient means of accomplishing this restriction.

Finally, it may be useful to make a technical comment on the methodology of tax analysis. One feature of the discussion in this section of the paper is our usage of one variety of an "equi-revenue" technique of comparison. These equi-revenue comparisons, however, involve separate base-rate combinations that yield the same *maximum* revenue. It is only within this stringently restricted subset of possible tax arrangements that we have permitted the application of the equi-revenue methodology, and that we have applied excess-burden criteria, appropriately derived from the constitutional perspective. Strictly speaking, even this limited use of the equi-revenue comparison is questionable, because *all* of the separate dimensions of tax selection (maximum-revenue yield, excess burden, and such "equity" effects as intrude) are aspects of the same general constitutional choice. It seems clear, however, that given our model of post-constitutional political process, maximum-revenue potential will be the predominant issue in the selection of tax institutions.

## 5. One Among Many

So far our discussion has been cast in terms of a single individual's choice calculus. This need not be nearly so restrictive as it might appear, particularly since we have examined choice in a constitutional setting, where the chooser is not expected to know just what his own position will be in post-constitutional periods. Nonetheless, we have neglected the problems that arise when the individual recognizes that regardless of what his own position will be, he will be one among many taxpayers, with differences among persons in both tax base and in preferences.

We may first consider whether or not our earlier results concerning tax-base limitations will hold in this setting. We may look at a simple two-person illustration. In fig. 3, we assume that the two persons, *A* and *B*, will earn an equal amount of money income and in the pretax or no-tax equilibrium, $Y_0$. (Recall that under our constitutional-stage assumptions, the individual will know only that the two persons *A* and *B* will have the characteristics depicted; he will not know which of the two positions he will, himself, occupy.) The persons are predicted to differ substantially, however, in their response to the imposition of a tax on the limited or money-income base, with leisure (or other valued end-products) exempted from tax. The differential responsiveness is indicated by the slopes of the "demand curves" for money income, as shown by $D_A$ and $D_B$.

The first point to be noted here is that so long as any responsiveness at all is predicted, the argument for the noncomprehensive base developed earlier holds without qualification. Each of the two persons whose preferences are depicted in fig. 3 will be protected against the exploitation potential of government that would be present under full-income as opposed to money-income taxation.

Let us now examine the revenue-maximizing government's predicted tax behavior in this two-person situation. If the government could treat *A* and *B* separately and differentially, and if it could levy a proportional tax on each (but not a regressive tax), it would impose a tax rate of $t_a$ on *A* and the higher rate, $t_b$, on *B*. Such differential treatment would clearly allow scope for the extraction of more revenue from the community than would be possible if the government were required to levy the *same* proportional rate on each person. The revenue-maximizing uniform rate, *t*, is determined in fig. 3 where the "market" marginal-revenue curve, $MR_m$, cuts the dollar-price line, with "price" set at the intercept of the vertical drawn from this intersection and the aggregate "demand curve" $\Sigma D$. This rate is such that $t_a < t < t_b$. The fact that revenue collections under the revenue-maximizing discriminatory rate structure $(t_a, t_b)$ exceed those under the uniform rate, *t*, suggests a further means of constitutionally restricting the revenue proclivities of Leviathan: by imposing

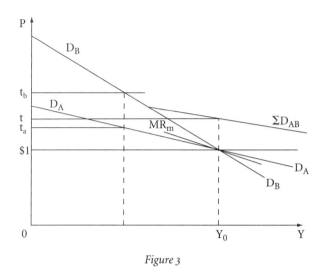

*Figure 3*

the constraint that tax schedules be *uniform* over persons. Such an argument for *uniformity*, which is related to but different from the more familiar "horizontal equity" norm, has not, to our knowledge, been developed anywhere in normative tax theory.[19]

The construction in fig. 3 can also be used to illustrate a proposition that seems at variance with that reached in models which assume institutional fixity. In the conventional framework, the behavior of individuals within the structure of given tax institutions is analyzed, and any attempt on the part of one person or group to avoid or to reduce tax payments, through recourse to nontaxable sources or uses of income, is interpreted as imposing an *exter-*

---

19. It is interesting to note that in this model no constitutional rationalization for "horizontal equity" as traditionally conceived emerges. A Rawlsian maximin rule, or generalized risk aversion, might generate a case for reducing the expected variance of the post-tax, post-expenditure income distribution in post-constitutional periods, but neither involves a specific, independent desire to tax those with identical pretax incomes identically. By contrast, in the more familiar model of constitutional choice in which the median voter's preference is decisive at the post-constitutional level, horizontal equity norms may be desired as a means of limiting distortions in public goods supply. A tax rule which levies burdens only on a small proportion of the population could be expected to generate levels of public goods supply which are significantly different from the optimum. In our model, however, the median voter is essentially irrelevant, and horizontal equity norms are simply subsumed by "vertical equity" ones.

*nal diseconomy* on less responsive taxpayers.[20] Behavior in reducing tax liability generates costs for others in the community by making higher rates of
tax and/or lower rates of public spending necessary than would otherwise be
required.

Consider the same issue in our constitutional framework. An individual
seeks to limit the revenue-potential of Leviathan, while remaining uncertain
as to his own position. In this case, he is benefited by the knowledge that at
least some taxpayers will be able to reduce tax liability by shifting to nontaxable sources (uses) of income. This may be shown easily in fig. 3. Compare the revenue-maximizing uniform rate, $t$, with that rate which would
be revenue-maximizing if the two taxpayers were predicted to be equally responsive in the manner indicated by $D_B$. The uniform rate would, of course,
rise to $t_b$, with a higher revenue potential. To the extent, therefore, that a person at the constitutional-choice level can predict that some members of the
set of taxpayers will be able to shift to nontaxable sources (uses) in post-
constitutional periods, his concern about the exploitative possibilities of Leviathan is correspondingly reduced.

Finally, we want to consider whether or not our earlier results concerning the relationship between progression and maximum revenue hold in
the many-person setting. It is perhaps intuitively appealing to suggest that
the results might not hold, since if low income persons should have particularly high elasticities of demand for leisure, it seems as if it might be revenue-
maximizing to levy lower rates of tax on their incomes while, at the same
time, levying higher rates on incomes above such limits. Progression offers
one means of making this sort of discrimination, while preserving uniformity.

Once more we begin with the simple two-person case, and for simplicity
suppose that for any positive tax rate individual $B$ has higher income than
individual $A$. Under the uniform-schedule restriction, will progression always yield less revenue than proportionality? We may answer this question
by examining the revenue-maximizing uniform rate schedule in our two-
person case. Only if this schedule is progressive will proportionality raise less
revenue than progression. To check this, let us suppose that the tax rate,

---

20. For an explicit discussion in such an externality setting, see James M. Buchanan,
"Externality in Tax Response," *Southern Economic Journal,* 33 (July 1966), 35–42.

$t_a$, is imposed on all incomes over the range from zero to $Y_a^1$, and rate $t_b$ on all additional income. In this case, total revenue, $R$, is given by:

$$R = 2t_a Y_a^1 + t_b (Y_b^1 - Y_a^1), \tag{16}$$

where $Y_i^1$ is individual $i$'s equilibrium income in the presence of taxation. Now we use the result

$$Y_i^1 = Y_i^0(1 - \eta_i t_i) \text{ for } i = a,b, \tag{17}$$

where $Y_i^0$ is individual $i$'s equilibrium income in the absence of taxation, and $\eta i$ is $i$'s elasticity of demand over the range $Y_i^0$ to $Y_i^1$, and define $\gamma$ so that

$$\gamma = \frac{Y_b^0}{Y_a^0}, \tag{18}$$

to obtain

$$R = Y_a^0[2t_a(1 - \eta_a t_a) + \gamma t_b(1 - \eta_b t_b) - t_b(1 - \eta_a t_a)]. \tag{19}$$

By maximizing $R$ with respect to $t_a$ and $t_b$, we determine $\hat{t}_a$ and $\hat{t}_b$ and can examine the ratio

$$\frac{\hat{t}_a}{\hat{t}_b} = \frac{4\gamma\eta_b + \eta_a(\gamma - 1)}{4\eta_a(\gamma - 1) + 2\eta_a}. \tag{20}$$

Clearly, the revenue-maximizing rate structure is progressive only if (19) is less than unity in value; or if

$$\eta_b < \frac{\eta_a(3\gamma - 1)}{4\gamma}. \tag{21}$$

Since $\gamma \geqq 1$, we know that

$$\frac{1}{2} < \frac{3\gamma - 1}{4\gamma} < \frac{3}{4}. \tag{22}$$

Thus, if there were no particular reason to assume that high income receivers have lower demand elasticities than low income receivers, we would expect (20) to be violated. In this case, the conclusion derived in our one-person model would carry over: progression would involve a revenue loss. But, it is also quite clear that (20) may hold; and in the case where $\eta_a$ is significantly larger than $\eta_b$ (by no means implausible), then the "right" degree of progression *could* generate more revenue than the revenue-maximizing proportional rate. The "right" degree of progression (from the revenue-maximizing government's perspective) does not, however, seem likely to be large. For example, it can be shown that the maximum revenue derived from linear progression of the type examined above (i.e., a rate schedule of the form $m = \beta \cdot Y^1$) is always less than that generated by the maximum-revenue proportional structure.[21]

## 6. Tax Limits and Tax Reform

As our analysis has suggested, the tax-base and tax-rate constraints imposed on governments at the constitutional level should, ideally, be such as to allow for the financing of some roughly efficient bundle of public goods and services. The danger of allowing governments access to revenue-raising instruments that will generate budgets in excess of these requirements is central to our whole model. We should, however, recognize that errors can be made in the opposing direction, that the constitutional tax constraints might, through time, prove to be overly restrictive. In this case, post-constitutional pressures will surely arise for escape through constitutional-style adjustments designed to widen the bases and to allow for more flexible rate structures, to move generally from specificity towards comprehensiveness. Empirically, it will always be difficult to distinguish between genuine constituency demands for a relaxation of such tax constraints, and the ever-present demands of the revenue-seeking politicians-bureaucrats. For the latter group, and their spokesmen, efforts will tend to be directed towards "loophole closing," towards increasing the number of sources that may be taxed. "Tax reform" advocacy on the part of the "bureaucratic establishment" will tend to

21. This paper is restricted to an analysis of the opportunities of imposing limits on the revenue-collecting potential of Leviathan through constitutional constraints on tax bases and tax rates. This would not, of course, be the only objective of an ideal "fiscal constitution," even if we remain within tax-side questions. To the extent that Rawlsian-like precepts of justice enter into the constitutional calculus, or even the more utilitarian motives of insurance and/or protection, a requirement that general public goods be financed at least partially by the imposition of progressive income taxes may emerge from conceptual agreement among all parties. In this context, our analysis may be viewed as complementary through its implication that progression may, independently, impose its own revenue limits.

be centered on "tax-base erosion." Indeed one indirect test of the empirical validity of our model of political process lies in the observed lack of reformist concern about relative rates of tax within existing tax-law limits. This offers some evidence to the effect that the revenue limits are indeed being approached.

In the discussion of proposed tax-base changes, the attitude of the traditional normative tax theorist and the members of the taxpaying public perhaps differ more sharply than anywhere else. Our analysis is helpful in "explaining" the attitudes of the taxpayers. For example, they are likely to react negatively and emphatically to proposals to move towards taxation on the basis of full income, as, for example, by including the imputed rental values of owned residences in the base for the personal income tax. The normative tax theorist, who advocates such inclusion always from reasoning based on equi-yield comparisons, responds to the taxpayers by arguing that overall rates of tax may be lowered simultaneously with the proposed widening of the base. But the taxpayers may be implicitly, but correctly, rejecting the equi-yield postulate, in their predictions that *any* widening of the tax base must open up further taxing possibilities for a revenue-seeking government.

Illustrations might easily be drawn from recent American fiscal experience. For example, in the early 1960s, a proposal was widely discussed which sought to replace part of the corporation income tax with a broad-based value-added tax. The proposal was quickly rejected, no doubt in part for the reasons suggested: it may have been predicted that ultimately the rates of value-added tax would reach heights that would greatly exceed those required to recover revenue forgone under the corporate income tax. In fact, of course, almost any widely advocated tax change tends to be justified in terms of its greater "efficiency" or its greater fairness, springing from the extension of the tax base. And as our analysis indicates, if our perception of post-constitutional political processes bears any relation to reality at all, it is precisely on such grounds that the change should be rejected!

We have, in broad and general terms, examined the basic issue of tax-base comprehensiveness in a constitutional-choice perspective, as opposed to the standard economists' perspective which is limited to single-period alternatives informed by familiar in-period efficiency criteria. We should emphasize, however, that our analysis does not involve a rejection of the efficiency norm, as properly understood. The rational person, who tries to predict his own position as a future taxpayer and as a beneficiary of public goods and services, will try to carry out some efficiency-like calculus in arriving at his choices among fiscal institutions at the constitutional stage, in the prediction that these institutions, once chosen, will remain as quasi-permanent features of the economic-political environment. As our analysis indicates, what is efficient at this level of choice may not be coincident with those institutions that seem to be efficient in the more restricted choice models usually discussed by fiscal theorists.

Our results depend critically on the assumed predictions about the properties of the political process. We have introduced a model of government as a revenue-maximizer limited by the tax constraints imposed in the constitution. This model is not to be confused with any one of the following models: the all-powerful government, subject to no constitutional constraints whatever; the benevolent and omniscient government, which provides the ideally efficient in-period quantities of public goods and "prices" these efficiently; the majority-rule democracy that makes fiscal decisions about public goods supply reflecting the preferences of the median voter—at least as traditionally conceived.

Each one of these alternative models of government (along with other variants not listed), as well as the one we have introduced in this paper, can be used to "explain" certain features of the institutional reality that we observe. Our claim is limited; the analysis based on the constitutionally constrained but revenue-maximizing government seems congruous with some fiscal institutions in existence that do command deference as "constitutional" elements, while at the same time the analysis seems consistent with many public, as opposed to academic, attitudes towards central issues in tax reform.

To the extent that our analysis does succeed in "explaining" both the institutions in existence and prevailing attitudes towards changes in these institutions, the contribution is positive. We should emphasize, however, that we are not primarily concerned with drawing a contrast between the "what is" of fiscal reality and the "what ought to be" that is contained in the traditional normative discussions of tax reform. Our analysis may well have a higher degree of positive explanatory content than the familiar alternatives. But our discussion is grounded squarely on a normative model of constitutional decision-making. Tax-base comprehensiveness is a reform objective that is almost never questioned in the traditional treatments. This paper suggests, first, that tax-base comprehensiveness may be rejected in a normative constitutional-choice calculus under certain political assumptions, and, secondly, that elements of the observed fiscal structure may well reflect this normative framework.

# The Logic of Tax Limits
## Alternative Constitutional Constraints
## on the Power to Tax

*Geoffrey Brennan and James Buchanan*

## I. Introduction

On Tuesday June 6th 1978, Californians voted overwhelmingly[1] for the Jarvis-Gann tax limitation proposal, Proposition 13. Several additional proposals were approved in the November 1978 state elections, and attempts to extend constitutional limits to the Federal budget were made in 1979. The "taxpayers' revolution" seemed to be genuine, and it was interpreted as such by politicians. Regardless of the ultimate outcome, the 1978–1980 period promises to go down as a truly fascinating episode in fiscal history.

For the public finance specialist in particular, tax limitation must be of extreme interest. Strangely enough, however, there is little in the standard analytic repertoire that would enable him to come to terms with what tax limitation is all about. He may indeed be able to analyze the effects of reductions in particular taxes to the extent that the revenue from those particular taxes is made up from other taxes. He may even be able to calculate, by appeal to the relevant benefit-cost analysis for the particular set of expenditure reductions involved, whether the implied "balanced budget" reduction is "efficiency increasing." But even this enormously ambitious—and, arguably, conceptually impossible—evaluation exercise hardly focuses on

From *National Tax Journal* 32 (June 1979): 11–22. Reprinted by permission of the publisher.
1. Virtually, a two-to-one majority to favor.

the crucial nature of "tax limitation" as an abstract notion. For what is at stake here is a general restriction on the use of particular taxes, or in some cases on the size of government, which is to apply *over the indefinite future.* For this reason, a full cost-benefit (or incidence) analysis requires an assessment not only of any current expenditure cuts, but also of all the future expenditures which government might have made if the tax limitation had not been operative.

In this sense, tax limitation has to be understood and interpreted in *constitutional* terms. Tax limits imply a change in the rules of the politico-fiscal game. Their explicit objective is to constrain government from taking actions that the citizenry predicts governments would or might have taken in the absence of tax limitations. If we are to make any sense of the tax limitation exercise at all, therefore, it is obligatory to offer some analysis of the nature of government—of the way in which the political mechanism operates.

Traditional public finance does not supply any such analysis. Implicit in the normative framework extensively used in policy discussion, however, is the notion of the benevolent dictator: government is effectively unconstrained beyond its internally imposed pursuit of ethical excellence, the true perceptions of which are obligingly supplied by the economics profession and other morally astute advisors. In this institutional setting, any constraints such as tax limitation (or electoral processes!) can be viewed only as undesirable restrictions, ranging from the mildly irritating to the wildly perverse. Tax limitation cannot be understood within such a political setting without retreat into the assumption of irrational electoral behavior.

Although modern public choice analysis provides explicit models of the political mechanism, it is also of limited value in treatment of tax limitation. The thrust of theoretical public choice analysis implies skepticism about the virtues of majoritarian political processes as a means of making "social" decisions, but much of the policy application exploits a simple median voter model in which political outcomes are broadly consonant with electoral wishes. In addition, the major focus in the public choice analysis of "government failure" is on the comparison of political and market institutions, rather than on ways in which political processes may be made to operate "better." To the extent that such improvements in political process have been sought, attention has been directed almost exclusively toward changes in electoral processes. The role of non-electoral constraints—and of fiscal rules in particular—as a means of moderating government behavior in directions that the citizenry desires has been almost totally neglected.

In this paper, we adopt a "constitutional perspective" in examining fiscal institutions. In this perspective, we introduce a model of political process in which electoral complications are explicitly excluded. This procedure allows us to offer an analytic setting within which the logic of tax limits can be understood, and by means of which alternative types of tax limitation can be evaluated. The structure of our argument is as follows. In section II, we present and attempt to justify the underlying model of government. In section III, we indicate briefly alternative forms that tax limitation might take and the means by which alternative constitutional adjustments might be evaluated. Sections IV, V and VI consider these alternative forms and represent the main analytic input of this paper. Section VII offers a brief summary and conclusion.

## II. Monopoly Government and the Power to Tax

To introduce the model of government that we wish to develop, it may be useful to reflect briefly upon the nature of government in a very abstract and broad-brush way. We may conceive of a world in which there is no government at all—an imaginative technique which in political theory dates back to Hobbes.[2] The Hobbesian insight was that in the absence of any collective enforcement of property rights, including the right to one's own life, life for anyone would be "poor, nasty, brutish and short." This Hobbesian state of nature could be characterized by complete "freedom of entry" in the use of coercive power. Individuals would be in a perpetual state of potential conflict with each other, and opportunities for mutual gains would not be exploited because even the simplest of trades would be too difficult to consummate.

From this setting, we might think of the rise of government as an emergent monopolization of coercive power, with government becoming the institution that is assigned that monopoly right. As Hobbes clearly recognized, however, although the presence of government makes it *possible* to define and enforce property rights to the advantage of all, major problems emerge concerning how government is to be prevented from exploiting its monop-

2. Thomas Hobbes, *Leviathan* (J. M. Dent, Everymans Library, 1943).

oly power for its own ends. In this perspective, government is naturally and inherently monopolistic—and the primary problem of constitutional design is to constrain the actions of government so that the outcomes which emerge are at least tolerable to the citizens who conceptually grant their consent to government in its exercise of monopoly power.[3]

One of the most familiar manifestations of the government's coercive power lies in the government's power to tax. This power to tax is the power which the government has to secure control over resources in which individuals hold nominal property rights. In itself, the power is held independent of taxpayers' consent and independent of any obligation to use the resources so obtained for purposes of which those taxpayers approve. In this sense, the power to tax is inherently coercive. And it is, of course, necessary that it be so. The ability of collective (as distinct from decentralized) action to circumvent the free rider problem in providing public goods[4] depends on the ability of the assigned authority to collect revenue independent of any current expression of willingness to pay.

In the absence of specific constitutional restrictions to the contrary, the power to tax is simply the *power to take*. If the government seeks to obtain a particular piece of property, it is of no account whether it does so simply by appropriating it directly, or by purchasing it, together with a tax *on the owner* for the full purchase price. In this case, taxing and taking are *identical*. Yet legally, they are not. Most constitutions severely limit government acquisition by direct appropriation, but the essentially equivalent power to tax is not restricted in anything like the same way. This apparent anomaly is explained once we recognize that the power to *tax* is (possibly implicitly) restricted in other ways. Uniformity requirements, for example, might require that others in the same circumstances as the property owner—perhaps with the same aggregate wealth—must pay the same tax. This could imply that

---

3. The language here reflects our implicit contractarian perspectives. It would be possible to conceive of government as wresting power by brute force. Historically, this origin of government may be descriptively accurate in many cases. But conceptually and normatively, it is more useful to think of government as emerging from voluntary agreement among the members of a group, and then to ask what the *terms* of that agreement might be.

4. Or, more accurately, goods for which price exclusion is infeasible or prohibitively expensive.

whereas taking the property directly would survive electoral scrutiny, the taxing alternative would not do so because more citizens are involved. Other rationalizations for the legal distinction between "taxing" and "taking" could no doubt be conceived, but the example here is instructive in one important sense. It indicates that purely fiscal requirements—restrictions on the generality of taxes in this case—may be necessary to ensure that electoral processes work within tolerable limits.[5] Apparently, *electoral* constraints are not the only form of restriction on government action; apparently, electoral constraints do not work particularly well in constraining government; and apparently, non-electoral constraints can be imposed which in some cases supplement and in others operate in lieu of normal electoral processes.

Tax limitation is, we believe, to be seen in this setting. In this connection, there are two aspects of the current tax limit history that are particularly striking. First, tax limitation proposals did not emerge out of normal political processes. Interparty competition and parliamentary procedures apparently failed to secure policies that the electorate desired. Normal electoral constraints were conspicuously inadequate. Second, the apparent objective of tax limit exponents was not to secure a once-and-for-all balanced budget reduction. Constitutional tax limits are explicitly designed to prevent governments from taking actions which, over an indefinite future, it is believed they would have taken, *electoral constraints notwithstanding*. Tax limitation is a *constitutional* affair.

In what follows, we shall adopt a model of monopoly government—of Leviathan—in which we abstract entirely from electoral constraints. In other words, we assume electoral constraints to be utterly ineffective. This is admittedly an extreme assumption. We believe it can be justified on both historical and à priori theoretical grounds. But we will not seek to offer any such justification here. Rather, we will defend the use of this assumption essentially as an analytic device. If one wants to focus on *non*-electoral constraints on government, it is useful to assume electoral constraints away. For those who remain skeptical, we appeal to John Stuart Mill—

... the very principle of constitutional government requires it to be assumed that political power will be abused to promote the particular pur-

---

5. Whether the requirement that taxes be general is itself sufficient to ensure acceptable political outcomes is, of course, dubious, as we show below.

pose of the holder; not because it is always so, but because such is the natural tendency of things, to guard against which is the especial use of free institutions.[6]

Accordingly, we assume that government possesses genuine coercive power which it uses—within the limits imposed by the constitution—for its own purposes. These purposes are not assumed to be more than normally benevolent; it is therefore logical to treat government as an income-maximizer in the way we typically treat private citizens. Leviathan's income, thus defined, is the excess of tax revenues over expenditures on public goods, i.e.,

$$Y = R - G, \tag{1}$$

> where Y is "income" to Leviathan (government)
> R is aggregate tax revenue
> and   G is expenditure on public goods.

On this basis, "natural" government would supply no public goods at all, unless constrained to do so under the constitution. Maximizing Y involves minimizing G. Thus, we would expect a basic ingredient of all voluntaristic constitutions to be restrictions on the *domain* of public spending. By this, we mean a set of rules concerning those things on which tax revenues may legitimately be spent, supplemented by restrictions on direct misappropriation of funds, "corruption" and such like. Such restrictions are a major part of most constitutions and are assumed throughout the discussion.

Although such rules exist, we would not expect them to be *entirely* constraining. Some leakage into the pockets of politicans-bureaucrats, in a variety of forms, can be expected. Thus, only a proportion of R, denoted by $\alpha$, will be spent on the public goods and services which the citizenry expects to want, and $\alpha$ will be characteristically less than unity. Hence, we can write:

$$G = \alpha R, \tag{2}$$

and therefore $Y = (1 - \alpha)R$.

In this simple model, there is a direct relationship between the maximization of Leviathan's income or surplus and the maximization of tax revenues. The central constitutional question for each citizen can now be simply

6. John Stuart Mill, *Essays on Politics and Society,* vol. 19 of Collected Works (Toronto University Press, 1977).

stated: how can each obtain the benefits of public goods supply[7] without exposing himself to gross exploitation by government—exploitation in the form of disastrously excessive tax burdens (and correspondingly excessive levels of public goods). One obvious answer to this question is the possibility of tax limitation, and, of course, our major task here is to examine and evaluate alternative forms that tax limits might take.

## III. Alternative Forms of Tax Limitation

Alternative tax limitation possibilities can be broadly categorized according to the aspect of the tax or tax system which is subject to restriction. Accordingly, we distinguish between limits imposed: first, on tax revenues; second, on tax bases; third, on tax rates.

1. *Revenue limits:* In this case, the constraint takes the form of specifying a maximum of the revenue which a government may obtain from a particular tax or tax system. The revenue maximum might involve an absolute magnitude, or perhaps more likely a share of the jurisdiction's total income or total product. The latter type we might refer to as "share limits," more commonly applied as restrictions on total budget size (or revenue from a total tax system, broadly defined) than as restrictions on particular taxes.

2. *Base limits:* In this case, limits take the form of restriction on the bases to which government may have access in acquiring revenue. These limits may specify the revenue instruments which government *may* use, or those revenue instruments which government may *not* use. The assignment of the property tax to local governments might be an example of the former; "balanced budget limitation" is an example of the latter in the sense that it denies government access to debt issue as a revenue-raising device.

3. *Rate limits:* Rate limits can take a number of forms. Restrictions may be placed on the *level* of rates—usually in the form of a maximum limit above which rates cannot extend. Alternatively, restrictions may be placed on the allowable rate *structure*—that it should be proportional, or that it should be uniform across individuals or across commodities.

---

7. Broadly interpreted to include the definition and collective enforcement of private property rights.

In what follows we shall examine these various possibilities in turn, with an eye both to how effective they might be in constraining a revenue-maximizing government and to how efficient they are in achieving a given degree of limitation. The use of these two criteria indicates the normative underpinnings of our evaluation procedure. We believe that that which emerges from consensus at the constitutional level has considerable normative authority, in line with the position we have taken elsewhere.[8] Thus, our predictions about what would emerge from the individual's calculus at the constitutional level become the means not only for understanding the current tax limitation movement but also of evaluating it.

## IV. Share and Revenue Limits

Understandably perhaps, share limits seem to hold a peculiar fascination for economists. The idea of specifying a limit to the size of government as a share of some economic aggregate (more or less well defined), such as gross product or total income for the relevant political jurisdiction, seems to offer a direct way of limiting public activity. But these ratio-type constraints are likely to be much more congenial to the professional economist-consultant than to the practicing politician or the average taxpayer. The economic sophistication required on the part of the citizens (and politicians) whose support must be organized to implement any constitutional change can represent a major barrier to the electoral success of this type of constraint. Taxpayers tend to think in terms of specific levies, and of their own treatment under such levies by the taxing authorities. They do not think in terms of such abstractions as total tax revenues or total spending, and surely not in terms of the ratio between two abstract entities, total budgets and total product or income.

But setting these problems of electoral psychology aside, are there any purely technical problems that ratio limits seem likely to pose? There are two that seem to us particularly important—one relating to whether the limits are effective, and the other relating to whether those effective limits are achieved in the most desirable way.

8. See, for example, J. M. Buchanan, *Freedom in Constitutional Contract* (Texas A&M University Press, 1977).

In the simple Leviathan model outlined above, government seeks to maximize its own surplus or income, measured by tax revenues, R, minus the necessary outlay on public goods and services, G. If it is constrained at R, either in absolute or share-of-income terms, it may seek to provide the necessary G indirectly rather than directly, and thereby increase its surplus, Y. One means of accomplishing this result would be to manipulate the structure of taxes while remaining within the overall uneven constraint. Consider, for example, some publicly provided good such as education. Clearly, the government can achieve a required level, either by direct provision of education (i.e., it can tax individuals and provide the service free of direct charge) or by subsidizing private provision. And the subsidy in question may take the form of vouchers (or direct subsidy of some other type) or tax concessions. In principle, each of these alternatives could produce precisely the same outcome, but they clearly involve quite different amounts of nominal tax revenue. The subsidizing of private activity will typically achieve a larger response per dollar of revenue raised than direct provision; obversely, for any given level of activity, subsidy will typically involve less tax revenue than direct provision. Subsidies given as direct payments will likewise involve more nominal tax revenue and a higher nominal government budget than tax concessions which induce an identical private response. At the very least therefore we should require that such "tax expenditures" be incorporated into the relevant measure of total revenue for "share limit" purposes.

But this in turn raises the question as to whether we ought also distinguish between subsidies and direct provision; for, as we have observed, an identical amount of revenue can involve a different level of government influence depending on the form of government action. Even if the implicit subsidy embodied in "tax expenditures" is made explicit, therefore, the problem associated with translating any given revenue figure into some measure of government "output" remains. And there are important conceptual issues at stake in this. Is it clear, for example, that we do wish to minimize government "output" or influence, independent of its revenue cost? Is there a distinction to be drawn between policies which involve revenues passing through the hands of government agencies, and those which do not? We do not attempt to answer these questions here. But it does seem clear that any share limit which accurately reflected what it is we wish to measure would be extremely complex and itself somewhat open to debate, and the problems of electoral ignorance would be correspondingly aggravated. Equally, the extent to which an aggregate revenue limit would succeed in achieving the objective of placing limits on government activity seems open to some doubt.

Suppose, however, that in the presence of this maximum share (appropriately defined), government is genuinely constrained. Nevertheless, government can achieve its maximum share in a variety of ways between which the citizen-taxpayer behind the veil of ignorance could not be expected to be indifferent. For example, different tax arrangements will induce different excess burdens: in the extreme case government could exploit tax instruments considerably beyond their maximum revenue limits and the excess burden induced by the tax could be many times greater than the revenue raised. There is nothing inherent in the nature of share limits which would give government the incentive to seek out broadly based, minimally distorting taxes. As we have already seen, the government, on the contrary, has the incentive to acquire its revenue limit by the application of very high rates to a base made narrow by strategic concessions.[9] Whether these high rates raise much or indeed any revenue is largely beyond the point: the associated excess burdens seem likely to be very substantial indeed.

## V. Base Limits

The possibility of constraining the activities of government by specifying the *bases* on which taxes may be levied is not one which seems to have attracted much attention in the tax limitation context. Perhaps the reason for this is that it seems to set much of the standard public finance literature on its head. The virtues of broad-based, "comprehensive" taxes are replaced by an explicit preference for the appropriately narrow tax base—"appropriate" in that when the maximum revenue rate is applied, the revenue yield is exactly that required to supply the level of public goods which citizens expect to desire in future periods. Yet it is clear that if the government is constitutionally

---

9. Craig Roberts and Richard Wagner have recently used an observation along such lines to explain why power-maximizing governments do not abolish tax loopholes. ("Tax Reform Mongering: Common Ignorance or Political Fraud," paper presented at the Southern Economic Association Meetings, Washington, 1978.)

restricted to particular taxes with well-defined bases, its revenue share is necessarily restricted, and especially so as the activities excluded from taxation are substitutable for those upon which taxes may be levied.

Consider an apparently extreme, but still relevant, example. Suppose that government is allowed to levy personal taxes on money incomes but that it is constitutionally prohibited from taxing income-in-kind. In such a setting, as income tax rates increase, taxpayers will, of course, shift toward income-in-kind. This shift generates an excess burden, familiar from analyses of welfare economics. What economists have overlooked, however, is the constraining influence that such potential shifts can exert on government's fiscal appetites. Faced with the prospect that taxpayers can, and will, shift to nontaxable options, even if at some cost, governments will find that maximal-revenue limits are attained at much lower budgetary levels than would be the case if the tax base should be fully "comprehensive."

The illustrative analytics of figure 1 may be helpful here. Suppose that $D_X$ indicates aggregate demand within the taxable community for some good X, and that X has been assigned to the government as *the* base. For analytic simplicity, we assume that $D_X$ is linear and that X is produced under conditions of constant costs. We define the units of X in terms of a "dollar's worth," so that marginal cost is everywhere one dollar, and $X_0$ is the total pre-tax expen-

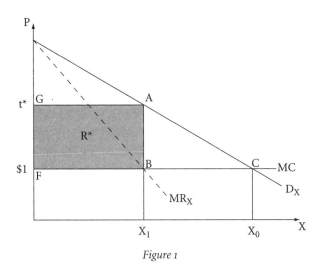

*Figure 1*

diture on X.[10] To avoid the possibility of various forms of "discrimination," we assume that the government is limited by a requirement that the tax rate structure be uniform both across units of X and between individuals.[11] What uniform proportional tax on X will government choose, given its revenue-maximizing proclivities?

This question is analytically identical to asking what price a profit-maximizing monopolist would charge for X if he were assigned a monopoly franchise in the sale of X: tax revenues in the one case are exactly equivalent to profits in the other. As is well known, we can determine the profit-maximizing output-price combination by constructing a marginal revenue curve, $MR_X$, which intersects the dollar MC line at $X_1$: this output is the profit-maximizing output and $AX_1$ the corresponding profit-maximizing price. Analogously, the tax revenue maximum involves a gross-of-tax price of $AX_1$, and a per unit *tax* of $(AX_1 - 1)$ dollars: the tax *rate* involved is $t^*$, given by $(AX_1 - 1)/1$, and the revenue obtained is $t^* \cdot X_1$, shown as the shaded area $R^*$ in figure 1.

We should note at this point that in this linear case, the $MR_X$ curve necessarily bisects the horizontal distance between the $D_X$ curve and the vertical axis at any price. In particular, $X_1$ is exactly one half $X_0$. It follows that the excess burden induced by the maximum revenue tax, the "welfare triangle" ABC, has an area exactly one half of $R^*$.[12]

Two things follow from this observation. First, if we consider assigning to government some broader tax base, it is clear that this same revenue $R^*$ could be obtained at a smaller welfare loss. This is the observation on which the traditional "efficiency" preference for broad-based taxes is founded. However, assignment of a broader tax base to government would, under Leviathan assumptions, simply lead to a larger maximum revenue yield. This not only would increase the level of public spending, possibly beyond desired

10. The significance of this assumption is that we can treat the tax per unit as a tax rate, t. The assumption is in no sense crucial.

11. We shall examine the significance of this assumption in the ensuing section on tax *rate* limitation.

12. While it is true that this result assumes linearity, it is also true that conventional measures of excess burden, such as those promulgated by Arnold Harberger, implicitly assume linearity by considering only first order terms in the relevant Taylor series expansion. ("Three Basic Postulates for Applied Welfare Economics," *Journal of Economic Literature* [September 1971]: 785–97.) The linearity assumption here, then, should not be regarded as unduly objectionable.

limits, but also would increase correspondingly the excess burden attributable to taxation (to one half of the *new* and *higher* maximum revenue yield). Thus, revenue limits imposed via the assignment of limited tax bases also set limits on the *welfare losses* attributable to taxation.

Second, the use of base limits, as opposed to share limits, ensures that the welfare loss attributable to taxation can never exceed one half of revenue raised. As pointed out in the previous section, it is conceivable that in the share-limits case tax rates may be pushed above their maximum revenue values, in which case welfare losses will exceed half the revenue obtained, and in the limit will absorb virtually all consumer surplus generated from X. If the practical relevance of this possibility is doubted, it needs to be asked whether one can be sure that the very high marginal rates of tax applying in some Western countries, above ninety percent in some cases, are not already above the maximum revenue limits of the relevant taxes.

The implications of this discussion for conventional tax policy should perhaps be underlined. The overwhelming preference for broad-based taxes which characterizes tax policy orthodoxy is exposed here as extremely dubious. To the extent that government behaves according to the Leviathan assumptions postulated here, or equally, to the extent that constitutional tax limitation is to be interpreted as a widely shared desire on the part of the citizenry to inhibit the growth of government, the familiar policy recommendations of tax economists must be recognized as heading in precisely the wrong direction. Broader-based taxes will ultimately lead to larger revenues being collected than otherwise, with concomitantly larger levels of public goods supply than the citizenry desires at current prices, and larger levels of fiscal exploitation.

There is one possible virtue of base limits which does not seem to be present under direct revenue limits or rate limits. This is the possibility of using appropriately chosen tax-base constraints to establish incentives for governments or governmental agencies to provide the goods and services valued by the taxpayers themselves rather than prerequisites of bureaucratic office. If the constitutionally allowable bases for taxation are chosen so as to be strongly complementary to the public goods to be provided, governments will find it necessary to perform with tolerable efficiency in order to collect tax revenues. A highway agency, for example, charged with producing and maintaining roads will be motivated to fulfill its assigned function if its revenue base is restricted to gasoline and vehicle levies, because the better the roads, the more gasoline will be purchased and the larger and more expensive the cars bought and hence the more revenue the surplus-maximizing agency will provide. Likewise, a government television network will tend to operate in viewers' interests if programs are financed by the sale of television-watching licenses. In the extreme case, this establishes an argument for public provision of services for direct fees and charges. By appropriate choice of tax base, the proportion of revenue expended by government on the goods which citizens want (the parameter $\alpha$ in equation [2]) can be increased, and this is, we believe, an important feature of base limitation as a means of constraining government.[13]

Although it is not possible to explore "balanced budget limits" in this setting, it should be clear that these may be interpreted as a form of base limitation. Under a balanced budget restriction, however, government access to allowable revenue sources is constrained not by specifying the tax instruments which government *may* use—but rather those which government may *not*. A balanced budget amendment *denies* government access to debt issue and restricts its access to new money creation as revenue-raising devices. An assessment of the virtues of such an amendment would involve both an evaluation of the peculiar vices of new money creation and debt issue under Leviathan assumptions—peculiar, in the sense that they do not apply to other revenue instruments—and of the influence that the removal of these instruments from Leviathan's armory would have on total revenue capacity of government. We do not attempt to discuss these issues here. We do, however, believe that this is the *setting* in which they should be discussed and understood.

Finally, it should be emphasized that the success of any form of revenue limitation, whether implemented by base limits or direct revenue limits, depends on the existence of additional constraints on governmental regulatory powers. Just as discretionary exercise of tax concessions can achieve government objectives at very low revenue cost, regulations—and the exercise of power by fiat more generally—can be used to substitute for budgetary ex-

13. This argument is developed more fully in Geoffrey Brennan and James Buchanan, "Tax Instruments as Constraints on the Disposition of Public Revenues," *Journal of Public Economics* (June 1978): 301–18.

penditures. One would expect that the direct exercise of legislative power would be used much more extensively as revenue limits, however imposed, are approached. Constitutional rules which limit government access to regulation could be devised. Some already exist. And it could be that, to the extent that reducing government revenues also reduces the size of the bureaucratic machine in which regulations and their enforcement are born, revenue limits and limits on rule by regulation are over some range complementary. For our purposes here, we simply note the need for such constraints in genuine constitutional reform.

## VI. Tax Rate Limits

Rate limits can take two forms: limits on maximum rates that can be imposed; and limits on the rate *structure*. We examine these in turn.

### A. MAXIMUM RATE LIMITS

Maximum rate limits are simple to comprehend and relatively easy to apply. In *conjunction* with base limits, they represent a direct and efficient means of restricting government access to revenue. In the *absence* of base limits, however, they are unlikely to be genuinely constraining. For suppose that a maximum rate limit were imposed in isolation. The immediate result would be that Leviathan would be forced into widening the tax base in order to secure revenues. At first glance, this may seem to be a desirable thing; by setting the rate limit low enough, the citizen-taxpayer could ensure that a genuinely comprehensive tax would raise the revenue required to finance the level of public goods supply he expects to want. And given the widely vaunted virtues of comprehensiveness in the tax system,[14] Leviathan would seem to have the incentive to provide a tax system that is genuinely desirable. Clearly, however, the forces that lead Leviathan to broaden the tax base do not stop when an acceptably broad base[15] is reached: the revenue-maximizing government cannot be expected to stop obligingly when some conceptual "horizontal equity" norm is achieved. A tax on *gross* rather than net income might, for

14. In a normative setting rather different from that adopted here.

15. Perhaps of the Simons type. See Henry Simons, *Personal Income Taxation* (University of Chicago Press, 1938).

example, be instituted. And as well as the maximum-rate income tax, we would expect the maximum-rate sales tax, the maximum-rate company income tax, the maximum-rate payroll tax, the maximum-rate wealth tax, the maximum-rate estate duty and so on. In the limit, government would appropriate revenue up to the natural limits set by individuals' preparedness to work, to save, to take risks and so on. In general, one would expect this level of revenue to go well beyond that which the citizen-taxpayer would desire—and, of course, these natural limits would be operative whether maximum-rate restrictions were imposed or not. Of themselves, therefore, rate limits do not, in any way, ultimately constrain the *level* of revenues—though they may force governments to collect the available revenue in expensive and inefficient ways.

It is clear, however, that when base limits are also operative, rate limits can be used to ensure revenue collection with minimal excess burden. Recall that with base limits used in isolation, the welfare loss under revenue-maximizing rates will be exactly half the maximum revenue.[16] Suppose we consider two alternative tax bases, X and Y, and Y is the larger; suppose further that X yields a maximum revenue, $R_x^*$, that provides the level of public goods supply citizens want. Under base limitation alone, X will be the preferred tax base since Y will yield too much revenue. But there is a tax rate, $t_y$, which when imposed on the larger base Y will yield the same revenue, $R_x^*$, as the maximum revenue from X. Assignment of base Y *together with a maximum-rate limit* of $t_y$ will, of course, yield that same revenue at smaller welfare loss, just as the traditional analysis assures us. The orthodox tax analysis, therefore, could be looked on as implicitly assuming an appropriate maximum-rate constraint: the appropriate maximum rate must however be jointly determined with the base to yield the desired level of revenue. The equi-revenue assumption familiar from orthodox tax analysis only becomes institutionally relevant if there are appropriate constitutional restrictions to ensure that revenue cannot increase.

## B. Rate structure limits

We have already noted the analogy between assigning Leviathan some taxable base X and assigning Leviathan a monopoly franchise in the sale of X. Carry-

16. As shown in Fig. 1 and the surrounding text.

ing this analogy further, we should note that a profit-maximizing monopolist can obtain larger profits from the sale of X than those indicated in figure 1, by various forms of discrimination: discrimination over units of X, or between different consumers of X. In the same way, the revenue-maximizing government can use the rate structure effectively to discriminate over units of X, and/or between different taxpayers. Such discrimination will increase public revenue—and therefore appropriate restrictions on the *rate structure* can be a means of tax limitation, just as maximum rate limits can be.

Consider the simple two-person example set out in figure 2. Individuals A and B have demand curves for the assigned tax base, X, designated by $D_A$ and $D_B$. The aggregate demand for X is $D_T$. Suppose there is a legal restriction which requires *uniformity* of tax treatment of A and B, in the sense that A and B must face the same rate structure. The revenue-maximizing rate chosen will be t*, derived from the aggregate demand curve $D_T$ and the associated marginal revenue curve. In the absence of the uniformity restriction, however, Leviathan could impose the proportional rate on A which maximizes the revenue obtained from A (shown as $t_A^*$ in figure 2, and determined from $D_A$ in the same way as t* is from $D_T$) and the corresponding rate on B which maximizes the revenue obtained from B (shown as $t_B^*$ in figure 2). This would increase tax revenues since, by definition, one is obtaining more revenue from each taxpayer than with t*. Requiring unifor-

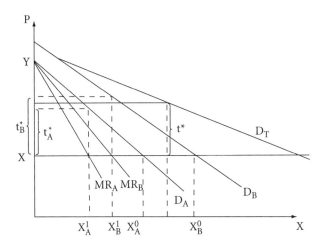

*Figure 2*

mity as between taxpayers is, therefore, one means of restricting total revenue.

We should note that discrimination *among individuals* under a proportional rate regime does not have any efficiency advantages. The welfare loss for A is exactly half the revenue obtained from A; likewise, for B. Hence, the aggregate welfare loss remains one half of aggregate revenue.

Another form of discrimination is, of course, possible—this is discrimination over units of X. In the monopoly case, "perfect" discrimination, appropriating the entire consumer surplus of all consumers, is an analytically familiar possibility. Here, precisely the same possibility appears. By setting a rate structure for each individual which follows that individual's demand curve,[17] Leviathan can obtain as tax revenue the entire consumer surplus from X of each taxpayer. The rate structure for A, for example, would involve an initial rate infinitesimally below XY for the first unit of X and decline over the range to a zero rate at $X_A^0$. Each taxpayer would face a different *regressive* rate structure, and virtually all consumer surplus would be appropriated as public revenue.

Constraints which outlaw regressive rate structures may be used to restrict government revenue take. Suppose that regression is permitted, but uniformity in the rate structure as between individuals is required. Then, the revenue-maximizing rate structure can be derived as in figure 3. We construct $D_A^+$ in this figure by taking twice the vertical difference between $D_A$ and the dollar marginal cost line and adding it to the dollar line. Thus, the distance XZ is exactly twice XY. This line depicts the revenue per unit of X obtained while the rate structure follows $D_A$—for B will consume the units taxed on this basis as well as A. Clearly, in the range up to F where $D_A^+$ and $D_B$ intersect, the revenue obtained from the rate schedule based on $D_A$ exceeds that obtained from the rate schedule based on $D_B$, because in the latter case only B would purchase units of X. Beyond F, the opposite applies. The uniform rate structure which maximizes revenue therefore follows $D_A$ up to H and $D_B$ thereafter and is depicted in figure 3 by the heavy line. We should note the sudden jump in the marginal rate at H. Under this rate structure, A will consume at $X_F$ and B at $X_B^0$: there is therefore a standard welfare loss im-

---

17. More strictly, his indifference curve corresponding to zero consumption of X given his consumption possibilities.

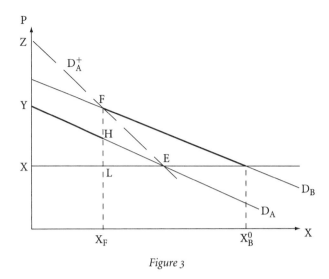

*Figure 3*

posed by the uniformity constraint—in this case equal to the triangle HLE.

What emerges clearly from this discussion is that requirements of uniformity in the rate structure applying to different individuals and requirements which restrict regressivity in the rate structure of particular taxes may be used to restrict the revenue capacities of a Leviathan government, along with or independent of base limits or direct revenue limits.

In evaluating the desirability of rate structure restrictions, however, a certain amount of care must be exercised. We should note that the perfectly discriminating regressive tax structure involves a zero welfare cost. Suppose that, under a proportional rate structure, the tax base assigned yields the level of public goods supply the citizenry wants. Since permitting a regressive rate structure would increase revenue levels, it might seem that this should be undesirable. However, it need not be. Consider figure 1. The maximum revenue $R^*$ obtained under the revenue-maximizing proportional tax, $t^*$, is exactly half the aggregate surplus given that $D_X$ is linear, and the total cost in terms of consumer surplus from X forgone, which includes the excess burden, is $(3/2) R^*$. Allowing the "perfectly discriminatory" regressive rate structure to be applied to X would therefore double the level of revenue and hence of public goods supply, and increase the cost in terms of consumer surplus forgone by one third. It seems that only if the demand for public goods supply is extremely inelastic will the imposition of restrictions to prevent regression be desirable. We should note, however, that this proviso is strictly applicable to the case where the perfectly discriminatory tax rate structure is feasible: if *imperfectly* discriminatory tax rates are likely to be applied, then restrictions on the rate structure are more likely to be desirable. In any case, the advantages of discrimination appear only when discrimination *over units* (i.e., via a regressive rate structure) is applied: discrimination *between individuals* in and of itself implies no reduction in excess burden per dollar of revenue, under revenue-maximizing government behavior.

## VII. Summary and Conclusions

There can be little doubt that tax limitation is and will remain an important issue of current economic policy.

In this paper, we have tried to suggest a setting within which the issue may be examined along with some indication as to how the public finance specialist may contribute to the analysis. The taxpayers' revolution can be satisfactorily understood only in constitutional terms and by appeal to a model of political process that is captured neither by the "benevolent despot" model of conventional policy analysis, nor by the median voter model that dominates the public choice alternative. We have suggested a *non-benevolent* despot model, that we have called "Leviathan." And in order to offer an analysis of alternative tax limitation possibilities, we need to examine ways in which Leviathan can be constrained by elements of the "fiscal constitution."

The formal analysis of the fiscal constitution, both in its positive and normative aspects, remains in its infancy. In this paper, we have done little more than set the stage for discussion.[18] We have, however, in the process attempted to indicate how the analytic discussion of tax limitation, in its diverse possible guises, might go.

If there is a policy conclusion to be drawn from this discussion it is perhaps that there is more than one way to skin the governmental cat, and the alternatives are not necessarily all equally good. And we need to be reminded

---

18. In our forthcoming book, we shall explore many of the relevant issues in greater detail. See Geoffrey Brennan and James Buchanan, *Taxation for Taxpayers: Constitutional Control of the Taxing Power* (forthcoming, 1979).

that much which passes for informed tax advocacy—indeed, much conventional analytics—is systematically eroding many of the natural tax limits embodied in our current system. Attempts to broaden tax bases, on ostensibly legitimate equity and efficiency grounds, lead in directions that the modern taxpayer apparently does not wish to tread.

# Proportional and Progressive Income Taxation with Utility-Maximizing Governments

*James M. Buchanan and Roger Congleton*

## Introduction

In the *Constitution of Liberty* (1960), F. A. Hayek suggested that proportional taxation of personal incomes is compatible with a social order in which individual liberties are preserved whereas progressive taxation is not.[1] He argued that proportional taxation, in itself, would exert a sufficiently constraining influence on the behavior of government in exploiting its inherent fiscal authority. We may infer from his discussion that Hayek would support a constitutional limit on the taxing power that would allow the levy of proportional income taxation but that would prohibit the imposition of progressive rates.

To our knowledge, the precise effects of such a constraint on the fiscal authority of government have not been fully analyzed. This paper is aimed at partially filling the gap. In highly simplified models, we shall examine the behavior of government under proportionality constraints, and we shall compare this behavior with that predicted under progressive taxation. We shall

From *Public Choice* 34 (1979): 217–30. Reprinted by permission of the publisher, Kluwer Academic Publishers.

We are indebted to Geoffrey Brennan and to Yew-Kwang Ng for helpful suggestions. Partial research support for Buchanan's work on this paper was provided by the National Science Foundation.

1. University of Chicago Press, 1960, chapter 20, 306–23.

analyze the effects of maximal rate constraints under both proportionality and progression. In the first part of the paper we shall ignore the effects of taxation on incentives to produce taxable income; incentive effects are introduced in the second part of the analysis.

Before we can make the analysis meaningful, some model of governmental decision-making is required, along with some specification of the nontax constraints on fiscal authority. We shall model governmental behavior in very general terms. We assume only that governmental fiscal decisions are made by some subset of the taxpaying citizenry, some less than all-inclusive coalition of the whole polity. The decision-making group may be conceived as a majority coalition representing one of two major political parties, with the total group of taxpayers being divided into members of this majority and members of the minority. Alternatively, we might consider the setting to be one where a ruling clique or committee (in the limit of one person) makes decisions for the polity, in which case the overwhelming majority of all taxpayers falls within the nonruling or potentially exploitable group. We do not need to specify anything about the relative pre-tax income levels of members of the ruling group and the ruled group. The "poor" may or may not be members of the ruling coalition. All that is minimally required for our analytical purposes is that the population of all potential taxpayers be divided into two distinct sets. In the formal analysis of subsequent sections of the paper, we shall use the simplifying two-person setting with one person designated as the "ruler," with the other person treated as the potential exploitee, the "ruled," who has no influence on his own fiscal situation.

It is evident that a constraint or limit on the taxing power or authority of government means little unless this constraint or limit is also accompanied by constraints on the spending power. If a government can implement direct transfers in a discriminatory manner, then members of any ruling coalition can capture for themselves any desired share of the total incomes of the exploited group independent of any structural tax-side constraints that might be constitutionally imposed. In the analysis that follows, we explicitly restrict the spending power of government to the financing of public goods and services, defined in the classic Samuelsonian sense as embodying both complete jointness in consumption and nonexcludability. This requirement may be relaxed to allow for the provision of both impure goods and even for fully divisible goods so long as we retain the assumption that all persons in the community share equally in the benefit flows of whatever goods and services government does, in fact, provide, and, further, that such goods and services are not retradable.

## Proportionality, No Rate Constraint, No Incentive Effects

Consider a highly simplified two-person (A, B) model with two goods, one private, Y, and one public, G. The public good is available at a constant per unit cost, C, defined in units of the private good. Initial or pre-tax production of the private good (income) are in the amounts, $Y_a$ and $Y_b$, per period, and through our assumption that incentive efforts are absent, persons will continue to generate private goods or incomes in these amounts per period regardless of the tax-spending decisions that are made, or by whom.

Assume now that the constitution specifies that the same uniform rate of tax, $r$, must be levied against the private goods incomes of both persons, A and B, and that the proceeds of this proportional tax must be used exclusively to finance the purchase-provision of G.

We shall initially assume that the tax-spending authority is vested exclusively in B, who becomes the "governor" or "ruler." We can now proceed directly to solve B's utility-maximizing problem in the setting postulated. Note that, under the assumptions of the model, A, the "ruled," confronts no choice. B's utility is a function of two arguments, his disposable income (private good) after tax ($Y_b - rY_b$) and public goods, G, as indicated in (1).

$$U_b = u_b[(Y_b - rY_b), G].$$ (1)

It is within B's power to choose the value of G that will maximize $U_b$, and we assume that B does this by selecting $r$, the rate of tax that is to be imposed on the incomes of both persons. The budget constraint of the polity is shown in (2).

$$rY_a + rY_b = cG.$$ (2)

Maximizing with respect to $r$, first-order conditions are satisfied in (3).

$$\frac{\partial u_b}{\partial(Y_b - rY_b)} \bigg/ \partial u_b/\partial G = \frac{Y_a + Y_b}{c} \bigg/ Y_b.$$ (3)

This solution is, of course, the familiar tangency requirement for individual equilibrium.

We may depict this solution diagrammatically in Figure 1, where the quantity of the public good, $G$, is measured on the ordinate and that of the private good, $Y$, along the abscissa. We set the relative pre-tax income levels at $Y_a$ and $Y_b$, with $Y_a$ being double $Y_b$. The opportunity locus confronted by $B$ is shown as the straight line connecting the point, $(Y_a + Y_b)/C$, at which point all of the private income of the community is used up in purchasing the public good, $G$, and the point $Y_b$, at which no $G$ is purchased and $B$ retains his full initial own production of the private good. $B$'s equilibrium is shown at $E$, where $0G$ units of the public good and $0y_b$ units of the private good are consumed by $B$.

We have looked directly only at the pre-tax and post-tax positions of $B$, whom we have assumed to be the decision-maker. Note, however, that the pre-tax position of $A$ enters into the determination of $B$'s utility-maximizing position through the intercept and slope of $B$'s opportunity locus. In the model under consideration here, this locus is fixed by parametric values for the cost of producing the public good, and for the pre-tax income levels of $A$ and $B$.

Consider now the position of $A$, the person who is subject to possible fiscal exploitation because of his powerlessness to influence the tax-spending

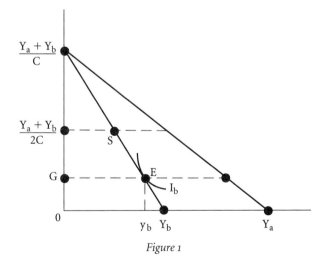

*Figure 1*

decision of B. If A should be identical to B, both in preferences and in initial pre-tax incomes, the delegation of decision-making authority to B will not harm A, even in an opportunity-cost sense, because A's most preferred position would be equivalent to B. In such a setting, the political decision rule would not really matter. The opportunity locus of A would, in this case, be coincident with that of B. In order to make the analysis more general, we allow pre-tax incomes of A and B to differ, while continuing to assume identical utility functions. In the construction of Figure 1, the pre-tax income of A, shown as $Y_a$, is two times that of B, shown as $Y_b$.

The opportunity locus facing A in Figure 1 is the straight line connecting the same intercept on the ordinate as that for B and the point $Y_a$ on the abscissa. As with the opportunity locus for B, this line is invariant for A once the values of C, $Y_a$, and $Y_b$ are set, given the proportionality constraint. A's opportunity set is not affected by the behavior of B in making the community's fiscal decision. If A's income is higher than B's, as drawn in Figure 1, the opportunity locus for A must lie outside that of B throughout the range. Further, as the construction demonstrates, the post-tax private-goods consumption of A in relation to the post-tax private-goods consumption of B must be equal to the ratio of pre-tax private incomes of the two persons. This is insured by the fact that both persons must share the same quantity of the public good; hence, regardless of the utility-maximizing choice made by B, both persons must be located along the same horizontal line in Figure 1, with the ratio of private goods remaining in the pre-tax two-for-one ratio. Consumption cannot be fully equalized as between the two persons so long as any private-goods consumption is allowed to take place.

To this point the analysis is fully symmetrical with respect to the identity of the ruler or decision-maker. We have initially assumed that B is the ruler; we may shift the decision-making power to A with similar conclusions. As the construction in Figure 1 indicates, no definitive conclusions may be reached concerning whether or not the utility-maximizing proportional tax rate will increase, stay the same, or decrease, as the decision-making power is shifted from B to A. Any one of these directions of change might be possible with the standard convexity properties of utility functions. The direction of change will depend on the combined income and substitution effects which work in opposition to each other under the assumption that G is a normal good, along with Y. If we stay within the assumption that the utility functions for *A* and *B* are identical, the location of the utility-maximizing position of *A*, along *A*'s opportunity locus, will depend on the ratio of the income and "price" elasticities of demand for *G*. Under proportionality, and because he has a lower initial income, *B* must face a lower tax-price per unit of the public good than *A* at all levels. *B*'s tax-price is defined by the slope of his opportunity locus. A shift of decision-making power to *A* from *B* would, due to the substitution effect alone, tend to decrease the demand for *G*. But such a shift also involves moving to a higher income level, and, if *G* is normal, this will tend to increase the demand for *G*. If the two effects are just offsetting, there will be no change in the amount of *G*, and in the proportional tax rate, *r*, as a result of the switch between persons in fiscal authority. In this case, the proportional tax rate will also guarantee the satisfaction of the normal efficiency conditions for public-goods provision; the utility-maximizing position of either person also insures satisfaction of the Lindahl conditions for public-good equilibrium.[2]

## Proportional Taxation, Maximum Rate Limits, No Incentive Effects

It is relatively easy to extend the analysis to show the effects of maximum rate constraints, while remaining within the proportionality restriction, and continuing to assume that there are no disincentives from taxes on behavior of the two persons in generating private-goods income, *Y*. The imposition of a maximum rate constraint effectively truncates the opportunity locus of both the rule and the ruled person, at the level of the constraint, drawn in Figure 1 as 50 percent. Such a constraint may or may not affect the utility-maximizing position of the ruler. If *B* is the decision-maker, and, prior to the new constraint, equilibrium is located along the segment of the locus below *S*, there will be no change. If, however, the initial position lies above *S*, the constraint will become binding, and the effective new rate of tax will be the maximum allowed, with *B* remaining in a corner solution at *S*. Note that in the proportionality setting there is no difference in effect between a limit

<hr/>

2. For an early discussion that concentrates strictly on the possible efficiency properties of proportional taxation, see James M. Buchanan, "Fiscal Institutions and Efficiency in Collective Outlay," *American Economic Review* 54 (May 1964), 227–35.

imposed on rates of tax and a limit imposed on total tax revenues, or total spending, in relation to income.

## Progressive Taxation, No Rate Limits, No Incentive Effects

We may now compare the results under the general proportionality constraint with those that might be predicted to emerge in the absence of such a constraint, while retaining the same model for political decision-making and the same spending-side restrictions. We cannot, however, simply assume the absence of all tax constraints on government. We want to impose the requirement that arbitrary discrimination, related, for example, to political power rather than income, is prohibited and, further, that tax payments be at least proportional to income.

In this model, we should anticipate that the results depend significantly on who is the government. There will be major differences in the utility-maximizing behavior of the "poor" if they are in the politically dominating coalition and the behavior of the "rich" if they are in such a position. This set of differences is not present under the proportionality constraint. An important element of potential political conflict is necessarily introduced by the institution of income tax progression.

As in our earlier treatment, we shall initially assume that $B$, who earns a pre-tax income only one-half that earned by $A$, is the ruler. Individual $B$ is free to select the tax structure he prefers, with the residually determined quantity of $G$. We assume, as before, that there is no utility interdependence.

So long as $B$ is not satiated with the public good at such a limit, we may predict that *all* income above the level of his own earning, above $Y_b$, will be taxed at the maximum 100 percent rate. Individual $B$ secures without cost that quantity of the public good, $G$, that is made possible by the revenues collected from $A$ over the $Y_a - Y_b$ income range. We depict these results in Figure 2, which is similar in construction to Figure 1. $B$'s position shifts from $Y_b$ to $T$ as a result of the imposition of the maximum tax on the income of $A$ above $Y_b$. Beyond this limit, the opportunity locus for both $B$ and for $A$ is defined by the line segment connecting $T$ and $(Y_a + Y_b)/C$. Note that, in this unlimited progression model, the final distribution of consumption of *both* the private good and the public good is fully equalized if the equilibrium so-

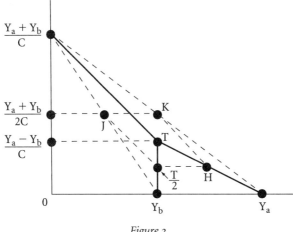

*Figure 2*

lution lies on or above $T$.[3] Hayek's implicit proposition to the effect that tax progression inherently implies post-tax income equalization is validated in this model, even when we restrict governmental fiscal activity to the financing of genuinely public goods and prohibit direct income transfers.

The opportunity locus for $B$, the person whom we have initially made the ruler, lies everywhere outside that which is available to $B$ under the proportionality constraint, which is shown by the dotted line from $Y_b$ in Figure 2. By contrast, the opportunity locus for $A$ lies everywhere inside that which is available to him under proportionality.

The model is clearly not symmetrical with shift in governorship. If $A$ is the decision-maker instead of $B$, he is better off by adopting a rate structure that defines the lowest allowable limit to progression, which is, of course, proportionality. In this case $A$'s opportunity locus remains unchanged from that available to him under the proportionality constraint.

Interesting comparisons emerge only when $B$ is considered to be decisive.

3. This result is related to that which is shown to emerge under an independent adjustment model by Jeremias and Zardkoohi. They demonstrate that consumption of all goods will be equalized among all persons in a public-goods interaction under certain configurations of preferences, even if there is no collective action. See Ronald Jeremias and Asghar Zardkoohi, "Distributional Implications of Independent Adjustments in an Economy with Public Goods," *Economic Inquiry* 14 (June 1976), 305–8.

Will more or less $G$ be provided under progression than under proportionality? As Figure 2 suggests, no definitive answer is possible merely from the standard convexity properties of preference orderings. If the solution lies above $T$, the ruler, $B$, is paying a higher marginal tax-price (the slope of his opportunity locus) than that which he confronts under proportionality. But he will also enjoy a higher level of private-goods income. Once again we have an income effect and a substitution effect working in opposing directions if we assume that both goods are normal.[4]

## Progressive Taxation, Maximum Rate Limits, No Incentive Effects

We may now examine the effects of imposing maximum rate limits in a progressive tax setting. In the simple two-person model analyzed, we have shown that in the absence of rate limits, if $B$ is the decision-maker the income of $A$ above that of $B$ will be subjected to a 100 percent marginal rate. The most plausible form of tax limit in such a setting may be one that restricts the allowable marginal rate. Suppose that the maximum marginal rate of tax is set at 50 percent. This limit guarantees that tax revenues collected from $A$, over the bracket range, $Y_a - Y_b$, will finance public-goods provision only up to one-half the amount financed under the fully confiscatory rate. Person B, whom we assume to be the collective decision-maker, finds his own position shifted to $T/2$ in Figure 2. But this position has not brought him into full equality with $A$, as was the case with unrestricted progression. After paying the maximum marginal rate on the income over the range, $Y_a - Y_b$, and financing $T/2$ in public goods, $A$ finds himself at $H$.

As in the earlier case, $B$ will confront an opportunity locus with a kink; now located at $T/2$ rather than $T$. From this point the locus will parallel that of $A$, drawn from $H$. At the maximum rate limit, $B$ would find himself at $J$ while $A$ would be at position $K$. Regardless of $B$'s utility-maximizing choice among his opportunity locus, $B$'s post-tax private-goods income will fall short of $A$'s by precisely the maximum marginal rate times the difference in

---

4. Geoffrey Brennan has emphasized the shift in marginal tax-price under progression as opposed to proportionality in a median voter model. See Geoffrey Brennan, "A Note on Progression and Public Sector Size," *Public Choice* 32 (Winter 1977), 123–29.

pre-tax incomes. As compared with the full equalization of incomes under no-limit progression, a differential will remain in the restricted-rate model so long as any private-goods consumption is allowed. Recall that, under proportionality, except at the limit where all resources are devoted to the public good, the post-fisc ratio of private-goods income or consumption remains identical to the pre-fisc ratio. With limited rate progression, by comparison, the post-fisc ratio shifts in favor of the low-income receiver, but the absolute differential remains as determined by the maximum marginal rate.

The construction suggests that the imposition of a maximum limit on marginal rates of tax may be a more effective means of restricting potential fiscal exploitation than comparable attempts to limit total tax revenues or total spending more directly. In the context of Figure 2, suppose that it is desired to restrict total taxation to one-half of total income, that is, to $(Y_a + Y_b)/2$. Further, suppose that this limitation might be imposed by explicit tax-rate constraints or by overall constraints on revenues. If, for example, the maximum allowable marginal rate of tax is set at 50 percent, clearly satisfying the overall objective, the opportunity locus faced by $B$ will be that discussed above, with the kink at $T/2$. On the other hand, under the more general total revenue constraints, the opportunity locus for $B$, the ruler, would be that which kinks at $T$. As the construction in Figure 2 indicates, the opportunity locus under the general revenue constraints lies wholly outside that defined by the tax-rate constraints. In this sense, the tax-rate constraint becomes more restrictive.

## Proportional Taxation, No Rate Constraint, and Incentive Effects

To this point, we have assumed that taxpayers' behavior in generating the tax base, income, is invariant under all possible rates of tax. That is to say, individuals continue to earn the same income, pre-tax, regardless of the rate of tax that is imposed. The analytical convenience of this assumption is clear; it enables us to construct models in two dimensions, quantities of public and private goods. As we relax this assumption to allow for incentive effects, we necessarily introduce a third "good," nontaxable "leisure" or other desired "outputs" of taxpayers' time than the generation of taxable base, $Y$.

Let us first examine proportional income taxation with only this one change made in the simple models developed earlier. The person in the two-person community who is subject to potential fiscal exploitation, who is the ruled rather than the ruler, will modify his behavior in producing $Y$ in some generally inverse relationship with the rate of tax that is exogenously imposed on him. As confronted by the ruler, this behavioral change involves a constriction of his opportunity locus. The ruler is, therefore, unambiguously worse off under the behavioral adjustment model than he is in the model in which the potentially exploited taxpayer cannot adjust in response to the tax. Contrariwise, the latter is in an unambiguously improved position. To the extent that he can "opt out" by shifting some part of his psychic earnings into nontaxable options, he is better off than he should be if he were somehow to be precluded from making such shifts.

The ruler, or decision-maker, solves his utility-maximizing problem much as in the simpler model, but he does so in this case by considering both his own opportunities to realize consumption benefits from the nontaxable activity, $L$, and the predicted behavioral adjustment of the potential exploitee under varying rates of tax.

These adjustments may be predicted by examining the optimization problem of the ruled, $(A)$, a problem that does not exist in the simpler model. The utility function for the person ruled contains arguments for after-tax, private-goods income, $(1 - r)Y_b$, government services provided, $G$, and nontaxable income, $L_a$. His task is to maximize:

$$U_a = u_a[(1 - r)Y_a, \left(\frac{r}{c}\right)(Y_a + Y_b), (L_a^* - \ell Y_a)]. \qquad (4)$$

The person ruled, $A$, has, in effect, only a single decision variable, $Y_a$, in this specification, since $r$ and $Y_b$ are determined by the ruler, and because a choice of $Y_a$ determines the amount of nontaxable income, "leisure," available, $L_a^* - \ell_a Y_a$, where $L_a^*$ is the maximum amount of the nontaxable good, $L$, and where $\ell_a$ is the rate of transformation between $Y_a$ and $L_a$. Maximizing with respect to $Y_a$, the first order condition is met in (5):

$$\frac{\partial u_a}{\partial(Y_a - rY_a)}(1 - r) + \frac{\partial u_a}{\partial G}\left(\frac{r}{c}\right) + \frac{\partial u_a}{\partial L_a}(-\ell_a) = 0. \qquad (5)$$

The usual strict convexity assumption thus implies that the amount of the tax base generated, $Y_a$, will be functionally related to the tax rate, $r$.

Given the adjustment function of the ruled, $Y_a = y_a(r, Y_b)$, the optimization problem faced by the ruler, $B$, is completely specified. $B$'s utility is, like that of $A$, dependent on his consumption of the tax-base good, $Y_b(1 - r)$, his consumption of government services, $G = r/c(Y_a + Y_b)$, and his consumption of the nontaxed good or activity, $L_b = L_b^* - \ell_b Y_b$. His utility function can be represented in (6).

$$U_b = u_b \left[ (1 - r)Y_b, \left(\frac{r}{c}\right)(Y_a + y_a), (r, Y_b), (L_b^* - \ell_b Y_b) \right]. \qquad (6)$$

In this formulation, the ruler has two decision variables: (1) the rate of the proportional tax, $r$, and (2) the amount of the taxable good, $Y_b$, that he will generate. The amount of government services, $G$, and the level of nontaxable activity, $L_b$, are determined by these two variables under his control. Maximizing with respect to $r$ and $Y_b$, the first order conditions are met in the following:

$$Y_b \frac{\partial u_b}{\partial (Y_b - rY_b)} = \frac{1}{c} \left[ Y_b + Y_a + r \frac{\partial y_a}{\partial r} \right] \frac{\partial u_b}{\partial G} \qquad (7)$$

$$\frac{\partial u_b}{\ell_b \partial L_b} = (1 - r) \frac{\partial u_b}{\partial (Y_b - rY_b)} + \frac{r}{c} \left( 1 + \frac{\partial y_a}{\partial y_b} \right) \frac{\partial u_b}{\partial G}. \qquad (8)$$

The solution is depicted in the three-dimensional Figure 3, for the case where, $y_a(1) = 0$, $\partial y_a / \partial Y_b \leq 0$, and $\partial y_a / \partial r < 0$. Note that regardless of the form of the adjustment function for $A$ the ruler's opportunity locus will lie below that available when the potential exploitee cannot or does not adjust (depicted in Figure 3 as the triangular surface above the curvilinear one) at every point save those where the tax rate is zero. To the extent that the person ruled, $A$, adjusts to changing tax rates, the ruler, $B$, is worse off, and the potential exploitee is better off.

If the ruler is the less wealthy of the two persons, the utility-equalizing effects of the proportional tax–public-goods package are less than those in the absence of adjustment. By shifting his effort away from those activities that generate taxable base, the potential exploitee reduces the utility-equalizing potential for public-goods provision. On the other hand, if the ruler should be the wealthier of the two, the utility-equalizing effects of public-goods provision may, in fact, be larger with adjustment than in the absence of adjustment. In this case the person ruled may, to some extent, "free ride" on the services provided by government largely at the expense of the ruler.

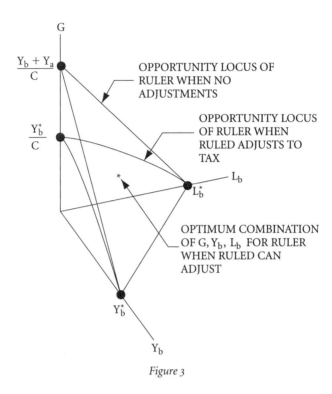

*Figure 3*

## Proportional Taxation, Maximum Rate Constraints, and Incentive Effect

The introduction of a maximum rate limit operates in this setting much as in the one without the behavioral adjustments. The details of analysis can be omitted. We should note, however, that the desirability of imposing any maximum rate constraint is lessened in the presence of the potential shift of taxpayers into nontaxable pursuits and away from the generation of taxable base. In this sense, preservation of the availability of nontaxable opportunities that yield utility to the taxpayer can serve as a good substitute for the imposition of rate constraints.[5]

5. In their first paper on tax constitutions, Brennan and Buchanan concentrated their analysis on the potential limits on total revenue that might be insured by the presence of nontaxable options or opportunities. See Geoffrey Brennan and James Buchanan, "Towards a Tax Constitution for Leviathan," *Journal of Public Economics* 8 (December 1977), 255–73.

## Progressive Taxation, No Rate Constraints, and Incentive Effects

We now shift the setting in which the ruler is allowed to impose progressive rates of tax on incomes, with no constraints as to rates, but now in the presence of behavioral adjustments on the part of those who are outside the ruling coalition. As noted earlier, the solution will be quite different with different rulers or decision-makers. The delegation of power to the high-income earners will tend to produce the proportional tax model already discussed. We can, therefore, limit analysis to the situation where the low-income earner is the ruler or governor.

In this political framework with the no-incentive model, we demonstrated that the ruler would maximize utility by levying a 100 percent rate of tax on all income higher than that which he himself earns. This dramatic result no longer holds when taxpayers have the ability to shift to nontaxable opportunities, and, indeed, in the case discussed above, an optimizing governor will never impose this confiscatory rate on any level of taxable income generated, no matter how high this might be. The utility-maximizing rate schedule over the income range above that received by the ruler, over the range $Y_a - Y_b$, will be that schedule which generates the highest revenue from $A$, given his predicted adjustment to nontaxable opportunities at alternative rates. As Brennan and Buchanan have shown in related analysis, with linearity assumptions, the rate schedule satisfying this maximum yield criterion will be proportional.[6] This implies that the ruler will levy a uniform rate of tax on all incomes above his own. He will not impose progressive rates for incomes over the higher range. Once the revenue-maximizing rate (or rate schedule) has been levied on incomes in those ranges beyond that received by the decision-maker, the latter finds himself at a kink in his opportunity locus; a specific quantity of public good, $G$, is available without cost. Whether the decision-maker will remain in this position or whether he will choose to expand the provision of $G$ beyond this point depends, of course, on both the shape of this utility function and the cost of the public good. Beyond this limit, he must pay a tax-price per unit of the public good and that is as high as that paid by the potentially exploited taxpayer. The decision-maker, in our

---

6. Brennan and Buchanan, op. cit.

political framework, is assumed not to be able to levy taxes discriminatorily; he cannot impose taxes on the income of $A$ below $Y_b$, while leaving $B$'s income over this range exempt from levy of tax.

## Progressive Taxation, Maximum Rate Limits, and Incentive Effects

The presence of nontaxable opportunities tends to limit the rates of tax that any utility-maximizing ruler will impose on taxpayers. In the model considered above, the revenue-maximizing rate of tax (or rate structure) on higher incomes may well be lower than any "reasonable" maximum that might be imposed constitutionally. The consumption-equalizing potential of the progressive rate–public-goods fisc, which is clearly present in the no-incentive setting where the ruler is the less wealthy of the two, is reduced where potential taxpayers can make behavioral adjustments by shifting into nontaxable options, even in the absence of explicit rate limits. To the extent that he can "opt out" in response to the tax, a taxpayer can guarantee to himself the consumption that he privately values, over and above any attempts at consumption equalization via the fiscal process. In terms of utility equalization, location of decision-authority in the wealthy person does not modify this basic result. As noted, the ruler will, in this case, opt for a proportional rate structure. But adjustment must make the ruled "poor" better off and the rich ruler worse off. If the elasticity of substitution between taxable-base generation and resort to nontaxable options is relatively low, maximum rate limits may be desired to restrict potential fiscal exploitation. As in the no-incentive model, effective maximum rates will guarantee the maintenance of differentials in the final consumption of private goods as between the potentially exploited high-income recipient and the low-income earner when the latter is the decision-taker. The additional opportunities for resorting to nontaxable options will, in this case, insure somewhat wider differentials of tax-base consumption than in the no-adjustment case.

## Conclusions

In a set of very simple models we have attempted to isolate and to analyze possible differences in the operation of proportional and progressive income tax systems, given specific assumptions about the political decision structure and public spending constraints. Other models could, of course, be developed under widely differing assumptions. In particular, other conclusions would emerge if we relaxed the public spending constraint and allowed for governments to carry out direct income transfers. In recognition of this restriction, our results should be interpreted as carrying implications only within limits. Nonetheless, the results are suggestive in themselves.

Any system of taxation that is more "progressive" than equal-per-head taxes, when combined with spending on genuinely public goods, must equalize final consumption of "goods" in some absolute sense. By definition, persons secure equal quantities of public goods. And if these are financed in any way other than with equal-per-head taxes, some consumption equalization must result.

With proportional taxation, and when taxpayers do not adjust pre-tax income in response to tax, the ratio of private-goods consumption between taxpayers at differing income levels remains the same before and after the tax, regardless of rate. Absolute differentials in private-goods consumption (or possibilities for consumption) are, of course, reduced in direct relationship to the rate of the proportional tax.

With progressive taxation, again when taxpayers make no behavioral adjustments, the final consumption of private goods tends to be equalized, both in a relative and in an absolute sense, and in direct relationship to both the quantity of public good financed and the progressivity of the structure. In the unrestricted utility-maximizing model, rates of tax on all incomes above those earned by the ruler will be fully confiscatory in this model.

If taxpayers make no behavioral adjustments to tax, the presence of constitutional limits on allowable maximum rates, under either proportion or progression, can check the tendency toward consumption equalization. However, such constitutional rate limits may be much less important if taxpayers can be allowed to retain opportunities for shifting into nontaxable utility-generating activities in response to taxes. The existence of such opportunities may well be a more important check to the fiscal powers of government than any formal limits. Hayek's principal concern about progressive taxation need not arise when nontaxable options are significant. The presence of such options does, of course, reduce the *generality* of the tax, whether proportional or progressive. But the admittedly desired features of generality, as an abstract goal, must be matched against the efficacy of nongenerality in limiting the degree of potential fiscal exploitation.

# The Ethical Limits of Taxation

*Abstract:* Normative tax theory has concentrated on the distribution of tax shares to the neglect of the absolute level of taxation.
The first Rawlsian principle of maximal equal liberty is introduced
to derive limits on the absolute level of taxation. The critical requirement is that the freedom of persons, singly or in coalitions, to
form new political associations be counted as a relevant liberty in
the Rawlsian array. Simple examples illustrate the argument, and
critical parameters are identified and discussed briefly.

## I. Introduction[1]

How should tax shares be allocated among persons? Normative tax theory
has been almost exclusively devoted to attempts to answer this question. The
early arguments about the shape of the utility function for income were

From *Scandinavian Journal of Economics* 86 (April 1984): 102–14. Copyright 1984 by The
Editors of *Scandinavian Journal of Economics.* Reprinted by permission of the publisher.

I am indebted to Geoffrey Brennan, David Levy, and Loren Lomasky for helpful comments on earlier drafts of this paper.

1. In several earlier papers, written separately and jointly, I have analyzed limits on taxation from a constitutional perspective. See James M. Buchanan, "Constitutional Constraints on Governmental Taxing Power," *ORDO,* Bd. 30 (Stuttgart: Fischer, 1979), 334–
59; "Procedural and Constitutional Constraints on Fiscal Authority," in *The Constitution
and the Budget,* ed. W. S. Moore and R. G. Penner (Washington: American Enterprise Institute, 1980), 80–84; "The Limits of Taxation," in *The Constitutional Challenge,* ed. M.
James (St. Leonard's, N.S.W.: Centre for Independent Studies, 1982), 113–30; and James
M. Buchanan and Geoffrey Brennan, "The Logic of Tax Limits," *National Tax Journal,* 32
(June 1979), 11–22. The justification of tax limits in this perspective was largely, if not exclusively, based on the predicted working properties of postconstitutional political processes.

aimed at justifying this or that degree of progression in the tax rate structure. More generally, vertical equity arguments have been addressed to the design of appropriately unequal treatment for unequals while horizontal equity arguments have involved the definition of equal treatment for equals. These discussions have been carried on in almost total neglect of the expenditure side of the fiscal process. Presumably, the same normative principles for the allocation of tax shares have been held to be applicable whether the total tax share in aggregate income is 10 per cent or 90 per cent, or anything between such limits. That is to say, traditional normative tax theory has been silent on the absolute level of taxation; it has contained no implied limits.

My purpose in this paper is to explore this unexamined question. Quite apart from normative criteria for the allocation of tax shares, are there normative criteria that may be introduced to set *limits* on the absolute level of taxation? I shall suggest that this question may be answered affirmatively, and I shall indicate that tax limits may be derived from the application of widely shared ethical norms. "Justice" in taxation involves how much of the national income is to be extracted for collective purposes as well as how that share which is extracted is to be allocated among different persons.

It will first be necessary, in Section II, to set the problem by summarizing alternative paradigms for analyzing the taxation-expenditure process. Section III introduces the normative treatment with a generalized discussion of the ethical legitimacy of taxation, a necessary way-station for any argument that seeks to establish some ultimate limits. Section IV advances the ethical precept upon which the derivation of tax limits is based, and Section V uses numerical examples to suggest the specific limits that are implied. The sensitivity of the results to critical parameter values is discussed in Section VI. Section VII places the whole argument in its general context.

## II. Alternative Paradigms for Taxation

Taxation may be, and has been, perceived and interpreted by citizens, and by tax economists, in several paradigms. (1) First of all, taxation can be viewed as the cost side of an inclusive fiscal exchange process, with taxes being treated as "prices" that persons pay for the benefits provided by collectively financed goods and services made available to them by the government. (2) Secondly, taxation can be thought of, and modelled, as the embodiment of fixed charges that the community is obligated to meet, charges that are made necessary by the financing requirements for politically determined outlays that are not directly related to individually imputable benefit flows. (3) Thirdly, taxation may be considered as a set of coercively imposed charges imposed on those who are politically weak by those who are politically strong (a ruling class, an establishment elite, a majority coalition, a party hierarchy) for the purpose of financing private goods and services enjoyed by the latter. (4) Finally, taxation may be conceived as a self-contained collective enterprise, characterized by positive and negative transfers that have as their ultimate purpose the achievement of collectively chosen patterns of post-tax, post-transfer distributions.

It is clear from the definitional listing alone that the relevance of ethical limits depends on the perspective from which the taxing-spending process is examined. In the first of the paradigms, the limits to taxation are those determined by the preferences of citizens themselves for collectively provided goods. In this model, the fiscal process is one of voluntary exchange, as it has been developed basically by Knut Wicksell and Erik Lindahl.[2]

In the second model, taxation is isolated from the political process, and the absolute level of revenues required to meet pre-determined fiscal obligations is considered to be outside of and beyond any application of ethical norms.

In the third perspective, there are no useful ethical limits, except those that might be advanced as guidelines for the ruling elites. Positive limits on the absolute level of taxation in this paradigm may be derived from the application of straightforward wealth-maximization models of sovereign behavior.[3]

Only in the last of the fiscal paradigms defined above does the question of ethical limits apply directly. To what absolute limits of taxation should the collectivity, as a unit, be restricted, when taxes, in part or in total, are levied expressly for the accomplishment of transfer or redistributive purposes?

2. Knut Wicksell. *Finanztheoretische Untersuchungen* (Jena: Gustav Fischer, 1896); Erik Lindahl, *Die Gerechtigkeit der Besteuerung* (Lund, 1919). See also my paper, "Taxation in Fiscal Exchange," *Journal of Public Economics*, 6 (1976), 17–29.

3. For such models, see Geoffrey Brennan and James Buchanan, *The Power to Tax* (Cambridge: Cambridge University Press, 1980).

How much fiscal redistribution should take place? How much fiscal redistribution is dictated by adherence to principles of justice?

## III. The Legitimacy of the Transfer State

To what extent does the collectivity, as a unit, hold an ethically justifiable claim against the income flow generated by individual effort in an economy that is characterized by specialization and trade? Within the appropriately functioning laws and institutions that protect property and contract, a distribution of valued end-products emerges from the interactions of demanders and suppliers in input and output markets. Independent of ethical considerations, individual owners of inputs tend to secure shares in aggregate value of output commensurate with the contributions of those inputs to such value. What claim, then, can the collectivity advance to a share of value, and, if any claim at all is legitimate, how can its extent be determined?

Some state claim against valued output of the economy must be acknowledged once the productivity of the legal-governmental framework is recognized. Without an institutional regime that protects property and enforces contracts, there might be little or no total output to be claimed. The economy of Hobbesian anarchy is not efficient by any standards, and those who dream of competitive protective associations in anarchy do precisely that, they dream. In a setting where there is no enforced and protected difference between "mine and thine," individuals will exert relatively little effort, and a large share of that which is exerted will be devoted to predation and defense.[4] The collective provision of order is productive. Hence, a claim on value of output by the institutions that provide such order, the collectivity or state, is established, even on the most extreme productivity ethic.[5]

---

4. For analysis, see *Explorations in the Theory of Anarchy*, ed. Gordon Tullock (Blacksburg: Public Choice Center, 1972); also my *The Limits of Liberty* (Chicago: University of Chicago Press, 1975).

5. J. R. Kearl has supported the collective claim to a share of valued output along essentially the lines sketched here. Kearl, however, explicitly states that the question as to the extent of this claim "has no quantifiable answer" (p. 80). See J. R. Kearl, "Do Entitlements Imply That Taxation Is Theft?" *Philosophy and Public Affairs*, 7 (Fall 1977), 74–81.

What measures the extent of such a claim? If the orthodox imputation process is carried out, the collectivity might claim a predominant share of total value. A conceptual experiment in which the legal-governmental order is removed would surely indicate that the "marginal product" of the state is extremely high. The payment of all input factors, including the state, in accordance with the values of internal marginal products, would more than exhaust the total product of the economy. The inclusive production functions exhibit increasing returns, due to the scale economies in the provision of protective-enforcement services. We seem to be plunged into the analogue to the classical joint cost problem, with a comparable indeterminacy in solution.[6]

One possible response is offered by the purely procedural contractarian. The patterns of distribution that emerge from whatever institutions that are agreed on in the conceptualized contractarian setting are defined to be "just" or "fair" because of the procedures through which they are produced. No further normative criteria are required or needed. In this setting, individuals are placed behind some veil of ignorance and/or uncertainty where they cannot identify their own positions under the operation of the institutions to be selected. The institutions so selected may include a transfer sector, and, with it, taxation that is outside any meaningfully defined exchange process. The absolute level of taxation is not, however, determinate. The limits on taxation are those that emerge from the idealized procedure, which itself becomes the object of the normative or ethical evaluative exercise.

The procedural criteria for justice or fairness may be retained as the ultimate test for any proposed set of institutional arrangements. The normative analyst may, however, seek to go beyond purely procedural restrictions and examine institutional alternatives that may be put to the procedural test. What ethical-moral precepts guide the choice among alternatives in the idealized contractual setting?

---

6. For more extended discussion, see my "Marginal Productivity, Maximal Equal Liberty, and the Limits of Taxation," mimeographed, Center for Study of Public Choice, June 1983.

# IV. The First Rawlsian Principle: Maximal Equal Liberty

This was precisely the task that John Rawls set in his highly acclaimed book, *A Theory of Justice* (1971).[7] He derived two basic principles of justice and suggested that these would guide agreement among parties in the idealized contractual setting. The two principles were these, first, *maximal equal liberty*, and, secondly, the *difference* principle for the distribution of primary goods. The Rawlsian argument generated lively discussion among economists as well as philosophers and other social scientists. Almost all of the economists' treatment was concentrated, however, on the second of the two suggested principles, the maximin or difference principle of distribution. Attempts were made to derive the taxing implications of satisfying this second principle. And, for the most part, Rawls was interpreted as having offered persuasive ethical argument in support of institutions that embody considerable redistribution of incomes and wealth among persons.

What these interpreters of Rawls' work overlooked, however, was the assignment of *lexical* priority to the first principle of maximal equal liberty. Rawls was careful to state that this first principle was to be met before the application of the second principle is attempted. Institutions that fail the test for satisfying the first principle are necessarily ruled out of consideration, regardless of their possible efficacy in seeming to further the objectives defined in the second principle.

I shall argue that limits on the absolute level of taxation are implied by the first of the two Rawlsian principles of justice, that of maximal equal liberty, and, hence, that the difference principle can only become relevant within these limits. Further, my argument suggests that the ethical support for the first Rawlsian principle, based exclusively on liberty, may be accepted even by those critics who may not go along with the second principle.

## EQUAL LIBERTY

There are two elements in the first principle of liberty. Institutions that are to be put to the procedural test must meet dual requirements. Liberties

---

7. Cambridge: Harvard University Press.

among persons must be *equal*, and these equal liberties must be *maximal*. Each one of these two conceptually separate requirements becomes important in any analysis-discussion of tax structure and tax limits. I shall not, in this paper, concentrate my attention on the equal liberty requirement. This neglect is prompted exclusively by considerations of space and not by any absence of challenging issues waiting to be analyzed. These issues are those raised in orthodox normative tax theory, noted at the outset, and the Rawlsian approach may yield helpful insights into familiar territory. In its broad sweep, however, the equal liberty proviso lends support for the standard precepts of generality in taxation, and rules out overtly discriminatory tax treatment. But in all this discussion, the concern is with justice or fairness in the allocation of tax shares among persons and not with the absolute level of taxation, within the confines of the equal liberty criterion. For example, a set of fiscal institutions might meet the equal liberty requirement and yet extract 90 per cent of valued output from the economy for collective purposes.

In the discussion that follows I shall assume that all institutions to be considered meet the equal liberty criterion, and that agreement has been reached on precisely how this requirement is to be defined. I shall be more precise and assume, without argument in defense, that taxes must be proportional to meet the equal liberty proviso, and that all transfer payments take the form of equal-per-head demogrants.[8]

MAXIMAL LIBERTY[9]

I shall demonstrate that the satisfaction of the maximal liberty criterion does imply a limit on the absolute level of taxation. In order to do this, I must first advance at least a working definition of liberty itself, and without getting bogged down into long-winded philosophical debate. I shall define liberty

8. In a paper in preparation, I hope to show that the equal liberty precept, alone, dictates *proportional* taxation along with *equal-per-head demogrants* as the basic institutions of the redistributive public sector.

9. I am particularly indebted to Loren Lomasky for pointing out to me the Rawlsian emphasis on maximal liberty. I had earlier, like many others, interpreted the first Rawlsian principle largely in terms of the equal liberty element. For a paper in which both these elements of the Rawlsian principle are used, see James M. Buchanan and Loren Lomasky, "The Matrix of Contractarian Justice" (draft paper prepared for Liberty Fund Conference, "Liberty and Equality," Key Biscayne, Florida, November 1983).

only in its negative sense; an individual is at liberty or free to carry on an activity if he or she is not coerced from so doing by someone else, be this an individual or group. Whether or not the individual has the ability or power to undertake the activity that he is at liberty to undertake is a separate matter, and it can only confuse discussion to equate liberty with ability or power or to extend its meaning to include these qualities.

My working definition can be illustrated in an example used by Amartya Sen. A person is at liberty to sleep on his back or his belly if no other person or group interferes with the exercise of such choice. A physical disability that may prevent one of the two options being chosen is not a constraint on the person's liberty, as such.

We may think in terms of a listing of all the activities that persons may be at liberty to undertake, subject only to the requirement that all persons in the relevant community be allowed the same or equal liberties. The familiar set of civil liberties comes to mind: liberty of speech, press, religion, voting, association. To these may be added the "economic liberties": consumption patterns, location, occupation, trade, property holdings.

Consider, now, two possible regimes, I and II. In Regime I, the collectivity, as an organized political unit, levies a tax of 90 per cent on valued output. From the revenues so collected, the collectivity supplies the legal-protective-enforcement environment, which requires an outlay of 10 per cent of total product. The remaining revenues are distributed to all members of the political community in a set of equal-per-head demogrants. (I assume away incentive effects feedbacks on output. Persons work equally hard at all levels of taxation and demogrants.)

In Regime II, by contrast with Regime I, the collectivity collects only 10 per cent of valued output, again through a proportional tax. Such tax generates revenues in the minimal amount required to finance the supply of the legal-political order. There are no demogrants.

In both regimes, individuals possess equal liberties to speak, write, vote, exercise religion, associate, and to choose their own consumption pattern, location, occupation, trading partners, and private assets. Is it then possible to state that individuals possess more liberty in II than in I? Clearly, persons have different abilities to satisfy their own desires in the two regimes, but it is not clear that individual liberties are different, under the definition posed earlier.

I suggest, however, that an inclusive list or array of activities might also include the liberty of individuals to *form new polities* from within the existing one, the liberty to secede. Singly, or in coalitions of any size, persons would be allowed to withdraw simultaneously from both the tax and benefit sides of the fiscal account, which would require that they provide *all* public services, including legal order, on their own. Such an internal exit option is a meaningful addition to the set of liberties normally considered, and a society in which this equal liberty of secession exists clearly is superior, on grounds of the first Rawlsian principle, to a society where this liberty does not exist.

The relationship of this particular liberty to the limits of taxation should be clear. The collectivity cannot ethically justify a claim on the economy's valued product that is over and beyond that level of taxation that would encourage any subset of the community membership to form their own separate polities. The idealized internal exit option places ethical limits on the absolute level of taxation, and it is only within these limits that the second Rawlsian principle, or indeed any other distributional principle, can be legitimately applied.

## V. Numerical Examples

The limits of taxation imposed by the equal liberty of secession may be illustrated numerically. Assume that there are 75 persons in the political community, made up of two separate groups, each one of which contains internally homogeneous members. There are 25 A workers, and 50 B workers, and an A worker is twice as productive as a B worker. Aside from these two qualities of labor, the only other productive input is the legal-governmental order. Workers are equally productive in any combination.

Since we have assumed away any incentive effects, suppose that the economy generates a total product of 100 units under any fiscal regime. These units are in the dimension of a single all-purpose consumable good. There is no saving or capital.

Withdrawal of a single A worker reduces total product by 2 units; withdrawal of a B worker reduces total product by 1 unit. For simplicity, suppose that abandonment of the legal-protective framework reduces total product to zero.

Consider, now, the situation in Regime I, described above, where the collectivity levies a proportional tax of 90 per cent on all valued output. From the 90 units in revenues that it collects, the state then uses 10 units to provide the legal-protective umbrella for the economy. The remaining 80 units are returned to all members of the community in equal-per-head demogrants, with each of the 75 members getting 1.067 units.

Positions of individuals in the two groups will be as follows:

| Individual | Pre-tax Wage | Tax | Demogrant | Net |
|---|---|---|---|---|
| $A_1$ | 2 | 1.8 | 1.067 | 1.267 |
| $B_1$ | 1 | 0.9 | 1.067 | 1.167 |

The 90 per cent level of taxation is *not* ethically justifiable on the principle of maximal liberty. To show this, consider the prospects for members of the A group. Assume that the legal-protection "good" is completely lumpy; it takes 10 units to provide this good for any level of community membership. Assume that there are no scale advantages to the size of the market as such.

By seceding and forming their own political unit, the A workers can generate a total product of 50 units, of which 10 units, or 20 per cent, will be required to provide the legal-protective umbrella. The 40 units that remain can be retained by the persons in the group, for a net value of 1.6 units per person, which is higher than that secured under the operation of Regime I. Any level of taxation that leaves a member of the A group with a net consumption capacity below 1.6 is not sustainable under the liberty of secession option.

Note, however, that the application of the principle of maximal liberty does *not* remove all indeterminacy in the level of taxation chosen, and it does *not* prevent the state from undertaking transfer activity through its fiscal structure. There is nothing in the argument that supports taxation at the minimal level required to finance the legal-protective order, or 10 per cent in the example. The range of indeterminacy extends from 10 per cent, at its lowest, to 40 per cent, at its highest.[10] Any level of absolute taxation within

---

10. In the examples here, I have left out of account any explicit strategic threat behavior on the part of the members of the potential secession coalition. By choosing the internal exit option, members of this group do, of course, impose costs on all persons who

this range satisfies the precept of maximal liberty in the conditions specified in the examples. Choice of the level of taxation within this range must be made on grounds other than the application of the first Rawlsian principle. And it is at this stage, and only at this stage, that the second Rawlsian principle, or some other principle of distribution, might be legitimately introduced. Application of the difference principle, within the range of values allowed by the principle of maximal equal liberty, would, of course, restore determinancy in the definition of the "just" tax-transfer structure.

## VI. Critical Parameters

The numerical examples are helpful in calling attention to the several critical parameters that become relevant in setting the limits on taxation that may be dictated by adherence to the principle of allowing equal liberty of secession to all persons in the economy, a liberty that I have suggested must be included in the array of activities along any Rawlsian dimension. Changes in the values for these parameters will clearly modify results.

Perhaps the most obvious parameter of critical importance that is suggested by the numbers is that which describes the relative sizes of the two groups in the economy. If, in the example, there should be only 10 A workers, along with 65 B workers, with all other conditions remaining as postulated, total product would, of course, be only 85 units. The minimal proportional tax rate required to finance the legal-protective services would be 11.8 per cent. And the maximal rate consistent with adherence to the maximal equal liberty precept increases to 100 per cent. The number of A workers, in this case, is simply too small to make the secession option economically viable. On the other hand, if the number of A workers in the total population of 75 persons should be 35 rather than 25, then, given the other parameters, the maximum tax rate with the liberty of secession option falls from 40 to 29.4 per cent. The arithmetic suggests that the ethical limit on taxation, dictated by the principle of maximal equal liberty, falls as the size of the group

---

remain as members of the original polity. And recognizing this set of tax externalities, threat potentials do exist which would need to be taken into account in any positive, predictive theory. My concern, however, is not with what a potential coalition might be able to enforce but is, instead, with what level of taxation can be ethically justified.

that is relatively more productive increases, and quite apart from any direct exercise of potential political power. So long, however, as there exist any economies of scale in the provision of the services of the legal order, there must remain some room for net fiscal transfers over and beyond the minimal tax limits.

As a second parameter, consider the public-goods characteristic of the provision of the legal-protective services. In the numerical examples, I have assumed extreme jointness, in that the same outlay is required for provision of such services independent of the size of the collective group. At the other extreme, of course, where there is no jointness, no scale economies, in provision of these services, we are back in the private or partitionable goods model. But, as previously noted, this anarchist Utopia is not intellectually recognizable. However, the scale economies may lie somewhere between the two extremes; equal outlays need not be required to provide legal-protective services for differing-sized communities. In the central example, the group of the 25 A workers might, say, be able to finance the required services here for a total outlay of 8 units, by comparison with the 10 units required for the inclusive community of 75 persons. In this case, the absolute limit to taxation that the inclusive community could impose, while honoring the liberty of secession requirement, would fall to a maximum of 28 per cent, by comparison to the 40 per cent indicated under the other model.

A third critical parameter describes the relative productivity of workers in differing combinations. In the example of Section V, I assumed that workers were equally productive in any input arrangement. If, by contrast, an A worker would be productive only if his efforts were combined with B workers, the standard imputation process would not apply. Secession on the part of the A workers would be precluded technologically, and there would be no limits imposed by the liberty of secession criterion. Again, however, something in between the extreme models might be plausibly considered. Suppose that in the central example, A workers might, indeed, produce independently, but that, outside the nexus that includes some B workers, each worker might generate a "marginal product" of only 1.8 units rather than 2 units. In such case, the liberty of secession requirement would be less restrictive on the absolute level of taxation, with the upper limit being raised to more than 65 per cent.

A fourth critical parameter is that which describes the economies of scale for the economic nexus in the large. If specialization and division of labor are such as to make a large economy necessarily more productive than a small economy, and if trade among persons in separate political units is prohibited, this parameter will become relevant. In the example, I assumed that such scale economies did not exist. If, however, we assume that the smaller economy of 25 persons is less productive, because of its size alone, we get results comparable to those introduced above by technological advantages of particular input combinations. It seems questionable, however, whether this particular parameter should be treated as potentially relevant. If a new polity forms within an existing unit, there need be no presumption that trade among members of the now-separated political units should cease. That is to say, the scale economies of the inclusive market area, if these exist, need not be lost through potential political separation.

A fifth critical parameter has been neglected because of simplicity in exposition. In the examples presented in Section V, I assumed that incentive-effect feedbacks on work effort, due either to the imposition of taxes or to the payments of demogrant transfers, did not exist. Clearly, the reaction of taxpayers-transferees to varying levels of fiscal activity would be relevant in any determination of the critical upper limit to levels of absolute taxation. To the extent that higher levels of taxation and/or higher levels of transfers affect work effort negatively, the upper limit on taxation imposed by the liberty of secession criterion is reduced.

Finally, I have not mentioned the potential barriers to political secession that would be imposed by the costs of organizing coalitions. There may exist groups of persons who would secure net gains from securing political independence in a separated unit, but these groups may never be formed because of organizational costs. Free-rider incentives may prevent the emergence of the entrepreneurs that would be necessary to get such coalitions effectively organized. As with the economy-wide issue of scale advantages, however, it seems questionable whether this parameter should be treated as relevant for my purposes. In any actual assessment of potential secession, these costs must clearly be reckoned. But for my purposes of discussing the secession option as an ethical principle for assessing levels of taxation, the organizational costs barrier is not necessarily relevant.

My intention in this section has not been to discuss the critical parameters exhaustively and in detail, but rather to indicate how the results are sensitive to changes in these underlying behavioral, technological, and economic characteristics of the political-legal-economic interaction. Any attempt to determine empirically the precise upper bounds that would be imposed by the operation of the liberty of secession principle would require an estimation of the values for each of the parameters noted, and many more in addition. My aim has been, instead, to indicate that, in any given setting, such an upper limit exists and could, at least conceptually, be empirically estimated.

## VII. Economics and Ethics

The last two sections suggest that the limits to taxation, which I advanced as being those dictated by adherence to an ethical norm, depend critically on *economic* characteristics, and the analysis seems to have shifted to areas familiar within economics: the theory of public goods, the theory of clubs, the theory of the core of an economy, and related subject matters. The demonstration of just such an integration between ethical precepts and the realities of economic process is, itself, a useful by-product of the exercise. The constitutional organization of a tax-transfer system based on adherence to the principle of maximal equal liberty will *not*, in itself, offer determinate guarantees for particular upper limits to taxes. It will do so only within the context of the parameters that describe the economy. Given any such values, however, or given any pre-constitutional estimates for the ranges of such values, upper bounds to taxation emerge. These limits provide ethical-normative criteria for fiscal structure that have been absent, to my knowledge, in normative fiscal theory.

The ethical justification for the upper limit to taxation emerges from the idealized application of the principle of maximal equal liberty. It does not require models of political reality that are, themselves, embodiments of the ethical idealization. In other writings, noted earlier, I have analyzed tax limits largely on the basis of predictions about how politics might work in practice. The results in this paper require no such political imperfection. Even if the fiscal structure chosen and put in place at the constitutional level should operate perfectly, the limits discussed here would remain fully applicable.

Further, the derivation of the ethical limits to taxation does not depend on any presumption that persons respond only to economic self-interest, as the numerical examples might have seemed to suggest. Given liberty of secession, members of particular groups may select the internal exit option, even if such action was counter to measured economic interest. Or, given a sufficient sense of inclusive community solidarity, individuals may remain within an organized collectivity even if economic self-interest should dictate secession. My concern is with a normative derivation of the absolute limits to taxation and not with any positive prediction as to when such limits may be reached. The argument carries through whether or not persons respond to measured self-interest.

The central argument is Rawlsian in that I have used his first principle to generate the results. But the argument does not require extension to or acceptance of the second Rawlsian principle of justice, the difference principle of distribution. The argument does depend on acceptance of the principle of maximal equal liberty behind the veil of ignorance and/or uncertainty as a basic precept of justice that might be used as a guide in the organization of a fiscal structure. And, as noted earlier, the results are presented in the form of hypotheses to be put to the conceptual contractarian test.

It is important to emphasize that my concern is with the organization of the tax-transfer system rather than with the larger and more extensive political organization of society. I have suggested that the equal liberty of secession is a measurable activity along the Rawlsian dimension. And this liberty, if it exists, imposes predicted limits on levels of taxation. But even if this liberty of secession does not, in fact, exist, the organization of the fiscal structure may be guided *as if it did*. In other words, there is *no* ethical-normative justification for extending taxation beyond the indicated upper limits because political reality does not itself allow an equal liberty of secession. My argument is precisely the reverse; because the equal liberty of secession may not, in fact, exist, its conceptualization as a norm offers guidelines for the organization of a fiscal structure that may lay claim to ethical-moral legitimacy.

The emphasis has been on the internal exit option, the equal liberty of secession. The economic analysis is, of course, analogous to the treatment of the external exit option, summarized under the rubric "Tiebout models."[11] To the extent that persons are free to migrate across boundaries of separate

---

11. See Charles Tiebout, "A Pure Theory of Local Expenditures," *Journal of Political Economy*, 64 (October, 1956), 416–24.

political jurisdictions, effective positive limits are placed on tax-transfer activities within any given political unit. And in many particular cases, these limits may suggest lower boundaries on taxation than those emergent from application of the internal exit option. The ethical-normative issues involved in the equal liberty of persons to migrate among separate polities are more complex and more extensive than those that are required to generate the results of this paper.

# Coercive Taxation in
# Constitutional Contract

## I. Introduction

Man does not, and possibly could not, exist in isolation, and most of that which we value depends critically on the presence of civil order, which only collective organization ensures. Man is not the state, but man versus the state is an equally inappropriate metaphor. Man depends on the state. The questions to be explored in this essay involve the implications of this dependence for the legitimacy of coercive taxation in a society that locates sources of value exclusively in its individual members.

How much can the collectivity coercively extract from individuals while satisfying broadly acceptable ethical norms? The libertarians offer a clear answer: *Nothing.* Any tax payment coercively extracted is equivalent to theft and should be labeled as such. This conclusion depends critically on the judgment that individuals have well-defined "natural rights" that are independent of existence in civil society. The contractarian cannot make such a judgment; his response to the question is necessarily more complex.

If Wicksellian contractual criteria are applied directly at the legislative stage of collective decision, and only at this stage, the response is fully consistent with that of the libertarian, but only because taxation becomes vol-

From *Explorations into Constitutional Economics,* comp. Robert D. Tollison and Viktor J. Vanberg (College Station: Texas A&M University Press, 1989): 309–28. Reprinted by permission of the publisher.

I am indebted to my colleague Viktor Vanberg and to Geoffrey Brennan, Australian National University, for helpful comments.

untary rather than coercive.[1] In the Wicksellian construction, the collectivity, as such, is justified in imposing fiscal charges on the citizenry only if there is general agreement (in the limit, unanimous agreement) on both the purpose of the outlay to be made and the distribution of the tax shares required to finance the outlay. The criterion for legitimacy lies in the process of agreement; it remains silent on both the absolute level of taxation and on the distribution of tax shares.

If the basic contractarian approach is extended to the constitutional stage and applied to the ultimate selection among alternative collective decision-making rules, the Wicksellian test of agreement at the in-period, postconstitutional, or within-rule stage no longer suffices.[2] There is nothing in the basic contractarian construction to suggest that some Wicksellian unanimity or near-unanimity rule would be adopted for each and every fiscal choice confronted by the organized collectivity. It seems possible to derive less-than-unanimity rules for making fiscal choices from conceptually unanimous agreement at the constitutional level of deliberation. Majority voting rules, both for the election of representatives and for decisions within a legislative body, may emerge from a constitutional agreement. In this case, what are the limits to the coercive taxation that legislative majorities may impose?

I shall take as given for my discussion that *some* limits on the taxing power of the collectivity would be laid out in the constitutional contract. Legislative majorities would never be granted fiscal carte blanche; claims made for unrestricted fiscal domain cannot find ultimate legitimization in any contractarian construction. I have presented the general argument for limits elsewhere.[3] My concern in this paper is with ascertaining what these limits might be.

In earlier work written jointly with Geoffrey Brennan, we analyzed the in-

1. See Knut Wicksell, *Finanztheoretische Untersuchungen* (Jena: Gustav Fischer, 1896); major portions of this book are published in translation as "A New Principle of Just Taxation," in *Classics in the Theory of Public Finance,* ed. R. A. Musgrave and A. T. Peacock (London: Macmillan and Co., 1958), 72–118.

2. See James M. Buchanan and Gordon Tullock, *The Calculus of Consent* (Ann Arbor: University of Michigan Press, 1962).

3. See my book *The Limits of Liberty* (Chicago: University of Chicago Press, 1975), esp. p. 73; and my paper "Taxation in Fiscal Exchange," *Journal of Public Economics* 6 (1976): 17–29.

dividual's choice of tax limits, but within the restrictions of a model that assumed away the problem that I now address. In our book, *The Power to Tax*,[4]
we posed the specific question: Given some postulated preferred outlay for
collective purposes, how must the taxing power granted to government be
limited so as to ensure that revenues collected remain as close as possible to
the levels dictated by the preferred outlay? We showed that the answer to this
question requires a modeling both of government's behavior in using the
taxing power assigned and the citizens' responsiveness to the imposition of
taxes. The different, and more difficult, question I examine in this paper involves the individual's constitutional choice of a desired or preferred level of
aggregate collective outlay, a question that must somehow be answered prior
to the onset of the Brennan-Buchanan analytical exercise.

My concern is not primarily with those taxes that must be imposed in order
to generate revenues sufficient to finance the "protective" or the "productive"
state. The first of these adjectives describes the activities of the collectivity that
are involved in maintaining the legal umbrella in which individuals interact
with one another. These activities include the protection of rights to property,
as these rights may be assigned in the basic contract, and the enforcement of
contracts made for voluntary exchanges of these rights. The provision of
these services to all members of the collectivity involves genuine "publicness."

In addition to these protective or minimal-state activities, however, government may also provide other genuinely public or collective consumption
goods and services, described technically as those goods and services that are
inherently nonrival in consumption and that are not amenable to efficient
means of exclusion. Both types of these goods and services require financing,
and taxes must be levied in order to secure the revenues.

Taxes required to finance the two sets of activities must, in one sense, be
coercive, since an individual may not voluntarily pay for goods and services
that are available to him whether or not he makes payment. There is no difficulty, however, in deriving a constitutional-stage contractarian justification
for the imposition of taxes for these activities, along with the minimal coercion that may be necessary. To the extent that the goods and services are genuinely "public," and, therefore, made available on equal-access terms to all

4. Cambridge: Cambridge University Press, 1980.

persons, there must be some means of assigning tax shares sufficient to finance an efficient level of provision that will meet a conceptual Wicksellian test of agreement in-period. The predicted difficulties of adjusting tax shares so as to secure actual agreement for each good in each period may, however, be such as to justify resort to decision rules that will allow some coercive taxation that fails even the conceptual unanimity test.[5] The restriction of the financing to genuinely public goods would, however, ensure severe upper limits to such taxation. In any case, the problem of deriving a contractarian justification for such taxation becomes minuscule in comparison with the problem that I propose to address in this paper. The specific question I want to address here involves the possible extension of coercive taxation beyond both protective and productive state limits. Can we derive a contractarian-constitutional authorization for the imposition of taxes to finance *purely redistributive transfers?*

In Section II, I describe a highly simplified model that allows the basic question to be examined in a setting that seems most favorable to fiscal transfers. Section III is devoted to a brief treatment of some of the underlying philosophical presuppositions. In Section IV, I look at the results that might emerge from the familiar Rawlsian construction. Section V presents alternative results through geometrical illustrations. In Sections VI, VII, VIII, and IX, the simplified assumptions of the initial model are relaxed, and the implications are analyzed. The whole argument is summarized in Section X.

## II. Restrictive Assumptions for an Initial Analysis

I propose to set out the conditions that are the most favorable possible for constitutional-stage agreement on high levels of coercive taxation motivated by the individual's constitutional-stage preference for postconstitutional reductions in income inequalities. Four restrictive assumptions are imposed on the initial model.

1. *All valued product is social rent.*

I assume that in the absence of collective or governmental activity in the provision of protective-productive state services (minimally, the protection

---

5. See Buchanan and Tullock, *Calculus of Consent.*

of rights and the enforcement of contracts) no production of value is possible. The life of persons in the Hobbesian jungle is poor, nasty, brutish, and short. As applied to individuals singly and in isolation, this assumption seems plausible enough. But, for this initial model, I shall assume that no production of value is possible in any organized community smaller or less inclusive than the polity's total membership. I also assume that there is only one polity. This set of assumptions ensures that all value produced is "social rent"; without organized collective activity, no product at all is generated.

2. *Full income is measurable independent of observed individual behavior.*

Like Assumption 1, this second assumption is technological in nature rather than behavioral. I assume that in any postconstitutional period there exist some means of measuring an individual's capacity to produce or to generate value, here called full income, whether or not the individual is observed to exercise such capacity. Such an independent measurement is required in order to assess the appropriate fiscal charges (either as taxes or transfers).

3. *No excess burden.*

The two remaining assumptions are behavioral rather than technological. I shall assume initially that there is no private-sector behavioral response to either taxation or public spending (including receipt of transfer payments). Persons consume, work, save, and in precisely the same patterns regardless of the level and structure of either the tax or spending side of the fiscal process. There are no incentive effects of the fiscal structure; excess burdens are zero.

4. *No rent-seeking.*

Finally, I shall initially assume that the Brennan-Buchanan reasons for imposing constitutional restrictions on the taxing powers of government are absent. I assume that in postconstitutional periods government operates precisely as the preferences of individuals at the constitutional stage might dictate, as reflected in the constitutional-stage agreement. There is no attempt, on the part of political agents, to extend revenue collections beyond those minimally required to meet the collective outlay needs that are predicted to occur. Nor is there any effort, on the part of such agents, to direct the patterns of expenditure away from those constitutionally desired by the citizens and toward those that meet the preferences of the agents. Further, in the case of taxes and transfers (negative taxes) there is no net slippage between collection and disbursement. The tax-transfer process is ideally efficient.

## III. To Whom Does Social Rent Belong?

As noted in the introduction, for either the libertarian or the in-period Wicksellian there is no basis for the constitutional authorization of tax financing of pure transfers.[6] The constitutionalist-contractarian may, however, be less negative toward a genuine transfer process. What elements will inform the thinking of a person who is placed behind a veil of ignorance and/or uncertainty in constitutional choice when he or she considers the possible authorization of pure fiscal transfers?

Recall the first extreme assumption introduced. Outside the umbrella of civil order; no person, individually or in coalition with any group less inclusive than the total membership, can generate value. In this sense, therefore, all valued product is imputable to the presence of that order, which is collectively rather than privately supplied. All product is social rent in this setting.

Given the presence of civil order, valued product will be generated through market interaction that will allocate pre-tax shares among persons roughly in accordance with relative productivities.[7] Some withdrawal of product must, of

---

6. Wicksell explicitly states that the procedural criteria he proposes are for the purpose of promoting justice in taxation, rather than in ultimate distribution of product. He does not pre-judge the pre-tax distribution, but he argues that any adjustment in this distribution belongs to the general sphere of law rather than taxation.

To the extent that general agreement emerges on a set of tax-financed transfers in a postconstitutional period, there is, by definition, no genuine transfer of utility involved. Those who agree to be taxed in order to make the transfers to others do so voluntarily, even if collectively rather than privately, and are not, therefore, coerced by the collectivity in the process.

7. Technically, this statement may be interpreted as a presumption about the organization of production in the economy, but it is a presumption that would not be seriously questioned. It amounts to saying that, given the establishment and enforcement of general rules of property and contract, production would be efficiently organized in many separate units (firms), which would exchange both with other units and with persons.

course, take place for the financing of the minimally required protective services and the preferred levels of genuinely collective consumption goods. Assume, for illustrative purposes, that this withdrawal amounts to roughly 10 percent of total product value. Will the person, behind an appropriately defined veil of ignorance and/or uncertainty, choose to restrict the levy of taxation to roughly this 10 percent range, or will there be some reason to authorize the postconstitutional levy of taxes beyond this range in order to finance redistributive transfers?

If the 10 percent level of taxation is all that is constitutionally agreed on and authorized, the remaining 90 percent of valued production in the economy will then be finally allocated among persons in accordance with productivities, as adjusted by some allocation of tax shares for the financing of the protective-productive state services. If, however, the social rent assumption is accepted, this particular set of imputations is only one set from among many that might be chosen, and, as such, it seems to be arbitrary. Behind the veil, would not a person consider that at least some share of this remaining 90 percent of value could appropriately be devoted to the financing of transfers with the purpose of achieving a more desirable final distribution, as evaluated at the constitutional stage? If we put the question differently, how could such a question be answered in the negative?

The model has been deliberately constructed so that the "productivity ethic" offers little or no support to the libertarian. To the extent that this ethic is supportable at all, it can possibly justify the sharing of value in accordance with *external* productivities. It cannot be extended in support of

---

The assumption that all valued product is *social* rent, in the sense defined, should not be taken to imply that the whole economy's production is most efficiently organized in a monolithic "team," ensuring that even with the general rules of property and contract there would be no means of measuring relative productivities of differing team components. In such a setting, all product would be rent, whether or not we add the word "social" as a qualifier. In the decentralized organization of production and exchange here postulated, payments to inputs need embody no intra- or interfirm or industry rent despite the classification of all valued product as *social* rent. The presumption that decentralized rather than centralized or monolithic organization of production would be efficient, given the general rules of property and contract, is necessary in order for the question addressed in this paper to arise. If the whole economy is best organized as a monolithic "team," there would be no "redistribution" problem, at least in the sense normally discussed.

sharing in terms of *internal* productivities in a model that necessarily involves collective organization and provision for civil order. In a functioning market economy (and ignoring the financing of the legal umbrella) that is fully competitive, payments to inputs tend to equal external marginal products rather than internal, and the allocation of rents measured by the differences between these two products is, in a sense, acknowledged to be arbitrary.[8] If we now introduce inclusive collective provision of protective state services as a necessary input to the generation of all value even in an economy with decentralized production, there is an inherent indeterminacy in the imputation of value shares in terms of productivities inclusively defined. The collectivity, as such, can make a claim to a share well beyond that measured by the mere opportunity cost of the inputs it provides, just as can other inputs.[9] Or, if we put the issue in the context of our analysis, individuals, at the constitutional stage of choice of institutional rules, may agree that the social rent is to be shared in accordance with some standard other than that which would dictate collective exaction of the minimal outlays that are required to finance the actual inputs employed in state services. There seems to be no plausible basis for suggesting that all of the social rent over and above this minimum should be institutionally allocated to those who offer the market rather than the collective inputs, especially since, by our assump-

---

8. The external marginal product of an input unit is defined as the value that unit could produce in its most highly valued alternative use; this external product value is that which is necessary to ensure that the input remains in the employment specified; this value becomes the opportunity cost of the input to the employing firm. Internal marginal product is, by contrast, the difference in the value of total product in the specified facility attributable to the presence of the input unit in question. This internal product measures the potential opportunity loss that the firm would suffer if the input unit is not employed, but unless the external marginal product is equal to the internal, the internal marginal product is not the necessary opportunity cost of the input unit to the firm. The difference between the internal and external marginal product values becomes genuine rent, and the sharing of such rent between the owner of the input and the employing firm is not determinate in the operation of the competitive market process.

For an example of a practical application of the differences between the internal and external marginal product as bases for input payments, see James M. Buchanan and Robert D. Tollison, "The Homogenization of Heterogeneous Inputs," *American Economic Review* 71 (March, 1981): 28–38.

9. See J. R. Kearl, "Do Entitlements Imply That Taxation Is Theft?" *Philosophy and Public Affairs* 7 (Fall, 1977): 74–81.

tion, the external productivity of these inputs is nonexistent. Without these inputs, the state can produce no value, but without the services of the state these inputs produce no value.[10]

## IV. The Rawlsian Solution

The most familiar attempt to answer the basic question that I have posed, and to do so from a basic contractarian perspective, is that of John Rawls.[11] Using a carefully defined veil-of-ignorance construction, Rawls sets up idealized contractors who are then predicted to agree on two principles of justice that will guide the organization of the society. The two principles are lexicographically ordered; the first is the principle of maximal equal liberty; the second is the maximin or difference principle for the distribution of primary goods.

Economists as well as other critics of Rawls have concentrated attention almost exclusively on the difference principle, and they have failed to recognize that the first principle of maximal equal liberty also has distributional consequences. Both external exit (migration from the polity) and internal exit (secession) must be listed as countable Rawlsian liberties, without which the first principle cannot be satisfied. Including the guarantee of these two

---

10. Care must be taken to clarify the distinction between the nature of the collective input, let us say, *order,* and the ordinary input units that may be employed to produce this collective input, units that may work in either the state or the market sector. There is no basis for suggesting that the ordinary inputs employed in the state sector should secure more than their counterparts in the market sector. But this does not amount to saying that the state, as the collective, may not be authorized, in the constitutional choice process, to collect something over and beyond the necessary market-related payments to its own inputs.

Consider a simple example of a ten-person community. Behind a veil of ignorance, each person knows that no value can be produced without the presence of one police officer, who must be hired by the collectivity as such and who might otherwise produce value in the private sector in the presence of some alternative person as police officer. The collectivity will never be authorized, at the constitutional level, to pay the person hired as police officer more than his opportunity cost. But the collectivity may well be authorized, by agreement at the constitutional stage, to withdraw from the private sector product a total value (taxation) more than the opportunity wage of the single police officer collectively hired.

11. *A Theory of Justice* (Cambridge, Mass.: Harvard University Press, 1971).

liberties in the agreed-on constitutional arrangements ensures that the second Rawlsian principle applies only to social rent, only to that share of value over and beyond the external marginal product of persons or of groups.

In the highly restricted set of assumptions summarized in Section II, all of value that is produced is social rent. Persons possess equal liberties to leave the polity or to secede and form new polities, but, by assumption, they can produce nothing of value in either case. In addition, full incomes can presumably be measured, and persons behave identically regardless of the level of taxes and transfers. In this rarefied setting, the application of the Rawlsian difference principle would equalize the distribution of value among all persons, if we define valued goods as the relevant Rawlsian primary goods. This full equalization result or solution would also emerge from a standard utilitarian stance or from a straightforward equalization norm. The individuals who are genuinely behind the veil of ignorance in this setting would agree to a set of constitutional arrangements that would instruct government, in-period, to implement a tax-transfer scheme that would bring all persons, post-tax and post-transfer, to the same position. Rawls gets differing results only because he does not impose the third restrictive assumption that I have introduced in this essay. His analysis implicitly accepts the three other restrictions.

## V. An Emendation of the Rawlsian Solution

I do not want to relax any of the four assumptions at this point. My purpose in this section is to suggest that, even under the highly restrictive assumptions, full equalization would not be predicted to emerge from constitutional-stage agreement among persons who place themselves behind the genuine Rawlsian veil. The Rawlsian exercise, like the utilitarian, omits a critically important element, which, when included in the model, must modify the solution, perhaps substantially. Contractual agreement would be predicted to emerge on arrangements that would embody less than full equalization of incomes among persons, post-tax and post-transfer.

Why would the idealized contractors ever agree to any arrangements that would not produce full equality? They are behind the veil; all product is social rent; full incomes can be assessed for fiscal purposes; there is no excess burden; political agents do not seek rents. The contractors will recognize, however, that any distribution of capacities to produce value along the decentralized production organization must involve some "natural" imputation to separable persons or groups, who can then exert at least nominal claims to the potential values that may be produced. This is to say, individuals will attach putative "rights" to the "natural" assignments.[12] Hence, any *re*distribution of these potential values among persons involves, for one set of persons, a coerced "taking" of valued product that they consider to be "their own" in some nominal sense. There will exist a distinct threshold difference between the predicted loss from a coerced taking of one unit of value by taxation and the predicted gain from the receipt of one unit through transfer. This threshold difference will be anticipated by the idealized contractors, and it must lead to agreement on arrangements that will embody less than full equality in the final distribution of values, even in this model where the extremely restricted assumptions remain in force.[13]

12. Consider an example where all product is agricultural and is produced separately by individual families on small plots. The extreme assumptions hold; no value can be produced outside of civil order; full incomes are measurable; excess burdens and rent-seeking are absent. But the person who plants, hoes, and digs the potatoes will come to attach a claim to those potatoes that "he produces," and he will react negatively to any collective "taking" of these for transfer purposes. This negative reaction will be predicted by the contractors who participate in the constitutional dialogue behind the veil of ignorance.

The agricultural example suggests, however, that as the economy's production processes move beyond those that embody the direct association of the individual or family with observable product, the negative reaction to "takings" by the collectivity will fall in comparison to the reaction under the more primitive structure. As the individual comes to be more and more alienated from the goods and services produced, in the Marxian sense, we should, therefore, predict that idealized contractors, behind the veil, will tend to agree on a higher level of distributive transfers. The linkage between the shift into the industrial society and the rise of the transfer state may, in this way, be conceptually derived from the contractarian calculus. As the economy shifts beyond industrialization toward the service society, the pattern may possibly be reversed.

13. For a general discussion of the difference between the choice of a distribution and the choice from among redistributive institutions, see "Distributive and Redistributive Norms," chapter 14 in my book *Liberty, Market and State* (London: Wheatsheaf Books, 1986).

The precise location of the agreed-on solution along the spectrum between some pretax, pre-transfer distribution and full equality will be dependent on other institutional choices that are made, notably those that establish the structure of the tax system. To the extent that taxes are imposed directly on bases that are measured on market-related earn-

## SOME UTILITY FUNCTION GEOMETRY

The general argument sketched above can be more conveniently expressed by resort to simple utility function diagrams. The contractor will predict that the preferences of each person (any person) in any postconstitutional period can be described by a utility function of the standard form. The contractor will not know what his capacity for generating market-related, pre-tax income will be and hence, what his utility level will be, pre-tax, pre-transfer. But the contractor will predict that whatever this location there will be a kink in the function that relates this position to those below and above it that are achievable by the tax-transfer process. There will be a predicted threshold difference between the marginal loss (through tax) of a unit of value and the marginal gain (through receipt of transfer) of a unit of full income.

In Fig. 24-1, the predicted marginal utility of potential market-related, pre-tax, pre-transfer incomes at all levels of income is shown by $MU_i$. The function is down-sloping throughout the range, and it is drawn as a straight line for simplicity, since the sign of the second derivative of the total utility of full income function is not relevant for my purposes. The reverse image of the function is shown as $MU_j$. If the relevant institutional choice should be that of some ideal distribution, in the two-person setting shown, the contractor would, of course, choose the position of full equality, shown at $Y_E$. As noted, however, the choice is not among distributions, since these are determined by elements not within control of the constitutional contractors. The relevant institutional-constitutional choice is among arrangements that will implement some redistribution from the potential market-related, pre-tax, pre-transfer distribution. Behind the veil the contractor cannot identify himself, postchoice; he does not know whether he will be i or j. He can, however,

---

ings, with rates differing among persons, the threshold difference noted will remain important. If, however, the collectivity should be authorized institutionally to extract revenues "off the top," so to speak, prior to any market-related imputation of values among persons, the threshold effect would become less significant. Such a structure would require proportionality in rates, and some gross nonpersonal income base. For my purposes here, I shall neglect these interrelationships.

For a sophisticated discussion of individuals' preferences among tax institutions, although not strictly within a veil-of-ignorance construction, see Charles J. Goetz, "Tax Preferences in a Collective Decision-making Context," Ph.D. dissertation, University of Virginia, 1964 (Ann Arbor, Mich.: University Microfilms, 1965).

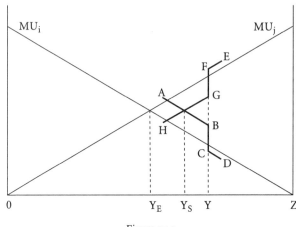

*Figure 24-1*

predict that the initial pre-tax distribution will be at Y, with Individual i receiving a full income of 0Y and Individual j receiving a full income of YZ, with the utility levels shown by the positions on $MU_i$ and $MU_j$.

The threshold effect is shown by the discontinuities in the tax-transfer curves traced out through the initial position on each basic utility function. For Individual i, the relevant function is that shown by ABCD, for Individual j that shown by EFGH. The idealized contractor, not knowing whether he will find himself in the position of i or j, will select a set of redistributive arrangements that will generate a position at $Y_S$. Note that, as drawn in Fig. 24-1, this agreed-on position will involve some shift from the potential market-related, pre-tax position, but that it will fall short of the position of full equality. As the construction suggests, quite independent of the particular configurations, if the discontinuities in the marginal utility functions are acknowledged to be present at all, the constitutionally preferred solution must fall short of the equal distribution in the direction of the market-generated, pre-tax, pre-transfer distribution. If the threshold differences are severe enough, relative to the inequality in the initial distribution predicted to emerge, the contractor may choose the uncorrected or market position, despite the fact that the ideal distribution would remain that described by full equality.[14]

14. In terms of the geometry of Fig. 24-1, the initial position will be constitutionally preferred if the vertical displacements (shown as BC on $MU_i$ and FG on $MU_j$) are suffi-

# VI. Secession, Social Rent, and External Marginal Product

As I have repeatedly emphasized, the results derived in Section V are those that emerge in the contractarian setting that is deliberately designed to represent the conditions that are most favorable for constitutional-stage agreement on high levels of coercively imposed postconstitutional taxation for the financing of pure transfers. As we relax the four highly restrictive assumptions outlined in Section II, idealized contractors can be predicted to agree on fiscal-political arrangements that will generate lower levels of transfer taxation.

I shall relax the four basic assumptions in the order presented. The first assumption involves the nature of the economy's "joint production function," which was so defined as to ensure that all value produced in the economy, despite decentralized organization of production, could be classified as social rent, because of the necessary dependence on collectively supplied order. Individuals in isolation may, plausibly, be modeled as being unable to produce value on their own and without some legal protection. But groups of persons may form coalitions that by seceding from the inclusive membership of the single polity may organize for the provision of their own separate legal-political order, within which value can be produced.[15] To the extent that such prospects exist, or are predicted to exist when persons behind the veil consider alternative fiscal arrangements, the pre-tax share of value that can properly be classified as social rent may be dramatically reduced.

---

ciently large to overlap. Note that as the market position, Y, is shifted toward equal distribution, and/or as the thresholds increase, this result is more likely to occur.

15. I shall concentrate on the possible existence of internal exit through the secession option, within the assumption that there is some initial all-inclusive polity. Much the same analysis can be extended to a setting in which persons or groups have external exit options, that is, where there exist many separate political units, between which migration can take place. The analysis of external exit is more complex because it must involve several units; in addition, this analysis is more familiar because of its discussion under the "Tiebout model" rubric in fiscal theory.

For a preliminary paper that develops further the analysis of internal exit through secession, see James M. Buchanan and Roger L. Faith, "Secession and the Sharing of Surplus: Toward a Theory of Internal Exit," presented at the Public Choice Society Meeting, New Orleans, February, 1985.

The point here can perhaps best be presented with reference to the existence and measurement of external marginal product of inputs. In orthodox price theory, the external marginal product of an input unit is the payment that unit can command in its best alternative use, its genuine opportunity cost to a potential purchaser-employer. In our initial restricted model, there is no external marginal product for any input when the "production function" for the whole economy is considered. No individual could produce value outside of the collectivity, either singly or in groups. If we now introduce a secession option and recognize that individuals may, in groups, pull out from the initially organized collectivity and form their own independent polities for the provision of civil order, the external marginal products of those persons who might think of themselves as potential members of such seceding coalitions clearly become positive.

A recognition that individuals will strongly feel that they are "morally entitled" to the value status that they might expect to secure in an alternative political setting will inform all contractors as they consider fiscal arrangements at the constitutional stage of decision. The prospect that a group of persons who must pay a net tax to finance transfers to others might form a seceding group by pulling away from the organized collectivity will clearly serve to limit the fiscal coercion that will emerge from any agreement behind the genuine veil of ignorance. In terms of the discussion in Section V above, the effect will be that of accentuating the predicted threshold differences between payment of net tax and receipt of transfers.

It is important to emphasize, however, that this modification in the assumption about social rent will not eliminate from constitutional consideration all fiscal arrangements that embody coercive taxes for the financing of redistributive transfers. So long as there exists differential advantage in the provision of protective-productive state services to the inclusive membership of the polity, as opposed to the provision of comparable services in potentially seceding units (or indeed in other external polities), there will remain a space over which the choice of postconstitutional tax-transfer institutions may range, a space that will include many alternatives. The prospect for advantageous secession on the part of a net taxpayer group may, in the absence of an actual secession option being exercised, tend only to reduce the agreed-on level of transfer taxes rather than to eliminate such taxation altogether. That is to say, some social rent will remain, and this rent provides a potential source for contractually accepted transfer taxation.

If an exit option does in fact exist, there will be a genuine limit imposed on the level of fiscal transfers for redistributive purposes. At best, in these settings, the net taxpayers can be forced to finance the full costs of protective-productive state services, plus transfers in the amount of the costs of forming a seceding coalition.[16] These essentially prudential considerations will enter the calculus of the idealized contractors as predictions concerning the institutional feasibility space within which choices of fiscal institutions can be made. As such, they are not my primary concern, which is that of placing bounds on contractually preferred levels of coercive taxation within any defined feasibility frontiers.

## VII. The Nonmeasurability of Full Incomes

I shall now relax the second of the set of restrictive assumptions in Section II, that which postulated the technological feasibility of measuring the separate capacities of persons to generate value independent of any observed behavior. Without some such assumption, whether or not in extreme form, there would seem to be no basis for any contractarian justification of a redistributive fiscal structure.

This point may be illustrated with reference to Fig. 24-1, the simple two-person example. As drawn, Individual i is expected to be able to achieve a full income level shown by 0Y; Individual j is expected to be able to achieve a full income shown by YZ. Utility levels are directly related to expected full incomes. Suppose, however, that full incomes, the capacities to produce values, cannot be measured; there is no way to estimate an individual's capacity to produce value independent of his observed behavior. Suppose that actual production of value is all that may be empirically measured.

In this setting, an individual's appropriate fiscal liability (either positive or negative) could not be determined by direct reference to observed income-producing behavior. In Fig. 24-1, 0Y and YZ, if now defined to measure ac-

16. It is possible to argue that persons behind the veil of ignorance will agree on the principle of maximal equal liberty, the first of the two Rawlsian principles of justice. In this case, it can be further suggested that the liberty of persons to secede and form new polities is a countable Rawlsian liberty, in which instance the community that meets standards of justice must allow such an option to exist. For a discussion of some of the implications of this point, see James M. Buchanan and Loren Lomasky, "The Matrix of Contractarian Justice," *Social Philosophy and Policy* 2 (Autumn, 1984): 12–32.

tual income produced, might well represent behavioral outcomes of choices made by persons with *identical* full incomes. Individual i might, by working more, generate income 0Y, while Individual j, by loafing, might generate income YZ. In this case, a tax-transfer system, based on observed income produced, would be perverse to almost any objectives that might be agreed on by idealized contractors.

If, however, independent measurability of full incomes is simply not technologically possible, must the prospect of some perverse fiscal transfers rule out possible contractarian agreement on all redistributive structures? No answer can be given to this question a priori. The response would depend on contractors' predictions concerning the empirical relationship between individuals' capacities to produce value and their observed behavior in exercising such capacities. If this relationship is strongly positive, that is, if most individuals who are observed to produce relatively low incomes do so because of relatively low capacities to produce, and vice versa for high incomes, a redistributive structure need not seriously undermine legitimate contractarian objectives. Nonetheless, the contractual agreement will be informed by the prospect that any such system will involve some persons who secure transfer payments undeservedly, along with some persons who are taxed undeservedly.

The direction of effect on the basic constitutional choice of redistributive arrangements seems clear. Any relaxation of the second restrictive assumption imposed on the initial model will have the effect of reducing the level of coercive taxation for the financing of transfers that would emerge from any agreement among idealized contractors at the constitutional stage of fiscal choice. The relaxation of the second assumption operates in the same direction as the relaxation of the first. In terms of the geometry of Fig. 24-1, the effect is to widen the relevant threshold between the anticipated utility loss of a dollar of tax, levied on observed income, and the anticipated utility gain of a dollar's transfer, based on observed income. To put this result more generally, to the extent that differentials in observed income levels in the economy are predicted to reflect individuals' voluntary choices rather than individually exogenous elements, contractually derived coercive taxation must be lower.

## VIII. Excess Burden Introduced

I shall relax the third restrictive assumption imposed in Section II, that which involves an absence of predicted behavioral response of persons as taxpayers and transfer recipients in postconstitutional periods of fiscal operations. It is first necessary to examine the possible absence of behavioral response in a positive economic framework rather than as an assumption imposed on the model for clarity and simplification. Under what conditions is behavioral response unlikely? And, in these conditions, are there direct consequences for the choice among redistributive institutions as evaluated constitutionally?

An individual, facing a coercive tax liability that is measured by some base or source over which he exerts nominal claim, will not modify his behavior if there exist, over the relevant stage of private choices, no nontaxable utility-yielding opportunities. If such opportunities exist, and there is continuous and unconstrained variation between these and taxable opportunities, the individual who attains private equilibrium, pre-tax, will respond behaviorally. An absence of response would indicate that there are no nontaxable opportunities. A tax that is levied "optimally" on full or potential income would meet this condition, in which case there would be no anticipated utility loss due to excess-burden effects. Institutionally, however, such generality in taxation is not possible with informational requirements alone, and this will be recognized by our idealized contractors. Taxes must be anticipated to generate behavioral responses; persons will react by shifting toward nontaxable opportunities, and this will involve utility losses.

Similar conclusions apply for the transfer side. Here the analogue to non-taxable opportunities for the net taxpayers is eligibility requirements for transfer receipt, which will again involve anticipated utility loss by comparison with that achievable under a conceptually ideal pure transfer scheme. The idealized contractors will take account of the anticipated utility losses summarized under the excess-burden rubric, and constitutional agreement will reflect institutional arrangements that will embody a lower level of taxation (and transfer payments) than would emerge in the no-excess-burden model.[17] Although the institutional arrangements chosen will embody a

17. In the setting here postulated, the contractors will also tend to agree on a selection of tax and transfer institutions that will minimize the predicted behavior responses, given

lower transfer budget than in the no-excess-burden model, there is no means of determining whether or not the final, post-tax, post-transfer position achieved will be characterized by more or less remaining distributional inequality. Since the effect of fiscal incentives is to reduce the level of value produced, overall, a lower level of transfer may generate a distributional position closer to that of equality than constitutional agreement would produce in the absence of response.

## IX. Rent-Seeking Introduced

I shall now relax the last of the four restrictive assumptions, that which states that governments in postconstitutional periods act ideally on the implementation of any fiscal institution passed along to them as instructions from the constitutional order. This assumption was imposed strictly for purposes of simplifying the earlier exposition, and such governmental behavior is implausible in any realistic model. The behavior of political agents in seeking to further their own interests, given the constraints within which they are allowed to act, must itself be modeled.[18] Again I shall not advance a specific model here; for my purposes I suggest only the hypothesis that there will be some predicted departure from the norms of political perfection previously assumed. There will be some anticipated wastage or loss of revenues in the fiscal process itself. Some share of tax revenues collected will not be channeled as transfer payments to recipients designated as such in the constitutional instructions. A share of these funds will, instead, be directed toward the provision of benefits (in kind or cash) to those who act as political agents or those whom such agents seek to benefit.

This change in the initial model has the same effect on the results as

a simultaneously determined level of transfer budget. They will do so because the utility losses measured by the excess burdens will themselves be anticipated at the constitutional stage, and efforts will be made to minimize these deadweight losses. Although the model is quite different in purpose from that introduced by Gary Becker, this conclusion emerges from analysis that is in many respects analogous to his. See Gary Becker, "A Theory of Competition among Pressure Groups for Political Influence," *Quarterly Journal of Economics* 98 (August, 1983): 371–400.

18. In our book *The Power to Tax* (Cambridge: Cambridge University Press, 1980), Geoffrey Brennan and I examined the implications of a single revenue-maximization model for the behavior of governments.

those that stem from the relaxation of the three other restrictive assumptions. Since the idealized contractor will now recognize that fiscal transfers, no matter how strongly these may be dictated by constitutionally agreed-on criteria of fairness, can never be modeled as dollar-for-dollar replacements of payments for taxes, there will be agreement on a lower level of transfers than would be approved under an ideally operating polity.[19]

We may refer to the simple geometry of the two-person model in Fig. 24-1. The expectation that there will be some slippage between revenues collected in taxes and those that are finally secured by designated transfer recipients will have the effect of increasing the size of the discontinuities in the relevant marginal utility functions.

## X. The Whole Argument Summarized

My objective in this paper is the ambitious one of deriving possible limits to the imposition of coercive taxes for the financing of redistributive transfer payments within a general contractarian framework for normative analysis. My intent was not to lay down precise limits, but to outline the directions of effect that might be exerted by several relevant technological and behavioral elements on the possible constitutional delegation of taxing authority to legislatures.

I commenced with a rejection of the libertarian assertion that all taxation is theft, and I extended the Wicksellian unanimity criterion to the level of constitutional choice which allows for the possible activities of an in-period or postconstitutional transfer state. The tax-transfer authority would be limited by constitutional constraints, but this paper does not contain arguments for such general limits, as I have discussed these in earlier writings. My concern in this essay is to analyze the content of such constitutional constraints.

Initially, I set up a model that seemed to be the most favorable possible for the constitutional authorization of fiscal transfers. There are four highly restrictive assumptions. All valued product is social rent in the sense that

---

19. The difficulty of implementing any desired tax-transfer policy, as dictated by the objective of justice, through operation of any political institutions is discussed in some detail in chapter 8 of *The Reason of Rules*, by Geoffrey Brennan and James Buchanan (Cambridge: Cambridge University Press, 1985).

without the presence of legal-political order, inclusively defined over the whole membership of the polity, no value is generated at all. Secondly, it is assumed to be technologically feasible to measure individuals' full incomes, in-period, independent of any observed behavior. Thirdly, individuals do not respond at all to taxes and transfers. And, finally, governments operate perfectly in carrying out the dictates of the constitutional agreements.

Even in this highly confined model, the analysis suggested that the full equalization of incomes, which might seem to be dictated by concentration exclusively on the idealized distributive norms, will never be agreed to by the constitutional contractors, who will consider utility losses consequent on any *re*distribution of value among persons. In this rarefied setting, constitutional agreement may be reached, although not necessarily, on arrangements that shift the final allocation of values away from the initial market-related, pre-tax, pre-transfer imputation toward equality, but never on arrangements that will promote full equalization.

The restrictive assumptions were then relaxed in sequence. The first assumption attributed all valued product to social rent, as defined. While this attribution may be plausible with respect to individuals in isolation, who can rarely produce value outside some community-collectivity, the restriction becomes invalid with respect to external exit, even for individuals, and with respect to groups of individuals for internal exit. Groups may be organized for the purpose of seceding from the inclusive political unit, in which case the seceding group would be required to provide its own protective-productive collective services. The analysis suggested that any attenuation of the social rent attribution with respect to either external or internal exit would lead constitutional contractors to reckon on enhanced utility losses when tax exactions exceed properly measured opportunity cost limits. This recognition will reinforce the direction of departure from equality already indicated in the initial pure model.

Relaxation of the second assumption, that which assumes the measurability of full incomes, points in the same direction, that is, toward lower levels of coercive taxation. Practically, incomes that are to be used as the bases for estimating fiscal liabilities must be behaviorally generated, ensuring errors in relating tax and transfer payments to full incomes, the appropriate contractarian base. The idealized contractors will recognize this departure from conceptually ideal measurement and will move toward minimizing errors by placing more weight on pre-tax, pre-transfer imputations.

The third assumption of no excess burden will, when relaxed, shift the results in the same direction as the first two considered. Finally, the relaxation of the assumption concerning the behavior of political agents, when added to the directional effects of the adjustments already noted, may call into question any significant departure from the pre-tax, pre-transfer allocation of shares in value, adjusted for some imputation of payments for the provision of protective and productive state services.

The analysis does not lend itself to laying down hard and fast limits. It does, however, advance the argument beyond that which stops at the criteria for the contractual process itself. That which does emerge from the idealized constitutional contract is, by construction, the "just" solution to the initial question posed. And this ultimate response must be allowed to include a whole set of possible fiscal arrangements. What the analysis of this essay does is to provide additional insights into the calculus of the individual contractor who participates in the constitutional exercise.

Environmental parameters are, of course, critical to any constitutional dialogue, and some directions of effect may be readily predicted. To the extent that persons think of themselves as members of the inclusive political community rather than as individuals in isolation or as members of potentially seceding groups, the range for coercive taxation is expanded. To the extent that genuine publicness in the provision of protective productive services extends over the inclusive membership, the same result holds. To the extent that individuals are homogeneous with respect to utilizing their capacities, the scope for measuring appropriate fiscal liability increases and with it the scope for coercive taxation. The same result follows from homogeneity in response to fiscal arrangements. And, finally, to the extent that agents behave in furtherance of the "public interest," as defined in the constitutional agreement, the threshold between the losses involved in taxation and the utility gains embodied in transfer receipts is reduced. Shifts in these critical parameters in the opposing directions will, of course, generate directionally opposite results.

# Constitutional Constraints on Governmental Taxing Power

> To distinguish effectively the legislation on general rules by which
> the tax burden is to be apportioned among the individuals from
> the determination of the total sums to be raised, would require
> such a complete re-thinking of all the principles of public finance
> that the first reaction of those familiar with the existing institu-
> tions will probably be to regard such a scheme as wholly imprac-
> ticable. Yet nothing short of such a complete reconsideration of
> the institutional setting of financial legislation can probably stop
> the trend towards a continuing and progressive rise of that share
> of the income of society which is controlled by government. This
> trend, if allowed to continue, would before long swallow up the
> whole of society in the organization of government.
>
> —F. A. Hayek, *Law, Legislation and Liberty,* Vol. 3,
> *The Political Order of a Society of Free Men*

## I. Introduction

In the passage cited above, Professor Hayek has pointed to the necessary distinction between the structure of taxation and the level of taxation. Implicit
in the Hayek position, in the citation and elsewhere, is the belief that effec-

From *ORDO* Band 30 (Stuttgart: Gustav Fischer Verlag, 1979): 349–59). Reprinted by
permission of the publisher.

I am indebted to my colleague Geoffrey Brennan for helpful suggestions.

tive control over the structure, by which Hayek means the allocation or dis-tribution of tax shares among persons, will insure adequate control over the level of taxation. That is to say, Hayek suggests that if the powers of governments to modify tax-share distribution through ordinary legislation are appropriately restricted, there should be no need to limit the powers of legislative-parliamentary majorities in setting the overall level of public out-lays, and, hence, of taxes.

Hayek's belief in the overall efficacy of democratic processes within the constraints imposed by general tax rules may not be shared by every observer of the fiscal Leviathan, and, in any case, it should be evident that Hayek's proposal is only one among a set of possible "fiscal or tax constitutions" that might be suggested. My purpose in this paper is to discuss, in very broad terms, the possible set of rules and arrangements that may be introduced to define the limits on the taxing powers of governments in modern Western democracies. The "tax constitution" may include constraints on the level as well as the structure of taxation. I shall explore questions that arise in any attempt to lay down some preferred set of tax rules.

## II. Why Are Fiscal Constraints Desired?

The first step in any discussion of fiscal constraints involves the basic reasons for imposing any restrictions of the power of governments to tax. At the practical level, and as indicated in the citation from Hayek above, mere ob-servation of the rates at which governments have grown, and notably in the decades since World War II, is perhaps sufficient to justify examination of the prospects for fiscal constraints. At the analytical level, the logic of fiscal constraint is relatively straightforward. If government should match the im-age of the benevolent despot that informs so many of the normative policy models used by modern economists, constitutional constraints on govern-mental behavior, in taxation or in any other respect, might not be necessary. Even under such an extreme assumption, however, the mere fact that sepa-rate persons have separate utility functions would insure that any govern-mental decision-process is necessarily inconsistent and unstable. A "social welfare function" cannot logically exist, given a set of reasonably desired properties for such a function. All of this is quite apart from the recognition that any governmental decision-makers must be assumed to have proclivities to act in accordance with their own, rather than some vaguely defined general, or public, interest. For both of these basic reasons, it is within any person's interest to impose some limits on the taxing power of governmental decision-making coalitions, regardless of how "democratically" such a coalition might be organized, and how inclusive the voting rule might be. The normative foundations for a tax constitution emerge directly from the utility-maximizing behavior of any, and hence all, persons in the polity.

The logical argument for tax constraints does not depend on the supposition that democratically selected ruling coalitions or legislative majorities will, in each and every budgetary period, raise the levels of taxing and spending beyond those deemed to be desirable or efficient by the average citizen. To the extent that checks imposed by competitive electoral politics hold taxing and spending within "reasonable" limits, the constitutional constraints may not become binding. But this is no argument against the existence of such constraints, which may well be designed to offer protection against undue fiscal exploitation in precisely those situations where the competition among politicians and parties fails to control tax-spending explosion. The internal controls of democratic politics and the constitutional controls imposed external to the ordinary legislative process are complements rather than substitutes.

## III. Existing Tax Constitutions

It is important to recognize that constitutional constraints on governmental powers to tax do exist in Western democratic societies, even if these constraints have been almost totally neglected by economists. In the United States Constitution there is a provision that requires that federal direct taxes shall be uniformly apportioned among the separate states, and this constitutional proviso was interpreted by the courts in such a way as to prohibit the levy of progressive income taxes throughout the first century and one-half of the national experience. In order for the federal government to secure the power to levy progressive taxes on personal incomes, the United States Constitution was specifically amended in 1913. The uniformity requirement would still prohibit federal government taxation of residents of specific geographic areas on any discriminatory bases. Further, and quite apart from the formal provisions in the written constitution, the more general requirements for due process would prohibit the levy of overly discriminatory taxes of many varieties, on the part of either the federal or the state-local govern-ments. Much the same conclusion would probably apply to almost all of the Western democracies, although I am not personally familiar with the consti-tutional law on taxation in countries other than the United States.

There are constitutional-legal restrictions on governmental powers to tax persons differentially. That is to say, a person is, to a degree, legally protected from the arbitrary fiscal exactions of government which might set him up as against equal treatment of his fellows. The more general principle of "equal-ity before the law" extends in this respect to taxation.

Such legal constraints against arbitrary or discriminatory treatment are to be contrasted with the almost total absence of constraints on the level of tax-ation that may be imposed on the body of taxpayers, on the overall share in total income or product that may be exacted by the fisc. Both formal consti-tutional law and the tradition of the common law are silent on the second type of constraint, which the accumulating evidence on the rapid growth in the governmental share in national incomes makes clear.

There is also an asymmetry between the legal-constitutional constraints on taxation and those on public outlays. Although no constraints on the overall levels of taxation exist, there are legal restrictions, as noted, on the differential tax treatment of persons and groups. No such constraints exist on the spending side of the fiscal account. Governments can, and do, dis-criminate in the pattern of outlays, proffering benefits to specifically chosen groups, whether these be classified geographically, occupationally, demo-graphically, or otherwise. The general principle of "equality before the law" has never been applied to the distribution of governmental benefits among citizens. This asymmetric treatment of benefits tends, of course, to under-mine the restricting influence of any tax-side constraints against overall fis-cal discrimination by governments. General taxes that are used to finance discriminatory benefits can produce distributional results that are almost equivalent to those produced by the use of discriminatory taxes.

While it is necessary to recognize that some constitutional-legal con-straints on governmental fiscal powers do exist, and notably on the powers to impose discriminatory taxes, it is also essential to avoid attributing effi-ciency to the existing legal structure in these respects. As suggested, the evi-dence of this century implies that existing legal rules have not been effective in curbing the fiscal appetites of governments. In this setting, it becomes appropriate to raise questions about additional and/or alternative tax rules and arrangements that might serve the long-term interests of taxpayers better than those interests seem to have been served by the legal institutions in being. The existing structure possesses little or no normative standing in such an evaluation sense; there is no basis for an argument to the effect that elements of such a structure are somehow the most desirable because they are observed to exist.

The existing structure does have methodological standing in that any improvement or suggestions for improvement must take that which exists as the starting point for change, the position upon which and from which any changes must be made.

## IV. What Is a "Good" Tax Constitution?

Before alternative suggestions for reform in the fiscal or tax constitution are examined, it is necessary to discuss the issue of normative criteria for judgment. We need some basis on which to argue that one proposed set of fiscal or tax constraints is better or worse than another. There may exist widespread agreement on the desirability for reform, on the need for some change in that which exists, but until and unless some criterion for evaluation is discussed, differing personal preferences may characterize the discourse.

Care is required at precisely this point, however, lest we impose too readily a strictly teleological straightjacket on the argument, a straightjacket that is not at all appropriate. In order to define a "good" set of tax rules, a "good" tax constitution, it is not necessary to have in mind, or even to postulate for purposes of argument, specific end-states that governmental decision-taking under such rules must produce. The appropriate criterion for "goodness" is to be found in the process of agreement on potential change among potential taxpayers rather than in the end-state that such change is intended to insure.[1] A change is defined to be "good" because it is agreed to by members of the community; members do not agree because a change is somehow independently "good."

---

1. For perhaps the best treatment of the distinction between process and end-state criteria, see Robert Nozick, *Anarchy, State and Utopia* (New York, 1974).

If, however, the test is agreement, how can a whole group of potential taxpayers-beneficiaries, even conceptually, be expected to agree on anything? The assignment of tax shares is a zero-sum game; agreement seems impossible on its face. It is here that a constitutional perspective becomes imperative. If tax rules, rather than the in-period distribution or assignment of tax shares, are discussed, it is possible to conceive of general agreement among all potential taxpayers. If a person is uncertain about his own economic position in a sequence of future fiscal periods, when the rules to be chosen are anticipated to remain in effect, he will be led, via his own self-interest, to opt for rules that seem "fair" in the sense that they offer plausibly acceptable or tolerable results regardless of economic position in the community.

In its extreme or limiting variant, the setting for individual choice postulated here is that made familiar by John Rawls.[2] Behind a genuine "veil of ignorance" and in some "original position," the individual knows nothing at all about his own role or position. In less extreme variants, such as that postulated by Gordon Tullock and myself in *The Calculus of Consent*,[3] the individual need only be assumed to be highly uncertain about his own future prospects. In any such choice settings, the only relevant choice is among rules that are expected to remain in effect over a sequence of periods.

Agreement among all persons will not necessarily emerge in such constitutional choice settings, even at some conceptual level. This much must be acknowledged. But the range for disagreement is necessarily narrowed, and dramatically so by comparison with that which characterizes the zero-sum struggle over in-period tax shares. Disagreement at the level of constitutional choice is not disagreement derived from divergencies of personal economic interests of the standard sort, at least in the limit. Disagreement may emerge as a result of differing assessments of the predicted working properties of alternative institutional arrangements. A "bargaining range" of sorts may exist, even in idealized constitutional choice.[4] From this it follows that there may be several possible sets of arrangements or institutions that might emerge, even from the most severely constrained contractual setting. For

2. *A Theory of Justice* (Cambridge, 1971).

3. Ann Arbor, 1962.

4. For a discussion of this bargaining range and the predicted results of contractual agreement, see James M. Buchanan and Roger Faith, "Subjective Elements in Rawlsian Contractual Agreement on Distributional Rules" (Working Paper CE 78-6-3, June 1978).

purposes of discussion, therefore, we must look to fiscal and tax constraints that may possibly satisfy the contractarian criterion while continuing to acknowledge that there may exist other sets of constraints which might equally qualify and which could, in whole or in part, substitute for the particular set under examination.

In the following sections of the paper, I shall examine alternative sets of constitutional constraints on the fiscal powers of government. In any normative evaluation of these constraints, the criterion should be the possible derivation from a genuine constitutional choice–contractarian calculus. Could this set of proposals have emerged from a contractual agreement among persons in the community, each one of whom is, at the moment of choice, uncertain about his own economic position during the sequence of periods in which the constraints are to be operative?

## V. The Generality of Fiscal Rules

The discussion in all of the preceding sections is, in one sense, preliminary to an examination of alternative institutional schemes or arrangements that have roughly the same objective, that of keeping governmental fiscal activities within some proximate relationship to the desires of taxpayers-beneficiaries. In this section, I shall discuss Hayek's proposal for the generality of fiscal rules. Following this, I shall examine proposals for modifying the political decision structure, notably those of Knut Wicksell, proposals that indirectly affect fiscal outcomes. Beyond these proposals, which may be classified as political, I shall then examine more explicit fiscal constraints. These may take several forms. Constitutional limits may be placed on the allowable rate structure of specific tax instruments. The total tax revenue, or level of public outlay, may be restricted to a defined maximum share or proportion of national income or product. Yet another variant involves constitutional restriction on the allowable bases of taxation. Finally, the political competition inherent in fiscal federalism may accomplish indirectly what explicit fiscal constraints are aimed for directly. Each of these alternatives will be examined in concluding parts of this paper.

As noted in the Introduction, Hayek has stressed the importance of generality in fiscal as well as other aspects of law. If the government is required to levy taxes in accordance with "general rules," protection against arbitrary fiscal exploitation may seem to be provided. But what does taxation in accordance with general rules mean in this context?

As I have suggested above in the discussion of existing fiscal constraints, the requirement for generality in taxation has little or no effect unless it is somehow accompanied by a like requirement with respect to the spending or outlay side of the governmental fiscal account. Generality in spending is perhaps easier to define than generality in taxation, even though real-world applications of the generality precept are much less prevalent. To say that government spending must be general would imply that all members of the political community, including the members of decision-makers for government itself, either secure or have access to the same level of publicly financed or publicly supplied goods and services. A restriction to the effect that government could finance only purely public or purely collective goods and services, defined technologically in the Samuelsonian sense of nonexcludability and nonrivalry in consumption, would meet such a requirement. Operationally, however, there is not and could not be any categorical distinction drawn between such goods and services, if indeed they exist, and other goods and services that government might finance or provide. The generality precept might still be satisfied, however, even with impure and partially or fully partitionable goods and services, if provision is such as to insure that each person, each member of the polity, receives an equal share. For example, government could, conceptually, finance the purchase and provision of, say, milk, which is clearly a partitionable "private" good. But the generality requirement would still be met if everyone in the community should be given an equal quantity.

Direct grants of money might even satisfy the generality criterion provided again that all persons get equal payments. Such equal-share grants may seem to negate the very purpose of most fiscal transfer programs, but such grants may, nonetheless, qualify under the Hayekian rule of general law.

The problems that arise with such grants are directly related to those that arise in any attempt to define generality in taxation. Let us suppose that the generality requirement is met on the spending side of the budget. What allocations of tax shares are permissible under the generality precept? Especially in *The Constitution of Liberty*,[5] Hayek argued in favor of proportional

5. Chicago, 1960. Chapter 20, 306–23.

taxation and in opposition to progressive taxation. He implied that proportionality in rates would meet the generality criterion. So long as those who take decisions on behalf of government should, themselves, be subjected to fiscal-tax costs in the same relation to personal incomes as others in the community, there would be some clearly felt restricting influence on expansive outlays, an influence that need not be present under a progressive rate structure.

If governmental outlays should be restricted to the purchase and provision of purely public goods and services, the Hayek argument would be valid. The argument would also hold for "private" or partitionable goods and services that are not retradable because of technological reasons (e.g., haircuts), provided that such goods and services are made available equally to all persons. However, if direct money transfers and/or spending on retradable private goods are allowed, even if such spending is general, proportionality in taxation is not sufficient to exert any constraining influence. Consider a very simple example where direct but general pecuniary transfers are financed through proportional income taxation. Suppose there is a three-person community, with pre-tax incomes of $1000, $100, $100. Constitutionally, transfers must be made equally per head and taxes must be proportional. The two-person majority can, in this setting, fully equalize post-tax, post-transfer incomes by levying a 100 per cent tax and transferring $400 to each of the three persons. (I neglect incentives in this example.) Much the same result could be accomplished even if direct cash transfers should be prohibited, while governmental outlays on partitionable and retradable goods and services are retained as permissible. The proportionality criterion for taxation, in and of itself, may do little or nothing to constrain the fiscal appetites of government, even in those settings where governmental decision-makers pay taxes like everyone else and secure nothing more than their pro-rata shares of governmentally financed benefits.

## VI. The Political Decision Structure

In *Law, Legislation and Liberty,* and notably in the third and concluding volume,[6] Hayek discusses changes in the basic institutions of political decision-

---

6. F. A. Hayek, *Law, Legislation and Liberty,* Volume 3, *The Political Order of a Society of Free Men* (Chicago, forthcoming).

making that might insure adherence to the general rule of law. With respect to fiscal decisions, and as indicated in the citation at the start of this paper, Hayek suggests that the structure of tax rates be set by a separate and distinct "law-making" body, members of which are selected for longer terms and from persons with more restrictive qualifications, while decisions on the levels of taxation (and spending) would remain with ordinary legislative or parliamentary bodies. As the simple numerical example above suggests, however, constraints on the rate structure, even if these should prove highly effective in preventing arbitrary manipulation of tax rates for partisan or short-term political advantage, may not be sufficient to insure against fiscal exploitation. It may be necessary to constrain both the rate structure and the level of taxes.

Constraints may, however, be indirectly exerted through changes in the political decision structure, in the rules for making fiscal decisions for the polity. It is at this point that Knut Wicksell assumes a position of special significance. He is unique among pre-modern economists in recognizing the proclivities of parliamentary majorities to thwart rather than to promote the desires of taxpayers. Wicksell did not, however, propose direct constraints on the taxing powers of government; indeed, he suggested that taxes should be even more flexible than those observed in his time. He sought to reform the rules for political decision-making by replacing majority voting in legislatures with a rule of unanimity. Wicksell recognized that only with an effective unanimity rule could there be any guarantee that governmental spending projects would return expected benefits in excess of costs, would be "efficient" in the standard sense. In order to implement a unanimity rule, to widen potential areas of agreement among all groups of taxpayers, tax-share distributions were to be left as wide open and as flexible as possible.[7]

There can be no quarrel with the claim that the Wicksellian constitution would constrain government's fiscal appetites. We need only to ask: "How much public spending could be observed if all taxes had to be approved unanimously in the legislature?" to get a feel for the answer. The problems with the Wicksellian reforms are the opposite of those suggested with the generality criterion. Governments may be so constrained as to prevent them from financing goods and services that may be desired by the citizenry and which only governments can provide. Wicksell himself recognized the overly

---

7. *Finanztheoretische Untersuchungen* (Jena, 1896).

restrictive nature of the strict unanimity rule, and he proposed departure from the extreme version when he came to practical implementation. He replaced strict unanimity with a qualified voting rule of something on the order of a five-sixths vote of the members of a legislative assembly.

Any shift away from the extremum of unanimity toward less-inclusive voting rules, however, must allow for the prospect of fiscal exploitation of persons and groups who do not accede to the decisions made. A five-sixths decision rule, standing alone as the only constitutional requirement, would not prevent the excluded one-sixth from suffering arbitrary taxation at the expense of the dominant or ruling five-sixths. There is a necessary trade-off between less-inclusive rules which allow for expanded fiscal activities by governments and the prospects for fiscal exploitation of groups that remain outside the ruling coalition. In any constitutional choice calculus, this trade-off must be explored and analyzed, but the predicted results in terms of taxing and spending levels predicted vary within wide limits.[8]

## VII. Tax Rate Limits

In modern Western democracies, little or nothing has been done toward moving toward the achievement of Wicksellian-type reforms in constitutional structure. Further, the fiscal experience of the twentieth century has exacerbated rather than resolved the problems that prompted Wicksell to advance his proposals. Simple majority voting continues to occupy a sacrosanct role in both the theory and the practice of modern politics, for the general electorate as well as in legislative assemblies and in committees. The constraints on fiscal outcomes that are exercised by the existing political decision procedures and/or by the existing legal rules are minimal. In the setting that we observe, therefore, more explicit constraints on governmental taxing and spending powers would seem to be dictated.

These explicit constraints may take any one of several forms. I shall first examine very briefly the possible efficacy of imposing maximum rate limits on specific taxes. Suppose, for example, the existence of a constitutional provision that restricts the taxation of personal income to some maximum

---

8. The analysis in *The Calculus of Consent* was largely concentrated on this trade-off. See James M. Buchanan and Gordon Tullock, *The Calculus of Consent* (Ann Arbor, 1962).

average rate, say, one-third. Such a provision would clearly constrain government's ability to raise revenues from this single source or base. Unless, however, such a restriction should be accompanied by bounds on the allowable bases for taxation generally, the net impact of the restriction on income-tax rate might be minimal. Faced with a maximum-rate limit on one taxable base, a revenue-seeking government could simply shift to alternative bases. Specific rate limits would not be wholly ineffective, and especially as applied to major revenue producers in modern fiscal systems, but such limits would have to be supplemented by other controls. On balance, specific tax rate limits are probably dominated by other forms of fiscal constraint when viewed from the perspective of a potential taxpayer's constitutional choice calculus.

## VIII. Tax Revenues and Total Spending as Shares in National Product or Income

Partly in recognition of the difficulties of constraining government effectively by maximum-rate limits, practical attention shifts to proposals for restricting the size of the government budget, measured in terms of either revenue intake or spending outlay. Absolute limits on total revenues or on total outlay are, of course, conceptually possible, but most proposals here take the form of allowable shares or proportions of the income or product generated in the community. Such ratio or share proposals reflect the view that the primary concern arises with respect to the proportionate rather than with the absolute size of the governmental sector in the economy. Under the ratio-type constraints, tax revenues and total outlays are allowed to increase, but only in line with general economic growth.

The imposition of this sort of fiscal constraint at some constitutional stage requires the substantive determination of a desired relative size of the governmental sector. Such a determination is not necessary in either of the first two constitutional reforms discussed, both of which are purely procedural. The difficulties in settling on an appropriate governmental share, even in terms of some maximal limit, are manifold. The preferred size of the governmental sector, as measured by either revenues or outlays, will vary over time as technology changes, as economic and social characteristics of the political community change, as the efficiency of government itself changes. And unless nonfiscal constraints on governmental activity are also present, the imposition of a binding revenue or spending constraint may do little more than shift the structure of government toward direct regulation and away from taxation.

A second major criticism of ratio- or share-type constraints on revenues or outlays arises from the tendency for maximal limits to become minimal. This feature can be illustrated by the ratio-type proposals that were widely discussed in the United States in 1978. Widespread frustration with the observed explosive growth in taxation and in public spending, and at all levels of government, provoked a varied set of proposals aimed at slowing down the relative increase in government's share in the economy. However, in order to reduce the disruption that might be threatened by overt reductions in budgets, proponents of constitutional ratio-type limits tended to settle on roughly status quo shares as those that would be maximally allowable. But, of course, if such constraints should be constitutionally implemented, any prospects for reducing government's share below status quo levels become very remote.

A further problem with ratio-type fiscal constraints lies in the economic sophistication required on the part of citizens and politicians whose support must be organized to implement any constitutional change. Taxpayers think in terms of specific levies, and of their own treatment under such levies by the taxing authorities. They do not think in terms of such abstractions as total tax revenues or total spending, and surely not in terms of the ratio between two abstract entities, total budgets and total product or income. At best, and even ignoring the difficulties noted above, ratio-type constraints seem much more congenial to the professional economist consultants than to the practicing politicians or to the average taxpayer.

## IX. Limits on Tax Bases

A more suitable approach may be some constitutional control over the bases upon which taxes may be levied, rather than control over either the specific rates of tax on the one hand or over total revenues on the other. Such control over the bases for taxation retains the advantage of the procedural limits in that no constitutional stage determination of the preferred governmental share in the economy is required, at least in the precise sense. To the extent that government is constitutionally precluded from levying taxation on more than a limited number of activities, its revenue share is necessarily restricted, and especially so as the activities excluded from taxation are substitutable for those upon which taxes may be levied.

Consider an apparently extreme, but still relevant, example. Suppose that government is allowed to levy personal taxes on money incomes but that it is constitutionally prohibited from taxing income-in-kind. In such a setting, as income-tax rates increase, taxpayers will, of course, shift toward income-in-kind. This shift generates an excess burden, familiar from analyses of welfare economics. What economists have overlooked, however, is the constraining influence that such potential shifts can exert on government's fiscal appetites. Faced with the prospect that taxpayers can, and will, shift to nontaxable options, even if at some cost, governments will find that maximal-revenue limits are attained at much lower budgetary levels than would be the case if the tax base should be fully "comprehensive."

Consideration of the possible efficacy of base constraints in imposing genuine fiscal controls on government tends to turn upside down precepts drawn from traditional normative theories of taxation, those which emphasize excess burden under equi-revenue models of analysis. "Noncomprehensiveness" rather than "comprehensiveness" becomes a possibly desirable attribute of a tax structure.[9]

Properly chosen tax-base constraints may also be effective in providing incentives for governments or governmental agencies to provide the goods and services valued by the taxpayers themselves rather than prerequisites of bureaucratic office. If the constitutionally allowable bases for taxation are chosen so as to be strongly complementary to the public goods to be provided, governments will find it necessary to perform with tolerable efficiency in order to collect tax revenues. A highway agency charged with producing and maintaining roads will be motivated to fulfill its assigned function if its revenue base is restricted to gasoline and vehicle levies.[10]

As noted with respect to overall constraints on revenues or on spending,

---

9. For a more formal analysis of constraints on bases of tax, see Geoffrey Brennan and James M. Buchanan, "Towards a Tax Constitution for Leviathan," *Journal of Public Economics*, 8 (December 1977), 255–73.

10. For a detailed analysis of this usage of tax-base constraints, see Geoffrey Brennan and James M. Buchanan, "Tax Instruments as Constraints on the Disposition of Public Revenues," *Journal of Public Economics*, 9 (June 1978), 301–18.

tax-base constraints could not, in themselves, be effective in controlling governmental intrusions into the economy until and unless these are accompanied by constraints on governmental regulatory powers. The latter can always substitute for fiscal powers; this is a simple fact that must be reckoned with in any discussions of constitutional reform.

## X. Geographic Limits on Tax Bases: Fiscal Federalism and Voting with the Feet

Political federalism offers a means of limiting tax bases, tax rates, total budgets, as well as the range and scope of governmental regulatory activity. To the extent that fiscal and regulatory powers can be lodged in governmental units smaller in geographic extent than the effective size of the interdependent economy, and with some minimal number of political units, competition among such political units will insure against undue exploitation of citizens, and without explicit constitutional controls. The rights of citizens to migrate freely, to vote with their feet or with their mobile resources, will limit the extent to which their demands for governmentally provided goods and services can be ignored by governmental units, regardless of the personal proclivities of the politicians.

If the central government, the political entity that is coincident in area with the economy (and which because of this coincidence assumes some role in policing the economy itself such as insuring free trade and migration among subunits), can be restricted constitutionally in its range of functions, explicit fiscal constraints may not be needed. And, indeed, the federal structure of the United States which vested residual fiscal as well as regulatory powers with the separate states throughout the early part of the nation's history, may have rendered additional constitutional constraints on government's fiscal proclivities unnecessary. As the central government has come to be more dominant, however, and notably during the middle years of the twentieth century, the need for additional constraints has clearly emerged. The devolution or decentralization of fiscal and regulatory powers, once these have been seized by the central government, may prove more difficult to achieve than the more direct constraints on the central government's exercise of such powers, in any of the forms examined above.

# XI. Conclusions

The formal analysis of such controls on government has scarcely commenced. Political economists must forgo their temptations to tell governments what they "should do," and spend more time predicting what governments "will do" under varying forms of constraint. Only on such analysis can solid proposals for constitutional reform be based. Wicksell led the way; both his and Hayek's proposals deserve a better hearing than they have got. Normative discourse must shift to the stage of constitutional reform.

The proposals for constitutional reform aimed at curbing the fiscal powers of modern Leviathan are not, of course, mutually exclusive. All of the proposals discussed in this paper, and others, deserve attention, analysis, discussion, and serious consideration as means toward accomplishing what should be accepted as a legitimate objective. Modern public choice, which has only been developed within the decades since World War II, now allows us to understand more about the way governments work. This understanding in turn suggests that governments, like markets, work effectively only if they are constrained by constitutional rules, by "laws and institutions" that serve to keep various natural proclivities to excess within bounds or limits.

## Summary

### Constitutional constraints on governmental taxing power

Hayek has suggested basic change in the fiscal constitution. He proposes to separate the collective decision concerning the allocation of tax shares and the collective decision concerning the overall level of taxation, assigning these decisions to different bodies. Hayek's proposal is only one among many possible changes in the fiscal constitution of democratic government, all of which may be aimed at limiting the abuse of the taxing power.

This paper examines, in broad and general terms, alternative constitutional means of limiting the taxing power of government. Limits on tax rates, on tax bases, and on total taxes as shares in income are evaluated against criteria for a "good" fiscal constitution.

## PART FOUR

# *The Fiscal Constitution*

# The Tax System as Social Overhead Capital

## A Constitutional Perspective on Fiscal Norms

*Geoffrey Brennan and James Buchanan*

## I. Introduction

The object of concern in this paper is the tax system.

This is, of course, a totally conventional preoccupation—some might say, the *central* preoccupation—of the public finance specialist. However, although our subject matter is orthodox, our perspective is not. We shall not be concerned with the question of what particular tax system is the "ideal" one. Nor shall we deal with the effects of particular tax changes on economic growth, an issue which for many doubtless represents the main focus of this Congress.

Our concerns are in a way more basic. Our aim is to bring to bear on the tax system a particular *perspective*—a perspective that is rather different from that implied by the reigning orthodoxy. For, within orthodox public finance, the tax system is conceived as a set of instruments by means of which "government" pursues certain policy objectives. Within our alternative "constitutional" perspective, the tax system is instead viewed as a *set of rules* under which the individuals who make up a polity pursue *their own* objectives, both those that are implemented collectively and those implemented

From *Public Finance and Economic Growth,* Proceedings of the 37th Congress of the International Institute of Public Finance, Tokyo, 1981, ed. Karl Roskamp (Detroit: Wayne State University Press, 1983), 41–54. Reprinted by permission of the publisher and the International Institute of Public Finance.

privately. This perspective not only provides a rather different conception of what the tax system really *is;* it also directs attention to some implications that the tax structure, and changes in it, have for economic growth—implications that are both significant and too often ignored.

Our central point is that the tax system, whatever its precise nature, represents *social capital.* It does so in the sense that a workable tax system is both costly to accumulate and costly to destroy. These costs arise primarily because tax law, like virtually all law, depends for its value on its predictability and its constancy. Frequent changes in the tax law destroy much of what it is that the tax law ought properly to provide. In other words, the tax system is to be viewed as having a *quasi-constitutional* status. That is, it represents not merely an *outcome* of the political process, but more particularly an important part of the *context* within which political and market decisions are made. In part, this "contextual" role derives from the fact that a whole range of private market decisions—what and when to consume, whether or not to take risks, how much to save, and how to hold one's savings—are all crucially dependent on the manner in which the tax structure is organized. Less obvious, but no less critical, the tax system also determines the *cost-sharing arrangements* for collectively provided goods and services, and thus the "price" that each voter-taxpayer faces in "buying" such goods and services through the political mechanism. In this sense, the tax structure is a more basic element in the social framework than are many other aspects of political reality which *derive from* the tax system rather than being determined along with it.

Once the quasi-constitutional status of the tax system is recognized, it seems natural to regard that status as something it is the special role of the public finance expert to protect. At the very least, one ought to require of the would-be fiscal reformer a certain sensitivity to the nature of that which he seeks to reform, and a certain attentiveness to the costs of change. Such sensitivity does not emerge so readily from a conception of the tax system as a "set of policy instruments for particular government objectives": rather, tax policy takes its place in the line-up along with subsidy policy, regulation, expenditure policy, wage policy, etc., as just another weapon in the policy armory—the special status of tax matters tends to be lost.

At the "policy" level, our general argument might be conceived as commending some set of rules or institutional arrangements that place limits on the frequency, and perhaps the extent of tax law changes. But our central object is not so much to generate policy conclusions as it is to hold up an alternative conception of what the tax system really is. Our fundamental conviction is that some sort of *"constitutional understanding"* is imperative in public finance; and that some form of *fiscal constitution* is a crucial ingredient in generating long-term sustainable economic growth.

It is useful to present our argument initially in the most general terms. In section II, we set out some of the language and conceptual apparatus that is preliminary to the main argument. In section III, by appeal to some simple game theory examples, we set out the case for a durable constitution, and then apply this to the fiscal context (sections IV and V) to spell out the implications for tax reform and tax change. Section VI offers some brief concluding remarks.

## II. Some Preliminaries

When we talk of a "constitution" in this setting, we will mean the set of rules which determine the ways in which individuals interact in the social structure. The standard analogy is with the rules of some parlor game (poker, chess, or bridge), which lay down such things as what plays are legitimate, how the winner is determined, and perhaps limits on stakes. Such rules do not, of course, represent a total description of any particular play of the game, still less of all possible plays: they simply describe the rules within which all *legitimate* plays must take place. Just as we can distinguish between the rules of bridge and the play of a particular hand so we distinguish between the "constitution" of a society (or *rules* for interaction) and the particular political and economic outcomes that might emerge from the *actual* interactions among persons and groups within that set of rules (or "constitution").

In its most general form, the constitution of a society can be depicted in terms of a number of central elements, which would include:

  i. a set of "rights," to both person and property;

  ii. a structure for enforcing such rights against other individuals;

  iii. a set of rules relating to how those rights might be exchanged;

  iv. a set of rules concerning how collective decisions shall be made;

v. a set of rules defining the range over which such collective decisions shall be applied.[1]

Any particular such constitution need not, of course, be written or explicitly codified: it may simply reflect an emergent and consensual understanding of "how things are done"—an understanding that individuals generally abide by, and which is enforced by appeals to attitudes widely shared.[2] In many cases, however, it will be important to have the constitution, or elements of it, rendered *explicitly,* and enforced via institutions that are created as an integral part of the constitutional order itself.

In this paper, we shall focus on aspects of any constitutional structure that bear directly on tax matters. In this connection, we shall define the *"fiscal constitution"* as those rules of the socio-economic game that describe the tax and expenditure structure of the public sector (broadly defined). In a sense, the fiscal constitution is one aspect of those rules which set out what individuals, acting *collectively,* may and may not do to one another (a subset of [iv] and [v] above). A restriction on the *taking* of property, for example, would be an element in the fiscal constitution, thus defined. Requirements for *uniformity* of taxation, specifications of what can (and cannot) be subject to tax, and any limits on rates that can be applied would be other examples. So would restrictions on the *domain* of government spending and on public budgeting *procedures* (including restrictions on the direct diversion of tax revenues for the private uses of politicians, administrators, or bureaucrats).

We should note that all these are examples of *rules* of the "fiscal game," and are not particular plays within such a "game." Under any such set of fiscal rules, a wide range of particular outcomes is possible, depending on the "plays" of the various actors in the political processes through which collective decisions are actually reached.

Orthodox public finance, in its normative variants, has been largely concerned with what these particular outcomes "ought to be," in terms of the familiar criteria of "efficiency," "equity," "employment," "economic growth," or some weighted combination of these. By contrast, the profession has not

---

1. Following James M. Buchanan, *The Limits of Liberty* (Chicago: University of Chicago Press, 1975).

2. See Lester Hunt, "Some Advantages of Social Control: An Individualist Defense," *Public Choice* 36, no. 1 (March 1981): 3–16.

paid very much attention to the "rules" under which such outcomes emerge. The constitutional approach focuses exclusively on these rules. Such a focus suggests that anyone who is to play the political game, including the would-be economic advisor, ought to pay attention to its rules, and have some sense of why such rules are important. It also suggests that the primary scope for better outcomes lies in the changing of the rules, and not in preaching to the players.

## III. The Significance of Rules

Why are *rules* so important? Why indeed is a *constitution* necessary at all?

In public finance (or indeed in economics and the social sciences generally), the subject matter for analysis is the interaction of persons within a framework of social order. The observed patterns of outcomes are generated by the separate actions of many individual actors. Outcomes *emerge*, as it were. They are not produced as if by the action of a single agent. For any one person who acts in such a process, his own preferred course of action depends on what he predicts other persons will do, and *vice versa*. Within some limits, the individual must remain uncertain as to how others will act, but chaos rather than order would surely be present if persons were required to act in total ignorance as to the behavior of others. Predictability is provided by *rules* for behavior which, taken as a set, provide a shell or setting within which the separately acting persons generate "social" results that are properly characterized as embodying meaningful order. For the individual actor, rules set limits on the uncertainties about the behavior of others: rules establish boundaries. And, by so doing, they greatly facilitate "social efficiency."

The elementary principles of what might be called a "normative theory of rules" or of "constitutions" can best be demonstrated through the use of a series of some highly simplified two-person, two-strategy interaction illustrations, or "games," presented in the subsections below.

### Symmetrical Self-Enforcing Rule

Two trains have just pulled into adjacent platforms at the station. Mr. A is on one train, and he wishes to change quickly to the other before it departs. Mr. B is on the other train, and wishes to change to the train that A is quitting.

B's action

|  | right | left |
|---|---|---|
| right | [10, 10] | [0, 0] |
| left | [0, 0] | [10, 10] |

A's action

*Figure 1*

Connecting the two platforms is an overhead bridge, just wide enough for two people to pass safely provided that each person takes a different side of the bridge. Within the time limits, there is no time for A (or B) to communicate by word or action which side of the bridge he is intending to use. Clearly, in this case, if there is a well-established rule that both A and B observe and expect the other to know and observe, each can catch his train successfully. If no such rule exists, or if one or other party is ill-informed, there is, let us say, an even chance that A and B will collide and both miss their trains.

We can depict this simple interaction in terms of the noncooperative game matrix of Figure 1. Each "player" has two strategies—left or right. The pay-offs to each outcome are indicated in the cells of the matrix, in which the first number is the return to A and the second number is the return to B.

The crucial feature of the interaction illustrated in Figure 1, and of those to be discussed below, is that the set of rules has value because it provides *information*—information that would be more costly to provide in other ways. The information thus provided depends partly on the *durability* of the rule. Consider, for example, the situation in Figure 1 if the rule should be determined, not once-and-for-all, but by a coin toss each morning—heads means left, tails right. The chances that A and B will know the prevailing rule seem slight, and the virtues of having a rule at all are almost entirely lost.

Note that, in this case, it does not matter to either player what the particular rule of action is—whether to keep to the right, or to keep to the left. All that matters is that there *be* a rule. There is, for this reason, no enforcement problem in ensuring that each individual will "play by the rules": once A believes that B will keep to the left, so will he. Neither individual can benefit from breaking the rule in any way.

## Non-symmetrical rules

The sorts of rules that are of most interest to the public finance specialist are *not* self-enforcing: they are ones that require the coercive power of the state to enforce. One example of an interaction in which such rules are required is the familiar prisoners' dilemma interaction, which underlies much of the modern theory of market failure. For our purposes here, however, it is not useful to rehearse the familiar analysis: we direct attention instead to a variant of the interaction in Figure 1, one that is, we believe, particularly relevant to the question of tax rules.

To do so, let us alter our initial example slightly. Let A and B now be the drivers of cars heading towards a one-lane bridge. Mr. A is travelling from north to south; Mr. B, from south to north. They arrive at the bridge simultaneously: one must give way or they will crash. But this time A and B are *not* indifferent as to who gives way. Nor are they necessarily indifferent as to the rule that ultimately prevails: each may *care* whether the "give way" sign is planted at the north or south end of the bridge. The nature of the interaction here can be depicted in the matrix shown in Figure 2.

As in Game 1 there is no unique "equilibrium" outcome in this game: each individual needs to know what action the other will take before he can make his own "best" choice. And as in Game 1, there are definite social advantages in having *some* rule—the miserable $[-10, -10]$ outcome can then be avoided entirely. Here, however, it is not clear that it is possible to secure agreement on any *particular* rule, because the opportunity cost of agreeing to any given rule, for the *relatively* disadvantaged player, is the forgone possibility of securing the rule much more advantageous to himself. For exam-

B's action

|  |  | give way | proceed |
|---|---|---|---|
|  | give way | $[-1, -1]$ | $[-1, 15]$ |
| A's action | proceed | $[10, -1]$ | $[-10, -10]$ |

*Figure 2*

ple, the cost to A of the rule that requires that he give way is the additional eleven utils/dollars that he might have received from the reverse rule that requires B to give way. Consequently, while both A and B might agree to the desirability of some rule *in principle*, they may not agree on any particular rule: an institutional procedure under which the rule to be imposed is determined, say, *at random* might secure unanimous endorsement, even though no *particular* rule could be agreed upon unanimously.[3]

Suppose that, somehow, the rule that emerges is the one that requires A to give way. Note that A has an incentive to break the rule if he thinks he can get away with it. If, for example, in a particular instance there is a *fifty-fifty* chance that B will reach the bridge after A does and hence that B will stop to avoid collision, then we can show that A will rationally violate the give-way rule and proceed. To see this, note that the expected return to A of violating the rule in this case is:

$E_A$ = probability of collision $\times$ cost of provision

+ probability of proceeding safely $\times$ benefit to proceeding safely.

By assumption, the relevant probabilities are 50 percent, and the relevant pay-offs can be read off from the lower row of Figure 2. Thus,

$$E_A = \frac{1}{2}(-10) + \frac{1}{2}(10) = 0,$$

but the return to giving way is $(-1)$, which is less than $E_A$. Consequently, if there is a fifty-fifty chance (or better) that A will not crash if he disobeys the give-way rule, he will proceed. The give-way rule will therefore have to be enforced if it is to act as a rule at all.

There is then a case for some enforcement agency being operative in this game, just as in the prisoners' dilemma case. But though individuals in the prisoners' dilemma case may seek to *break* the law, there is never a benefit to

3. In our illustrative example, we assume that side-payments or compensations, in money or other goods, are not possible. To the extent that such payments are possible, A and B might, of course, agree on one of the nonsymmetrical rules. Side-payments in effect convert the nonsymmetrical pay-off structure into one that is, at least potentially, symmetrical. For purposes of our generalized analysis, we want to remain within the non-symmetrical pay-off example.

either party in *abolishing* the rule or inhibiting enforcement generally. Nor, in the conventional case, is there any advantage to be gained to either party from a *change* in the law.

In our example here, by contrast, order is precarious for a reason over and beyond the familiar free-rider incentive problem in the standard prisoners' dilemma. In Game 2, individuals have an incentive not merely to break the law unilaterally but to *subvert the rule of law* itself. One or another player (whichever one happens to be the relatively disadvantaged in pay-offs) may expect to gain from a total breakdown of law followed by a return to the state of nature, from which he might expect a new recontracting to occur. If, in such recontracting, he expects that there is some positive probability that a *different* rule will emerge—this time more favorable to him—the subversion of the originally prevailing law may seem a fully rational course of action.[4]

Equivalently, although both parties recognize the importance of the rule's *stability* in serving the desired information-providing role, the relatively disadvantaged party will always seek to have the rule changed—even though this involves a "period of adjustment" in which there will be necessary uncertainty over the prevailing set of rules. Over this adjustment period, there will be expected net damage to *all* parties: cell 4 in Figure 2 will prevail more than otherwise.

Our discussion is not intended to show that changes in the law or the rules are never desirable. What the analysis does indicate is the logical coherence of the "conservative" view that there is a presumptive case against changing the rules, except where such change is no more than an accommodation to widely established practice. Such a case springs naturally out of a recognition of the "information-creating" role that law plays in human interactions. The law is a form of public capital: it depends in part on its durability for its value.

What the discussion also indicates is that we can expect continual pressure to "reform" the law, even when everyone would agree *ex ante* that law

---

4. Something of this sort seems to have underlain Hobbes' anxiety about the fragility of the rule of law. In this sense, to conceive of the Hobbesian analysis of political order as an application of the prisoners' dilemma interaction and of "free-rider" problems as traditionally posed in public goods theory seems somewhat misconceived.

should be stable and even where the prevailing law is no worse than any alternative. Furthermore, even where law reform may possibly involve a change in rules that represents a genuine improvement on the *status quo,* the change may still not be desirable once it is recognized that change itself destroys a capital value. It is as if the individual recognizes, after a time, that the house he has built on his estate is not the best house that he might have built with the money—but this recognition is not sufficient generally to induce him to knock down the existing house and start again. Likewise, the recognition that the prevailing law is not the "best" is not sufficient grounds for law reform.

## IV. The Tax Law

The general "principles" that emerge from an understanding of rules (from a constitutional perspective) can be captured in a few simple propositions:

1. rules provide for regularity in actors' behavior, regularity that has value because of the information that it conveys;
2. changes in rules violate that regularity and are hence inherently costly;
3. although the presence of some rule has value, there may be no one *particular* rule regarded as best by all actors—hence, many actors may want a change in rules though they cannot agree as to what change they want;
4. even where there *is* a single "best rule," it will not be costless to achieve a change from some "inferior" rule—hence, an "inferior" rule may in fact be best if it happens to be what prevails.

All these propositions seem to us to be totally valid in the particular application to tax law. Consider each proposition in turn.

### TAX LAW AND CERTAINTY

It has long been recognized that the entire structure of the modern economic system—depending as it does on accumulation, investment, and complex exchange—requires the existence of well-defined and well-protected property rights. In the absence of such rights, life would indeed be "solitary, poor, nasty, brutish, and short," as Thomas Hobbes reminded us. The justification for the powers of the state lay, in Hobbes' view, precisely in the need to create and defend recognizable rights to property and person. Yet, the protection of individuals and their property from the ravages of others will not ensure the security from which accumulation and complex exchange might spring, if those private rights remain at risk from the ravages of the *state* itself. Limits must be set on the power of the state to *interfere* with the property rights the state is supposed to protect. Such limits involve restrictions on the state's power to *take*. They may also incorporate restrictions on the state's power to tax *in toto,* and on the ability of the state to adjust its taxing arrangements with excessive frequency. Effective limits may, of course, be embodied in the operative rules concerning collective decision-making. It may be argued that electoral competition under simple majority rule may be sufficient to constrain outcomes within tolerable bounds. Whether this is so or not,[5] it seems clear that a tolerable social order requires secure property rights—property rights secure *both* from private predation and theft *and* from the whimsies of an arbitrary state.

## THE COSTS OF TAX CHANGE

To illustrate the significance of all this in the tax law context, consider two possible regimes. In the first, the tax system is liable to "reform" annually: a lump-sum poll tax one year gives way to a tax on profits the next, which in turn is replaced by a beer and spirits excise, and then a wages tax, and so on. In this regime, the citizen can never know what the tax rate on any activity that he undertakes will be; he knows only that there is some nonnegligible chance that he will lose virtually the entire value of anything he accumulates, that the particular industry in which he seeks to invest will be obliterated and so on. In the second regime, by contrast, any tax system decided on must prevail for two decades: the individual can plan his economic future over a twenty-year time horizon in full knowledge of what tax arrangements he will face. It seems difficult to imagine that accumulation, entrepreneurship, and consequent growth would be higher in the first of these societies than the second, almost irrespective of what the particular tax chosen in the second regime happens to be.

---

5. See Geoffrey Brennan and James M. Buchanan, *The Power to Tax: Analytical Foundations of a Fiscal Constitution* (New York: Cambridge University Press, 1980), chap. 2.

## THE PRESSURE FOR TAX CHANGE

It almost goes without saying that the tax system is always vulnerable to the workings of special interests. Virtually every citizen would like a tax break in his own favor—and as anyone who has been involved in any tax reform exercise will no doubt testify there is never any shortage of special pleading for concessional tax treatment from almost every quarter.

What is a more germane consideration for the profession, however, is the pressure for tax reform that arises from the "tax reform specialists"—members of the revered profession of public finance experts whose training and interests equip them so well for the tax reform exercise. Nor is the pressure for tax reform among this group solely to be explained in terms of income maximization (though that helps). Every good public finance man worthy of his salt would surely like to feel that he has had "an influence" on the tax structure—to bequeath to society a sample of his fiscal creativity. These are, after all, the terms in which we justify our existence to ourselves.

Yet it does seem at times as if tastes for alternative tax systems among the cognoscenti are a little like tastes in hats. One man likes accruals taxation of capital gains, another the integrated company income tax, another the exemption of mortgage interest, another the inclusion of imputed rent. Some are pure Haig-Simons men; others extol the consumption/expenditure tax. And so on and so on.

Now, it can be queried whether our record, in terms of effective reforms implemented as a profession, is particularly distinguished. But the question our discussion here poses, is whether, if we had had much more influence, it would have mattered much to anyone but ourselves. The simple truth is probably that a certain amount of what we urge so forcefully is pure self-indulgence. Certainly it is difficult to find within the profession any widespread sympathy for the idea of leaving well enough alone. There seems to have been relatively little basic understanding of the point that the tax system *is* a piece of social capital, and that changing it involves *destroying* social capital.

To be sure, any tax policy advocate will talk *as if* the particular "reforms" that *he* is proposing will be the last ever to be effected—that *his* system will prevail for the foreseeable future. But any change in the tax law implies that the tax law is *susceptible* to change—and the pressure for reform necessarily implies a shift towards more change rather than less. On balance, the profession has, possibly implicitly, stood for more change: the ancient wisdom to the effect that "an old tax is a good tax" seems to have been pretty much forgotten.

## V. Tax Change and the Fiscal Constitution

Whether or not the costs of excessive change in the tax law are recognized by the tax policy experts, they do seem to be recognized in the rules and procedures of prevailing tax reform arrangements. For in most countries, tax reform is accorded a quasi-constitutional status. In the English-dominated part of the world, for example, tax reform is largely entrusted to specially assigned "Royal Commissions" or Committees of Enquiry (the Carter Commission in Canada and the Asprey and Mathews Committees in Australia exemplify).[6] Such committees operate explicitly *outside* the arena of regular parliamentary politics. Neither politicians, nor professional bureaucrats, are (typically) members of such bodies.

Apparently it is recognized that the determination of relative tax burdens and the structure of the tax system more generally are not matters that should be dealt with simply in the context of annual budgetary deliberations. Moreover, although a "call for submissions" from interested parties and "public hearings" are part of the normal tax reform committee's procedures, it is clear that the committee's task is not simply that of weighing up a whole array of special pleas and deciding which should prevail. The task is rather to provide recommendations as to which tax system is best for the community in the light of abstract normative criteria—often enough laid down in the terms of reference. In that sense, the standard normative framework for orthodox tax analysis could be viewed as providing a set of *constitutional* rules by which tax systems can be evaluated. The notions of "horizontal and vertical equity," "neutrality," and "simplicity" take on, in this view, status as elements of a fiscal constitution.[7]

6. J. G. Head, "Issues in Australian Tax Policy for the Eighties," Anzaas Conference Paper (Brisbane, 1981, mimeographed).

7. As in James M. Buchanan, "Taxation in Fiscal Exchange," *Journal of Public Economics* 6 (March 1976): 17–29.

More important for our purposes, however, is the implication that the tax system should not be decided merely as a part of regular political processes—that effective "limits" on both the nature and frequency of tax reform are required, over and above limits embodied in majoritarian electoral constraints. And it is the limits on the *frequency,* rather than the *nature,* of tax changes that deserve particular emphasis here, precisely because it is the frequency aspects that the profession seems not to have emphasized.[8]

None of this is, of course, to deny the necessity of occasional tax reform exercises: tax systems do tend to decay somewhat over time, partly in response to parliamentary/Congressional "fiddling" and partly in response to the creative responses of imaginative taxpayers and their advisers who exploit ambiguities and omissions in the tax law. There may even be changes in common notions of what fiscal justice requires, and genuine advances in professional understandings of the workings of alternative tax regimes.

Nor is it to deny the importance of doing the occasional tax reform "properly"—of getting the tax system reasonably efficient and tolerably fair. In this connection, it should perhaps be noted that not only does fairness have an intrinsic value, it also seems likely that tax systems that are patently unfair are unlikely to survive for long periods—at least without potentially costly enforcement and/or social unrest. In that sense, tax systems that are widely regarded as inequitable are themselves likely to be less than optimally "durable" and, to the extent that they encourage taxpayer dishonesty, tend to breed a disrespect for the law in general that can enormously depreciate the overall social fabric.

Nevertheless, it can hardly be denied that the public finance profession has been one of the most consistent and vocal lobbies for tax reform over the last thirty years or so in almost every country. And this has no doubt given the impression to the public at large that the "experts" believe that tax re-

---

8. In the third volume of *Law, Legislation and Liberty* (*The Political Economy of a Free People* [Chicago: University of Chicago Press, 1979]), Professor F. A. Hayek recognizes the constitutional nature of the tax-share structure. His reform proposals include the assignment of the authority to determine tax-share allocation to a "senior" special representative assembly devoted to making "laws," that would, once chosen, be expected to remain in being for relatively long periods. The "lower" representative assembly would "govern" in the standard way, and would be empowered to set budgetary levels, and hence, tax rates, within the determined tax-share structure.

form is necessarily and desirably a continuous on-going process. Nor is such an impression entirely unjustified. Orthodox analysis cultivates a view of the tax system as a set of "policy instruments," through which "governments" can pursue their various objectives; as those objectives change, so ought the tax instruments through which their achievement is sought.

Indeed, in tax advocacy rhetoric, reformist zeal often seems to imply the view that the current situation is so bad that *any* change would be a change for the better. It needs to be stated categorically therefore that precisely the opposite presumption is the appropriate one. Unless we can be sure that the tax system finally emerging from the tax reform process will be distinctly better than what we have—and maybe not even then—it may be best to do nothing.

# Tax Reform without Tears

### James Buchanan and Geoffrey Brennan

This paper traces the distributional implications of departures from an idealized tax base. Orthodox public finance specialists operating within the conventions of tax orthodoxy have traditionally been preoccupied with this question. Seeking the twin objectives of efficiency and equity, the standard analyst tries to specify both an ideal tax base and a rate structure that should be applied to that base in order to distribute the cost of public expenditures equitably. In theory nondistorting taxes make it possible simultaneously to achieve "perfect" vertical and horizontal equity (however defined) with no efficiency loss induced by the tax system. In practice these various objectives conflict with one another because perfectly nondistorting taxes do not exist. For example, a more progressive rate structure will distort leisure-effort choices more severely; it will discriminate more between people according to the time pattern of their income streams; and a minimally distorting tax will vary between otherwise economic equals according to their elasticities of demand for leisure.[1]

By a kind of perverse luck the tax system contains so many distortions that some reforms advance all objectives. Closing some of the major loopholes in the personal income tax is one such reform. Such loopholes not only reduce efficiency and discriminate unfairly among economic equals but also violate common norms of vertical equity by offering chinks in the

From *The Economics of Taxation,* ed. Henry J. Aaron and Michael J. Boskin (Washington, D.C.: Brookings Institution, 1980), 33–53. Reprinted by permission of the publisher.
1. Given that averaging schemes are characteristically imperfect.

fiscal armor through which the incomes of many of the richest taxpayers all but disappear.

Empirical support for this latter contention is not hard to find. Even the most cursory glance at the relevant statistics indicates that the rich use these loopholes far more than do the poor. In fact, some commentators see the departure of actual income tax payments from those implied by the nominal rate structure as a prime reason why the U.S. tax system as a whole is roughly proportional rather than progressive.[2] If such loopholes do indeed undermine the major instrument of progression in the federal tax system, hope for any genuine overall progressivity is scant. It is conceivable, moreover, that the effect of loopholes on vertical equity is more significant than the effect on horizontal equity; if people within income classes make much the same use of loopholes, and the major differences are among income classes,[3] then loopholes undermine *vertical,* not horizontal, equity. On this basis it is tempting to make vertical equity considerations a major—perhaps *the* major—justification for tax reform; many commentators over the past decade have yielded to such a temptation.

At the same time, popular discussion of tax reform has tended to relegate efficiency considerations to a secondary place. "Excess burden" issues, it is claimed, involve allocative losses that are "small and difficult to measure."[4] And even where excess burden is discussed it is often treated as if efficiency losses fall only in general and not on anyone in particular.

In this paper we explore the distributional impact of excess burdens. We claim that a direct relationship exists between the extent to which taxpayers exploit loopholes and the size of the excess burden those loopholes induce. We hold that this excess burden falls precisely on the exploiters themselves. Several conclusions follow. First, the empirical measures of effective progression that are based on the ratio of actual tax payments to an idealized tax

---

2. See Joseph A. Pechman and Benjamin A. Okner, *Who Bears the Tax Burden?* (Brookings Institution, 1974), for much of the relevant data; and George F. Break and Joseph A. Pechman, *Federal Tax Reform: The Impossible Dream?* (Brookings Institution, 1975), for related commentary.

3. An outcome consistent with the scenario envisaged by Martin Feldstein in "On the Theory of Tax Reform," *Journal of Public Economics,* vol. 6 (July–August 1976), 77–104.

4. Pechman and Okner, *Who Bears the Tax Burden?* 3.

base (for example, total income) are themselves misleading; the nominal rate structure offers a measure of true progression that is not obviously inferior to these estimates of "effective" rates. To the extent that the nominal rate structure is progressive, so generally will be burden sharing. Second, and for the same reason, empirical estimates of horizontal equity exhibited by different taxes or tax regimes may be rather misleading. Third, far from being "small and difficult to measure," allocative losses must be concomitantly large if the exploitation of tax loopholes is as significant as the standard discussions relate; and the measurement of such losses presents few problems not also present in estimating effective progression.

This analysis suggests that failure to include the excess burden attributable to loopholes leads to exaggerated estimates of their distributional effects. By contrast, arguments for tax reform resting on inefficiencies caused by loopholes receive too little attention.

In fact, *efficiency* considerations allow ample scope for legitimate tax reform, and arguably they are ethically superior and politically more practical than arguments based on equity considerations. Instead of emphasizing the injustice or unfairness of the existing system, as evidenced by the alleged failure of the "rich" to pay their "fair shares," tax reformers should place more stress on economic waste, the burden of which is borne largely, if not exclusively, by those who find it advantageous to make behavioral adjustments in response to tax loopholes. Moreover, emphasis on increased progression, as an end in itself, may possibly represent a strategic mistake on the part of the reform protagonists. Tax reform may become a "possible dream" when it is recognized that after taxpayers have adjusted to loopholes, those who avail themselves of special rules and regulations are not materially better off than they would have been in the absence of such rules and regulations. *All* taxpayers might agree on a reform that improves the post-tax position of all parties, by reducing excess burdens. Meaningful tax reform can be, and should be, examined and discussed as a "positive-sum game" and not as the "zero-sum game" that it is often made out to be. A corollary, obscured in the standard reformist emphasis on increased progression, is that a reduction in excess burden and an accompanying increase in revenue collections could make possible lower marginal rates of tax, quite apart from any shift toward comprehensiveness of the tax base.

Very little in this paper is new. Most of the points are implicit in orthodox discussion, and for the purposes of this paper we accept that logic completely.[5] We merely emphasize certain oversights in traditional tax reform literature and urge a more thorough integration of equity and efficiency norms. When this integration is made, the importance of those efficiency norms emerges.

Our argument proceeds as follows. First, we illustrate the problem by appeal to two simple, rather stylized, numerical examples. Then, we present a more general algebraic/diagrammatic treatment and introduce our central results. Next, we demonstrate the possibility of tax reform via marginal rate reduction, and then we refer to the strictly horizontal equity problems posed by consensual changes. Finally, we offer a brief conclusion.

Perhaps, however, one clarifying comment should be offered here. Not *all* departures from an ideally neutral comprehensive tax base induce adjustments by *all* taxpayers to minimize tax payments. But we do believe that all such departures have that tendency. We do not argue that all taxpayers can adjust equally easily. Thus we do not—and need not—argue that the horizontal and vertical equity case for closing tax loopholes is entirely inappropriate, except in the limiting cases that our numerical examples illustrate. For this reason our discussion is cast in terms of the "exploitation" of tax loopholes by "rich" taxpayers—the object of much indignation on the part of many tax reform specialists—although it is in fact somewhat more general. Both the horizontal and vertical equity cases for closing tax loopholes are overstated *to the extent that there is any behavioral adjustment to tax loopholes at all.* On that basis the relative importance of efficiency arguments correspondingly grows, and the possibility of genuinely consensual tax reform increases, together with its political practicability and ethical desirability.

## Two Numerical Examples

We first present two numerical examples based on highly restrictive assumptions with sharply contrasting results. In each example we assume that peo-

5. We *have* attacked it in another place. See Geoffrey Brennan and James Buchanan, "Towards a Tax Constitution for Leviathan," *Journal of Public Economics*, vol. 8 (December 1977), 255–73.

ple are indifferent to alternative sources of income, that they face linear rates of transformation among these alternative income sources over relevant ranges of choice, and that the tax rate structure is a simplified two-bracket schedule. As noted below, the examples differ from each other in one critically important assumption.

The pre-tax setting is identical in the two examples. Consider a two-person model (which may be extended to include many persons so long as each additional person is assumed to be identical to one of the two described here). Person 1 earns $10,000 per period from some standard income source, while Person 2 earns $20,000 per period from the same source. A progressive tax of 10 percent on the first $10,000 and 20 percent on the second $10,000 is imposed on personal income. The government expects to collect $4,000— $1,000 from Person 1 and $3,000 from Person 2.

After a period of behavioral adjustment the results are different. Person 2 locates a source of nontaxable income and shifts some of his efforts to earning income from this source.[6] Person 1, by assumption, continues to earn $10,000 in pre-tax income from the taxable source and to pay the anticipated tax. Actual tax payments made by the two persons, when measured, prove to be roughly proportional to measured gross incomes (from both sources) rather than progressive.

Under what conditions can we properly infer that Person 2 has escaped his "fair share" of the tax and that an increase in the effective rate of progression is indicated, something that might be accomplished by taxing the nontaxable source?

### THE EQUITY MODEL

Consider the following post-tax equilibrium. Suppose that Person 2 secures $15,000 from the taxable source and pays a total tax of $2,000; in addition he

---

6. Preferential tax treatment of income sources or income uses is often based on the actual or alleged presence of such external benefits. Legislatures may deliberately create tax-reducing options for the purpose of modifying private behavior. The analysis of this paper can readily be extended to include this, but to attempt to discuss the implications here would distract from the main argument. In any case the conventional emphasis has been on the absence of such spillover benefits or, more correctly, on the inappropriateness of such considerations for the structure of income taxation.

can earn $5,000 from a nontaxable source. His labor input is unchanged and his gross pre-tax income remains at $20,000. But he has increased post-tax income from $17,000 to $18,000 by shifting some of his income receipts to the nontaxable source. The government finds itself with $1,000 less than anticipated. Note that the government's loss is equal to Person 2's gain. From this it follows that there is *no* excess burden of the tax; there is no net allocative inefficiency involved in the tax-induced shift between income sources, because Person 2's productivity is the same in both the taxable and nontaxable activities.

## THE COUNTERMODEL

Suppose now that the nontaxable source of income is only four-fifths as productive as the taxable source. Suppose further that after a period of adjustment, Person 2 earns $18,888—$14,444 from the taxable source and $4,444 from the nontaxable source. In this situation, note that the tax actually collected from each person is 10 percent of gross income ($1,000/ 10,000 = 1,888/18,888).

But what is the distribution of the tax *burden* in this case? It is now wholly misleading to infer from the proportionality of actual revenues collected to gross incomes that the distribution of burden is also proportional, as it was in the equity model. To look at the tax burden, one needs to look at post-tax positions. The position of Person 1 is defined by a post-tax income of $9,000, as before. The government anticipated that Person 2 would have a post-tax income of $17,000 owing to his expected payment of $3,000 to the government. After adjustment, Person 2 still ends up with $17,000. Person 2 is no better off than he would have been without the nontaxable option, yet the government collects $1,112 less in revenue. This loss in economic value arises exclusively from the shift in Person 2's earnings from the more productive taxable source to the less productive nontaxable source. The revenue loss measures the difference between the total value of output produced in the no-tax and the post-tax situations, a difference that is generated solely by the imposition of the tax. It measures the excess burden of the tax, if excess burden is defined as the loss in social value as distinct from the actual payment to the government.

This counterexample has, of course, been deliberately contrived to demonstrate our central point while yielding the proportionality results. At a minimum this counterexample should give pause to those who try to assess relative tax burdens on the basis of statistics measuring actual tax payments.[7]

## General Analysis

Both numerical examples contain extreme discontinuities. In this section we offer a more general model that reaches the same conclusion—reduction in excess burden is a more appropriate justification for tax reform than is increased progressivity, and it is equally feasible.

We continue to assume that potential taxpayers have no preference for one kind of work over another; it follows that normal utility-maximizing behavior will dictate an equalization of net-of-tax marginal rates of return in alternative employments. If the wage rate in a taxed activity, $W_T$, exceeds the wage in an untaxed activity, $W_U$, people will shift effort from taxed to untaxed labor as long as $W_U > W_T (1 - t)$, where $t$ is the marginal tax rate. Only when $W_U = W_T (1 - t)$ will a person be indifferent between additional work in the two activities. If the wage rates measure marginal productivity, it is clear that *at the margin* the difference in productivity between the two income sources (the "excess burden") must be negligibly different from the tax saving, as determined by the marginal tax rate. Equally, in the pre-tax situation (that is, when the tax rate is zero), the difference in the productivity of the two sources is also negligibly different from zero: in the tax-free situation the individual is also indifferent between the sources at the margin. Over the

7. In the example, given the simplifying assumptions, Person 2 will remain in the same post-tax position with income at $17,000 at *any* level of taxable income between the $10,000 and $20,000 limits. The break between taxable and nontaxable income chosen in the illustration is the only one within these limits, however, that will precisely mirror the proportionality results where tax payments made by the two persons are proportional to gross incomes, despite the progressive rate structure. If Person 2 had remained wholly unresponsive to the tax, his post-tax income would have been the same, but actual payments to government would have been higher, and a conventional "effective progression" measure would have yielded progressive results. On the other hand, if Person 2 had reduced taxable income to $10,000, the conventional measure would have suggested a *regressive* structure of revenue payments to government, despite the *progressivity* of the underlying tax burden.

entire range of substitution, therefore, the excess burden would be roughly half the tax avoided, given that there are no discontinuities or nonlinearities.

Precisely the same reasoning applies if particular expenditures are tax-favored. Rational behavior dictates that a person be indifferent between a dollar's worth of nondeductible and deductible outlays both before and after the tax is introduced. Hence he will make expenditures on tax-favored commodities that would not be worth making if expenditures on that commodity were treated equally with other expenditures. Once again a reasonable approximation to the excess burden under normal circumstances seems to be half the tax avoided.

The point can be made by appeal to the geometry of figure 1. To focus on the substitution of tax-exempt activities for taxable ones, we assume in figure 1 that the total amount of income-generating activity (this could be thought of as labor input) is fixed at $\overline{Y}$ units. The horizontal axis depicts how this total is divided between activities that are potentially taxable and activities that will not be subject to tax. Along the vertical axis we depict the return to the individual, per unit of labor effort, in the earning of taxable income. We define units of income-generating activity in such a way that the pre-tax return per unit of time spent in the taxable activity is $1.

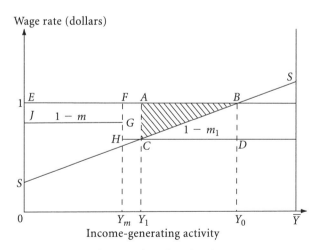

*Figure 1.* Labor supply with and without taxation

The curve $SS$ shows the allocation of income-generating activity to taxable sources as the marginal return from those taxable sources changes. Read from right to left, therefore, $SS$ depicts the marginal productivity of the individual in deriving income from nontaxable activity.[8] (The demand for the worker's services in potentially taxable activities is taken to be infinitely elastic at the initial dollar wage.)

In the absence of tax the individual would devote $Y_0$ units of income-generating activity to those activities that are to be taxed, and $\overline{Y} - Y_0$ units to those activities that are to be tax free and will earn income from those sources accordingly. His total initial income therefore consists of $\$Y_0$ from taxable sources, plus the area below $SS$ beyond $Y_0$ (area $SBY_0\overline{Y}$) from nontaxable sources.

Suppose that the tax to be introduced is a progressive income tax consisting of two rates (in line with our earlier examples): the tax rate $m$ applies over the first $Y_m$ dollars of taxable income earned, and the rate $m_1$ over all subsequent taxable earnings. The lines $(1 - m, 1 - m_1)$ depict this tax regime: tax revenue is given by the area between that line and the horizontal dollar line over the relevant range. Because the return on taxed income sources has declined as a result of the tax, the individual will substitute activity in nontaxed areas for activity in taxed areas, until the marginal return in each pursuit is once more identical: this occurs when the level of activity in the taxed area is $Y_1$, where $SS$ cuts the line $(1 - m_1)$. The individual's gross taxable income falls in response to the imposition of the tax from $Y_0$ dollars to $Y_1$ dollars. His nontaxable income increases from the area under $SS$ from $Y_0$ to $\overline{Y}$, to the area under $SS$ from $Y_1$ to $\overline{Y}$—an increase measured by area $BCY_1Y_0$. The tax he avoids paying is therefore $m_1 (Y_0 - Y_1)$ dollars, or equivalently the area $ABDC$. Note that this amount is not the same as the tax revenue forgone by the exemption of the tax-free income sources, because the individual was earning some income from the tax-exempt income source before the imposition of the tax. Rather, $ABDC$ measures the amount of revenue forgone as a result of the taxpayer's behavioral response to the imposition of the tax.

---

8. We ignore the possibility that the supply curve is backward bending, due to income effects, as an unnecessary complication. Because our major focus is on loopholes and their exploitation, the shape indicated seems most plausible to us.

The crucial point of this construction is that on the basis of *SS* as drawn, the value of the redirected income-earning activity to the taxpayer is *not* $(Y_0 - Y_1)$ dollars. The taxpayer is induced by the tax to move to less efficient income-earning activities—activities that return him an amount equal to the area under the *SS* curve over the range of adjustment. This is less than $(Y_0 - Y_1)$ dollars by the amount *ABC*; the taxpayer thus bears a burden of *ABC* in addition to the tax revenue received by government. This is the excess burden, and assuming *SS* to be linear over the range of adjustment, this is exactly one-half of the tax revenue the taxpayer avoids paying, that is, $ABC = \frac{1}{2}[m_1(Y_0 - Y_1)]$.

Within a similar geometric construction, we can set forth the extreme assumptions that are implicit in both the equity-oriented and the counter-equity arithmetical examples above. In both examples there is presumed to be *no* earning from tax-free sources before tax: that is, $Y_0$ and $\overline{Y}$ are identical. In the equity model the "rich" person is assumed to secure the full value of the tax avoided. Figure 2 depicts this situation. As in figure 1, *SS* in figure 2 depicts the allocation of the taxpayer's activity between the taxed and untaxed forms of income as the marginal tax rate varies (or equally, read from right to left, the marginal productivity of untaxed income-earning activity). In the absence of tax the taxpayer earns $20,000 in the form of "taxable" income; in the presence of the tax with marginal rate $m_1$, he earns $15,000 in that

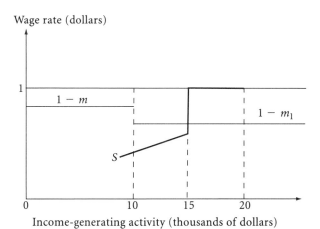

*Figure 2.* Labor supply: equity example

form. Because *SS* takes the shape it does, however, there is no excess burden induced by the adjustment: the tax-free earnings source generates virtually identical gross returns to those from the taxed source over the entire range to $15,000 and then drops to intersect the $(1 - m_1)$ line at that point. The line *SS* must intersect $(1 - m_1)$ at $15,000, since otherwise the taxpayer would substitute untaxed for taxed activity over a different range. For example, if *SS* were horizontal over the range from zero to $20,000, the taxpayer would never pay tax at all given this definition of taxable income; he would avoid tax entirely. In the case depicted in figure 2 (as in the numerical example) the activities substituted for taxed activities yield virtually a full $5,000 worth of value to the taxpayer.

The counterequity case is depicted in figure 3. In this case, productivity in the tax-exempt activity is no higher than $(1 - m_1)$ per unit of work effort. The taxpayer responds to the tax by substituting tax-free income-generating activity over the range from $20,000 to $14,444. Although he maintains his full input of income-generating activity, his gross income has fallen to $18,888 because income-generating activity in the tax-exempt area earns him negligibly more than he would receive net-of-tax from the taxed area. The individual is virtually indifferent between the two income sources over the range from $14,444 to $20,000. The key point of figure 3 is that each dollar of tax saved creates virtually one dollar of inefficiency and brings virtually no benefit

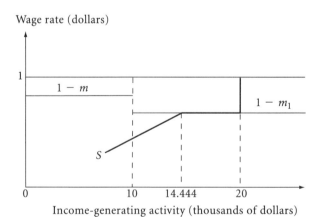

*Figure 3.* Labor supply: counterequity example

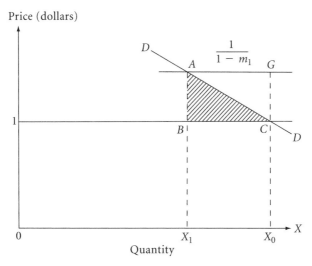

*Figure 4.* Excess burden resulting from commodity taxation

whatsoever to the tax avoider. In this case, the excess burden and the tax saving are virtually identical.

Similar diagrammatics can be used to illustrate tax avoidance on the expenditure or "uses" side of income. In figure 4 expenditures are taxed at the rate $1/(1 - m_1)$ and the amount of commodity $X$ demanded is $X_1$. If the commodity $X$ becomes tax exempt, demand rises to $X_0$, where the price by assumption equals 1. Tax avoidance will be area $ABCG$, or $m_1(X_0 - X_1)$; and the excess burden associated with that outlay shift, given the assumption that $D$ is roughly linear over the relevant range, will be area $ABCG$, or $m_1(X_0 - X_1)$; and the excess burden associated with that outlay shift, given the assumption that $D$ is roughly linear over the relevant range, will be area $ABC$ or $\frac{1}{2}[m_1(X_0 - X_1)]$ as before.

It may be useful at this point to investigate some of the assumptions in the discussion so far. One assumption in both the numerical examples was that the lower-income individual did not adjust his behavior in response to the imposition of the tax on $Y$—an assumption that is inconsistent with the generalized continuity assumption adopted here. Denoting tax avoidance as $A$, where $A = m \cdot \Delta Y$, and using a definition of the elasticity of the supply curve, $SS$ in figure 1, as $\varepsilon = (\Delta Y/Y_0)/(\Delta p/p)$, it follows that $A = m^2 \cdot \varepsilon Y_0$

because the initial price is defined to be unity, and $m$ is the marginal tax rate.

If the elasticity, $\varepsilon$, is taken to be the same at all income levels, then it follows that tax avoided will be *more than proportionately* larger for the rich than for the poor. For example, in the numerical illustration above, where Person 2's marginal tax rate (postadjustment) is twice Person 1's, then tax avoidance by Person 2 will be *four times as large a proportion* of his initial taxable income as tax avoidance by Person 1 is of 1's taxable income, even if there is no other difference. Given that 2's income is twice 1's, the absolute reduction in income earned in the taxed form will be four times as large for 2 as for 1, and the tax avoided eight times as large.

Thus the analysis explains why tax avoidance is particularly appealing to the rich and justifies in part the assumption made in the examples given above that tax avoidance by lower-income persons can be effectively ignored.

Until now we have assumed linear supply curves (on the sources side) and demand curves (on the uses side). We have also assumed that the marginal tax rate is unchanged over the relevant ranges. This assumption is much less reasonable. Generally the marginal tax structure consists of a considerable number of steps, or conceivably it could be smoothly progressive (as in figure 5). Although in such cases the excess burden remains as the area $ABC$ or $\frac{1}{2}[m_1(Y_0 - Y_1)]$, the tax forgone is given by the area between the tax curve, labeled $(1 - m)$, and the horizontal unit price line and exceeds $m_1(Y_0 - Y_1)$ because the marginal rate at $Y_0$, $m_0$, is larger than that at $Y_1$. We can approximate tax forgone by the change in $Y$ times the *average* of $m_0$ and $m_1$.

Hence $A = \frac{1}{2}(m_0 + m_1)(Y_0 - Y_1)$ and the excess burden, $W$, equals $\frac{1}{2}[m_1(Y_0 - Y_1)]$.

Then, the ratio of excess burden $(W)$ to tax avoided $(A)$ will be

$$W/A = m_1/(m_1 + m_0). \tag{1}$$

This expression depends on the rate of change of marginal tax rates as income rises rather than on the level of marginal rates, and this varies throughout the progressive rate scale. Because marginal rates are bounded at the upper end (at something below 100 percent), the ratio in equation 1 will tend to fall as one moves higher up the progressive rate scale. For the richest tax avoiders, those whose income after tax avoidance is subject to tax at rates near the maximum, $W/A$ is near the value of $\frac{1}{2}$ applying in the earlier discussion.

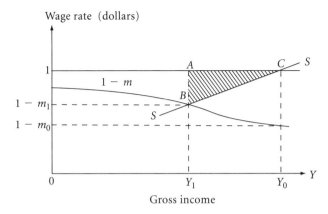

*Figure 5.* Labor supply and excess burden with continuously variable wage schedule

This theory generates two central conclusions. First, where tax avoidance is substantial, excess burdens in general will also be substantial. This conclusion implies that the scope for tax reform that makes virtually everyone better off is broader than the standard discussion seems to imply. The second conclusion is that the total tax burden, including excess burden, is distributed in a more progressive fashion than is normally indicated. Comparing, for example, any two persons whose post-tax taxable incomes are the same, the one who avoids the more tax (that is, whose pre-tax income was higher) endures a larger total burden.[9] If a tax structure that is progressive at pre-tax levels of $Y$ is transformed via tax avoidance into a structure in which actual tax payments are *proportional* in terms of initial levels of $Y$, then the true distribution of burdens (including excess burden) lies somewhere be-

9. We should note that it is not necessarily the case that for individuals whose *initial* levels of taxable income are identical, the one who avoids the most tax will have the largest excess burden. Whether or not this is so depends on the elasticity of the marginal tax rate structure because larger tax avoidance implies both a larger value of $(Y_0 - Y_1)$ and a *smaller* value of $m$. If the marginal rate reduction is proportionately greater than the increase in income diverted, excess burden will fall.

Since $W = \frac{1}{2} [m(Y_1)] [Y_0 - Y_1]$, we can show this by differentiating $W$ with respect to $Y_1$, with $Y_0$ identical for both. Then $dW/d(Y_0 - Y_1) = \frac{1}{2} [m(Y_1)] + \frac{1}{2} (Y_0 - Y_1) dm/dY_1 [dY_1/d(Y_0 - Y_1)]$. Because $dY_1/d(Y_0 - Y_1) = -1$, $dW/d(Y_0 - Y_1) > 0$ if and only if $1 > (dm[Y_1]/dY_1) (Y_0 - Y_1)/m(Y_1)$.

tween the nominal and effective rate structures—and may not be too far removed from a simple average of the two. The tax burden, of course, would be precisely equal to that simple average if excess burden equaled *half* the tax avoided; the smaller the ratio of excess burden to tax avoidance (that is, as the elasticity of the marginal rate structure increases over the relevant ranges), the greater the weight that should be given to the effective rate structure.

## Tax Reform via Marginal Rate Reduction

Reformers who stress equity and seek to increase the effective progressiveness of tax payments try to ensure that the "rich" pay their "fair shares" of the total costs of government. In practice this approach leads to attempts to close loopholes, to eliminate the tax shelters, and to end the use of deductions or credits to shield income sources or income uses from taxation. This type of reform advocacy obscures an important avenue to genuine tax reform via *reduction* in the rate of tax progression.

In the counterexample shown in figure 3 the nontaxable income source is demonstrably less productive than the taxable source. In this setting a reduction in the top bracket rate can result in a complete elimination of excess burden as well as tax avoidance because the less productive tax-exempt source of income ceases to be worth pursuing. The tax becomes effectively comprehensive because no actual income source escapes tax. And most important, *all* parties may be made better off. The post-tax incomes of the "rich," who previously resorted to the nontaxable opportunity, increase, and the government collects *more* revenue from these same taxpayers. A conventional measure of tax payments would suggest progressivity, as desired by the reformists; furthermore, in this case payments would measure tax burdens.

The equity-oriented reformer might emphasize the possibility that in order to accomplish the same results, the effective marginal rate of progression might have to be cut so far that the tax structure would not yield the desired revenues. While this possibility exists, so do the opportunities for improved productivity that the efficiency-oriented reformer emphasizes.

The contrasting implications here may be illustrated readily in numerical terms. If the tax-exempt income source is only half as productive as the taxable source, any top bracket rate below 50 percent will eliminate the nontaxable source, without any explicit action toward making income from this source taxable. With appropriate adjustment to inframarginal rates of tax, the taxpayer could find his post-tax position improved by a shift to exclusive reliance on the taxable source; the government could collect more revenue than before the tax reduction, and almost as much as it had anticipated before it considered the existence of the nontaxable opportunity. There need be no loss in economic value produced by the tax under the appropriately revised rate schedule.

By contrast, if the tax-exempt income source yields 90 percent of that available from the taxable source at the pre-tax earnings position of the taxpayer, the top marginal tax rate would have to be less than 10 percent to ensure that there be no resort at all to the nontaxable opportunity. In this case, rate adjustment alone, sufficient to eliminate both excess burden and tax avoidance, might make it impossible for the government to raise as much revenue as in the prereform situation. If the taxpayer is in equilibrium at the margin and is earning some nontaxable income, and if the rate structure is progressive, some reduction in marginal rates must exist along with appropriate inframarginal rate adjustment that will simultaneously improve the position of the taxpayer, increase governmental revenues, and reduce excess burden.[10]

Given that individuals with differing incomes must in practice face the

10. The requirement that the taxpayer be in equilibrium at the margin rules out the possibilities of corner solutions analogous to those required for the numerical example of the equity-type model discussed earlier in the text. Consider a situation where two income opportunities are *equally* productive over a limited range but where beyond this the nontaxable source is not productive at all. In this case, regardless of the rate structure, the taxpayer will engage in the nontaxable activity up to the point where it ceases to be productive, regardless of the tax schedule. No change in tax rates can induce him to alter his effort in the nontaxable activity. On the other hand, if the tax schedule is everywhere progressive, the government can increase its revenue collections by increasing inframarginal rates of tax. But the taxpayer is necessarily made worse off in the process. No positive-sum game between government and the taxpayer can be constructed in this setting.

If the nontaxable source is nearly as productive as the taxable source over some range and significantly less productive beyond this range, there always exist tax adjustments that raise revenue, increase the taxpayer's welfare, and eliminate excess burden. In many cases, however, mutual gains may require a regressive rate schedule. If we rule out regressive rates, severe discontinuities in the productivity schedules for nontaxable options may preclude tax reform that reduces excess burden.

*same* tax schedule, and given the assumption of continuity, the scope for tax reduction that increases public revenue, reduces excess burdens, and benefits all taxpayers is limited. Any inframarginal tax increases must in this scenario increase tax burdens imposed on people lower down the income scale who do not benefit from reductions in high marginal rates. In some cases it is conceivable that revenue collected from an individual would increase due to a reduction in marginal tax rates without any increase in inframarginal rates. This situation arises if the reduction in marginal tax rates induces an increase in income from the taxable source $(Y)$ sufficient to offset the loss in revenue caused by the marginal rate reduction; then revenue collected from that individual would go up, but the excess burden would go down sufficiently to leave him better off.

Suppose the marginal rate, $\bar{m}_1$, applies over the range from $Y_2$ to $Y_1$ and beyond. Then, the revenue $(R)$ due to the excess of $m_1$ over some alternative marginal rate $(m)$ that might have prevailed (say the rate applying on incomes over the previous range to $Y_2$) is $R_m = (Y_1 - Y_2)(m_1 - \bar{m})$. Then

$$dR/dm_1 = (Y_1 - Y_2) + m_1 \cdot dY_1/dm_1.$$

Now

$$Y_1 = Y_0(1 - \varepsilon m_1),$$

where $Y_0$ is the income that would be earned from the taxable source in the absence of tax, $Y_1$ is income from the same source after imposition of tax, and $\varepsilon$ is the elasticity of earning taxable income with respect to the wage net of tax; so

$$dR/dm_1 = Y_0(1 - \varepsilon m_1) - Y_2 + m_1(-\varepsilon Y_0)$$
$$= Y_0 - Y_2 - 2\varepsilon m_1 Y_0.$$

This $dR/dm_1$ is less than zero if and only if

$$\varepsilon > (Y_0 - Y_2)/(2m_1 Y_0).$$

Note that if $m_1 = 50$ percent, $\varepsilon > 1$ is sufficient if $Y_2 > 0$; the implication is that for higher marginal rates the condition is not so very stringent.[11]

Beyond this possibility, however, the main policy thrust of the excess

---

11. Note that this result is predicated on the assumption that the person in question is the highest-income taxpayer, since otherwise revenue lost exceeds $m_1(Y_1 - Y_2)$.

burden perspective accords with that of the equity view—a shift toward a comprehensive tax base reduces efficiency losses due to the tax system (although as we have pointed out, a move toward comprehensiveness need not be the only means of decreasing tax-caused inefficiencies). Where the equity-oriented and the consensus philosophies may diverge, however, is in the use each would make of the revenue gained thereby. The equity-oriented reformer is likely to urge cuts in tax rates on lower-income groups to increase the effective progressivity of the tax system. In our alternative consensus perspective the distribution of the incremental revenue is constrained by the requirement that no one is made worse off. Even within this constraint, however, there remains scope for alternative distributional allocations of the gains from tax reform.[12]

12. A simple example will illustrate. Suppose that the tax rate schedule applicable to income from source $Y$ is 10 percent on the first $10,000, 20 percent on the second $10,000, and 30 percent on the third $10,000. In the absence of taxation, Individual 1 would earn $10,000 from income source $Y$ and $2,000 from other sources, pre-tax. Individual 2 earns $20,000 from income source $Y$ and $4,000 from other sources, pre-tax. The elasticity of supply of labor to earn income from source $Y$ is 1.64 for both individuals. The post-tax equilibrium involves Individual 1 earning $8,333 from income source $Y$ and $3,664 from other sources; and Individual 2 earning $13,333 from income source $Y$ and $10,664 from other sources. As a result, Individual 1 pays $833 in tax, while 2 pays $1,666; the effective rate of tax is proportional (at a rate of 8.3 percent if measured as a proportion of income earned from source $Y$ before tax was imposed, or approximately 7 percent if measured against income of *all* sources).

The *actual* burdens (including excess burden) are $916.70 for Individual 1 and $2,333 for Individual 2.

Suppose we now move to a comprehensive tax system and that as a first step we leave the tax rates unchanged. Income sources will revert to their pre-tax proportions; $1,400 will be raised from Individual 1 and $4,200 from 2. In order to maintain revenue at the same aggregate level of $2,500, one possibility would be to opt for maximum progression and to cut the rate on the first $10,000 to zero, leaving Individual 2 to pay the full $2,500. Since this would necessarily leave 2 worse off, it lies outside the limits imposed by consensus-type criteria.

Within those consensus limits, however, very considerable variation remains possible. Consider, for example, the following tax schedules:

a.  1 percent over the first $10,000        Individual 1 pays $200; Individual 2 pays $2,300
    10 percent over the next $10,000
    30 percent over the next $10,000

b.  5 percent over the first $20,000        Individual 1 pays $600; Individual 2 pays $1,900
    22.5 percent over the next $10,000

c.  Proportional at 7 percent              Individual 1 pays $840; Individual 2 pays $1,680

## Rate Reduction and Horizontal Equity

If tax reform that increases revenue, reduces excess burden, and raises the welfare of all is possible, an explanation is required of the apparent dominance of reformist emphasis on increased progression. Why has the approach to reform that promises gains to all and that therefore holds a potential for agreement among all parties been so neglected? Presumably one response to this query would refer to the limited applicability of the analysis. Our analysis is restricted by the implicit assumption that everyone in a single income class or category responds identically to the imposition of tax. That is to say, we have taken no account of differences among the responses of taxpayers in the same income class to the advantages of nontaxable earning opportunities or income uses. In fact, only certain members of an income class respond to a tax through shifts to sources or uses of income that are fully or partially tax exempt. Those who exploit or exercise nontaxable options may seem to escape their "fair shares" relative to those within their own defined income class who fail to exercise such options.

But what does equality for tax purposes mean? Are taxpayers who respond differently to a tax, reflecting either differential tastes or differential capacities, to be arbitrarily defined as "similar" for tax purposes? Since Martin Feldstein has recently explored some of these questions in some detail, his argument will not be reviewed here.[13] General standards of "equal treatment" may nonetheless place severe limits on the adjustment in marginal and inframarginal rates of tax that may be worked out in the complex political bargaining process.

Within-class adjustment has received insufficient attention in the reformist discussion on the potential tax reduction that movement toward tax-base comprehensiveness would make possible. As noted, the emphasis has been placed almost exclusively on general rate reductions, over all classes, that

---

*All* raise approximately the same revenue as the initial tax on $Y$ alone; *all* leave both individuals better off (that is, enduring smaller total burdens) than the initial arrangement. Where the schemes differ is in the breakup of the total allocative gains, which the shift toward comprehensiveness makes possible. These total allocative gains are $750—$83 from Individual 1, and $667 from Individual 2—and this $750 can be divided between 1 and 2 in any manner desired.

13. Feldstein, "On the Theory of Tax Reform."

would seem to become possible on the elimination of preferential treatment accorded to various income sources and uses. This emphasis is misplaced in the context of the alternative reform perspective that has been suggested in this paper. Marginal rate reductions, along with the appropriately designed inframarginal rate changes, are instrumental to the elimination of excess burden without necessary legal changes in the definition of income categories. Such reductions may, in the event, require that the spillover benefits of total tax cuts accrue to nonresponsive taxpayers who perchance are members of the classes most responsive to nontaxable options. To the extent that this is the case, the tax reduction prospect that is inherent in any tax reform may be largely if not wholly concentrated on members of those general income classes for which the nontaxable options are quantitatively important.[14] Tax reform viewed in this alternative perspective cannot readily be utilized as a handy means of implementing generalized rate reductions, and especially in such a manner as to further the liberal objectives of ever-increasing progressivity, as measured over income classes.

## Conclusion

The most important practical aspect of the alternative perspective suggested lies in its political rather than in its economic features. To the extent that those who suffer the excess burden of income tax by resort to preferentially treated sources or uses can be induced voluntarily to shift toward socially efficient behavior patterns, they will support rather than oppose reforms in the pull and haul of the legislative process. Agreement can emerge on genuine compromise solutions. Bargaining, of course, will continue to take place, but the object becomes the division of the net gains rather than the gains that are

---

14. This may be illustrated in the numerical example of note 12. Suppose that all or almost all of the behavioral adjustments to the prereform tax are made by persons in the same class as Individual 2 in the example. These persons can be made better off by the appropriate rate adjustments while moving to a more comprehensive income level. But these same rate adjustments must also be made available to those persons within the same income class who did not utilize nontaxable sources or uses of income before the reform. These persons will gratuitously benefit by a reduction in their tax payments. But this spillover effect dictated by principles of horizontal equity will constrain the set of distributional outcomes somewhat more than the arithmetical example of note 12 indicates.

secured from the imposition of losses on members of losing political coalitions.

The alternative perspective outlined here also has ethical advantages that are too often neglected. Regardless of income level, those persons who have adjusted their behavior to the existing structure of taxation, and have done so legally, could be argued to have ethically legitimate expectations that the structure will not be arbitrarily modified. To impose damages on such persons through reform measures designed to attain some idealist version of comprehensiveness violates widely accepted equity norms. Ethical arguments against imposed reforms become stronger when it is recognized that essentially equivalent results can be attained by consensus. Agreement is surely preferred to conflict, whether within or without the arena of democratic politics.[15]

---

15. To a limited extent this approach is embodied in U.S. Department of the Treasury, *Blueprints for Basic Tax Reform* (Government Printing Office, 1977), largely through the emphasis on transitional problems involved in any major tax-law changes.

# The Political Efficiency
# of General Taxation

*Abstract:* If political decisions are made by legislative majorities, a constitutional constraint requiring generality in the imposition of taxes will be economically efficient. In the absence of such a constraint, majorities will tend to impose differentially high taxes on members of political minorities, and such differentiation opens up several sources for resource waste. This argument lends support for a uniform proportional rate of tax on all incomes.

## Introduction

There is a normative argument for general taxation that stems from a recognition of the interdependence between the rules of politics (the constitution as inclusively defined) and the patterns of outcomes generated by the behavior of persons who act within such rules. The argument is based on the criterion of economic efficiency, defined in the standard sense. A tax structure is inefficient to the extent that it reduces economic value below that which might be potentially achievable within given resource and technology constraints and within the particular political-legal order that exists. The efficiency ranking of tax institutions will differ among separate sets of political-legal rules. An institution that is classified to be relatively efficient in one constitutional order may be ranked quite differently in alternative settings.

The present discussion proceeds from the assumption that the constitutional regime is described by individual liberty, private ownership of prop-

From *National Tax Journal* 46, no. 4 (1994): 401–10. Reprinted by permission of the publisher.

erty, and a market economy, subject, however, to politicization through the operation of majoritarian democracy that is relatively unconstrained regarding range and scope of governmental outlay or level and distribution of taxes. In this setting, a tax structure characterized by *generality* in the treatment of persons or other objects of imposition will involve a lower wastage of economic value than alternative structures.

The economic case of generality in taxation is quite distinct from the familiar case that can be advanced on equity grounds as one extension and application of the norm of equality before the law.

In the next section, I shall compare and contrast the setting for normative tax analysis introduced here with that which describes the conventional framework of fiscal economics. In the third section, I examine the working of majoritarian democracy in a highly simplified construction, the purpose of which is to show that departures from generality, with predicted efficiency consequences, must remain characteristic of such politics, until and unless specific constraints are imposed constitutionally. The fourth section addresses some of the difficulties that arise in defining and applying the generality norm to taxation. The final section brings the discussion to bear on the United States fiscal experience of the 1980s and 1990s.

## The Institutional Reality of Political Taxation

For most automobiles, the efficient fuel is gasoline; for most farm tractors, the efficient fuel is diesel oil. In each case, efficiency is a measure of the ratio between desired or valued output and valued input. In this illustrative example, it becomes folly for some putative "efficiency expert" to recommend diesel fuel for automobiles and gasoline for tractors. That which is efficient depends on the process through which inputs are transformed into outputs.

Unfortunately, normative economists rarely act as if they understand the elementary principle that this example clarifies. Despite Wicksell's warning issued a century ago, normative economists continue to proffer advice as if the state, or collective agency, is all-powerful, monolithic, and benevolent.[1] Nowhere is this stance more in evidence than with reference to taxation. When asked the question: "What is the efficient tax system?" fiscal econo-

---

1. Knut Wicksell, *Finanztheoretische Untersuchungen* (Jena: Gustav Fischer, 1896).

mists have proceeded almost exclusively on some presumption that politics does not matter and that the government both aims for efficiency in taxation and is able to implement whatever it seeks to accomplish.

Even within the conventional limits of discourse, however, there have been two quite distinct approaches to normative tax analysis. The first, and more traditional, concentrates attention on the distribution of taxation in isolation from the spending or outlay side of the fiscal account. This approach is based on some implicit assumption that the size and composition of the government budget are beyond the competence of normative advice and, further, that the distribution of taxation exerts little or no feedback, whether positive or normative, on those forces that do, in fact, determine the allocation of outlay for the polity. This approach became the starting point or base for the nineteenth-century utilitarian norm that dictated tax distribution in accordance with the principle of equimarginal sacrifice, a distribution that produces "least-aggregate sacrifice" in utility as aggregated over all members of the politically organized community. With plausibly acceptable notions about the similarities among persons as utility generators, this principle of least-aggregate sacrifice was used to justify differentiation in rates of tax by income or wealth classification, that is, progressive taxes.

The normative argument for progression in rates survived the demise of utilitarianism as an internally coherent philosophical position with practicable implications. The central elements of the nineteenth-century normative exercise reappeared in a much more sophisticated form in the "optimal tax" theories of the 1970s and 1980s. Again, these normative exercises can be used to justify differentiation in rates of tax on persons with differing incomes or endowments. And, importantly, the same normative structure is available to suggest that there are possible efficiency gains from differentiation in rates among commodities when the tax base is shifted to goods.

As noted, there is an alternative approach that also falls within conventional normative analysis, although this approach is somewhat less familiar. In this second approach, the distribution of taxes is not treated in isolation from the outlay side of the budget, and an explicit attempt is made to make the bridge between taxation and spending. The question posed here is not simply about the efficient distribution of taxes for some exogenously determined revenue total. Instead, the question becomes: What is the efficient size of the government budget? The answer emerges from a straightforward extension and application of the welfare economics of the market or private sector of the economy. A necessary condition for efficiency in the public sector is present when the marginal costs of extending public goods provisions are equated to the marginal evaluations of persons, summed over all persons in the relevant sharing group. In its modern form, this solution was presented by Samuelson in his seminal 1954 paper. Earlier origins are found in works by Wicksell and Lindahl.[2] This approach offers normative justification for differentiation in taxation in accordance with the separate demand intensities for publicly provided goods and services and especially at the appropriately defined margins. The implied differentiation here may be broadly consistent with that which emerges from the utilitarian construction in some cases but may be quite inconsistent in others.[3] The divergencies between the normative implications of the two approaches have prompted some modern tax analysts to suggest that the two precepts be applied to separate sectors of the governmental budget.[4]

My purpose here is not to review in detail either of these two conventional approaches to tax norms. Instead, my purpose is to suggest that neither approach, as sketched out above, embodies the necessary attention that must be paid to the politics through which any taxation must be processed and implemented. If government is indeed accurately modeled as a monolithic and benevolent entity, the two conventional approaches may be interpreted to yield diverse, yet useful, normative advice as to the allocation of taxes among the citizens in a polity. But if such a model of politics and governance is not descriptively accurate, even to some first approximation, then the specific ordering of tax institutions that emerges from either of the two approaches may be misleading and, if introduced into political argument, may be counterproductive.[5]

2. Paul Samuelson, "The Pure Theory of Public Expenditure," *Review of Economics and Statistics* 36 (November 1954): 387–89; Wicksell, *Finanztheoretische Untersuchungen;* Erik Lindahl, *Die Gerechtigkeit der Besteuerung* (Lund: Gleerupska Universitets-Bokhandeln, 1919).

3. James M. Buchanan, "Fiscal Institutions and Efficiency in Collective Outlay," *American Economic Review* 54 (May 1964): 227–35, and "Taxation in Fiscal Exchange," *Journal of Public Economics* 6 (1976): 17–29.

4. Richard A. Musgrave, *A Theory of Public Finance* (New York: McGraw-Hill, 1959).

5. I shall not discuss here an alternative construction that was introduced by Geoffrey Brennan and James M. Buchanan in *The Power to Tax* (Cambridge: Cambridge University

This point was recognized by Wicksell, but it was not widely understood in the sense stressed here because he sought to remedy the inconsistency between tax norms and democratic decision structures by modifying the latter rather than by reexamining the former.[6] That is to say, Wicksell proposed to change the rules that allowed legislative majorities to make taxing-spending decisions. He sought to secure increased economic efficiency in the fiscal process by requiring a more inclusive legislative majority for collective action. In the conceptual limit, he suggested a rule of unanimity. In practice, Wicksell suggested a qualified majority of some five-sixths of the members of the legislature. With such a change in the decision rules, neither the distribution of taxes nor the distribution of program benefits need be general or uniform. There is no argument for generality in the Wicksellian scheme.

An alternative means of moving toward some reconciliation of the inconsistency between political reality and tax norms, and the one I suggest in this paper, is to use the same starting point as Wicksell but to accept the institutions of majoritarian democracy as quasi-permanent constitutional parameters. Given the existence of such decision structures, we can then ask the question posed earlier. What is the tax structure that seems most likely to yield the relatively most efficient pattern of outcomes?

There are two alternatives to be considered: legislative majorities may be empowered to impose taxes without specific constraints; or legislative majorities may be constrained constitutionally to the imposition of general taxation, with such a constraint applying only to the distribution of taxes among persons and groups. The level of taxation remains subject to majority determination.

In this political setting, I suggest that the requirement for general taxation is politically or constitutionally efficient in the sense that such a constraint will produce patterns of legislative outcomes that will tend to minimize the destruction of economic value through the operation of the fiscal process. In this more realistic perspective, general taxation becomes first-best constitu-

---

Press, 1980). In that construction, government was modeled as a revenue-maximizing Leviathan, in which case the implications for the fiscal constitution are, of course, quite different from those that might be derived from either of the conventional approaches or from the model of majoritarian politics introduced in this paper.

6. Wicksell, *Finanztheoretische Untersuchungen.*

tionally, even if it is recognized that such taxation remains second- or third-best from the idealized perspective of benevolent governance.[7]

## Majoritarian Democracy

The reason why general taxation is constitutionally preferred to differential or discriminatory taxation in political democracy is that the very structure through which political decisions are made prevents any attainment, even approximately, of the type of tax differentiation that might be defined to be "optimal" or "ideal" in a stylized setting of benevolence. That is to say, majoritarian decision processes cannot, by their nature, be expected to generate patterns of outcomes that embody the tax discrimination among persons and groups or over goods that correspond to that which might be yielded through some economists' exercise of proffering advice to a despot.

Majority rule means what it says: rule by a majority coalition. And this fact alone guarantees that there must be discrimination in treatment between persons who are members of the majority coalition and those who are not unless discrimination is constitutionally constrained. This discrimination holds for the distribution of taxes as it does for all other activities under the authority of government.[8]

With generality in taxation present as a constraint, majoritarian politics can work more or less as it is modeled to work in much of standard public choice theory. Under such constraint, majority voting tends to generate outcomes that reflect the preferences of the median voter for the overall level of

---

7. Dwight R. Lee and Arthur Snow criticize conventional tax analysis for its neglect of political incentives, but they do not explicitly develop a model of political process (*Political Incentives and Optimal Excess Burden* [Athens, University of Georgia, 1993, mimeographed]).

8. Objections may be raised to the argument that majority politics must embody discrimination. Why would it not be possible for members of a majority coalition to behave nondiscriminatorily? If, however, politicians tried to behave in this fashion, they would surely lose out in electoral contests with others who would promise to secure differential benefits for another coalition. The political leader who genuinely tries to promote the overall or general interest simply does not survive in democratic electoral politics. For further analysis, see James M. Buchanan, "How Can Constitutions Be Designed So That Politicians Who Seek to Serve 'Public Interest' Can Survive?" *Constitutional Political Economy* 4, no. 1 (Winter 1993): 1–6.

taxation and, by inference, the size of the budget. In the absence of the generality constraint, however, majority voting tends to insure that one part of the inclusive constituency is maximally exploited through the fiscal process while members of the majority coalition secure substantially all of the net benefits from collective action.

The logic of the analysis here is straightforward, and it is perhaps surprising that public choice theorists have not concentrated more attention on majoritarian exploitation relative to their emphasis on median voter dominance. In part, this neglect may stem from a failure to recognize that fiscal politics is not analogous to committee deliberations and that the alternatives for collective choice are endogenous to the process of selection itself rather than exogenously determined. Unless constrained otherwise, majorities must coalesce around alternatives that embody differential treatment among members of the collectivity.

Consider a highly simplified three-person political community, the constitution for which dictates that collective decisions are to be reached by majority voting. Further, suppose that there are three discrete rates of taxation that might be imposed on each person, with the level of collective public goods provision being residually determined by the tax inputs forthcoming from the three persons. We designate the three rates of tax as H (high), M (medium), and L (low).

There are 27 possible distributions of taxation here; only three of these reflect symmetry or nondifferential treatment for the three parties:

$$(\text{HHH}), (\text{MMM}), (\text{LLL}) \tag{1}$$

If the effective fiscal choice should be restricted to these three options, majority voting would produce an equilibrium that represents the preference of the median voter, provided that all preferences could be arrayed to exhibit single-peakedness.[9] But without a generality requirement, majority voting could produce outcomes that range over any and all of the whole 27 prospects that are within the possible. And even if there should exist a majority

---

9. In the absence of single-peakedness, there is no majority equilibrium, even with consideration limited to symmetrical or general treatment alternatives. In the example here, nonpeakedness would appear bizarre, since this feature would require that one person rank a medium tax rate lower than both a high rate and a low rate.

equilibrium among the three general tax prospects, there must exist alternatives outside the symmetrical set that dominate any solution within the set for a majority coalition.

Suppose that preferences are such that (MMM) would, in fact, be the majority equilibrium if the options are constrained to satisfy a generality norm. This imputation would tend to be dominated for some majority by any one of the following sets of rates:

$$(LLH)(LHL)(HLL) \qquad (2)$$

This group of imputations may, following von Neumann and Morgenstern, be called the solution set for our unconstrained majoritarian game, as sketched out above.[10] A person would prefer that his or her own rate of tax be lowered while those of the minority member of the group be raised to the maximal possible limit. Far from producing some "middle" or "compromise" outcome, majority voting must, in the nonconstrained case, guarantee maximal differentiation between individuals who are members of the majority and the minority.

An important efficiency implication may be drawn from the comparison between assumed median preference outcome under the generality constraint and the set of outcomes (2) under nonconstrained majoritarianism. Given a generality constraint, so long as underlying preferences remain stable, the symmetrical solution, MMM, remains in equilibrium. Particular persons may, of course, prefer one of the other possible solutions; one person might prefer the symmetrical low tax regime, LLL, while another person might prefer the high tax regime, HHH. But if MMM is the majority equilibrium under generality, and if any person expects preferences to remain stable, he or she will not find it worthwhile to invest resources in efforts to modify the majoritarian outcome that determines the distribution of taxes. Investment in political rent seeking on the tax side will be minimal.

We can contrast this relative quiescence with the situation confronted by a single person in one of the imputations included in 2 when there is no generality constraint. Even if preferences are not predicted to change, the person who finds himself or herself in the exploited minority position has a contin-

---

10. John von Neumann and Oskar Morgenstern, *Theory of Games and Economic Behavior* (Princeton: Princeton University Press, 1944).

uing incentive to persuade one of the other two persons to leave the majority coalition and to join in an alternative one that will then exploit the party left out. At the same time, each person in the successful majority will retain an incentive to persuade his or her partner in the coalition to remain loyal. The incentive to invest resources in political rent seeking is present for all persons at all times, and these efforts may take on several forms, including side agreements for adjustments on the spending side of the account that may be aimed explicitly to attract and retain persons in majority coalitions for tax-side decisions. The prospect for majoritarian cycling among tax structures appears here in its near-classical sense, and we should not be at all surprised to observe that legislative majorities are almost always engaged in alleged "tax reform."

The abstracted model here suggests continuous cycling along with subsequent instability in tax distribution among persons. This implication is mitigated in effect when the model is changed in order to allow for differential exploitability of the separate voters-taxpayers. If rates of tax are applied to, say, an income base, and if income is unequal, pretax, then that majority coalition which maximally exploits the high-income recipient tends to be more stable than either of the other maximal exploitation alternatives. The reason is simple: members of the exploiting majority have more to gain from tax discrimination against rich persons than against middle-income or poor persons. The cyclical prospects reemerge, however, when, as, and if the rich recognize their vulnerability here and invest in innovative cross-budget adjustments along with other politically effective "bribes."

A second related, but much more familiar, source of relative inefficiency in discriminatory as compared with general taxation is located in the necessary administrative costs that are imposed both on government as tax collector and on the individual as taxpayer. With differentials in rates of tax on different persons and/or different sources, identification and classification become necessary; complex enforcement schemes become essential if individual response patterns include efforts to reduce liabilities to tax. Taxpayers, on the other hand, undergo costs in these same efforts to limit liabilities for tax. The ancient precept for simplicity in taxation is increasingly violated as the structure moves away from generality.

An additional source for inefficiency generated by the workings of majoritarian politics is found in the differential excess burdens that arise from the predicted high-tax exploitation of members of political minorities. In the three-person example used here, the solution set includes only those imputations that involve maximal tax rates for one of the three persons, along with minimal rates for the others. If either of the imputations in 2 is compared with the symmetrical MMM result, which we assumed to reflect median preference under the generality norm, there will be an increase in excess burden due to the asymmetry between the loss and gain functions traced out by increases and decreases in rates.[11] This conclusion, strictly speaking, depends on an assumption that the three persons are identical, but a less rigorous statement of the relationship tends to hold even in the presence of inequality. Excess burdens of tax increase at an increasing rate with tax rate increases. General and uniform rates of tax tend to produce lower excess burden than the differential taxation that would likely emerge from majoritarian decision processes, although there will always exist some ideally abstracted schedule of differentiation that would minimize excess burden.[12]

When a dynamic perspective is adopted, the inefficiency-generating properties of majority decision making become more pronounced. Members of any temporary majority coalition will have an incentive to use the taxing power to exploit maximally members of the minority. But precisely because any majority coalition is impermanent, members will not act to maximize present values of the revenues that might be extracted. Instead, rates of tax imposed will be higher than those that would maximize present values. The short-term Laffer curve relationship dictates higher rates of tax than any long-term relationship.[13] The unconstrained fiscal operation of majoritarian

11. Geoffrey Brennan and James M. Buchanan, "The Normative Purpose of Economic 'Science': Rediscovery of an Eighteenth Century Method," *International Review of Law and Economics* 1 (December 1981): 15–66, and "Predictive Power and Choice among Regimes," *Economic Journal* 93 (March 1983): 89–105.

12. Gary S. Becker has argued that the politics of competing interest groups will tend to generate a distribution of taxation that corresponds to that which will be optimal in the stylized model of the welfare economist ("A Theory of Competition among Pressure Groups for Political Influence," *Quarterly Journal of Economics* 98, no. 3 [August 1983]: 371–400). Becker's construction does not distinguish between majority and minority influences on outcomes. His analysis does not incorporate the workings of majoritarianism, as such.

13. James M. Buchanan and Dwight R. Lee, "Tax Rates and Tax Revenues in Political Equilibrium: Some Simple Analytics," *Economic Inquiry* 20 (July 1982): 344–54.

democracy will almost surely insure lower rates of growth in the economy than would be the case under *ceteris paribus* conditions except for the introduction of a generality requirement for taxing.

To this point, I have identified and discussed several sources of economic inefficiency directly associated with an absence of a generality constraint on the taxing authority of government in majoritarian democracy: first, the incentives provided for wasteful resource commitment in political rent seeking; second, the related increases in costs of administration, both for government and taxpayers; and third, the additional excess burdens involved in any discriminatory tax structure emergent in a majoritarian setting, particularly in dynamic perspective. A fourth possible source for inefficiency to be considered concerns predicted effects of nongenerality in taxes on the size and composition of the public or collective sector of the economy, that is, on the budget itself.

Early public choice arguments to the effect that majority voting rules tend to generate budgets that are "too large" by efficiency standards were themselves based on the presumption that taxes are levied generally, or at the least are more general in their incidence than the distribution of benefits.[14] If discrimination among both taxes and benefits (including transfer payments) is nonconstrained, the tendency for excessively large budgets would seem to be more pronounced, since the members of the majority coalition would, in this setting, confront lowered tax costs for any public program, whether for public goods or for transfers, than would be the case under general taxation.

## The Meaning of General Taxation

I have discussed the efficiency-enhancing properties of a generality norm in taxation without specific definition of what generality must mean in the context analyzed. In one sense, the generality norm must be defined operationally. Since the ultimate purpose is to constrain majoritarian politics in order to prevent its natural tendency toward differential or discriminatory usage of the taxing authority, generality must be defined to extend uniformity in treatment over all members of the inclusive voting constituency. Any general

14. James M. Buchanan and Gordon Tullock, *The Calculus of Consent* (Ann Arbor: University of Michigan Press, 1962).

tax must apply to all persons who are eligible to cast votes in electoral processes.

Uniformity is somewhat more difficult to define precisely. In the abstract model discussed in the previous section, uniformity in tax treatment was assumed to be met by a standard or flat tax on some designated source, itself tied to the individual who is made personally liable. Such a definition is acceptable, provided that it is understood to require that the exemption or exclusion of any particular subsource or person becomes equivalent to the levy of zero rates and hence must violate any generality precept. If, for example, income is to be the basis on which taxes are levied, generality implies the imposition of the same rate on all sources of income, to all persons, with no exceptions, for any reason. The presence of any deduction, exclusion, or exemption must act to drive a political wedge between those who are subjected to the positive rates, even if these are identical over all members of the group that is taxed, and those persons who are differentially favored by the zero rates. One of the most disturbing features of several modern income tax "reforms" has been the removal of persons from the tax rolls, a step that necessarily sets up the parameters for exacerbated distributional politics.

A major issue in normative tax theory has been bypassed to this point by my assumption that income, if used as a base for taxing persons, can itself be readily defined in such a way as to command universal acceptance. This standard remains far from achievement, however, with reference to an income definition deemed appropriate for the levy of taxes. Specifically, should "income as received" or "income as spent" become the base for general taxes on persons and families? The advocates of spending-based taxation have long argued that saving must be excluded in order to avoid discriminatory double taxation. On the other hand, to the extent that persons secure utility from accumulation, any exclusion of saving sets up a differential rate structure, as defined operationally in terms of potential political behavior. Strict adherence to the generality principle would seem to argue against any exclusion, including saving, from the base for personal income tax.

A closely related argument involves the treatment of capital gains. As the value of an asset increases, the wealth of the owner increases. But is this increase properly counted as "income" for computation of tax liability? As with the tax treatment of saving, the indicated response here seems affirmative. Each of the sources of political inefficiency comes into play if special treatment is accorded to capital gains. Differential treatment of such income reduces the political efficiency of the tax structure. This judgment does not, of course, imply that the inclusion of capital gains in the tax base exerts no negative economic effects, especially when dynamic considerations are introduced. The overall rate of capital accumulation, and subsequently the rate of economic growth, may be higher in a fiscal regime that includes differentially favorable treatment for capital gains. But one of the costs of such a provision is a decrease in the political efficiency of the fiscal structure, for the reasons noted.

The principle of generality may, of course, be applied to other sources of tax than income. The imposition of taxes on the production, sale, or usage of goods and services can also be general or discriminatory over the whole set of possible items. Rates of tax can be uniformly levied on all goods and services, or rates may be applied differentially to separately identified goods and services, with zero rates included in the range of prospects. As with an income base, the "efficient" set of rates that might be put in place by a benevolent authority would include differentiation. But in majoritarian politics, the dominant coalition of interests represented in majority governance need not match the particular combination of interests that the optimal tax mix would require in support. For more or less the same reasons as with the income tax, there is an argument from efficiency that suggests the superiority of general taxation.

In sum, the general tax system that would meet criteria for political efficiency would, in income taxation, closely correspond to the Hall-Rabushka flat tax proposal advanced in the early 1980s,[15] which was introduced into the 1992 primary campaign by Jerry Brown, who seemed to understand the basic argument based on political efficiency. The politically efficient system of income taxation would involve a flat rate, proportional tax on all sources of income, without deduction, exclusion, or exemption. And if taxation of goods and services is required, the rate of tax would be levied uniformly over all potentially eligible items.

I should note, in particular, that the flat tax would not remove the redistributive aspects of the fiscal structure. Persons with higher incomes would,

---

15. Robert E. Hall and Alvin Rabushka, *Low Tax, Simple Tax, Flat Tax* (New York: McGraw-Hill, 1983).

of course, pay higher taxes. If more redistribution than that offered by the equal access to publicly provided goods and services were desired by the majority, this objective might be attained by the appropriate arrangement of transfer payments. The flat tax would make the intake side of the fiscal account politically efficient in a relative sense. The principle of generality might, of course, also be extended to the spending and transfer side of the account, in which case the argument could be made for a set of demogrants along with provision of equal access of all public goods programs for all citizens. Even with a politically efficient fiscal structure, as outlined, we might expect redistributional coalitions to emerge in the workings of majoritarian politics. But the generality constraints would in such a setting force majoritarian outcomes toward those patterns that would genuinely reflect the median preferences of the whole voting constituency rather than the differential class exploitation made possible by nongeneral fiscal treatment.

## Politics and Taxes in the 1990s

The efficiency-based argument for general taxation suggests only one avenue for reform in the operation of domestic politics in the United States in the 1990s. This politics seems to have become increasingly distributional, and members of Congress have come to be increasingly occupied in promoting particular interests, whether these be geographically or otherwise defined. "The politics of pork" dominates considerations of any all-encompassing or general interest. Traditionally, however, pork-barrel politics has been associated with the distribution of spending projects and the distribution of regulatory and protective governmental measures. Traditionally, the presumption has been that there remains sufficient generality in taxation to warrant a relative absence of concerns like those examined in this paper.

Only in the decades since World War II has the recognition emerged that distributional politics also tends to become dominating in tax reform policy. The basic structure of taxation has been subjected to almost continual change over these decades, and the precepts of generality came to be increasingly violated, with the results that have been indicated above. In the early and mid-1980s, considerable support seemed to mount for tax reform in the direction of restoring greater generality. And somewhat surprisingly to observers, a coalition between the leaders of the Reagan administration and the

Congress produced the major tax legislation of 1986. This reform shifted the tax structure of the United States toward generality and neutrality. The bases for both personal and corporate income taxes were broadened; many tax shelters and loopholes were closed. Rates of tax were lowered, and the number of differentials was reduced. Normative tax theorists, of almost all ideological persuasions, hailed the 1986 reforms as a substantial shift toward a more desirable tax system.

To public choice economists, however, the 1986 legislation seemed almost certain to be politically vulnerable. It became relatively easy to predict that the 1986 reforms would not remain in place for many years and that efforts would be made to reintroduce both increases in rates on the more comprehensive bases for tax and new differentials in rates for particular persons, groups, and sources.[16] The ink was scarcely dry on the tax bill before Republican politicians commenced to call for a special reduction in rates of tax on capital gains. These early efforts came to nought, but the 1990 budget agreement between the leaders in the Bush administration and the Congress acted to increase differentiation in rate structure and hence reflected an unraveling of the 1986 direction of change.

The tax proposals embodied in the Clinton "deficit reduction" package enacted in 1993 reflect quite an explicit reversal of the generality thrust of the 1986 legislation. These proposals include a new set of tax rate differentials by income level, which were advanced quite directly under rhetoric that seemed designed to stimulate majoritarian between-class antagonism. At the same time, special treatment was to be accorded to persons, groups, and sources of income that were deemed worthy of such discrimination.

The tax lobbyists and tax lawyers who seemed, ever so slightly, to have suffered their own recession in the late 1980s, looked forward to a renewed period of high prosperity in the mid-1990s. The status of the generality principle for taxation seemed relatively low in 1993, but the argument for general taxation, based on the political-constitutional efficacy of this institution in the operation of majoritarian democracy, has in no way been affected by the ebb and flow of electoral politics.

The American economy would be made more productive if American

---

16. James M. Buchanan, "Tax Reform as Political Choice," *Journal of Economic Perspectives* 1, no. 1 (Summer 1987): 29–35.

politics could be effectively constrained by some constitutionally required adherence to a generality principle in taxation. It may be appropriate here to borrow a term from modern physics and to think of the economic value that is destroyed by discriminatory taxation as disappearing into a "black hole" before it is allowed to come into existence at all.[17]

17. Stephen P. Magee, William A. Brock, and Leslie Young, *Black Hole Tariffs and Endogenous Policy Theory* (Cambridge: Cambridge University Press, 1989).

# Rational Majoritarian Taxation
## of the Rich
### With Increasing Returns and
### Capital Accumulation

*James M. Buchanan and Yong J. Yoon*

## I. Introduction

In the United States political setting of 1993, the dominant majority coalition effectively excluded high-income recipients (the rich) from participation in fiscal decisions and sought to increase the differentially high taxation of members of this group under a rhetoric of "fair shares." This real-world fiscal environment motivates our analysis in this paper. We address the question: What rate of taxation should the political majority rationally impose on high-income recipients if this majority is motivated strictly in the interest of its members?

We shall use highly abstracted models of the political economy that incorporate several simplifying assumptions. We suggest, however, that the results attained are relevant for the decision calculus of the leaders of the majority coalition. And in particular, we suggest that the possible presence of generalized or economy-wide increasing returns along with saving and the accumulation of capital make such decision calculus more difficult than that which would be implied in modern normative tax analysis that may involve maximization of a specific social welfare function. More specifically, our

From *Southern Economic Journal* 61 (April 1995): 923–35. Reprinted by permission of the publisher.

analysis indicates that the rational fiscal exploitation of the rich may involve *lower* tax extraction than orthodox fiscal theory would suggest. Or, in summary terms, the middle- and low-income members of the dominating majority may secure more fiscal gains as well as *non-fiscal* benefits from the income-producing behavior of the rich than is recognized in the traditional analyses, and these benefits should be taken into account in any comprehensive reckoning. One implication involves the strengthening of the case for expenditure based taxation, even from the perspective of members of non-saving classes.

We shall proceed as follows: we shall first, in section II, summarize the straightforward response to the question posed in a simple model that assumes all income is derived from current labor supply and that the economy operates under universalized constant returns. In section III, the constant returns assumption is replaced by one of generalized increasing returns. A central contribution in the paper is that of tracing out the effects of this change in the model. In section IV, we include income from capital, which adds complexity to the analysis of both earlier models, and introduces implications of its own that are challenging quite independent of the presence of increasing returns. In section V, we examine the prospects for an expenditure tax rather than an income tax. Finally, in section VI we discuss some extensions and qualifications on the analysis.

## II. The Political Economy under Constant Returns: The Benchmark Model

Consider an economy in which production is specialized and in which exchanges of goods and services are made through an interlinked set of markets. Politically, the community has a "democratic" constitution, and government adequately meets its protective state obligations to protect property and contract against private predation. There is universal franchise and majority voting. There are no restrictions on the fiscal authority of the majority coalition, either in imposing taxes or in allocating benefits from government spending, including direct transfers. All taxes are levied against an income base, and persons cannot be taxed on their potential rather than their observed income receipts. Leisure, as such, cannot be taxed.

For initial simplicity in exposition, we assume that all income is derived from current supplies of labor services. There are no capital goods that yield income, and labor, itself, cannot be made more productive of income by investment in either general or specific skills. The community is made up of three distinct groups of individuals, classified by value productivity. There are no non-producers in the economy. For simplicity, assume that, within each of the three groups, all persons are equivalent. We designate the groups as $R$ (rich), $M$ (middle), and $P$ (poor), and individual members of these groups as $r$, $m$, and $p$. The economy, which we assume to be closed, is characterized by constant returns, in each industry, in each industrial category, and for the inclusive size of the network of production-exchange.

Given the parameters of the basic or benchmark model as described, we now assume that a majority coalition emerges that is made up of all members from the middle- and low-income classes or groups, from $M$ and $P$. Members of the high-income group, $R$, are relegated to minority status and are unable to influence political decisions. We assume that members of the dominant coalition are motivated only by their own economic interest; they are not altruistic toward members of $R$.

More restrictively, we also assume that members of the majority are not concerned about possible defections in the coalition membership through a series of subsequent electoral periods. We explicitly abstract from issues of potential instability in the majority coalition due to the defection of members in response to possible side-payments from non-coalition members. This assumption allows us to avoid discussion of the whole set of problems that involve rotating sequential majorities and cycles.

Since, by assumption, all members of $R$ are identical, little could be gained by differential taxation among separate members of the exploited minority. The tax rate structure confronting each person may take many forms. Initially, consider proportional taxation. What rate will the majority coalition impose on all members of the high-income group? Note that this question may be analyzed independent of whether or not members of the majority find it advantageous to impose taxes on themselves. If revenues sufficient to meet collective purposes can be raised from the rich, no residual taxes will be accepted by members of $M$ and $P$. And if revenues raised from $R$ are more than sufficient to meet collective goods demands, as determined by members of $M$ and $P$, the taxation of members of $R$ will still be used to finance direct transfers to those persons in $M$ and $P$.[1]

The rate of tax that will be imposed on all members of the high-income group, $R$, will depend on the predicted responses of members of this group to differing rates. If no response at all is predicted to occur, that is, if income-producing behavior of the rich is not predicted to change as a result of changes in tax rates, the majority will impose confiscatory taxes on all incomes of the group over some subsistence minimum.[2]

If any behavioral response to taxation on the part of the taxed persons is anticipated to occur, the optimal levy for the majority to impose will be that rate that maximizes total revenue extraction. Under the simplifying assumptions here, where all income is from currently supplied labor services, and further, where the coalition is not concerned about voter defections from its own ranks, there will be a uniquely determinate solution to this maximization problem. This will be attained at the extremum of the "Laffer curve" or function that relates tax rates directly with revenue totals.

More formally, and stated in terms of the taxation of a single member of $R$, the majority's problem is to maximize:

$$V_r = ty_r \tag{1}$$

subject to

$$y_r = f(t), \tag{2}$$

---

1. The usage of revenues collected from persons in $R$ may, of course, be used to finance direct transfers to members of $M$ and $P$ before the "efficient" level of collective goods is financed, if "efficiency" is defined to include the evaluations of members of $R$. (Marilyn Flowers and Patricia Danzon, "Separation of the Redistributive and Allocative Functions of Government: A Public Choice Perspective," *Journal of Public Economics* [August 1984]: 373–80.)

2. More plausibly, although it would not emerge from the behavioral calculus postulated in the model here, we might expect that the incomes of the rich would be taxed so as to bring post-tax levels down to equality with the incomes of the members of the middle-income group. (James M. Buchanan, "The Political Economy of Franchise in the Welfare State," in *Capitalism and Freedom: Problems and Prospects,* ed. R. T. Selden [Charlottesville: University Press of Virginia, 1975], 52–77. In *The Economics of Legal Relationships,* ed. H. B. Manne [St. Paul: West Publishing Company, 1975], 78–97. As "The Political Economy of the Welfare State," in *The Theory of Public Choice—II,* edited with Robert D. Tollison [Ann Arbor: University of Michigan Press, 1984], 174–93.)

where $t$ denotes the tax rate and $V_r$ revenue extraction from a single member of $R$. The income of a minority member $y_r = f(t)$ in (2) is determined by utility maximization: given tax rate $t$, work effort is chosen to maximize

$$v(c, L)$$

subject to

$$c = (1 - t)y_r$$
$$y_r = F(e - L), \qquad (3)$$

where $c$ is consumption, $L$ leisure, and $v$ is the utility function of member $r$; $e$ is member $r$'s input endowment, and $F$ is the production function the individual member $r$ faces. The first order condition for the majority's solution is met when

$$dV_r(t)/dt = 0, \qquad (4)$$

and the maximum tax revenue can be extracted at the tax rate at which income $y_r = f(t)$ attains unit elasticity.[3]

We want to call attention to one feature of this model. There is no *non-fiscal* interest on the part of the members of the majority in the incomes of the rich. These incomes matter to the members of the majority only as potential sources of tax revenue. The contribution to national income made by

---

3. Brennan and Buchanan have written extended treatments of the determination of the optimal rate of tax in a revenue-maximizing model. In their analysis, they assumed that a monolithic government, separate from the taxpayers, seeks to maximize revenue collections. They did not examine the calculus of the majority in its imposition of taxes on the minority, although the same analysis can be readily applied to this case. (Geoffrey Brennan and James M. Buchanan, "Towards a Tax Constitution for Leviathan," *Journal of Public Economics* [December 1977]: 255–73, and *The Power to Tax: Analytical Foundations of a Fiscal Constitution* [New York: Cambridge University Press, 1980].)

Buchanan and Lee examined some of the implications of temporal adjustments and differential rates of discounts in determining the rate of tax that would be imposed by government. As in the Brennan and Buchanan analysis, however, they did not extend the model to consider majority imposition of taxes on the minority. (James M. Buchanan and Dwight R. Lee, "Tax Rates and Tax Revenues in Political Equilibrium: Some Simple Analytics," *Economic Inquiry* [July 1982]: 344–54. In *The Theory of Public Choice—II*, edited with Robert D. Tollison [Ann Arbor: University of Michigan Press, 1984], 174–93, and "Politics, Time, and the Laffer Curve," *Journal of Political Economy* [August 1982]: 816–19.)

the rich in earning high incomes is totally irrelevant to the majority except through the fiscal interdependence described.

## III. The Political Economy under Generalized Increasing Returns: The Effect of Non-fiscal Interdependence

We now change only one element in the basic model outlined in section II. We drop the assumption that the economy operates under constant returns and replace this with the assumption that there are increasing returns to the size of the network of market production and exchange. For our purposes it is sufficient to assume that as the size of the economy increases, the value productivity of inputs increases as measured in units of output.

This assumption of generalized increasing returns is not a radical departure from the central idea of economic theory. Adam Smith's widely cited principle that the division of labor is limited by the extent of the market is an early statement of the relationship. As the economy increases in size, increased specialization is made possible with consequent increases in the efficiency of resource usage. Subsequent to Smith's initial insight here, other economists have variously urged their peers to replace the constant returns postulate with that of increasing returns. Notable among these critics have been Allyn Young and Nicholas Kaldor. And one of the most interesting developments in economic theory of the 1980s and 1990s has been the return of economists' interest to increasing returns models.[4]

It is not our purpose here to mount a general criticism of orthodox usage of the constant returns postulate. A summary statement of the analytical efficacy of this postulate may, however, be helpful in understanding why economic theorists have seemed so reluctant to introduce generalized increasing returns, even for the limited objectives of examining the full implications of the change in the basic model of the economy. Under constant returns, the

---

4. We have attempted to bring together the major contributions in the increasing returns tradition in economic theory, from those of Adam Smith, through Alfred Marshall, Allyn Young, Nicholas Kaldor, and including modern contributions in several areas of application. (James M. Buchanan and Yong J. Yoon, *The Return to Increasing Returns* [Ann Arbor: University of Michigan Press, 1994].)

explicit interdependence among the separated activities of participants in the inclusive market economy is effectively *minimized.*

In the idealized model of general equilibrium,[5] persons react independently and separately to the parameters they confront, and their behavior does not, in itself, affect the economic well-being of others in the nexus, except in those well-identified instances where the activities enter directly into utility or production functions of those other than the actors. In the stylized economy without the presence of these familiar externalities, there is no behavioral interdependence among participants. This sort of interdependence is eliminated because, under constant returns, the market distribution of payment to inputs in accordance with marginal productivity exhausts total product.

Fiscal interdependence is, of course, present, even under constant returns, once a tax system embodying an income base is in place. A person's behavior in earning or not earning income affects others in the economic-fiscal nexus through the effects on revenues,[6] and it is, of course, precisely these effects that are incorporated in the revenue-maximizing calculus traced out earlier. Over and beyond this fiscal linkage, however, under constant returns, the individual who chooses voluntarily to earn less income in response to the imposition of a tax suffers the full consequences of his/her action. There are no non-fiscal spillovers that affect the utilities of others in the economy.

Consider an example. The young radiologist who earns $200,000 per year and works full time when, say, the rate of tax is 20 percent, responds to an increase in the rate to 50 percent by reducing income earnings to $100,000. The revenue shortfall of $20,000 on the $100,000 of income now forgone is reckoned in the revenue maximizing calculus that dictates the imposition of the 50 percent rate on the income that is earned, on the non-forgone $100,000. The fisc gains (by $10,000); the income loss in the aggregate economy ($100,000) exerts no negative impact on the utilities of those who impose the tax increase.

The radiologist loses the value of post-tax marginal product of one-half

---

5. For instance, Gerard Debreu, *Theory of Value* (New Haven: Cowles Foundation, 1959).

6. See James M. Buchanan, "Externality in Tax Response," *Southern Economic Journal* (July 1966): 35–42, and "Pareto Superior Tax Reform: Some Simple Analytics," *Eastern Economic Journal* (Winter 1994): 7–9.

his effort ($80,000 out of $100,000) minus the value placed on the added leisure (say $60,000) for a net loss of $20,000. The majority members gain through the enhancement of fiscal revenue ($10,000), but there are no other gains or losses after sufficient time for adjustment takes place. All under the presumption of constant returns.

The results become quite different when we replace the constant returns postulate with generalized increasing returns. The behavior of anyone who changes the supply of input to the market affects the size of the total economy, as before. But such changes generate spillover benefits or damages to all other participants, and these effects are transmitted outside the fiscal process. The person who earns less income, whether as a result of a tax change or simply as a shift in preferences for leisure, exerts an external diseconomy on all others in the production-exchange nexus.[7]

The decrease in the size of the aggregate economy, measured in total income earned through the market process, reduces the potential for exploiting specialization. The effect is that the output price vector increases relative to the input price vector. Any input is made less productive of value than it would be had the reduction in the economy's size not occurred.

The presence of such *non-fiscal* interdependence among the income-earning activities of all participants in the economy modifies the decision calculus of the political majority which, in our model, seeks to determine the optimal fiscal exploitation of members of the excluded minority. By assumption, the only available instrument is the rate of tax that may be levied on incomes earned through market activity.[8] But the rate that will maximize revenues is not optimal for the majority when non-fiscal interdependence exists. The objective function of the majority is not restricted to revenues collected from the minority. Because they are also participants in the aggregate economy, members of the majority now have an independent economic interest in the total amount of income generated in the economy and, hence, in the income earned by each individual member of the taxed minority.

---

7. Buchanan, alone and with Yoon, has analyzed the economic content of the work ethic in essentially this framework. (James M. Buchanan, *The Economics and the Ethics of Constitutional Order* [Ann Arbor: University of Michigan Press, 1991], and *Ethics and Economic Progress* [Norman: University of Oklahoma Press, 1994]; Buchanan and Yoon, *Return to Increasing Returns.*)

8. Brennan and Buchanan have discussed the choice of base as well as rates (*Power to Tax*).

In this setting, the optimal tax rate for the dominant majority to impose on the members of the minority must be lower than that rate that will maximize revenue collections. The majority's maximizing solution will describe a tax rate–total revenue position that is located on the upsloping part of the "Laffer curve" relationship rather than at the extremum.

The member of the majority coalition tries to maximize a utility function determined by own income ($y$) and the tax revenue:

$$u(y, \ V_r). \tag{5}$$

The income level $y$ is determined by economy-wide productivity, which is a function of the aggregate income under generalized increasing returns. Since the tax rate affects aggregate income through the income of a minority member ($y_r$), we can express $y$ as a function of $y_r$,

$$y = g(y_r), \tag{6}$$

where $g$ is an increasing function.

The first order condition for the utility maximization (5) is met when

$$u_1 dy/dt + u_2 dV_r/dt = 0,$$

or

$$dV_r/dt = -(u_1/u_2)(dy/dt), \tag{7}$$

where $u_1$ and $u_2$ are partial derivatives of the utility function with respect to income $y$ and tax revenue $V_r$. The sign of $dy/dt$ is negative by the chain rule

$$dy/dt = (dy/dy_r)(dy_r/dt) < 0, \tag{8}$$

where the term $dy/dy_r$ is positive because of the generalized increasing returns, and the next term $dy_r/dt$ is negative because of tax induced incentive on the behavior of the minority members. We conclude that the sign of $dV_r/dt$ in (7) is positive. Total tax revenue is not maximized in this solution.

## IV. Capital Introduced

The models of the economy analyzed in sections II and III above are restricted by the simplifying assumption that all income is derived from currently supplied labor services. We now drop this assumption and introduce a model that allows income from both human and non-human capital to make up some share in market returns, and, further, that allows the accumulation of capital generating such income to take place by withdrawal of income from spending on current consumption. With this single change in the assumptions, we can treat the constant returns and the increasing returns cases in sequence.

## CONSTANT RETURNS

We continue to restrict the majority's decision-makers to the single control variable, the rate of tax that may be levied proportionately on all income from market activity earned by members of the minority group, $R$, whether this income be from the sale of labor services or lease or sale of capital goods.

If some share of market income represents a return to capital, then any tax on income will reduce the net return on investment in capital accumulation. This reduction in rate of return may or may not reduce the proportion of income that is saved. But since the tax (or any increase in the rate of tax) reduces the net income available for consumption and saving, the effects on the amount of saving are clear. The rate of capital accumulation in the economy will be reduced as the rate of tax on income increases.

Because of this predicted effect on capital growth, the income stream in all future periods is reduced as the tax rate is increased. In this feature, the model differs from the all-labor income model analyzed earlier, in which the rate of tax imposed in one period has no effect on the income potential for subsequent periods. Does this feature make the decision calculus of the majority taxing authority different?

Consider an example in which, say, the revenue-maximizing rate of tax, after full adjustment, on all market income earned by members of the minority is 50 percent, and where the fully adjusted pre-tax income under this regime is $100,000. From this income pre-tax, the fisc extracts $50,000 and the taxpayer retains $50,000. Assume that from the retained $50,000 the taxpayer saves 22.77 percent, or $11,390. For simple exposition, we assume that the saving is the only source of future income.

Now compare this fiscal regime with an alternative one that involves only a 40 percent rate of tax, with a pre-tax adjusted income of $120,000, with revenue of $48,000 to the fisc, and taxpayer retention of $72,000. If the rate of saving out of income is invariant at 22.77 percent in the two regimes, a total of $16,390 would be saved. In a summary comparison, revenues are higher in the first regime by \$2,000 (\$50,000 − \$48,000), while savings are higher in the second by \$5,000 (\$16,390 − \$11,390).

Under what conditions would the majority be led to select the second regime rather than the revenue-maximizing solution in the first? In the comparison as set up in the example, the majority should be indifferent as between these two regimes if future tax revenue is discounted at the market rate of interest. The second regime generates \$2,000 less in current revenue to the fisc, but increases savings by \$5,000. This measures the present value of the future income that will be generated when the savings are invested. From this income stream, the 40 percent rate of tax will yield a present value of \$2,000, which is equal to the current revenue shortfall the replacement of the first regime creates.

We have, of course, rigged the arithmetical example in order to demonstrate the underlying logic of the differences in the decision-makers' maximizing calculus when capital income is introduced. Nonetheless the example is helpful in suggesting several relationships. If the rate of saving from income by the rich is increased (decreased) or if the income response to taxation becomes larger (smaller), the majority's optimizing rate of tax decreases (increases) relative to the strict current revenue-maximizing rate. But this statement must be read with caution. The majority member may still try to maximize tax revenue as defined in present-value terms.

On the other hand, an increase in the majority's discount rate makes strict or current-period revenue maximization more likely.[9] We have assumed that the majority coalition is not concerned about the defection of minority members to newly emergent majorities in electoral succession. Dropping this assumption would, of course, dramatically shorten the effective time horizon for the decision-makers. But, even under such a restriction, there is no reason why the rate of time preference for majority decision-makers need be equal to that reflected in the market.[10]

The discussion is perhaps sufficient to suggest that once capital income is included in the tax base the dominance of the revenue-maximizing solution in the majority's decision calculus no longer exists in the strict sense, even

---

9. Geoffrey Brennan and James M. Buchanan, *The Reason of Rules: Constitutional Political Economy* (Cambridge: Cambridge University Press, 1985).

10. Linda Cohen and Roger Noll have related work on this issue (*The Technology Pork Barrel* [Washington, D.C.: Brookings Institution, 1991]).

within the restrictive limits imposed by the constant returns postulate. There are no non-fiscal interdependencies of the sort treated in section III. But the fiscal interdependencies themselves may operate to temper somewhat the current-period exploitation of the minority, provided only that the members of the majority are rational in pursuit of their own economic interest.

## Generalized increasing returns

The extension of the analysis to apply to an economy that operates under generalized increasing returns is straightforward. As the discussion in section III above indicated, the majority decision-makers will, in the presence of increasing returns, have a positive economic interest in the total income generated by the activity of members of the rich minority, over and beyond that interest that is effected through the fiscal process.

To the extent that the imposition of a tax on the income of the rich, or any increase in such a tax, impacts on the absolute amount of income that would have otherwise been saved, and ultimately made available for capital formation, the flow of income in future periods is reduced. And this shortfall in future-period income will, in itself, forestall the potential for the exploitation of specialization that a larger market might have brought into being.

The majority decision-maker must include in the maximizing calculus both the effects of the tax on savings and capital formation and the non-fiscal effects that measure the influence of economy-wide increasing returns, directly in the current period and indirectly in present-value terms for all future periods. Only if all of these effects can either be ignored altogether or be swamped in significance by a very high discount rate will the solution dictate adherence to the strict revenue-maximizing rate of tax. A formal statement of the decision-maker's maximizing calculus is indicated.

## Formal model

The fiscal interaction between majority and minority members can be formulated as a Stackelberg game in which the majority is the leader and the minority is the follower. The majority member tries to maximize intertemporal preferences,

$$u(y, V_r) + \beta u(y^f, V_r^f)$$

subject to

$$V_r^f = tI;$$

with

$$I = y_r^f + (1 + r)s. \tag{9}$$

Here $\beta$ denotes the subjective time discount factor, $r$ denotes the net interest rate, and superscript $f$ indicates next period variables; the next period income $I$ is the sum of the earned income $(y_r^f)$ and the capital income from the saving. We express saving $(s)$ as a function of income $y_r$. But this saving function is the result of the optimal decision by the minority member in response to the given tax rate $t$.

Given the tax rate $t$, the minority member chooses current and future income levels, $y_r$ and $y_r^f$, and the saving $s$ so as to maximize intertemporal preferences

$$v(c) + \beta_r v(c^f)$$

subject to

$$c + s = (1 - t)y_r$$

and

$$c^f = (1 - t)I = (1 - t)[y_r^f + (1 + r)s], \tag{10}$$

where $\beta_r$ is the time discount factor of the minority member, $c$ and $c^f$ are current and future consumption levels; superscript $f$ indicates future variables. The first order condition for the majority's utility maximization problem (9) is

$$u_1 dy/dt + u_2 dV_r/dt + \beta u_1^f dy^f/dt + \beta u_2^f dV_r^f/dt = 0, \tag{11}$$

where $u_1$ indicates the partial derivative with respect to the current income $(y)$, $u_2$ the partial derivative with respect to tax revenue $V_r$, and $u_1^f$ indicates the partial derivative with respect to future income $y^f$, etc.

Under constant returns, the income of the majority member is not affected by the size of the economy. In this case $dy/dt = 0$ and $dy^f/dt = 0$, because the tax rate is the only parameter that affects the size of the economy in the model. And the first order condition (11) reduces to

$$u_2 dV_r/dt + \beta u_2^f dV_r^f/dt = 0$$

or

$$dV_r + \beta(u_2^f/u_2)V_r^f/dt = 0. \tag{12}$$

The first order condition above indicates that the present value of revenue is maximized according to the time discount factor $\beta u_2^f/u_2$ of the majority member.

Under generalized increasing returns, however, the assumption ($dy/dt = 0$ and $dy^f/dt = 0$) does not hold. Instead, to the majority member, his own income is a function of the size of economy and thus is a function of $y_r$, the income of the minority member; $y = g(y_r)$ and $y^f = g[y_r^f + (1 + r)s]$ where $g$ is an increasing function. Then,

$$dy/dt = g'(y_r)(dy_r/dt) < 0;$$

and

$$dy^f/dt = g'(\cdot)[dy_r^f/dt + (1 + r)ds/dt] < 0,$$

where $g'$, the derivative of $g$, is positive, and the derivative $ds/dt$ is negative.

Therefore, the optimal level of present value of tax revenue is on the up-sloping part of the related and appropriately defined Laffer curve. From equation (11),

$$d[V_r + \beta(u_2^f/u_2)V_r^f]/dt > 0.$$

The tax rate on the income of the minority that is optimal for a member of the majority lies below that rate which maximizes the present value of the revenue stream, which, in return, lies below that rate which will maximize current-period revenues. This relationship holds regardless of the discount rate used by the majority, even when this rate is infinity; that is, the majority does not care about the future.

## V. Expenditure Tax and Income Tax

The formal model introduced above lends itself to an examination of the question: Under what conditions might members of the majority rationally choose to allow minority members to exempt saving altogether from taxation? That is, will a spending tax be selected rather than an income tax?

Assume, first of all, that the discount rate that informs the majority member's fiscal choice is equal to the market rate of interest which, in turn, measures the return on capital investment in the economy. In this setting, as usual, a dollar's worth of saving also measures the present value of future income that can be generated by that saving, as discounted by the market rate.

Even in this restricted model, the presence of economy-wide increasing returns will tilt the balance toward the expenditure tax. Because this tax increases saving relative to that generated under the income tax, the economy's size is increased. There will be some non-fiscal benefits to the majority from the spending tax even if the two taxes are equivalent fiscally.

Under the income tax, equation (10) in section IV describes the consumption saving decision of the minority. The first order condition characterizes the saving decision

$$-v'(c) + \beta_r(1 + r)v'\,(c^f) = 0, \tag{10a}$$

where $c = (1 - t)y - s$, and $c^f = y^f + (1 + r)s$; and $\beta_r(1 + r)$ is 1 by assumption. The relative price of saving is 1. Under the spending tax, given the tax rate $t^*$, the minority member chooses consumption and saving to maximize his intertemporal utility,

$$v(c) + \beta_r v(c^f)$$

subject to

$$c + s = (1 - t^*)y + t^*s$$

and

$$c^f = y^f + (1 + r)s. \tag{13}$$

The first order condition is

$$-v'(c)(1 - t^*) + v'[y^f + (1 + r)s] = 0. \tag{13a}$$

The relative price of saving is $(1 - t^*)$ which is less than 1. This will induce a substitution of saving for current consumption. Since the tax rates, $t$ and $t^*$, are chosen so that tax revenues are the same under the two tax regimes, the outlay on consumption and saving will be the same; the tax revenues being equal, $ty = t^*(y - s^*)$, it follows that $(1 - t)y = (1 - t^*)y + t^*s^*$ where $s^*$ is the saving under the expenditure tax.

Under the standard assumption of concave utility function, the marginal utility of future consumption $v'[y^f + (1 + r)s]$ falls as saving increases. Thus we obtain $s < s^*$, the minority member saves more under the spending tax, thereby increasing the size of the economy with consequent non-fiscal benefit to the majority.

If the current income-generating response to taxation is lower under the spending tax, the majority will prefer to levy the expenditure tax on the minority, even under the constant returns postulate. The maximal present value of tax revenue is larger under the expenditure tax. This pattern of response is suggested when it is recognized that saving, itself, generates utility, to the person who saves. The spending tax, which exempts this utility-enhancing use of income, allows the prediction of a somewhat lower negative income-earning response than under the income tax.[11] If we introduce the increasing returns postulate in this setting, the relative superiority of the expenditure tax is increased.

The results sketched out above depend critically on the assumption concerning the discount rate used in the majority's calculus of choice. If this rate is higher than the market rate, then the choice is biased toward the income tax base, which will, of course, always generate higher maximum revenues in immediate periods. The simple fact that we do not observe more majoritarian support for the spending-tax alternative in political discussion may itself suggest, at least indirectly, that the implicit discount rate in fiscal choice is higher than any market rate, perhaps substantially so.

## VI. Qualifications, Extensions, and Conclusions

To this point, we have concentrated attention on the majority's optimizing decision in levying a *proportional tax* rate on either the income or the spending of the rich members of the political minority. Empiricist critics will immediately point to the irrelevance of the analysis to any real-world polity due to the fact that the tax structures are skewed to incorporate progressivity rather than proportionality in rates. Two comments are in order.

---

11. James M. Buchanan and Yong J. Yoon, "Income Tax and Expenditure Tax," working paper (Fairfax, Va.: Center for Study of Public Choice, George Mason University, 1993).

First, the analysis applies, almost without qualification, if we replace the uniform proportional rate with the effective marginal rate of tax, thereby allowing for lower rates over inframarginal ranges of tax base. Behavioral adjustments by taxpayers are made, almost exclusively, in response to effective marginal rates, rather than to average rates of tax. Secondly, the widespread existence of progressive rate structures, accompanied by a political rhetoric that seems to reflect deliberate majoritarian intent to exploit the rich fiscally, suggests that majorities are not rational in their choice behavior. Pareto-superior rearrangements may often be possible that include *reductions* in effective marginal rates (which may often be beyond optimal limits) along with *increases* in rates on inframarginal units of base. Majorities can thereby gain revenues, in current- and present-value terms, while at the same time securing the spillover benefits from an expanded economic nexus. At the same time, members of the class that is differentially taxed can possibly secure the benefits that emerge from a reduced distortion in relevant margins of behavioral choice.[12]

The thrust of our argument has been one of demonstrating that the political majority need not exploit the richer members of the polity to the extent suggested in the elementary models of revenue maximization. We suggested, in section III, that the presence of economy-wide increasing returns requires the recognition of the non-fiscal benefits, to members of the majority, that stem from the income-generating activities of the rich. This effect becomes more pronounced as the share of income received by the rich increases and as the predicted negative response to taxation increases.

In section IV, we suggested that even in an economy with constant returns the interdependencies produced by capital accumulation may offer rational bases for majoritarian limits on strict revenue-maximizing tax rates and, in some settings, for explicit exemption of savings from taxation altogether.

An important additional qualification on our analysis becomes necessary when we allow for particular differentiation among individuals within each income category. We explicitly assumed that members of the majority (of $P$ and $M$) are not concerned with electoral sequences involving shifting coalitions. But, also, we implicitly assumed that individual members of these politically dominant groups do not expect to shift economic status over time

---

12. Buchanan, "Pareto-Superior Tax Reform"; Brennan and Buchanan, *Power to Tax*.

and thus the majority coalition makes taxing decisions in each and every period. If we drop these assumptions, the analysis will, of course, be changed.

Consider a person who is, say, a member of $M$ (middle income class) in period $t_0$, but who expects to be able to move to a higher income class ($R$) in period $t_1$ and beyond. Further, this person recognizes that tax rates put in place in $t_0$ will tend to remain in place in $t_1$ and beyond. In this setting, and depending in part on the subjective rate of discount adopted, the person in question will be reluctant to levy the rate of tax on members of $R$ in $t_0$ which would satisfy the conditions for optimality stated formally in our analysis. The implication is that the greater is the upward mobility expectation in the economy, the lower will be the rate of taxation of the rich.

Finally, we shall note again two critical framework assumptions of our whole analysis. First, the economy has been assumed to be closed. In effect, the inclusive production-exchange nexus has been assumed to be coincident in participation with membership in the political unit. Second, the macro-economic stabilization instruments have been assumed to operate so as to maintain nominal aggregate demand, thereby insuring that employment remains near its natural rate.

If the economy, or parts thereof, is open to external trade, the scale efficiencies that arise from the presence of increasing returns are less pronounced. And a fully rational tax-imposing majority could, in principle, offset the scale effects that result from taxing the rich by, simultaneously, opening up the economy so as to create an expanded scope for specialization. For example, the combined Clinton program of increasing tax rates on the rich and approving NAFTA (North American Free Trade Agreement) may be mutually offsetting along some dimension of effective scale. Whether or not any political majority could be consistently rational over such disparate dimensions of policy may, of course, be open to question. And the successful political history of protectionism does not suggest extensive collective rationality, regardless of the composition of the decision-making authority.

In public and media discussion, the macroeconomic impact of fiscal adjustment, whether in taxation, expenditure, or government borrowing, commands primary attention. An increase in rates of tax on the members of the high-income minority is often assessed for its effects on levels of aggregate demand, and, through these effects, on rates of employment and economic growth. The rich will, of course, generate less income, pre-tax, than before the rate increase; the return of tax revenues to the income stream is not sufficient to offset the initial income reduction.

Efficient macrostabilization policy can insure the isolation of this "excess burden" effect, keeping the reduction in aggregate demand in line with the tax-induced reduction in aggregate supply and concentrating net losses on those who are directly subject to the tax rate increases, *provided* that the economy is described by a constant returns technology. Under increasing returns, however, this conceptually simple demand-supply equation is disrupted, making macroeconomic adjustment more difficult.

Whether or not the macroeconomic framework parameters operate so as to guarantee even tolerable approximation to stabilization objectives is, of course, a question that we need not address here. We should acknowledge, however, that the "taxation of the rich" that is optimal for the political majority does depend on the actual rather than the idealized operation of the macroeconomy. We have basically followed conventional procedure in this respect. We have attempted to analyze the taxing calculus of the majority in isolation from any interdependence with the stabilization calculus.

## PART FIVE

*Confessions of a Burden Monger*

# Debt, Public

Public debt is an obligation on the part of a governmental unit to pay specific monetary sums to holders of legally designated claims at particular points in time. The sums owed to creditors may be defined in standard monetary units of the debtor government or in units of an external currency. The United States national debt represents, predominantly, an obligation of the federal government to pay specific sums of United States dollars to creditors. On the other hand, national debts may, and local debts must, be defined in units of external currency. The monetary obligation may be that of paying either interest or a return of principal, or both. Specific issues of debt may or may not be characterized by definite maturity schedules. Consols, which represent obligations to pay interest in perpetuity, involve no obligation for a return of principal.

Public debt must be distinguished from currency outstanding. The obligation on the part of a money-issuing governmental authority to the holder of currency is not public debt, since the claim can also be met in currency units.

Public debt is created by the act of public borrowing, or, in other words, the act of floating public loans, the act of selling government securities. This is a process through which governmental units, in exchange for money (currency or demand deposits) give promises to pay, this exchange being normally voluntary on the part of the lender. For governments the purpose of the exchange is that of securing current purchasing power with which they may purchase resource services, or final products. The issue of public debt is

From *International Encyclopedia of the Social Sciences,* vol. 4 (London and New York: Macmillan, 1968), 28–34. Reprinted by permission of the publisher.

one means of financing government expenditures, alternative to taxation and to direct currency creation.

Public debt is amortized, or retired, by a reverse transfer in which government gives up money for debt instruments, either through purchase on the open market or through scheduled maturity payments.

## Measurement

Public debt is normally measured in nominal maturity values. This does not represent the "size" of the public debt in such a manner as to make comparisons over time and among separate governmental units fully accurate. Varying composition of debt can affect its degree of liquidity for holders, as well as other characteristics. To the extent that debt instruments are valued for these nondebt features, the effective size of public debt, as such, is reduced. A more accurate measure of debt is produced by capitalizing the annual interest charges at some appropriate rate of discount, normally that rate which approximates the return on risk-free investment in the economy. An example will clarify this point. In terms of nominal maturity value, national debt may be of equal size, say $300,000 million, at two points in time. In the one case, however, if the debt is composed primarily of short-term issues possessing a high degree of "moneyness," the annual interest charges may amount to, say, only $6,000 million. In the other case, if the debt is largely funded, the interest charges may be as high as, say, $12,000 million. Clearly, the "size" of the public debt is not identical in the two cases; other dimensions than nominal maturity values must be included in any appropriate measure. For purposes of making intertemporal and international comparisons, the most appropriate measure is perhaps the ratio of annual interest charges to gross national or gross domestic product.

Public debt may characterize both national and local fiscal systems. Data are much more readily available for national debts, and that of some selected countries may be introduced for illustrative purposes. Table 1 shows the national debts of several selected countries in 1960, defined in nominal maturity values, local currency units being converted into United States dollar equivalents at official exchange rates. The right-hand column of Table 1 indicates the ratio of national debt to gross national product of the issuing country.

*Table 1.* National Debt in Selected Countries, 1960

|  | National Debt, 1960[a] *(in millions of dollars)* | Ratio of Debt to GNP[b] *(Per cent)* |
|---|---|---|
| Brazil | 4,911 | 19 |
| Canada | 17,679 | 49 |
| France | 24,925 | 40 |
| Germany | 611 | 1 |
| India | 13,159 | 35 |
| Japan | 2,551 | 7 |
| Norway | 1,293 | 29 |
| United Kingdom | 77,652 | 124 |
| United States | 286,471 | 57 |

a. Includes introgovernmental debt. Converted to U.S. dollars at official rates.

b. Rounded to nearest percentage point.

Source: International Financial Statistics

The most significant fact that emerges from any comparative survey of national debts in the various countries, and one that is indicated from the data summarized in Table 1, is that no single country was, in 1960, dangerously "overburdened" with national debt. Among the major countries of the world, only for the United Kingdom was the size of the national debt larger than GNP. And for relatively few countries, developed or underdeveloped, is the ratio of national debt to GNP more than 50 per cent. There are several reasons for these results, some of which make their significance less than it might initially seem to be.

Countries that are characterized by large national debts, measured proportionately to GNP, tend to be those that have enjoyed reasonably stable governments, that have been victorious in wars, and that have experienced reasonable monetary stability over a relatively long period. Great Britain and the United States, both victorious in two world wars and both characterized by political stability and relatively moderate inflation, carry relatively heavier national debts than most other countries. Causality seems to work in only one direction here, however. Political and monetary stability do not result from large national debts; instead, large national debts emerge only in conditions of reasonable political and monetary stability. In the absence of these conditions, public borrowing will rarely be important as a means of financing public spending, and, even when it is successfully carried out, the creditors of the state may be subject to confiscation through inflation or through default.

Historically, the large increases in national debts have been associated with the financing of war emergencies. This is illustrated by the growth of the United States national debt, shown for selected years in Table 2.

## Composition

Public debt assumes many forms, ranging from consols at the one extreme to treasury bills of very short maturity at the other, with other characteristics not relating to maturity schedules. The form in which debt is marketed affects the interest rate that must be paid, since various features, desired in themselves, may be offered complementary to what may be called "pure debt." Consols, which have no maturity and which obligate the issuing government only to pay a specific interest charge periodically and in perpetuity, provide a useful benchmark for comparative purposes. These come close to representing "pure debt," and as other features are added the cost of carrying debt tends to decrease. The fixing of a definite maturity, which obligates the government to return the principal to the holder of claims, increases the li-

*Table 2.* Growth of United States National Debt, Selected Years

| Year | Nominal Maturity Value (In millions of dollars) |
|------|--------------------------------------------------|
| 1917 | 1,023 |
| 1919 | 26,349 |
| 1930 | 15,774 |
| 1940 | 42,376 |
| 1946 | 277,912 |
| 1949 | 249,509 |
| 1960 | 286,471 |
| 1965 | 317,270 |

Source: U.S. Treasury Department data

quidity of the claim, especially as maturity is approached. Hence, as maturities are shortened, liquidity is increased to the point at which short-term treasury bills take on a high degree of "moneyness." For this reason bills can normally be sold at considerably lower rates of interest than long-term bonds.

Certain countries have been successful in floating issues of debt that obligate the government to return monetary sums of fixed purchasing power to holders of claims. These constant-value bonds, which provide holders with apparent protection against inflationary erosion in value, have been marketed at very low rates of interest. Great Britain, in the years since World War II, has successfully introduced "premium bonds," which incorporate certain features of a lottery.

The terms "funded debt" and "floating debt" have been used, historically, to refer to long-term and to short-term debt, respectively. Any definitions are, to an extent, arbitrary, but all issues of more than five years' maturity are generally called "long-term," and all issues with shorter maturities are called "short-term." The rubric "floating debt" is most explicitly used with reference to issues of less than one year maturity.

The names given to specific debt instruments reflect the maturity category. Bonds are securities issued for long term. Notes and certificates are intermediate term, and treasury bills are short term. The term "government securities" is used to refer to the whole range of public debt instruments.

## Ownership

The pattern of ownership of public debt is an important factor in determining its impact on the national economy. In almost all countries national debt is held in significant amounts by various governmental or quasi-governmental agencies. For some purposes it is desirable to include only debt held outside the governmental sector in measuring total debt. For other purposes intragovernmental debt should be included. Insofar as the agencies holding debt are, in fact, treated as being independently accountable units, both in their investing and in their paying functions, the public debt that these agencies hold is not different in effect from that held by the nongovernmental public. However, insofar as these agencies holding debt are not independent of direct treasury control, their holding does not constitute debt at all and could as well have been canceled at the outset. For the most part, intragovernmental debt represents some combination of these two institutional situations.

It is also important to distinguish between the debt held by the nonbanking public and that held by the banking system and by certain categories within the banking system. To the extent that government securities are held by the central banks, they provide reserves for the commercial banking system, and changes in central bank holdings are indicative of important monetary movements in the economy. To the extent that commercial banks hold securities, potential reserves are available to them.

Traditionally, debt held internally and debt held externally have been sharply distinguished. In a national accounting sense, the servicing of internally held debt does not require the transfer of income resources out of the national economy, whereas, of course, such a transfer is required for the servicing of an externally held debt. This point is relevant, even though it must be kept in mind that, other things being equal, the income base from which the transfers are to be made must be larger in the case of externally held debt, precisely by the amount of the necessary interest transfer.

## Management

Public debt management may be defined as that set of operations required to maintain an existing nominal debt. Again, consols provide a useful reference point; if all public debt should consist of consols, management reduces to the payment of interest charges. Significant problems of management arise because issues must be refinanced, must be "rolled over," at periodic intervals. These problems become more difficult as the proportion of floating debt in the total becomes larger and also as economic conditions over time become less stable.

Recognition of management difficulties explains the traditional policy objective of funding the national debt to the maximum extent that is possible. This objective may conflict with other objectives that have been introduced into public policy. As national debts grow in importance, the annual interest payments assume relatively large shares of the governmental expenditure budget. This fact prompts recognition of the minimization of interest cost as an objective of debt management, one that is sharply in conflict with funding. Modern developments in the theory of macroeconomic policy have also forced the recognition that debt management exerts significant over-all effects on the economy. This produces a third possible management objective, that of supplementing macroeconomic policy in promoting stabilization-growth aims.

In a period of threatened inflation both the funding and the macroeconomic objectives would dictate a shift out of short-term into long-term issues, but this would increase interest costs. By contrast, during a period of recession both the interest-cost and the macroeconomic objectives dictate a shift into short-term issues from long-term, but this runs afoul of traditional notions about funding. The experience of the United States since World War II suggests that the best explanatory hypothesis is that management has been directed toward maintaining substantially the same maturity structure over time.

## Monetization

Interest costs on national debt could, of course, be reduced to zero through direct monetization of public debt. This is a process through which interest-bearing issues are refinanced through the issue of money, currency, or bank deposits. Because of the interest saving alone, monetization is always to be recommended insofar as it can be accomplished without inflation. Only the threat of inflation provides a barrier to monetization.

As the national economy grows, an increasing stock of money is required in order to maintain a constant level of product and service prices. One means of injecting increments to the money stock into the system is through debt monetization. Given the improbability that modern governments will retire public debts through the deliberate creation of budgetary surpluses, monetization provides the primary means through which national debts will be reduced. Monetization of debt is possible only for governmental units that possess independent money-creating powers.

## National Debt and Fiscal Policy

There is no simple connection between fiscal policy and the issue or retirement of national debt. Budgetary deficits need not be financed by the issue of debt, defined in a meaningful way. And, if such deficits are generated purposefully for the supplementing of aggregate demand, national debt should not be used as the means of financing. Instead, money should be directly created, which is always an alternative means of financing. In such a setting, the issue of debt exerts a deflationary, and undesirable, impact on total demand.

The elementary confusion about all this arises because, institutionally, national governments tend to disguise money creation through so-called "borrowing" from the central banks, and "public debt" is, nominally, created in this money-creating process. It is essential, however, that these two methods of financing deficits, which are conceptually quite different, be distinguished in the analysis.

The same analysis applies, in reverse, when budgetary surpluses are created. If the purpose of generating the surplus is that of reducing total demand, debt held outside the central banks should not be retired. Instead, the surplus should be disposed of by drawing down treasury balances or retiring debt held by central banks, which is the institutional equivalent of destroying money.

## Principles of Public Debt

The preceding sections of this article summarize the institutional elements of "public debt," on which there exists broad agreement among professional experts. It is the "theory," or "principles," of public debt that has traditionally generated controversy, and the debate shows little sign of being resolved, although essentially the same arguments have been advanced for two centuries. For those who remain skeptical about the progress of economic science, the debt-theory controversy provides ample corroboration.

Nominally, the central question has been: *Who* bears the burden of public debt, and *when?* Analysis is clarified if this question is more carefully stated as follows: Who bears the real cost, or burden, of the public-expenditure projects that are financed by the issue of public loans, and when is this real cost incurred? What is sought is the incidence of debt, and the problem is comparable to that of locating the incidence of taxation, should this alternative financing device be employed.

This question is important because only if it is answered properly can a rational choice be made between debt issue and alternative financing devices. When should government borrow? This ultimate policy question cannot be answered until and unless the consequences of public borrowing can be predicted. Public spending may be financed in any of three ways: (1) taxation, (2) public borrowing, and (3) money creation. The appropriate situations for the use of the second alternative cannot be identified until the differences between this and the remaining alternatives are analyzed.

For *whom* is the central question relevant? Failure to clarify this point has also led to ambiguity. In any broadly democratic political structure, "government" is the institutional process through which people make "public" decisions. Therefore, "When should government borrow?" becomes merely a shorthand manner of asking, "When should individual citizens, as participants in the governmental decision process, as prospective taxpayers, borrowers, or beneficiaries, borrow?" The question of the appropriateness of public debt issue becomes analogous to the question concerning private debt issue for the individual in his private capacity.

The answer to the central question posed above seems obvious. Public borrowing should take place when it is desirable to put off or to postpone the incurring of real cost until some later period, in return for which, as in any act of borrowing, an interest charge must normally be paid. The desire to postpone the incurring of real cost or incidence of the public expenditure project may or may not be related to the characteristics of the project itself. Public or collective consumption may, in some cases, be legitimately financed from public loans, just as private consumption may be legitimately financed from private loans. A more normal or standard reason for public borrowing is found, however, in the temporal pattern of benefits that are expected to be produced by the public spending project. If the project involves a large and concentrated outlay that is anticipated to yield benefits over a whole sequence of time periods in the future, considerations of both efficiency and equity suggest resort to public loans, provided only that direct money creation is predicted to cause inflation. Traditionally, public debt has been discussed with reference to the financing of extraordinary expenditure needs, and specifically with reference to public capital formation. Historically, national debts have been created largely during periods of war emergency, when spending needs have indeed been extraordinary, even if the result has not been public capital formation of the orthodox variety.

## The controversy

Little more would need to be said with respect to the "principles" of public debt were it not for the fact that the straightforward analysis has been recurrently challenged, and by economists of great eminence. Ricardo's logic led him to enunciate the proposition that the public loan and an extraordinary tax of equivalent amount exert identical effects on the rational individual. Under conditions of perfect certainty, perfect capital markets, and under the assumption that individuals act "as if" they will live forever, the future tax liabilities that are inherent in a public debt obligation will be fully capitalized at the time of debt issue, and the effects on individual behavior patterns will be identical to those that would be produced by a tax of the same capital sum.[1] Within his own restricted model Ricardo's basic proposition cannot be challenged, but its validity does not contradict the elementary notions on public debt outlined above. The individual, as prospective taxpayer-borrower-beneficiary, confronts two financing alternatives—current taxation and public debt issue. And to the extent that he interprets these two alternatives correctly, he knows that each of the two will impose upon him a real cost, a burden that in a present-value sense is substantially the same. This Ricardian equivalence does not suggest, however, that the objective pattern of cost payments remains the same over the two alternatives. Taxation and debt issue remain different, not similar, financing institutions, between which the individual may choose, for the simple reason that taxes require a transfer of resource services from the individual to the fisc during the initial period, whereas debt issue postpones such transfer until later periods. Whether or not the individual, under debt financing, correctly or incorrectly anticipates or "capitalizes" future tax liabilities as he "should" in the normative Ricardian model, is not relevant to the determination of the objective pattern of real cost payments over time.

## A common fallacy

The most pervasive and recurring fallacy in the discussion of public debt has been that which summarizes the theory of internally held debt by the state-

---

1. David Ricardo, *On the Principles of Political Economy and Taxation,* vol. 2 of *Works and Correspondence* (1817; Cambridge: Royal Economic Society, 1951).

ment, "We owe it to ourselves." The fallacy here is not a new one; it was widely held by both scholars and publicists in the eighteenth century. It almost faded out of the literature during the nineteenth and early twentieth centuries, only to reappear and to gain predominance after the so-called Keynesian revolution of the 1930s. In the immediate post-Keynesian decades the fallacy came to be almost universally accepted by economists. Therefore, if for no other reason, the importance that this fallacy has held in the literature warrants some consideration of it here. For purposes of discussion it may be labeled the "national accounting fallacy."

If the government borrows funds internally, so the theory goes, the public expenditure project is financed from internal resources. These cannot be brought from future time periods into the present; hence, the opportunity costs of the public project, regardless of the method of finance, must be borne during the period in which the resources are actually used. Public debt involves no postponement of cost or burden in time, and the view that it does so is based on a crudely drawn analogy with private debt. In periods after public debt issue, the required interest payments represent nothing more than transfers from taxpayers to bondholders, and, so long as both groups are members of the community, no real cost is incurred. External public debt, by contrast, because of the necessity to transfer interest payments to outsiders, is seen as wholly different from internal debt and analogous to private debt.

This conception of national debt contains a fundamental flaw in its failure to translate opportunity cost or burden from aggregative components into something that is meaningful to individual members of the community. What is the behavioral relevance of the fact that the resources actually used up in the public project are taken from current consumption or investment within the community until and unless those members of the community who must undergo the sacrifice of alternatives can be identified? Once this question is raised, however, and such identification is attempted, the fallacy is clearly revealed.

The members of the group who actually surrender purchasing power, command over current resource services, which is used by the government to carry out the public purpose, are those who purchase the public debt instruments, the government securities. No other members of the group sacrifice or "give up" anything directly during the initial period. But do the bond purchasers bear the real costs or burden of the project? That they do not becomes clear when it is recognized that their surrender of current funds is a wholly voluntary and private transaction in which they exchange current purchasing power for promises, on the part of the fisc, of income in future periods. These bond purchasers, or persons acting in this capacity, do not in any way consider themselves to be exchanging purchasing power for the benefits of the public spending, which would be the case if they should be really bearing the real cost. If, however, it is acknowledged that bond purchasers do not bear the real cost of the public spending, and if no other members of the group bear such cost during the initial period, who does pay for the project that is debt-financed? If, as the national accounting fallacy suggests, none of this cost is shifted to future periods, public debt might seem to provide for "fiscal perpetual motion," since a means would have been located for financing beneficial public projects without cost.

The core of the fallacy lies in the equating of the community as a unit, in some aggregated national accounting sense, with the individuals-in-the-community, in some political sense as participants, direct or indirect, in collective decision making. In their capacities as prospective taxpayers-borrowers-beneficiaries, individual members of a political community can postpone the objective real costs of public spending through resort to debt finance, even though they may sell the debt instruments, bonds, to "themselves," acting in a wholly different capacity as bond purchasers. There are two exchanges, not one, involved, and it is the neglect of this basic duality that has clouded much of the discussion and analysis. Individuals, as taxpayers-borrowers-beneficiaries, through the political decision process, "exchange" the future tax liabilities that debt issue embodies for the promise of expected benefits of the public spending, current or in future. They are enabled to do this because individuals, in their capacities as prospective bond purchasers, are willing to exchange current purchasing power for the promise of future payments. The second group makes an intertemporal exchange that is the opposite of that made by the first group. And it is grossly misleading to think of these two exchanges as canceling in effect merely because the two groups may be partially coincident in membership.

The alleged differences between internal and external debt disappear in a model that corrects for this national accounting fallacy. In either situation individuals in their roles as participants in collective fiscal choice secure command over resource services initially without the necessity of giving up purchasing power. Whether other parties to the exchange be foreigners or some subset of individuals acting in their private capacity as bond purchasers makes no essential difference, secondary transfer considerations aside.

For individuals as they participate in fiscal choice, public debt is the institutional analogue to private debt as these same individuals act privately. Basically, the same principles apply in each case, despite all the disclaimers made by economists. This is not, of course, to equate public finance with private finance in all respects. The important difference lies, however, not in the effects of borrowing but in the fact that national governments possess powers of money creation whereas private persons, and local governments, do not. The power to create money allows national governments to generate budgetary deficits without at the same time issuing debt. The principles of public borrowing, which are at base simple, have been obscured by the failure of economists to make this elemental point clear. In part, as suggested before, this has been the result of institutional complexities present in modern fiscal-financial structures. Modern governments create money through issuing what they commonly call "public debt"; they do so by "borrowing" from central banks. This disguised money creation does not, of course, have the same effects as genuine debt issue.

The analysis of public debt which was dominant in the 1940s and 1950s, as a result of the Keynesian and post-Keynesian emphasis on deficit financing combined with the confusion between debt issue and money creation, was subjected to critical attack in the late 1950s and early 1960s. Predictions as to the development of analysis or the acceptance of ideas are risky at best, but it seems reasonable to suggest that the principles of public debt are on the verge of synthesis. Undue optimism is, however, surely to be avoided, especially if the history of debt theory is to be used as a guide.

BIBLIOGRAPHY

Adams, Henry C. *Public Debts: An Essay in the Science of Finance.* New York: Appleton, 1887.
Bastable, Charles F. *Public Finance.* 1892. 2d ed. London and New York: Macmillan, 1895.
Buchanan, James M. *Public Principles of Public Debt: A Defense and Restatement.* Homewood, Ill.: Irwin, 1958.

de Viti de Marco, Antonio. *First Principles of Public Finance.* 1934. London: Cape, 1950. First published in Italian.

Ferguson, James M. (editor). *Public Debt and Future Generations.* Chapel Hill: Univ. of North Carolina Press, 1964.

Great Britain, Committee on National Debt and Taxation. *Report.* London: H.M. Stationery Office, 1927. Known as the Colwyn Committee Report.

Harris, Seymour E. *The National Debt and the New Economics.* New York: McGraw-Hill, 1947.

*International Financial Statistics.* Published monthly since January 1948 by the International Monetary Fund.

Lerner, Abba P. "The Burden of the National Debt." In *Income, Employment and Public Policy: Essays in Honor of Alvin H. Hansen,* 255–75. New York: Norton, 1948.

Leroy-Beaulieu, Paul. *Traité de la science des finances.* Volume 2, *Le budget et le credit public.* 1877. 8th ed. Paris: Alcan, 1912. Volume 1 is entitled *Des revenues publics.*

Maffezzoni, Federico. "The Comparative Fiscal Burden of Public Debt and Taxation." *International Economic Papers.* Vol. 11, 75–101. First published as "Ancora della diversa pressione tributaria del prestito e dell'imposta" in Volume 9 of the *Rivista di diritto finanziario e scienza delle finanze.*

Ricardo, David. *Works and Correspondence.* Volume 1, *On the Principles of Political Economy and Taxation.* 1817. Cambridge: Royal Economic Society, 1951.

# Confessions of a Burden Monger[1]

Who bears the cost, and *when,* of public expenditure projects that are financed by public loans? This is the central question that has been, and is, at issue in the debt-theory discussion that E. J. Mishan continues with his recent paper. Whether the expenditures themselves are wasteful, marginally, or highly productive is irrelevant. What is sought is the incidence, the pattern of distribution, interpersonally and intertemporally, of the cost, which must exist in any of the models under consideration.[2]

My own argument has been, and remains, the naïve one that "cost" or "burden" remains meaningless until and unless it can be translated into effects on some *persons* in the group *at some time.* Mishan appears to accept the point that those persons who voluntarily purchase the debt instruments (government securities) offered for sale by the treasury are not made "worse off" in any welfare sense. Yet these persons, or persons acting in this capacity, are surely the only members of the group who, during the initial period of loan-financed public spending, directly "give up" or transfer to the government purchasing power, command over resource services. It is irrelevant to my own central argument whether this purchasing power is drawn from

From *Journal of Political Economy* 72 (October 1964): 486–88. Copyright 1964 by The University of Chicago. All rights reserved. Reprinted by permission of the University of Chicago Press, publisher.

1. The term "burden monger" has been explicitly introduced into the debt-theory discussion by E. J. Mishan in his recent paper, "How to Make a Burden of the Public Debt," *Journal of Political Economy* 71 (December, 1963), 541.

2. If some of Mishan's remarks on this score are taken seriously, they would seem to imply that he considers it improper to speak of either a tax burden or a debt burden because, in either case, the costs of the project may be more than offset by the benefits of the combined fiscal operation. Hence even to speak of "tax burden" may "tacitly condemn" tax financing of public expenditure projects. Even "the great Pigou" might have bridled at such normative linguistic advice.

funds otherwise destined for private consumption or private investment.[3] Individuals, in their roles as taxpayers-beneficiaries (in a voluntaristic political setting), give up nothing. They may be said to suffer a cost, to "pay for," the benefits of the public project only to the extent that they *anticipate* the necessity of making future payments of real goods and services. Any current or initial period bearing of cost, for the taxpayer, is exclusively "subjective," and, as such, it is nonobservable.

Mishan is correct when he argues that under conditions of perfect certainty and perfectly working capital markets these individuals, as taxpayers-beneficiaries, will act identically under either tax or loan financing of similar projects. Insofar as the taxpayer anticipates fully his future tax liabilities under debt and chooses to discharge these in the initial period to the same extent that he would in response to the comparable current tax, he may do so. In this case, he also bears some *objective cost* of the public project during the initial period, defined in terms of the real transfer of resource services from those uses to which they would normally be devoted. However, in a voluntaristic political setting, the "representative" taxpayer-borrower-beneficiary could never be observed to respond to debt in this manner since he could, much more simply, resort to tax financing directly. The essence of public debt, as a financing institution, is that it allows the objective cost of currently financed expenditure projects to be postponed in time. For the taxpayer, public debt delays the necessity of transferring command over resource services to the treasury.[4]

Despite all argument to the contrary, therefore, taxation and borrowing are alternative, not similar, means of financing public expenditures. This is surely an elementary proposition. The question is: Why have some economists, of recognized professional competence, refused to accept its validity?

In this respect, Mishan's paper brings into the open an important aspect

3. The source of funds is of importance in the models developed by Modigliani, Vickrey, and certain other participants in the debt-burden discussion.

4. A failure to distinguish between the subjective cost and the objective cost or burden of debt-financed public projects has been the source of much of the ambiguity that has characterized the discussion on public debt. In a forthcoming paper, "Public Debt, Cost Theory, and the Fiscal Illusion," I attempt to clarify this important distinction in some detail. This paper is included in a forthcoming book, *Public Debt and Future Generations*, ed. James M. Ferguson (Chapel Hill: University of North Carolina Press). This volume collects many of the recent contributions to the discussion.

of the whole controversy that has seemed to lie just beneath the surface. Mishan explicitly suggests that those economists, whom he has classified as "burden mongers," have somehow been immoral in that their arguments may be interpreted wrongly by politicians and the public.[5,6] By implication, Mishan is suggesting that economists, even in their formal analysis, should try to predict the ultimate effects of this analysis in promoting their desired social objectives. This attitude presumes that the general public must be protected against its ignorance, or at least against its inability to reason logically. If widely held, this attitude would, of course, produce effects on scientific advance, in economics or in any other discipline, that need not be elaborated here. The relevant question is why need this attitude arise with respect to the public debt problem at all? Basically, this problem remains a simple one, and discussion should be purely technical.

With all due apologies to students of Henry Simons and Lloyd Mints (and Abba Lerner for that matter), it is necessary to state once again that debt issue is not equivalent to money creation. Taxation, public borrowing, and

---

5. Note that the last section of Mishan's paper is entitled "The Moral of the Story," and that this section (p. 542) contains the following statements: "If increasing the public debt is to become associated in the minds of economists with a burden on the future, it is hardly likely that the interested public will look upon it with an open mind.

"But presidents as well as former presidents, treasury officials, administrators, politicians, and journalists do not as a rule read ingenious arguments with professional vigilance, particularly if it seems, on the surface, to bear out a favorite prejudice. It soon becomes current that well-known economists have written a book, or a paper, 'proving' that the public debt is, after all, a most grievous burden. In this way a presumption against increasing the public debt becomes established in respectable and influential circles, a presumption which may well act as a brake on swift remedial action by the government when it faces a decline in economic activity."

6. The same point is made, less explicitly, by Emile Benoit: "In recent technical literature, attempts have been made to revive, on a more sophisticated basis, concerns already abandoned by most economists about the 'burden' of an internally held debt. This burden, in its new form, assumes a somewhat metaphysical character, not incompatible with everyone being absolutely better off than if the debt had not been acquired. It is devoutly to be hoped that in facing the very real dangers ahead, we shall not have our vision clouded by chimeras of this kind. Economists should be especially careful, I feel, not to permit their abstruse professional speculations to be misinterpreted as providing support for popular economic fallacies. And of all such fallacies, the belief in the burdens and perils of the public debt seems to me the most widespread and the most dangerous." "The Propensity to Reduce the National Debt Out of Defense Savings," *American Economic Review*, 51 (May, 1961), 459.

money creation are *three,* not two, alternative means of financing public services. The failure to distinguish between money creation and debt issue, which are two conceptually different fiscal operations, has been, and remains, pervasive, as Mishan's paper clearly illustrates. Public debt issue is an operation in which the treasury transfers to bond purchasers promises to pay income in future periods, as interest or principal or both, in *exchange* for current purchasing power, currency, or bank deposit claims. Money creation, by contrast, involves no such exchange.

Public debt creation is always deflationary. Hence, it becomes fully appropriate, as a fiscal device, only in two possible circumstances. First, it may be used as a means of mopping up excessive liquidity during periods of threatened inflation. Second, it is a means of financing real public expenditures during periods when money creation is anticipated to produce undesirable inflationary consequences. Debt issue is never appropriate as a means of financing budget deficits if the purpose of such deficits is to shore up total demand in the economy. Money issue, not public debt, is the proper reflationary device. This is not to deny that second-best instruments must sometimes be accepted, and these are not necessarily ineffective because they are second best. However, the fact that the desired results of deficits may overcome, in some cases, the deflationary effects of the debt financing of such spending, should not suggest that either the deflationary effects or the real-cost effects of public debt be ignored. Surely the institutional confusion between the public borrowing and the money issue alternatives does not justify *analytical* confusion.

It is, of course, wholly inappropriate for politicians, or anyone else, to infer from the discussion on the burden of public debt anything at all, pro or con, about the desirability of budget deficits. The fact that politicians and the public do make such inferences obligates the economist to clarify the analysis, and to distinguish carefully two separate questions. In my opinion, the economist should not retreat ever further into technical and terminological obscurity while refusing to accept the obvious conclusions of very simple analysis.

# The Icons of Public Debt

The theory of public debt remains a "murky battleground." My own attempts at clarifying some of the elementary principles, along with those of my supporters-defenders, have failed to convince large numbers of professional economists. Professor James Tobin, in his recent review article[1] of the book edited by James Ferguson, has acutely if indirectly noted the reason for this failure through his reference to my "iconoclastic writings." An iconoclast is defined as a destroyer of religious images or icons. To win the day, the iconoclast must provide more than straightforward logical argument; he must also shatter faith.[2] My notions about debt burden seem to counter images that are more than intellectual constructions, more than scientific paradigms. If this is true, some excuse is provided for repetition and clarification of basic propositions, especially when such a competent economist as James Tobin can seem so fundamentally confused about my own admittedly "simplistic view."

This view, according to Tobin, "throws away the whole 'incidence and effects' literature of public finance." No statement could be more in error. My aim in the whole discussion has been, and remains, that of answering the fundamental question: Who pays, and when, for public expenditures that are financed by debt issue instead of taxation or money creation? This is precisely the incidence question. Who pays the income tax; what is the inci-

From *Journal of Finance* 21 (September 1966): 544–46. Copyright 1966 by American Finance Association. Reprinted by permission of the publisher.

1. James Tobin, "The Burden of the Public Debt: A Review Article," *Journal of Finance*, Vol. 20, No. 4 (December 1965), 679–82.

2. Perhaps Nietzsche's statement is relevant here. "Faith means not *wanting* to know what is true." Nietzsche in *Antichrist*, cited by Walter Kaufmann, *The Owl and the Nightingale* (London: Faber and Faber, 1959), 173.

dence of the income tax? These are mere shorthand versions of: Who finally pays for the public expenditures that are financed through the income tax? Precisely contrary to Tobin's charge, my efforts can best be interpreted as attempts to bring the theory of public debt back into the incidence framework.

"Stripped of all embellishment, it [Buchanan's view] reduces to the assertion that payment of taxes is *per se* a burden—whether or not the taxes affect incentives and resource allocation. Since debt finance postpones the levy of taxes, it obviously shifts Buchanan's burden to future generations." With this statement I have no quarrel, and, as I have asserted, the point is elementary, obvious, and self-evident. Which makes all the more mysterious the continuing refusal of highly competent economists to acknowledge it. Tobin follows the above with: "The justification for this definition is that taxes are compulsory and involuntary. In contrast, market transactions, including the purchase of public debt, are voluntary agreements." Why does Tobin consider the initial statement to require any justification? There is nothing in my analysis that connects the elementary point with compulsion or coercion of tax payments. In its broadest sense, the underlying political model for my analysis is democratic, and, at some level, individuals can be said to agree to pay taxes in exchange for public goods. Whether the individual, in the actual moment of payment, feels himself coerced or whether he feels that he is voluntarily contributing to a worthwhile collective purpose is wholly irrelevant for the validity of my central proposition concerning the temporal location of burden. The fact that *taxes are payments* is, in itself, sufficient. In this sense, taxes are no different from prices paid in market transactions. The payment of prices for ordinary goods and services is also, *per se,* a burden. This we all accept without the sophistication of economic theory.

Why the confusion here, which Tobin seems to share with other contributors to the debt-burden controversy? As he suggests, the "political theory is questionable," but it is the unstated political theory implicit in the neo-Keynesian debt analysis and not my own. In the latter, individuals, acting as members of a democratically organized collectivity, choose to finance specific public outlays through debt issue, the sale of interest-bearing obligations. In so doing, these same persons, explicitly or implicitly, act to postpone the payment for these outlays through time. In quite a separate, and wholly different, capacity, individuals, domestic or foreign, purchase the interest-bearing bonds. In this strictly individualistic setting, individuals give up current command over resource services in exchange for future income. The point is that *two*, not one, transactions are involved here. In one the individual acts as a member of the collectivity; in the other he does not. Unless this fact is recognized, debt issue stands in danger of being touted as the fiscal equivalent of the perpetual motion machine which will allow beneficial public programs to be financed without cost on anyone at any time.

There are, of course, secondary effects of debt issue, such as the effects on interest rates, the effects of taxes on allocation, etc., and these may be important. My objective has been, and is, to clarify the primary effects before complicating the analysis with these secondary ones. This comment applies also to the Modigliani-Vickrey analysis of the effects of debt on capital accumulation. This whole aspect of the discussion is not germane to the primary analysis of shifting or postponing the burden of payment through time that debt, public or private, facilitates.

Both Tobin and Musgrave,[3] in their reviews of the Ferguson volume, suggest that the whole analysis is applicable only when full employment is assumed to be present. If this were valid, the analysis would, indeed, be severely limited in scope. The postponement of cost or burden that debt issue facilitates is, however, as valid for unemployment as for full-employment models. Throughout the debate, and through most of the post-Keynesian fiscal policy discussion, there has been a consistent refusal of economists to make the vital distinction between money creation and debt issue. Failing to make this distinction, they have equated deficit creation with debt issue directly. Had they been familiar with the teachings of Henry Simons, which, to my knowledge, have not yet been refuted, they would have acknowledged that the issue of interest-bearing debt is never optimal when the aim is to shore up aggregate demand. In the classic Keynesian situation, there are no real costs of employing otherwise idle resources. Money creation is clearly indicated; there are no costs to bear, no burden to be shared, currently or in later periods. If, because of error in analysis or rigidity in institutions, interest-bearing debt is used in such situations, the postponed cost may, in-

---

3. R. A. Musgrave, "Review" of Ferguson, *Public Debt and Future Generations*, *American Economic Review*, Vol. 55 (December 1965), 1226–28.

deed, be a small price to pay for the benefits that are secured by the outlay. This fact does not, however, remove the costs on future-period taxpayers, costs which, in this case, are wholly excessive and unnecessary.

Tobin concludes by stating that "nothing . . . —unless one accepts Buchanan's identification of burden with tax payments—disturbs economists' customary insistence on the essential difference between internal and foreign debt." With this statement I am in accord, since, presumably, Tobin would allow his orthodoxy to be disturbed if my definition of burden should prevail. The question concerns whether or not burden or cost can be identified with tax payments in the primary sense. If tax payments are not made by individuals in some sort of exchange for public services, in present, past, or future periods, what are they made in exchange for? If we can secure public goods and services without paying taxes (including inflation) then why not private goods without prices? This remains the Tobin mystery upon which we have a right to seek enlightenment. Until I am shown otherwise, I shall continue to hold that many of my fellow economists have been, and remain, wrong in their elementary understanding of public debt.

But, please, fellow iconoclasts, no more references to President Eisenhower! Our task is difficult enough, and the icons will be shattered much more quickly by the opposing procedure. Let us try to invent more complex and abstruse means of stating the simple propositions; only then can we perhaps carry conviction with the majority of modern economists.

# Public Debt and Capital Formation

> The practice of contracting debt will almost infallibly be abused
> in every government. It would scarcely be more imprudent to give
> a prodigal son a credit in every banker's shop in London, than to
> empower a statesman to draw bills, in this manner, upon posterity.
>
> —David Hume

## A Summary History of Some Ideas and Their Consequences

To the Victorians, the consumption of capital was venality itself, and even full consumption of income was prodigal in the extreme. Ordinary prudence demanded that some share of income be put aside for adding to the capital stock. In their world, capital, once created, was indeed permanent, whether it was measured separately in each family's portfolio or jointly in the national aggregates. Further, there were no essential differences between the precepts for fiscal prudence applicable to the family and those applicable to the nation. Basically these same attitudes carried over into the Victorians' approach to the institutions of law, politics, and the economy. The Gladstonians did not really expect to live forever, but they acted as if they did, and their moral precepts matched their behavior. (The Ricardian theorem on the equivalence of public debt and taxation may, indeed, have been descriptive of at least some of the Victorians.)

From *Taxation and the Deficit Economy: Fiscal Policy and Capital Formation in the United States*, ed. Dwight Lee (San Francisco: Pacific Research Institute for Public Policy, 1986): 177–94. Reprinted by permission of the publisher.

I am indebted to Geoffrey Brennan, Australian National University, for helpful comments.

We are a century away from "capitalism's finest hour," if we restrict our definition of "capitalism" to refer to prevailing public attitudes on the accumulation and maintenance of "the capacity to satisfy wants stored up in things."

How distant these Victorians seem to us now!

We have passed through several shifts in ideas and attitudes. Even before Keynes, economists had challenged the classical (and Victorian) equivalence of public and private debt. Fallacies of aggregation antedate the Keynesians, and the argument that "we owe it to ourselves" was ushered in early in this century. This aggregation fallacy, to the extent that it gained acceptance, served to loosen somewhat the precepts of fiscal prudence for governments, although the principle of budget balance kept public-debt creation within bounds of reason. Norms for private capital accumulation and preservation remained pervasive, however, until Keynes and the Keynesians promulgated the "paradox of thrift." With this step, even the norms for private, personal prudence came to be undermined. Spending, not saving, spilled over to benefit society. Alongside this inversion of private norms, the Keynesian theory of public policy directly undermined any intellectual basis for the maintenance of balance in governmental budgets. The modern era of profligacy, public and private, was born.[1]

Through their effects on public and political attitudes, ideas do have consequences. But these consequences emerge slowly and with significant time lags. After Keynes, the anticlassical, anti-Victorian ideas were firmly in place in the academies and in the dialogues of the intellectuals. Politics, however, reflects the behavior of politicians, whose ideas change but slowly. Hence, during the years immediately after World War II, many politicians adhered to the old-fashioned precepts for fiscal prudence, only to be treated condescendingly and with scorn by academics and intellectuals. Some of us now recall with both amusement and sadness, the derision that greeted President Eisenhower's reference to public debt as a burden on our grandchildren.

By the late 1950s, there was a marked shift in the thinking of economists,

---

1. For more extended treatment of the divergent classical and Keynesian attitudes toward public debt, see James M. Buchanan, *Public Principles of Public Debt* (Homewood, Ill.: Richard D. Irwin, 1958); for extended treatment of the impact of the Keynesian theory of policy on governmental creation of deficits, see James M. Buchanan and Richard E. Wagner, *Democracy in Deficit* (New York: Academic Press, 1977).

characterized by a revival of essentially classical ideas on the incidence and effects of public debt. These then-novel notions were by no means universally accepted by academic economists, but the challenge to the aggregation fallacies was not refuted. Among academic economists, the discussion of public debt changed, slowly but surely, toward the earlier verities, a change that took place over the 1960s and 1970s.

As with the onset of the Keynesian ideas three decades earlier, however, public and political attitudes lagged behind those emerging in academia. And the politicians who made the policy decisions of the 1960s and 1970s had fully absorbed the Keynesian lessons on both macroeconomic policy and public debt. They were ready and quite willing to apply the policy messages appropriate for the 1930s to the policy environment of the 1960s and 1970s, because these messages offered apparent intellectual support for their natural proclivities to spend and not to tax. The era of seemingly permanent and increasing governmental deficits was upon us, an era from which we have not yet escaped.

In 1986, we can only hope that the political decision-makers of the 1980s and 1990s will have become familiar with the post-Keynesian challenges to the aggregation fallacies and that something akin to the classical Victorian precepts for private and public prudence will come to inform the observed politics of these decades. The restoration of old ideas that have been for a long time displaced by fallacies is, at best, more difficult than acceptance of ideas that have been carried forward in an unblemished tradition. We can hope that such restoration goes forward. As of 1986, there are both encouraging and discouraging signals to be observed. The financial politics for the remaining years of this century remain unpredictable.

## The Elementary Logic

A debt instrument (bill, note, or bond) is a contractual obligation, on the part of a person or entity, that promises payment of stipulated amounts of things (or claims on things) over a sequence of designated periods subsequent to the period in which the instrument is signed. That is to say, debt is an obligation to pay *later*. Taken separately, therefore, the contracting of debt by an owner of a portfolio of assets amounts to a claim against the anticipated stream of net returns from those owned assets. This claim must reduce the present value of the assets, which is determined by discounting the anticipated stream of net returns. At this level of very elementary logic, the issue of debt is identical to the destruction of capital value.

This basic relationship between debt issue and the destruction of capital value tends to be obscured or overlooked because of the mind-set imposed upon us by double-entry bookkeeping or balance-sheet accounting. The issue of debt, the incurrence of the obligation to make payments in future periods, is more or less automatically treated as only one side of a two-sided transaction. The issuer of debt is a borrower, who receives a transfer of payment during the period of the contract itself. This payment *now* is that which is received in exchange for the promise to make payments *later*. In this two-sided treatment, the balance sheet of the borrower is adjusted by adding the present value of the debt instrument to the liability side of the account and the present value of the current payment received to the asset side. There is no change in net worth. There seems to be no destruction of the capital value of the whole portfolio or enterprise.

The legitimacy of this double-entry procedure is based on the implicit presumption that the funds secured currently in exchange for the debt instrument will be used productively, at least in some prospective or anticipated sense. Such a presumption is invalid when the borrower simply uses up or consumes the funds that are currently received in exchange for the promise of future period payments. In this case, the separated or one-sided model of debt issue is more helpful than the double-sided model. Debt issue becomes equivalent to the "eating up" of capital value, pure and simple.

This elementary logic of debt applies, of course, to any intertemporal contract. There is no difference between individual, firm, agency, or public borrowing. In all cases, the issue of debt for the purpose of financing current-period use or consumption is equivalent to the destruction of the capital value of the asset stream that is anticipated. This basic proposition holds independent of the value of the portfolio. If there is no capital value, the creation of debt will, in this case, produce negative capital. If the capital value is initially negative, debt will merely increase the negative total.

## Public Debt and Public Consumption

What connection has the elementary logic of the above discussion with the summary history of ideas sketched out at the very beginning of this chapter?

And, indeed, with the title and purpose of the chapter? The connection and relevance should be clear enough. The public debt incurred by the U.S. government during the regime of ever-increasing, and apparently permanent, budgetary deficits has financed public or government *consumption* rather than public or government investment. The classical rules for fiscal prudence have been doubly violated. Not only has government failed to "pay as it goes"; government has also failed to utilize productively the funds that have been borrowed. There has been no offsetting item on the asset side to match the increase in net liability that the debt represents. The capital value of the income stream of the national economy has been reduced, dollar for dollar, with each increase in present value of liabilities represented by the debt instruments issued.[2]

Proper accounting would, therefore, require that any estimate of "national capital stock" derived by discounting the net national income be written down or reduced by the present value of the outstanding national debt instruments. A somewhat different way of putting this point is to say that a share of the anticipated national income over future periods has already been precommitted for the payments of amortization and interest charges on the debt. This share is simply not available for free disposition, either privately or publicly, in accordance with the preferences of persons who nominally "earn" the income in the periods to come. The national debt obligation is an overload, a burden, that carries forward with it no compensating asset or claim. For U.S. citizens, the national debt is fully analogous to a private debt that has been incurred to finance a consumption spree in some past period.

Objections may be raised to my simplistic approach to such weighty issues of national fiscal policy. An initial, if unsophisticated, argument might suggest that federal government outlays (that have, admittedly, been partially financed by debt) have not been "wasteful" and that any analogy to a private consumption spree is misleading. After all, or so such an argument might

---

2. The present value of the liabilities presented by the debt instruments may not be so high as the maturity values of the debt. There will be a difference here to the extent that government borrows at rates of interest lower than the rate appropriate for discounting future tax liabilities, which would normally be the market rate of return. To the extent of this difference in present values, the government has not issued what we may call "real debt" but has, instead, imposed a tax on persons living during the period of the public consumption. The extreme case is, of course, that in which the government "sells" bonds to the central bank at zero or very low nominal rates.

run, these outlays financed spending on the provision of goods and services that were deemed to be collectively beneficial, including transfers to the needy and to those who hold legitimate entitlement claims.

My analysis does not, however, imply that the outlays made by the government were "wasteful" in any such sense of the term. The spending that was debt- or deficit-financed during the 1970s and 1980s may well have provided benefits of a higher value than the then-present value of the debt instruments required to finance such spending. But precisely the same point may be made about the spending made by an individual during a private consumption spree. The pitiable character who, after having blown his whole week's wages, borrowed still more funds to finance last Saturday's spending at the local pub, may well have enjoyed Saturday-night benefits that he estimated, *then,* to be higher than the opportunity costs of the debt obligation that he assumed. The rationality or irrationality of the choices made last Saturday night cannot, however, affect the burden of the debt obligation at next week's payday. The improvident one may, of course, have warm memories regarding last Saturday's pleasures, and he may sigh that "it was worth it all," but, come Friday, he will have fewer dollars of net income available for current spending than he would have had if last Saturday's binge had not taken place at all. The fact that the benefits or pleasures then enjoyed may have been more than, equal to, or less than the properly estimated choice-influencing opportunity cost becomes irrelevant to the temporal location of the postchoice costs. The benefits, no matter how great or small they might have been, *have been enjoyed.* The postchoice consequences must be suffered *now.*[3]

## Public Debt and Public Investment

A more sophisticated argument may commence with an explicit denial that federal outlays financed by debt have, in fact, been exclusively devoted to current public consumption. It may be suggested that some share in federal government outlays represents investment spending on long-lived capital as-

---

3. For a generalized discussion of costs that makes the distinctions between prechoice and postchoice costs, see James M. Buchanan, *Cost and Choice* (Chicago: University of Chicago Press, Midway Reprint, 1975).

sets. To the extent that federal outlays are investmentlike, it is appropriate that these be financed with debt issue. Government practice in this respect is no different from ordinary business procedures, and responsible financial planning must allow for borrowing to finance the purchase of genuine asset items. A practical suggestion that often emerges from this argument is that the government's fiscal account should be improved by the introduction of a categorical separation between consumption and investment items, between the current consumption and the capital budget, sometimes referred to as above-the-line and below-the-line items. This distinction does characterize public accounting procedures in several countries.

Cursory examination suggests that this argument warrants close consideration. If, in fact, the share of federal government outlay financed by debt should be roughly similar to the share that might appropriately be classified to be investment in public capital, there would be an offsetting item on the asset side of the nation's balance sheet that would match the liability that the present value of debt represents. In this setting, when *both* sides of the transaction are recorded, both the issue of debt and the purchase of the assets, there need be no net change in the present value of the national capital stock. And, indeed, if the investment outlay should prove productive in some net sense, a properly measured present value should record some increase.

The question would seem to be empirical. How much federal spending during the observed era of deficits can properly be classified as public capital investment? And does this estimated share in total outlay come close to that share that has, in fact, been financed by debt?

Care must be taken, however, to specify precisely what is required for an item of budgetary outlay to be classified as a public capital investment. The durability of an asset alone is not sufficient to make its purchase qualify as capital investment for purposes of the exercise here. In order that an item of governmental outlay be labeled a net asset, with a positive present value to be entered on the balance sheet as offsetting the debt liability, there must be an increment to the net income stream directly attributable to that asset.

As an example of a long-lived asset that cannot qualify as public capital for our purposes, consider a monument that is designed to last forever. There is no measured income flow associated with the monument. While there may be benefits anticipated from the monument over the whole sequence of future time periods, these anticipated benefits cannot be appropriated as a source for the tax payments that may be required to service the debt if the initial outlay is debt-financed.

In terms of criteria for tax equity, the anticipated flow of benefits over time may seem to suggest the appropriateness of debt- rather than direct-tax financing. In this sense, the outlay on public "capital," like monuments, is quite different from that on current public consumption, the benefits from which accrue during the period when the public goods are actually consumed. The anticipated benefits from the monument add to the stream of psychic income or utility. And a measure of utility levels in any future period should, ideally, include some imputed value for these particularized benefits. Note, however, that persons receiving these benefits have no choice as to the form that these take, and there is no prospect of converting income benefit flows into other channels that might be helpful in covering amortization and interest charges on the debt.

Public "capital," like monuments, which does seem to include much durable investment of government (public buildings, defense hardware), may be likened to personal, private investment in specific human capital designed to yield consumption benefits over time. Consider, as an example, outlays for a course in music or art appreciation. The anticipated benefits extend over a lengthy sequence of periods, and utility streams over these periods are higher than they would otherwise be without the initial investment outlay. But once the initial outlay is made, these benefits are "locked in," so to speak; they are inalienable in the sense that there is no prospect of converting them into realizable monetary equivalents. The person who has incurred a debt obligation to take the course on art appreciation may enjoy knowing all about art, but the enhancement in his utility in this respect will not reduce the burden of the debt overload during the relevant payout or debt retirement periods. If double-entry books were kept in utility dimensions, the inclusion of an offsetting asset value to the debt liability might seem appropriate. Double entries in accounts normally, however, refer only to realizable values and enforceable obligations. Unless this elementary precautionary precept for prudence is followed, persons who might indeed be wealthy in the utility dimension will find themselves in the bankruptcy courts.

For governments, this precept for fiscal prudence would suggest that assets be classified as "public capital," and hence introduced as offsetting items on the balance sheet, only if measurable and realizable money income flows are anticipated. For example, if government constructs a toll highway or an urban transport network, it is appropriate to discount the expected stream of anticipated facility revenues or fees to produce a capital value of asset that the facility represents. This asset value should, however, be limited to the discounted value of the fees that are actually expected to be collected. It should not include the full cost outlay on the facility if fees are not expected to cover these costs. Government's announced or expressed unwillingness to collect fees from a debt-financed facility's users sufficient to cover full costs becomes equivalent to precommitment of a share of nonfacility income. The result is precisely the same as if the funds secured in exchange for the debt instruments are used for current public consumption.

Since we know that a relatively small share of governmental outlays reflects "public capital investment," even in the broadest definition, and since even within this share there are precious few facilities or projects that carry an associated direct income stream, the analytical treatment of all public outlays as current public consumption does not seem far off the mark, and surely not far enough off to yield wildly misleading conclusions. This result should not be surprising in itself, since federal fiscal accounts are not arranged or discussed in terms of the distinction between current and capital outlays, and decisions on the sizes of the deficit are never related to the composition of the budget.

## But, After All, We Do Owe It to Ourselves

The elementary logic carries through. The issue of public debt to finance the great and continuing fiscal spree of the 1960s, 1970s, and 1980s has been equivalent, in all relevant respects, to the destruction of capital value. A substantial and ever-increasing share of our future income has been precommitted. There are no offsetting asset items in the national balance sheet.

As I suggested in the first section of the chapter, this spree is at least partially the result of the widespread acceptance of aggregation fallacies, a set of ideas that were in the air long before Keynes, but which were putatively legitimized intellectually by the Keynesian macroeconomic methodology. It seems useful at this point to see precisely how this methodology served to undermine the classical Victorian theory of public debt.

To do this, let us return to the elementary logic of the personal consumption loan. An individual, let us call him *B* for borrower, desires funds in excess of those available to him during time period, $t_0$. To secure these required funds, he contracts a loan; he issues debt and proceeds to finance current spending for consumption in $t_0$. Having consumed the funds, but with the contractual promise to pay later still before him, *B* has suffered a reduction in his net wealth position. He has, in effect, eaten into his capital; he has precommitted some share of his anticipated future income.

The funds that *B* used in $t_0$ were obtained from *L*, whom we shall call the lender. She gives up funds in $t_0$ in exchange for *B*'s debt instrument, *B*'s promise to pay later. Let us now look at the balance sheet adjustment for *L*. At the time of the contract, in $t_0$, she writes down the *Cash* item and writes up the *Notes Receivable* item, both on the asset side of the ledger. There is *no* change in *L*'s net worth in the transaction.

Let us now make *B* and *L* man and wife, and combine their two separate balance sheets to create a single family account. The combined balance sheet will record the debt liability item of *B* and the notes receivable item for *L*, which seem to offset each other. But the balance sheet, struck as of $t_1$ after the marriage, will not directly reflect the history of the transaction. By comparison with the family balance sheet that might have been had *B* not engaged in the consumption spending spree, the net wealth of the family is lower by the size of the debt liability.

Straightforward, simplistic, elementary. Indeed so. But it is the failure to go through these very simple steps that has led many fine intellects to go wildly wrong in their analyses of public debt. The central failure was that of comparing irrelevant rather than relevant alternatives. In our highly simplified two-person example, the macroeconomic methodology would have involved taking a balance sheet snapshot of the combined account of *B* and *L*, whether or not the conjectural marriage had taken place. Such a snapshot would have revealed the debt liability of *B* and the offsetting claim of *L*. From this simple offsetting balance, the conclusion emerges that there is no net debt for the community as a unit. To be sure, or so the argument would have proceeded, *B* holds a present-value liability, and *L* a present-value claim. But these are precisely canceling in the net. There can, then, be no community "burden" of debt. The conclusion appears totally absurd in this two-person model. It is not the two-person "community" that has incurred the debt; *B* has, and *B* must pay *L*. And it is not the "community" that has enjoyed the consumption spree; *B* has done so. Indeed, *L* has financed the spree by voluntarily giving up command over resources in $t_0$, but only in explicit exchange for the debt commitment.

The aggregation fallacy surfaces when the "community" in the form of a government that acts for all citizens assumes the role here of *B*, the borrower in the two-person example. Here it is the government, acting on behalf of the whole "community," that spends beyond its means in $t_0$, and, in so doing, incurs the debt obligation. The fact that the lenders, the *L*s, may also be members of the community is totally irrelevant to the calculus. These persons, the lenders, sacrifice or give up purchasing power over goods or other assets in exchange for the promises of future payment written into the debt contract. In this latter capacity, these *L*s act privately, and not at all for the "community." A proper combination of private and public accounts can only record a net decrement to the community's net wealth as a result of the consumption spending–debt issue transaction. Analytical clarity requires that the macroeconomic aggregates be broken down into relevant components attributable to private and to public or governmental accounting records.

## Is Public Debt Equivalent to a Tax on Capital?

The elementary logic of our second section cannot be challenged. The financing of public consumption outlay by government borrowing is equivalent to reducing the income stream available for private and/or public disposition in all periods of time subsequent to that period in which the funds are initially transferred from lenders and the revenues utilized. If the national capital stock is measured as the present discounted value of the anticipated future income stream, debt-financed spending of this sort amounts to a destruction of this stock.

This simple result must stand. But this result is not identical to the related, but different, proposition to the effect that public-debt financing and capital taxation are equivalent. These two revenue-raising instruments become equivalent in all respects only under a particular set of circumstances. And these circumstances are not the ones usually associated with the two alternatives in practical fiscal operation.

In the first place, capital taxation, as this fiscal instrument is normally discussed, does not often include the present value of anticipated income from labor in the tax base. In other words, human capital, or the value thereof, is often not subject to the capital levy. Unless it is so subjected, however, the so-called capital tax is only partial. Such a tax is in no sense identical in effect to the issue of debt if the interest and amortization charges on the latter are to be financed by general taxes on income flows. The important difference is suggested in the above statement. This difference lies in the fixing of the pattern of incidence in the one case and the effective postponement in the other. With a tax on capital, whether this be entirely general or limited to particular forms of capital, the imposition of the tax defines, once and for all, the distribution of the burden. With public-debt issue, by contrast, there is no immediate or first-period definition of the ultimate pattern of incidence. To make the debt equivalent to the tax, it would be necessary to assign to each current asset-holder a specific share in the liability that the public debt represents. Through such a procedure, any public debt could be converted into an instrument that is fully equivalent to any tax on capital, whether this be general or specific. Unless such first-period assignment of liability is made, however, the actual incidence of debt would seem to be highly unlikely to be equivalent to that resulting from the levy of the equal-revenue capital tax that might have been imposed in lieu of debt issue.

## Debt Retirement and Capital Creation

The elementary logic is fully symmetrical. If an issue of debt to finance current consumption is equivalent to a destruction of capital value, then the retirement of existing debt that is financed by the drawing down of current consumption must be equivalent to the creation or restoration of capital value. This simple result holds for either private or public debt. To retire outstanding debt from current consumption is identical to the financing of new income-yielding investment. In balance-sheet terms, the value of the liability item measured by the debt is reduced; there is no explicit change on the asset side of the account. Net worth, or capital value of the enterprise, be this of a person, firm, or nation, is increased, dollar for dollar, by the net pay-off of debt.

The symmetry carries through, however, only if both sides of the account are analogous. Debt creation to finance current consumption destroys capital value; debt retirement financed from current consumption creates capital value. But debt retirement out of current investment does no such thing. If a debt-amortization program is financed from funds that would otherwise be destined for investment, the effect is neutral with reference to the value of capital. From this result it follows that the explicit retirement of outstanding national debt by the imposition of a once-and-for-all capital levy will not affect the properly measured value of the national capital stock.

The analogy with capital taxation to finance outlay in lieu of debt applies in reverse here. There will normally be significant differences between the effective distributional incidence of any capital levy aimed at debt retirement and the distributional incidence of the continuing liability that an existing debt embodies. The explicit imposition of a capital tax will fix, once and for all, the final incidence of the aggregate charges for the outlays that were initially debt financed. On the other hand, and by contrast, the carry-forward of the debt allows such final incidence to be in part postponed. *Someone* in the polity, now or in some future period, owes the full liability value of the debt that is on the books. But *no one* has an *assigned* share in this liability. A person may behave under the expectation that successful political strategy can remove, from himself, all or most of the debt-measured liability. The debt liability is a continuing zero-sum game.

There is a direct public-choice implication in this comparative incidence of the two institutions. Precisely because any tax levy, whether on consumption or investment, fixes the distribution of the ultimate charges, there will be directed political opposition by those persons and groups on whom the tax incidence falls. Politically, therefore, the choice is far from neutral. There will be a natural bias against any proposal to retire debt from tax-financed revenues. Those who are to be taxed will oppose; those who may be the net beneficiaries may not exist (future generations) or, if they do, may not treat the aggregate reduction in liability as personally experienced increases in their own net wealth. For the same reasons that politicians find it much easier to finance outlays with debt rather than with taxes, they also find it much easier to carry forward debt, once issued, than to retire debt from tax sources. In a very real sense, the Victorian model has been reversed. National capital, once destroyed by debt creation, will not be restored. Or, to put this point differently, public debt, once created, is *permanent*, regardless of the initial usage to which the funds might have been devoted.

## Default, Inflation, and Capital Value

The only means through which public or national debt is likely to be "retired" is via default, whether this be explicitly or implicitly carried out. But default does absolutely nothing toward restoring the capital value destroyed when the debt was created and the resources used up. Default is equivalent to the levy of a discriminatory tax on those persons and entities, internal and external, who hold debt instruments in their investment portfolios. Consider, first, a model in which all holders of debt are citizens of the issuing jurisdiction. Repudiation of the government's debt obligation will reduce to zero the liability item in the imagined balance sheets of all future taxpayers. It will also reduce to zero the capital value of the debt instruments carried in the balance sheets of all holders of the relevant securities. Since these two items, aggregated over the whole community, are precisely offsetting, there is no net effect on capital value. Some persons are made better off; others are harmed. There is no increase in the expected value of the national income stream over future periods, and, hence, no increase in the value of the national capital stock.

The crudest of aggregation fallacies must be avoided here. Because default does not, in itself, affect capital value in the aggregate, it should not be concluded that the debt itself had no effect. Again, the relevant alternatives must be examined. If the debt had not been issued and the funds used up, those who invested in government debt instruments could have invested in income-yielding assets. The net income stream, and therefore the capital value, would have been greater in the absence of the debt. The fact that explicit default neither increases nor decreases the value of the national capital stock, in the aggregate, suggests only that there is no miracle of fiscal process that will remove the burden of error once made. Indirectly, of course, explicit default may reduce the effective value of the government's exploitable capital value. If, because of a past default on debt, government cannot borrow at or near market rates, government's own net worth is reduced. But in such case, government, as an entity, becomes distinguishable from the community.

If some holders of government-debt instruments are foreigners, default can, by repudiating the capital values of these external holders of claims, increase somewhat the net wealth of the members of the internal community.

This international redistribution of burden is fully analogous to the internal redistribution of burden in the previous model. It becomes somewhat arbitrary to aggregate only within national boundaries. And, in this model of externally held debt, the indirect effects of repudiation are likely to be more severe than with internally held debt. Default is likely to make it difficult for governments to borrow in international markets except on unfavorable terms. If the potential for foreign borrowing is included as an asset item in a national balance sheet, default on debt will reduce the capital stock.

Implicit rather than explicit default is the much more likely consequence of government debt. History provides more than sufficient evidence to suggest that governments find it relatively easy to default on their real-valued debt obligations through inflation. With access to money-creation powers, governments find it almost irresistible to destroy capital values of debt holders. Nominal obligations are honored; real-valued obligations are ignored and capital values confiscated. The basic analysis is almost identical to that for explicit default sketched out above.

But there are important differences. As public debt continues to increase in a deficit-financing regime, interest charges on this debt increase. The share of total budgetary outlay devoted to the service of previously issued debt increases. At some point, political pressures will ensure resort to inflationary financing, if this avenue of revenue creation is possible. Through inflation, the real value of current government outlays may be maintained, and possibly even expanded, in the face of ever-mounting interest charges on the debt, charges that are denominated in nominal monetary units rather than in real values.[4] This result would be impossible in a regime that honored the real value of the debt claims.

So long as the inflation is unanticipated, in whole or in part, government can continue to be responsive to demand pressures for expanded outlay on goods, services, and transfers, and to counter pressures against tax increases, while appearing to remain "responsible" in meeting its interest charges on the debt that is outstanding. Through the inflationary process, the government may, over a considerable period of time, succeed in confiscating the real values of previously issued debt claims, while, at the same time, it may

---

4. For an analysis of such a sequence, see my paper "Debt, Demos, and the Welfare State" (Presented at the CIVITAS Conference, Munich, Germany, October 1982).

continue to issue new debt to finance flows of current outlays. Open and explicit repudiation of public debt would confiscate values at one moment, but because of the explicit signal such repudiation would provide, the potential for exploitation would be much more limited than with the implicit repudiation through inflationary financing. As the inflationary process continues, default risk will, of course, come to be incorporated in borrowing rates. As such rates increase, the weight of interest charges in the budget grows, generating, in turn, political pressure for still further inflationary financing of outlay, including debt service. An equilibrium of sorts is attained only when government becomes unable to borrow at any rate, a position that is then identical to that reached immediately with open and explicit default.

As the basic analysis suggests, default on public debt as such neither destroys nor creates capital value in the aggregate, except through the indirect effect on government's potential borrowing capacity. Other indirect effects may emerge, however, through incentives on private decisions to create capital. If the government defaults, explicitly or implicitly, if it levies what amounts to a discriminatory tax on the holders of its own debt instruments, individuals who might be potential investors may become concerned about potential government seizure of other forms of capital, through the fiscal structure or otherwise. The direction of effect on capital creation seems clear; individuals will tend to put aside relatively fewer resources for investment than they would in a regime characterized by government dedication to honor its own debt obligations.

Default through inflationary financing has, in this respect, even more severe incentive effects than open default. With inflation, the discriminatory tax cannot be levied exclusively on holders of public-debt claims. Inflation tends to destroy the value of all assets and claims that are denominated in monetary units, including the holders and users of cash balances. In this setting, therefore, individuals who might be potential creators of capital will predict that government will, indeed, destroy such values once they are created. That which remains only a fear with open default becomes a predictable consequence of continued inflationary financing. In terms of criteria for capital accumulation and preservation, therefore, explicit repudiation of public debt seems clearly preferable to default by means of inflation.

## Constitutional Conclusions

In 1986, we live with a large and ever-increasing national debt. Funds secured in exchange for the government securities that make up this debt have been used, largely if not exclusively, to finance public consumption. The resources so commanded by government have already been used up. Whether or not these resources were "worth" the value that the debt liability now embodies is an irrelevant question. Capital value that cannot be restored has been destroyed. We live with a capital stock that is permanently lower than that stock might have been had the government not embarked on the great fiscal spree of the 1960s, 1970s, and 1980s.

If we look at political reality, it seems unlikely that we shall act to restore the national capital stock by retiring debt out of funds drawn from current consumption. We shall not deliberately reduce the flows of goods and services, public or private, that we enjoy. We may, and presumably will, continue to default on real-debt obligations through inflation, but this behavior will in no way restore capital value already lost.

Realistically, we can at least hope to "stop the bleeding." We can stop the continuing destruction of capital value through deficit-debt financing. As our institutions are now organized, however, we cannot hope to accomplish even this minimally desired result. The temptations of ordinary pressure or interest group politics are simply too overwhelming for those who hold elective office, whether in the executive or legislative branch of government, to resist. The response behavior exhibited in ordinary politics cannot be behavior that would satisfy the demands of reasonable fiscal prudence.

What to do? Our politicians will not be reconverted easily to the Victorian fiscal religion, especially since the Keynesian alternative fits so closely with their natural proclivities to spend without taxing. But we can, as politicians, as academicians, and as laymen, recognize what is happening. And diagnosis is the first step toward cure. Once sufficiently recognized, fiscal profligacy can be contained by appropriate *constitutional* remedies. Ordinary politics will simply not allow fiscally responsible outcomes to emerge from modern democratic institutions. But ordinary politics operates within a set of *constitutional rules,* and these rules have been and may be changed so that more desired patterns of outcomes will emerge.

In this respect, the proposed constitutional amendment that would require budget balance on the part of the national government becomes the most important fiscal reform that has been discussed in the century. Such an amendment, considered as a *general rule* of fiscal prudence, can be discussed, evaluated, and possibly approved largely in independence from the demand-side pressures of day-to-day politics. The fiscal outcomes of ordinary politics now resemble the behavior of the compulsive gambler who finds himself in Las Vegas or Atlantic City. Who can expect the gambler to refrain from "irresponsible" behavior, given the temptations that he faces? But just as the compulsive gambler can know his own proclivities and stay home, so can those who ultimately make political decisions, the citizens, know the proclivities of our ordinary politicians and keep their fiscal activities within bounds of prudence by the enactment and enforcement of constitutionally restraining rules.

No such rule can be expected to work miracles. But an effective balanced-budget constraint, along with some accompanying rule that limits access to money creation as a financing device, could make the U.S. economy the genuine "fiscal wonder" of the late 1980s and 1990s. We cannot undo the damage that has been done. But we can move to levels of economic activity undreamt of in our philosophy.

Do we possess the requisite political understanding, along with the courage, to implement a new fiscal regime? I shall wait upon the answer.

## PART SIX

# Ricardian Equivalence

.

# Barro on the Ricardian
# Equivalence Theorem

Is public debt issue equivalent to taxation? This is an age-old question in public finance theory. David Ricardo presented the case for the affirmative.[1] Professor Robert J. Barro reexamines the question in his recent paper without, however, making reference to Ricardo or other early contributors.[2] Although his discussion is carefully qualified to allow for exceptions under specified conditions, the thrust of Barro's argument supports the Ricardian theorem to the effect that taxation and public debt issue exert basically equivalent effects.

Barro's central emphasis is on demonstrating that under reasonable conditions which involve overlapping generations of persons with finite lives taxpayers will capitalize the future obligations that public debt issue embodies. To the extent that this capitalization occurs, government bonds do not

From *Journal of Political Economy* 84 (April 1976): 337–42. Copyright 1976 by The University of Chicago. All rights reserved. Reprinted by permission of the University of Chicago Press, publisher.

I am indebted to my colleagues Gordon Tullock, Nicolaus Tideman, and Richard Wagner for helpful comments.

1. The basic Ricardian discussion is contained in David Ricardo, *Works and Correspondence,* ed. Piero Sraffa (Cambridge: Cambridge University Press, 1951), vol. 1, *On the Principles of Political Economy,* 244–49, and "Funding System," vol. 4, *Pamphlets and Papers,* 149–200. Antonio de Viti de Marco elaborated the Ricardian thesis in a somewhat modified setting. His analysis was first developed in de Viti de Marco, "La Pressione tributaria dell'imposta e del prestito," *Giornale degli economisti* 1 (1893): 216–31. Essentially the same analysis appears in de Viti de Marco, *First Principles of Public Finance,* trans. E. P. Marget, bk. 5, chap. 1 (New York: Harcourt Brace, 1936), 377–98. For my own summary discussions, see Buchanan, *Public Principles of Public Debt* (Homewood, Ill.: Irwin, 1958), 43–44, 114–22.

2. Robert J. Barro, "Are Government Bonds Net Wealth?" *Journal of Political Economy* 82, no. 6 (November/December 1974): 1095–1117.

add to the perceived net wealth in the economy. From this Barro infers that the substitution of debt for tax finance will exert no expansionary effect on total spending. There are two questions here. Are the future tax liabilities fully capitalized? And, even if they are, does this necessarily imply that the fiscal policy shift exerts no effect on total spending? To establish the second result, it is necessary to examine the differential impacts of taxation and debt issue, quite apart from the question of the capitalization of future taxes. Barro wholly neglects this necessary part of any comparative analysis of the two fiscal instruments, and, because of this neglect, his conclusion is not nearly so relevant for policy as it seems to be. This neglect may stem from Barro's failure to specify properly the inclusive set of transactions that debt issue represents.

After constructing his overlapping-generations model with no government sector, Barro then superimposes an issue of public debt without offsetting or compensating changes. He states, "Suppose now that the government issues an amount of debt, $B$, which can be thought of as taking the form of one-period, real-valued bonds. . . . It can be assumed, for simplicity, that the government bond issue takes the form of a helicopter drop to currently old (generation 1) households."[3] We are immediately prompted to inquire why any government would undertake such an activity. If the purpose is to increase total spending in the economy, this might be done much more readily by the straightforward issue of money, which does not involve future payment obligations. Or, if the purpose is to finance public spending without current taxation or money creation, bonds must be sold in the private capital market, and persons who purchase these bonds must draw down private investments or reduce private consumption. Under this condition, it is impossible that "the increase in $B$ implies a one-to-one increase in the asset supply. . . ."[4]

There are two alternative interpretations of Barro's seemingly bizarre model of bond issue. The first and more constructive interpretation suggests that Barro introduces the model only because of his concentrated interest on the wealth effect of debt issue within the strictly Ricardian or differential-incidence framework. The second interpretation suggests that

3. Ibid., 1101.
4. Ibid., 1103.

Barro's analysis applies only when governments do, in fact, incur future payment obligations without securing command over funds in the initial period, a setting which does not apply to public debt as ordinarily conceived but which may apply to the operation of the social security system in the United States.

These quite separate interpretations may be discussed briefly in turn. Barro directly follows the first statement cited above with the following: "Equivalently, it could be assumed that the bonds were sold on a competitive capital market, with the proceeds of this sale used to effect a lump-sum transfer to generation 1 households."[5] Superficially, the two operations are not at all equivalent. If, however, the bonds dropped from the helicopter are marketable, those who get them may, as desired, convert them into currency. The net effects are the same as the government's sale of bonds to voluntary purchasers along with the lump-sum transfer of the proceeds to the same persons who would have received the bonds in the first model. In either case, the government bonds will replace private bonds or other assets, and the net-wealth effects of this substitution must be considered along with the wealth effects embodied in the capitalization of future tax liabilities. Why might Barro have felt that he could neglect the first of these considerations? He could have done so if his interest is exclusively on determining the differential effects of debt and tax financing, and he is willing to make the severely restrictive assumption that the source for the ultimate purchase of the government bonds is identical to the source from which the alternative taxes would be drawn.

This may be clarified by the following simple *t*-account comparison. Under the tax alternative, the *t*-account adjustments appear as in figure 1a. Under either of the debt-issue alternatives, the final *t*-account adjustments are as shown in figure 1b. If we are interested only in comparing the differential effects of tax and debt finance for a given level of spending, and if we are willing to make the heroic assumption that the direct impact of these two fiscal instruments is identical, then the part of figure 1b below the dotted line represents the net difference between the two combined fiscal operations.

In this interpretation, Barro is simply not concerned either with the independent effects of debt-financed spending on net wealth or with the effects of public debt issue in a modified differential-incidence framework. Does the

5. Ibid., 1101.

(a)

Taxation

| Assets | Liabilities |
|--------|-------------|
| Public assets (+) | |
| Private assets (−) | |

(b)

Debt Issue

| Assets | Liabilities |
|--------|-------------|
| Public assets (+) | |
| Private assets (−) | |
| - - - - - - - - - - - - - - | - - - - - - - - - - - - - - - - |
| Government bonds     (+) | Present value of tax liabilities (+) |

*Figure 1*

financing of public spending by genuine public debt increase aggregate demand in the economy? This is a meaningful and relevant question that has been more widely discussed than the one which Barro analyzes. In terms of figure 1, this question requires us to look at the adjustments in figure 1b only, without regard to any comparison with 1a. Provided that we do not go beyond the simple *t*-accounts, the net-wealth effect of debt financing of public outlay seems to depend on the degree to which future taxes are discounted. But this neglects the possible effects of the sale of bonds on displaced private borrowers. To the extent that these borrowers, those who would have secured the funds had not the government done so, would have applied the same discount factor to the future payment obligations as that applied by the public borrowers (the taxpayers), net wealth will not be modified regardless of the degree of capitalization of future taxes. It seems reasonable to suggest that perceived net wealth, as relevant for spending behavior, increases with increases in either private or public debt. But there are offsetting changes, and the direction of net effect depends on the differences.[6]

6. In a strict accounting sense, future obligations that are implicit in any debt issue, public or private, may be fully capitalized, while at the same time behavior may reflect the

Perhaps the most familiar setting is one that compares the effects of debt financing with explicit money creation for a given increment in public outlay. This, too, is a differential-incidence model but one that is quite separate from the Ricardo-Barro model. The analysis here requires all of the considerations noted above with respect to independent debt issue but has the advantage of emphasizing the specific deflationary impact of debt sales quite apart from the question of future tax capitalization.[7] This latter aspect assumes primary importance, of course, when the principal objective for fiscal policy is to generate an expansion in aggregate spending.

Barro's analysis may be interpreted in a second and more restrictive way that takes his explicit model for debt issue at face value and makes no attempt to generalize it toward meeting the expressed purpose of the paper. In this view, Barro analyzes the issue of debt by a government which does not secure funds in the initial period and which does not allow its debt obligations to be resold in markets. Something analytically analogous to this sort of operation may take place when legislation is enacted which commits the government to pay old-age pensions without at the same time fully financing such obligations with current levies of taxes. Barro does, in fact, refer to the applicability of his analysis to social security financing, and he may have been led to generalize too readily from this somewhat singular example. In this setting, the aggregate economic effects depend strictly on the relative discounting of future benefits on the one hand and future taxes on the other.

To this point my criticism of Barro's paper has been confined to the ambiguities in his setting for public debt issue along with the possible incompleteness of his analysis. I have not challenged his basic conclusion that future taxes will tend to be fully discounted save under the exceptions that he notes. Nonetheless, this conclusion may be questioned on empirical grounds. What evi-

---

rational intent of borrowers to accelerate spending. In this context, a lending-borrowing transaction must affect aggregate spending quite apart from the absence of change in measured net wealth. See R. N. McKean, "Liquidity and a National Balance Sheet," *Journal of Political Economy* 57, no. 6 (December 1949): 506–22. Reprinted in *Readings in Monetary Theory,* ed. F. A. Lutz and L. W. Mints (New York: Blakiston, 1951), particularly p. 75.

7. See R. A. Musgrave, *The Theory of Public Finance* (New York: McGraw-Hill, 1959), 538. For particular emphasis on the deflationary impact of debt issue, see Earl Rolph, "Principles of Debt Management," *American Economic Review* 47 (June 1957): 302–20.

dence might be adduced to suggest that individuals do not, in fact, modify their behavior fully to adjust for the present values of the future tax obligations that public debt issue implies?

Consider, first, the social security system which, as indicated, fits more closely with the narrow interpretation of Barro's results. One implication of his analysis would be that the social security system as it has operated should not have modified the rate of private saving in the economy. This runs counter to the result that has been observed by Martin Feldstein, who estimates that the rate of private saving has been reduced by some 38 percent.[8] Additional evidence may be indirectly available from the historical record if the basic public choice paradigm is accepted. If politicians are ultimately responsive to the desires of their constituents, we may infer something about constituents' evaluations by observing the behavior of politicians. The 40-year history of social security financing yields ample evidence that politicians are extremely reluctant to adopt anything which smacks of full funding for the system. Under the Barro hypothesis, there should be roughly indifferent public reactions to a fully funded and to an unfunded pension system.

If we shift to the more general model, governments should be roughly indifferent as between financing current outlays from taxation and from genuine debt issue. There should be no effect of debt-financed deficits on aggregate spending. Direct testing of this hypothesis is difficult because of the fact that budget deficits are normally financed by some combination of genuine debt issue and money creation.[9] Again, however, the behavior of legislators seems to offer indirect evidence against the capitalization hypothesis. Can anyone in the post-Keynesian world of 1975 seriously question the proclivity

8. See Martin Feldstein, "Social Security, Induced Retirement, and Aggregate Capital Accumulation," *Journal of Political Economy* 82, no. 5 (September/October 1974): 905–26. It should be noted that even with full lifetime discounting of future taxes, a life-cycle model of utility maximization would produce a negative effect on private saving under a pay-as-we-go public pension system. But, of course, the life-cycle model itself implies that debt financing necessarily differs from tax financing to the extent that debt is not retired within a generation.

9. Levis Kochin, "Are Future Taxes Anticipated by Consumers?" *Journal of Money, Credit and Banking* 6 (August 1974): 385–94, attempted to estimate empirically the impact of deficit spending on private consumption. His conclusions tend to support the capitalization view.

of politicians to expand public debt in preference to tax increases? At the state-local level, where the money-creation powers do not exist, why should we observe constitutional constraints on public debts?[10] With public as with private finance, the very creation of debt suggests that borrowers desire to accelerate spending.

10. Admittedly, the out-migration prospect for citizens in local jurisdictions offers an offsetting influence to full discounting.

# The Logic of the Ricardian Equivalence Theorem

*Geoffrey Brennan and James M. Buchanan*

## I. Introduction

The classical Ricardian theorem on the equivalence of taxation and debt has experienced a surprising resurgence in modern economic policy analysis. This interest springs in part from traditional concerns over the differential effects of tax and debt financing for macroeconomic policy purposes,[1] and in part from questions relating to the effects of future social security obligations on current capital accumulation.[2]

From *Finanzarchiv* 38 (1980): 4–16. Reprinted by permission of the publisher.

The specific origins of this paper stem from a discussion between the authors that was directly stimulated by a conversation between Buchanan and Randall Holcombe, Auburn University. We are indebted to Holcombe for rekindling our interest in the Ricardian theorem. A part of the construction of Section II is developed, in a different application, in a chapter of our book *The Power to Tax: Analytical Foundations of a Fiscal Constitution* (Cambridge University Press, forthcoming).

1. See Robert J. Barro, "Are Government Bonds Net Wealth?" *Journal of Political Economy*, Vol. 82, 1974, 1095–1117; R. Barro, "Unanticipated Money Growth and Unemployment in the United States," *American Economic Review*, Vol. 67, 1977, 101–15; James Tobin, "Government Deficits and Capital Accumulation," *Cowles Foundation Papers*, No. 502, October 1978; William Buiter and James Tobin, "Debt Neutrality: A Brief Review of Doctrine and Evidence," *Cowles Discussion Paper*, No. 497, September 1978.

2. See Robert J. Barro, "Reply to Feldstein and Buchanan," *Journal of Political Economy*, Vol. 84, 1976, 343–49; Martin Feldstein, "Perceived Wealth in Bonds and Social Security: A Comment," *Journal of Political Economy*, Vol. 84, 1976, 331–36; M. Feldstein, "Social Security and Private Savings: International Evidence in an Extended Life-Cycle Model," in M. Feldstein and R. Juman (eds.): *The Economics of Public Services*, London,

Our concern in this paper is not so much with the current policy discussion, but rather with aspects of the Ricardian theorem which are logically prior and which must be settled before the lines in the various policy debates can be properly drawn. Our objective is to examine the basic logic of the Ricardian theorem and to clarify certain ambiguities in that logic which seem, so far, to have been almost totally overlooked.

We commence by stating the theorem itself along with the set of conditions that the literature appears to take as necessary for the validity of the theorem in the strict sense.

The theorem states that *taxation and public debt are exactly equivalent in their effect on the economy.*

The conditions that are allegedly necessary for this theorem to hold are:

1. Public expenditure in the initial period is invariant as between the two financing instruments;
2. Public debt issued in the initial period must be serviced and/or amortized from the proceeds of taxes levied in later periods;
3. Capital markets are perfect, and persons may borrow and lend at the same rate as government;
4. Individuals are certain as to both current- and future-period income earning prospects;
5. Individuals, as current taxpayers and as potential future taxpayers, behave in terms of infinite planning horizons—they act "as if" they plan to live forever;
6. Individuals fully anticipate the future-period tax liabilities that are embodied in debt issue;
7. All taxes are lump-sum.

For purposes of our discussion, the first four conditions set the problem. We shall not discuss these requirements, although our neglect does not, of course, imply that these conditions are unimportant.[3] We concentrate only on questions raised by the last three of the conditions listed.

---

1976; Levis Kochin, "Are Future Taxes Anticipated by Consumers?" *Journal of Money, Credit and Banking,* Vol. 27, 1974, 385–94; Randall Holcombe and Asghar Zardkoohi, "The National Debt Controversy," Mimeographed, Auburn University, November 1978.

3. Conditions (3) and (4) in particular warrant considerable defense. In his general critique of the theorem, Tobin challenges both of these requirements.

It is perhaps not surprising that attention has been concentrated on conditions (5) and (6) above, since these conditions seem to impose very restrictive behavioral and informational assumptions on actors in the economy. And, indeed, Ricardo himself appears to have challenged the validity of the equivalence theorem on these grounds.[4] In the modern resurgence, as represented in the debate between Robert Barro and Martin Feldstein on the effects of the implicit social security debt, these conditions are taken to be the critical elements in determining whether the equivalence theorem will ultimately be corroborated or falsified empirically. Barro's introduction of an intergenerational bequest and transfer motive was designed as a means of offering a plausible behavioral model in support for condition (5). And it is condition (5) that seems perhaps most important for long-range issues relating to saving and capital formation. On the other hand, condition (6) raises the issues concerning possible fiscal illusion and has a more direct bearing on a large range of questions concerning the possible efficacy of debt-financed deficits in influencing rates of spending.

## II. "Lump-Sum" and Other Taxes

In order to set the terms for our own discussion, we begin with the simple observation that debt is a means of altering the time pattern of the imposition of taxes. Setting aside the precise implications of this fact, all the current writers are at least agreed on the fact itself—that financing a current project by debt issue implies that taxes will be higher in future periods (and lower in the current period) than they would be if that project were financed by current taxes.

Now, suppose that all taxes imposed are "lump-sum." What does this mean in this setting? It must surely involve the requirement that the effects of the tax are independent of the time period in which that tax happens to be levied. If that were not so, any anticipated tax liability would be reflected in attempts to avoid it. All possible taxpayer response is ruled out by the lump-sum assumption. But if the lump-sum requirement is interpreted in this way then the Ricardian theorem is a pure tautology—*lump-sum* taxa-

---

4. See Gerald O'Driscoll, "The Ricardian Non-Equivalence Theorem," *Journal of Political Economy*, Vol. 85, 1977, 207–210.

tion requires that a tax now is exactly equivalent to a tax next year which raises the same present value of revenue by assumption. Debt and taxes *must* be equivalent. And failure to allow fully for the future by virtue either of finite horizons or of fiscal illusion is inconsistent with the lump-sum assumption. Any lump-sum tax must be intertemporally neutral, *both* in the sense that it does not distort between present and future consumption when used in all periods at a constant rate *and* in the sense that a tax differential between periods does not induce any taxpayer response. Consequently, the Ricardian equivalence proposition follows directly from the assumption that taxes are lump-sum: and assumptions (5) and (6) are logically irrelevant.

A more modest, somewhat looser definition of "lump-sum" taxation[5] may be seen to require only that there is no *current* adjustment which will alter tax liabilities. A labor tax (such as a payroll tax), when the elasticity of labor supply is zero, might seem to exemplify this. This clearly does not in any sense require infinite time horizons or perfect foresight. But even *with* infinite time horizons and perfect foresight, such a tax institution will not guarantee a Ricardo/Barro result.

In fact, once we replace the assumption of taxation that is lump-sum in the strict sense indicated earlier, with plausible tax institutions, the equivalence theorem will not hold in general even given all the other assumptions. Given this, it seems important to examine the Ricardian theorem in a more reasonable tax setting, and this for two reasons. First, it seems desirable to place the Ricardian theorem in some analytic environment where it is not merely an elementary tautology. Second, to the extent that empirical tests are being applied and interpreted, and policy conclusions derived from the empirical results, it seems important to be clear as to what those empirical results imply. Our aim therefore in what follows is to reassess the Ricardian theorem assuming more or less familiar, perfectly feasible tax institutions.[6]

5. No doubt somewhat closer to what Barro had in mind; Robert J. Barro, "Are Government Bonds Net Wealth?" op. cit.

6. Only James Tobin seems to have discussed this dimension of the Ricardo theorem and, even in his analysis, the relaxation of the assumption of "lump-sum" taxation is not recognized as crucial. Our analysis was developed independent of Tobin's, and is in part contained in a chapter of our forthcoming book, *The Power to Tax*, op. cit. One of us (Buchanan) had seen a draft of Tobin's paper "Government Deficits and Capital Accumulation" before the specific subject analysis of this paper was completed, but only after

The central thrust of our discussion can be indicated by appeal to a simple example. We assume, in this example, that the tax in question is a conventional income tax. We consider two archetypes. Individual A is a professional boxer, who earns substantial current-period income but who expects a substantially lower income in future periods. By contrast, Individual B is a medical student whose future income is expected to be much above his current income. Individual A will, of course, prefer that the public outlay be financed by debt, that the aggregate tax on income be postponed. Individual B will prefer that the outlay be financed by current taxation. These preferences will exist not because the two persons differ in their basic utility functions, but more simply, because their own liabilities are related to their expected incomes in each period.

Of course, the equivalence theorem may be valid even if differing persons in the community expect differing time streams of income, *provided* that these time streams, for all persons, are invariant. If, however, we allow for some exercise of choice as among differing time patterns of income receipts, the theorem no longer holds. If the debt alternative is selected, *all* persons in the community will have some incentive to try to become like Individual A in the example rather than Individual B—an incentive that will typically be reflected in their choices between current consumption and saving or accumulation.

What is at stake here is the recognition that with a fixed total revenue requirement each individual faces a tax liability that he considers to be contingent, both upon his own response behavior and on that of all other taxable individuals in the community.[7] It is this fact that, in the absence of lump-sum taxation in the strict sense indicated earlier, establishes a necessary dis-

---

our own model (written in November 1978) was substantially worked out (largely by Brennan) did a return reading of Tobin's paper indicate the similarities with his discussion. Tobin's treatment of the lump-sum requirement remains, however, considerably less rigorous than the analysis of this section, and Tobin does not advance the criticism of the Ricardian logic developed here at all.

7. In earlier work, Buchanan's *Public Finance in Democratic Process* (Chapel Hill, 1967) introduced a "contingent liability" argument to explain a possible preference for taxation over debt financing under essentially Ricardian assumptions. But the Ricardian equivalence theorem was not explicitly discussed in this connection, and the relation of the whole "contingent liability" notion to the behavioral analysis of elementary tax theory was not emphasized.

tinction between private debt and public debt, and between public debt and taxation. The *appropriate* analogy is between public debt and an income-related private debt—one in which the liability is some fraction of the person's future income (e.g., student loans). Such an income-related private debt is different from a fixed-liability private debt, and hence from a current tax, for obvious reasons.

Under the current ($T_1$) tax alternative,

$$D_i = R \frac{Y_i}{\Sigma Y_i}, \tag{1}$$

where $D_i$ is the present value of the $i$th individual's tax liability, where R is the revenue requirement, $Y_i$ is the $i$th individual's current-period income (or tax base more generally), and where $\Sigma Y_i$ is the total current income in the community (or tax base). Under our assumption that all persons are identical, $\Sigma Y_i = nY_i$.

Under the public debt alternative,

$$D_i = R \frac{X_i}{\Sigma X_i}, \tag{2}$$

where $X_i$ is i's income in the period in which the debt is redeemed from the proceeds of taxes.

To make the central point of this section in its most severe form, suppose that there is no current leisure-effort trade-off at all. That is, $Y_i$ cannot be adjusted in any way: the $i$th individual will not adjust his work effort to the tax in the initial period. However, since public debt is necessarily a tax on future income, and since future-period income is, in this model, determined by the individual's own decisions as to saving in the current period, it follows directly from elementary analysis that, when he fully discounts future taxes, the taxpayer will seek to shift income from the future to the present. The individual will save *less* under debt than under the current-period tax that generates equivalent revenue in current-period terms.

## III. Some Simple Geometry

These general remarks can be elucidated by appeal to a more explicit model, and some simple geometry. We assume specifically that:

a. there is a community of $n$ individuals, who are all exactly identical in all respects—in particular, they have identical consumption possibilities in all periods, and identical tastes as between present and future consumption;

b. there are two periods only—$T_1$ and $T_2$—and debt issued in $T_1$ must be amortized in $T_2$;

c. the rate of interest, r, is unaffected by debt issue;

d. the total revenue to be raised over the two periods is an amount R in present-value terms, and it is to be expended in the current period.

In addition, we take as given the assumptions 1 to 6, set out in Section I. Some discussion of the assumptions of our model may be called for. By virtue of assumption (a), we can take it that any of the standard tax institutions which we examine below will impose a tax burden of $(1/n)R$ on each individual. We can therefore abstract from differential income effects. Assumption (c) together with (a) is sufficient to require *external* borrowing, since all taxpayers in the model allocate their consumption intertemporally in the same way. However, the old Keynesian distinction between internal and external debt is not relevant here (as all parties to the debate agree), and this characteristic of the model should therefore not be offensive to anyone. Assumption (d) is for convenience; in fact, the time period of expenditures does not matter here, because it will be the same for both financing alternatives—debt *and* current taxes. But it should be emphasized that under the tax alternative *all* public expenditure over the two periods is being *financed* in period one, whereas under the debt alternative it is all financed in period two. The real-world analogue can be thought of as the "extraordinary expense" if need be, but it is clear that the analysis would be in no way affected if there were *additional* spending financed by taxes imposed at the same rate in the two periods. We simply abstract from these other balanced-budget operations.

We depict this analytic setting in the familiar diagrammatics of Figure 1. In this diagram, we depict the typical individual's income/consumption in the initial or current period $T_1$ along the vertical axis and his income/consumption in the future period $T_2$ along the horizontal axis. Total consumption possibilities over the two periods in the absence of the revenue operation is given by XY, and is linear by virtue of the assumption of interest

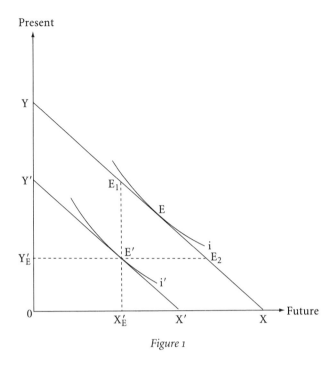

*Figure 1*

invariance. The associated consumption equilibrium is at E and involves positive net savings.

Let us consider in this diagram the imposition of a "lump-sum" tax under which all individuals pay an identical amount, $(R/n)$. Under truly lump-sum taxation, consumption possibilities fall to $X'Y'$, where $Y'Y$ is equal to $(1/n)R$, the individual's share in the present value of the revenue requirement $[X'X$ is equal to $(1/n)R (1 + r)]$. By the definition of "lump-sum" taxation in the strict sense, the revenue extraction induces only a negative income effect and the new consumption equilibrium is at $E'$; and it is so, irrespective of whether the tax is levied in the current period, or in the future period as under the debt alternative. Under the current tax, the pretax position required to achieve $E'$ is $E_1$; the current tax is imposed, and present consumption is $Y'_E$ with gross savings of $Y'_E Y$; when the future tax is imposed, the level of future consumption $Y'_E E_2$ generated by those savings is reduced by the amount of tax in period 2, $E'E_2$. In either case, the final consumption equilibrium is at $E'$—and under the debt alternative, gross private savings are larger than under the current tax alternative by exactly the current value of the debt, Y'Y. The Ricardian theorem holds, and does so by virtue of the assumption that all taxes are lump-sum: E' is the only postoperation equilibrium consistent with that assumption.

Suppose we consider some more plausible tax institution—one in which a rate of tax is applied to some economic magnitude to generate the revenue required. In order to make our basic point in a fairly striking way, consider a situation in which taxes are imposed on consumption expenditure—an income tax with strongly concessional treatment of savings, a conventional value-added tax, a general sales tax, or a pure Kaldor-Mill-Andrews personal expenditure tax all exemplify. Here, unlike the "lump-sum" case, the current tax and the debt—future tax alternatives are quite different.

Let us look first at the current tax, under which R is to be raised by a proportional consumption tax in $T_1$, with no tax at all in $T_2$. Clearly, the individual will have an incentive to postpone consumption to the second period, to $T_2$, when the tax rate is expected to be lower (to be zero). In this setting, the rate of tax on consumption in $T_1$ required to generate R/n in revenue is Y"Y/0Y, producing the equilibrium at $E_T$, as indicated in Figure 2.

Analogously, under debt financing, there is no tax in $T_1$; the liability is postponed via debt to $T_2$, the period in which $(1 + r)$ R/n must be raised.

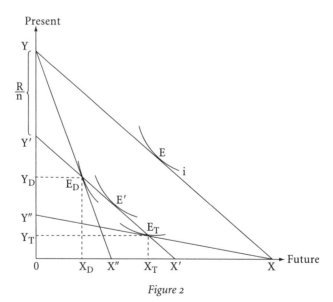

*Figure 2*

The tax rate on consumption in $T_2$ required to raise $(1 + r) R/n$ will be $X''X/0X$, with an equilibrium at $E_D$ in Figure 2. In neither case will any person succeed in avoiding his pro rata share of total revenue liability; each person will pay $R/n$ in present value under each of the alternatives. This result does not, however, imply that behavior is the same under each alternative. It is privately rational for each person to try to reduce his liability by modifying his behavior. These are precisely the same results that would emerge from a comparison of any two *current* tax instruments under the world-of-equals, equi-revenue assumptions of our model. For example, suppose that a tax on whiskey is compared with a tax on beer. In such a model each person would pay $R/n$ under each tax, but there will be relatively more consumption of beer under the whiskey tax than under the beer tax.

The situation in which individuals find themselves under either the tax or the debt alternative is fully analogous to that familiar in game theory as the prisoners' dilemma, or in public goods theory as the free-rider dilemma. In a behavioral sense, it is rational for the individual to adjust to the alternatives that he privately confronts, and to do so independent of the actions of other persons, even if he recognizes the nature of the interdependence. If, instead of this privately rational behavior, an individual tries to behave as he would prefer that all persons behave (that is, if in the presence of the acknowledged interdependence, the individual tries to behave in accordance with some version of a Kantian generalization principle), he would become vulnerable to "exploitation" by others in the sense that his relative share in the aggregate fiscal liability would be increased.

The differing effects of the taxation and public debt alternatives are most clearly evident in terms of private capital accumulation or savings. Under current taxation, savings are $Y_TY'$ in Figure 2; and the debt alternative with taxes imposed in the second period, gross savings are $Y_DY$—while savings *net* of bond issue are $Y_DY'$ in Figure 2. Clearly, net savings are smaller in the latter case. The difference is directly attributable to the attempt by the individual (each individual) to minimize his aggregate tax liability.

We should note that this response to the intertemporal pattern of tax rates does not depend on any current leisure-effort trade-off, which might also be induced by the consumption tax. The possibility of shifting leisure consumption intertemporally so as to consume more leisure in the period with higher tax rates would, of course, increase the effect of the timing of tax imposition, even if aggregate leisure consumption stayed constant over the two periods. But here we abstract from any leisure-effort trade-off: for simplicity, the consumption tax is assumed not to generate any excess burden at this behavioral margin.

It is perhaps arguable that these intertemporal effects are considerably overstated by examining taxpayer response under a *consumption* tax. Under a tax on labor income, for example, the opportunities for taxpayer adjustment may be distinctly less striking—particularly if we rule out the possibility of intertemporal shifts in leisure consumption. However, qualitatively the same taxpayer response can be predicted. To the extent that the acquisition and running down of *human* capital alters the level of labor income receipts, the timing of tax imposition will affect incentives to acquire human capital: under the debt alternative individuals will have the incentive not to acquire human capital in period one and may even run down existing human capital, so as to avoid the future taxes implied by debt—fully anticipated, by assumption. Under the current tax alternative, the opposite incentives apply. We can therefore expect that human capital accumulation will be smaller under the debt than under current taxation. An interesting implication of this is that to the extent that physical capital is a substitute for human capital, we might reasonably expect that physical capital accumulation would *increase* under the debt alternative. By saving (buying physical capital), the taxpayer can reduce labor income in the future period when high tax rates prevail without a corresponding reduction in his future consumption. On this basis, given labor income taxes, debt would tend to generate *larger* accumulation of physical capital; and since it is typically only physical capital accumulation that is measured in empirical investigations, empirical tests of the effects of debt on total capital accumulation may, under labor income taxes, generate profoundly misleading results.

Consider finally a conventional income tax, which falls equally on property and labor incomes. Here, the incentives with respect to the accumulation of both physical and human capital are identical: the higher the tax rate applying in the future period, the smaller the incentive to acquire capital. For this reason, debt will involve a smaller net accumulation of capital than current taxes do. As in the consumption tax case, debt *reduces* capital accumulation of all types.

The discussion of this section should be sufficient to establish the simple proposition that, under plausible tax institutions, the Ricardian equivalence theorem will not in general hold. It also suggests that the particular tax institutions that apply may be significant in determining both the magnitude of the effects that debt issue has on capital accumulation, and whether that magnitude can be captured by conventional empirical examination.

## IV. Neutral Arrangements

It is clear that in a regime in which taxes are imposed at some rate on consumption or labor income[8] the requirement for intertemporal neutrality is that tax rates be identical in both (all) periods. With an "extraordinary expense" of the type we have been discussing here, neither debt nor current taxation meets this criterion—either will distort intertemporally. In the case of a stream of expenditures spread over the two periods, the same requirement of identical tax rates applies—but, of course, may be satisfied by "current" taxes *in each period* under annual budgeting, if expenditure levels happen to be the same in each period.

There is a quite distinct efficiency argument for equalizing tax rates as between periods—that minimizing the present value of *current* excess burdens, say between effort and leisure, also requires equalization of tax rates. This follows directly from the fact that excess burden is a convex function of the tax rate applied. Barro himself has used this line of reasoning to develop a "theory of public debt" (which, of course, would be a contradiction in terms if debt and taxes were identical).[9] But it needs to be emphasized that this line of reasoning, although it involves a relaxation of the "lump-sum taxation" assumption, *is* quite distinct. The more obvious possibility that differential tax rates over time will generally distort intertemporally, which is the argument developed here, does not in any way depend on taxes distorting choices within a given period.

Once this more general requirement for neutrality—the identity of tax

---

8. As is widely recognized, the conventional income tax is not intertemporally neutral in a setting where all saving is for future consumption by oneself or one's heirs, even if the tax is imposed at the same rate in all periods, because of the "double taxation" of savings embodied in property income taxation.

9. Robert J. Barro, "On the Determination of the Public Debt" (University of Rochester Working Paper, Rochester, N.Y., 1978).

rates between periods—is recognized, however, the significance of any empirical findings tends to pale. Given recent history, it would be quite reasonable for taxpayers to expect tax rates to rise—largely independent of reliance on debt. Of course, *ceteris paribus,* the use of debt will imply larger tax rates in the future—but it is by no means clear how large a role explicit debt plays in expectations about future tax rates.[10]

To the extent that future expenditures are expected to exceed current levels, then the neutral arrangement would, of course, involve creation of a "sinking fund" so as to ensure that tax rates in future periods will be equal to current rates. For the "extraordinary expense" of the foregoing model, on the other hand, the appropriate debt-tax mix is required. One possible real-world institution that would meet the neutrality requirement for such a "once-and-for-all," totally unexpected expenditure is the sale of consols—debt obligations that involve no amortization and that require the tax financing equal interest charges in each period, *including that of the initial issue.*[11]

As far as the strict Ricardian comparison is concerned, however, the message is clear: the debt and current-tax alternatives imply *differing* rates of tax between periods—neither is neutral, and each distorts in a different direction.

## V. Fiscal Illusion and Finite Horizons

It is useful here to ask what effect fiscal illusion and finite horizons may have on the differential effects of debt and taxes in our model, as opposed to the pure lump-sum model.

It is, as we have noted, difficult to specify exactly how debt illusion might intrude into the pure Ricardian model without violating lump-sum assumptions. Presumably what writers have had in mind is that the future "lump-sum" tax liability implied by debt is underestimated by citizens-taxpayers, so that under the debt alternative the negative income effect induced by future

10. The implicit social security debt may, for well-known demographic reasons, play a much more significant role. Tax limitation may also have significant effects in encouraging accumulation to the extent that it encourages taxpayers to believe that future tax rates will be lower than they would otherwise have been.

11. The possible sale of consols in meeting the neutrality requirements was first passed on to us by Professor John Bossons of the University of Toronto.

"lump-sum" tax obligations is believed to be less than it actually is. Individuals are taken to act as if they locate on the income-consumption curve $E'E$ in Figure 3 above $E'$—say at $E_D^P$—in the debt case, whereas they locate at $E'$ in the tax case. If present consumption is not inferior, then net savings will be lower in the debt case, and the debt *consumption* equilibrium will be $C_D^P$ involving lower future consumption than anticipated. Under this interpretation, the effect of debt illusion on capital accumulation is unambiguous: net capital accumulation must decline.

In our model, however, the zero illusion equilibrium is at $E_D$ under the debt alternative. If debt illusion induces the taxpayer to believe that future tax rates will be lower than they actually are, he will act so as to locate at some point on the price-consumption curve $E_D E$ to the right of $E_D$, say at $E_D^L$. Here there is an imagined income as well as a substitution effect at stake, but it is quite conceivable that net capital accumulation may go *up* in response to debt illusion, as in Figure 3. The actual consumption equilibrium associated with $E_D^L$ will turn out to be at $C_D^L$, in this case with *lower* current consumption and higher future consumption than the disillusioned taxpayer would have preferred, or would have chosen under perfect foresight. Of

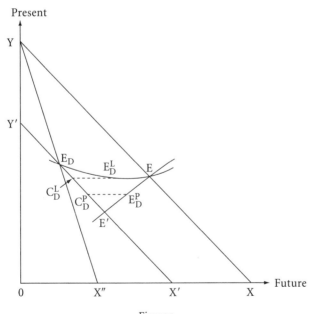

*Figure 3*

course, $C_D^L$ *could* lie on X'Y' above $E_D$, but the effects of fiscal illusion here are quite ambiguous. If debt fails to induce a detectable response in net capital accumulation (i.e., net of bond issue), it could be *because* of fiscal illusion rather than because of its absence.

## VI. Summary and Conclusions

We have demonstrated that the Ricardian equivalence theorem is untenable in any meaningful sense that might serve as a basis for fruitful empirical investigation. What does this conclusion imply for the methodology of further research? Clearly, the effects of public debt issue, relative to the effects of taxation, warrant investigation, both analytical and empirical.

Given the logical ambiguities in the equivalence theorem as currently used, it would seem useful to drop condition (7) from the list of requirements of the idealized model. An internally consistent set is provided in conditions (1) through (6). This procedure will allow both current taxation and future-period taxation to be discussed in terms of recognizable and realistic tax institutions rather than idealized analytical benchmarks. As the analysis of this paper shows, the two financing instruments generate different effects under the conditions specified. There is no equivalence theorem to be tested. Debt issue will tend to discourage savings and capital accumulation relative to that which would be generated under tax financing of the same public expenditures. In the context of the current debate, the analysis supports the Feldstein results with Barro-like assumptions.

The hypothesis to be tested would be one which states that debt issue does discourage savings, rather than the opposite. But what explanation might be sought if empirical results suggest that such an hypothesis is falsified? In this case, one could look to conditions (5) and (6), those relating to planning horizons and to possible illusion, or to the nature of the taxes involved and failure to include human capital in savings measures, as providing plausible explanations as to why savings might not be reduced by debt. We may explain some offsets to the effects on saving indicated in the full model, as the analysis of Section V suggests. We may move somewhat closer to the Barro empirical results for Feldstein-like reasons. If individuals do not fully recognize the future tax liabilities that are implicit in debt issue they may save more, not in order to provide for future heirs, but much more simply, in order to take advantage of what they think are more advantageous terms of trade between present and future incomes net of tax. Of course, this is only a possibility: it depends on the perceived substitution effect outweighing the perceived income effect due to the imagined lower future taxes.

As noted in the Introduction, one of our purposes in this paper is methodological. The modern discussion of the classical Ricardian theorem has been marred by a failure of the protagonists in the controversy to examine the basic structure of the comparative tax analysis with sufficient care. Equipped with a mastery of the powerful techniques of empirical testing, economists have been prone to advance hypotheses prematurely. As a consequence, the empirical findings may, in fact, corroborate or refute hypotheses, which, when properly formulated, are almost the opposite to those that are allegedly tested by the data.

# The Incidence and Effects
# of Public Debt in the
# Absence of Fiscal Illusion

## James M. Buchanan and Jennifer Roback

*Abstract:* This article clarifies several points concerning the effects of public debt. First, the article clarifies the distinction between the Ricardian equivalence and Barro neutrality theorems. Second, the article develops a voting model with two types of families, neither of whom has fiscal illusion. We show that debt may have redistributive consequences and that some voters will rationally prefer debt to taxes. In this way, we develop a rudimentary positive theory of debt issue. We also verify the proposition that debt issues that redistribute income are not neutral with respect to savings and consumption.

With the publication of his 1974 paper "Are Government Bonds Net Wealth?" Robert J. Barro initiated a separately identifiable research program in the theory of macroeconomic policy.[1] Barro's analysis on public debt was itself

From *Public Finance Quarterly* 15 (January 1987): 5–25, copyright 1987 by Sage Publications, Inc. Reprinted by permission of Sage Publications, Inc.

We appreciate the encouraging suggestions advanced by participants in the Public Choice Center conference on deficits in September 1985, particularly Michael Parkin. We also got helpful comments from participants when an early draft of the article was discussed at a University of Chicago economics department seminar in November 1985.

1. R. J. Barro, "Are Government Bonds Net Wealth?" *Journal of Political Economy* 82, no. 6 (1974): 1095–1117.

contained within the more comprehensive research program summarized under the rational expectations rubric, the hard core of which allows no relaxation of strong informational-expectational postulates of rational behavior. Barro's conclusion was to the effect that government bonds do not, in any aggregative sense, constitute positive net wealth. From this conclusion, the inference has been drawn that public debt issue, as such, imposes no net costs. As we shall demonstrate, such an inference is incorrect, even in the absence of fiscal illusion, except in the unique fiscal operation that precisely balances off assets and liabilities in each person's account. In all other fiscal policy shifts involving debt issue, net wealth in the economy may be increased, decreased, or unchanged, depending on the temporal and distributional imputation of the spending benefits.

There is a difference between the Ricardo theorem and the stronger proposition that we shall call the Barro neutrality theorem, a difference that has not been fully recognized. Clarification of the distinction here allows us to show the extreme restrictiveness of the neutrality hypothesis while remaining within the methodological boundaries required for the validity of the equivalence hypothesis. Our analysis has direct implications for a theory of public debt issue itself, implications that differ from those derived by Barro.[2]

## Ricardian Equivalence and Barro Neutrality

In his comment on Barro's original paper, Buchanan observed that Barro's result has been widely discussed in the traditional public finance literature under the rubric of the Ricardian equivalence theorem.[3] This characterization was misleading in its failure to recognize that while the Barro theorem necessarily incorporates the Ricardian it goes considerably beyond the latter. The Ricardian proposition concerns the equivalence of debt issue and taxation as alternative means of financing public outlay. The theorem states that these two financing methods exert identical effects on the economy and, in particular, that savings and consumption patterns are invariant as between

2. R. J. Barro, "On the Determination of the Public Debt," *Journal of Political Economy* 87, no. 5 (1979): 940–71.

3. J. M. Buchanan, "Barro on the Ricardian Equivalence Theorem," *Journal of Political Economy* 84, no. 2 (1976): 337–42.

the two alternatives. The Barro theorem, on the other hand, asserts that the issue of public debt, as such, is neutral in its effects on the economy; it does not affect the rates of consumption and saving.[4]

The logic of the Ricardian theorem is straightforward. Assume that individuals are connected to future generations so that they are effectively infinitely lived. Each individual has some intertemporal utility function that yields a time path of consumption and savings when maximized subject to an intertemporal budget constraint.

$$\max u \, (x_1, x_2 \ldots x_n)$$

$$\text{s.t.} \sum_{i=0}^{n} \frac{y_i}{(1 + r)^i} = \sum_{i=0}^{n} \frac{x_i}{(1 + r)^i} \tag{1}$$

This budget constraint simply says that the present value of the earnings stream, y, must be equal to the present value of the consumption stream, x. A time path of savings is implied by any solution to this maximization problem.

Now suppose that government makes an expenditure in the amount of $E_0$, an outlay that can be financed either through debt issue, $D_0$, or current taxation, $T_0$. The debt issue has associated with it some stream of future taxes, $T_1 \ldots T_n$, required to service and amortize the debt. Obviously the present value of this tax stream is exactly equal to the amount of the debt issue, which in turn is equal to the amount of the expenditure, that is,

$$\sum_{i=1}^{n} \frac{T_i}{(1 + r)^i} = D_0 = E_0 = T_0.$$

4. In one sense, it is not entirely fair to attribute this view to Barro, who argues in his reply to Buchanan that his argument was "directed toward fiscal questions that involve shifts between tax and debt finance for a given volume of public expenditures. Shifts in the expenditure level have real effects that depend on the degree of substitutability between public and private expenditures in individual utility functions . . . and on the direct productivity of public expenditures . . . and it did not seem necessary to become involved in these issues" (R. J. Barro, "Reply," *Journal of Political Economy* 84 [April 1976]: 343–49). However, actual debt issues in the real world involve some combination of substitution of debt for taxes and finance of new expenditures. Thus, one is necessarily involved in these issues. The purpose of this section is to clarify the conditions under which the full neutrality result holds.

Assume the government finances $E_0$ by the sale of bonds, and that the present value of an individual j's share of the future tax liability is $D_{0j}$. (Persons are denoted $j = 1, \ldots k$, hence $\Sigma D_{0j} = D_0$.) Assume that the individual correctly assigns to himself this liability item. His budget constraint becomes

$$\sum_{i=0}^{n} \frac{Y_{ij}}{(1 + r)^i} = \sum_{i=0}^{n} \frac{X_{ij}}{(1 + r)^i} + D_{0j}. \tag{2}$$

Alternatively, suppose the government finances $E_0$ by current taxation, $T_0$, with the individual's share being $T_{0j}$. The individual's budget constraint is then:

$$\sum_{i=0}^{n} \frac{Y_{ij}}{(1 + r)^i} = \sum_{i=0}^{n} \frac{X_{ij}}{(1 + r)^i} + T_{0j}. \tag{3}$$

Budget constraints 2 and 3 are identical in present-value terms as long as $D_{0j} = T_{0j}$. The Ricardian theorem states that with perfect capital markets the consumption and saving streams implied by [2] and [3] are identical for the economy as a whole. That is, if the government issues debt, individuals lend while the government borrows. If the government levies taxes, individuals borrow in order to smooth their consumption stream and still meet their current tax obligation.[5] The consumption paths are the same in the two cases since the overall budget constraint has not changed, and the capital markets allow costless intertemporal transfers. The only difference in the two cases is that in one case the individual borrows while the government "saves," and in the other case the reverse is true. Note, however, that the Ricardo theorem has nothing at all to say concerning the effects of the combined fiscal operation on the levels of consumption and saving. This theorem states only that such effects will be invariant as between debt and taxes.

The Barro neutrality theorem is stronger in precisely this respect. The neutrality theorem states that savings and consumption levels are invariant upon debt issue. This result depends on a crucial assumption in addition to those made with respect to the Ricardian theorem. Full neutrality requires that the budget constraint in [1] be identical to that in [2] and [3]. This condition implies that the expenditures are distributed to the taxpayers in such a way

5. A. de Viti de Marco, *First Principles of Public Finance*, trans. E. P. Marget (New York: Harcourt Brace, 1936).

as to balance precisely their tax or debt liabilities. With debt issue, the required condition for an individual is

$$\sum_{i=0}^{n} \frac{Y_{ij}}{(1 + r)^i} + E_{oj} = \sum_{i=0}^{n} \frac{X_{ij}}{(1 + r)^i} + D_{oj}. \tag{4}$$

It is clear from [4] that only a set of cash transfers to persons allocated so as to balance precisely their correctly assessed shares in the present value of the debt-induced liability can ensure the full neutrality result. That is, $E_{oj} = D_{oj}$, for all j.

Consider, first, a setting in which the public outlay is in the form of cash transfers that are allocated among persons on some basis that does *not* correspond to the allocation of the debt-induced liabilities for future tax payments. In this case, some persons in the economy will experience net-wealth increments as a result of the debt-financed transfer operation; other persons will experience net-wealth decrements. The neutrality result will hold in this setting only if the effects on the consumption-saving patterns of the two groups are precisely offsetting. While there is no justification for making such an assumption on a priori grounds, the directional offset may suggest that the neutrality result remains a reasonable approximation for macro-economic considerations. The aggregate budget constraint still satisfies:

$$\sum_{j=1}^{k} \left( \sum_{i=0}^{n} \frac{Y_{ij}}{(1 + r)^i} + E_{oj} \right) = \sum_{j=1}^{k} \left( \sum_{i=0}^{n} \frac{X_{ij}}{(1 + r)^i} + D_{oj} \right), \tag{5}$$

where k = the number of individuals in the economy/polity.

A second setting more damaging to the neutrality result involves the use of the public outlay to finance the provision of public goods and services. In this case, neutrality would require that persons judge themselves to be neither better nor worse off after receiving the benefits of the debt-financed good or service than they would have been if the fiscal operation had not taken place. The strict distributional requirement discussed in the preceding paragraph remains relevant here, but, over and beyond this requirement, persons may place values on public goods benefits that exceed, fall below, or just equal the present-value liability of the future taxes that they have, correctly, assigned to themselves.

For example, if the debt is used to finance a pure public good in an idealized voluntary exchange model of the fiscal structure, then absent fiscal illusion, all persons in the economy would respond to the debt-financed outlay just as they would to the current-period levy of a set of Lindahl tax prices.[6] Each person would enjoy some fiscal surplus, and, hence, some net increment to properly measured wealth. In the other extreme, in which the funds raised from the sale of bonds are totally squandered on exotic foreign travel for members of Congress, all citizens experience net decrements to their perceived wealth. In either of these extreme models, or with any that fall between these, there may be effects on patterns of consumption and saving in the economy. The direction of such effects cannot be predicted without knowledge of each individual's intertemporal utility function.

## The Macroeconomic Setting
## for the Neutrality Theorem

Before proceeding with further implications of our argument, it may be useful to review the context within which Barro's paper appeared. Barro was responding to the once-dominant Keynesian proposition that the substitution of debt finance for tax finance of public outlay exerts stimulatory effects on the economy, and, specifically, that such a fiscal policy shift would increase consumption at the expense of saving. Since, in such an operation, funds given up by bond purchasers are, in effect, transferred to taxpayers, at least in the aggregate, the only residual portfolio entries are the bonds in the hands of persons who bought them from government. Why should this whole operation make people consider themselves better off? The orthodox response incorporated fiscal illusion in that people were presumed not to reckon fully on the future tax liabilities that the very existence of government bonds implies.

Barro openly challenged the fiscal illusion presumption and argued that so long as persons relate themselves to future taxpayers, as is empirically indicated by the observations of bequests among generations, a rational behavioral calculus would require that future tax liabilities be recognized. The present value of the future tax liabilities is matched by the present value of the claims to these payments. The lifetime budget constraint of the represen-

---

6. See M. J. Bailey, *National Income and the Price Level: A Study in Macroeconomic Theory* (New York: McGraw-Hill, 1971).

tative household is unchanged. Government bonds are not net wealth. There is no effect on levels of current consumption or saving in a shift from tax finance to debt finance. In the analysis of this article, we shall, with Barro, remain within the hard core of the rational expectations research program. We shall assume that persons are not subject to fiscal illusion and that the utility of parents depends on their children's welfare.[7] They recognize that current-period issue of public debt does, indeed, embody future-period tax liability. We also assume, with Barro, that the debt finances pure cash transfers. Hence, we have no quarrel with Barro's basic result, within the stylized distributional assumption of his model. Our analysis concentrates on the implications of this assumption.

## Why Is Public Debt Issued?

Why is public debt issued? Barro in his later paper has recognized this question to be important.[8] If fiscal illusion is absent, and if the distribution of the values of the benefits from public outlay precisely matches the distribution of the accurately assessed present values of future tax liabilities, why should government borrow? Some model of government itself is required to answer this question; we shall adopt a modern public choice approach here by reducing political decisions to those made by economic actors.

This approach immediately suggests analogy with private borrowing.[9] Why do individuals borrow? They do so when they desire to shift the temporal relationship between their expected earnings or income streams and their anticipated spending streams: *As borrowers,* individuals are, in effect,

---

7. Other critics of Barro's position relax these assumptions. Lindbeck and Weibull, for example, abandon the perfect altruism assumption of the Barro model and connect the generations by assuming that wealth holdings enter the utility directly and that individuals supply labor in more than one period (A. Lindbeck and J. W. Weibull, "Intergenerational Aspects of Public Transfers, Borrowing and Debt," Seminar Paper no. 299 [Stockholm, Sweden: Institute for International Economic Studies, 1984]). Stiglitz also relaxes the perfect altruism assumption (J. E. Stiglitz, "On the Relevance or Irrelevance of Public Financial Policy: Indexation, Price Rigidities and Optimal Monetary Policy," Working Paper no. 1106 [Cambridge, Mass.: NBER, 1983]).

8. Barro, "On the Determination of the Public Debt."

9. J. M. Buchanan, *Public Principles of Public Debt: A Defense and Restatement* (Homewood, Ill.: Irwin, 1958).

drawing down the capital values of their expected income streams in ex-change for enhanced levels of spending in the initial period. (These same persons may, of course, utilize borrowed funds, *as investors,* to restore and even to enhance capital values. Our concern here is with the effects of the borrowing per se.)[10] By the act of borrowing, considered in isolation (and separately from any disposition of funds that are borrowed) individuals are "eating up" or destroying capital. In terms of intergenerational relationships, borrowing for the financing of current consumption amounts to a decision to reduce bequests.

When we shift attention to public or collective borrowing that is carried out on behalf of the citizenry through the agency of government, there is no clear motivation for borrowing in the context of Barro's idealized model.[11] It is evident that all persons whose behavior is analyzed in this model of a fiscal policy shift must remain indifferent as between the borrowing and taxing methods of financing ongoing public outlay or on an expansion of public outlay to finance an idealized set of cash transfers. The individuals' budget constraints are not affected, and they have no basis for departing from estab-lished intertemporal equilibria as a result of the change in policy. Barro has resorted to a second-order smoothing argument in an attempt to clarify this ambiguity that emerges as a consequence of the full neutrality proposition.[12] We suggest that there is a much simpler response to the question: Why do governments borrow?

The key to understanding the analysis that follows is to recognize that an increase in the national debt while holding private bequests constant is an exact substitute for a direct decrease in private bequests. For an individual, the reduction in his or her level of bequests made possible by public debt issue is measured precisely by the present value of the future tax liabilities

---

10. Drazen explicitly considers the possibility that parents may borrow (either publicly or privately) to finance human capital investments for their children (A. Drazen, "Gov-ernment Debt, Human Capital and Requests in a Life-Cycle Model," *Journal of Political Economy* 86, no. 3 [1978]: 505–16). We abstract from these interesting issues here.

11. Stiglitz ("On the Relevance") argues that debt (or social security) can be used as a means of spreading risk across generations. He abstracts from altruism, however, and ar-gues that the risk sharing is mutually advantageous to all generations and hence would be agreed to.

12. Barro, "On the Determination of the Public Debt."

that will be assessed against his or her heirs. If persons wish to reduce their bequests, they can use public debt as a means of doing so.[13] They can use public debt to increase their current consumption. The future taxes required to service and amortize the debt are charges against future consumption. It is a direct consequence of the Barro theorem that this operation will be equivalent to a decrease in private bequests.

Suppose that we classify persons in the polity into two sets: (A, or "Ants"), those whose intertemporal equilibria embody positively valued bequests to heirs and assigns, and (G, or "Grasshoppers"), those whose intertemporal equilibria embody no such bequests.[14] In this setting, the full neutrality result will carry through only if, for instance, the tax reductions financed by debt issue are exclusively concentrated on members of the first set of persons who plan to leave positively valued bequests. If, by contrast, the shift from tax to debt finance involves *any* reduction in the tax shares of persons in the second set, these individuals will experience an increment in their net wealth. As a general proposition, it is clear that rational choice on the part of people in the second set dictates a clear preference for the debt-financing option, as long as they currently pay any taxes for the financing of public outlays.

Precisely the same results emerge when we examine the possible issue of government bonds to finance incremental spending. Only if the benefits of such outlay are exclusively concentrated on persons in the first (A), or Barro, set, could we expect indifference on the part of members of both groups as between the debt-financed outlay proposed and the no-action alternative. If any benefits from spending are expected by members of the second (no positively valued bequests) (G) set, these persons must rationally prefer that the fiscal action take place.

Recall that people in this second set (G) are classified by the absence of any desire to leave positively valued bequests. Only a small number of this group would, presumably, solve their intertemporal maximization problem by optimally selecting the corner solution described by zero-valued bequests. Most members of this second set would, if feasibility constraints allowed it, choose to leave negatively valued bequests in varying magnitudes. The insti-

---

13. Drazen ("Government Debt") makes this point in a somewhat different context.
14. Either one of the two sets may, of course, be empty. The Barro model can be interpreted as one in which the second set contains no members.

tution of public borrowing brings the possibility of making negatively valued bequests within the feasibility set, an alternative that is not readily available to people in their private economizing capacities. In existing legal structures, heirs are responsible for the private debts of decedents only up to the extent of the decedent's positively valued private assets.[15] On the other hand, for persons who plan to leave no positively valued bequests to heirs, public-debt-financed reductions in taxes and/or increases in spending benefits may become equivalent to preferred negatively valued bequests. Public debt may allow these persons to dictate a time path of consumption that is rationally preferred to anything available in the no-debt setting.

## The Aggregative Consequences

We have offered an explanation of why government issues debt to finance current public consumption, including transfers, but we have not yet examined the consequences of this public choice model for the macroaggregates that command the attention of most economists. What are the implications of our analysis for the whole "crowding out" issue? What are the predicted effects on the rates of saving in the economy?

We want to remain strictly within the informational-expectational-market perfection confines of the Barro-type analysis here. Specifically, all persons in the economy are presumed to recognize that an issue of public debt in the amount $D_0$ embodies a present-value future tax liability of precisely the same amount. Suppose, now, that the Gs succeed in securing political approval of such an issue of debt, with the revenues devoted either to a tax reduction or to a new spending program where some of the benefits are to be enjoyed by the Gs. (We will discuss below the factors that will increase the probability of the Gs securing such approval.) Careful analysis here requires some specification of the setting within which members of the A group attempt to respond to the politically imposed fiscal operation.

---

15. Buiter makes this point but regards it as a variety of market failure. (W. H. Buiter, "Theory of Optimum Deficits and Debt," in *The Economics of Large Government Deficits*, Federal Reserve Bank of Boston Series no. 27). That is, since individuals cannot impose binding financial obligations on the unborn, the set of forward capital markets is incomplete.

## CASE I. TAXES ON BOTH AS AND GS CURRENTLY
### AND IN FUTURE PERIODS; PROGENIES OF EQUAL SIZE

Suppose that, prior to the fiscal policy shift, taxes are levied on persons in both the A and G groups. For simplicity, assume that taxes are shared equally between these two groups, on a per capita basis, that the groups are of equal size, and, further, that persons within each group are identical to one another. Assume, further, that both groups expect equal-sized progenies and, also, that taxes will be equally shared by the two progeny groups in all future periods.

The public debt finances, say, an equal per head cash transfer to all persons in the polity during the initial period when the borrowing operation takes place. The members of the G set do not concern themselves at all with the taxes that will be levied on their own progeny, although, by our assumption, these members of the G set fully recognize that such taxes will indeed be imposed. Ricardo-like adjustment behavior is limited to members of the A group. They seek to leave positively valued bequests to their heirs, and they will reckon on incorporating the full present value of future tax liabilities anticipated to be imposed on these heirs in their postdebt equilibria. Under the specifications of this model, the budget constraints of persons of this A group have not been modified by the fiscal policy operation. New saving in precisely the amount of the present value of the future tax liabilities anticipated to be imposed on A's *progeny* will be generated. In this model, however, at least to a first-order approximation, this new saving will only be one-half of the value of the debt that is issued, one-half of the present value of future tax liabilities for all persons in the polity. Since, however, the Gs do not save at all, either before or after the fiscal operation, and since the rate of saving of the As increases, private saving in the economy increases.

Note, however, that aggregate consumption (public and private) also increases. The As maintain previously attained consumption levels; they use all of the cash transfers returned to them in generating the new saving. The Gs, by contrast, utilize all of their received cash transfers in expanding consumption. The new saving by the As will be sufficient to purchase only one-half of the debt that is issued to finance the transfers. In other words, the increase in public borrowing, which may be regarded as a decrease in public saving, is not completely offset by the increase in private saving by the As. The aggregate of private and public saving falls.

The source of the increased consumption on the part of the Gs is a reduced flow of funds available for private investment. There is a necessary crowding out of investment opportunities. This will, of course, generate second-order effects on interest rates, but our concern is not with these second-round effects here. The first-order effect is that the present value of the earnings stream for the whole economy is reduced by one-half of the size of the debt that is issued.[16]

Note that in the fiscal setting described in Case I, neither the Ricardian equivalence theorem nor the Barro neutrality theorem is valid. The financing of the set of equal-per-head cash transfers by taxation exerts different effects from the financing by debt. With taxes levied on members of both the A and G sets, there is no net increase in the Gs' consumption. The transfers finance the required tax payment for both the As and the Gs. The fiscal operation is totally neutral in its effects under tax financing whereas, as indicated above, there is a necessary reduction in the present value of the economy's earnings stream under debt financing.

## Case II. Taxes on As only, both currently and in all future periods; progenies of equal size

Consider, now, a different specification, one that might, at the outset, seem somewhat more favorable to the generation of the full neutrality results of the Barro analysis. Assume that the persons in the A set, those who desire to pass along positively valued bequests, pay *all* of the taxes in the polity in the initial period, and, further, that they also expect their own progeny to pay all of the taxes that are to be imposed in subsequent periods. The members of the G set pay no taxes initially, and they expect that their own progeny will also escape all taxes in the future.

The Gs do, however, possess the franchise, and they succeed in securing

---

16. The results of this section are similar to those reported by Stiglitz ("On the Relevance"). In a somewhat different model, Stiglitz shows that debt issue is neutral unless it generates intergenerational redistributions of income.

political approval for a debt issue that will finance the set of cash transfers allocated equally per head among all persons in the polity, both As and Gs. In this case, the As will indeed incorporate the full value of the anticipated future liabilities in their portfolios. But they will experience a net decrement to their wealth, and unless their intertemporal equilibria require target levels of bequests for their heirs, the new saving that the fiscal operation will generate will fall short of the full value of the debt. If the As adjust to the experienced decrement in their wealth by marginal shifts among all of the dated arguments, we should predict that saving will increase only by some share of the full value of the debt that is issued. There will be some crowding out of productive investment opportunities. The present value of the economy's expected income stream will be reduced. In one sense, this result is hardly surprising. The debt issue amounts to a transfer from the As who pay taxes to the Gs who do not. Because the As have a higher propensity to save than the Gs, a transfer from As to Gs almost certainly reduces aggregate savings in the economy.

It is useful to note that, in this model, the fiscal operation described is fully equivalent to the imposition of a capital levy to finance the same outlay. Since, by assumption, only the As possess capital, and only the As pay taxes both initially and in all future periods, a capital levy will fall exclusively on the As, who will adjust their intertemporal consumption-saving patterns to the net decrement in wealth identically to the adjustment that takes place under the debt-financing alternative.

Note that in the fiscal setting described in Case II, the Ricardian equivalence theorem remains valid while the Barro neutrality theorem is invalid. This model brings out the differences between the two propositions. There is no differential effect on the economy exerted by the tax- and debt-financing alternatives (the Ricardian theorem), but there is an effect of the combined financing-spending operation on the present value of the economy's earnings stream.

## CASE III. CURRENT TAXES ON BOTH As AND Gs; ONLY As HAVE PROGENIES

This setting has qualities of both Case I and Case II. Recognizing that all future-period taxes must be paid by their own heirs, the As must capitalize the full expected value of future tax liabilities and make the indicated equilibrating adjustment in their planned rates of consumption and saving over all periods. As in Case II, there will be some current-period crowding out of private investment opportunities.

Case III differs from Case II, however, in that the Ricardian equivalence theorem, which was satisfied in Case II, no longer holds in Case III. Here the financing of the transfers by debt does differ from the financing of taxation because the Gs effectively pay nothing under the debt otherwise. As with Case I, the tax-financing–transfer-spending operation is neutral in its effect on the economy. The debt-financing–transfer-spending operation reduces the rate of saving. Neither the Ricardian nor the Barro theorem is valid in this setting.

## Intertemporal Utility Gains and Losses

The simple models introduced in the preceding section may be used to examine the intertemporal incidence of the fiscal operation examined. In Case I, where the As secure a return of transfers equal to the taxes that they pay, this group suffers no utility gain or loss from the imposed fiscal change. On the other hand, the Gs who live in the initial period gain by the receipt of the transfers. In subsequent periods, the heirs of the As do not lose, by comparison with the utility levels that they might have experienced in the absence of the initial-period fiscal operation, because the enhanced bequests they receive will just offset the increased taxes they will be required to pay.[17] By contrast, the heirs of the Gs, who will also be required to pay taxes, will receive no positively valued bequests. They must suffer utility losses. A share of the "burden" of the debt-financed transfers must be shifted to members of this group.

17. To say that the heirs of the As suffer no net utility loss in the setting postulated here requires some qualification. These persons will be coercively required to give up some share of their earnings to pay for servicing and amortization of the previously issued public debt. They will surely experience some utility loss to the extent that they have attached some putative psychological claim to the total earnings stream produced from the assets bequeathed to them by their antecedents. Utility loss, in this sense, could be avoided only if those shares of the asset earnings required for debt service and amortization could have been somehow sequestered and removed from the psychologically relevant domain over which A's heirs exercise putative ownership.

Case II is different in that we assume that all taxes are levied on the As, and their heirs, those persons who both make and receive positively valued bequests. As with Case I, the Gs who live during the period of the initial debt-issue transfer operation secure positive utility gains; they enjoy the benefits of expanded consumption. Their own heirs pay no taxes in subsequent periods; hence, their utilities are not affected. For the As, however, there is a net utility loss or burden imposed in both the initial and in all future periods. As the analysis indicated, the As who live during the period of the initial debt-transfer operation will suffer net utility loss; the transfers they receive are not sufficient to offset fully the value of the future tax liabilities that the debt issue embodies. But the heirs of the As will also suffer utility losses because they will, except in the target-bequest solution, receive lower-valued positive bequests than they would have done in the absence of the initial-period borrowing operation. Some share of the "burden" of debt is passed along to members of this "generation" who receive bequests less than adequate to meet fully the service and amortization charges on the debt.

In Case III, the members of the Gs have no progeny, which justifies-explains their preferred zero or negative bequests. If government borrows to finance the set of equal-per-head transfers, or to reduce the previously existing equal-per-head taxes, all Gs secure net utility gains through their enhanced rates of current consumption. All members of the As who prefer to leave positively valued bequests to their heirs suffer current-period reductions in wealth and will, in response, reduce both consumption and savings rates. The heirs of the As will secure lower bequests and, hence, will also suffer utility losses in comparison with the relevant fiscal alternative. In terms of the pattern of intergenerational effects on utility levels, Case III is identical to Case II.

In each of the cases examined, there is a shift of some share of the "burden" of payment for the public outlay onto members of "generations" who do not participate in the fiscal decision-making process. These persons, whether among the later-period Gs, as in Case I, or the later-period As, as in Cases II and III, suffer utility losses. The welfare implications may be ambiguous, however, since our whole analysis has been conducted within a setting where initial-period persons, whether As or Gs, take into account the prospects for their progenies, and, indeed, act as if their own lives are infinite.

Consider, first, the private borrowing context, in which an individual chooses to reduce the level of positive bequests. In so doing, the person maximizes utility on behalf of his own infinitely lived family. The currently living member of the family judges himself better off as a result of reordering the time path of the family's consumption. The disutility of the future generation due to the reduction in consumption is more than offset by the gains in utility to the person currently alive. Hence, through a utilitarian cost-benefit calculus of the person currently alive, total utility increases as a result of the borrowing.

The ambiguity arises precisely because the evaluation made by the currently living would almost certainly not be identical to the evaluation made by their progeny in future periods. The utility of these future persons does enter into the utility function of those currently living, by assumption. But that does not imply that the present person regards the utility of the future person as a perfect substitute for his own. That is, suppose the utility function of the present person is

$$U_p(C_p, U_f[C_f]),$$ (6)

with subscripts denoting "present" and "future" persons. Then the marginal utility of a change in the consumption of the future person is evaluated by the present person to be

$$\frac{\delta U_p}{\delta U_f} \frac{\delta U_f}{\delta C_f}.$$ (7)

But the future person evaluates the change in his consumption as

$$\frac{\delta U_f}{\delta C_f}.$$ (8)

These are clearly not equivalent unless

$$\frac{\delta U_p}{\delta U_f} = 1,$$ (9)

which is obviously an exceptional case.[18]

Moreover, the persons who live in later periods will always prefer a larger

18. Drazen ("Government Debt") considers similar issues in the context of examining the likelihood of individuals choosing positive bequests.

to a smaller bequest. The future person regards the utility of his ancestors as being totally beyond his own realm of experience or possible influence. The future person would always be better off if the member of the earlier generation had sacrificed more of the earlier consumption in favor of increased bequests. Hence, there is a necessary ambiguity in making any welfare evaluation of private intertemporal transfers.[19] With private borrowing, however, individuals who reduce requests basically draw down their own potential capital stock. Hence, despite the ambiguity in any formal welfare evaluation, there is little expressed concern, at least directly, with the "socially optimal" path of intergenerational transfers in some aggregative sense.[20]

Can such relative moral indifference be extended to the evaluation of public borrowing in the setting where all participants in the collective decision process are modeled in Barro-Ricardian terms? In Case I, the analogy with the private borrowing model seems to carry through. The members of the Gs, those initial persons who secure enhanced consumption, do so at the expense of *their own* heirs and no one else. In Cases II and III, however, this analogy breaks down. In each of these cases, the Gs may, by debt financing, succeed in imposing utility losses not on their own heirs, whose utilities the Gs do incorporate in their intertemporal adjustment (by assumption), but rather on the As, both those who live in the initial period and in all later periods. In these two cases, the welfare or moral evaluation that is relevant becomes that which applies to any coercive transfer, whether this is inter- or intratemporal.[21]

## The Simple Politics of Public Debt

We have suggested that public debt issue can be explained by resort to simple public choice models of political action. If there are persons who prefer to make zero or negative bequests to their heirs and/or who prefer to shift the costs of financing public outlay onto others than themselves, the institution

19. See R. H. Strotz, "Myopia and Inconsistency in Dynamic Utility Maximization," *Review of Economic Studies* 23, no. 3 (1956): 165–80.

20. However, see Stiglitz ("On the Relevance") and Buiter ("Theory of Optimum Deficits") for recent exceptions to this general statement.

21. See J. M. Buchanan, "The Moral Dimension of Debt Financing," *Economic Inquiry* 23, no. 1 (1985): 1–6.

of government borrowing allows them to accomplish such an objective. We have not yet discussed how such persons, the Gs, in our models, achieve political dominance.

In Case I, it is interesting to note that the As, who plan to leave positively valued bequests, have no incentive to oppose debt financing. The Gs, however, will support debt issue, either to reduce current taxes or to finance new transfer programs. In this setting, almost any model of political process will predict resort to debt issue.

In Cases II and III, the As will stand opposed to public borrowing while the Gs will support it. In these situations, political approval for debt financing emerges readily from majoritarian models in which there are more Gs than As. Note, however, that *any* relaxation of the strict informational-expectational assumptions here will generate some lessening of the opposition on the part of the As with no offsetting shift in the support of the Gs.

This point may be illustrated with reference to Case III, in which the Gs have no progeny. Here, the As, who want to leave positively valued bequests, and who are required, under the restrictive rationality postulates, to take the full value of future tax liabilities into account, may not possess the information required to determine the size of Gs progeny. To extend the full informational postulate to such limits may give pause to many who would accept the more straightforward future tax capitalization required in Case II.

Other political decision models that allow for the influence of interest groups over and beyond the interaction of voters in voting models may be introduced, almost all of which bias results toward government borrowing.[22] Even in a setting where a large proportion of persons may prefer to leave positively valued bequests to their heirs, the implied opposition to debt financing may be overwhelmed by any number of breakdowns in the requirements necessary for such opposition to emerge as a political force.

## Conclusions

Throughout the analysis in this article, we have explicitly accepted the informational-expectational assumptions of the basic research program

22. J. M. Buchanan and G. Tullock, *The Calculus of Consent: The Logical Foundations of Constitutional Democracy* (Ann Arbor: University of Michigan Press, 1962).

within which the modern discussion, initiated by Barro, has been conducted. This acceptance should not be taken to imply any particular position concerning the applicability of these assumptions to real-world consequences of debt and deficits. One of us, at least, is on record as having called several of these assumptions into question.[23] Our purpose in this article has been the more limited one of examining the effects and incidence of public debt squarely on the turf of those modern macroeconomists who work broadly within the rational expectations research programs.

We have demonstrated that the full neutrality theorem, advanced by Barro, holds only in a much more restricted fiscal setting than may have been inferred. Our analysis does not, of course, carry direct implications concerning the quantitative significance of the indicated departures from the full neutrality results. Clearly, to the extent that persons behave in accordance with Ricardian theorem postulates, the impact of any debt-financed public spending is mitigated. We claim to have shown only that there remains an impact, even within the assumptions of this theorem. Any departure from these postulates would, of course, increase the effects of debt-financed deficits of the relevant macroeconomic aggregates and, also, would modify the incidence of debt issue, both intra- and intergenerationally.

23. Buchanan, *Public Principles*; J. E. Ferguson, *Public Debt and Future Generations* (Chapel Hill: University of North Carolina Press, 1964); G. Brennan and J. Buchanan, "The Logic of the Ricardian Equivalence Theorem," *Finanzarchiv* 38, no. 1 (1980): 4–16.

## PART SEVEN

# The Constitution of a Debt-Free Polity

# Organization Theory and
# Fiscal Economics
## Society, State, and Public Debt

*Viktor Vanberg and James M. Buchanan*

## 1. Introduction

Both the magnitude and the apparent permanence of budgetary deficits have refocused economists' attention on the basic theory of public debt. Although the issues are different in the debates of the 1980s from those that were central in the debates of the late 1950s and early 1960s, a common element in both discussions is the dominance of a macroeconomic methodological perspective. Buchanan's 1958 challenge to the Keynesian macroeconomists, which was only partially successful, applies with equal force to much of the macroeconomic policy discussion of the 1970s and 1980s.

Our purpose in this paper is not to prolong or to extend the debate on the basic economic theory of public debt. We shall not examine the respective macroeconomic consequences of debt versus tax financing, an issue that has occupied much of the received debate. Our purpose is the different one of demonstrating that elementary organization theory can be used to draw attention to relevant dimensions that remained implicit in the arguments that separated Buchanan from his critics.[1] While the thrust of our analysis sup-

From *Journal of Law, Economics, and Organization* 2 (Fall 1986): 215–27. Copyright 1986 by Yale University. Reprinted by permission of the publisher.
1. J. M. Buchanan, *Public Principles of Public Debt* (Homewood, Ill.: Richard D. Irwin, 1958); J. Ferguson, ed., *Public Debt and Future Generations* (Chapel Hill: University of

ports Buchanan's criticism of the macroaggregation embodied in the orthodox view, the arguments used here are quite different from those advanced
earlier by Buchanan.[2] The main target of our criticism is not the organic fallacy implied in certain macroaggregationist notions that treat the economy
or the community as a unit. Our departure from the orthodox treatment is
based, instead, on the latter's failure to distinguish properly between "the
state" and "the society" or "the economy," a failure that obscures crucial dimensions of the whole public debt issue. As we shall argue, if the state is
properly recognized as an *organization* and distinguished as such from "the
society" or "the economy," a reinterpretation of central notions of the public
debt debate commends itself, in particular, with respect to such issues as the
distinction between "internal" and "external" debt, the relevant effects of
public debt, and the debt burden.

## 2. The State as an Organization

Organizations like clubs, associations, unions, and firms can meaningfully be
treated as operating *units* without departing from a methodologically individualistic framework for analysis. Within an organization, persons are typically related in ways that allow for joint decisions and concerted action. This
capacity for joint effort reflects the fact that as a member of the organization
the individual is submitting a part of his resources to the organization's system of control or authority. The essence of organizational membership is
subjection to the authority system (however this system may be constructed)
as it applies to whatever resources are defined to be within the organization's
domain. Within an organization, the resources that are pooled by the individual members are subjected to unitary control. And, as this control is ex-

---

North Carolina Press, 1964); J. M. Buchanan and R. Wagner, *Democracy in Deficit: The Political Legacy of Lord Keynes* (New York: Academic Press, 1977).

2. A main target of Buchanan's criticism of what he called "the new orthodoxy" is a macroeconomic perspective that, by focusing on "the aggregate totals which make up the national balance sheet" (*Public Principles*, 41), implicitly adopts an organic conception of the nation or community, a conception that is inherently inconsistent with the individual-istic economic tradition (ibid., 36). Buchanan's emphasis is on the fallacy of aggregation that is committed by treating "the economy" ("the society," "the community") as the unit for which the relevant trade-offs between costs and benefits of public debt are to be assessed.

ercised, the organization can meaningfully be treated as a decision-making, acting unit. The unifying principle is that which is embodied in the rules that describe the organization's authority structure.

Individuals are members of particular organizations under specific resource commitments, such commitments varying over types of organizations. In this sense, the difference between, for instance, a golf club, a business firm, and a political party can be specified in terms of the kind and extent of resources committed to the respective organization. The *constitution* of an organization, whether explicit or implicit, states the terms of membership, including a specification of the share of an individual's resources subject to the control of the organization. The constitution also defines the individual's rights of participation in the system of organizational control over the combined resource shares of all members.[3]

"The society" or "the economy" is not an organization. "The society" (or "the economy") is a conceptual construction, a useful name for the totality of socioeconomic relationships among a group of persons, with the group being typically defined by geographical dimensions. The society (or the economy) is not an organizational unit that controls resources somehow pooled by its members. Although the phrase "members of a society" is often used in practice, the sense in which a person can be said to be part of a society (economy) is quite different from what applies to membership in an organization. The society (or the economy) does not exist as a system of authority to which the individual, as member, has submitted some share of his resource endowment.

In contrast, the state *is* an organizational unit in the strict sense defined above. The state is the political organization of persons who live in the society, and it normally holds a monopoly position in its role as a "protective" agency,[4] establishing and enforcing the legal framework within which social interaction takes place. It is an organization through which joint collective actions are taken. As with any organization, individuals are members only

3. J. S. Coleman, *Power and the Structure of Society* (New York: Norton, 1974), 38 ff.; V. Vanberg, *Market und Organization* (Tuebingen: Siebeck [Mohr], 1982), and "Organizations as Corporate Actors," Working Paper, Center for Study of Public Choice, George Mason University, 1984.

4. J. M. Buchanan, *The Limits of Liberty: Between Anarchy and Leviathan* (Chicago: University of Chicago Press, 1975).

with defined shares of their resource endowments, and the legitimate do-main of the state extends only to those resources that individuals, as citizens, submit to the state's authority. As with most organizations, the dividing line between resources committed to the control of the organization and those remaining outside the organization's domain may be blurred, and there may be slippages between private and public domains, with accompanying am-biguities. Nevertheless, aside from the limiting case of a perfectly totalitarian structure, for all states, as for all other organizations, a meaningful distinc-tion can still be drawn between those resources that individuals, as citizens, commit to the state's potential control and those resources that they retain for private disposition, individually or in non-state organizations.[5]

In terms of this distinction the dividing line between "the state" and "the society" can be clearly specified: The state comprises all the relations in which individuals engage in their capacity as citizens, and the society com-prises all these plus those relations in which individuals engage in their pri-vate capacity.

To interpret the state as an organization does not, or course, ignore the unique features that distinguish the state from other organizations. Since the state is the agency through which the "rules of the game" are established and enforced, the state controls to an important extent the institutional environ-ment within which persons act in all private capacities, either individually or organizationally. However, despite the fact that the legal umbrella for the whole society is provided through the auspices of the state, there remains a

---

5. The constitutionally defined demarcation between an individual's resources com-mitted to an organization and those of his resources remaining outside the organization's domain is an issue different from the distinction between full versus limited liability. A business firm, for instance, has in its domain those resources that, according to the firm's constitution, the owners-members have committed to the firm's authority system. Whether limited or full liability, the firm's authority to dispose over its owners-members' resources is restricted to the resources constitutionally committed and does not extend to any other resources owned by its members as persons. The question of whether the owners-members are fully liable for external claims held against the firm does not affect the definition of the firm's legitimate domain as an organization.

In this context, it seems to conform to common understanding, as well as to inter-national legal practice, to view the state as a "limited liability" organization. The state's members, the citizens, are not held personally responsible for the state's debts. A creditor could not shift a legal claim against, say, Argentina to an Argentinian citizen as a private person.

crucial distinction between what citizens do (or may be required to do) as citizens, as members of the organization "the state," and what persons do in their private capacities, within the constraints of the legal umbrella.

## 3. Public Debt and Private Claims

There is a straightforward implication of the distinction made above for central issues in public debt theory. Both in the dominant Keynesian macroeconomics of the 1950s and—often more implicitly—in the macropolicy discussion of the 1980s, there is a categorical distinction made between internal and external public debt, with the words *internal* and *external* referring to the distinction between debt held by citizens of the borrowing state as opposed to debt held by foreigners. The inference typically is that public debt obligations held by persons within the economy are, somehow, less burdensome than those held by persons outside the economy, that the former are, somehow, not net debts, due to the offsetting claims held by persons within the economy.

If we consider an organization like a golf club or a trade union, it would seem clearly fallacious to suggest that debt incurred by the organization, as such, should be meaningfully balanced off against the private savings of those persons who are members. A strict dividing line is drawn between those resources that are subject to the organization's domain (which persons, as members, have submitted to the organization's control) and those resources that are outside this domain, although still owned by the persons who make up the organization's membership. Those resources that remain outside the organization's defined domain are *external* to the organization, no less than resources owned by nonmembers. If, for example, the bonds issued by a country club for the financing of a swimming pool should be purchased by members, the debt so created remains external to the club except in the special case where members were somehow obligated, *in their capacities as members,* to purchase debt obligations. If members are, as a condition of membership, so obligated to purchase the club's debt instruments, financing an outlay by "debt" of this kind and financing the same outlay by direct contributions of members would be equivalent in many respects.

If, by contrast, members have no such obligation to purchase the bonds issued by the club, and, instead, purchase these securities (make the loans) on a strictly voluntary basis, the debt financing and the contribution financing alternatives are quite different in effect. If a distinction is made between "internal" and "external" borrowing by the organization, the relevant demarcation line is between loans that might be secured from members *as obligations of membership* and loans that are negotiated with nonmembers or with members in their strictly private capacities. It would be misleading to label as "internal borrowing" funds that are loaned to the organization by members in their private capacities, with "internal" suggesting that the relevant transactions all remain within the collectivity of persons who hold membership in the organization. Such a usage of terms here would ignore the basic fact that only the organization does indeed exist as an accounting unit, the obligations and claims of which can be meaningfully compared. The same cannot be said for the particular group of persons who hold membership in the organization. This group does not exist as a collective unit that inclusively embodies the total resource endowments of the organization's members.

These arguments apply to the organization "the state," notwithstanding the special character of this particular organization. If the government finances outlays by exercising its constitutional authority to impose taxes on citizens or to *require* citizens to purchase bonds as a condition of continuing membership (forced loans), the fiscal operation is clearly "internal," and the two methods of financing would be equivalent in many respects. That is to say, taxation and forced loans are properly classified as internal means of financing for the organization "state."[6]

If, however, government borrows from persons who happen to be citizens but who act only in their private capacities and voluntarily (that is, not as part of their obligations as citizens) purchase the debt instruments, this borrowing would be just as external to the organization, as such, as would be borrowing from persons who are not citizens (from foreigners). Different

---

6. Conceptually, three different types of such forced loans can be distinguished: first, *nontransferable* loans, generating claims tied to the original purchaser; second, *transferable* loans, generating claims that can be transferred—e.g., by bequest—to other members of the organization, but not to nonmembers; and third, *tradeable* loans, generating claims that can be sold or transferred to anybody, including nonmembers. The differences between these types of forced loans may be of interest in some context, but they will be ignored here, in order not to complicate our analysis.

from the way the internal-external distinction is de facto defined in the public debt debate, the organizational conceptual framework used here suggests that the relevant distinction between internal and external public debt is not that between loans made by citizens on the one hand and loans made by foreigners on the other. The distinction is between those loans that citizens must advance according to the terms of citizenship, that is, forced loans levied upon them by government in the exercise of its duly constituted fiscal authority, and those loans that are made through wholly voluntary purchases of debt instruments, whether by citizens or noncitizens. As stressed above, individuals who, as citizens, are members of the organization "the state" are not identical to individuals as described in terms of *all* their resource endowments, save in those settings where there exist no limits on governmental authority.

In all settings where there are constitutional limits on the exercise of governmental powers over the individual, it becomes misleading, and ultimately inappropriate, to aggregate claims and obligations across "the society" or "the economy" in some national balance-sheet sense of accounting.[7] Balance sheets may be constructed for individuals and for organizations, including the state. The economy, however, is simply not a social unit for which claims and obligations can be meaningfully discussed.

As our discussion suggests, the state, as an organization, is equally obligated and the terms of membership for citizens in the future are equally affected, whether the debt is held by citizens or by foreigners. So long as debt instruments are voluntarily purchased, the source of the loans remains irrelevant for the state's balance sheet; all debt is external. The claims of those who hold the debt instruments, be they persons within the economy or out-

---

7. To argue, as Abba P. Lerner (see Buchanan, *Public Principles*, 12) did, that "for national debt which is owed by the nation to citizens of the same nation . . . [there] is no external creditor . . . We owe it to ourselves . . ." is to blur the fundamental distinction between the organized unit "state" and "the society" or "the economy." If by "nation" Lerner meant *the state,* and by "we" all the citizens in their capacity as members of the state, then for what is called "national debt" there is an "external creditor," namely, citizens in their *private capacity,* i.e., with those of their resources that remain outside the state's domain, and the statement "We owe it to ourselves" is simply misleading. The imputed collectivity "we" ("the society," "the economy") simply does not exist as a "unit of account." Only in the limiting case of a perfectly totalitarian system would the proposition "We owe it to ourselves" make sense.

side, enter into private balance sheets, which are beyond the domain of the political organization.

## 4. The Effects of Public Debt: The Burden Issue

A core issue in the long-standing public debt controversy has been the equivalence of, or difference between, taxation and borrowing as means to finance public expenditures, particularly with respect to the question of who bears the burden of the expenditures made. The traditional discussion focused on the macroeconomic consequences of the two financing instruments on savings and capital accumulation in the economy, notably on the realism of the assumptions involved by the Ricardian equivalence theorem or its modern restatement, the Barro neutrality theorem.[8] The organizational theoretical framework used here suggests a different emphasis. Since the state as an organization is the borrowing unit, the effects of using this financing instrument that should be analyzed first are those concerning the current and future members of the organization. For a discussion of these effects, and notably of the effects on future generations of members, a few terminological remarks should be helpful.

If we use the term "corporate action" to define those activities that are attributed to the organized unit as such (to a club, a union, a firm, a state), then the act of borrowing by such a unit may be called "corporate borrowing." Utilizing the analysis of section 3, we can refer to "internal corporate borrowing" when loans are advanced to the organization by its members *in their capacities as members,* and we can refer to "external corporate borrowing" when loans are advanced to the organization by persons who act voluntarily in their private capacities, whether or not they are members of the organization. Drawing an analytical distinction between the membership

---

8. Compare D. Ricardo (*The Works and Correspondence of David Ricardo,* 10 vols., ed. P. Sraffa, with the collaboration of M. Dobb [London: Cambridge University Press, 1951–55], 1: 244–46, 4: 149–200) and R. J. Barro ("Are Government Bonds Net Wealth?" *Journal of Political Economy* 82 [1974]: 1095). For a discussion with further references to the literature, compare R. G. Holcombe, J. D. Jackson, and A. Zardkoohi, "The National Debt Controversy," *Kyklos* 34 (1981): 186. For a careful distinction between the equivalence theorem and the neutrality theorem, see J. M. Buchanan and J. Roback, "The Incidence and Effects of Public Debt in the Absence of Fiscal Illusion," *Public Finance Quarterly,* forthcoming.

groups in the organization at the time of and subsequent to the act of corporate borrowing, the term "future members" can be used as a name for the latter group.[9] It is obvious that corporate borrowing implies obligations for future members to amortize and service the debt and, hence, that deficits imply financing current public expenditures by future payments. In this sense corporate borrowing in general and public debt in particular clearly imply that, independent of benefit considerations (alternatively: independent of the character of the expenditure so financed), a burden of *payment* is shifted to future organization members or citizens-taxpayers.

How such a temporal shift of burden is to be judged will depend on the particular circumstances. If, over the relevant period of debt service, the membership group remains the same as at the time the debt was created, the financing arrangement simply involves a postponement of cost within the same group, comparable to a situation where an individual finances current expenditures by borrowing. If, however, the membership group changes within the relevant period of time, this means that—depending on how, exactly, the composition of the group changes—some or all of the beneficiaries of the debt-financed expenditure are able to shift the burden of payment, in part or even in total, to other persons. In this sense corporate borrowing has a negative impact on the terms of future membership in the respective organization, except in the case where productive investments have been financed that generate sufficient benefits over the relevant period to compensate for the debt burden.[10]

Since corporate borrowing might allow the current beneficiaries of cor-

---

9. The "future members" in an organization, according to this definition, may include current members to the extent that they remain within the organization after the debt has been incurred, as well as new members who join the organization after the creation of the debt.

10. In this sense, and except for the situation specified, public debt imposes a cost on future generations, a cost that cannot be eliminated. If the future generations should choose, either explicitly or implicitly (by inflation), to repudiate the debt, the effect is only to shift the ultimate distribution of incidence, not to eliminate it.

Note that the intertemporal shifting of a net burden to members of the organization in their capacities as members depends only on the productivity of the debt-financing outlay relative to the state's borrowing rate. Possible adjustments in saving by members, in their private capacities, aimed at offsetting the personal impact of future payments does nothing to affect the debt-created obligation for future payments by members in their organizational roles.

porate expenditures to shift the costs, at least in part, to other persons, the use of such a financing instrument would seem to be a tempting option in an organization's budgetary practice. The extent, however, to which this temptation actually can be effective is obviously dependent on the constraints under which the organization's budgetary decisions are made.

## 5. Principles of Corporate Borrowing and Opportunity Costs

The potential of an organization to finance corporate outlays by debt is contingent on two sets of conditions. First, there must be some (explicit or implicit) constitutional provisions that allow the organization to borrow and that stipulate the decision-making procedures to be followed when borrowing is considered. Second, there must be present potential creditors who might purchase the debt instruments. The willingness of potential creditors to lend to the organization will depend on the perceived prospect that loans will be repaid and on the opportunity costs of making the funds available. The opportunity costs are basically different to potential creditors as between internal corporate borrowing and external corporate borrowing. For the external creditor, the opportunity costs of lending to an organization equal the value of the best alternative use of the funds provided, possibly a loan to another organization. For the internal "creditor," the member who is forced to subscribe to the loan as a condition of continuing membership, the choice faced is not among alternative uses of funds, but is, instead, between accepting the compulsory loan in order to remain within the organization and dropping membership and leaving the organization entirely (or facing whatever sanctions are imposed within the organization for failing to meet one's membership obligations). The member can avoid providing the internal loan only by removing himself from the organization where the loan is a requirement of continued membership.

There are structural features of *private* organizations that tend to discourage external borrowing to finance wasteful investments or consumption. Current members, deciding on the organization's financial practices, and/or potential creditors, typically have good reasons to take the impact on future membership conditions into account when deciding on borrowing or providing a loan to finance corporate expenditures. Where membership rights are tradeable (as, for instance, shares of stock in a corporation), antic-ipation of negative effects on future terms of membership, which can be ex-pected to decrease the value (price) of membership rights, will limit current members' inclination to use corporate borrowing as an instrument to fi-nance unproductive expenditures. Where membership rights are not trade-able, but where, for other reasons, current members are interested in keeping the terms of membership sufficiently attractive to draw new members and to retain present members, a similar argument applies. In both cases current members face a trade-off between potential gains from debt financing and potential losses, either in terms of a decreasing value of tradeable member-ship rights or in terms of disadvantages resulting from the organization's in-ability to attract new and/or to keep old members in periods subsequent to the debt creation.

Independent of the organization's current members' inclination or reluc-tance to finance unproductive expenditures by borrowing, potential credi-tors—whether members of the organization or nonmembers—have their own reasons to pay attention to the consequences the debt-financed expen-ditures will have on the future attractiveness of the terms of membership. The probability that the loan they provide will be properly repaid depends on the existence of members who comply with the organization's debt obli-gations over the relevant repayment period. The more current expenditures and the way they are financed tend to make future terms of membership less attractive, the greater the risk that there may be no members in the future willing to fulfill the organization's obligations (notice that bankruptcy is one way for "future members" to evade the organization's debt obligations), and the less inclined potential creditors will be to provide a loan to the organi-zation. Consequently, in private organizations we can identify mechanisms that on one side tend to provide current members a motive to curb their temptation to finance unproductive outlays by debt, and, on the other side, set external limits to their capability to engage in such a financial practice.

## 6. Public Debt and the State as an Organization

In the case of private organizations, the freedom of entry (or refusal of en-try) and exit essentially limits the potential exploitation of future members (members in periods subsequent to the debt creation) through the debt financing of wasteful outlay. Individuals may simply refuse to join and, thus, to take on the debt obligations of financially shaky organizations or, if they are members of such an organization, they may exercise their option to leave the membership group. As a general rule, the easier it is for persons to refuse entry and to exit from an organization once entered, the better the interests of future members are protected.

It is precisely the weakness of this self-enforcing feedback mechanism that characterizes the state, considered as an organization. Membership rights in a state are typically not transferable,[11] and they are typically not acquired by explicit decision. Potential entrants who are born into citizenship do not have the option of refusing entry into the organization, as such, and by the time they are old enough to make a deliberate decision to stay or to leave, the costs of exit will be high, compared with the typical exit costs for private organizations. The principal reason for the comparatively high exit costs is, of course, that *citizenship* and *residency* are typically coupled, that one cannot, as a rule, quit one's membership in a state without moving one's residence outside the state's geographical boundaries.[12] Because of these high exit costs, however, decisions to leave or to stay will be relatively unresponsive to changes in the attractiveness of the terms of membership, and, accordingly, the temptation of any group of current members to shift costs temporally is enhanced. By financing outlay with debt, with the proceeds used to produce current-period benefits, the current-period membership group can effectively pass on the net costs of the combined fiscal operation.[13]

The obverse of the same point involves the possible behavior of creditors

11. A. Alchian, "Some Economics of Property Rights," in *Economic Forces at Work* (Indianapolis: Liberty Fund, 1977), 127–49, especially 137 ff.

12. In principle, citizenship and residency are, of course, separable, a fact which may have, as the editors of this journal reminded us, interesting implications for the present issue. As a *nonresident-citizen,* a person may be able to escape certain membership obligations (notably, for instance, payment of taxes) without giving up citizenship. On the other hand, a *resident-alien* may be burdened with what are typical membership obligations (again: notably, tax payment) and he may be able to escape these burdens only by relocating his residence.

13. States will, of course, differ with respect to the exit costs faced by citizens. Local units of government are less able than more centralized units to exploit either current-period or future-period taxpayers (see G. Brennan and J. M. Buchanan, *The Power to Tax: Analytical Foundations of a Fiscal Constitution* [Cambridge: Cambridge University Press, 1980]).

in their expressed willingness to lend to the organization. When they consider loans to a private organization, they must reckon on the future impact of current budgetary practice on the attractiveness of membership and/or the transfer prices of shares in the organization. When the same creditors consider loans to the state, as an organization, the same concerns are not present. The high exit costs along with the compulsory entry of future members offer assurance that there will be a set of persons who will necessarily be members of the organization. The risk of default will still be present, as it would with private organizations, but the relative weakness of the entry-exit option for citizens remains an important differentiating characteristic of the state, one that will surely influence the behavior of potential creditors.

A somewhat different, if closely related, aspect of the creditor's attitude toward state debt is grounded in the recognition that the future members cannot isolate themselves wholly from charges incurred by past members. Public debt allows past members of the state to leave enforceable claims against income of future members, which may exceed, in total, the value of the assets transmitted to those persons as members of the state.[14] In contrast, negatively valued bequests are not legally possible for families, and they are ruled out practicably for voluntary private organizations. Potential creditors of the state need not, therefore, be concerned with the temporal "productivity" of the debt-financed outlay, so long as the limits of the state's taxing authority have not been reached.

## 7. Exit, Voice, and the Democratic State

The interests of persons who will be members of the state are not protected from potential fiscal exploitation to the same extent that they would be in organizations characterized by voluntary entry and exit. This fact alone does not, of course, imply that such exploitation must occur. What remains to be examined is the potential effect of the voice option, which in A. O. Hirschman's classic book is mentioned as the second principal means for individuals to control an organization's performance.[15] The dynamics of the inter-

14. Buchanan and Roback, "The Incidence and Effects of Public Debt."
15. A. O. Hirschman, *Exit, Voice, and Loyalty* (Cambridge, Mass.: Harvard University Press, 1970).

nal decision-making process remain to be analyzed. The rules that define procedures through which organizational decisions are reached make up a part of the constitution of any organization.

Implicitly, in references to such procedures earlier in our discussion, we have presumed that membership implies potential participation; that is, we have presumed that the organizations are, in some sense, ultimately "democratic." Such a structure embodies the constitutionally defined rights of members to exercise the decision-making authority of the organization, either directly through some voting procedures or indirectly through a delegation of authority to a designated agent or group of agents. This basic presumption of democratic decision making need not apply, generally, to all states, as organizations. Since, however, our primary concern is with Western countries, we shall restrict attention to those states that do embody democratic processes in the sense indicated. We want to examine the extent to which democratic decision processes act to reflect the interests of persons who will be members of the community in periods after that in which fiscal decisions are made.

For any organization, the membership group at the time of debt creation and the membership group in subsequent periods are typically different, due to the exit of old members and/or the entry of new ones. But there is always an intersection of these two membership sets. To the extent that there is a mix of old and new members, and to the extent that their time horizons *as members* vary, some being more concerned than others about the impact of current organizational decisions on future terms of membership, the interest of future generations of members should have some voice in current organizational decision making. For the state this means that the temporal shift of debt burden is restricted to the extent that current-period members themselves anticipate they will be affected themselves in subsequent periods and also to the extent that they take into account the interests of their own heirs.

However, as with the entry-exit dimension of membership, there are also special characteristics of the state, as an organization, that are relevant for the "voice" dimension. One such feature is the discrepancy between the set of *voters,* participants in decision procedures for the organization, and the set of *members*. In private organizations that embody democratic rules, the right to vote (to participate) is typically acquired on entry into membership. Hence, the set of voters is typically coincident with the set of members.

With the state, however, persons typically become citizens, or members, by birth, while voting rights are attained only on maturity. Those who are franchised make up only a subset of those defined as members.

The implication of this discrepancy for the public debt issue is straightforward. It is precisely those members who should exhibit the most long-range or farsighted interests who are the disenfranchised. The decision process is biased toward the temporally characterized interests of those members who participate. These interests will necessarily exhibit somewhat shorter time horizons than those that would emerge if all members could be treated as full participants. The effect here is accentuated by the necessary shortening of the time horizons for all members (and voting participants) as they approach or pass retirement age.

As indicated earlier, the interests of persons who are currently not franchised but who will become members of the state will be, to some extent, incorporated within the interests of those who do participate in current-period decisions. Persons are not indifferent to the interest of their children, grandchildren, nieces, nephews, and even the children of strangers. These interests in future citizens will, of course, mitigate the willingness of present members, as voters, to transfer the cost of public outlays forward in time. There seems to be no reason, however, to expect that such caring for future members would totally offset the effects of the nonrepresentation of future interests in the overall political process.

Reform aimed at insuring more direct representation of future interests runs afoul of other problems. Reduction in the voting age immediately raises questions of competency, and the weighting of adult votes to take account of minor dependents violates basic norms of political equality. Analogous to the legal representation of a minor by a guardian, a "political guardian"—presumably one parent, who could vote on behalf of a "political minor"—is a conceivable arrangement, but there are obvious difficulties. There seems to be no escaping the conclusion that, whereas for private organizations the typical interests of current members and/or potential creditors can be expected sufficiently to constrain the use of borrowing, the dynamics of interests cannot be expected to do the same for the state. Explicit constitutional constraints may be needed as a safeguard against the temporally biased interest of the franchised members.

Such constitutional constraints could, of course, take several forms. A simple prohibition on deficit financing or some requirement that super-majorities in legislatures are necessary to authorize such financing may prove workable. (Most versions of the proposed balanced-budget amendment to the United States Constitution involve the requirement that three-fifths of both houses of Congress approve any departure from projected matching of revenues and outlays.) A rule limiting government's debt instruments to forced loans only may be a much more effective constraint. Alternatively, required administrative differentiation between consumption and capital outlay in the state's budget, with debt financing restricted to the latter, might seem to offer prospects for improvement, despite observed failure of such procedures in several European countries.

## 8. The Limited State and the Theory of Macroeconomic Policy

We have deliberately eschewed entering the lists on either side of the various arguments among economists on the macroeconomics of public debt and deficits, especially in the economists' own terms. Our purpose has been restricted to the demonstration that some of the elementary principles of organization theory can point toward a clarification of some of the apparent ambiguities that remain in the economists' arguments. While our chosen area of inquiry has been that of public debt, there are evident implications of the analysis for wider and more inclusive issues in the theory of macroeconomic policy.

Our central proposition is that the "state" should be defined as an organization with *limited* claims on the resource endowments of its members, and that this organization, as such, be distinguished categorically from "the society" or "the economy." This proposition may be of more relevance for normative than for positive analysis, but its normative thrust applies at the level of fundamental political philosophy rather than at alternative methodological presuppositions for macroeconomic theory. And we submit that the definition of the state as being subjected to some limits on its potential command of resources is a normative model that finds widespread acceptance among social scientists and philosophers in Western societies. As our discussion may suggest, however, much of the theory of macroeconomic policy may be based, albeit unconsciously, on quite a different normative model of the state, one that even its practitioners would never explicitly adopt.

# The Economic Consequences
# of the Deficit

## 1. Introduction

I appreciate this opportunity to present my ideas on the economic consequences of debt-financed budgetary deficits. I say this because my ideas are
not widely accepted by my fellow economists, and, indeed, my ideas are
much closer to those that emerge from the common sense of the ordinary
citizen. These ideas were initially developed in my 1958 book, *Public Principles of Public Debt*,[1] which challenged the then-orthodox Keynesian notion
that public debt involves no temporal shift of burden because "we owe it to
ourselves." My basic ideas have not changed over the course of three decades;
but the importance of the subject matter has changed. It is far more important in 1986 than it was in 1958 to get the fundamentals of analysis correct.
My second major effort was a book, *Democracy in Deficit*,[2] written jointly
with Richard E. Wagner and published in 1977. This second book did not examine the economic consequences of debts and deficits; it did, instead, explain why modern or post-Keynesian democratic decision process generates
quasi-permanent deficit financing. Whereas the first book was an attack on
the Keynesian macroeconomic theory of public debt, the second book was
an attack on the Keynesian presuppositions about democratic politics.

From *Economia delle scelte pubbliche* 3 (1986): 149–56. Reprinted by permission of the
publisher.

Presented at Symposium on Budget Balance, New York, The Plaza Hotel, 9–11 January
1986.

1. Homewood, Irwin.
2. New York, Academic Press.

It is not surprising that my efforts in both cases ruffled the feathers of economists, who continue to remain dominated by the macroeconomic mindset imposed by the mid-century Keynesian "revolution" in economic thinking. I shall not, in this paper, continue my ongoing argument with other economists, but some mention of my adversary stance is helpful as background for the subsequent discussion.

## 2. The Elementary Principles

In its simplest terms, the economic consequences of a debt-financed budgetary deficit are equivalent to the economic consequences of a debt-financed deficit in the account of any economic-financial unit, whether this be a person, a family, a corporation, a club, a church, or a labor union. When current revenues fall short of current outlays or expenditures, a deficit emerges, and if revenues are not increased or outlays decreased, the deficit or shortfall must be financed by borrowing. (With national governments, which possess money-creation authority, budget deficits may also be financed directly by money issue. I shall leave this possible revenue source out of the discussion here, since the relevant subject matter involves the consequences of debt-financed deficits. These consequences may, in themselves, make some ultimate resort to monetization more likely, a point that I shall touch on briefly below.)

For both the borrower and the lender, the sale and purchase of debt instruments involve a temporal displacement in the availability of funds. The borrower is enabled to *spend more* than revenue or income in the initial budgetary period, but is obligated to *spend less* than revenue or income in some future period. The lender *spends less* than revenue or income in the initial period but is enabled to *spend more* than revenue or income in periods during which the debt is amortized. And, as I have argued for three decades, the government is not different in these respects from any other borrower.

A return to the primer is required because of the massive confusion in much of the discussion of public debt and deficits. If we rule out default (and I shall return to discuss possible default later), the primary economic consequence of debt-financed spending by government is the guaranteed necessity that we must, as citizens–taxpayers–program beneficiaries, give up some part of our incomes in future periods in order to meet interest and amortization charges on debt. A share of our future incomes is obligated to meet the legitimate claims held by creditors of the government. And it makes no difference whatsoever whether these creditors are themselves citizens or foreigners.

The financing of current government spending by debt is equivalent to an "eating up" of our national capital value. If we define a capital value by discounting an expected stream of future incomes, then any offset against such future incomes reduces this value. And it does so in precisely the same way that consumption of a capital asset would. By financing current public outlay by debt, we are, in effect, chopping up the apple trees for firewood, thereby reducing the yield of the orchard forever.

The analogy between debt-financed public consumption and the destruction of capital value is often rejected because, it is argued, with internal debt held by citizens, the obligations against future incomes embodied in public debt are just matched by the claims held by those who have purchased the government's securities. In this simplistic macroeconomic logic, therefore, there is no effect on capital values summed over the economy. The absurdity of this argument is demonstrated once we recognize that those who purchase the securities do so in a wholly voluntary exchange transaction, and that, precisely because the purchase is voluntary, these same persons *might have* used the funds either to purchase other income-yielding private assets or for initial-period private consumption. In either case, the capital values of claims held by those who purchase the government securities cannot be counted as positive offsets to the negative capital value that is necessarily embodied in the obligation to meet future interest and amortization charges. This negative value is a charge against the portfolio of citizens, *as members of the political unit,* and it is not matched by any offsetting positive increment to the capital value appropriately assigned to this same portfolio. This result holds quite independent of the sources of the initial funds loaned to government.

## 3. Domestic and Foreign Debt

This basic logical error in analysis informs the familiar argument that debt claims held by foreigners, so-called "external debt," is more onerous than those debt claims held by citizens or domestic organizations. The error here stems from a failure to consider the alternatives initially faced by the purchasers of securities. If debt instruments are bought by citizens, alternative uses of funds *in the domestic economy* are foreclosed. If the bonds are bought by foreigners, these alternatives in the domestic economy remain open. The claims against future income held by foreigners in the second case here are precisely equivalent to the value of the uses of the funds that remain available for exploitation in either private investment or consumption opportunities. As citizens, as members of the political organization of government, we are in exactly the same position whether the national debt is held by persons inside or outside of the national economy.

It is often suggested that the 1980's regime of massive deficits has been sustainable without major economic damage only because foreigners have purchased large blocs of the securities issued to finance the deficits. Otherwise, it is suggested, budget deficits of the magnitude experienced would have exerted unacceptable upward pressures in interest rates. My conclusion about the equivalent effects of foreign and domestic debt does not contradict such a suggestion. The impact of a debt-financed deficit, of any given size, on the rate of interest will depend on the supply of loanable funds, and if foreign investors supply for domestic loan markets, public or private, the rate of interest will be lower than it would be if such foreign investment funds were not made available. It makes no difference at all as to whether foreigners purchase private or governmental securities.

## 4. Crowding Out

A second major source of confusion, or at the least, of ambiguity, involves the "crowding out" issue. Since debt financing requires government to *sell* securities in exchange for funds supplied by lenders, funds that are then used up when government spends, it seems evident that these funds might have been used by the lenders to purchase income-yielding private claims. Prospective sellers of private securities (e.g., firms seeking to expand capital facilities by floating new issues of stocks or bonds) are "crowded out." Private securities can be marketed only at interest rates that are much higher than those which would prevail in the absence of the government borrowing operation.

This seemingly straightforward argument has been challenged by some economists who suggest that the issue of public debt, in itself, stimulates new savings. According to this argument, citizens will recognize the future-period tax liabilities that are embodied in any issue of public debt. They will, accordingly, adjust their behavior so that these future tax payments, which will be imposed either on themselves or on their descendants, can be more easily met. In this scenario, persons who observe government borrowing will put aside additional savings by reducing current rates of consumption spending. The additional saving will, to the extent that it takes place, match the additional demands on loanable funds that the public borrowing operation represents. In the limit, if the new saving offset is complete, there is no "crowding out." And, even if not complete, any new saving generated as a result of public debt issue will make the crowding out of private capital formation less than the initial argument might suggest.

My own position is that whether or not debt financing of budget deficits "crowds out" private investment and capital formation is essentially a *secondary* rather than a *primary* consequence. By labeling this issue to be secondary, I am not suggesting that it is unimportant. I am suggesting, instead, that economists' undue concentration on this question, to the almost total neglect of the more important primary effect or consequence of debt, is inexcusable. In order to emphasize my position here, let me, strictly for the purposes of discussion here, assume that no crowding out occurs at all. Assume that there is no effect of debt-financed deficits on the rate of interest, and, hence, on the rate of capital formation in the economy. This result would require that new savings are generated just sufficient to finance fully all of government's debt instruments offered.

The primary *economic* consequence of debt-financed deficits would still be present, even in this extreme, and totally unrealistic case. There will be a net claim against future private income flows in the economy, a claim held by creditors of the government, all those persons, individuals, or organizations, domestic or foreign, who hold government securities. Taxes, which are by their very nature coercive, must be levied against persons in order to generate the revenues that are required to finance the interest charges on the debt. The share of private incomes that must be devoted to tax payments cannot, by definition, be available for private disposition as individuals might desire, acting in either their private or their public capacities. The burden of having to make the tax payments from personal income streams will be present, quite independent of the behavior of those who make the initial-period decisions as to how much to save and to consume. The person faced with a tax bill to finance interest charges will not make any relationship between the saving that his father may not have made because the debt was issued earlier. The person, faced with such a tax bill, will reckon only on the simply observed fact that income that he might otherwise use is taken away in taxes. The result is precisely analogous to the apple orchard example introduced earlier. If the yield of three trees under a person's nominal ownership is committed to debt service, it is fully equivalent to having an orchard with three fewer trees.

## 5. How Long Can We Tax the Future?

The descriptive implications of the elementary analysis are clear. The federal government has embarked on a debt-financed spending spree that cannot be permanently sustained. The fact that the government cannot go bankrupt in any sense analogous to a person or business firm does nothing to modify the central proposition. Government's ultimate taxing and money-creation powers can, of course, guarantee that all nominally valued debt claims will be honored, but neither an ever-increasing interest share of tax revenues nor an inflationary monetization of nominal debt claims offers a viable option for permanent reform.

The budgetary deficit must be reduced. But what are the consequences of this reduction? Current rates of government spending must be cut back, perhaps dramatically, and/or current rates of tax must be increased, perhaps dramatically. Either of these steps, or any combination of the two, must also have serious economic consequences. Spending cuts will reduce expected benefits to all those persons and groups that have come to anticipate continued program expansions. Tax increases will reduce incomes available for private disposition by individuals, some share of which would be devoted to private investment.

A reduction in the deficit, financed by either a cut in rates of government spending or an increase in rates of tax, could be predicted to lower, somewhat, the rate of interest, because the reduction in government's demand for loanable funds would not be fully offset by a reduction in the supply of such funds. This effect on the rate of interest is, again, a *secondary* consequence of the reduction or elimination of the deficit. The primary consequence is the shift of the incidence of payment for government programs from future-period taxpayers to those taxpayers who are around during the period when the government outlays are actually made.

At some point, this shift in the temporal incidence of government spending must be made. Real growth in the national economy can postpone the day of reckoning, but interest charges cannot permanently take up an increasing share of the federal budget.

## 6. Do We Need to Change the Rules?

But is there much prospect that our democratic decision procedures will accomplish this shift in incidence? Must we not predict that these processes will operate to insure that the deficit dilemma gets much worse before it gets better? Having embarked on the debt-financed spending spree, will our political structure, as it is currently organized, measure up to the challenge that it faces?

I do not think that it can do so. Or will do so. As we can all observe, there seem to be almost insurmountable political costs involved in either spending cuts or tax increases. Modern American politics operates in accordance with a set of rules that makes effective resolution of the deficit issue almost impossible. The implication should be clear. Improvement or reform can be expected to occur only *if the rules are changed.* It is on this conviction that I have long been a strong supporter of proposals for a constitutional amendment to require budget balance.

I shall not develop the argument for such an amendment here. I have done that many times before, and that is not my assignment. I want, instead, to take a "realistic" perspective and to examine what seems now, in 1986, to be the most probable scenario. Despite what I might, personally, hope for, I do not now predict enactment of an enforceable balanced-budget amendment to the constitution within the next decade. Further, I do not think that congressional precommitments in the general Gramm-Rudman form will prove effective. There may well be quasi-successful short-run congressional attempts to reduce the size of the budget deficits, without changes in the basic decision procedures or rules. These efforts may, however, actually be counterproductive over the long term because they may, to the extent that they are successful in the short term, serve merely to distract attention from the structural-procedural reform that is required. Any such short-term congressional restoration of effective fiscal discipline could be and probably would be dissipated rapidly by return to fiscal profligacy. Recognizing this prospect, why should political leaders incur both political and economic costs now for the benefit of political leaders and constituents who come along later?

## 7. Prospects for Default

What then, can we realistically expect? Continued expression of concern about debt-financed deficits with little observed success in doing much about them? Mounting interest charges that consume larger and larger shares in federal budgetary outlay?

At some point in such a sequence, default or repudiation of the national debt must become a central political issue. Since the United States national debt is almost exclusively denominated in dollars, the real value of this debt can be reduced dramatically, in the limit to zero, by money issue. There are two ways that default through monetization might take place. First, the Federal Reserve monetary authority could simply purchase all outstanding government securities with newly created dollars. All creditors would, in this setting, be guaranteed full nominal values of their claims. The inflation generated by the new money issue would reduce the real values of all fixed claims in the economy; the operation would be equivalent to a tax on all holders of such claims. Alternatively, the monetary authority could generate inflation by issuing additional money through ordinary channels, and in this way reduce the real values of all nominal debt claims outstanding, public and private. The effects would be almost equivalent to the first operation; the effective incidence will be on all holders of fixed claims. The second of these operations is more likely to take place than the first, and with accompanying denials by all concerned that there is any explicit intent to default on the national debt.

The relationship between national debt and another round of inflation deserves somewhat closer attention. Inflation will act to reduce the real value of national debt outstanding; the debt as a share of GNP might level off and even fall. For this reason, all comparisons between sizes of national debt and

GNP are highly suspect, since the ratio of debt to product can be reduced dramatically by massive inflation. Such a policy thrust must, however, prove much less effective (from the government's perspective) in the late 1980's and early 1990's than it did in the 1970's. Outstanding debt is now more concentrated in short-term issues, and inflationary expectations would very quickly be incorporated into interest rates. As the government would attempt to roll over and refinance maturing issues of debt, interest charges would rise to match the anticipated inflation. The apparently beneficial fiscal results would be largely short term in nature.

At some point in the sequence, more explicit repudiation of the national debt would surely enter into political discussion. And the failure of almost all commentators on the deficit, including economists, to seriously examine debt repudiation seems to me analogous to whistling past the graveyard. When we do consider default seriously, the arguments against such a drastic policy change are not nearly so strong or self-evident as many of us might hope they were. I cannot fully develop these arguments here, on either side, but let me put the question as follows: Why should taxpayers-beneficiaries who live in the year 1990 or 2000 be coerced into paying for the public program benefits that we, as taxpayers-beneficiaries in the middle 1980's, have used up? Why should these future-period taxpayers (which may, of course, include many of us) pay for the spending spree? I have looked at this question in some detail, and the strongest argument I can find against default lies in the acknowledged legitimacy of the claims held by the creditors. Those who are purchasing the government securities, and who have purchased them in the past, do and have done so in the expectation that their claim will be honored. To repudiate such claims would amount to a violation of contract, and we like to live in a legal system in which contracts are honored. But governments have often broken contracts before, and, when all is said here, with whom did the creditors contract? I do not want to suggest that the arguments in favor of repudiation of the national debt will become politically dominant. I do suggest that default will become increasingly discussable as the debt-financed spending spree continues.

Default would, of course, call a halt to new borrowing, at least for a time, since lenders would become quite scarce. Note, however, that repudiation of the debt would eliminate the large interest component in the budget. Hence, once we get past the threshold point where the annual interest charges exceed the annual deficit (which is not far off), it will actually be in the short-term interest of current-period taxpayers-beneficiaries to default.

## 8. Conclusion

Both our fiscal and our monetary structures are currently in disarray. And, as members of the body politic, we are all behaving irresponsibly in our unwillingness to look at, analyze, and ultimately to support structural reforms that offer the only prospects for permanent improvement. We have allowed a quasi-independent monetary authority to accidentally attain a monopoly over fiat money issue without effective market or political control. Who can predict a random walk, which is the best modern characterization of the sort of monetary system we endure? Alongside this random-walk monetary authority, we have a fiscal structure from which almost all pretense of balancing off the costs of taxes against the benefits of spending has been removed. The problem is not, however, with irresponsible political leaders, in either the executive or legislative branch of government. The problem is that the rules of the game are such as to make fiscal responsibility and fiscal prudence beyond the limits of the politically feasible. Constituents enjoy the benefits of public spending; they do not enjoy paying taxes. The politics of the deficit is as simple as that.

The tragedy is that so many of us recognize full well what is happening and remain powerless to do anything about it. I have often called for a genuine "constitutional revolution," but how can we move toward its realization?

Let me finish, however, on a somewhat more optimistic note. The proposed amendment for budget balance has been seriously discussed for a decade, and at relevant political levels. Gramm-Rudman at least expresses a recognition of the necessity of fiscal precommitment of some variety. Economists, finally, are coming around to examination of basic structural changes in our economic and political institutions, and notably in our monetary and fiscal structure. These are all probably necessary precursors to reform in fiscal and monetary rules. If, and this is a big if, we can only get on with such reform before it is too late.

# Budgetary Bias in Post-Keynesian Politics
## The Erosion and Potential Replacement of Fiscal Norms

## 10.1. Introduction

In the post-middle decades of this century, modern governments have sustained historically high levels of public consumption in part by resort to debt financing. Ordinary public outlays have been debt financed in all phases of the cycle, and with no reference to the recurring nature of the demands for such spending. In behaving in this way, governments have totally disregarded classical fiscal precepts. They have done so because previously existing moral constraints have been effectively destroyed. This extended era of public profligacy may be nearing its end, and, indeed, the logic of compound interest must ultimately impose a limit. But the prospective utility loss consequent to the departure from fiscal discipline cannot now be avoided. The regimen of fiscal austerity that would be required to restore the pre-Keynesian *status quo*

From *Deficits*, ed. James M. Buchanan, Charles Rowley, Robert D. Tollison (New York: Blackwell, 1987), 180–98. Reprinted by permission of the publisher, Blackwell Publishers Ltd.

An early version of this paper was initially prepared for presentation at the Nobel Symposium on "Growth of Government," Stockholm, Sweden, 14–17 August 1984. I am indebted to my colleagues Frank Forman, David Levy, Charles Rowley, Viktor Vanberg, Karen Vaughn, and Jack Wiseman for comments on the earlier draft presented at the Stockholm conference. I am also indebted to both my formal critics (Karl Brunner and Johann Myhrman) and to other participants in the conference (especially Assar Lindbeck) whose comments have led to substantial changes from the initial draft.

*ante* may be neither politically feasible nor economically efficient, but a regimen of fiscal prudence must soon become both politically necessary and economically rational. From some date within this century, the welfare-transfer state must be financed from a potentially disposable public income flow that is permanently lower than that which might have been sustained (and from which a larger welfare-transfer-state outlay might have been permanently maintained) in the absence of the departure from the Victorian budgetary norms.

Several parts of the summary thesis outlined above must be separately discussed.[1] I shall argue:

1. that modern regimes of debt financing have had effects that are substantively equivalent to a destruction in the value of national capital, particularly as measured in utility dimensions;

2. that this result stems, at least in part, from a breakdown in moral constraints;

3. that the prior existence of these constraints need not have reflected the results of a rational choice calculus, although the constraints served, in effect, a value-maintaining purpose;

4. that the restoration of such constraints, or their more formal legal-constitutional equivalent, may be supported readily on moral grounds, but not readily on the economic efficiency criteria of normative welfare economics;

5. that a distinction must be made between the adoption of a constitutional rule for budget balance and an in-period budgetary adjustment that moves toward budget balance;

6. that the political compromises necessary to secure agreement on a regime

---

1. I have addressed separate elements of the central thesis in several previous works. These works have not, however, addressed either the moral dimensions or the prospects for working out Pareto-Wicksell improvements from the deficit-financing status quo.

For earlier material, see James M. Buchanan, *Public Principles of Public Debt* (Homewood: Irwin, 1958); James M. Buchanan and Richard Wagner, *Democracy in Deficit* (New York: Academic Press, 1977); James M. Buchanan, "Debt, Demos, and the Welfare State," presented at CIVITAS Conference, Munich, Germany, October 1982, in *Liberty, Market and State* (London: Wheatsheaf, 1985); and "Public Debt and Capital Formation," prepared for Pacific Institute, San Francisco, California, 1984, in *Liberty, Market and State.*

for budget balance must embody recognition of the effects of the inter-temporal transfer process.

## 10.2. Analytical Clarifications

Modern regimes of debt-deficit financing for public consumption emerged from the heritage left by the Keynesian theory of macroeconomic policy. For my purposes in this paper, I need not take a stand concerning the efficacy or inefficacy of budgetary deficits, *per se,* in stimulating the economy, and, hence, in reducing unemployment and/or generating inflation. Even in the idealized Keynesian setting, there is no basis for an argument that govern-ment should issue interest-bearing debt to finance deficits or retire debt to dispose of surpluses. To the extent that the Keynesian prescription works, the argument is to spend without taxing which can, of course, be financed most effectively by direct money creation, or, in the converse setting, to tax with-out spending, which can be most effectively carried out with monetary neu-tralization of the excess revenues.

For purposes of analytical clarity, I shall assume that money creation aimed at the accomplishment of macroeconomic or stabilization objectives is wholly divorced from money creation, debt issue, or taxation as alterna-tive means of financing governmental outlays on real goods and transfers.[2] Viewed as a revenue-raising instrument, money creation can best be treated as a particular form of tax. My concentration in this paper is on the choice between taxation and genuine government borrowing, as alternative instru-ments for financing public outlays independent of stabilization purposes.

I shall assume initially that governmental outlays are exclusively devoted to the provision of currently consumed goods and services (including trans-fers) and that political agents are under continuing pressures from constitu-ents for expansions in these outlays. On the other side of the fiscal account, different sets of constituents (or perhaps even the same persons differently organized) continually oppose increases in taxes.

2. The analysis need not incorporate an explicit "full-employment" assumption. All that is required is the assumption that explicit macroeconomic or stabilization policy in-struments remain separate from those here discussed.

Conjecturally, I introduce a setting in which public borrowing has not been invented, at least for financing public consumption. The current budget is balanced at the point where constituency pressures for expanded rates of outlay and those for reduced rates of taxation come into political equilibrium.[3] Let us now impose on this equilibrium a "new technology" of government borrowing. Political agents will treat this new technology as a shift outward in their feasibility space, since they can now respond favourably to constituency pressures for more outlays without the offsetting pressures against tax increases. So long as constituencies respond less negatively to debt issue than to taxation over some range, this result must hold.[4] The size of the outlay budget expands; deficits are created; and a specified portion of the future income flow is obligated for the service and amortization of public debt. The size of the deficit, and hence of new debt issue, is determined by the position of some new political equilibrium where constituency pressures against the combined levy of taxes and the issue of new debt offset those for expanded outlays.[5]

The first point to be emphasized is that the incurring of public debt to finance current public consumption is substantively equivalent to an "eating up" of capital. This statement holds regardless of the source of the borrowed funds; that is, regardless of the possible "crowding out" effect of government debt issue. To the extent that domestic lenders to government reduce private investment, that is, to the extent that crowding out occurs, the value of the economy's capital stock is reduced, in terms of the standard measures. However, even if, in an extreme case, no such crowding out takes place, and all funds come from lenders' sacrifice of current consumption, the combined

3. The equilibrium postulated here is similar to that which has been analysed more formally by Gary Becker. See his "A Theory of Competition among Pressure Groups for Political Influence," *Quarterly Journal of Economics* 98 (1983): 371–400.

The "equilibrium" concept is introduced with reference to the balance between offsetting political forces; it does not imply temporal stability even in the sense applicable to the standard economists' usage of the term.

4. Note that there is no need to make a particular assumption about the degree to which some constituents in the polity discount future taxes that are embodied in debt issue. So long as some constituents fail to discount fully, the results carry through.

5. I have discussed this equilibrium, its dynamic sequence, and its consequences, in some detail elsewhere, and I shall not repeat the analysis here. See my paper "Debt, Demos, and the Welfare State," cited above.

spending-borrowing operation increases aggregate utility in the initial period at the cost of reduction in aggregate utility in later periods, which is precisely the trade-off made in any activity involving capital consumption. Lenders, whether domestic or foreign, suffer no current-period utility loss (and presumably secure some utility gain) in voluntarily acquiring debt instruments; beneficiaries of current spending by government secure utility gains. Those who face tax obligations in subsequent periods suffer net utility loss.[6]

I suggest that the conjectural model sketched out in this section offers a basis for examining the regime of debt-financed public consumption that we have observed in Western, as well as developing, nations in the decades since the Second World War. No one could argue that the observed deficits have been justified economically by governmental capital investments. At best, capital-budget accounting adjustments could produce only slight modifications on the public consumption model. Further, the inflation-generated effect that holds down the ratio of debt to GNP cannot legitimately be interpreted as a signal of fiscal discipline.

## 10.3. The Victorian Moral Constraints

In several places, I have referred to the Keynesian repeal of the effective fiscal constitution, but I have not examined this repeal in depth. Why did the politicians of the post-middle decades consider debt-financed deficits to shift outward the frontier of their fiscal space? There was no explicitly adopted constitutional amendment that allowed budgetary imbalance as an institutional innovation.

The Keynesian arguments were effective in providing politicians with excuses for acting out their natural proclivities to spend without taxing, as they responded to constituency pressures. These proclivities had previously been held in check, both for politicians and for constituency groups, by moral constraints. To finance public consumption by debt was immoral in the pre-

---

6. For a sophisticated modern analysis of the intertemporal effects of public debt issue, see Assar Lindbeck and Jörgen W. Weibull, *Intergenerational Aspects of Public Transfers, Borrowing, and Debt* (University of Stockholm, Institute of Economic Studies, 1984, mimeographed).

Keynesian political world. But why were these moral constraints so vulnerable to the Keynesian persuasions?

I suggest that the peculiar vulnerability stemmed from the fact that the norms for public fiscal prudence were, in a sense, aberrant, and they may have reflected non-functional transfers of precepts for private economizing. In making such a statement, I am marrying Keynesian and Hayekian insights. What I have called the set of Victorian moral constraints on behaviour, many of which we still carry around with us and which still influence much of our everyday behaviour, is the product of biological evolution, cultural evolution, and, possibly, rationally calculated moral precommitment. Hayek has emphasized those norms for conduct that are transmitted in a course of cultural rather than biological evolution. He has suggested that culturally evolved norms, like their genetically evolved counterparts, are largely unconscious and are not really understood by those who act in accordance with their dictates.[7] These culturally evolved moral norms have proved to be highly useful in the sense that the behaviour produced has facilitated the expansion of the possibilities for human interaction over wider and more inclusive communities, in part transcending the geographical boundaries of organized polities.

For my purposes, the important norm that constrained behaviour is that which dictated that capital, once accumulated, should be maintained and transmitted to future generations. The treatment of capital as permanent, in a behaviourally relevant sense, has been important in allowing economies to make provision for growth and development over time, included as a necessary function of an economic organization in the classic Knightian listing.[8] With respect to privately owned capital, the utility functions of individuals reflect this norm in the arguments that describe bequest motives in their various forms. In this setting, the capital preservation norm presumably contains some mixture of biological as well as cultural components.

A Victorian extension of this norm was reflected in the rules for fiscal prudence that emerged in the years in which the financing of modern nation-

---

7. See F. A. Hayek, *Law, Legislation and Liberty,* vol. 3 (Chicago: University of Chicago Press, 1979), especially the Epilogue.

8. See Frank H. Knight, *The Economic Organization* (Chicago: Harper Torchbooks, 1933).

states became important. These rules were, however, almost exclusively the result of cultural evolution. There seems to be little or no direct linkage between the extended family, which may be the focus of biologically evolved moral norms, and the nation-state. Nothing remotely akin to a bequest motive for the collectivity, as a unit, enters the individual's utility function.[9] The immorality of behaving collectively in a manner that effectively "eats up" a portion of the income or utility stream that would be otherwise available to future citizens was a very real constraint on the Victorians. But, in a sense, this constraint was artificial and unnatural. Hence, this particular norm was highly vulnerable to the apparently rational arguments of the Keynesians, who sensed, quite correctly, that the Victorian behavioural transference from private to public economizing reflected little valuational content. The norm was ripe for destruction, especially when it was recognized that its overturn could pander to the natural proclivities of the politicians and their constituency groups. Gladstonian fiscal prudence was proven to have relatively little sticking power.

## 10.4. Moral Constraints as Social Capital

We must recognize, however, that the Victorian constraints themselves were assets with a capital value to the members of the community. We live today at a standard that would have been impossible had our predecessors not treated both private and public capital value, to an extent, as permanent. The rules for fiscal prudence, once abandoned, cannot be readily restored. It is as if a valuable and income-yielding asset has been smashed, one that will be difficult if not impossible to replace.

Moral rules, like more formal legal rules, are public capital, and they may carry positive weights in a properly constructed national balance sheet.[10] Investment in some replacement rules or constraints, even if these would have to be more formal and be made legally constitutionally binding on political

9. For a discussion of the limits of man's moral capacities, and especially as related to large political communities, see my "Markets, States, and the Extent of Morals," *American Economic Review* 68 (1978): 364–68, reprinted in *What Should Economists Do?* (Indianapolis: Liberty Fund, 1979).

10. For further and more general discussion, see my *The Limits of Liberty* (Chicago: University of Chicago Press, 1975), chapter 7.

behaviour, would seem to be suggested, once a positive capital value is placed on the previously existing moral constraints. However, the mere fact that the Victorian norms for fiscal prudence carried positive value tells us nothing about the rate of return on the "investment" that might have gone into the "production" and "maintenance" of those norms. The moral dimension it-self suggests the inappropriateness of modelling some conceptualized "social investment" in familiar cost-benefit terms. Comparative rate-of-return con-siderations need not have entered, even vaguely, in the origination and pres-ervation of such rules for behaviour. There is, therefore, no direct implica-tion to be drawn concerning the potential rate of return on some more explicit "investment" in the establishment of formal, legal constraints that might be introduced as replacements for the previously existing moral rules.

It would be illegitimate to infer that simply because there did exist a norm for budget balance, and this norm had a capital value, it is collectively ra-tional to replace this norm with some enforceable amendment to the politi-cal constitution that would dictate pre-Keynesian behaviour patterns on the part of politicians. The question of the rationality or irrationality of mov-ing to a regime of budget balance must be addressed on its own, and inde-pendent of the pre-Keynesian fiscal history.

## 10.5. Intertemporal Preference: Private and Public

I have suggested above that borrowing to finance current consumption in-volves essentially identical results, whether carried out by an individual in his private capacity or by a collectivity of individuals, who act through govern-ment in their "public" capacity. The question to be addressed now is whether or not such activity can be judged non-optimal in any meaningful sense. Or does such activity reflect merely an expression of intertemporal preference? Or is there some categorical distinction to be drawn in this respect as be-tween the private and public choice models?

Consider, first, the intertemporal choice problem faced by the individual in a private-economizing role. Consumption flows in different periods enter as positively valued arguments in the utility function. There would seem to be no a priori basis for assigning utility weights so as to make intertemporal consumption patterns correspond with anticipated patterns of income re-ceipts. There would seem to be no significance attached to the zero saving (lending)–zero borrowing position within a single arbitrarily defined period. It would seem that the individual might choose to create an in-period deficit or surplus without violation of standard rationality norms. Hence, any criticism of observed profligate behaviour would seem to require resort to moral rather than efficiency criteria. By a more or less natural extension, the same inference would seem applicable to persons, who, as agents for the collectivity, express intertemporal preferences that weight current-period consumption relatively higher than future-period consumption.

Even at the individual economizing level, however, some current-period choices that reflect relatively high weighting for current-period consumption may be judged to be inferior in an intertemporal sense, and to reflect myopia when considered in terms of a life plan. We need some means of distinguishing or identifying those patterns of choices that may pass muster on meaningful rationality criteria. I suggest an intertemporal or multiperiod model of a Wicksellian contractual setting.

Consider the "individual" as a series of separate persons that exist in separate periods: person 1 in period 1, person 2 in period 2, person 3 in period 3, etc. We need not enter into complex philosophical discussion over problems of personal identity to recognize that, at least to some extent, the person that exists at one moment is different from the one that exists at another moment.[11] Suppose, now, that the effective status quo set of "rights" for each period is defined by the in-period income flow. All decisions that are to involve differences between an in-period consumption flow and the in-period income flow must be reached through the conceptually unanimous agreement of the persons over the whole sequence. Clearly, all decisions to create budgetary surpluses will meet this test, given ordinary *Homo economicus* assumptions. Decisions to create a budgetary deficit, however, and hence to increase some in-period consumption flow above that period's income flow, and, in consequence, insuring the opposing result for another period of periods, may pass the multiperiod Wicksellian test only if there exist particular configurations of income flows and consumption flows over time and relative to each other that will generate conceptual acquiescence on the part of persons who know that they will be saddled with debt burden with no di-

---

11. For just such philosophical discussion, see Robert Nozick, *Philosophical Explanations* (New York: Basic Books, 1982).

rectly compensating flow of services. In reality, some life-cycle income and preference parameters may be such as to meet these requirements. The behaviour of the medical student who borrows to finance current consumption (even beyond a human capital investment complement) may well be approved by the conjectural present shadow of the rich doctor in future years. But, equally clearly, there are many possible patterns of profligacy that will totally fail the multiperiod unanimity test.

We do not especially concern ourselves with departures from broad rationality norms in the private behaviour of individuals as they express their intertemporal preferences. One reason for this relative neglect is the recognition that "personal identity" does have intertemporal significance, that the person who is profligate remains effectively the same person who must bear a large share of the costs of such profligacy in subsequent periods. In a very real sense, each one of us is necessarily placed behind something akin to a Rawlsian veil of ignorance with respect to our intertemporal choices.

When we shift attention to public rather than private economizing, the separation of persons by time period becomes clearly more relevant. Age differences exist, even if each "person" is assumed to remain a single identity over a lifetime. The same multiperiod Wicksellian test may be applied to determine whether or not an observed departure from the status quo, defined in this case as budget balance, could have been conceptually agreed to by all potentially affected parties. It seems evident that an observed regime of debt-financed profligacy in public consumption could not so readily be rationalized on some collective or group life-cycle considerations as could some comparable regime of profligacy in private consumption. It is difficult to conceive of a situation in which those persons in future periods, whose disposable consumption opportunities are restricted to levels below income flows because of debt overhang, would have willingly given up such claims in some conceptualized Wicksellian agreement with those current-period beneficiaries of public outlays.[12] This conclusion is reinforced when the pat-

---

12. Care must, of course, be taken not to slip into the familiar aggregation fallacy with respect to debt that is held internally. Debt claims against future income streams may be held by citizens, and these claims precisely offset the interest-amortization charges. Since these are balancing items in the national aggregates, they may be treated as transfers rather than as net claims. Such an argument is confused by its failure to treat relevant

tern of public consumption outlays exhibits no temporal lumpiness, that is, when there exists no "extraordinary" outlay requirements expected to be short-term in nature.

In summary, there seems to be a strong presumptive argument to the effect that the debt-financed public consumption we have observed can be criticized in terms of the criteria derived from an idealized multiperiod Wicksellian contract. That is to say, the decision to finance public consumption by debt can be judged to be Pareto-Wicksell inferior in an intertemporal sense, a judgement that carries its own normative thrust.[13]

All contractarian arguments depend, however, on the definition of the initial set of "rights" among the potential contractors, upon the status quo from which all conceptual contracting begins. If the collectivity of persons who exist in future periods (in their capacities as members of the political "club") is considered to have no "right" to the flow of income that their own efforts generate in the environmental setting of those parties, there is no basis for the conceptualized Wicksellian veto that this collectivity might exercise against those who seek to advance current-period claims against the future income flows.

It is precisely such claims that are being made in the accumulation of continuing deficits that we now observe as the political status quo. Persons in the acting generation, now, through the auspices of their government, are apparently exercising what they deem to be legitimate claims on future- as well as current-period income flows. We have, in most Western democracies, observed regimes of debt-financed public consumption for two or more decades. The fiscal-political status quo involves continuous deficit financing.

---

choice alternatives. Those citizens who initially purchase public debt instruments voluntarily could have otherwise invested in private capital claims or, possibly, could have maintained higher levels of consumption. In either case, in post-loan periods they could have held private claims that are income-yielding claims that do not exist. The asset sides of lenders' balance sheets are, therefore, equivalent with and without the public borrowing. On the other hand, borrowers' (citizens') balance sheets are different with public borrowing because liabilities have been increased (because of debt service and amortization), while there are no additional publicly owned assets that yield a positive return in the model of public consumption examined here.

13. The moral content of the efficiency criterion, and especially if the Paretian construction is interpreted in the Wicksellian consensus setting, seems to be a subject worthy of more examination than has been given it by either economists or moral philosophers.

To demonstrate that there may be no intertemporally efficient shift from budget balance, when balance is the status quo, is a wholly different matter from demonstrating that a shift to budget balance from a deficit status quo is itself Pareto-Wicksell superior in an intertemporal sense.

With currently observed putative claims being made to future income flows, can we mount a contractarian efficiency-based argument for a reduction in the deficit? The answer seems clearly negative. There is no scheme that may be worked out, even conceptually, such that all persons living now could be compensated or bribed sufficiently to secure their unanimous agreement to reduce spending benefits or to accept increased taxes as means of reducing the deficit.[14] In the absence of intertemporal altruism, the normative welfare economics of the deficit becomes quite simple. Debt-financed current public consumption outlay accomplishes a straightforward intertemporal transfer; those persons who are recipients are members of the "current generation"; those who are the transferors or losers are the persons who will live in future time periods. The latter persons, and only these, will find their potentially disposable income reduced.[15]

Economists, as such, are at a loss in condemning the continuing regime of debt-financed public consumption outlay (including transfers). Because of the negative result of the simple normative exercise just outlined, economists cannot advance efficiency based arguments for change, even if these arguments are extended to the limits of the multiperiod conceptual Wicksellian contract. Beyond this, however, economists continue to find the ele-

---

14. This conclusion might be mitigated in a model of behaviour in which rent-seeking reaches extreme limits. If, given the prospect of financing some predicted quantity of programme benefits from debt, individuals and groups are expected to compete wastefully for these benefits and, in the process, to overexhaust, in the aggregate, the benefits value, some scheme might be worked out that would secure agreement to forgo the debt-financed programme benefits. Prospects for any such scheme would depend, however, not only on the extreme level of rent-seeking behaviour postulated, but also on the generalized recognition by parties engaged in such behaviour that the overall effort is wasteful.

For a set of papers that develop the theory of rent-seeking in varying applications, see *Toward a Theory of the Rent-Seeking Society*, edited by James M. Buchanan, Robert Tollison, and Gordon Tullock (College Station: Texas A&M University Press, 1980).

15. I am assuming that the debt obligations are honoured. If default occurs, holders of debt instruments will, of course, suffer reductions in capital values, and, hence, in disposable income.

mentary logic of the intertemporal transfer process difficult to accept. As I noted in my 1958 book,[16] most economists define opportunity costs in resource rather than utility dimensions, a fundamental error that makes impossible any understanding of the intertemporal transfer of cost that borrowing facilitates, either privately or publicly. Because they do not feel at all easy with the intertemporal transfer argument, economists cannot move easily into moral condemnation of the fiscal behaviour that they observe.

The first step toward clarification of the discussion involves the explicit acknowledgement of the intertemporal transfer that has been taking place in modern fiscal politics. On this point, as I have often emphasized, the attitude of the citizenry is more sophisticated that that of most economists. Once the intertemporal transfer is recognized for what it is, the second step of the discussion is the direct introduction of moral argument. The financing of current public consumption by debt issue is unjust because it shifts income from those who are not and cannot be beneficiaries of the outlay and who do not and cannot participate in complex political process that generates the observed results. "Taxation without representation" is literally descriptive of the plight of those who will face the debt-burden overhang in future periods.

## 10.6. Deficit Reduction and Constitutional Reform

Once the elementary principles are fully understood, however, there remains the necessity of separating categorically two policy questions. The first involves policy toward deficit reduction without change in the procedural rules under which budgetary decisions are made. The second involves policy toward changing these rules, that is, toward possible constitutional reform. Specifically in the United States setting, the second question involves the prospects for an amendment to the constitution that would mandate budget balance.

Consider the first of these two questions. From a status quo that embodies debt financing of a portion of public consumption outlay, what arguments may be adduced for a reduction of the deficit? As suggested, arguments that the intertemporal transfer is unjust on some Rawlsian-like basis may be persuasive for some constituents. Also, quite apart from arguments directly

16. *Public Principles of Public Debt,* cited above.

from criteria for justice, genuine intergenerational altruism may describe the attitudes of large numbers of persons. Further, the mere fact that many persons now living expect to be around for a long succession of time periods may make for an enhanced consideration of future-period costs in any budgetary calculus.

Individuals who share the attitudes of either of these groups, separately or in some combination, may support efforts to reduce the size of the deficit, through some combination of spending-rate reduction and tax-rate increase. They must, however, also reckon on the characteristics of the political decision structure. These characteristics were of relatively little import when the Victorian norms were more or less generally shared throughout the citizenry. Once these norms were eroded, however, the fiscal consequences become critically dependent on how the political decision structure is organized. Budgetary decisions are not made in an "as if" setting of Wicksellian contract. The political process is by no means unanimitarian, quite apart from the non-representation of the yet unborn.

The individuals who might, for any of the several reasons noted, support a reduction in the deficit, must also recognize that effective majority coalitions in subsequent budgetary periods may negate any current-period action toward deficit reduction. What would be the force, say, behind any major reduction in the size of the U.S. Government deficit for 1985 when we recognize that a dominant political coalition in, say, 1986 or 1987, may once again dissipate the capital value restoration that deficit reduction in 1985 would represent?

There is a much stronger basis for generating support for binding constitutional commitment embodied in a rule for budgetary balance than there is for simple reduction in the size of the continuing deficit without any change in the procedural rules. If they can somehow be assured that their current-period sacrifice, measured by lowered public consumption benefits and/or higher current-period taxes, are to be reflected in permanent and long-continuing increases in future-period disposable income, private and public, larger numbers of constituents will support proposals for deficit reduction than in the case where no such assurance is given.

Even if the choice is posed in terms of support for constitutional reform in budgetary procedures, and specifically in terms of a balanced-budget requirement, change from the existing regime of continuing deficits cannot be

easily accomplished. Large constituency groups must oppose any move toward budget balance on self-interest grounds. Think only of those persons
whose time horizons are quite limited, the aged or near-aged, and who do
not exhibit strong intergenerational altruism. A deficit-reducing tax increase
inversely related to age and directly related to the number of direct heirs
might be considered here, but we need only to think of such a proposal to
imagine the opposition that would emerge. A lag in the implementation of
the budget-balance requirement, say over a five-year term, might prove of
some value in softening the opposition, but, again, the sources of opposition
can be readily defined.

## 10.7. Debt Retirement and Default

To retire any portion of national debt by the generation of a current-period
surplus of tax revenues over current public consumption is equivalent to a
restoration of some of the present value of the future-period utility stream
that has been drawn down in prior periods. But why would members of any
taxpaying or beneficiary group suffer the net reduction in disposable income
flow, the benefits of which would be enjoyed exclusively by persons in future
periods?

It seems clear that widespread political support for in-period debt retirement will not emerge. What assurance could be offered current-period taxpayers that the value so restored would not immediately be dissipated by
relapse into deficit financing, perhaps with some change in the dominant
political coalition? If concerns for justice, along with intertemporal altruism,
are sufficiently present to warrant the adoption of a rule requiring budget
balance, some long-term scheme of debt retirement might be possible provided that it includes some guarantee against value dissipation.

Realistically, of course, given the history of fiscal regimes in Western as
well as in developing nations over the decades after the Second World War,
default on existing national debt is much more probable than any retirement
or even, perhaps, any move toward budget balance, save that which becomes
necessary in a post-default era. As debt-financed public consumption continues, as interest charges mount, and at an increasing rate, the collectivity,
in its political embodiment, will come to be increasingly attracted by the
prospects of wiping out, at one fell swoop, the major liability item on the

governmental balance sheet. The temptation here is relatively higher the larger the share of the debt that is held by foreigners, and the more concentrated the ownership among the citizenry. Explicit repudiation of debt obligations will, in any case, dramatically reduce the capital value of the national government "as a going concern" and will act to close off the borrowing option for some time, but the short-term gains promised by the elimination of interest and amortization charges may come to be irresistible beyond some limits.

Default through inflation of the money stock is more likely than default through explicit repudiation, especially for those governments that have issued debt nominally defined in their own currencies. The apparent gains that government can secure through the effect of inflation on the real values of outstanding debt instruments must stand as a continuing attraction to politicians, who must reckon always with public reactions. If inflation can be rationalized on economic stabilization, growth, and employment arguments, and/or the public fooled into locating the responsibility for inflation in nongovernmental agents, the fiscal account of government will seem to undergo improvement in real terms, and without the recrimination that would surely accompany any explicit default. The experiences of the 1970s, however, when government did default on a large scale through inflation, will make a repeat exercise more difficult, and especially as default risk is built into the interest rates required for turnover of the outstanding debt.

## 10.8. Modern Fiscal Politics

We have reaped and are reaping the fiscal whirlwind that resulted from the Keynesian destruction of the Victorian norms for fiscal-budgetary prudence. These norms were highly vulnerable to the apparently rational arguments advanced by the Keynesians. Unfortunately for us all, the Keynesians made two critical mistakes, one involving elementary macroeconomic policy and the other involving a total neglect of public choice implications.[17] They failed

---

17. I need not enter the lists on one side or the other concerning additional possible analytical errors in the Keynesian structure. My identification of the two errors relevant for my analysis does not imply that no further errors exist.

to distinguish real debt issue from money creation, and, accordingly, failed to stress that demand-enhancing deficits, to the extent that these might be justified, would always be more efficiently financed by straightforward money issue than by interest-bearing debt, which does load future-period taxpayers with wholly unnecessary charges.

Surely the most important Keynesian mistake was, however, the gross neglect of politics and political process. The Keynesians, as a set of policy advocates, refused to heed Knut Wicksell's early advice. They continued, despite Wicksell's warning,[18] to act as if they were proffering advice to a benevolent despotism that acts always in the "public interest," as the latter is defined and formulated by the economists.

Policy advocacy must always be placed squarely in a political setting, and it must be cognizant of the incentive structure that faces persons in their varying public choosing roles, as voters, as party leaders, as elected politicians, as bureaucrats. The most elementary prediction from public choice theory is that in the absence of moral or constitutional constraints democracies will finance some share of current public consumption from debt issue rather than from taxation and that, in consequence, spending rates will be higher than would accrue under budget balance.

Some strength yet remains in the Victorian budgetary norms, and effective rhetoric may reinforce this component of the political decision calculus on fiscal matters. But norms that evolved over centuries cannot be "turned on" in years, or even in decades, if at all. Explicitly chosen constitutional constraints offer a more plausible avenue for reform, but both the initial adoption and the subsequent enforcement of such rules must surmount almost every one of the problems that public choice theory has identified. These problems emerge from collective decision models that incorporate the self-interested behaviour of individual participants.

Self-interest need not, however, be exclusively short term. The hope for reform must lie in the prospect that, in evaluating alternative rules for social order, individuals will, once again, adopt the time perspective of the Victorians, that they will, as persons with finite lives, act as if both themselves and the institutions that they construct, will live forever.

---

18. See Knut Wicksell, *Finanztheoretische Untersuchungen* (Jena: Gustav Fischer, 1896).

## 10.9. Conclusion

The erosion of the constraints reflected in the morally based classical rules of debt issue introduced a budgetary bias that has shifted the observed political equilibria to somewhat higher levels of governmental outlay than we might have experienced under the influence of such constraints. At least some part of the explosive growth in government spending, especially in the post-middle decades of this century, can be attributed directly to this shift. To the extent that opposition to deficit financing takes the form of effective pressures on the monetary authorities rather than on corrections through the budget itself, there may be effects on the rate of inflation which may indirectly generate a further impetus toward budgetary expansion.

I have concentrated on the budgetary bias toward deficit financing. I have not discussed the influence of the Keynesian theory of policy on expansions in government outlay generally and apart from deficits. To the extent that governments have assumed new responsibilities for stabilization, and that these have given support for a shift from private to public spending, there is an additional explanatory element to be introduced.

The erosion in the classical norms for fiscal-budgetary prudence can do nothing, of course, toward explaining public-sector growth prior to the middle years of this century. And, even for this period, the explanatory reach of the elements here discussed falls short of any inclusive hypothesis.

Finally, I should note that to the extent that the erosion of the budgetary norms is explanatory the effect on the rate of public-sector growth will necessarily be limited in time, even if there are no explicit institutional changes. The simple logic of compound interest guarantees that the share of public spending that is debt financed must reach a limit, beyond which no further increases in the rate of outlay attributable to the deficit-financing political bias can be expected. Since, however, in the political equilibrium defined by such a limit, a large share of outlay must be for debt interest (in the absence of default) net public spending for public goods and transfers must be lower than that level which might have been politically sustained had the post-Keynesian deficit-financing regime never occurred.

# Dialogues Concerning
# Fiscal Religion

*James M. Buchanan and Richard E. Wagner*

## 1. Introduction

In writing and in publishing *Democracy in Deficit*, we were aware that we would arouse antagonism from many camps. We attacked the Keynesian orthodoxy in macroeconomic policy, yet for expository purposes we accepted the central features of the Keynesian model. We did this because we wanted to focus on the manner in which the Keynesian precepts would be applied within democratic political institutions. The Keynesian theory of policy proceeds as if policy is enacted by benevolent and omniscient despots. Our primary inquiry concerned the probable conduct of policy once we allowed for the obvious reality that results emerge through democratic processes. Our main emphasis was not with macroeconomic analysis as such, though aspects of our presumptions about macroeconomics appear in several places in *Democracy in Deficit*. As we acknowledged in the book, we do not deny that major unsettled issues remain in macroeconomic analysis, treated independent of the implementation of policy. And, of course, these issues deserve the efforts and attention of economists. But does not the "political economy" of policy also merit notice?

Our macroeconomic position cannot be simply described by Keynesian, Monetarist, or Marxist. It is not, therefore, surprising that we have attracted the attention of a disparate set of critics. Before responding to the critics spe-

From *Journal of Monetary Economics* 4 (August 1978): 627–36. Copyright 1978. Reprinted with permission from Elsevier Science.

cifically, we should express our gratitude to Professor Karl Brunner for organizing this symposium, as well as to the critics who have made contributions. When all is said, the worst treatment authors can receive is neglect. Intelligent criticism carries its own mark of mutual respect. We hope that this brief response lives up to the standards of our critics.

## 2. Who Were the Keynesians?

Professor Tobin reacts personally to our criticism of American Keynesians and in so doing he seriously misinterprets our argument. If we can be allowed the occasional rhetorical flourish that may well have been misleading, we did not intend to suggest that Keynesianism arrived full-blown in Washington in 1961. Keynesian economics was not really brought in denim carpetbags from Cambridge, Minneapolis, and New Haven. The policy advice of the *1962 Economic Report* did not sweep out the long-stagnant swamps in one blow. Had this interpretation described our reading of the historical record, we should have named more names, given credit where due, and we should have tried to cite line and verse. But surely such an interpretation gives far too much influence to the particular policy advisors of the early 1960s or of any other time. Keynesian economics came to Washington and to the consciousness of our politicians in fits and starts from the 1940s, through the 1950s, and into the 1960s. It came via the textbooks read by budding politicians of the whole postwar era; it came in the academic and intellectual discourse of the 1950s; it came in the financial and economic journalism of this period.

We do not suggest that the Camelot economists pulled off a monumental coup and took control over the implementation of economic policy, as Tobin seems to think we do. Camelot economics merely represented the culmination of a process in which the understanding of economic reality that informs public policy changed essentially from the classical vision to the Keynesian. The dominant belief about our economic order came to be Keynesian. Our critique, therefore, was aimed at a generation of economists rather than at a handful of readily identifiable persons who, perchance, may have been in the vanguard when the politicians finally began to act out the repeated messages they had been receiving.

## 3. The Theory of Public Debt

At least three of our critics question the theory of public debt that our book embodies. Tobin charges that our argument is "factually false" in attributing the "no future burden" position to the Keynesian economists. This charge is again related in part to Tobin's misinterpretation of our targets. We challenge anyone to read the elementary textbooks of the 1945–65 period and to find more than the occasional passing reference to the future burden of public debt. The overwhelming preponderance of the discussion is on the other side, discussion that suggests the fallacy of the classical position rather than its elemental truth. Interestingly, in this respect, we could scarcely do better than to cite Tobin himself who, in 1965, asked, and answered: "Does debt-financing . . . place a 'burden' on future generations? The answer has long been . . . 'no' among academic economists."[1]

Exegesis aside, however, do the Keynesians, even today, accept the theory of debt burden that we have tried to present in *Democracy in Deficit* and elsewhere? If Tobin correctly summarizes the Keynesian view, it seems clear that they do not. He acknowledges the presence of "future burden" only to the extent that capital accumulation is affected adversely by debt issue. But this possible effect of debt finance is only a by-product of its primary influence. By comparison with taxation, debt issue reduces the charges on current-period taxpayers, on voters, on legislators who are sensitive to voters' wishes, and increases charges on persons who will live and vote in future periods. This fact is too elementary to warrant repetition save for the continuing refusal of highly sophisticated economists to accept its logical consequences.

Robert Barro fully appreciates the central issue in debt theory, and we welcome his constructive criticism of our thesis. We are encouraged that the long-forgotten Ricardian Equivalence Theorem has found an elegant modern defender. Barro's suggestion that our own model of public debt is closer to the Keynesian than to the Ricardian is only partially correct, however, for the relations among the Ricardian, the Keynesian, and our theories of debt entail consideration of two separate dimensions. The Ricardian as well as our

---

1. James Tobin, "The Burden of Public Debt: A Review Article," *Journal of Finance,* 20 (December 1965), 679.

own says that public debt will shift the temporal location of the tax burden from taxpayers in the present to taxpayers in the future. In this respect, we stand with the Ricardians in opposition to the Keynesians. Taxpayers in the future will, of course, be either the same people as taxpayers in the present, only older, or children of taxpayers in the present. Barro suggests that present taxpayers will take full account of the future tax liability entailed by debt finance, in which event debt finance will be indistinguishable from tax finance in its impact. This identity results because present taxpayers will increase their saving in response to debt finance and will do so in an amount sufficient to amortize the debt when it comes due.

We differ from the Ricardians because we do not think that future taxes are fully discounted. We think that public debt is different from taxation precisely because we, unlike Barro, do not think that people act with an infinite-lived perspective. While the debate between us and the Ricardians should be open to empirical examination, let us be careful to avoid adding to existing confusion here. We are not concerned with the differential impact of these alternative financing instruments on the private economy. Our main concern is with how the issue of debt differs from taxation in its impact on the *public economy*. Niskanen is correct in noting that our proposition that debt finance will increase public spending because of its effect in reducing the perceived price of government entails the proposition that debt finance will increase aggregate spending. Nonetheless, our book is about the public sector import of debt finance.

Our thesis suggests that an expanded use of debt finance will lower the perceived price of government, thereby producing a larger public budget. Niskanen presents evidence to support this thesis. Within a model of federal spending, Niskanen finds that a relative decrease in the importance of tax finance (a relative expansion in the use of debt finance) lends to an increase in federal spending, and with an elasticity of about 0.6, meaning that a $100 replacement of taxation by debt would increase public spending by about $60.

Where does Niskanen's evidence leave Barro's proposition in support of the Ricardian Equivalence Theorem? If debt is viewed as less costly than taxation, why would tax finance be used at all? Perhaps we should distinguish between average and marginal perceptions here. If public expenditure is viewed as less costly when financed by debt than when financed by taxation, there would seem to be strong tendencies for borrowing to take place. Suppose we postulate the reasonable proposition that the perceived cost of any source of revenue rises with the use made of that source. An equilibrium distribution between debt and taxation would result when the marginal perceived costs were equal. At this margin, the Ricardian Theorem would come into effect. Yet in total terms debt finance will have increased public spending.

In closing this section we may discuss briefly the empirical indications that are used to signify a proclivity toward debt finance. Both Barro and Gordon suggest that we have interpreted the post–World War II period incorrectly because the ratio of debt to GNP has been declining over this period. Barro further suggests that the identical pattern of or declining debt/GNP ratio holds for all postwar periods, and uses this observation to suggest there has been no change in the historical pattern of debt finance.

We contend that debt/GNP ratios are inappropriate for the analytical task at hand, and that actual amounts of debt are the appropriate magnitudes. What we are concerned with is action by individuals in a political context. The patterns of a debt/GNP ratio is irrelevant to such rational political action. What is relevant is that the ability to borrow reduces the price of government below what it would have been had only tax finance been used. This, and only this, is what is relevant to our thesis. That the ratio of debt to GNP is declining is of no behavioral relevance.

The observed behavior of politicians and the observed patterns of policy discussion also support our central hypothesis. We do not find politicians generally indifferent between tax finance and debt finance. This absence of indifference would seem to suggest that the Ricardian Equivalence Theorem is not fully descriptive of economic reality. Historically, the discussion of public debt in the pre-Keynesian era was accompanied by discussion of sinking funds to provide for debt amortization. A sinking fund is, in fact, an institutional arrangement that has the effect of approximating the results described by the Ricardian Theorem. Moreover, we still observe debt limits at all levels of government. These considerations suggest that, in all ages, political action has been on our side of the issue in question, recognizing the need for constitutional-institutional arrangements to constrain the tendencies toward debt finance.

## 4. Rational Expectations and Public Choice:
## A Cautionary Criticism

Barro's reconstruction of the Ricardian Theorem on public debt is derivative from the rational expectations hypothesis in the theory of macroeconomic policy, a development to which Barro himself has made major contributions. As we noted in our book, we do not accept the thesis that the implications of rationality are the same for both private choice and public choice. We submit that the particular manifestations of rational economic conduct depend on the institutional setting within which choice takes place. People may be basically rational in all conduct, but the outcomes of choice will still vary as between market choice and public choice.

We shall limit our remarks here to Barro's extension of rational expectations to public-debt theory. In the theory of market exchange, so long as a sufficient number of participants possess the knowledge to act efficiently, the results are equivalent to those that would emerge if all participants should possess this knowledge. So long as a sufficient number of traders possess information and act in response to it, the marginal adjustments will insure movements toward equilibrium positions that are indistinguishable from those produced under universal omniscience over all traders.

When, however, we extend the usage of economic tools to the explanation of behavior in nonmarket situations, the generalization of the rationality postulate must be made with considerably more prudence. Not that people are necessarily less rational, but that the informational foundations for economic conduct are weaker. Relatedly, the absence of a profit motive in government weakens the incentive to act on the knowledge that is possessed. These differences mean that there may not exist opportunities which enable those participants who possess the appropriate information to act so as to generate equilibrium results equivalent to those produced by universal omniscience.

Consider a simple example. In a competitive labor market for carpenters and plumbers, there may be no more than five percent of the workers in the total community who may detect a difference in returns to the two occupations, and be willing to change occupations in consequence. But the willingness to shift to this small number may be enough to insure that wage rates of carpenters and plumbers will be equalized, a result that would, of course, also be produced if all workers in the community should know about the wage difference and be willing to shift employments in response. Consider now, however, a setting in which individuals must "vote" on a pair of alternatives, say, between the debt-financing and the tax-financing of a specific governmental outlay. Assume, as in our market example, that five percent of the voters are fully informed in that they, and only they, realize that the two alternatives are equivalent in present-value terms. The remaining ninety-five percent of the voters do not sense the equivalence, but instead view the debt alternative as being less costly than tax finance. Do there exist opportunities through which those whose actions correspond with the predictions of economic theory can bring the results into equivalence with those that might be forthcoming in a market setting? It seems to us that such opportunities are indeed limited, and that the median voter will likely be among the uninformed in the public choice that must be made as between taxation and debt creation.

We should never lose sight of the fact that traditional economic theory works so well, in spite of the questionable status of the usual presumptions about knowledge, because values are set at the margins. In public choice theory, by contrast, there is little scope for arbitrage through the actions of a few people at the margin, at least in the simple models of democratic process. A recognition of this basic difference between market and political institutions suggests that propositions derived from a model of market choice cannot be applied automatically to public choice. Consequently, much more attention should be given to the way in which information flows, learning motivations, and institutional constraints may make political or public choice outcomes different from those that would be predicted to emerge under market choice.

## 5. The Two Hypotheses

William Niskanen empirically examines two hypotheses that are suggested in our book. While his evidence supports the thesis that deficits increase public outlays, it rejects the thesis that deficits produce inflation via the stimulus given to money expansion. Barro similarly finds no support for the proposition that deficits influence the supply of money. Ultimately, of course, we need a theory of the money supply process if we are to understand the relation between deficits and monetary expansion. Our examination of the relation between Federal Reserve actions and the desires of the legislature is not, of course, a theory of the money supply process. Rather, our observations on this topic simply express the importance of recognizing that the Federal Reserve is not truly independent of the legislature. Hence, legislative desires to spend in excess of the revenues will not, when combined with a desire not to let the increased demand for loanable funds that results from the government's borrowing requirements drive up interest rates and crowd out private investment, generally be neutralized by the Federal Reserve. In our framework, the rate of expansion in the supply of money will be elastic with respect to public deficits. Other variables would also go into a full model of the money supply process.

Questions of the interpretation of empirical evidence depend, of course, on the acceptability of the model used for testing. While we have some questions about the models of the money supply process advanced by Barro and Niskanen, this symposium is not the place to initiate an examination of the theory of money supply. It suffices to say here that we find Barro's and Niskanen's results and formulations suggestive, though not definitive. Barro finds a positive relation between deficits and the supply of money until he introduces a variable to account for the impact of the difference between actual and "normal" expenditures upon the supply of money. While Barro interprets this variable as accounting for wartime increases and recessionary falls in spending, it also picks up a period of rising expenditure because of the adaptive lag structure he uses. This gets us right back to the question of the relation among deficits, money, and government spending. Niskanen similarly found a positive relation between deficits and the supply of money. By bringing in a dummy variable for the period since 1966, Niskanen also found the relation between deficits and the supply of money to disappear. But what accounts for the shift in the money supply process that occurred in the mid-1960s? Perhaps the three of us are not in that much disagreement after all. We will need more work on the theory of the supply of money before we can tell.

There are some other questions that can be raised about the causal relationship between budget deficits and the growth of government. In his paper, Donald Gordon identifies a vulnerable aspect of our argument, an aspect that had also been emphasized by Victor Goldberg in his comments on a prepublication draft of the manuscript. Our hypothesis does not "explain" the observed explosion in state-local spending in postwar decades, even after we have made adjustments for central government grants, matching requirements, administrative and judicial mandates, and other federal pressures. Niskanen's evidence supports our reasoning that debt finance will lead to expanded government spending because debt reduces the perceived price of government. This proportion would seem as true for local government as for the federal government. But the money-creating power of the federal government would also seem to give an added impetus to expansions in federal spending. Yet the growth in state-local spending remains a puzzle.

Once again, of course, we must not mistake a particular coefficient for an entire model. Spending increases for many reasons, with debt finance being only one reason. It is always possible that these other factors required to describe a complete model would operate to increase state-local spending more rapidly than federal. In the absence of such a model, the implications of different rates of spending growth for our theory about debt finance must remain open-ended. Perhaps Gordon is correct: perhaps even with strict budget balance and without the Keynesian theory of economic policy, we should have had roughly the spending explosion we have observed. Perhaps history cannot be "explained," even in part, by the influence of the ideas of academic scribblers. If this is the case, we had as well join those of our colleagues who engage in the escapist worlds of puzzles, theorems, and proofs. But in some final sense, we simply refuse to believe that people, and their ideas, cannot exert some control over events.

## 6. The Model of Political Process

Craig Roberts accuses us of political naiveté. He offers an alternative explanation of the factual record by postulating a model of a monolithic government bent on furthering its own interest, which translates directly into maximization of the size of the public sector. Keynesian economics, in Roberts' view, was used merely as the apologetics for the massive power grab that we have witnessed since the close of World War II. His explanation requires no resort to error, illusion, or institutional influence. The actors in his model are coldly rational, and they know quite well what they want and how to get it.

The last part of Donald Gordon's paper finds common ground with Craig Roberts' critique. Gordon suggests the possible contradiction between the position taken in *Budgets and Bureaucrats*,[2] and that represented in *Democracy in Deficit*. In the former, the behavior of a partially independent and uncontrollable bureaucracy in generating the observed acceleration in the growth of government was the focus of attention. The existence of this force need not, however, preclude the complementary element discussed in our book. We make no claim that the Keynesian bias is the only significant explanatory factor. Our purpose was to isolate this factor and to examine its influence critically. There seems to us to be no inconsistency in examining other factors, at other times and places, that may either offset or complement the one that was treated in our book.

We do not deny the apparent correspondence of many aspects of the monopoly-government model and the reality that we observe. But we share with Tobin the view that such a fully closed model leaves no room at all for normatively inspired policy discussion. If all that we can do is describe the behavior of self-seeking agents who act on behalf of the government, what is the point of our activity as economists? Surely, there must be improvement that is possible, and surely there is some role for economists in achieving this. At this level of discussion, our position is somewhere between Tobin on the one hand and Roberts on the other. We do not despair of offering normative policy advice, as Roberts' model implies we should. But we do not expect ordinary politicians to have the wisdom of saints, as Tobin's position implies we should. We are neither elitist nor authoritarian, unless these labels should be attached to anyone who honestly tries to evaluate the limits of representative democracy in economic policy management. When these limits are acknowledged (and we suggest that they must be), we take a stand quite explicitly for the introduction of constraining rules, for an explicit *fiscal constitution*, that will keep the political excesses within bounds. It is toward the development and implementation of such rules that our own normative channels for improvement lie. Roberts would, if put to it, have to call the existing situation hopeless; Tobin would have to look for wiser men in politics; we hope for constraining rules based on reasoned consideration of political reality.

We do not suggest that the constraining rules advanced in our book are

---

2. See *Budgets and Bureaucrats: Sources of Government Growth*, ed. T. E. Borcherding (Durham: Duke University Press, 1977).

optimal in any orthodox sense of this term. (We do not quite know what "optimal" means in such contexts, and we are simply at a loss when Gordon starts talking about the "optimal" size of public debt.) We agree with Tobin that much analysis and dialogue are required, but we do insist that normative policy discussion shift to the level of alternative rules as opposed to alternative policy expedients within the existing political process. We do not think that an effective fiscal-monetary constitution would resolve all of the difficulties of our time, nor do we think that its absence caused the Viet Nam war. Our claims are much more modest; an effective fiscal-monetary constitution can exert directionally desired influences on political decision-makers, and through a recognition of such influences, can introduce stabilizing elements in the economy.

## 7. The Question of Macroeconomic Perspective

Barro and Tobin suggested that we should have made more of a direct contribution to macroeconomics. To do this would have been to adopt a quite different purpose for our analysis than the one we chose to adopt. Our main interest was simply in treating seriously the straightforward observation that politicians, not economists, make economic policy. The economic impact of the economic policy that emerges from the political process does, of course, depend on the character of the economic order. In considering this impact, we do possess a macroeconomic perspective, and this perspective was revealed at several places in our book.

Indeed, it is recognition of the political implementation of economic policy as filtered through our macroeconomic perspective that allows us to portray the economic consequence of Keynesian policy to be harmful. In our view the economic order is essentially stable, and monetary disturbance operates in nonneutral fashion in the short run.[3] An institutional framework that promoted monetary and fiscal stability would facilitate the coordinative properties of the market economy. The implementation of economic policy within the existing institutional framework, however, acts to generate eco-

---

3. See, for instance, Richard E. Wagner, "Economic Manipulation for Political Profit: Macroeconomic Consequences and Constitutional Implications," *Kyklos*, 30, no. 3 (1977), 395–410.

nomic instability. The price signals in the market economy are distorted by policy, so economic discoordination results. When the observed state of economic circumstances is filtered through the Keynesian vision of the economic order, however, economic management to correct the economic discoordination seems to be called for. An economy that is distinctly non-Keynesian in nature can appear to be Keynesian through the implementation of economic policy. Our views on macroeconomics, in other words, enable us to describe the political biases of Keynesian economic policy as something distinctly harmful and responsible for economic malaise.

## 8. Conclusion

*Democracy in Deficit* was completed in the summer of 1976. Since that time, we have had two additional years of budgetary history. These years have not refuted the book's central hypothesis that the United States has embarked on a regime of permanent deficit financing of significant, and possibly accelerating, scope. We acknowledge in the book, and we reaffirm here, that our purpose was, and is, in part that of constructive dialogue. Only by predicting the consequences of observed processes in advance can these consequences be avoided if they are deemed to be undesirable. We do not need to fall off the cliff in order to convince ourselves that, empirically, the cliff is there. Is it not far better to find out in advance that the cliff is ahead and that we still might prevent disaster if we can reverse direction?

We do not accept the charge that we presented no *analysis,* as such, in the book. We attempt to analyze the workings of political institutions through which macroeconomic policy has been made in the post-Keynesian era. We invite other economists to do the same thing. Our analysis may be incorrect, in the large or in the small. We may not be cynical enough in modeling the behavior of public choosers, as Craig Roberts suggests. Or we may not attribute a sufficient degree of rationality (and political control) to the ultimate taxpayer-voter, as Barro urges. Or perhaps the quantitatively measurable record does not bear our analysis empirically, in some respects, as both Niskanen and Gordon suggest. We are institutionalists in the sense that we think that arrangements or rules do affect outcomes. Ultimately the test of our analysis of politics, and our interpretation of the historical record will stand or fall on empirical grounds. But our concern is that the evidence required to convince recalcitrant professional colleagues may arrive too late to allow the necessary constitutional reforms to be introduced in time to be effective. Quite frankly, we are more interested in opening a dialogue that may generate preventive steps than we are in achieving simon-pure empirical credentials or in being labeled as belonging to this or that camp or school. There is, indeed, a deal of ruin in a nation, as Adam Smith assured us. But defensive dialogue is essential to preserve that which remains vulnerable to those forces that would do the dealing.

# The Moral Dimension of Debt Financing

## I. Introduction

Economists have almost totally neglected moral or ethical elements of the behavior that has generated the observed modern regime of continuing and accelerating government budget deficits. To the extent that moral principles affect choice constraints, such neglect is inexcusable. It is incumbent on us, as economic analysts, to understand how morals impinge upon choice, and especially how an erosion of moral precepts can modify the established functioning of economic and political institutions. A positive, empirical theory of the operation of moral rules is in order even if we want to leave the preaching to the moralists.

An understanding of how moral constraints affect patterns of political outcomes need not require comparable understanding of the origins of moral rules themselves. Indeed, one of the arguments I want to develop depends critically on the "non-rational" attributes of such moral rules. The effects of moral constraints are, of course, fully symmetrical. If moral rules constrain choices, that is, if there exists what we may call a moral feasibility frontier, then it is the case that an erosion or destruction of moral norms relaxes the constraints and thereby shifts the frontier locus "outward," with consequences that we, as economists, can analyze.

From *Economic Inquiry* 23 (January 1985): 1–6. Reprinted by permission of Oxford University Press.

This paper was presented as the Presidential Address at the Western Economic Association International conference, Las Vegas, June 28, 1984.

I shall argue that the explosive increase in debt or deficit financing of public consumption outlays can be explained, at least in part, by an erosion of previously existing moral constraints. The political decision makers did not "discover" a new technology of debt financing midway through this century. Their rational self-interest has always dictated resort to non-tax sources of public revenues. What happened in this century was that debt financing ceased to be immoral. We have here an almost perfect example of the harm that "rationalist constructivism" (to use this term pejoratively in the Hayekian sense) can produce. The attempt to impose "rational choice" behavior on those who were constrained by previously existing and culturally evolved moral rules has, in fact, allowed a reversion to the more primitive instincts that previously were held in check.

This moral dimension of the modern fiscal dilemma must be appreciated if there is to be any hope of escape. Abstract rules that have evolved unconsciously cannot themselves be rationally restored. However, rationally chosen constraints can be introduced to serve, in part, as substitutes for the eroded moral rules. Balanced budgets formerly dictated by moral standards, were never explicitly mentioned in formal constitutional documents. Without such standards, however, balanced-budget constraints must be explicitly chosen, imposed, and enforced.

## II. The Tribal Heritage

I am neither ethnologist nor anthropologist, and I make no claim to more than minimal lay knowledge of such areas of inquiry. Hence, my remarks should be treated as conjectural rather than as recorded history. With this disclaimer made, let me suggest that there is nothing in our genetic or biological "nature" which dictates an abiding interest in the abstract future of the human species, or even in the future of the arbitrary collectives which include large populations and claim dominion over large territories. Biologically, we remain tribal animals, and our natural instincts have not evolved beyond those which emerged in very small human communities. Precepts for behavior which we call moral often reflect merely our communitarian sense of loyalty to fellow members of the tribe.

The evolution of post-Enlightenment attitudes toward the formation, accumulation, and maintenance of capital (stored up capacity to satisfy wants) reflected a continuing perception of the extended family as the relevant tribal unit. Through the process of group selection, those families whose members exhibited financial prudence survived and prospered. Generalized norms for human behavior with regard to the accumulation and maintenance of wealth and property were unconsciously directed toward family interests, not primarily those of individuals and not at all to the interests of political entities akin to modern nation-states.

## III. From Moral Community to Moral Order

I have found it useful to employ the terms "moral community" and "moral order" to distinguish between the two sets of human interaction relevant for the discussion here.[1] Persons belong to a moral community if they share loyalties to the group, as such. They participate in a "moral order" if they share commonly accepted codes of conduct that enable productive interaction to take place between persons of differing moral communities. Norms for fiscal prudence on the part of persons who act on behalf of political entities are norms for a "moral order" rather than norms for a "moral community." In a very real sense, these norms for collective fiscal prudence run counter to basic genetic drives. As Hayek in particular has emphasized, especially in his more recent writings, the norms for "moral order" have emerged in a long process of cultural rather than biological evolution.[2]

Modern man gradually came to adopt modes of behavior that enabled him to escape the limits imposed by his tribal heritage; he learned to behave in accordance with moral norms that are not of genetic origin, but which, nonetheless, are not learned consciously or rationally. As he did so, he was able to develop what Hayek has called "the great society," which is equivalent to what I have called "moral order." Man came to behave *vis-à-vis* persons who were not members of his own tribe in such fashion that reciprocal dealings became possible. In this way, ownership rights came to be mutually respected, even between members of wholly separate tribes. Trade and ex-

---

1. See James M. Buchanan, "Moral Community, Moral Order, or Moral Anarchy," Abbott Memorial Lecture no. 17, in *Colorado College Studies* (Colorado Springs: Colorado College, 1981).

2. See F. A. Hayek, *Law, Legislation and Liberty: The Political Order of a Free People,* Vol. 3 (Chicago: University of Chicago Press, 1979).

change as we know it in all its forms, from the simplest to the most complex, emerged; the specialization of labor was extended, and the miracle of coordination of modern markets was achieved.

My purpose here is neither to criticize nor to elaborate the Hayekian story. My purpose is the more limited one of suggesting that we can see an example of a move from moral community to moral order in the shift in the norms for fiscal prudence on the part of those who make decisions for the relevant polities. There is nothing in our tribal heritage that compels respect for our "national capital stock," any more than there is nothing that compels respect for the lives and property of persons whom we do not include and have never included in our moral community. Individual behavior that evinces respect for the capital stock of the nation, as a unit, is (or was) a product of *cultural* evolution, not an outgrowth of any genetic heritage. The fiscal norms of the Victorians, which we may now view as praiseworthy, were culturally derived norms. The shift from a prudent attitude toward family capital, which may be at least partly of biological origin, to a comparable attitude toward national capital was a shift resulting from cultural evolution. It is of considerable interest that this shift was well under way when Adam Smith decided upon the very title of his book.

## IV. Keynes as a Moral Revolutionary

The Victorian fiscal morality, a set of behavioral precepts which dictated adherence to strict budget balance, to a limited absolute level of taxation, and to a self-enforcing monetary regime, was neither rationally nor biologically derived. It was an outgrowth of a cultural evolutionary process which was not understood by those who shared the morality. It existed in continual tension with the tribal morality which remained essentially indifferent to the Victorian rules for fiscal behavior; indeed allegedly rational arguments for fiscal-monetary debauchery were introduced on occasion.

On the moral dimension that is my emphasis here, Keynes may be viewed as a successful revolutionary who destroyed the Victorian precepts. He did so for rationally based reasons, and he sought to replace the strong but essentially unconscious adherence to long-standing rules by what seemed at the time to be a well-reasoned "logic of policy." However, Keynes totally failed to recognize that the long-standing rules for fiscal-monetary prudence were required to hold the tribal instincts in check, and that, once the Victorian precepts were eroded, the tribal instincts would emerge with force sufficient to overwhelm all rationally derived argument.

The debt finance we observe today we might have predicted from the simple public-choice analysis of political behavior. Constituents enjoy receiving the benefits of public outlays, and they deplore paying taxes. Elected politicians attempt to satisfy constituents. There is little need here to elaborate on this simple model of public choice, which now seems so straightforward. As you know, I have discussed this model in the book I wrote with Richard Wagner several years ago.[3] This paper goes beyond the model in that book by offering an explanation as to why the natural proclivities of citizens and politicians alike emerged only in the post-Keynesian era. I have previously referred to the fact that the Keynesian theory of economic policy essentially repealed the implicit fiscal and monetary constitution evident in the Victorian era.

## V. The Vulnerability of Culturally Evolved Norms

Why did these implicit rules exist and why were they so vulnerable? It is useful to consider here the Hayekian distinction between culturally evolved codes of conduct and biologically driven instincts. The human animal, in modern political structures, has chosen to "eat up" the capital stock of his nation. (For let us make no mistake about it: this is precisely what the debt financing of public consumption is, an "eating up" of national capital.) This choice has been taken because of the shift in moral standards that the Keynesian revolution embodied. It is no longer immoral to mortgage the future flow of the national income, at best an abstraction which commands little moral assent.

The erosion of the standards of fiscal morality applied to political units has exerted predictable spillover influences on the standards of morality applied to family and personal portfolios. There remains, nonetheless, a major difference in the vulnerability of the two sets of standards. To some extent at least, the immorality of destroying family or personal capital stems from biological origins. Public profligacy now seems almost unlimited because of the

---

3. James M. Buchanan and Richard Wagner, *Democracy in Deficit: The Political Legacy of Lord Keynes* (New York: Academic Press, 1977).

destruction of moral standards that were clearly produced in a cultural evolutionary process. Private profligacy continues to be held in check by moral standards that are only in part culturally determined.

From the perspective taken here, it is interesting to observe that attempts by modern economists to de-emphasize the consequences of our changed behavior with respect to public debt issues have included the revival of the Ricardian equivalence theorem, which involves the conversion of public debt into its private debt equivalents. To the extent that such conversion does, in fact, take place, individual standards of morality for the consumption of family or private capital stocks are implicitly extended to the aggregate national capital stock. These models are deficient, however, in precisely the same sense as the simple public-choice models. They provide no explanation at all for the explosion in public debt financing of ordinary public outlays during middle decades of this century. If, indeed, individuals act in a suprarational Ricardo-Barro manner, why did the financing mix between taxation and debt shift so dramatically in the post-Keynesian era?

## VI. Culturally Evolved Norms as Public Capital

If my basic diagnosis is correct, that we have lived through a period in which culturally evolved rules of fiscal prudence as applied to the behavior of public choosers (in all capacities) have lost their previously existing moral force, it is necessary to acknowledge that we have destroyed a valuable portion of our public capital stock. The metaphor is useful in that it suggests that there is a quasi-permanency involved here, even if it were possible to "reconstruct" that which has been destroyed. If moral rules must evolve slowly and without deliberate construction, then there is little hope for any attempt at restoration. We can take a somewhat more optimistic view, however, if we recognize that there is always some substitutability between rules for behavior which reflect moral norms and those which are explicitly chosen as constraints.

If this substitutability is accepted, then an observed erosion in constraining moral norms can be offset, at least in part, by deliberate adoption and enforcement of behavioral constraints. If, in our varying capacities as public choosers (as voters, as members of benefit-receiving special interest groups, as taxpayers, as members of political parties, as elected politicians, as bureaucrats), we are not constrained by moral sanctions against the accelerating destruction of our national capital stock through the deficit financing of public consumption, we must look to the more formal rules of the political institutions within which we make public decisions. It is not at all contradictory or inconsistent to recognize that the rules under which we choose may be non-optimal while at the same time we behave within those existing rules in accordance with rational utility-maximizing norms. Given the absence of moral constraints and given the observed open-ended rules for fiscal decisions, rational behavior on the part of public choosers insures the regime of continuing and accelerating budget deficits.[4] In view of the difficulty if not the impossibility of any deliberative restoration of moral precepts, we must indeed look to explicit rules if reform in the pattern of results is to be expected.

I think that the discussion on the constitutional amendment to require governmental budget balance offers the most constructive advance in policy reform in several decades. Having lived through the destruction of fiscal morality by the Keynesian mind-set, we must make every effort to replace this morality with deliberatively chosen constraints which will produce substantially the pre-Keynesian pattern of results. Economists, in particular, need to bring their own thinking up to date on all such matters and to rid themselves, once and for all, of the notion that they need only proffer advice to a benevolent government which eagerly pays heed.

---

4. There are, of course, limits to deficit financing. Continued increase in debt-service charges cannot be characteristic of economic or political equilibrium. Explicit default, or default through inflation, will, of course, impose such limits. Even fear of such default may, however, be sufficient to generate the requisite political support for *temporary* reductions in deficit size. But there is nothing in modern democracies to generate permanent changes in the pattern of results.

# The Balanced Budget Amendment
## Clarifying the Arguments

*Abstract:* From the perspective of a supporter, this paper responds to the several criticisms that have been raised to the proposed constitutional amendment to require budget balance. Economists have concentrated on the loss of fiscal flexibility. This objection is countered by reference to the political inefficacy of attempted budgetary manipulation. Lawyers have concentrated on problems of enforcement. This objection is countered by reference to observed respect to other constitutional rules.

## *Part One*

## 1. Introduction

On 26 January 1995, the U.S. House of Representatives approved a proposed constitutional amendment that requires balance in the budget of the federal government by the year 2002. On 2 March 1995, the U.S. Senate, by a single vote, failed to approve such an amendment. As this monograph is written (March 1995), the proposal for constitutional constraints on deficit financing appears certain to occupy the attention of the public and politicians alike over several years.

This monograph is intended as a possible contribution to the ongoing

From *Public Choice* 90 (1997): 117–38. Reprinted by permission of the publisher, Kluwer Academic Publishers.

discussion, at several levels of dialogue, during 1995, 1996 and beyond. It is prompted specifically by the recognition that much of the expressed opposition to the amendment for budget balance is based on serious misunderstandings rather than upon interest-motivated desires to maintain high levels of debt-financed governmental outlay.

As early as 1954, in an unpublished paper, I identified a political flaw in Keynesian macroeconomic policy, and I predicted the regime of continuing fiscal deficits that we have witnessed over the half-century. I did not call explicitly for a constitutional amendment, but by the time I published my 1958 book on public debt, the constitutional implications were clear. In the early 1960s, Gordon Tullock and I examined the constitutional foundations of democracy in general terms, and also in the early 1960s, I discussed more explicitly the proclivity of democratic process to generate regimes described by "easy budgets and tight money." As we came to observe continuing deficits, Richard Wagner and I spelled out both the history and the analysis in our 1978 book, *Democracy in Deficit*. Various proposals emerged in the 1970s, 1980s and 1990s, all aimed at constitutional correction. I expressed my personal support in legislative hearings, documents, papers and books.

I do not parade this long record of personal involvement to promote my books or to establish my bona fides. I do so to suggest that my current position, along with that of a relatively small number of coauthors, colleagues and students, does not reflect some belated recognition of the deficit as an issue, born out of concern about the fiscal profligacy of the 1980s. The structural flaw in our fiscal politics did not arise in the 1980s, and it will not go away in the ordinary politics of the 1990s and beyond. The structural flaw requires structural correction, that is, constitutional constraint that will, effectively, change the basic rules for the fiscal game.

I shall proceed as follows. In Section 2, I summarize the history of attitudes toward budget balance in order to tell us where we are and how we got to the here and now. In Section 3, I show that the ordinary politics of majoritarian democracy cannot get the deficit under control, despite the noblest of efforts. The incentive structure of this politics is such as to insure the dissipation and any gains that might be achieved temporarily. Section 4 presents the basic analysis of the constitutional rule for budget balance, with emphasis on the necessary distinction between choices among rules and choices within rules—a distinction that is missed by many in the current political dialogue. More specifically, stress is put on the intertemporal feature that makes any budget balance rule especially difficult to put in place. In Section 5, the critical distinction between the fiscal adjustments that the adoption of such a rule makes necessary over a transition period and the adjustments that are required on a permanent and continuing basis is examined. And I advance the argument for temporally lagged implementation of any constitutional rule for budget balance.

Part Two shifts attention to possible criticisms that have been advanced against adoption of the constitutional amendment. The first argument, treated in Section 6, is the one that suggests rejection of the proposed amendment based on the notion that it is inappropriate for inclusion in the general constitutional structure. In this section, I make a separation between the "clean" amendment for budget balance and the sometime proposals that include constitutional requirements for qualified majorities in tax legislation. I suggest that complementary advocacy of such tax and/or spending limits serves to sow confusion—even among those who have been among the strongest advocates of the basic amendment.

In Section 7, I move on to consider the argument most often advanced by economists—an argument that suggests academic residues of the Keynesian rationale for fiscal fine-tuning. Section 8 examines the arguments that emerge from legal-political sources that defend the status quo by reference to issues involved in the enforcement of any fiscal rule. In Section 9, I briefly analyze a sophisticated "supply-side" argument that was advanced in the 1980s and which reappeared in the 1990s in support of the complementary tax and spending limit supplements in the basic rule. Section 10 briefly discusses capital budgeting as it may apply to the proposal rule. Section 11 examines the specious social security argument that was used by opponents to defeat the amendment in the U.S. Senate in early 1995.

In Part Three, Section 12 returns to positive discussion with examination of some of the macroeconomic implications of an operative regime of budget balance. In Section 13, the monograph is concluded with a general discussion of the symbolic significance of the adoption of a constitutional rule for budget balance.

## 2. How and Why We Got Here

The budget of the United States federal government has not been balanced since 1969. And despite rhetoric about fiscal responsibility and despite occasional short periods during which the size of the deficit has been reduced (the Gramm-Rudman years of the second Reagan term and the Clinton years after the 1993 budgetary legislation), there is little or no expectation that a regime of budget balance will somehow emerge to replace the quasi-permanent regime of fiscal deficits.

How and why did the United States political structure get into this pattern of acknowledged fiscal irresponsibility? If we understand how and why we got here, we may begin to understand how we might get out.

The first century and one-half of our national political history did, indeed, embody a norm of budget balance. This rule was not written into the constitutional document, as such, but rather it was a part of an accepted set of attitudes about how government should, and must, carry on its fiscal affairs. Politicians prior to World War II would have considered it to be immoral (to be a sin) to spend more than they were willing to generate in tax revenues, except during periods of extreme and temporary emergency. To spend borrowed funds on ordinary items for public consumption was, quite simply, beyond the pale of acceptable political behavior. There were basic moral constraints in place; there was no need for an explicit fiscal rule in the written constitution.

The balanced budget norm is ultimately based on the acceptance of the classic principles of public finance. Government borrowing offers a means through which burdens of paying for current public spending can be transferred forward through time and placed on the shoulders of those "future generations" who will be subjected to the taxes required to service and amortize public debt.

These elementary principles were overlooked in the Keynesian macroeconomic theory developed in the 1930s and 1940s. The government budget was seen to offer an instrument through which a wise and benevolent government could fine-tune the economy so as to promote the commonly desired objectives of full employment and economic growth. In this vision, any constraint on the exercise of governmental discretion in setting rates of taxes and spending could only reduce the efficacy of the macroeconomic enterprise.

In order to sell the Keynesian policy prescriptions, the moral onus on government debt and deficits had to be exorcised from public consciousness. For this purpose, the intergenerational effects of public debt–financing had to be denied. Such a denial was allegedly accomplished by concentration on macroaggregates to the neglect of the necessary reduction of costs and benefits to the individuals who lose and gain. By the claim that debt financing did not impact negatively on future-period taxpayers, the moral constraint that had acted to insure fiscal responsibility was eroded and nothing emerged to take its place. The natural proclivities of democratically elected and constituency respondent politicians to spend and not to tax were allowed free play.

The economists were converted to the Keynesian mind-set by the 1940s, and they launched their advocacy of fiscal profligacy in the name of the potential achievement of widely acclaimed objectives, while wearing romantic blinders concerning the motivations of those who must make fiscal choices. The politicians themselves were, at first, reluctant to cast off the shackles of the old-time fiscal religion, but, by the 1960s, they too had come to realize that there were no dramatic negative feedbacks. The regime of permanent and accelerating deficits became a part of our political reality.

Understanding why and how we got here is easy. How to get back to where we were, as described in our moral attitudes toward imposing burdens on future taxpayers, becomes central to the whole debate about the proposed constitutional amendment.

## 3. Why Ordinary Politics Cannot Balance the Budget

If fiscal irresponsibility could, indeed, be laid at the feet of particular politicians or parties, there might be some expectation that with electoral rotation those who stand for fiscal integrity might eventually replace those who are fiscally profligate. But such expectation could only be utopian. The fault lies not in ourselves, as participants in the ordinary politics of modern majoritarian democracy, but in the structural rules within which this politics takes place.

As they now exist, these rules allow our political agents to escape the discipline of opportunity cost. Government spending for a wide array of "goods" may be authorized, and every one of these "goods" may be valued positively by some or all constituents. The approval of these rates of spending may, however, proceed without explicit regard to the genuine opportunity cost that must ultimately be measured in the sacrifice by someone, sometime, of other values that might have been produced. It is not the public spending, as such, that is the proper focus of attention here. (The normative question of the dividing line between political and private resource use may be important in its own right, but its introduction into the argument on the decision structure can only be misleading.) That which makes the existing rules generate patterns of outcomes that we deem to be irresponsible is the political agents' authority to *spend without taxing*. Little or no sophistication is required to recognize how different the dynamics of fiscal choice would be in a constitutional setting that forced politicians to levy taxes to cover outlays.

The residual Keynesians in our midst, who remain locked into macroeconomic illusion, may continue to suggest that the opportunity costs of public spending must always be borne contemporaneously with the spending itself. They suggest that the valued resources are used up as the outlays are made. But they forget that those who actually give up resources do so in exchange for valued claims (interest-bearing government securities) against future taxpayers.

A more sophisticated denial of the simple logic of deficit financing is located in the argument that citizens, and their political agents, do, indeed, face the full opportunity cost of debt-financed outlay because they will, quite rationally, discount the future tax obligations that any issue of public debt embodies. In this argument, the temporal displacement of the costs of public spending need not affect fiscal choices. Within this "Ricardian logic," there need be no concern about failures in the basic rules of fiscal politics.

Politicians may be observed to spend without taxing, while the shortfall is made up by public borrowing. But, it may be asked, why is government different in this respect from a private person, or a firm, who may also be observed sometimes to borrow in order to meet spending needs? An important difference lies in the absence of any assigned liability for future payment for servicing and amortizing public debt. The owner of a government bond holds a claim against the general tax base of the political community, not against the income or assets of some identified person or group. There is no effective presence of future-period taxpayers in current-period political choice settings, a presence that might exert some rough balance into the fiscal benefit-cost calculus.

The incentives are such as to generate a regime of fiscal deficits as a necessary consequence of fully rational responses of political agents to the demands of their constituents. This result remains quite robust under many possible variations in the definitions of political rationality and in the composition of political coalitions. There are, of course, upper limits on the natural proclivity of constituency responsive political agents to create fiscal deficits. But the margin between tax and debt financing that comes to be established in a political equilibrium is well beyond any margin that might be dictated by choices that fully incorporate the present-period interests of future-period taxpayers.

To this point, I have discussed only the direct incentives that exist to bias fiscal choices toward deficit financing of public outlay. These incentives are supplemented by a secondary set which serve to make efforts to behave responsibly in some long-term fiscal sense seem folly. Assume, heroically perhaps, that a majority of elected political agents, acting on behalf of their constituents, comes to acknowledge the long-term damage of continued deficit financing, and that this majority takes effective action toward reducing or eliminating the imbalance in the budget. Such praiseworthy enterprise would necessarily remain vulnerable in the face of electoral rotation. If the responsibly acting majority coalition could be assured permanence or quasi-permanence in positions of fiscal authority, the deficit-reduction effort might well succeed. But, with constitutionally guaranteed electoral periodicity, there is no assurance that deficit reducing actions (tax increases or spending cuts) taken currently will not be dissipated, wholly or in part, by the actions of other majority coalitions in future periods.

To reduce the budget deficit, costs must be imposed on current-period taxpayers and/or current-period beneficiaries of governmental programs. Taxes must be increased, and/or rates of spending must be reduced. There will be predictable electoral feedbacks on those political agents who impose such burdens. Why should current-period agents, even those who fully acknowledge the long-term damage generated by continuous deficit financing, take on the political costs of deficit reduction if they, at the same time, fear that all of their current-period efforts are vulnerable to dissipation by differing political coalitions in future periods? In ordinary majoritarian politics, there is no way through which currently serving political agents can "lock in" or make secure the salutary effects that any action might produce.

This set of secondary incentives reinforces the primary ones. The natural proclivity to spend without taxing becomes even more dominating an influence on choice when current-period political agents recognize that the same proclivity exists for and will possibly be influential on those political agents who will become their replacements in later periods.

## 4. The Relevance of Rules

Political choices are made within rules. Elections to the U.S. House of Representatives take place every other year. This rule is only one among many that describe the operation of our politics. Who could deny that political outcomes would be different with congressional election cycles of, say, one year, or four years? This illustration suffices to show that rules matter. And because they do matter, we are obligated to consider changes in rules as well as particular policy options available within the set of rules that exist.

We must make a careful and categorical distinction between *choices among rules* (constitutional politics) and *choices within rules* (ordinary politics). The whole discussion about the constitutional amendment for budget balance is marred by a failure to recognize the importance of making this distinction. The proposal is aimed at changing the rule for the game of ordinary fiscal politics. Supporters of the change predict that, under the new rule, fiscal outcomes will be different, and better, than those outcomes now observed to emerge under existing rules that do not require budget balance.

The point of emphasis is simple. Rules constrain the set of admissible choice alternatives. Different constraints (different rules) must thereby generate different patterns of outcomes. And this direct relationship holds even with no change in the identification of the decision makers. The person who sets her alarm clock (a rule) gets up at a different hour from the person who does not set the clock (another rule). It is, therefore, little more than obfuscatory confusion to suggest that, because we shall have the same or similar political agents in authority with or without a formal balanced budget rule, there will be no predicted difference in fiscal behavior.

The rule for budget balance is, however, different in one critically important respect from ordinary rules for ordinary games. Consider an illustrative comparison. Think of a set of poker players who have been playing for some time under a rule that allowed for only stud games. Someone proposes that the rules be changed to allow draw poker to be called by the dealer. The proposed change may or may not be approved, but the point to note is that the *same* persons who played under the old rules are considering the new rules under which they will also expect to continue playing.

A budget balance rule differs in the temporal composition of membership as between the operation of the existing rules and that of proposed alternatives. Under the rule that allows for the generation of continuing deficits, those citizens and their legislative agents who enjoy the current benefits of spending without paying current taxes impose costs on all taxpayers who will be around in future periods. The rule for deficits allows current players in the fiscal game to secure differential gains at the expense of future-period players. A change in fiscal rules that would require budget balance removes such differential gains for current-period citizens. The primary beneficiaries of such a change are all those persons who will hold membership in the political community in future periods.

This temporal differentiation among prospective losers and gainers under alternative rules for fiscal politics makes any change from the status quo rule for deficit financing difficult to achieve. It is not as if the same set of players are changing the rules under which play will continue. Those persons who expect to leave the game soon—those who have high rates of time discount, and, in particular, those who benefit most directly from debt-financed spending—will oppose any change that promises its benefits only in future periods. The aged pensioner, or her political agent, must oppose the constitutional amendment for budget balance if her position is motivated by economic self-interest.

## 5. Lagged Implementation and Transitional Adjustment

It is clearly more difficult to secure agreement on a change in the rules of any game while the game is being played than it is to secure agreement on a set of rules before play begins. This relationship applies to the rules of fiscal politics as well as ordinary games. To the extent that is possible, alternative rules should be considered in a setting where individual positions cannot be identified in terms of prospective gains and losses under the operation of particular rules. Ideally, basic change in rules, constitutional change, should be made only behind some veil of ignorance and/or uncertainty that is sufficiently thick to allow the individual to choose among the alternatives without explicit consideration of the particularized distributional impacts.

This consideration alone suggests that proposals for constitutional change should be lagged in the time for full implementation, that they should never be applied immediately when identified distributional effects are maximally predictable. Critics of the balanced budget amendment who suggest that the introduction of time lags for implementation reflect political cowardice either misunderstand the simple logic of constitutional choice or deliberately seek to sow confusion.

Time lags for implementation should be distinguished from extensions in the time period allowed for transition to a new rule. All of the proposals for the balanced budget amendment include a specific period of transition, and, in the version passed by the U.S. House of Representatives in January 1995, this adjustment period was set at seven years. The purpose of a transition period is to allow for a gradual adjustment in rates of spending and taxing so as to minimize disruptions in established expectations of citizens, whether as program beneficiaries, taxpayers or their political agents.

There is no logical argument that suggests, say, a seven-year lag in implementation of a balanced budget rule. Clearly, uncertainty about distributional effects will be reduced as the time period for adjustment is extended, and, relatedly, there will be less required adjustment during each particular period. With a deficit of, say, $210 billion, a $30 billion first-year adjustment becomes reasonable with the proposed seven-year lag, provided that the constitutional rule operates to insure a continuance of the initial year discipline.

## Part Two

## 6. Budget Balance as a Procedural Rule

In Part One, I have laid out the arguments in support of the proposed constitutional amendment that requires the federal government to balance its fiscal budget. In Part Two, I propose to discuss separately and in some detail the most prominent objections and criticisms that have been advanced in opposition to the amendment, or in favor of the status quo, which we may think of as the rule for deficit financing. In this section, I shall address the argument based on the claim that a rule for budget balance is inappropriate for inclusion in the "law of the land" that the U.S. Constitution is supposed to represent, and that adoption of any such rule would amount to constitutionalizing a specific economic philosophy. I shall defer until Section 8 the more familiar economists' objection that the proposed rule embodies a particular stance on macroeconomic policy.

The essential distinction that must be made is that between a rule that acts on the *procedures* through which participants are allowed to reach and to carry out decisions and a rule that acts directly on the *outcomes* that any such decisions might describe. A simple example: A rule that all motor vehicles must drive on the right side of two-way roads in the United States is *procedural*. It does not, in any way, dictate or prohibit any particular pattern of road usage. By contrast, a rule that prohibits large trucks from usage of residential streets is nonprocedural or *substantive* because it operates directly on the set of permissible outcomes that may be generated by the behavior of the vehicle operators.

In the context of democratic politics, most of the rules that we normally classify to be constitutional are procedural. The constitutional rules define the processes within which political action takes place. Every citizen is granted the voting franchise; legislative agents are chosen by pluralities or majorities in elections that are scheduled regularly on predictable calendars. Once these and other procedural conditions are met, the basic rules remain silent on the wide ranges of outcomes that may be produced within their limits.

When viewed in this perspective, a constitutional rule for budget balance is procedural rather than substantive. Such a rule does not constrain either the overall size of the public sector (the budget) or the composition of the activities within that sector. Outcomes are allowed to emerge from the interaction of the various cooperative and conflictual pressures that describe the workings of ordinary majoritarian politics. Both proponents and opponents of the balanced budget amendment may, of course, apply their own evaluative standards to specific patterns of outcomes, however these may come about. But it is not legitimate to introduce evaluative criteria applicable for outcomes when directly assessing alternative procedural constraints.

The proposed balanced budget amendment lays out a new rule for making fiscal choices; it does not lay down guidelines for what these choices might be. In one sense, the proposal may be too simple to be understood. In its bare-bones formulation, the amendment requires only that congressional majorities, within the other constraints through which they are authorized to act, pay for what they spend, with "pay for" being defined in a willingness to levy taxes on those citizens who make up the current membership of the polity. By extension from everyday private life, the procedural norm here is simple indeed. Each person or family knows that it must pay for what it buys, and the background law that enforces this precept seldom enters into private consciousness.

Why should the body politic, through government, be allowed to behave differently? They are enabled to do so, in the absence of a constraining rule, only through the legally recognized organic life of the collectivity. A person or family cannot place future persons in indebtedness. Existing claims on a decedent are honored only against the value of assets held at death. There is no burden of private debt that may be transmitted intergenerationally.

Not so with government or public debt. Government remains alive through time, and their obligations are legally honored and enforced, even as the membership of the polity transforms itself through birth, life and death. Recognition of this basic distinction between the private and the collective economy provides the ultimate foundation for the budget balance rule which converts the collectivity into an analogue of its private counterpart.

At this point it is appropriate to discuss briefly that version of the balanced budget amendment that was debated, but not passed, by the U.S. House of Representatives in early 1995—the version that included the supplementary constitutional provision that all taxes should be approved by a three-fifths majority in both houses of Congress. Advocates of this version failed to make the procedural-substantive distinction that I have noted in this section. A constitutional rule that requires a three-fifths majority for *all* fiscal actions would remain procedural, since there is nothing constitutionally sacrosanct about simple majority decision making as such. But, as presented, the qualified majority was aimed to apply only to taxing decisions, a requirement that clearly represented an attempt to introduce substantive direction as to how the federal budget was to achieve and to maintain balance. Such a supplementary rule would have been inappropriate for inclusion in a constitutional structure that is best confined to procedural rules. And this evaluative conclusion holds quite independent of any separate judgment about the urgent need to keep the growth of the public sector within bounds.

## 7. Politics, Policy and Budget Imbalance: Response to the Keynesians

The argument that is most frequently advanced in opposition to the amendment centers on the loss of flexibility under a regime that requires budget balance. There is no dispute about the claim that the proposed rule would act to constrain fiscal choices. At issue is whether or not such constraint is desirable.

Whose choices are constrained by the enforcement of a balanced budget rule? The direct influence is exerted on the choices of those persons who are placed in the roles of fiscal agents for the collectivity, the politicians and bureaucrats who are authorized to make decisions on taxing and spending. The question to be resolved concerns the model to be used in understanding and predicting the behavior of these political agents, both individually and as they interact in complex institutional structures.

There is a long philosophical tradition in which the whole activity or enterprise of politics is modeled in an idealistic way. Political agents are implicitly presumed to be both benevolent and omniscient. They seek only to further "the public interest" in some inclusive, aggregative sense, and, perhaps more importantly, they are presumed to know precisely what this interest is. In the extreme version of this conceptualization of politics, *any* constitutional constraint on potential choices of agents must act to forestall or prevent some actions that would otherwise be beneficial for members of the community. Why, for example, should benevolent and omniscient governments ever be required to seek electoral approval for their actions? And, of course, such political agents should never be constrained in their access to particular institutional tools that might be used to further the public interest, as defined. Clearly, the budget, described as the composition of taxing and spending flows chosen on behalf of the collectivity, is a tool that might be used, in whole or in part, to achieve designated objectives. Any constraint imposed constitutionally necessarily reduces the ability of political agents to use the budgetary tool. By the very presupposition of this romantic model of politics, a constitutional constraint *could never* improve patterns of fiscal outcomes; at best, such a constraint would simply be ineffective.

It is from within this time-honored tradition of idealized politics that the whole Keynesian theory of fiscal policy emerged during the middle decades of the twentieth century. Keynes did not seriously think about the political institutions through which budgetary decisions are implemented. The "presuppositions of Harvey Road" embodied the notion that macroeconomic policy is to be made by a small, select and sophisticated elite, whose members are both fully informed and personally disinterested in securing private advantage.

The Keynesians—the whole group of economists, publicists and politicians who adopted the proffered nostrums as guidelines for practical policy—were particularly naive in their extension of the norms to the American political setting described by the division of power between the executive and legislative branches and without the party discipline of the British parliamentary regime. In a post–public choice retrospective evaluation, it is difficult to understand how anyone could have imagined that fiscal fine-tuning could be within the politically possible.

Quite apart from the neglect of political-institutional practicability, basic macroeconomic obstacles to the efficacy of fiscal fine-tuning were recognized early in the post-Keynesian dialogues. The fiscal budget, even if all issues of political pressures are overcome, remains a crude instrument, and the effects of budgetary manipulation emerge only after significant time lags. An observed deficiency in aggregate demand may prompt tax cuts or spending increases, thereby increasing the deficit, but by the time the effects of such changes take place, other forces may obviate the presumed need for the fiscal action.

A more persistent, and coherent, source of opposition to the balanced budget amendment is concentrated on the potential efficacy of built-in budgetary flexibility. If elements in the tax and expenditure structures are such that increased or reduced deficits (reduced or increased surpluses) emerge as a matter of course during either recessions or inflations, these budgetary changes serve as stabilizing forces that influence the macroeconomy to return to its predisturbance equilibrium.

This argument has considerable persuasive force if the balanced budget rule is framed and interpreted so strictly that *ex post* or end-of-period accounting equality between revenue intakes and outlays is enforced. If the rule requires that in the event of an *unanticipated* shortfall of revenues behind outlays, due to a reduction of anticipated revenue collections or to an unanticipated increase in rates of outlay, corrective adjustment must be introduced retrospectively as it were, then the operation of the rule would exacerbate the macroeconomic disturbance that might have generated the budgetary shortfall in the first place.

A more acceptable, and less stringent, interpretation of budget balance as a basic choice rule to be constitutionally implemented involves no such difficulty. The rule might require only that the final budget resolution, as approved by the Congress and the President, contain revenue and outlay estimates that are equal, as based on competently prepared and unbiased projections at the time of fiscal choice. If, subsequent to choice, that is, to the approval of the budget, the macroeconomic setting should change so as to generate shortfalls or surpluses, these shifts, in themselves, need not be considered to violate the constitutionally mandated rule for maintaining budgetary balance.

In the event that the budget for subsequent periods must be chosen under modified macroeconomic circumstances, implementation of the rule, as such, might require budgetary tightening (on either the taxing or spending side) relative to the prior period, whereas the standard Keynesian prescriptions dictate the opposing direction of change. But the whole hypothetical scenario here can be grounded only on some presupposition about the inefficacy or inoperability of monetary policy instruments in combination with assumptions about the tendencies of the economy toward macroeconomic instability. In a setting in which the central bank fulfills its primary responsibility and keeps the value of the monetary unit stable (within narrow limits) and in which the government budget is balanced, major internal sources for instability are eliminated. The balanced budget rule would, in itself, be an important stabilizing element that would provide an expectational anchor against the fiscal adventurism of impermanent political coalitions.

## 8. Enforcement and Implementation

The opposition to the proposed constitutional amendment for a balanced budget discussed in Section 7 stems directly from economists who have not fully escaped from the intellectual straitjacket imposed on their discipline by the Keynesian revolution of mid-century. A second main source of opposition emerges primarily from the legal community, from constitutional lawyers and legal practitioners, whose human capital has been invested in understanding and interpretation of the constitutional status quo. To members of this group, *any* change in existing rules of the political-legal order must act to create a setting that remains unexplored and unfamiliar. Natural instincts suggest opposition to any radical change, which, indeed, the proposed amendment represents.

At the intensely practical level, the legal opposition to the balanced budget rule targets the alleged ambiguities surrounding the enforceability of the amendment. Much of the argument here seems to be deliberately obfuscatory and appears to be a smoke screen for suppressed ideological objections. By contrast with the economic arguments discussed above—arguments that do express serious misgivings about how the proposed rule might work in its effects on macroeconomic policy—the enforceability arguments seem, at base, to be relatively empty and not worthy of consideration except for their apparent success in introducing uncertainties in the attitudes of persons who might otherwise support the amendment.

The first, and elementary, point to be made is that any rule (law, constraint), once put in place, will necessarily provide incentives for violation, either openly or covertly. This effect is inherent in the notion of a rule. The logical grounds for imposing a rule for budget balance is the need to constrain government's proclivity to spend without taxing. The enactment of the rule will not, directly, reduce or eliminate the pressures brought to bear on fiscal decision makers. They will remain vulnerable to demands for spending increases and tax cuts. Faced with the presence of an operative rule for budget balance, these political agents will try to accomplish their purposes by avoidance and evasion when opportunities permit. Efforts will be made to shift programs off budget and to secure regulatory objectives through nonfunded mandates aimed at both private and public units. The acknowledgement that a rule for budget balance would increase the activities of political coalitions along avoidance-evasion dimensions does not, however, support the conclusion that such a rule would not succeed in imposing fiscal constraint. No law could pass that demands perfect enforcement.

A more suspect argument against the amendment takes the form of scare stories about possible means through which enforcement might take place. At issue here is not the predicted efforts of legislative and executive officers to avoid the force of the rule, but rather the processes that may be called into being when and if such agents openly defy or disregard the constitutional prohibition on deficit financing of governmental outlay. What would happen if the Congress and the President simply proceed to approve a budget that violates the constitutional prohibition on deficits? Would the Supreme Court then act on its own and order cuts in rates of spending and increases in taxes? Or would it direct the President to impound funds as necessary to bring the budget into compliance with the constitutional requirement?

When such concerns as these are raised, the implications for the ultimate division of political authority may seem to become threatening. Who could support a constitutional change that promises to open up yet another area for judicial intrusion?

Such concerns seem misplaced when we look at the operational experience of American democracy. The institutions of governance—executive, legislative, judicial—have long operated within established, and time-honored, constitutional limits. The basic "rules of the game" have only rarely been breached. Elections are organized on schedule; majorities or pluralities effectively determine outcomes; the electoral succession of political representatives occurs peacefully; military authority defers to civilian control.

Why should anyone predict that the Congress and the President would behave differently under the constraints imposed by a new rule that requires budget balance? Why should a Congress defy this rule any more readily than it would refuse to honor electoral results? The very fact that such a rule would be *constitutional,* and understood as such, would seem to be sufficient to guarantee basic adherence.

## 9. Budget Deficits and Tax Increases

In this section, I shall examine an argument that was important in persuading the Reagan administration against promoting a balanced budget amendment in the early 1980s—an argument that also fostered acquiescence in the mounting fiscal deficits of that period. The same argument resurfaced in support for the inclusion of direct tax or spending limits in the amendment as proposed in 1995. For identification of the argument addressed here, the fiscal stance associated with Milton Friedman may be noted.

In a sense, the argument is not correctly classified among those advanced in opposition to the constitutional amendment for budget balance. The argument is less direct, and it is aimed at reasons for advocacy of the rule. The argument challenges the basic presupposition behind the support for the rule of budget balance—the presupposition that budget deficits, as such, are the center of normative concern. Instead, the claim is that deficit financing, in itself, is irrelevant. The modern variant of the ancient Ricardian theorem is adduced—a theorem that equates debt and tax financing of public outlay through the rational calculus of citizens who fully discount the expectations of future-period taxes that any issue of debt embodies. The variable that deserves exclusive attention is the rate of government spending rather than the manner of its financing. Will aggregate outlay be larger or smaller under debt financing? The argument of the early 1980s was to the effect that the Congress might fear increases in the deficit more than increases in taxes, and, as a result, deficit financing might actually slow down rates of approval for ever-larger budgets.

This position is seriously flawed on at least three counts. First of all, and as noted earlier, it ignores the burden that the payment of interest charges places on future-period taxpayers. Second, it presumes, quite naively, that political agents are more willing to levy current taxes on constituents than they are to authorize public borrowing. Finally, there is the implicit failure to separate fiscal choice-making at the postconstitutional and the constitutional level.

In retrospect, the political-fiscal experience of the early 1980s seems bizarre. The diversion of attention from budget imbalance almost guaranteed that the deficits would increase rather than decrease over time. In the 1995 discussion, the Friedman argument offered analytical encouragement to those who sought to append the proposed amendment with tax or spending limits, thereby shifting the proposal from the procedural to the quantitative category and providing occasion for totally different sources of opposition.

## 10. The Case for Capital Budgeting

Critics of the balanced budget amendment often identify the failure to include an exemption for capital spending as a major flaw. Such critics suggest, at least by inference, that the constitutional amendment for balance in the current budget might deserve serious consideration upon the establishment of a separate capital budget account.

The classical (pre-Keynesian) theory of public debt included a normative argument in support of debt financing of lumpy or extraordinary spending on projects that promise to yield benefits over some finite sequence of periods subsequent to that in which the initial outlay is made. By analogy, individual families and business firms finance long-lived assets with debt extending over the income-yielding lives of the assets. Persons finance consumer durables, including houses, by debt, and mortgage payments are a large share in household budgets. Firms finance capital improvements by bonds. The argument suggests that governmental units should be constitutionally empowered to behave under roughly similar rules.

Two issues emerge, however, that suggest caution in setting too much emphasis on capital budgeting. First, a distinction must be made between capital assets that will yield income to government (via the taxable income base) over some effective life, and those assets, although physically durable, that may not yield measurably productive increments to the income stream. Such assets should, in principle, be treated quite differently from the first sort in any sound accounting. The argument for separate treatment applies only to the first sort of capital investment assets. Servicing and amortization of debt used to finance the second sort of assets impose net burdens on future-period taxpayers that are indistinguishable from burdens imposed by servicing the debt used to finance ordinary public outlay. The fact that there may exist marble monuments that last forever offers no basis for a claim that such edifices are appropriately financed by debt issue.

A second problem emerges even if the capital budget is defined to include only those public investments that do, in fact, generate streams of income, thereby providing sources for debt service. The classical theory of public finance supported debt issue for capital projects only when the spending was predicted to be extraordinary rather than continuous over a whole sequence of budgetary periods. If rates of spending on capital projects that are fully eligible for exemption from period-by-period budget balance requirements are roughly uniform over time, the operation of separate current and capital budget accounts, with only the first subject to the balance mandate, would not be different, in effect, from combination into a unified account—all of which is subject to the balance requirement. In this setting, which seems empirically descriptive of modern fiscal institutions, the argument for the establishment of a separate capital budget, with exemption from the constitutional rule for balance, seems much ado about nothing.

## 11. Social Security Trust Fund Accounting and the Amendment for Budget Balance

This section was not in the initial outline for this monograph. It has been added only as a response to the U.S. Senate debates in February–March 1995 that resulted in a one-vote failure of the proposed amendment to secure the votes necessary for approval. Opponents of the amendment justified their position by introducing alleged threats that ultimate implementation of the constitutional change would carry for social security programs.

There are two, quite different, claims advanced. The first is to the effect that trust fund revenues should not be used to balance the fiscal budget. This claim is bizarre at best, since all estimates for the size of deficits for the 1990s do include OASI revenues, which, in isolation, generate a surplus over outlays (some $60 billion in 1995). To move to budget balance in seven years, or by 2002, as projected in the program advanced in the U.S. House of Representatives proposal of 1995, both revenues and outlays under the social security program are included. To argue for exclusion of trust fund accounting revenues from the achievement of the initial target for budget balance is to argue that the objective be made more rather than less difficult to achieve.

A second, and quite different, argument is both more direct and more reflective of interest-group pressures on political choices. If the amendment, as proposed, should be ultimately approved, both by the Congress and the required number of states, reductions in rates of projected federal outlays and/or increases in rates of taxes will be necessary over the years of transition. Opponents sought to secure specific exemption of social security outlays from any spending reductions made necessary under the generalized austerity regime that implementation of the balanced budget rule would cause. The debate over the efficacy or inefficacy of a constitutional rule for budget balance, a debate that is properly joined along the dimensions already discussed above in Sections 6 through 10, was effectively shifted to argument about budgetary composition, argument that seems totally inappropriate at the level of constitutional discourse.

## Part Three

### 12. Budget Balance and Macroeconomic Stability

Opponents of the constitutional amendment for a balanced budget have "pulled out all the stops" in describing the horrible consequences that the rule could produce. As discussed earlier in Section 7, much of the argument is grounded in outdated Keynesianism, as this shows up in nonsophisticated models of the economy and in naive models of democratic politics. In part, however, the generalized macroeconomic opposition to the balanced budget rules stems from an elementary misunderstanding of the positive feedbacks on macroeconomic stability that the presence of such a rule would exert. In the language of competitive sports, "the best defense is a good offense." The most effective counter to the macroeconomic opposition arguments may be that which traces how the operation of such a rule will, first, introduce a stabilizing force in the economy and, second, will make the task of the monetary authorities much easier.

Who could challenge the claim that, if it were not for the expectation of continuing deficits, with the ever-present danger-threat of ultimate monetization of public debt, the efforts of the Federal Reserve authorities to squeeze the inflationary premium out of long-term interest rates would be more successful. Lower long-term rates would almost surely accompany implementation of the balanced budget rule, not only because of reduced inflationary expectations, but also because governmental demand for loanable funds would be reduced. And, with lower long-term rates, private investment would be encouraged.

A regime of budget balance, by comparison with a regime of continuing deficits, must embody lower rates of government spending and/or higher rates of taxation. Both of these changes reduce aggregate demand for consumption, private and public, and allow resources adjustment toward increased investment. Given any specified level of macroeconomic activity, under the two regimes compared, the postrule composition of resource use must involve a shift toward more investment and less consumption. Only if the "secular stagnation" thesis of the 1930s and 1940s should be revived could such results be denied.

It is perhaps too easy to become strictly provincial in discussions and debates about the possible efficacy of the constitutional rule for budget balance in the United States. Rudimentary attention to the historical experience of other countries and in other times may offer new insights. In almost all cases where economic-social-political stability has been undermined by hyper- or near-hyperinflation, generated by disproportionate increases in the quantity of money, the source has been fiscal. Governments have been motivated to spend revenues at rates in excess of their willingness or ability to collect taxes from constituents. To meet emerging revenue shortfalls, governments have, first, made efforts to borrow funds, that is, to finance deficits, by issue of public debt. As revenue shortfalls accelerate, however, lenders of funds (both domestic and foreign) have become wary of governmental credit worthiness. At this juncture, governments face increasing difficulty financing deficits with interest-bearing debt. Faced with such a dilemma, governments have, almost everywhere, resorted to the printing presses, subverting the allegedly independent monetary authorities (national central banks) for political purpose.

These historical experiences from other places and times should never be forgotten when we engage in current constitutional policy discussion in the United States. Participants on all sides of the debates are likely to presume that "it cannot happen here." But the potential macropolitical disaster that threatens when and if we fail to correct the structural flaw in our decision-making procedures must inform any reasoned attitude.

Finally, related observations concerning possible default on public debt are in order. As interest charges mount under the regime of continuing deficits and in the absence of corrective action as reflected in the proposed amendment, more and more questions must be raised about the moral-ethical status of those claims against productive income earners. Why should taxpayers in, say, 2010, be obligated to pay for public use of resources in, say, 1995? Why should future-period taxpayers be coerced in order to meet fiscal charges that are incurred by present-period program beneficiaries?

These questions, once posed at all, themselves suggest that the moral and, hence, political bases for "fiscal responsibility," as defined by both historical tradition and international agencies, become increasingly insecure as the regime of continuing deficits persists. It is scarcely an exaggeration to suggest that the collective choice is starkly simple: Adopt the constitutional amendment that requires budget balance *now,* or face fiscal-economic-political disaster in the rapidly approaching day of reckoning. Sooner or later, the piper must be paid.

## 13. The Rule as Symbol

The symbolic significance of a constitutional rule for budget balance should not be overlooked. Each person constructs her own image of the society in which she lives, and of her own role in that society relative to those of others through the use of symbols. And these symbols may only in some part mirror the realities that may be revealed by empirical science in its ordinary sense. In the United States, we presume that our society embodies "the rule of law," which, in its familiar representation, means that all citizens are subject to equal treatment under the law. But we also recognize that this interpretation of the rule of law remains in part only symbolic, as expressive of an idealized conception, and that, in the reality of legal practice, the equality norm is often violated. "The law" for O. J. Simpson in 1995 is not that which would have been faced by an ordinary citizen, black or white.

Recognition of the divergencies between the observed realities of social interaction and the idealization of these realities through their symbolic representations does not, however, offer legitimate grounds for rejecting the value of the latter. It may be suggested that the principle for budget balance, as such, remains symbolic of governmental fiscal responsibility. With few exceptions, even the most ardent opponents of the constitutional rule express adherence to budget balance as a norm for sound fiscal policy. And, prior to the Keynesian epoch, the symbolic status of budget balance, as an ideal, was in itself sufficient to limit violation of the implicitly accepted rule in political reality. There was then little, if any, need to formalize that which was almost universally accepted as a practicable norm.

Viewed from this perspective, approval of the proposed constitutional amendment becomes a reaffirmation of the symbol for governmental fiscal responsibility. The emplacement of this rule, interpreted as a fiscal norm, in the actual written constitution serves dual purposes. Such a rule positively modifies public expectations about the fiscal stance of government in future periods, and, at the same time, modifies the personalized cost-benefit calculus of those politicians who must make ordinary fiscal choices.

In the political climate of the 1990s, before any approval of the constitutional amendment for budget balance, the politician who responds to constituency pressures toward increased spending does so with some conscious recognition of the effects of his or her action on the size of the deficit, and, indirectly, in the burden thereby placed on future-period taxpayers. Continued deficit financing does, indeed, impose *some* opportunity cost on those whose decisions produce such results. But who can challenge the claim the constitutionalization of the moral norm of fiscal responsibility would act so as to increase such cost dramatically? To violate a moral norm is one thing, and especially as one decision maker in a large group. To violate a moral norm that also involves breaking a constitutional law is quite another.

PRIOR WORKS BY JAMES M. BUCHANAN ON
PUBLIC DEBT, DEFICITS AND THE CONSTITUTIONAL
AMENDMENT FOR A BALANCED BUDGET

Buchanan, James M. *Public Principles of Public Debt: A Defense and Restatement.* Homewood: Richard D. Irwin, 1958.

———. *Fiscal Theory and Political Economy.* Chapel Hill: University of North Carolina Press, 1960.

———. *Public Finance in Democratic Process: Fiscal Institutions and Individual Choice.* Chapel Hill: University of North Carolina Press, 1966.

———. "Concerning Future Generations." In *Public Debt and Future Generations,* edited by J. M. Ferguson, 55–63. Chapel Hill: University of North Carolina Press, 1964.

———. "Public Debt, Cost Theory, and the Fiscal Illusion." In *Public Debt and Future Generations,* edited by J. M. Ferguson, 150–63. Chapel Hill: University of North Carolina Press, 1964.

———. "Critique of the Public Debt." In *Economic Issues and Policies,* edited by A. L. Grey and J. E. Elliot, 185–90. New York: Houghton-Mifflin, 1965.

———. " 'Fiscal Policy' and Fiscal Choice: The Effects of Unbalanced Budgets." In *Public Finance in Democratic Process,* 98–112. Chapel Hill: University of North Carolina Press, 1966.

———. "Public Debt." In *International Encyclopedia of the Social Sciences.* 1968. Vol. 4: 28–34.

———. "The Economic Consequences of the Deficit." In *Symposium on Budget Balance*, edited by C. Cox, 11–18. Washington, D.C.: Committee for a Responsible Federal Budget, 1986.

———. "Public Debt and Capital Formation in the United States." In *Taxation and the Deficit: Fiscal Policy and Capital Formation in the United States*, edited by D. Lee, 177–94. San Francisco: Pacific Institute, 1986.

———. "First, the Academic Scribblers—Democracy in Deficit: The Political Legacy of Lord Keynes." In *The Federal Deficit*, edited by A. C. Kimmins, 42–54. *The Reference Shelf*, vol. 57, no. 4. New York: H. W. Wilson Co., 1986.

———. "The Fiscal Constitution." In *The Politics of American Economic Policy Making*, edited by P. Peretz, 225–28. New York: M. E. Sharpe, 1987.

———. "Keynesian Follies." In *The Legacy of Keynes*, edited by D. Reese, 130–45. New York: Harper and Row, 1987.

———. "The Political Economy of the Budget Deficit." In *Essays on the Political Economy*, 1–12. Honolulu: University of Hawai'i Press, 1989.

———. *Politiek schuldbesef* ("Political Debt Consciousness" and "The Deficit and American Democracy"). Rotterdamse Monetaire Studies, Erasmus University, Rotterdam, no. 16, 1984. 39 pages.

———. "External and Internal Public Debt." *American Economic Review* 47 (December 1957): 995–1000.

———. "The Real Debt." *Challenge* 7 (July 1959): 58–61.

———. "Easy Budgets and Tight Money." *Lloyds Bank Review* 64 (April 1962): 17–30.

———. "The Icons of Public Debt." *Journal of Finance* 21 (September 1966): 544–46.

———. "Democracy in Deficit." *Manhattan Report* 4 (1984): 6–9.

———. "The Moral Dimension of Debt Financing." *Economic Inquiry* 23 (January 1985): 1–6.

———. "The Political Economy of the Deficit: A 1987 Perspective." *Florida Policy Review* 3 (Summer 1987): 5–10.

———. "Debt—An Economic and Moral Crisis." *IPA Review* (May–July 1987): 56–57.

———. "The Deficit and Obligations to Future Generations." *Imprimis* 16 (January 1987): 1–6.

———. "Reining in the Deficit." *The Owen Manager* 9 (Spring 1988): 27–31.

———. "The Budget Balance Amendment: Statement to the New Hampshire House of Representatives, 2 April 1979." *Congressional Record*, 4 April 1979, S-3858.

———. "In Defense of Budget Balance." *Congressional Record* 125 (30 April 1979), no. 51, S4940-S4944.

———. Statement. House Judiciary Committee, 5 January 1995.

———. "Budget Balance Proposal." 1984. Unpublished paper.

———. "The Deficit and American Democracy." 1984. Unpublished paper.

———. "Budgetary Bias in Post-Keynesian Politics: The Erosion and Potential Replacement of Fiscal Norms." 1984. Unpublished paper.

———. "The Secondary Economic Consequences of the Deficit." 1985. Unpublished paper.

———. "The Budget Deficit in Modern Democracy." 1987. Unpublished paper.

Buchanan, James M., and Geoffrey Brennan. "Toward Authentic Tax Reform: Prospects and Prescriptions." In *The Power to Tax: Analytical Foundations of a Fiscal Constitution.* New York: Cambridge University Press, 1980.

Buchanan, James M., and Marilyn Flowers. "Public Debt and Public Finance." 1987. Unpublished paper.

Buchanan, James M., and Jennifer Roback. "The Incidence and Effects of Public Debt in the Absence of Fiscal Illusion." *Public Finance Quarterly* 15 (January 1987): 5–25.

Buchanan, James M., Charles Rowley, and Robert Tollison, eds. *Deficits.* New York: Blackwell, 1987.

Buchanan, James M., and Robert Tollison, eds. *Theory of Public Choice: Political Applications of Economics.* Ann Arbor: University of Michigan Press, 1972.

———. *Theory of Public Choice II: Political Applications of Economics.* Ann Arbor: University of Michigan Press, 1984.

Buchanan, James M., and Gordon Tullock. *The Calculus of Consent: Logical Foundations of Constitutional Democracy.* Ann Arbor: University of Michigan Press, 1962.

Buchanan, James M., and Viktor J. Vanberg. "Organization Theory and Fiscal Economics: Society, State, and Public Debt." *Journal of Law, Economics, and Organization* 2 (Fall 1986): 215–27.

Buchanan, James M., and Richard E. Wagner. *Democracy in Deficit: The Political Legacy of Lord Keynes.* New York: Academic Press, 1977.

———. *Public Debt in Democratic Society.* Washington, D.C.: American Enterprise Institute, 1966.

———. "Dialogues Concerning Fiscal Religion." *Journal of Monetary Economics* 4 (July 1978): 627–36.

Buchanan, James M., Richard E. Wagner, and John Burton. *The Consequences of Mr. Keynes,* Hobart Paper 78. London: Institute of Economic Affairs, 1978.

# The Ethics of Debt Default

> . . . for among democratic nations each generation is a new people.
>
> —Alexis de Tocqueville

## 19.1. Introduction

The budget deficit dominates economic policy discussion in the mid-1980s. Modern national governments demonstrate an inability to eliminate the excess of spending over tax rates. As a national collectivity, the United States (along with many other nations) finances a large share of current public consumption (including transfer payments) by borrowing. In the process, legal claims against disposable income flows in future periods are created, claims that are not matched by the accumulation of income-yielding assets.

There is widespread recognition that this pattern of fiscal behaviour cannot be sustained permanently. So long as the rate of increase in interest-bearing public debt exceeds the rate of economic growth, the interest charges on the public debt as a share of total product must increase. Either total public outlay must increase as a share of total product or interest charges as a share of total budgetary totals must increase. At some point, the annual interest charge will come to equal, and then exceed, the annual deficit. Once this critical threshold is passed, the simple economics of default come into play. If government is unable to borrow funds that are sufficient to meet annual interest charges on accumulated debt, default on existing obligations

From *Deficits*, ed. James M. Buchanan, Charles Rowley, and Robert D. Tollison (New York: Blackwell, 1987), 361–73. Reprinted by permission of the publisher, Blackwell Publishers Ltd.

will allow current rates of spending on goods, services, and transfers to increase and/or current rates of taxation to decrease. At this juncture, it is apparently to the short-run self-interest of citizens, as taxpayers-beneficiaries, to default on existing public debt, either directly through explicit repudiation or indirectly through inflation.

This straightforward self-interest argument is mitigated somewhat when it is recognized that any repudiation of government debt, either directly or indirectly, will tend to close off, at least for a time, prospects for further financing through borrowing. A government that has explicitly defaulted could not readily sell its bonds, and a government that has inflated its currency with the accompanying destruction in the capital values of debt claims would be faced with a high premium for inflationary risk. In either case, governments would be unable to respond to genuine fiscal emergencies without resort to oppressive taxation. And the ability to make such a response may retain a residual value. To the extent that this consideration enters the citizen's calculus, the self-interest motivation for default may not become effective until well past the threshold point described above. At some point, however, the relevant behavioural threshold will be passed, and economically motivated political pressure for default would seem decisive.

Citizens within the jurisdiction are also possible lenders to government, that is, holders of debt obligations. In this role, they would be opposed to any default, and their interests would also be reflected in the political debate. My concern in this paper is not, however, with the conflicts among pressure groups seeking default and those who seek to insure that public debt obligations are honoured. My concern is, instead, with the ethics of default, rather than with either the politics or the basic economics.[1]

To the extent that ethically based argument can be brought to bear, on one side of the issue or the other, or indeed to the extent that ethically based argument can be shown to be irrelevant, the behavioural predictions that emerge from the economic and political models can be either dampened or strengthened in application and possibly can even be directionally modi-

---

1. I have discussed these economic and political issues elsewhere, perhaps to an extent that my critics would label excessive. See my *Public Principles of Public Debt* (Homewood: Irwin, 1958); James M. Buchanan and Richard Wagner, *Democracy in Deficit* (New York: Academic Press, 1977).

fied. To my knowledge, there has been almost no discussion of the issues here among fiscal economists, public choice theorists, or ethical-moral philosophers. These issues are, however, almost certain to become increasingly relevant in the remaining years of this century and beyond.

The paper is organized by the differing, if related, arguments that might be advanced in support of and against adherence to the fiscal obligations that outstanding public debt represents. Section 19.2 discusses the quid pro quo argument against default in the context of a stylized model that will provide the benchmark for analysis in later parts of the paper. Section 19.3 examines the argument from moral community and from the moral legitimacy of law. Section 19.4 raises the intertemporal aspects of political choice. Section 19.5 utilizes a contractarian approach to examine both the morality of debt issue in the stylized setting and the morality of adherence to past commitments. Section 19.6 analyses the moral status of claims against the state, and the possible reciprocal obligations that those claims embody. The effects of the inclusion of a default risk premium in the contracted yields on debt instruments are examined for the moral-ethical implications toward default. The arguments are summarized in the concluding section 19.7.

## 19.2. Public Debt in Intertemporal Fiscal Exchange

Classical normative principles for public debt issue authorized governments to borrow required revenues when the outlay to be financed was expected to produce or purchase durable income-yielding or utility-yielding assets. That is to say, governments might legitimately borrow to finance genuine public capital investments. Simple principles of tax equity suggested that taxpayers during the immediate period of revenue use should not be saddled with the full costs of public projects that promised to yield benefits over a whole sequence of time periods. In this setting, debt service and amortization payments, presumably to be raised by taxes in periods subsequent to debt creation, were considered to be a necessary part of the intertemporal fiscal exchange that the collective decision to finance the capital project implements.

In this setting, there would seem to be a powerful moral-ethical argument in support of adherence to the debt contracts, even if some of the considerations to be examined in later parts of this paper remain relevant, and even if an initial decision may, when viewed ex post, prove to have been made in error. The basic moral argument is equivalent to that which might be advanced in support of adherence to any contract initiated on what seemed to be genuine quid pro quo terms.

I have put this argument against default on debt contracts first in my listing because it becomes irrelevant in the stylized setting of debt issue on which I want to concentrate attention in this paper. In the modern fiscal regime, debt is not used specifically to finance capital investment projects; debt is used as a means of financing ordinary, recurrent, public consumption. The citizens-taxpayers-beneficiaries in periods subsequent to debt issue are faced with contractually committed interest and amortization charges that are not offset by any income or utility yielding public assets. There may, of course, be borderline cases in which the investment and consumption components of public outlay may be difficult to distinguish. My concern is not with making a fine classification. For my purposes, I shall assume that there is agreement that some part of the debt issue finances outlays on programmes that everyone would agree to be pure public consumption.

This assumption does not imply that the debt-financed outlays finance non-beneficial programmes. Benefits may well exceed the costs. The assumption does imply that the benefits are concentrated in time; they are enjoyed exclusively by beneficiaries (and/or taxpayers in an opportunity cost sense) who live during the period when the debt is created. There are no benefits that accrue to persons living in subsequent periods.

## 19.3. Political Community, Morality, and the Law

To what extent is the state a "moral unit," defined as that unit which potentially commands the loyalties of the individual sufficiently to implant a sense of personal responsibility for the consequences of action taken by anyone who serves as agent? More generally, what are the conditions under which a person includes others than himself in "moral community"?[2] It seems evi-

2. For further discussion of moral community, as contrasted with moral order, see my *Moral Community, Moral Order, and Moral Anarchy,* Abbott Memorial Lecture (Colorado Springs: Colorado College, 1981) and my paper "Markets, States, and the Extent of Morals," *American Economic Review* 68 (1978): 364–68.

dent that within appropriate limits almost everyone acknowledges membership in several intersecting moral communities, as defined. The nuclear family offers the obvious example: persons accept moral responsibility for the behaviour of a spouse, a minor child, or an aged parent. As this very example suggests, however, the acceptance of such responsibility decreases with genetic distance and with time. Consider the debts of your uncle or even of your father if contracted before you were born. (Note that I am not concerned here with the limits of legal responsibility.)

In some cultural, social, and historical circumstances, "the family," as the important and inclusive socio-political unit, may assume a much more significant role than it does in modern Western societies. And, in such circumstances, the interests of the family, as a unit, may motivate the behaviour of each member; potential conflict between individual and group interest may not exist. But any extension of this sense of moral community to all members of a modern nation-state seems far-fetched and even bizarre. It is only under conditions of external threat (wars or expectations of war) that individuals feel morally attached to the group that defines its membership by citizenship in the nation-state. Under more ordinary conditions, the political unit is best conceived as the organizational structure that provides the means through which persons and small groups cooperate to secure separately defined objectives. The modern state is clearly not a "moral unit" in the sense defined above. An individual citizen does not feel morally responsible for the behaviour of other persons who happen to hold membership in the same polity, even if the latter may be acting as agents on behalf of the whole membership. Any argument based on moral community seems, at best, neutral with reference to the whole question of adherence to public debt contracts.

A different, even if related, argument offers support to such adherence. The basic moral value of the legal order is widely acknowledged, and this value may be invoked to validate almost any act, or set of acts, taken on behalf of the collectivity. So long as a decision has been made, and action taken, by legally authorized agents of the polity, the results should be respected, independent of either the specific content of the action or the specific process through which the decision might have been taken. The law, as such, warrants moral support by citizens simply because it is the law.

This familiar conservative argument may, of course, be used to lend putative moral strength to almost any political action, quite separately from the morality of the action itself. But the force of the argument should not be underestimated. Unless there is a general set of attitudes that embodies respect for past legal commitments, the very existence of an ongoing legal-political order is called into question. If each new legislature should simply repudiate the enactments of its predecessor, political chaos would quickly replace political stability and continuity.

Note that the point under discussion here is not the behaviour of the individual in abiding by or in violating the dictates of law which he or she may, possibly, consider to be unjust or immoral. The question here is, instead, the behaviour of the citizen as he or she considers lending support or opposition to political parties, representatives, or agents who propose, through constitutionally authorized legislative action, to repudiate contractual commitments made by prior governmental bodies. That is to say, I am not concerned with the person who might think about refusing to pay taxes to service debt as an individual expression of displeasure. I am concerned only with the moral stance of the citizen as he contemplates support or opposition to proposed collective default on outstanding debt claims.

It seems clear that there is moral value, over and beyond economically measurable worth of socio-legal stability, in membership in a polity where promise-keeping extends to the government as well as to citizens in their personal capacities. Almost any person will assign moral worthiness to his government's adherence to its commitments, including those made to creditors. Other things being equal, almost any person would prefer to be a citizen of a polity where promise-keeping characterizes governmental behaviour than to be a citizen of a polity where government reneges on its contracts.

These conclusions emerge, however, only when discussion is at the level of abstract principle. In particular cases, the results may be substantially mitigated. A collective decision to repudiate debt need not, in itself, pull down the whole legal-political house of cards, especially if it is accompanied by a basic change in the rules designed to insure against recurrence of the necessity for repudiation. The marginal effect of a single default on a contracted commitment is important, and recognition of this effect points directionally toward adherence to debt claims. But care must be taken not to make a single commitment carry the full weight for all political-legal-social stability.

## 19.4. Individual Responsibility for Collective Decisions

The citizen may accept some moral responsibility for generalized adherence to results that are generated through a collective decision rule, procedure, or structure, in which he or she is allowed full rights of participation. Consider a simple case where a political unit is to make a yes-no decision, e.g., to finance or not to finance a municipal swimming facility. The decision is to be made in a majority-rule referendum. Even for the person whose preferences might be over-ruled by a majority of his peers, the collectively chosen outcome may be accorded legitimacy and deemed worthy of support.

As this model is extended to incorporate representative rather than direct democracy the sense of participation is attenuated, but the thrust of the argument carries through. So long as the individual considers himself as a possible participant in the process through which collective decisions are reached, with his or her preferences equally weighted with those of others, even if the results run counter to interests, such results may be granted support for moral reasons.

Consider, however, a different setting in which the individual is not allowed to participate in the decision process, either directly or through the election of representatives. Political decisions are reached through the operation of some process that denies entry to the individual, and these decisions are then implemented on behalf of the collectivity, which, for such non-participatory purposes as taxation and regulation, treats the individual as a member. In this setting, an individual may, of course, abide by decisions from self-interest reasons. But any moral support for such decisions that might stem from membership itself would seem unlikely to be present, again save in the case of major emergencies.

When we examine the question of possible support for or opposition to default on outstanding public debt from this participatory argument, it is necessary to classify persons by age and by origins of citizenship. In the stylized fiscal model here, the benefits of the debt-financed spending have been enjoyed in past periods; the taxpayers in the post-spending periods face deadweight interest and amortization charges. Some of these taxpayers will, however, have also been participating members of the collectivity at the time the initial fiscal decisions were made. For this group, there is surely some sense of moral responsibility for carrying out the terms of the contracts made by the collectivity. These taxpayers-citizens will be in the position of persons in the participatory setting discussed above.

Other persons in the post-spending, post-borrowing periods will not have been present during the time of the initial fiscal actions. These persons will not have been born in time either to participate in the decisions or to enjoy the experienced benefits of the governmental spending. Persons in this "next generation" will not assign much, if any, moral legitimacy to decisions made for them by others, and they are quite likely to support arguments for repudiation of past claims.

To this point, I have implicitly assumed that the polity is closed and that new entrants are born into the membership. If we drop this assumption, and allow for new entrants by immigration, the argument is somewhat different. A prospective immigrant, who arrives in the post-spending periods, will recognize the existence of the debt claims as a liability against the expected income flows of future periods. In a real sense, these claims against the collectivity are a part of the contract between the new entrant and the polity. There is a moral legitimacy to such claims for the immigrant that is stronger than that which applies to the member of the "next generation," who did not participate in the initial decisions and who did not voluntarily choose to become a member of the political community.

## 19.5. Contractarian Reconstruction as a Moral Criterion

Governments, with general support from the citizenry, have often repudiated commitments made earlier by legally authorized political agents. Moral support for such repudiation arises when the initial action comes to be judged, subsequently, as having been itself immoral. The moral evaluation of the initial action clearly becomes relevant in any argument in support of or against repudiation.

In the fiscal model we are examining, we must ask the question: Was (is) the financing of recurrent public consumption (including transfer payments) by public borrowing in itself immoral? An initial effort at response might introduce an analogy with private borrowing. Is it immoral for a person to borrow to finance ordinary or recurrent consumption spending when there is no anticipated increase in income flows over time? Can the genuine profligate be judged immoral? This specific question need not be analysed in depth here, since, for many purposes, the direct relationship between action and consequences suffices to make the issue moot. Moral precepts are usually reserved for application to behaviour that affects other persons than the one who takes the action. In the case of individualized personal consumption, the "other persons" are later-period embodiments of the same person. It is precisely because of this continuing identity through time, as a commonsense notion, that we do not normally apply moral censure severely to the person who spends beyond his means, a behaviour pattern that must, by necessity, be short-lived. The actor suffers the consequences of his action. More significant moral issues are, of course, raised in personal consumption behaviour that affects the well-being of family members.

The analogy with personal finance breaks down when we consider individual behaviour in collective choice. Issues of morality necessarily emerge because, by the very nature of collective decision-making, each individual participates in a selection among alternatives that are to apply over all members of the community. Even if the consequences are concentrated in a single time period, there is no individualized relationship between action and result akin to that which characterizes private choice. The person who chooses (votes) is not necessarily visited with the consequences (costs and benefits) of his act. There is an essential externality introduced, and this carries an essential moral dimension that is wholly absent in private choice.

Recognizing the necessary interdependencies of individual choices in any collective decision process, and further recognizing that, with debt-financed public consumption, there is no individual-as-participant context, can we judge the act of public borrowing to be immoral? We require some criterion, and, to the individualist, the potential for contractual agreement provides the only alternative that is available. To apply this criterion intertemporally, it is necessary to conduct a thought experiment. We must imagine an individual who is placed behind an intertemporal veil of ignorance such that generational position cannot be identified. Will a group of several persons in this position reach agreement on the issue of public debt to finance recurrent public consumption?

Note that this thought experiment may yield results that lend legitimacy to collective action that imposes net utility losses, ex post, on designated persons. A person may well acquiesce in a structural arrangement that involves income redistribution, even if this arrangement involves takings from his own nominal stock of claims, evaluated ex post, if he considers the operative arrangement one that might have been reached by the conceptual contractual agreement of all persons in the original position, and before economic positions come to be identified.

Applied to the fiscal question posed here, is it possible that the taxpayer-beneficiary in the post-debt, post-spending periods might, conceptually, have agreed to the initial decision to finance spending by debt if he could have been present and could have participated in the decision process? Behind the intertemporal Rawlsian veil, is it possible that agreement might emerge that would authorize government, in any period, to finance ordinary public consumption by borrowing?

Faced with the debt overhang in periods subsequent to debt issue, the individual will, in any case, think that things "might have been better" had the debt not been created and the benefits of the spending dissipated. But the conceptual contract criterion requires that this sort of temporal identification be ignored and that the thought experiment be carried out as indicated. In such a setting, the individual would, of course, know that the first-period utility gains would be offset by later-period utility losses. The question reduces to the tradeoffs; are there situations in which the promised utility gains to the borrowing-spending "generation" more than offset the utility losses for those persons who will live in later periods? Note that considerations of time preference cannot enter the calculus here since the individual remains ignorant as to generational location.

This thought experiment suggests that agreement might indeed be possible on the authorization of debt financing of extraordinary and temporary demands on the collectivity (e.g., wars and disaster relief). As with the case of public capital investment, this sort of debt issue was permitted under classical fiscal norms. In the stylized model specifically examined here, however, the debt financing supplies revenues for ordinary and recurrent public consumption. In this case, agreement would not seem even conceptually possible. Debt financing fails to meet the test of conceptual contract. There is no way that an agreement between members of the separate "generations" could be worked out in support of financing benefits for persons in one generation at the costs of persons who live later. In welfare economics terms, there is no multi-period Pareto-superior move that can describe a shift to a regime of debt-financed public consumption. And this failure of the contractarian test does carry moral weight.

To this point, the argument may seem convincing. But we have implicitly assigned "rights" to individuals in the discussion immediately above, and a critic might here suggest that any such assignment is arbitrary. We may hold that the external imposition of costs on persons who live in periods after those in which the debt-financed benefits are enjoyed becomes immoral only if we, somewhat arbitrarily, assume that these later-period persons have rights to the income streams that they nominally earn or command. Whether or not this implicit imputation of rights accords with prevailing moral standards becomes an empirical issue of its own.

The issue here is made complex because of the confused state of analysis that stems ultimately from attempts at macroaggregation in total disregard of institutional parameters. Do persons, in their collective-political capacities, as voters-taxpayers-beneficiaries, in, say 1986, have a possible moral claim against the income streams that will be nominally claimed by persons who will be around in, say, 2010? The total income stream in 2010 may well be higher than that in 1986, even on a per person basis, because of private decisions to save, invest, and accumulate productive capital over the ensuing periods, actions that may, in total, more than offset the negative capital formation of the governmental sector. In this case how can the action of the "borrowing generation" be judged immoral *vis-à-vis* the interests of those who will live in 2010?

In my view, the reasoning behind this sort of question is confused because it fails to distinguish the institutional differences between private and public decisions. Persons who save and invest privately do not do so for the purpose of improving the well-being or utility levels of "future generations," as defined by membership of the polity. Persons save and invest privately, to the extent they do so over and beyond life-cycle planning at all, for the purpose of improving the well-being or utility levels of their own progeny or its designed surrogate. Whether or not such behaviour, in some aggregate sense, offsets the future-period weight of the claims created by debt-financed public consumption is irrelevant to the question concerning the basic morality of the initial fiscal action. Only if there should exist some direct institutional bridge between the privately bequeathed holdings of capital assets and the generalized claims against future-period income streams embodied in public debt obligations could the aggregate size of the anticipated future income flow, pre-tax, be an important consideration in moral-ethical arguments for or against default.[3]

In sum, there are plausible grounds for judging the debt financing of ordinary public consumption to be immoral by the contractarian standard, even if the "degree of immorality" falls far short of the level attained in, say, the early-nineteenth-century enforcement of slavery contracts. The questionable moral status of public borrowing under the conditions postulated at the least removes any moral basis for opposing default that might be grounded in the putative moral worthiness of the initial action.

## 19.6. The Moral Status of Claims

The strongest moral argument that can be adduced in support of adherence to government's contractual commitments and against default lies in the legitimacy of the claims that are held by the polity's creditors, whose rights would be violated if the commitments are not respected. In one sense, the attribution of moral legitimacy to the claims in itself creates an obligation on the part of members of the collectivity that such claims be respected. The familiar correspondence between rights and duties seems applicable here. If members of the collectivity fail to meet contractual obligations agreed on by agents for the polity in prior periods, they behave unjustly toward those persons, whether domestic or foreign, who hold claims against the polity, as an ongoing entity.

Even if, by the contractarian criterion discussed in section 19.5, the act of borrowing under the circumstances described may be judged immoral, there need be no implication that the act of lending to government deserves moral censure. Those persons who gave up command over resources during the

---

3. If an institutional bridge should exist such that persons in the initial borrowing-spending period are assigned specific shares in the aggregate liability, private choices on the part of these persons to bequeath income-yielding assets sufficient to allow their heirs to meet these assigned, and inherited, liabilities when due would place on such heirs some moral obligation to honour the debt claims. Such behaviour on the part of the initial generation would, however, seem internally inconsistent with the decision to initiate the whole borrowing-spending operation.

initial period of debt-financed spending did so in a wholly voluntary exchange transaction. These persons gave up purchasing power in explicit exchange for the governmental commitment to meet interest and amortization payments in subsequent periods. To deny these claims when due seems fraudulent when viewed from the perspective of those who hold the debt instruments.

The strength of this argument may be mitigated somewhat when the prospect of default risk is introduced. Individual creditors purchase debt instruments voluntarily in a market where prices are competitively determined. But especially as government's fiscal position becomes increasingly precarious in the regime of continuing deficit financing, lenders to government (buyers of government debt) may begin to anticipate the possibility of default. To the extent that they do so, a share of the market-determined yield will reflect a default risk premium. Such a premium would be less likely to emerge if borrowed funds could have been observed to finance income- or utility-yielding assets. In private loan markets, we observe higher interest rates on consumption than on investment loans.

How does the inclusion of a default risk factor in the yield on debt affect the attitude of the citizen-taxpayer-beneficiary toward the legitimacy of the contract? In legal terms, of course, the inclusion of default risk in the rate of return does not, in any way, mitigate the strength of the contractual obligation. But my concern is with the moral terms rather than the legal. If the government contracts a loan at 10 per cent, with a 5 per cent premium for default risk over a risk-free rate of 5 per cent, the creditors have a legally based entitlement to the full 10 per cent. But citizens in post-contract periods face the moral question of adherence to or default on the contract. To the extent that these "debtors" recognize that the built-in default risk forms part of the yield, their sense of moral obligation toward holders of debt claims is attenuated. If, indeed, creditors expected with a 50 per cent prospect that government would default, why should not "debtors" act so as to guarantee that these expectations of creditors are fulfilled? Why should not a policy of default on some randomly selected one-half of the debt meet the moral requirements of debtors toward creditors? Or, if default risk is generalized over all issues, why would not a reduction of yield by one-half, with a corresponding promise against further default, be morally justifiable? Moral argument for adherence to contracts cannot readily be made to include elements of return based on stochastic predictions made about such adherence itself at the time the initial contracts were negotiated between government and its bond purchasers.

## 19.7. Summary and Conclusions

I have tried to lay out and to examine critically the several arguments that may be made for and against a policy of direct or indirect repudiation of governmental debt obligations over and beyond arguments that are based on economic self-interest as it might operate in observed political structures. I have termed these arguments ethical or moral, used interchangeably here. The analysis is motivated by the prediction that these arguments must become increasingly important as economic self-interest dictates default. I have worked within a stylized fiscal setting that essentially eliminates classical justification for debt financing and, indirectly, for adherence for the contracts embodied in such financing. The deficit regimes of modern governments have come increasingly to fit the description of the stylized setting that I have introduced.

There seems no basis for moral support for debt obligations that can be grounded on the sense of "moral community," as such. By contrast, the argument based on the moral legitimacy of law, and on the government as a component of the legal order, may offer a significant motivation to continued adherence to contractual commitment made on behalf of the collectivity. The second possible basis for support of adherence to contracted commitments is the sense of individual responsibility for collective action stemming from participation. With public debt, it is necessary to classify persons by age, by generation, and by origins of citizenship. As the accumulating debt overhang increases through time, larger numbers of voters move into the group that feels no sense of having participated in the financing decisions or of having shared in the spending benefits.

In straightforward economic terms, the debt financing of public consumption involves an intergenerational transfer, with utility gains in financing-spending periods matched by utility losses in later periods. Once temporal identification is established, there can be no contractual justification for such transfers. However, as with other sorts of transfers, justification may be attempted by removing such identification through veil-of-ignorance recon-

struction of a possible contract. The analysis reveals, however, that no justification emerges from such an exercise. Debt financing of ordinary public
consumption must, therefore, be judged immoral, or, at the least, amoral by
contractarian criteria.

The strongest moral basis for adherence to debt contracts, even in the
stylized setting examined, lies in the possible acknowledgement of the standing of the claims. Creditors purchased debt instruments under expectations
that governments would keep their promises. And to the extent that these
claims are accorded legitimacy, there arise offsetting obligations that they be
met. Even this argument loses some of its force, however, when default risk
premiums are included in yields.

On balance, the moral arguments against default on public debt do not
seem so strong as seems to be assumed in the observed neglect of the question. Economic self-interest will surely dictate default, either directly or
through the inflationary process, in the real-world politics of the next decades unless democratic governments reform themselves dramatically. At
this stage of our fiscal history, a major issue of public policy will move directly into the domain of moral philosophy.

# Name Index

Alchian, Armen A., 16n. 21, 440n. 11
Arrow, Kenneth J., 11–12

Bailey, Martin J., 413n. 6
Barone, Enrico, 7, 101n. 1, 102, 103
Barro, Robert J., xv, 385–90, 392nn. 1,2,
  394–95, 403, 406, 408–11, 413–16, 426,
  436n. 8, 475–77, 478, 479–80, 483
Bartlett, Randall, 16n. 23
Bastable, C. F., 72n. 5
Becker, Gary S., 245n. 17, 314n. 12, 458n. 3
Benit, Emile, 359n. 6
Bergstrom, Theodore C., 7n. 7
Black, Duncan, 11–12, 26–27, 75n. 11
Borda, J. C. de, 12
Bowen, Howard R., 8, 11
Bowman, Ward S., Jr., 74n. 10
Bradford, David F., 152n. 2
Break, George F., 71, 103, 285n. 2
Brennan, Geoffrey, xiinn. 2,3, xivn. 8,
  xivn. 9, xvn. 11, 47n. 1, 51n. 3, 67, 98n. 7,
  188n. 13, 194n. 18, 204n. 4, 208n. 5, 209,
  212n. 1, 214n. 3, 229–32, 246n. 18, 247n.
  19, 263nn. 9,10, 279n. 5, 287n. 5, 308n. 5,
  314n. 11, 325n. 3, 328n. 8, 331n. 9, 337n.
  12, 426n. 23, 440n. 13
Breton, Albert, 16n. 23
Brock, William A., 320n. 17
Buiter, William, 392n. 1, 417n. 15, 424n. 20
Burkhead, Jesse, 71
Burstein, Meyer L., 74n. 10, 84n. 15

Carroll, Lewis, 12
Coase, Ronald H., 122n. 1
Cohen, Linda, 331n. 10
Coleman, James S., 431n. 3
Condorcet, Marquis de, 12
Congleton, Roger D., xivn. 8

Danzon, Patricia, 96n. 5, 324n. 1
Davis, Otto A., 123n. 3
Debreu, Gerard, 327n. 5
Demsetz, Harold, 16n. 21
de Viti de Marco, Antonio, 6, 7, 26, 385n.
  1, 411n. 5
Downs, Anthony, 15
Drazen, Allan, 415n. 10, 416n. 13, 423n. 18
Due, John, 135–36, 147n. 6

Einaudi, Luigi, 8, 112n. 13, 125

Faith, Roger L., 241n. 15, 255n. 4
Farrell, Michael J., 105n. 7
Feldstein, Martin, 22n. 29, 285n. 3, 302,
  390, 392n. 2, 394, 406
Ferguson, James E., 426n. 23
Fisher, Irving, 112n. 13
Flowers, Marilyn, 96n. 5, 324n. 1
Foley, Duncan, 7n. 7
Friedman, Milton, 103, 509–10
Furubotn, Eirik, 16n. 21

Girard, Marcel, 72n. 5
Goetz, Charles, 15n. 17, 238n. 13

# Subject Index

This book is set in Minion, a typeface designed by Robert Slimbach specifically for digital typesetting. Released by Adobe in 1989, it is a versatile neohumanist face that shows the influence of Slimbach's own calligraphy.

This book is printed on paper that is acid-free and meets the requirements of the American National Standard for Permanence of Paper for Printed Library Materials, z39.48-1992. ♾

Book design by Louise OFarrell, Gainesville, Fla.
Typography by Impressions Book and Journal Services, Inc., Madison, Wisc.
Printed and bound by Worzalla Publishing Company, Stevens Point, Wisc.